WHAT THE BIBLE TEACHES

Contributor

JAMES ALLEN

Brought up in Lurgan, Northern Ireland, Jim Allen was saved at the age of 17. After graduating with first class honours in Science, he taught for four years in Ballymena Academy before going to Malaya as Headmaster of a Grammar School and then Principal of the Specialist Teacher Training Institute in Kuala Lumpur. Returning to Northern Ireland when Malaya gained its independence, he became Vice-Principal of Larne Grammar School.

In 1968 he was commended by the Cloughfern Assembly, Co. Antrim to serve the Lord in Malaysia. Since 1973, when missionary visas were no longer granted by the Malaysian Government, he has visited Malaysia frequently to encourage the believers and preach the gospel. Today he preaches the gospel and ministers the Word of God throughout the British Isles as well as the United States, Canada and many other parts of the world. He is highly valued and appreciated for his ministry and especially his studies on Creation and Prophecy.

WHAT THE BIBLE TEACHES

with
Authorised Version
of
The Bible

IN ELEVEN VOLUMES
COVERING THE NEW TESTAMENT

VOLUME 10

JOHN RITCHIE LTD
KILMARNOCK, SCOTLAND

ISBN-13: 978 1 904064 47 3
ISBN-10: 1 904064 47 7

WHAT THE BIBLE TEACHES

40 Beansburn, Kilmarnock, Scotland

www.ritchiechristianmedia.co.uk

Re-typeset and printed 2007

Typeset at John Ritchie Ltd., 40 Beansburn, Kilmarnock.
Printed by Bell and Bain, Glasgow.

CONTENTS

Page

ABBREVIATIONS

AV	Authorised Version of King James Version 1611
JND	New Translation by J.N. Darby 1939
LXX	Septuagint Version of Old Testament
Mft	New Translation by James Moffat 1922
NASB	New American Standard Bible 1960
NEB	New English Bible 1961
Nestle	Nestle (ed.) Novum Testamentum Graece
NIV	New International Version 1973
NT	New Testament
OT	Old Testament
Phps	New Testament in Modern English by J.B. Philips 1962
RSV	Revised Standard Version 1952
RV	Revised Version 1881
TR	Textus Receptus or Received Text
Wey	New Testament in Modern Speech by R.E. Weymouth 1929

PREFACE

They follow the noblest example who seek to open the Scriptures to others, for our Lord Himself did so for those two dejected disciples of Emmaus (Luke 24:32). Whether it is the evangelist "opening and alleging that Christ must needs have suffered and risen from the dead" (Acts 17:3) or the pastor-teacher "expounding ... in all the scriptures the things concerning himself" (Luke 24:27) or stimulating our hope "through the patience and comfort of the scriptures" (Rom 15:4), he serves well in thus giving attendance to the reading of the Scriptures (1 Tim 4:13).

It is of course of equal moment to recognise in the exercise of able men, the continued faithfulness of the risen Head in giving gifts to the Church, in spite of her unfaithfulness. How good to recognise that "the perfecting of the saints ... the work of the ministry...the edifying of the body of Christ" need not be neglected. Every provision has been made to ensure the well-being of the people of God. And every opportunity should be taken by the minister of Christ and those to whom he ministers to ensure that the saints "grow up into him in all things which is the head, even Christ" (Eph 4:15).

At various times in the post-apostolic period, certain teachers have come to prominence, sometimes because they succumbed to error, sometimes because in faithfulness they paid the ultimate price for the truth they had bought and would not sell. Some generations had Calvin and Luther, others Darby and Kelly, but in every generation God's voice is heard. It is important that we hear His voice today and recognise that He does speak through His servants. The contributors to this series of commentaries are all highly-respected expositors among the churches of God. They labour in the Word in the English-speaking world and have been of blessing to many throughout their years of service.

The doctrinal standpoint of the commentaries is based upon the acceptance of the verbal and plenary inspiration of the Scriptures so that their inerrant and infallible teachings are the only rule of conscience. The impeccability of Christ, His virgin birth, vicarious death and bodily resurrection are indeed precious truths worthy of the Christian's defence, and throughout the volumes of this series will be defended. Equally the Rapture will be presented as the hope of the Church. Before the great Tribulation she will be raptured and God's prophetic programme will continue with Jacob's trouble, the public manifestation of Christ and the Millennium of blessing to a restored Israel and the innumerable Gentile multitude in a creation released from the bondage of corruption.

May the sound teaching of these commentaries be used by our God to the blessing of His people. May the searching of the Scriptures characterise all who read them.

The diligence of Mr. J.W. Ferguson and, for the reprint of this volume Mr. L. Slater, in proof-reading is gratefully acknowledged. Without such co-operation, the production of this commentary would not have been expedited so readily.

T. WILSON
K. STAPLEY

REVELATION

J. Allen

REVELATION

Introduction

1. **The Author of the Book**
2. **The Date of the Book**
3. **The Purpose of the Book**
4. **Interpretation of the Book**
5. **Bibliography**
6. **Outline**

1. The Author of the Book

On three occasions in the first chapter (vv. 1,4,9) and in 21:2; 22:8 the author identifies himself simply as John as if he required no further introduction to the churches of Asia, the first recipients of this book. While it is the author's authority as a prophet that is particularly stressed (1:3; 22:6-10, 18-19) there can hardly be any doubt that apostolic authority is inherent in the writing; just to read the book is to catch something of the authority that the author expects his readers to recognise. The author's use of the OT (278 of the 404 verses in this book have some allusion to or an echo of an OT Scripture) and his evident intimate knowledge of tabernacle and temple ritual, display a mind stored with the Hebrew Scriptures as well as Jewish teaching. Known intimately to the churches of Asia and with a Hebrew cast of thought, although expressing himself in Greek, the author scarcely needs any further identification. Add to these clues the fact of a banishment to the isle of Patmos (1:9) on account of his testimony to Christ and the case is virtually unanswerable for the authorship of John the apostle, son of Zebedee, and the one who leaned on the breast of the Saviour (John 13:23).

The earliest traditions support overwhelmingly the authorship of John the apostle. Justin Martyr (c.100-165) who lived at Ephesus within a generation of John gives unquestioning testimony to John the apostle as writer. Irenaeus (c.175-195), a native of Smyrna who had listened to Polycarp, a disciple of John, gives a like testimony. Relatively recent discoveries (1945) in papyrus documents from Egypt (dated c.150), quote 1:19 and then claim that this was written by "John the brother of James, these who were the sons of Zebedee". Many other early writers, amongst whom is Clement of Alexandria (200) and Origen (233), testify to the fact that John was accepted as the author from the earliest records available. There is no record of any dissenting voice until the third century when Dionysius of Alexandria (died c.264) raised a doubt as to the apostolic authorship on the ground of the dissimilarity of language between John's Gospel and Epistles and this book. There is a suspicion that Dionysius was not entirely without prejudice in his judgment for he bitterly opposed the majority of teachers of his day who believed in a literal millennial reign of Christ. It is not uncharitable to suggest that the clear teaching of this book as to a literal millennium may have had something to do with his raising a question as to the authorship. His main point was that its difference in language from the Gospel of John, as well as a different presentation of some theological concepts, show that it could not have been written by the writer of the Gospel of John. He first suggested that the writer could have been John Mark (Acts 13:5) but then appears to dismiss his own suggestion on the ground that John Mark did not go with Paul and Barnabas into Asia. Many modern commentators, using the same arguments as Dionysius, favour an old conjecture of Eusebius of Caesarea, the church historian (who died c.339), that the writer was probably John the Elder. This is based on a very doubtful remark by Papias (died c.130) who appeared to distinguish between John the Apostle and John the Elder in the assembly at Ephesus and secondly, very dubious archaeological evidence posing the possibility of two tombs in Ephesus with the name "John" on them. R.H. Mounce sums the matter up when he writes, "It is difficult to see how a single reference in an obscure fragment can supply any convincing basis for establishing authorship". It might be added in confirmation that history knows nothing of John the Elder and recent scholarship supports the traditional claim that this book came through John the apostle.

That there are differences in vocabulary, style and very particularly, in grammatical structures, is certainly true. The Gospel is written in very exact Greek while there are many divergences from accepted grammatical structures in Revelation. This argument has the inherent flaw that it insists that an author writes in a particular pattern no matter what his subject. Competent scholars have argued convincingly that while the five writings from the hand of John have striking differences they all have very striking similarities and that they all have come from the same geographical, cultural and theological background. R.H. Charles argues that John's Greek, for all its idiosyncrasy, is not ungrammatical, but has a grammar of its own, unparalleled in any other ancient writing, but nonetheless real and consistent, the hybrid grammar of a man thinking in Hebrew while writing in Greek (ICC p.cxvii). G.B. Caird builds on this argument and writes, "Because a man writes in Hebraic Greek, it does not inevitably follow that this is the only Greek he is capable of writing. He may have adopted this style quite deliberately for reasons of his own" (Black's *N.T. Commentaries* p.5). It may be suggested that John adopted this difference in style to deal with the difference in the nature of his book of Revelation and because of the vision style in which it is given to Him. G.B. Caird writes again, "John's Greek may be all his own, but it is not the product of incompetence, for he handles it with brilliant lucidity and compelling power, so that it cannot be held accountable for any of our difficulties of comprehension".

Other scholars have pointed out the strong correspondence between matters raised in the Gospel and this book. The word *logos* used only by John as a title of Christ (John 1:1, 14; 1 Jn 1:1) is used again of Christ in 19:13. The prophecy of Zech 12:10 is quoted in John 19:37 and in 1:7 and uses the same Greek word for "pierced" (*ekkenteō*) which is neither used in the LXX at Zech 12:10 nor elsewhere in the NT. H. B. Swete concludes an extensive survey of such correspondences with the remark that, "The evidence creates a strong presumption of affinity between the fourth gospel and the Apocalypse" (p.cxxx). The internal evidence supported by unusually strong and very early external evidence leaves no doubt that the writer of this final book of the Bible is John the apostle, son of Zebedee and disciple of Christ.

2. The Date of the Book

There are only two dates that have merited serious consideration for this book: an early date just after the reign of Nero (54-68) and a date a generation later near the end of the reign of Domitian (81-96).

The proposed early date has been based on the following assumptions:

1. that the persecution of believers in which John shared (1:9) refers to the Neronian persecution and that his banishment was in that reign.
2. that the references to the deadly wound of the beast (13:3) incorporate the *Nero redivivus* myth in which a revived Nero would be the incarnation of the evil genius of the Roman Empire.
3. that the beast was the symbolisation of the Roman Empire and its Caesar.
4. that Babylon was the code-name for Rome in the first century.
5. That the measurement of the temple (11:1-2) demanded a literal temple in Jerusalem so this would have to take place before its destruction in 70 AD.

The external evidence for this early date is virtually non-existent depending almost solely on a casual reference in the Muratorian Fragment (170-190) which claimed that Paul wrote to seven churches on the pattern of the messages to the seven churches in this book – thus placing its writing before Paul's Epistles. Support for this early date is confined now to expositors who propose a "preterist" interpretation (see under *Interpretation*) for the book and who insist that it has had its fulfilment in the history of the first century.

The later date of 96 AD near the end of the reign of Domitian has overwhelming support both internally and from writings that are almost contemporary with it.

The earliest reference is in the writing of Irenaeus (c.185), the friend of Polycarp the disciple of John, who when writing of the Apocalypse says, "For it was seen, not long ago, but almost in our generation, near the end of Domitian's reign". Since Domitian reigned from 81-96 this places the date around 96. The internal evidence in support of this date may be summarised as follows:

1. Persecution is affecting the churches in Asia (1:9) and further imperial persecution is expected (2:10). Apart from sporadic attacks on the christians in Rome under Claudius and then under Nero, there was no general persecution of Christians throughout the empire until the reign of Domitian.
2. John has been banished to Patmos. While various Roman emperors had used *relegatio* (banishment) to deal with political opponents, Domitian appears to be the first to use it against christians and also to use the isle of Patmos as a location. A very strong tradition, quoted by Clement of Alexandria (c.155-c220), insists that during the reign of Domitian John was banished to Patmos, and the same tradition claims that on the death of Domitian (96) John was released and returned to Ephesus and died there as a very old man.
3. It is probable that churches in the Roman province of Asia were founded about 50 AD or within the following decade. The degeneration and departure revealed in Christ's letters to those churches (chs. 2-3) would require some time to develop. It is unlikely that these conditions could have developed so rapidly as to require such scathing rebuke by the Lord as early as c.68.

There is no doubt that the weight of internal and external evidence supports a date of around 96 for the writing and distribution of this book. There is also no doubt that this late date and the authority of John, the last of the apostolic company, contributed to the wide distribution and early recognition of the book. Each of the seven churches would have served as a distribution centre for its area. With the darkening skies of imperial persecution its message would have been most relevant and would have meant that copies would circulate quickly far beyond pro-consular Asia. R.H. Mounce concludes a wide-ranging survey of the spread of the book with the words, "By the close of the second century the Apocalypse had circulated throughout the empire and was widely accepted both as Scripture and as the product of the apostle John" (p.38).

3. The Purpose of the Book

a. The Prophetic

The words of H. B. Swete are often quoted with approval: "In form it is an epistle, containing an apocalyptic prophecy; in spirit and inner purpose, it is pastoral" (p.xv). While there is considerable truth in this statement it should not be forgotten that the main purpose of the book is given in the opening words, "to shew unto his servants the things which must shortly come to pass". In other words the main thrust of the book is prophetic and, as the final book in the NT, it gives detail of events yet to take place on earth. That these events centre on the person of Christ is made clear in the introductory words, "The revelation of Jesus Christ". Around Him unfold matters related to the churches (chs. 2-3), the cosmos (4:1-19:10), the conquest (19:11-20:15) and the consummation (21:1-22:5), and as He Himself is "unveiled" the future is unfolded. In the first century to be associated with Christ meant to be treated in your own land as an alien with the possible loss of position and property, even of life itself, as the inevitable consequence. This book shows to believers, not only to those of the first century but to believers of all ages, that when the future is taken into account, nothing can be lost by their link with Christ; infinite gain is the result and the future holds only glory for believers. God has a plan and programme that "must shortly come to pass" – it is this that is made known in this book. The revelation in this book completes the NT writings with the unfolding of God's programme for earth.

b. The Pastoral

Faith grasps this revelation granted by God to Christ, and through the angel to John for the church; this will necessarily have pastoral implications in the message it brings to believers. That message will include both comfort and challenge. At the close of the first century the believers were learning by bitter experience the truth of the words of the Lord in the upper-room (John 15:19 R.V.), "If ye were of the world, the world would love its own: but because ye are not of the world, but I chose you out of the world, therefore the world hateth you". The tolerance with which Rome had treated the early church soon changed to suspicion as Jewish leaders attempted to bring charges of treason against Paul and the Christians in general. Slanderous attacks by those identified with "the synagogue of Satan" (2:9;3:9) stirring up the magisterial arm of imperial Rome from early in the reign of Nero had led to the deaths of a multitude of martyrs including Peter and Paul. The Caesar-cult from the days of Augustus and seen particularly in Domitian in the time of John had spread throughout the empire. The Christians were now treated as enemies of the state, subversives who must be eliminated. Under these circumstances it is clear what comfort this book would bring since it shows that:

i. Christ despised and hated now, would return triumphantly to reign on earth;

ii. the Christians, despised and few in number now, would share in this triumph of Christ;

iii. While Rome appeared so world-dominating and all-powerful there would arise another Empire with a mightier than Caesar at its head which would be overthrown by this triumphant Christ;
iv. The kingdom that Christ would establish would last for one thousand years;
v. Even the millennial kingdom, glorious as it would be, would be only the introduction to a state of bliss in a new heaven and a new earth which would be eternal.

While there was infinite comfort in this glorious unfolding of the future for the believers, there was also an inescapable challenge. Despite the growing hostility of the world there were still those who would have sought accommodation with that world. Whether in the church age, as shown in chs. 2-3 in Christ's messages to the churches, or in the tribulation age to follow, this book carries uncompromising warnings against lack of separation from the world. Those who are identified with the world must share its doom; in fact those who do not overcome in their circumstances in the church age will prove that they are but professors, having "a name to live" (3:1), and not possessors of eternal life; they will remain for the judgments on earth after Christ comes for the church. The challenge in the tribulation time is that those who take the mark of the Beast (14:9-10) must share his doom. Thus in the pastoral purpose there is both comfort and challenge.

c. The Theological

Another purpose can be discerned quite clearly in the book. The prophecies that permeate Scripture would have been left without a final consummation if this revelation had not been given. Prophecies concerning the "seed of the woman" (Gen 3:15), "the star out of Jacob" (Num 24:17), "the sceptre of thy kingdom" (Ps 45:6) relating to Christ would not have been brought into clear focus as to the time of their fulfilment. The prophecies relating to Israel as to their missionary purpose, their divine preservation, their period of terrible tribulation and their final restoration would have been left to raise many unanswerable questions. This book consummates the ministry of Isaiah, Jeremiah, Ezekiel and indicates how their words had a meaning far beyond their own apprehension. In a very special way Revelation completes what God has intended for men from Genesis – without this book the edifice of Scripture would be without its "top-stone". In particular the book of Genesis, the book of "beginnings", would be left incomplete; matters introduced in that book would be left without their final outcome. For illustration some of these matters may be listed thus:

	In Genesis	In Revelation
1.	Paradise is closed to man	Paradise is opened to man
2.	Man is barred from the tree of life	Tree of life is available to man
3.	Sin entered bringing sorrow and pain	Sin banished with sorrow and pain

4.	The first murderer, drunkard and rebel appear	The last murderer, drunkard and rebel are banished
5.	The first tears are shed	The last tear is wiped away
6.	The curse enters and brings death	The curse is removed and death is banished
7.	Satan enters the world stage	Satan banished to the lake of fire.

To turn the pages of this final book of the Bible is to see all the divine purposes of God fulfilled with reference to heaven and earth where His Son and His saints will share eternal glory. The full revelation of deity has been unfolded and the record of Scripture closes with God "all in all" (1 Cor 15:28).

4. Interpretation of the Book

The interpretation of any document or writing demands certain basic rules that apply automatically as the writing is studied; it is on the application of these basic rules that understanding depends. These rules, or "hermeneutics", are applied every time a book or document is read.

Grammatical interpretation demands the study of the words used and the sentence structure (syntax) in which thoughts are presented. Unless the grammatical structure is correctly interpreted the final interpretation will not reveal the meaning intended by the author. The reader has no right to impose his own understanding of the grammar; this is established by the author in his date and culture.

Historical interpretation demands the study of the historical and cultural circumstances that surround the different books in the Bible and give them their own individual setting. This involves consideration of the author, the date at which he wrote, and the current meanings of the words that he used in his own time. (Etymology does not always determine the meaning of a word historically for meanings change with time.)

Theological interpretation demands that the special claim of the Bible is recognised that in fact God is its Author and, indeed, the Interpreter of His own Book.

Thus as the infallible word of God the Bible is a unit in which each individual book is an integral part and no part will contradict any other part. Furthermore, the OT and NT are related to each other as type and antitype, as prophecy and fulfilment so that each throws light upon the other. Therefore allusions and echoes of previous writings will occur and recur since the author of both testaments is the same God.

The *Golden Rule of Interpretation* (suggested by Dr. D. L. Cooper and quoted by T.F. LaHaye (p.4) is: "When the plain sense of Scripture makes common sense, seek no other sense; therefore, take every word at its primary, ordinary, usual literal meaning unless the facts of the immediate text studied in the light of related passages and axiomatic and fundamental truths indicate clearly otherwise."

When applied to Revelation this method will interpret words and numbers literally unless the context demands a figurative or symbolic sense, something that is generally apparent in the passage. It recognises figures of speech, but insists that every figure has an intended correspondence to literal facts which can be ascertained according to rules of common sense and scriptural evidence. H.A. Ironside wrote in this connection (p.13), "This book is a book of symbols. But the careful student of the Word need not exercise his own ingenuity in order to think out the meaning of the symbols. It may be laid down as a principle of first importance that every symbol used in Revelation is explained or alluded to somewhere else in the Bible".

When the golden rule of interpretation given above is not strictly observed different schemes of interpretation may be developed. This has been true of the book of Revelation; four basic modes of interpretation have resulted. These may be briefly surveyed in very general terms as follows:

a. ***The Preterist Interpretation***

The preterist ("past") approach looks upon the content of the book as factual but claims that everything in it up to ch.20 had already been fulfilled by the time of John's writing at the end of the first century. In other words, the book presents history and not prophecy. The main guidelines of this method of interpretation were set by a Spanish Jesuit priest Alcazar in 1614 but many able theologians gave it credence. F. W. Farrar (1830-1903) writes, "The Apocalypse is what it professes to be – an inspired outline of contemporary history, and of the events to which the sixth decade of the first century gave immediate rise" (quoted by G. Cohen p.16). The beasts of ch. 13 are interpreted as imperial Rome with its imperial priesthood vested in the Caesar, while the second advent of Christ is interpreted as the fall of Jerusalem in 70 AD. This was the theory that demanded an early date for the writing of the book. This kind of interpretation carries its own refutation and all who acknowledge the claim of the book to be a genuine prophecy (1:1) find little of substance in it.

b. ***The Historical Interpretation***

The historical approach, like the preterist, takes the events of the book to be real but asserts that chs. 4-19 are a prophetic unfolding of church history from the time of the apostles to the second advent. Conflicting schemes have been proposed to link history with the events of the book but one common element in most of these schemes is that Babylon is interpreted not only as pagan Rome but as papal Rome. This meant that Luther, Calvin and many of the reformers came to adopt this view. The basic problem of this mode of interpretation is that the world-dominating period in the career of the beast lasts only 1260 days. To deal with this fatal limitation the theory, without the slightest warrant from Scripture, changes the 1260 days into a similar number of years. A. Barnes (p.244) makes the 5 months of the locust plague (9:1-11) last 150 years. Such schemes reveal great ingenuity, but the large variety of possible interpretations and the arbitrary nature of them means that few present-day expositors give much weight to the interpretation.

c. ***The Topical Interpretation***

This is sometimes called the Idealist Method or the Cyclic Method. Like the historicist approach this method understands the book to cover all of church history but differs from it in that it sees in chs. 4-19 a series of parallel visions each presenting an aspect of church history and climaxing in the second advent of Christ. In other words the method does not present the prediction of specific historical events but sets forth timeless truths in the battle between good and evil throughout the church age and leading up to the return of Christ to earth in conquest. This method is also sometimes referred to as the "spiritualising" or "allegorising" method as, of necessity, it must treat everything as symbolic and look for a non-literal meaning behind the visions. Like the preterist and historical interpretations the fatal weakness of this method is that it places the church on earth during the tribulation period to endure the "wrath of the Lamb" (6:17) when many Scriptures make it plain that the church will not face such wrath (Rom 5:9; 1 Thess 1:9, 10; 5:9). While appealing to a certain type of mystical mind and while emphasising certain spiritual truths there is no scriptural foundation for interpretation of this kind.

d. ***The Futurist Interpretation***

The futurist interpretation sees that the key to the book is given by Christ in 1:19 when He commanded John to write:

i. The things which thou hast seen – a reference to the vision of Christ (ch. 1)

ii. The things which are – a reference to Christ's messages to the churches (chs. 2-3)

iii. The things which shall be hereafter – a reference to things occurring after the church age (chs. 4-22)

Using this key given by Christ it becomes clear that only chs. 2-3 cover the church age and the whole of the book from ch. 4 onwards describes the happenings after the church has been removed from earth. Chs. 6-19 describe particularly events during the seven-year tribulation period leading up to the return of Christ to earth as Sovereign.

It will be shown in the commentary that this futurist view offers:

i The only scheme of interpretation where the grammatical-historical-theological golden rule of interpretation given above can be employed throughout without special pleading. In fact Scripture is allowed to mean exactly what it states without "spiritualisation" or "allegorisation".

ii The only feasible explanation that incorporates the OT and NT prophecies in perfect harmony and confirms the basic truth of the consummation character of this last book of the Bible. While there have been partial fulfilments and foreshadowings of many OT prophecies, it is only in the future events described in this book that they find their complete fulfilment, many of them in the seven-year tribulation preceding the coming of Christ to earth.

iii The only logical explanation of the chronological phases that mark the onward movement of the book expressions such as "after these things" (4:1) which will be shown to give the sequence of the future events.

The application of the golden rule of hermeneutics to this book has led to the acceptance of the futurist interpretation as the only possible scheme to fit the evidence presented. However among those who accept the futurist position three distinct groups of expositors emerge, depending on their interpretation of the millennial reign of Christ and the relation of the rapture of the church to that reign. The three basic positions are as follows:

i *The Amillennialist teaching*

Discarding one of the cardinal precepts of the golden rule of biblical hermeneutics amillennialists teach that there will be no literal reign of Christ on earth (the *a* before "millennialist" negatives the concept). Augustine of Hippo (354-430) rejected the scriptural teaching on the imminent return of Christ and refused to believe in a literal reign of Christ on earth for a thousand years. He believed that the millennium was the present age between the first and second comings of Christ, and that when Christ comes it will be to introduce a general resurrection and a general judgment followed by the commencement of the eternal state. He further taught that Satan had been bound at the cross. Faced with the reality of sin, paganism and unbelief and recognising that there was neither universal peace nor righteousness on earth, he spiritualised all the promises and prophecies into the blessings enjoyed by the church in this age. He taught that Israel, because of their rejection of Christ, were under the curse of God and there could never be any national recovery or restoration.

Changes have taken place in amillennialism since the time of Augustine but it still remains basically the teaching of the Roman Catholic church and, embraced by the reformers, it passed into the majority of protestant denominations; many evangelical christians have accepted its tenets. It has no place for the rapture of the church and insists that the coming of Christ has only one stage – His coming to earth.

ii *The Postmillennialist teaching*

This view of the millennium may best be presented in the words of a contemporary post-millennialist teacher (Lorainc Boettner): "Post-millennialism is that view of last things which holds that the Kingdom of God is now being extended in the world through the preaching of the gospel and the saving work of the Holy Spirit, that the world eventually will be christianised, and that the return of Christ will occur at the close of a long period of righteousness and peace commonly called the millennium .... It should be added that on post-millennial principles the second coming of Christ will be followed immediately by the general resurrection, the general judgment, and the introduction of heaven and hell in their fulness". This view was popularised by Daniel Whitby (1638-1726) as a reaction against liberalism and humanism and while rejected by the Anglican Church (his books were burned as heretical) it gained widespread acceptance. It is clear that post-millennialism has no room for the rapture or for the distinction that Scripture makes between Israel and the church. Two world wars have served to show the error of such teaching and post-millennialism is no longer widely taught.

iii *The Premillennialist teaching*

Standing in contrast to either the denial of a literal millennium in amillennialism or its introduction by means of gospel preaching as in post-millennialism is premillennialism. This was, in fact, the clear teaching of the early centuries of church history down to the time of Augustine (4th century). This presents the scriptural fact that the promised kingdom will be established in Christ's dramatic return to earth with the violent overthrow of the armies of Satan (19:11-21). The millennial kingdom thus established will be of a period of exactly one thousand years, when Christ and His saints will rule on earth from His capital city of Jerusalem. Israel as a nation will be reconciled to God and be the leading nation on earth. Peace and righteousness will be evident in the changed environment of earth; all the OT promises to Israel and the nations will be literally fulfilled. There will be no open sin permitted and the whole earth will be filled with the knowledge of God.

On the same principle of interpretation, it is asserted that the church will be removed from earth at the rapture before both the millennium and also the tribulation as summarised in the following statements:

1. Christ will come to earth literally and personally with power and great glory to establish His thousand-year kingdom on earth (Isa 2:2-4; Dan 2:44; 7:13, 14; Matt 25:31-46).
2. Before this happens there will be a seven-year period of tribulation to fulfil the seventieth week of Daniel (Dan 9:24-27). Israel in particular and the nations in general will suffer the providential, the retributive and the penal judgments from God in these years (Jer 30:4-7; Dan 7:7, 8, 15-28; 8:23-25; 9:20-27; Matt 24:3-31; John 5:23; 2 Thess 2:1-12). This will be described on earth as the day of the Lord.

3. Before the tribulation Christ will come for His church and remove her from earth (1 Thess 4:12-18) to heaven where the day of Christ ensues which includes the judgment seat and the marriage ceremony of Christ and the church. Christ brings His church with Him on His return to earth and she shares the millennial reign with Him.

5. Bibliography

a. ***Vocabulary and Grammar***

1. Abbott-Smyth *A Manual Greek Lexicon of the NT* 3rd Edition Clark T & T Edinburgh.
2. Berry G.R. *A Dictionary of NT Greek Synonyms*. 1979. Zondervan.
3. Bauer, Arndt and Gingrich *A Greek-English Lexicon of the NT* 10th impression. Cambridge
4. Dana and Mantey *A Manual Grammar of the Greek NT* S.P.C.K. London. 1928.
5. Hanna R.A. *Grammatical Aids to the Greek NT* 1980 Edition, Baker Book House.
6. Kittel and Friedrich *Theological Dictionary of the NT* (one volume edition). 1990. Eerdman's
7. Louw J.P. and Nida E.A. *Greek-English Lexicon of the NT* UBS 1988
8. Rienecker *The Linguistic key to the Greek NT* Reprint 1980 by Zondervan. – cited as Rienecker
9. Robertson A.T. *A Grammar of the Greek NT in the Light of Historical Research*. 4th Edition Broadman Press, Nashville.
10. Robertson A.T. and Davis W.H. *A New Short Grammar of the Greek NT* 10th Edition, Baker Book House.
11. Robertson A.T. *Word Pictures in the NT* 1933 reprint. Broadman Press.
12. Trench R.C. *Synonyms of the NT* MacMillan & Co. 1865.
13. Vincent M.R. *Word Studies in the NT* 1946 reprint. W. B. Eerdman's Pub. Co.
14. Vine W.E. *An Expository Dictionary of NT Word*s Oliphants 1952 – cited as Vine.
15. White W. *Theological and Grammatical Phrasebook of the Bible*, 1984 Moody Press.
16. Wilson W. *Old Testament Word Studies* Kregel 1978.

b. ***History***

1. Anderson Sir R. *The Coming Prince* Kregel 16th Ed. 1967
2. Broadbent E.H. *The Pilgrim Church*. Marshall Pickering (1931) 1985 reprint
3. Bruce F.F. *The Dawn of Christianity* Paternoster Press 1950
4. Bruce F.F. *The Growing Day* Paternoster Press 1950

5. Bruce F.F. *Light in the West* Paternoster Press 1950
6. Cunliffe Barry *Rome and her Empire* BCA Press 1994 Ed
7. Eusebius *An Ecclesiastical History* (translated by C.F. Cruse) S. Bagster 1838
8. Ferguson J. *The Religions of the Roman Empire* Thames and Hudson 1970 (1982 Reprint)
9. Frend W.H.C. *The Early Church* SCM Press Reprint 1994
10. Grant Michael *The Fall of the Roman Empire* Nelson and Sons Ltd. London 1976
11. Hislop A. *The Two Babylons*. Paternoster, London 1903
12. Kuiper B.K. *The Church in History.* W. B. Eerdmans Pub. Co. (1951) 1989 reprint
13. Latourette K.S. *A History of the Expansion of Christianity (7 vols)*. Paternoster 1971 Ed.
14. Latourette K.S. *A History of the Christianity in the 19th and 20th Century (5 vols.)* Paternoster 1970.
15. Massie Allan *The Caesars* Cardinal Press 1983
16. Miller A. *Miller's Church History (3 vols.)* Pickering and Inglis (undated)
17. Newton B.W. *Babylon and Egypt. Their Future History and Doom* S.G.A.T. 1890
18. Pember G.H. *The Antichrist, Babylon and the Coming of the Kingdom*. Schottle Pub. Co.
19. Pember G.H. *Mystery Babylon the Great*. Schoettle Pub. Co. Miami Springs (reprint 1988)
20. Salmon E.T. *A History of the Roman World* (30BC to AD138) Methuen, 6th Ed. 1968
21. Smith M.A. *From Christ to Constantine* IVP 1971
22. Smith M.A. *The Church under Siege* IVP 1976
23. Suetonius *The Twelve Caesars* (translated by Robert Graves) revised and illust. 1979
24. Wand J.W.C. *A History of the Early Church to AD500*. Routledge reprint 1994
25. Westcott B.F. *The Two Empires* Macmillan and Co. 1909 Ed.
26. Woodrow R. *Babylon, Mystery Religion.* R. W. Evangelistic Association 1981

c. ***The Seven Churches***

1. Barclay W. *Letters to the Seven Churches* SCM Press 1957
2. Davies J.M. *The Lord and the Churches* Pickering and Inglis Ltd. 1967
3. Grant F.W. *The Prophetic History of the Church* Loizeaux Bros (undated)
4. Hemer C.J. *The Letters to the Seven Churches of Asia in their Local Setting* Sheffield Academic Press (reprint 1989)
5. Morgan G.C. *The Letters of our Lord* Pickering and Inglis (undated)
6. Ramsay W.M. *The Letters to the Seven Churches of Asia* Hodder and Stoughton 1904

7. Smith Hamilton *The Addresses to the Seven Churches* Central Bible Truth Depot, London.
8. Stott John *What Christ thinks of the Church* Word Publishing 1990
9. Tatford F.A. *The Patmos Letters* Prophetic Witness Publishing House 1969
10. Trench R.C. *The Seven Churches in Asia* Macmillan 1867

d. ***General Commentaries***

That the following have been consulted or quoted on various points does not confer approval on the teaching of the commentary in general.

1. Alford H. *The Greek New Testament* (Vol. 4) Moody Press 1958
2. Baines T.B. *The Revelation of Jesus Christ* G. Morrish 5th Ed. 1911
3. Barnhouse D.G. *Revelation – an Expository Commentary* Zondervan 1971 (Reprint 1985)
4. Beckwith I.T. *The Apocalypse of John* Baker Book House, Reprint 1967
5. Benson E.W. *The Apocalypse* Macmillan & Co. 1990
6. Bullinger E.W. *Commentary on Revelation* Kregel Publications Reprint 1984
7. Caird G.B. *The Revelation of St John the Divine* Black's NT Commentaries 2nd Ed 1984
8. Coates C.A. *An Outline of the Revelation* Stow Hill Bible and Tract Depot (undated)
9. Cohen G.G. *Understanding Revelation* Moody Press 1978
10. Criswell W.A. *Expository Sermons on Revelation* Zondervan. One volume printing 1969
11. Dake F.J. *Revelation Expounded* Dake Bible Sales, Georgia. Enlarged Edition 1950
12. Darby J.N. *Synopsis of the Books of the Bible* Stow Hill Bible and tract Depot. 1943
13. Dunnett W.M. *Revelation – God's Final Word to Man* Meridian Publication 1991
14. Eller Vernard *The Most Revealing Book in the Bible* Eerdmans 1974 (reprint 1975)
15. Ellul J. *Apocalypse – The Book of Revelation* The Seabury Press. N.Y. 1977
16. Flanigan J. *Notes on the Revelation* Gospel Tract Publications. Glasgow 1987
17. Gaebelein A.C. *The Revelation Our Hope* Press (undated)
18. Govett R. *The Apocalypse Expounded by Scripture* Charles J. Thynne 1920
19. Grant F.W. *Revelation The Numerical Bible* Vol. 7 Loizeaux Bros. 1932
20. Grant F.W. *The Revelation of Jesus Christ* Loizeaux Bros (undated)
21. Hadjiantoniou G.A. *The Postman of Patmos* Zondervan 1961
22. Heading John *From Now to Eternity* Everyday Publications Inc. Toronto 1978
23. Hendriksen W. *More Than Conquerors* The Tyndale Press (1940) 1969 Reprint

24. Hughes P.E. *The Book of the Revelation* IVP 1990
25. Hoste W. *The Visions of John the Divine* John Ritchie Ltd. (undated)
26. Ironside H.A. *Revelation* Loizeaux Bros. 1920 (38th reprinting 1987)
27. Jardine S. *The Unsealed Book* John Ritchie Ltd. Kilmarnock 1966
28. Jennings F.C. *Studies in Revelation* Bible Truth Press, New York 1937
29. Johnston A.F. *Revelation* Bible Study Commentary. Zondervan 1983
30. Kelly W. *Lectures on the Book of Revelation*. Morrish (undated but c. 1886)
31. Ladd G.E. *A Commentary on the Revelation of John* Eerdmans Pub. Co. Reprint 1991
32. Lang G.H. *The Revelation of Jesus Christ* The Paternoster Press 1948
33. Lange J.P. *Commentary on the Holy Scriptures* Zondervan 1958
34. Larkin C. *Book of Revelation* Printed by E.W. Moyer Co. Philadelphia 1919
35. LaHaye T.F. *The Revelation of Jesus Christ* Zondervan 1973
36. Lincoln W. *The Book of the Revelation* Pickering and Inglis (undated)
37. Mauro P. *Of Things Which Soon Must Come to Pass* Reiner publications 1971
38. Morris H.M. *The Revelation* Record Tyndale House publications. 4th reprint 1986
39. Morris L. *Revelation* The Tyndale NT Commentaries. IVP 2nd Ed. 1987
40. Mounce R.H. *The Book of Revelation* The New International Commentary of the NT Eerdmans 1977
41. McDowell E.A. *The Meaning and Message of the Book of Revelation* Broadman Press. 1951
42. Newell W.R. *The Book of Revelation* World Bible Publishers 1935 (Reprint 1987)
43. Newton B.W. *Thoughts on the Apocalypse* Sovereign Grace Advent Testimony (1904)
44. Nicholl W.R. *The Expositor's Greek Testament (Vol. V)* Eerdmans 1967
45. Ottman F.C. *The Unfolding of the Ages* Kregel Publications (1905) Reprint 1967
46. Page J.B.D. *Christ in the Apocalypse* Gospel Tract Publications, Glasgow 1991
48. Phillips John *Exploring Revelation* Moody Press 1987 reprint
47. Pentecost J.D. *Things to Come* Zondervan 6th printing 1969
49. Scott W. *Exposition of the Revelation of Jesus Christ* Pickering and Inglis Ltd (undated)
50. Scroggie W.G. *The Great Unveiling* Zondervan 1979
51. Seiss J.A. *The Apocalypse* Marshall, Morgan and Scott. (15th Ed. undated)
52. Smith J.B. *A Revelation of Jesus Christ* Herald Press, Scottdale 1961
53. Still W.A. *A Vision of Glory* Bell and Bain Ltd, Glasgow 1987
54. Strauss L. *The Book of Revelation* Loizeaux Bros. 1964 (Reprint 1987)
55. Swete H.B. *The Apocalypse of St. John* Kregel Publications 1980 reprint

56. Tatford F.A. *The Final Encounter* Christian Outreach Book Centre 1983
57. Tatford F.A. *Prophecy's Last Word* Pickering and Inglis 1947
58. Tenney M.C. *Interpreting Revelation* Pickering and Inglis Ltd. 1958
59. Tenney M.C. *The New Testament – a Historical and Analytic Survey* IVP 1954
60. Thomas R.L. *Revelation – An Exegetical Commentary* (2 vols.) Moody Press 1992
61. Thompson J.L. *That Glorious Future* Morgan and Scott (undated)
62. Tregelles S.P. *Remarks on the Prophetic Verses in the Book of Daniel* Seventh Ed. 1965 Sovereign Grace Advent Testimony
63. Tucker W.L. *Studies in Revelation* Kregel 1980
64. Vigeveno H.S. *In the Eye of the Apocalypse* Regal Books Ca. USA 1990
65. Walvoord J.F. *The Revelation of Jesus Christ* Moody Press 1966
66. Welch C.H. *This Prophecy – an Exposition of the Book of Revelation* Berean Pub. Trust
67. Wilcock M. *The Message of the Revelation* The Bible Speaks Today IVP 1975
68. Zahn T. *Introduction to the NT (Vol. 3)* Klock and Klock reprint

6. Outline

I.	*Prologue*	
	Christ Communicating	1:1-8
II.	*Vision 1: Christ and the Churches*	1:9-3:22
	Christ Lives – The Priest	
	1. The Writer Introduced	1:9-11
	2. The Christ Revealed	1:12-20
	3. The Messages to the Churches	2:1-3:22
III.	*Vision 2: Christ and the Cosmos*	4:1-19:10
	Christ Acts – The Lamb	
	1. The Throne Scene in Heaven	4:1-5:14
	2. The First Six Seals Opened	6:1-17
	3. The First Parenthesis	7:1-17
	4. The Seventh Seal	8:1-5
	5. The First Six Trumpets	8:6-9:21
	6. The Second Parenthesis	10:1-11:13
	7. The Seventh Trumpet	11:14-19
	8. The Third Parenthesis	12:1-14:20
	9. The Seven Bowls Poured Out	15:1-16:21
	10. The Fourth Parenthesis	17:1-19:10

IV.	*Vision 3: Christ Conquering*	19:11-20:6
	Christ Comes – The Sovereign	
	1. The Revelation of the King	19:11-21
	2. The Establishment of the Kingdom	20:1-6
	3. The End of Earth History	20:7-15
V.	*Vision 4: Christ in Consummation*	21:1-22:5
	Christ Reigns – The Throne of God and The Lamb	
	1. The New Creation	21:1-8
	2. The New City	21:9-22:5
VI.	*Epilogue: Christ Challenging*	22:6-21
	Christ Speaks – The Morning Star	
	1. Human Responsibility	22:6-11
	2. Divine Reward	22:12-17
	3. Spiritual Responsibility	22:18-21

Text and Exposition

CHAPTER 1

I. The Prologue (1:1-8)
Christ Communicating

v.1 "The Revelation of Jesus Christ, which God gave unto him, to shew unto his servants things which must shortly come to pass; and he sent and signified it by his angel unto his servant John:
v.2 Who bare record of the word of God, and of the testimony of Jesus Christ, and of all things that he saw.
v.3 Blessed is he that readeth, and they that hear the words of this prophecy, and keep those things which are written therein: for the time is at hand.
v.4 John to the seven churches which are in Asia: Grace be unto you, and peace, from him which is, and which was, and which is to come; and from the seven Spirits which are before his throne;
v.5 And from Jesus Christ, who is the faithful witness, and the first begotten of the dead, and the prince of the kings of the earth. Unto him that loved us, and washed us from our sins in his own blood,
v.6 And hath made us kings and priests unto God and his Father; to him be glory and dominion for ever and ever. Amen.
v.7 Behold, he cometh with clouds; and every eye shall see him, and they also which pierced him: and all kindreds of the earth shall wail because of him. Even so, Amen.
v.8 I am Alpha and Omega, the beginning and the ending, saith the Lord, which is, and which was, and which is to come, the Almighty."

1. *The Introduction*
1:1-2

(a) *The Subject of the Book*

The first three words of the Greek text give the inspired title of the book and are the divine introduction to the following chapters. The words are "The Revelation of Jesus Christ". The word *apokalupsis* simply means the removal of a veil or covering and could readily be translated "unveiling" or "uncovering". The NT usage includes both an uncovering to the mind, as in Rom 16:25, and an uncovering to the physical eye, as will be the case when Christ is revealed at His second coming (1 Cor 1:7; 2 Thess 1:7; 1 Pet 1:7,13). Necessarily implied in the word is the thought of the prior hiddenness of the person or truth up to the point of revelation. This book will remove the veil from Christ; first for the spiritual and mental apprehension of the believer, and then it will anticipate the moment when physically "every eye shall see him" (v.7).

It may be argued that the words "of Jesus Christ" are subjective, i.e. that Christ is the possessor of the revelation and hence is the Person giving it. In English the simple possessive would express this: Jesus Christ's revelation. There is a measure of truth in this view for Christ does act as Revealer in the book: He reveals the conditions within the churches (chs. 2-3); He opens the seals of the seven-sealed book to reveal God's judgment on earth (chs. 6-16). Nevertheless this is only part of the full truth. When all the occurrences of the phrase are examined (1 Cor 1:9-11; Gal 1:12; 1 Pet 1: 7,13) it will be clearly seen that Christ is invariably the object of the revelation. There seems no reason why this occurrence should be treated differently. Christ Himself is the glorious Person to be revealed; other attendant matters will necessarily be involved (note the reference to "the things which must shortly come to pass") but He takes the centre stage and all will be seen in relation to His Person. That the angel is seen as simply a channel through (*dia*) whom the revelation was given, supports this interpretation. The person of Christ is to be unveiled with dire consequences for this earth where men once gave Him a cross. This unveiling is the subject of the book. The One who walked as man on earth (Jesus) and who fulfilled messianic expectation (Christ) is now glorified, and the day is coming for earth when the veil will be removed and all will be compelled to acknowledge His claim. In anticipation of that day God gives a preview to His servants. The glorious person of Christ in His various relationships is its central theme: Christ in the churches; Christ in the cosmos; Christ in conflict. See pages 18-19 for breakdown. These give kaleidoscopic pictures that must stir the hearts of saints who as yet have never seen the Saviour. His greatness and glory will occupy the heart as the book is studied. The ofttimes conflicting and confusing interpretations that men have imposed on this book have frequently led believers to avoid the very reading of it. God meant it to be clear and simple; He meant it to be a revelation.

(b) *The Source of the Book*

If the subject of the book is Christ the source of the book is God. It is in perfect harmony with the perfect manhood (Jesus) and the messianic claim (Christ) that God should give to Him this revelation of how God will vindicate this earth-rejected, yet heaven-anointed Man. John in his Gospel has set forth how the Son, in perfect manhood and in keeping with redemptive purpose, acts in holy submission to the Father. The explanation of the Lord is that the Father "hath given to the Son to have life in himself" and "hath given him authority to execute judgment" (John 5:26-27). The past tenses show that these relationships are not to be linked to a particular point of time but belong to His eternal relationship as Son of the Father. Here another past tense in the statement "God gave unto him" shows that in the execution of divine purpose in redemption Christ is the recipient of a gift that He mediates manward. In these contexts the verb "give" means "to entrust". This is the revelation that God entrusted to Christ. As the perfect Mediator He now communicates it to others. In contrast with the gifts of John 5:26-27, this gift lies within His relationship with God as the dependent Man. In keeping with Phil 2:9, it is to be seen as the recognition of His completed work of redemption. The truth of dependent manhood was emphasised by the Lord Jesus Himself with regard to His doctrine (John 7:16), His works (John 14:10) and His words (John 17:8); so now in glory He is still the dependent man until the purposes of God have been fully realised on earth (1 Cor 15: 24–26). This first verse of the book shows us that the Man Jesus Christ, while despised on earth, is honoured of God and now in heaven. The glory associated with that risen Man is about to be revealed.

(c) *The Substance of the Book*

There are two verbs which sum up the substance of the book: "to shew" and "signified". These verbs deal with two things: the matter of the book – its content; and the method of the book – its communication.

The first verb "to show" (*deiknumi*) is used in the NT of both mental apprehension (Matt 16:21) and visual revelation (Matt 8:4). A study of its seven occurrences in this book will show that both the verbal and the visual are involved as the revelation of Christ unfolds.

What is to be revealed is defined in the phrase "things which must shortly come to pass". The repetition of this expression in the first verse of the epilogue (22:6) is one of the things that bind the whole book into a unitary whole. The word "must" repeated throughout the book shows that however unexpected, unforeseen and unwanted by men there is an inescapable programme that will be carried into effect. "Must" can generally be understood as "it is necessary" or "it is binding". God would alert His servants ahead of time to the events that lie in His purpose for earth.

In Dan 2:45, speaking of the coming kingdom Daniel uses the expression, "what shall come to pass hereafter". John's expression here is similar but replaces the word "hereafter" with the word "shortly" which translates the phrase *en tachei*. This phrase, which if literally translated would be "in brief (time)", is used seven times in the NT. A study of these occurrences suggests that the primary thought is not so much the proximity of the event, but the absolute certainty of the event and the rapidity of fulfilment once the action is commenced. This can be seen very clearly in Luke 18: 7-8 where the rhetorical question "And shall not God avenge his own elect though he bear long with them?" is followed by the statement "I tell you that he will avenge them speedily (*en tachei*)". Both certainty and rapidity of action are involved here. Whatever seeming delay there is, action is certain and it will be swift. It is this thought of certainty that has brought comfort to believers in all ages. The thought of imminence will come more fully into the picture when the closely-related word *tachu* is used. This word occurs seven times in this book and is always translated "quickly". The time measurements of earth are meant for men (cf. 2 Pet 3:8), nevertheless comfort is brought to tested saints by the consciousness that God has said of the events that climax the age they will be both "soon" and "sudden". The tense of the verb "come to pass" shows both the certainty and finality of the end-time events. JND's margin gives this idea in the translation "be accomplished".

The previous verb *deiknumi* has shown that the revelation in this book will be both verbal and visual. This second verb *sēmainō* will stress the method by which the revelation will be communicated, the verb is related to the noun "sign" (*sēmeion*) which is used seven times in the book. The Newberry Bible margin explains the word as "signified, made known by signs or symbols". Some expositors, building on this idea, explain the word in its English translation as if it meant "to sign-ify", that is to communicate by the use of signs. It is a little simplistic and somewhat misleading to derive from this the idea that this book is all signs and symbols. While the verb may mean this in certain contexts it is not always so as the study of the NT usage in the following passages will show: John 12:33; 18:32; 21:19; Acts 11:28; 25:27. Its more general meaning, as given by Kittel, is "to make known", "to indicate", or "to declare". W. E. Vine balances these meanings helpfully when he states with reference to this verse "where perhaps the suggestion is that of expressing by signs". It is important to keep this in mind lest we imagine the whole book is symbolic. It is certainly true that there are many symbols in the book but they are there to illuminate the meaning. It will be an axiom of interpretation that the book is to be taken literally unless clear indications are given of the use of a symbol. This preserves from human imagination.

(d) *The Servants in the Book*

Those for whom this unveiling is given are described as "his servants", strictly "his slaves". The word "servant" (*doulos*) shows believers in relation to their master, it stresses not so much their activity (this would be *diakonos*) but His authority. His absolute authority and their obedience go hand in hand. In the Roman world it was never even considered that a slave had any rights whatever, either to privacy, possessions or even his own person. It was not an unusual thing for masters to put a slave to death. For a slave to be taken into the master's confidence would have been most unusual. Yet the NT has ennobled this word in using it of the relationship of a believer to God and to Christ. In the epistles believers are called both "servants of God" (Rom 6:22; 1 Pet 2:16) and "servants of Christ" (Eph 6:6). Here a case could be made for understanding "his servants" in either way. The grammar cannot be absolutely decisive but the word order and the thought of the verse suggest that the expression should be understood as "servants of God".

(e) *The Signature of the Book*

The channel of communication from Christ to John is through (*dia*) His angel. John thus stands in the tradition of Daniel (8:16; 9:22) and Zechariah (1:9) who both received their visions through an angel intermediary. Although the angel holds a most glorious and dignified office as channel of communication for Christ, he is but a fellowservant of John (19:10; 22:9); Christ alone is the source of the revelation. The necessity of an angelic intermediary arises from the nature of the communication. As one who lay in the bosom of the Saviour, John was as near as anyone could possibly be to Christ while here on earth, and he put on record his testimony in his Gospel. In a later day, still in communication with Christ through the Holy Spirit, John communicated teaching in his Epistles. Now it is the person of Christ in the full glory of His offices on earth that is to be unveiled. Christ will be seen as Priest (chs. 2-3), as Prophet (chs. 4-19:10), and as King (19:11-22). This unveiling will take place in a series of visions and movements between earth and heaven. Such a communication requires an attendant or conducting angel or, as some have called him, an interpreting angel. *Apostellō* (translated "he sent") shows that this angel is the accredited envoy of Christ. The sending and signifying are contemporaneous; that is to say we are not to limit the activity of the angel to his specific appearances in the book; he is the agent of the whole unveiling.

The final link in the chain of communication is one spoken of as "his servant John". As the bondservant of Christ, John is the chosen amanuensis to convey this revelation to men. The line of communication is clearly set out thus: God – Jesus Christ – His angel – John – God's servants. John is mentioned by name five times altogether in the book, twice more in this chapter (vv. 4,9) and in 21:2 and 22:8. The discussion regarding the author has shown that this is John the apostle, "the disciple whom Jesus loved" of the Gospel record. The emphatic "I John" in v.9 opening the main body of the book, after the prologue, is answered by the "I Jesus" (22:16) in the epilogue as the Master sets His seal upon the work of the bondservant.

(f) *The Summary of the Book*

The "who" (v.2) has John as antecedent. The basic meaning of the verb "bare record" (*martureō*) is "to bear testimony to" (but see comment on the noun at v.5). Testimony may be borne to what is either seen or heard and John's use of the past tense is simply an epistolary aorist. Some commentators have thought that in using the aorist tense John is referring back to the Gospel that bears his name. This interpretation is not necessary. Epistolary aorists (where the writing is viewed from the reader's point of view) were commonly used to refer to the current writing (an example is seen in Gal 6:11). A number of other commentators, who insist that the aorist tense be understood very strictly, suggest that John could have added the prologue after the main body of the book was completed.

This deduction again is unnecessary. Ordinary literary convention of the day would be clearly understood by the readers.

Testimony is borne in this book to two matters: 1. the word of God; 2. the testimony of Jesus Christ. "The word of God" is frequently used in Scripture of the scriptures in general (Acts 13:5; 18:11; Rom 9:6; 1 Cor 14:36; 2 Cor 2:17; 4:2; 1 Thess 2:13 etc.). Here it is used, however, in the way that is common in the OT – of a special, specific or prophetic word from God. In 1 Sam 9:27 Samuel speaks to Saul "stand thou still a while that I may show thee *the word of God*". Many examples show the same expression used of prophetic ministry as in 1 Kings 12:22; 1 Chron 17:3. In the following verse this whole book is described as "the prophecy". This revelation conveyed to John was, indeed, the word of God for the special needs of the time and, by inference, for the needs of all subsequent time. It is suggested that the other occurrences of this expression in the book as 1:9; 6:9; 20:4 should be interpreted in the same way.

Since the "word of God" has been interpreted as showing that God is the source of the Word then, unless there is contrary evidence, "the testimony of Jesus Christ" should be treated in the same way. The phrase means therefore the testimony borne by Christ; and this is best understood as the testimony that Christ bears, not directly now as in the Gospels (Matt 24-25; Luke 17:20-38; John 14:1-6) but indirectly through John to the servants of God.

In the Greek text there is no conjunction "and" before the final phrase "all things that he saw". The RV puts an italicised "even" which thus interprets the phrase as explaining the two previous clauses. The word of God and the testimony of Christ are borne through the angel to John in the visions that are to follow. It will be noticed that the book as a whole is marked by the repetition of the verb "I saw" and descriptions of the visions will form the basis of the subject matter of the book. The verb summarises the book as a unit. In all John's writings he stresses the personal experience of which he writes. He closes his Gospel with this note (John 21:24) and opens his first epistle with the same note (1 John 1:3).

2. *The Benediction*
1:3

This last book of the Bible is unique in the special blessing it carries for those who read, hear and keep "those things which are written therein". This is the first and the most comprehensive of the seven beatitudes in the book (see 1:3; 14:13; 16:15; 19:9; 20:6; 22:7,14). While the subsequent beatitudes convey a blessing for saints in the tribulation period (14:13; 16:15; 19:9), in the millennium (20:6) or in the eternal state (22:7,14), this one carries a blessing for saints in this present dispensation. W. Lincoln comments, "Now here it is well, in the first place, to remember that the same Spirit has been pleased to encircle the whole book of Revelation with special promise of blessing to him that 'reads and keeps' it;

having placed one such promise at the beginning of its opening chapter, and the other at the very last (1:3; 22:7)". The singular "he that readeth", followed by the plural "they that hear" has doubtless in view the first century practice of one public reader in the assembly. This was Jewish synagogue practice (Luke 4:16-20; Acts 13:14,27; 15:21) which in light of Paul's instruction to Timothy "give attendance to reading" (1 Tim 4:13) seems to have been carried over into the NT assemblies. Despite the availability of copies of scripture and the general literacy today this is still a very useful practice to follow.

The statement, which reads literally "the ones hearing ... and keeping", shows that there is but one group in view. "To hear" implies not physical hearing alone, but includes a positive response on the part of the hearer. To hear responsively will make changes in the life of the believer. John is echoing the Lord's ministry in the upper room when He said, "He that hath my commandments and keepeth them, he it is that loveth me" (John 14:21). The Hebrew idiom of keeping when used with commandments (1 John 5:2) means to do them. When used with "faith" (2 Tim 4:7) it means "to preserve intact". When used as here in the statement "keep those things which are written therein" it means to allow them to direct and control the life. In the idiom of English this would be "to act and live in the light of the truths revealed". This positive response brings the promised blessing. *The Expositor's Greek Testament* has a helpful note on those responding to the word – "carefully heeding the warnings of the book, observing its injunctions and expecting the fulfilment of its predictions instead of losing heart and faith [they enjoy the blessing]".

The "things that he saw" of v.2 have become through John the "things which are written". The latter expression views the completed revelation from the reader's point of vantage. Rienecker points out that "the perfect tense stresses the state or condition and often the authority of a legal document". This book carries the authority of God and saints responding to the truth contained in it come in for special blessing. Satan has an interest in keeping saints from even reading it and a special interest in obscuring its truth.

The final sentence of the benediction gives the reason for the special blessing being attached to this book: the time of which it speaks is at hand. The season has arrived when the events of which this book speaks are imminent; in other words "impending" or about to take place without any further warning. (See note on the difference between "immediate" and "imminent".) The word "time" (*kairos*) refers not to time in general (as would *chronos*), but to a season as marked out by certain conditions. When we speak of the winter *season* we draw attention to its characteristic conditions (cold, wet, stormy); this is not the case when reference is made to winter *time*. Several grammarians have pointed out that in scripture the use of the expression "the time" takes on a special meaning. Thayer states categorically ... " *ho kairos* alone, the time when things are brought to a crisis, the decisive epoch waited for". He gives as references Mark 13:33; Luke 21:8; Rev 1:3; 22:10. With this Bauer, Arndt and Gringrich agree, giving as one meaning of the word, "One of the chief eschatological terms, *ho kairos*, the time of crisis, the last times". Prophecy up to the cross and the death, burial, resurrection and ascension of Christ has all been fulfilled. The next prophecy awaiting fulfilment is the rapture of the church which is thus imminent (i.e. it does not await the fulfilment of any intervening event). The rapture thus opens the way for the end-time events on earth. To respond to the testimony of this book is to order the life in light of these events and this carries the special blessing. The expression "at hand" (*engus*) simply means "near". The word may mean near in space (Mark 13:28-29; John 6:4) or near in time. When time is involved the preferred translation is "at hand". In many references there are eschatological overtones as in Matt 26:18; Luke 21:31; Phil 4:5; Rev 22:10. This book unfolds the impending earth crisis and it is "at hand". Those who live in the light of this truth will be blest. The intervening centuries since this was written have done nothing to lessen the imminence of the end time crisis. It is still impending and the words "shortly" and "at hand" bring it very near.

Notes

It is important that the difference between "immediate" and "imminent" in the English language be understood. "Immediate" as defined by the *Oxford English Dictionary* means "taking effect without delay". Thus an immediate return would not allow any intervening events. "Imminent", on the other hand, means "impending" – it may happen at any time. Other events may intervene but this does not affect the impending nature of the return. The coming of the Lord in the NT is presented as imminent rather than immediate. If it had been spoken of as immediate saints would have cause for disappointment as years have now run into decades and decades into centuries since the promise was given and the Lord still has not come. But the imminent return has been the hope of the church from apostolic times since it did not await the fulfilment of any intervening scriptural event. God, with events in His own hands (Acts 1:7) could have so ordered matters that the return of the Saviour could have occurred at any stage. The perfect tense of James 5:8 which can be literally translated "the coming of the Lord hath drawn nigh (*ēngiken*) – shows that with the incarnation, crucifixion, resurrection and ascension of Christ now history, the next event on the divine calendar is His coming. It does not have to be immediate but it is certainly imminent. Believers in each succeeding age enjoy the glorious anticipation of His coming. This truth of imminence demands that a moral and ethical answer be seen in the life (1 John 3:3). God designed it so. Sadly, in successive ages misinterpretation of scripture has robbed many saints of the joy and stimulus of the imminence of this glorious hope.

3. *The Salutation*
1:4-5a

Reminiscent of the greetings in the NT epistles the salutation has three elements: the author, the addressees and the greeting. John, the last survivor of the apostolic company, needs to mention nothing more than his name when he writes to the churches in Asia. To stress his apostleship would scarcely be in keeping with being called a "servant" in the first verse. A quiet dignity becomes one who has lain on the Saviour's breast and is now the channel of this revelation of Christ.

The addressees are "the seven churches of Asia". Asia is neither the continent of Asia nor what has become known in more recent history as Asia Minor. It is the Roman province of Proconsular Asia comprising at the close of the first century Phyrgia, Mysia, Caria and Lydia. The seven churches, which will be named in v.11, are located in a rough crescent in the western area of this province (see map). Intriguing questions arise immediately concerning these seven churches:

1. Why are they addressed as *the* seven churches?
2. Why are only seven churches addressed?
3. Why are these particular seven churches selected?

The answers to these questions will be considered in the comments on the final verse of this chapter (v.20).

The consistent salutation of Paul in all his letters to churches is "grace and peace". In the personal letters to Timothy and Titus he adds "mercy". Peter too uses this form of greeting to the saints. In this closing book this greeting from divine Persons becomes a benediction. It may be observed that the book in which are heard the thunderings of divine judgment on earth opens with the word "grace" that speaks of unmerited favour manward. The book in which the tramp of gathering armies is prophesied opens with the stillness of a heavenly benediction "peace". These words define the heritage of believers despite conditions around.

John is only the channel; the source of the grace and peace which comes to men is God. Three statements unfold tremendous truth concerning deity. The threefold repetition of the preposition "from" (*apo*) shows the triune God in operation in redemptive purpose. Within deity there is unity, eternity, equality with individuality. The statements may be set out as follows:

1. From (*apo*) Him which is, and which was, and which is to come (v.4b)
2. From (*apo*) the seven Spirits which are before His throne (v.4c)
3. From (*apo*) Jesus Christ … (v.5)

The Eternal Father, the Holy Spirit and the incarnate Son join in a divine benediction upon men redeemed from an earth about to be judged.

The Eternal Father: "Him which is, which was, and which is to come". This is God the Father called in Isa 9:6 "The everlasting Father". He is presented as One who transcends all time. This title reflects the truth expressed by the OT name Jehovah. The Newberry Bible footnote is illuminative: "This title corresponds with the Hebrew name "Jehovah". "Which is"; present participle which always is; which was; imperfect tense which ever was. And participle which is to come; which always is the coming one". Time is an essential and inherent feature of creation, but the Creator is outside of time. The three expressions which make up the title bring the ineffable within the realm of human thought as far as language can. When the Eternal One blesses then this is blessing indeed. The participle translated "which is to come" is not a reference to the eschatological coming but reminds earth-bound creatures that He will ever be "the coming one". The title is repeated in v.8 and, with minor variations, occurs again in 4:8; 11:17; 16:5.

The Holy Spirit: "the seven Spirits (*pneuma*) which are before the throne". If the eternity of deity is shown in the first title then the energy of deity is shown in the reference to the Holy Spirit. The word for "spirit" (*pneuma*) is twice used in scripture for angelic beings (Heb 1:7, 14) but to interpret it in this way here would be a serious mistake. Angels in this book are never described by *pneuma* but *angelos*. A far more serious objection to such an interpretation is that it is inconceivable that created beings should be joined with persons of the Godhead in the benediction of grace and peace upon men. This would place them on an equality with the Father and the Son, which is unthinkable. The reference is to the Holy Spirit in all the perfection of His person and the plenitude of His power. In subsequent passages there is explicit identification in the full statement "the seven spirits of God" (3:1; 4:5; 5:6). Reference is often made to Isa 11:2 to illustrate the seven-fold character of the ministry of the Holy Spirit: "And the Spirit of the Lord shall rest upon him, the spirit of wisdom and understanding, the spirit of counsel and might, the spirit of knowledge and of the fear of the Lord". The problem is, that unless the title itself is counted, there are only six characteristics listed. The more probable reference (pointed out by R. L. Thomas), is to Zech 4:1-10 where the "seven lamps" (see 4:5) are supplied by the oil which typifies the Holy Spirit in His ministry (Zech 4:6). This ministry is referred to again in Zech 4:10 as "those seven; they are the eyes of the Lord, which run to and fro through the whole earth". The number seven denotes perfection or completeness; it does not denote seven Holy Spirits but refers to the perfect and complete ministry of the Holy Spirit in grace or judgment. The fact that the Holy Spirit has been the bringer of grace and peace to repentant men in all the ages past is a matter of scriptural record. Now, as seen before the throne, He shares in the divine benediction ere the impending judgment bursts upon unrepentant men.

The Son: "Jesus Christ." Messianic claims have been realised in a Man who stepped into history as Jesus. In this book the public demonstration of His

Lordship earthward awaits the coming of 19:16 when He will be shown to be "King of kings and Lord of lords". His three titles which follow show, in a special way, His relationship with time. Yet time must not be unduly stressed for what He became in time He ever will be; He has taken manhood back to glory.

In the past he was "the faithful Witness". This age of realisation commenced when Christ came to earth as a witness to God and for God. The word "witness" is *martus* which in early usage meant a "witness of" an event. It soon had another facet added to its meaning and was understood as a "witness to", in the sense of testimony borne to a person or event. Very early in church history the word developed a third meaning, to describe those who witnessed faithfully for Christ up to the point of death. This is the origin of the English word "martyr". The noun is used in this sense throughout the book (2:13; 3:14; 11:3; 17:6). Antipas died for his witness (2:13) and in 17:6 the meaning is made very clear when reference is made to "the blood of the martyrs". Thus the faithful witness of Christ on earth must include His death. A full-orbed witness to deity is seen in the life and death of Christ on earth.

In the present He is "the firstbegotten of the dead" (*ho prōtotokos tōn nekrōn*). Five times in the NT the word "firstborn" (*prōtotokos*) is used of Christ. The other references are Rom 8: 29; Col 1:15, 18; Heb 1:6. In Hebrew thought, while priority in time is certainly involved the main emphasis falls on primacy of rank. This can be seen in regard to creation (Col 1:15-18) where He has priority in time: "he is before all things"; but also primacy in rank: "by him were all things created". In this passage Christ has both priority in time and primacy of rank in resurrection and redemption. The One who, because of His faithful witness for God, suffered so grievously at the hands of men, has been gloriously vindicated in resurrection. He has ascended to glory there to implement God's purposes in redemption. The first to rise from the dead He has become the pattern of that which God will do for redeemed men. He is and always will be the firstborn: all firstborn rights belong to Him.

In Col 1:18 the expression is "the firstborn from the dead" (*prōtotokos ek tōn nekrōn*) to show that His resurrection was an *out*-resurrection: others were left in the graves. This is the kind of resurrection to be enjoyed by all sharers in the first resurrection (20: 5-6). Some MSS include "from" (*ek*) in this passage, but the weight of MSS evidence is against the reading. JND does translate "from the dead" but shows in a footnote that this is an interpretation when he makes the comment "literally 'of the dead'". The idea is that of the whole class of the dead Christ is the first to be raised out of it. It is a mere quibble to point to those whom Christ while on earth restored to life (Lazarus, Jairus' daughter, the widow's son), as contradicting this statement. These individuals were restored only to life on earth, where in the normal way, they subsequently died. Biblical teaching on resurrection shows the body is not only raised from the grave but changed and fitted for a subsequent state (1 Cor 15:51-54); whether eternal bliss (the first resurrection) or eternal judgment (the final resurrection).

In relation to the future He is "the Prince of the kings of the earth". The word translated "prince" (*archōn*) is more frequently translated "ruler" in the NT. These three titles have links with Ps 89. The faithful witness echoes the words of v. 37: the firstborn, echoes the truth of v. 27 and this third title of Christ echoes again this same Psalm where God promised to one of David's line, "Also I will make him my firstborn, higher than the kings of the earth" (v. 27). Christ is this now, but His primacy will be demonstrated on earth when he comes as "King of kings and Lord of lords" (19:16). The titles show that Christ is seen as great Prophet of His God as He witnessed on earth, as great High Priest of His people in resurrection now and as the great King who comes to reign.

4. *The Doxology*
1: 5b-6

The benediction that comes from the triune God and, very particularly, the supreme glory of the Lord Jesus as the One who has brought this within reach of men evokes from John a doxology of thanksgiving. In this he not only speaks for the churches but echoes the heart cry of the redeemed of every age. The RV "to Him that loveth us" translates the present participle of the verb *agapaō* which is a better attested reading than the past participle. It is not our experience of His love that is in view, as in Gal 2:20, but the unchanging character of One who is age-abiding in His love to men. This love is the basis of the actions that are the foundation of the blessing of the redeemed. "He washed us" translates the aorist participial expression "having washed us" (*lousanti hēmas*), the vital foundational action in conversion for the cleansing of sinners. The RV reading "loosed us" gives weight to some older MSS which read *lusanti* (aorist participle of the verb *luō*, to loose). Metzger supports this reading when he writes, "The reading *lusanti* (loosed) is to be preferred because it has superior manuscript support, because it is in accord with OT imagery (e.g. Isa 40:2 LXX) and because it suits better the ideas expressed in v.6(a)". However, other textual scholars disagree on the weight of MSS evidence and point out that in transmission it is always easier to drop a letter than to add one, and for this reason, they retain the word "washed". JND translates "hath washed us".

It should also be pointed out that the Hebrew imagery of washing is certainly in Ps 51:2,7; Isa 1:16,18 while in Titus 3:5 "the washing of regeneration" conveys the same idea of complete cleansing (as in John 13:10). The once-for-all washing of Aaron (Exod 29:4) at the inauguration of the priesthood is in keeping with the idea presented in v.6a. This washing was in water and was typical. The AV is almost too literal at this point to convey the meaning in English; the "in" (en) must be taken as instrumental ("by"), not as defining the element, but as describing the means of cleansing. It cost Christ His blood to effect this essential cleansing from our sins. "Blood" refers to the value of the death of Christ applied to sinners. The reading "washed us" is therefore to be preferred.

6 The second action, based on the first, is more accurately conveyed by the translation "and he made us to be a kingdom, to be priests unto His God and Father" (R.V.). The tense points to a standing that washed sinners already possess. Echoes of Exod 19:6, a promise made to national Israel, are unmistakable: "ye shall be unto me a kingdom of priests and a holy nation". What was confined to one nation in history is dispensational now, as John becomes the spokesman for the redeemed of this age. In the same way the truth of 1 Pet 2:9 goes beyond the nation of Israel to the redeemed from all nations to make them what they have never been before, "a kingdom" owning one dominion and one ruler. *The Expositor's Greek New Testament* has a useful note on the use of the word "kingdom" here, pointing out that it may well have carried an implicit anti-Roman Empire allusion, so that believers in John's day may well have consoled themselves with the thought that "We Christians, harried and despised, are a community with a great history and a greater hope. Our connection with Christ makes us truly imperial". It should be made clear that while the picture of the past national priesthood of Israel is used to illustrate a present spiritual reality, many other scriptures make it plain that the promises to the nation of Israel are not abrogated by this use; those promises to Israel will be literally fulfilled in the millennium.

The explanatory phrase "priests unto his God and Father" shows that while the kingdom is a unit the individual citizens have access to God and act for God as priests. While priestly functions are exercised by all believers now in our worship (Heb 13:15; 1 Pet 2:5; Rom 12:2; Phil 4:18) the word "priest" is not used in the Gospels or epistles to describe believers. Its use in this book (see also 5:10; 20:6) makes it clear that the public exercise of such a function belongs to the kingdom in manifestation. Believers now enjoy access to God in priestly capacity but in the millennial kingdom will act for God in a public way. The idea is illustrated by the expression in 2 Sam 8:18, "David's sons were chief rulers" (Newberry margin reads "priests"). In the millennial day of kingdom glory all the redeemed of this age will have the majesty of kings and the ministry of priests; they will be associated both with the throne and with the temple.

To the One who accomplished such a mighty work it is fitting that notes of praise should rise. Other notes will be added in subsequent doxologies throughout the book (5:13; 7:10) but two things belong to Christ eternally. Glory, which is best defined as revealed excellence, belongs to Him intrinsically. That which is essentially personal, through incarnation and the cross is seen now to be displayed positionally and officially in kingdom glory. Dominion (*kratos*) is His essentially. Now it will be displayed manifestly. The dominion of Israel, refused when He came the first time, will be shown to belong to Him. The dominion of earth when He rules from the river to the ends of the earth (Zech 9:10) will be given to Him. Eternally He will share the eternal throne of God (22:1). Truly dominion is His!

There is no verb expressed in the doxology so it is in order, as in most translations, to supply "be", thus making the doxology a prayer or wish. It is arguably better to see this as a statement and supply "are" in the sense of "belong". To Him "glory and dominion" belong; they are His by right.

"Forever and ever" (*eis tous aiōnas tōn aiōnōn*) translates admirably an expression unknown in the classical Greek writers. It actually imitates a Hebrew idiom for a period that is undefined, a period that has no end and thus, a period that is eternal. The expression is repeated twelve times in this book (omitting the slightly variant expression in 14:11); it allows the mind to scan the unlimited vistas that lie beyond the time horizons of earth.

"Amen" occurs ten times in this book (1:6,7,18; 3:14; 5:14; 7:12 (twice); 19:4; 20:20,21). It is the transliteration into English of the Greek *amēn* and this, in turn is the transliteration of the Hebrew. In the Gospels it is used only by the Lord Jesus. John in his Gospel records the double "amen" translated "Verily, Verily" twenty five times. In the epistles it occurs at the close of prayers as a benediction. It appears to have been used congregationally to signify acquiescence with the prayer uttered (1 Cor 14:16). It thus carries the thought of "so be it". Here John is expressing the acquiescence of the whole company of saints of this dispensation.

5. *The Theme of the Book*
1:7-8

The dramatic moment to which the whole action of this book is directed, the Lord Jesus as the sovereign Lord coming to dispossess the usurper from earth (19:11-16), is summarised in this verse.

7 "Behold" is a most fitting introduction to the climactic moment here described. It is a dramatic word calling attention to something unexpected that grips the whole attention of the speaker. The unexpected revelation may be either visual or mental as the truth breaks upon the consciousness! Drama is inherent in the words – Behold! Lo! See! Look for yourself! John under direct inspiration speaks oracularly of the dramatic coming of Christ. A truth so dramatic, and so far from natural thinking demands the Lord's personal confirmation in the following statement. The word drama is not too strong for the tremendous scene unfolded. "Behold, he cometh with clouds and every eye shall see him" presents the Person of Christ with the veil removed, at the very moment of His return to earth. All in this book that precedes this moment, is but a prelude and preparation; all that follows is but a postscript. The present tense in the verb "cometh" (as in John 14:3) dramatises that moment but allows the eye of faith to fasten upon Him as if actually on the way.

"With clouds" describes the parting of the atmospheric clouds to reveal Him. This is the fulfilment of Dan 7:13-14: "I saw in the night visions, and, behold, one like the Son of man came with the clouds of heaven ... and there was given him dominion and glory, and a kingdom, that all people, nations, and languages should serve him; his dominion is an everlasting dominion, which shall not pass away, and his kingdom that which shall not be destroyed". In Acts 1:9 when the Lord Jesus was taken up was a literal cloud that shut Him from the gaze of His disciples. When He returns, the literal clouds will part to reveal the once rejected but now glorified Christ. Clouds are associated with both the rapture (1 Thess 4:17) and the manifestation. All seven references to clouds (*nephelē*) in this book (1:7; 10:1; 11:12; 14:14 (twice); 14:15,16) are to be taken literally. The only NT reference where "cloud" would seem to be used metaphorically is in Heb 12:1 where it is not this word *nephelē* but a synonym *nephos* which is used (see Thayer).

The scriptures that refer to the rapture of the church (John 14:1-4; 1 Thess 4:13-18; 1 Cor 15:50-58) give no indication that anyone other than the raptured saints will see the Saviour. This moment of manifestation to earth is entirely different. "Every eye shall see him" embraces every eye on earth at that moment; the veil that now hides Him from men will be removed and He will be shown to be "King of kings and Lord of lords" (19:16). This is the climax to which the book moves: the unveiling of Jesus Christ.

There is, however, one particular nation of earth for whom this will be a specially traumatic moment. They are spoken of as "they also which pierced him". The inclusion of the italicised "also" in the AV is an attempt to convey the idea, implicit in the word order, of this one nation being singled out for particular mention. The "and" (*kai*) in this expression must be ascensive (giving a progressive effect) and thus points to a nation that bears special guilt. The aorist tense goes back to the cross and the guilt of the nation of Israel. The use of the verb "pierced" (*ekkenteō*) reminds us that John was an eye-witness of that dark scene (John 19:37). The verb links the author of the Gospel and the author of this book. This is the moment of revelation to the nation of Israel of the One who was pierced (Zech 12:10). The individuals who actually took part in that piercing are, of course, long dead; they await their personal judgment at the great white throne (20:11-15). However, the nation who accepted their guilt in the cry before Pilate, "His blood be on us, and our children" (Matt 27:25), will be confronted with the One they pierced!

There is a parallelism between the two parts of the verse as may be shown in the literal translation. Following the word order the verse reads in two parts:

1. and will see Him every eye – and (even) those who Him pierced
2. and will wail over (*epi*) Him all the kindreds (*phulai*) of the earth.

It is possible to explain the scene in two different ways. With Zech 12:10-14 in mind it is very possible to see the wailing here as describing the national mourning of Israel, tribe by tribe, in their confession and repentance, as the truth of the cross dawns upon them in a national conversion. However the weakness of this view is that "every eye" must be much wider than Israel. Further, the word "kindreds" (*phulai*) certainly cannot be restricted to the twelve tribes of Israel; its occurrence in 5:9; 11:9; 13:7; 14:6 demands a worldwide setting. Neither can "the earth" (*gē*) be confined to the land of Israel.

The Lord's use of the same Zechariah background in Matt 24:30 gives a better interpretation of this scene. The same verb for "wail" (*koptomai*) is translated "mourn": "and then shall all the tribes of the earth mourn, and they shall see the Son of man coming in the clouds of heaven with power and great glory". The immediate context of worldwide judgment in this passage fits in with the tribulation judgments associated with the Lord's coming (14:6; 15:4). The same verb is translated "lament" when describing the reaction of kings to the fall of Babylon (18:9) where there can be no thought of repentance. It is clear that the mourning here is not mourning in repentance but mourning in the bitter remorse (9:20, 21; 16:9, 11) that accompanies the disclosure of inevitable coming judgment. For those who have given allegiance to the satanic usurpers the revelation of Christ will mean all hope is finally gone, judgment is coming and the result is an earth-embracing wail.

The verse ends with a double affirmation. The first is the Greek affirmation *nai* translated "even so" and the second is the Hebrew *amen*. Taken together they confirm the absolute certainty of what has been prophesied. They are used in the same way in the last chapter of this book (22:20) with the meaning "it is so, Amen".

8 The identity of this coming One is made clear by the Lord Himself. While many, perhaps the majority of commentators, take the speaker in this verse to be God the Father, it is much more in keeping with the context to hear the Lord Jesus identify Himself. In the cross suffering was His portion, now in the act of coming to earth, sovereignty is shown to belong to Him! First, the tears, now, the triumph; first He came to redeem now He comes to reign but the Person is the same! This Person has all the attributes of deity; He is God manifest in flesh. Three titles manifest His deity. "I am Alpha and Omega". Alpha and omega are the first and last letters of the Greek alphabet. Idiomatically it is used to indicate a "whole", something included from beginning to end. Most languages have similar expressions: in English the expression would be used "he knows something from A to Z", in other words his knowledge of that subject is not partial or fragmentary but complete. Using an alphabet all the knowledge and wisdom of the ages may be stored in written records; through the alphabet, by use of the letters in words and sentences in inexhaustible combinations, thoughts and messages are communicated from mind to mind. Christ is the total message and conveys the whole revelation of truth from God to man. There is nothing revealed before Him, nothing after Him, nothing without Him. In Him is the sum total of divine revelation. To Him belongs the omniscience of deity. This title occurs again at the close of the book (21:6; 22:13). (The textual authority for the inclusion of the title in v.11 is weak, see comments *in loc* and its omission by RV and JND.)

Competent textual editors are satisfied that the next expression "the beginning and the ending" has very little MSS support, and, in keeping with this judgment it is omitted by the RV, JND and most translators. The similar title "the first and the last" is in 21:6; 22:13, with full MSS authority.

"The Lord God, the Almighty". The textual support for the inclusion of "God" is indisputable. The intervening words "which is, and which was, and which is to come" are a separate title. The noun (the Almighty) at the end of the sentence is part of the full title. Christ in resurrection is acknowledged as "Lord" (Phil 2:9-11). "The Almighty" describes deity as revealed in His working on earth, and occurs ten times in the NT. One reference is a quotation (2 Cor 6:18) and the other nine are found in this book (1:8; 4:8; 11:17; 15:3; 16:7, 14; 19:6,15; 21:22). That which belongs inherently to deity is revealed in Christ. In Him is displayed the *omnipotence* of deity.

"Which is, which was and which is to come" is a title which has been used of God the Father in v.4. The comments there apply with equal force to Christ. He is the One in whom *omnipresence* is seen – the One who transcends time. He belongs to eternity and thus as to time, He always is, He ever has been and He shall ever be the coming One. Infinite in knowledge (omniscient) He reveals God; infinite in power (omnipotent) He acts for God; infinite as regards the time/space relation He is God (omnipresent).

II. Vision 1: Christ and the Churches (1:9-3:22) Christ Lives – the Priest

1. *The Writer Introduced*

1:9-11

v.9 "I John, who also am your brother, and companion in tribulation, and in the kingdom and patience of Jesus Christ, was in the isle that is called Patmos, for the word of God, and for the testimony of Jesus Christ.

v.10 I was in the Spirit on the Lord's day, and heard behind me a great voice, as of a trumpet.

v.11 Saying, I am Alpha and Omega, the first and the last: and, What thou seest, write in a book, and send it unto the seven churches which are in Asia; unto Ephesus, and unto Smyrna, and unto Pergamos, and unto Thyatira, and unto Sardis, and unto Philadelphia, and unto Laodicea."

9 The words "I John" are as emphatic as they are at the close of the book (22:8). They call to mind the emphatic personal imprimatur of Daniel in the apocalyptic book of the OT (Dan 8:1; 9:2; 10:2). To the saints of Asia the last of the apostles needs no introduction other than his name. John not only identifies himself to the saints, he identifies himself with them. The ecclesiasticism, seen early in post-apostolic days, that distinguished between clergy and laity is noticeably absent in John's introduction of himself to his readers. The spiritual link in the family of God "your brother" is strengthened in a real way by what is shared in Jesus Christ. The word "companion" or, as rendered in the RV "partaker" (*sunkoinōnos*), denotes a sharing in the experiences of life. It is used on only three other occasions in the NT when it is translated "partaker" (Rom 11:17; 1 Cor 9:23; Phil 1:27).

That which believers share is expressed more clearly in JND: "in the tribulation and kingdom and endurance in Jesus". The single article shows that the three things are shared by all believers because of their standing " in Jesus". This expression "in Jesus" may be compared with the expression "in the Lord" (14:13) and contrasted with the Pauline expression "in Christ" (Eph 1:3) or the Petrine equivalent "in Christ Jesus" (1 Pet 5:10). John expresses the consequences of this standing in a threefold way. "Tribulation" (*thlipsis*) describes pressure or trouble arising from a hostile world. The Lord had warned of this in John 16:33 and anticipated that all believers would suffer this in some way. To equate this general experience of every believer with "the great tribulation" of 7:14 is faulty exegesis. There is no connection. In contrast to shared experience of trouble there is the compensation of being in a kingdom far greater than that of Rome, and under a Sovereign mightier than the Caesar. It is true that believers await the physical changes to take place when the King is revealed in millennial glory, but in the meantime, the spiritual aspects are theirs to enjoy. Under pressure from the world, yet with the prospect of the coming King there is developed the character trait of "endurance" (*hupomonē*) so valued by the Lord Himself (see 3:10). Sharing the same tribulation as other saints, under the same spiritual sovereignty and expecting the same Saviour develops this character in all believers. John shared with the believers their experience of trouble, their enjoyment of citizenship in the kingdom and their triumphant endurance in light of the triumph in Jesus.

The spiritual blessings shared with other saints "in Jesus" stands in graphic contrast with his physical isolation and loneliness. The island of Patmos is a rocky islet of approximately thirteen square miles, in the Dodecanese Islands group in the Icarian Sea. About thirty five miles from the coast of Asia, it is roughly crescent shaped with the horns facing westwards. The high cliffs and white crags of the shoreline against the dark seascape give it, particularly in winter storms, a wild magnificence.

From the time of Julius Caesar banishment to an island, preferably as inaccessible as possible, was an accepted form of punishment for well-connected "undesirables" who were thought to pose a threat to those in power. The Latin word for this sentence was *relegatio* and many of the great names in Roman history endured this kind of banishment for various periods. It is on record that Patmos was such a penal settlement. Domitian (AD 81-96), one of the most cruel of the Roman Emperors, used this power against Christians who refused to give him the divine honours he demanded. Unknown believers were simply burned at the stake or thrown to the beasts in the circus, but others of local standing, whose public martyrdom magistrates judged could stir up civil strife, were banished. Early church tradition is clear and surprisingly consistent (see introduction under "Date of the Revelation") that John was banished to the island of Patmos in the reign of Domitian and was released on the death of the Emperor. Tradition, thought by competent authorities to be reliable, says that John died at Ephesus in the reign of the Emperor Trajan (AD 98-117). Missing is any reliable tradition of what charges were laid against John to banish him to this lonely isle but, whatever they may have been, they were but the instruments of the outworking of an over-ruling divine plan that would be for the blessing of the church.

Why John was in Patmos is briefly stated. Because of the similarity of expression with v.2 the suggestion is sometimes made that John came voluntarily to Patmos to receive the revelation now given to him. However the preposition "for" (*dia* with the accusative) in similar phrases in 6:9 and 20:4, where it must be translated "because of" or "on account of", make it impossible to believe that John had taken up voluntary residence on Patmos to receive this revelation. Rather it is clear that John's faithful teaching of the word of God and fearless testimony to Jesus Christ had led to his banishment. In this way he becomes an illustration of, and sharer with, the saints in their time of trouble.

10-11 The normal condition of all believers is expected to be "in the Spirit" (Rom 8:9), but when God uses men as channels of communication there is a specially given enablement envisaged in Eph 3:5: "It is now revealed unto his holy apostles and prophets by the Spirit" (literally "in Spirit"). The expression "in spirit" describes that exaltation and detachment of spirit brought about by the Holy Spirit that enables John to become a channel of divine communication. He is carried beyond the realm where physical and natural senses dominate into the realm where can be known what is normally beyond the realm of human experience. The same expression will recur again in 4:12; 17:3; 21:10. The omission of the article draws attention to the character of the state produced by the Holy Spirit.

Having shown his physical location and his spiritual state John notes the day on which he received the revelation; it was given "on the Lord's day" (*en tē kuriakē hēmera*). It is easy to understand how the meditation and preoccupation with Christ of this surviving apostle in the loneliness of his exile, on the first day of the week, would be a fitting prelude for the granting of this revelation. That John uses the adjective "lordly" (*kuriakos*) to describe the day called in the NT "the first day of the week" (Matt 28:1; Mark 16:2,9; Luke 24:1; John 20:1,19; Acts 20:7; 1 Cor 16:2) is beyond question. The only other occasion of its use in the NT is helpful, for it is used to describe "the Lord's supper" (*kuriakon deipnon*) in 1

Cor 11:20. This adjective as shown by A. Deissman, noted archaeologist and linguist, marks the Lord's distinctive claim to His supper and His day. Without being directly stated this adjective sets these precious things in direct opposition to the "imperial" cult of the Caesars (see note for a full discussion). The fact that the term is not used for the first day of the week in any other place in the NT, or in the christian writings of the first century known to scholarship, is not an argument against this interpretation. John in using this term may be introducing it to believers or, perhaps more likely, simply authenticating its common use.

Many commentators equate "the Lord's Day" with "the day of the Lord" and teach that John in his ecstatic state was mystically drawn down amongst the scenes of that eschatological day. This cannot be sustained and, in fact, is most improbable. The first problem is that chs. 2 and 3 patently belong to this dispensation and are not part of "the day of the Lord". E.W. Bullinger, however false his premise, is at least consistent in his exegesis, and insists that these churches are Jewish synagogues in the tribulation period. Such an unjustifiable deduction needs no detailed refutation since it is clearly untenable. Further, if the Holy Spirit inspiring John's writing had meant to draw attention to that eschatological period the common expression "the day of the Lord" (*hē hēmera tou kuriou*) with its OT background was available: there was no need to coin a new expression. This is the expression used in 2 Thess 2:2, while the similar expression (*hēmera kuriou*) is used 1 Thess 5:2 and 2 Pet 3:10. Instead of this usual expression being used the adjective ***kuriakos***, not available in Hebrew, was coined. There is no doubt that in its very form it was designed to link "the Lord's supper" and "the Lord's day" in the minds of saints. The "lordly, dominical or imperial" supper places this supper in contrast to all other suppers and, in a similar way, one day of the week is distinguished from every other as "belonging to the Lord".

The trumpet-like voice from behind John is quite specific in its command, "what thou seest write in a book". The identity of the speaker is more open to question. The titles used by the speaker in the AV point without question to Christ. There is considerable doubt as to the reliability of the supporting manuscript evidence, a doubt that is reflected in the omission of the titles in both the RV and JND. Both titles are used of Christ, one in v.7 and the second in v.17. That the voice of the Son of Man is described in v.15 as "the sound of many waters" is not a valid argument against this being His voice since the situations are different. A trumpet-like voice demands attention, it cannot be ignored, while a voice "as the sound of many waters" drowns every other voice. However, with the weakness of the manuscript evidence, it is better to hear in this command the voice of the conducting angelic messenger giving John specific instruction as to what he is to do with the revelation given. This view is supported by the fact that this trumpet-like voice is heard again at the next stage of the vision in 4:1. There it is spoken of as "the first voice".

The summons from behind by the trumpet-voiced angel is in keeping with the experience of Ezekiel (Ezek 3:12). This dramatic method of arresting attention speaks of solemn matters that must have the undivided attention of the recipient. The one thing you cannot do with a trumpet sound is ignore it; it certainly speaks with authority and claims attention. The suggestion that the apostle was looking in the wrong direction, while not explicit in the text, may be a legitimate deduction since he had to turn round. The trumpet in Israel's history (Num 10:1-10) was synonymous with divine authority. The command that reaches John certainly carried divine authority. The command "write" is an imperative that will be repeated twelve times throughout this book. What John sees is to be written into a book and sent to the churches mentioned. The whole of the book is in question; it is a unit and must be sent as such. There is never any suggestion that the individual messages to the churches were to be separated from the book as a whole; their individual messages had to be seen in the context of the seven and of the book as a whole. It is an interesting note of history that there never seems to have been any real question raised about the canonical credentials of this book; it was immediately accepted for what it claimed to be – a divine revelation.

The completed revelation was to be sent to the seven named churches in the Roman province of Asia. The expression "what thou seest" with the present tense of the verb embraces the whole of the revelation. If John stood on the curve of the crescent-shaped Isle of Patmos looking eastwards (the horns of the crescent pointing westwards) the seven churches would lie in a rough semi-circle (see map) toward the sunrise. They are named in clockwise order. This is also the order in which they would be readily accessible by the roads of that day. Ephesus on the coast was the regular point of entry for the province, from which the road ran forty miles northward to Smyrna. A further forty miles north/north east would bring the traveller to Pergamum. From this point, turning generally south-east the distance to Thyatira was about forty five miles. At Thyatira the highway turns directly south with about forty miles to be travelled to Sardis. Moving on from Sardis in a south-easterly direction forty miles would bring a traveller to Philadelphia and after a further forty miles he would reach Laodicea. The reason for the selection of these churches will be discussed in comments on v.20.

Notes

10 Many commentators would equate the expression "the Lord's day" (*hē kuriakē hēmera*) with the similar phrase *hē hēmera tou kuriou*. Seiss states "I see no essential differences between *hē kuriakē hēmera* – the Lord's day – and *hē hēmera kuriou* – the day of the Lord. They are simply the two forms for signifying the same relations of the same things". A little further on he makes his meaning clear: "In a word, he was *en pneumati*, in spirit – a condition wholly loosened from the earth – transported by means of the Spirit *ēn tē kuriakē hēmera*, into the Lord's day – stationed as a spectator amid the very scenes of the great judgment itself". (Seiss *in loc*).

Support for this view has been thought to lie in the fact that the phrase "the Lord's day" as referring to the first day of the week is found neither in the NT nor in any literature of the period until a hundred years after this writing. This argument was answered as long ago as 1910 by A. Deissman, the noted antiquarian, when he pointed out that the adjective ***kuriakos*** (Lord's) had a very specialised meaning; he is worth quoting ***in extenso*** "The parallelism between the language of christianity and the official vocabulary of Imperial law shows itself in the use of the adjective ***kuriakos*** – belonging to the Lord, Lord's. Familiar to every reader of the NT from 1 Cor 11:20 and Rev 1:10, where it occurs in the phrases "the Lord's supper" and "the Lord's day" (i.e. probably Sunday) it may certainly be described as a very characteristic word of the early language of christian worship, and it was formerly considered as a specifically Biblical and ecclesiastical word, some even going so far as to regard it as a coinage of St Paul's. But, as a matter of fact Paul took it from the language of contemporary constitutional law, in which it meant 'imperial'". After quoting examples of its usage from various inscriptions going back as far as AD 68 to establish the point, Deissman goes on to draw attention to the idea of "Emperor's day" (called *Julia Sebaste*) in the Roman Empire and states, "I said that this name, formerly after some Hellenistic model was analogous to the primitive christian 'Lord's Day' as a name for Sunday. But the more I regard this parallel in connection with the great subject 'Christ and the Caesars' the more I am bound to reckon with the possibility that the distinctive title 'Lord's Day' may have been connected with a conscious feeling of protest against the cult of the Empire with its 'Emperor's day'". If this argument is valid, and most historians accept its truth, then the Holy Spirit through this writing is bringing into the vocabulary of believers another term to mark them out from the Roman Empire. The term "first day of the week" with its Hebrew background is now superseded by that title that links the day specifically with the risen Lord."

A case can be made for contrasting the "the Lord's day" with "man's day" (*anthrōpinē hēmera*) of 1 Cor 4:3. In "man's day" assessments are made in the light of human understanding and knowledge, but in "the Lord's day" assessments are made in light of His understanding and knowledge. Since judgment is the subject of this book and John is to be transported into those scenes, some argue that this expression simply means "viewing earth matters through the Lord's eyes". John on this view is allowed to see the Churches, the Cosmos, the Conflict, the Conquest and the Consummation from the viewpoint of the Lord Himself. See pages 18-19 for breakdown. While attractively simple, this argument takes no account of the presence of the article, or of the way the adjective ***kuriakos*** is used in 1 Cor 11:20. The whole argument is very weak and "The Lord's day" must be "the first day of the week". It is the fact that, from shortly after John's time, this became the familiar term in christian writings for the "first day of the week" and by the end of the second century was the normal term in use.

2. *The Christ Revealed*

1:12-20

v.12 "And I turned to see the voice that spake with me. And being turned, I saw seven golden candlesticks;

v.13 And in the midst of the seven candlesticks one like unto the Son of man, clothed with a garment down to the foot, and girt about the paps with a golden girdle.

v.14 His head and his hairs were white like wool, as white as snow; and his eyes were as a flame of fire;

v.15 And his feet like unto fine brass, as if they burned in a furnace; and his voice as the sound of many waters.

v.16 And he had in his right hand seven stars: and out of his mouth went a sharp two

edged sword: and his countenance was as the sun shineth in his strength.
v.17 And when I saw him, I fell at his feet as dead. And he laid his right hand upon me, saying unto me, Fear not, I am the first and the last:
v.18 I am he that liveth, and was dead; and, behold, I am alive for evermore, Amen; and have the keys of hell and of death.
v.19 Write the things which thou hast seen, and the things which are, and the things which shall be hereafter;
v.20 The mystery of the seven stars which thou sawest in my right hand, and the seven golden candlesticks. The seven stars are the angels of the seven churches: and the seven candlesticks which thou sawest are the seven churches."

12 Five verbs from John's pen bring the scene graphically to light "I heard" (v.10); "I turned" (v.12); "I saw" (v.12); "I saw" (v.17); "I fell" (v.17). John's reaction to the trumpet-like voice was natural: "I turned to see the voice that spake with me". He found an unusual scene: seven lampstands were before him and in the midst of the lampstands "one like unto the Son of man". The AV and RV translation "candlestick" has nothing to commend it but religious tradition (see JND). The word for "oil lamp" is *luchnos*; while *luchnia*, the word here, is the lampstand.

Whether the lampstands are placed in a circle around the Son of Man, as traditionally assumed, or placed asymmetrically is not stated. The important point is that Christ is "in the midst" of the lampstands. He is the focal point of the whole scene. It will be explained to John (v.20) that what he sees is the symbolic representation of the relationship between Christ and His church in testimony on earth during this dispensation.

The seven-branched single-based lampstand of the tabernacle (Exod 37:17) has been used in the OT as a symbol of Israel nationally in their testimony for God on earth. Failure in testimony had led to the removal of that lampstand to Babylon (2 Chron 36: 17-21). The restoration of the nation of Israel, seen in a partial way in the recovery from Babylon under Zerubbabel, awaits complete fulfilment in millennial conditions as symbolised by the lampstand in the ministry of Zechariah the prophet (Zech 4:11). In a far deeper sense the lampstand is a symbol of the person of Christ as the true testimony for God on earth. Only Christ could answer fully to the lampstand in Exodus (Exod 25:31-40). Its material (pure gold), its features (beaten work), and dependence on the oil, all speak plainly of the dependent Man in testimony for God seen in Christ personally while He was on earth (1 Tim 3:16). In this present dispensation Christ, rejected on earth and received in glory, has left a testimony for God during the time of His physical absence. The seven lampstands symbolise that testimony.

That the testimony is complete is emphasised in the fact that the lampstands are seven in number; that it is no longer a national unit but is composed of independent congregations is clear from the fact that they are single, free-standing lampstands. The fact that Christ is "in the midst" rules out any idea of a single-based lamp. In addition the single lamps are in harmony with the NT teaching on the autonomy of each local assembly. They are united by their common relationship with Christ.

These congregations have already been called churches (v.11). The word "church" (*ekklēsia*) etymologically is composed of *ek* (out of) and *klēsis* (a calling) (see Vine). The emphasis lies in the summons that gathers the company to Christ and it is the NT word for a company of believers gathered to Him. The Lord Himself used the term in Matt 16:18 to describe the whole company of the redeemed in this dispensation. Christ identified Himself as the foundation of this dispensational gathering when He said, "Upon this rock I will build my church". This is sometimes called the "universal church" but a much better term would be "the church of the dispensation". The Lord used the term again in Matt 18: 15-20 to describe a company of believers in a district called out to Himself locally in testimony. He gives a plain instruction about the problem that has arisen when He says, "tell it to the church". That church He defines in the following terms, "where two or three are gathered together in (*eis*) my name, there am I in the midst of them". Local companies like this are spoken of in the NT in the plural as "churches of Christ" or in the singular as "the church of God" in a district. For these churches Matthew's Gospel presents the dispensational background; the Acts of the Apostles gives the historical development as congregations were established across the Roman Empire from Jerusalem to Rome; the function and features of such companies, under a number of figures are explained doctrinally in the Epistles. It is therefore scarcely surprising that such assemblies as the Lord anticipated should have some place in this prophetic book. It would be a matter of surprise if this aspect of testimony was to be totally omitted.

That the lampstands around Christ as centre are seven in number stresses that the completeness of testimony is in view. Unlike the nation of Israel, the church in testimony on earth cannot be represented by a single lampstand as if it had an earthly base and centre. The gold speaks of the divine composition (the saints) and divine constitution (the scriptures) of each assembly. The fact that lamps are dependent on oil, typical of the Holy Spirit, is not stressed but implied. While each lampstand is an individual unit of testimony without any visible link they are united in that each is responsible to Christ. W. Scott writes: "They represent separate and independent assemblies, each one in its place responsible to cast its beams of light athwart the gloom" (p.42).

Some have argued that since the lampstand in the tabernacle stood in the Holy Place that this must be a scene in heaven. This is a mistake; the lamps and stars show it is a night scene on earth. Such a night scene, in a symbolic way, describes the period of the Lord's absence from earth. When He comes again to earth the day will break (2 Pet 1:19) and the sun arise (Mal 4:2); the time for lamps and stars will have gone forever.

13 It is part of divine reticence that no physical description is ever given of the Lord in all the NT. Not even John the beloved disciple attempts to gratify mere curiosity. Nevertheless in this final book we get glimpses of His glorious person filling various offices that unfold His majesty and glory. Three major pictures govern the chapters that follow:

1. Christ – as Priest walking in the midst of the lampstands
   (Christ and the Churches chs. 2-3).

2. Christ – as the Lamb standing in the midst of the throne
   (Christ and the Cosmos 4:1-19:10)

3. Christ – as the Word seated on the white horse
   (Christ in the Conquest 19:11-21)

Three matters set forth the royal dignity of Christ: His manhood glory; His priestly garment; His royal girdle. In spite of the glory John recognises the One who walks in the midst of the lampstands. He uses the title that the Lord Himself used eighty-one times in the Gospels (this number includes two occasions when others quoted Him). "Son of man" identifies Christ as true man, as representative man, man as God intended man to be. It does more; with the word "like" included it parallels Dan 3:25 where Nebuchadnezzar cried in wonder as he viewed the fourth form in the fiery furnace, "the form of the fourth is like the Son of God"; there the surprise is to see deity in manhood; now John recognises that judgment, the prerogative of deity, is demonstrably in the hands of a Man. The wonder is that John sees a Man acting as God. This latter point explains the use of the title "Son of man" rather than the more usual title, when the church is in view, of "Christ" or "Lord". In a key passage in John 5:18-30 Christ is seen as the Son of God (v.25) and, as the only begotten Son He is the sole life-giver. To hear His voice is to live. In v.27 of the same passage He is called Son of man. As Son of man His prerogative is to judge; "And hath given him authority to execute judgment also because he is the Son of man". The absence of the article before the title both in John 5:27 and in this passage, is to stress the point that it is the fact of His manhood that qualifies Him to judge men. The judgment entrusted to Christ is not a result of mediatorial office nor messianic claim but simply because He (the Son of God) is also characteristically a man. God has entrusted judgment to a Man, and this is the Man. The work entrusted to Christ in this passage is that of priest-judge. He judges not Israel, nor the nations but the churches on earth. Since judgment is in view and churches on earth are the subjects it is fitting that His title should be "Son of man". This title is absent from the Epistles because the church is heavenly in origin and destiny but occurs here because the Lord exercises this judgment while the churches are on earth.

It is true that the title "the Son of man" is a messianic title going back to Dan 7:13-14. It is, however, a serious mistake to confine it to His links with the nation of Israel and a greater error to say that it has nothing to do with the church. W. Scott writes: "The title is one which expresses a wider range of dominion and glory than that of king of Israel (compare Pss 2 and 8)". Ps 8 understood in the light of Heb 2:5-9 shows that in the title the stress is on the humanity of Christ. He is linked with all mankind. This link of deity and humanity in the person of Christ, revealed in incarnation, will never be relinquished. Through resurrection and ascension He has taken manhood back to the throne. This is the Man through whom life is given and judgment is exercised towards all mankind. Here the judgment is restricted to the churches.

The One who was wrapped in the swaddling bands, who wore the seamless robe and the scarlet tunic, is now clothed with "a garment down to the feet". This garment reflects official dignity. It is the word *podērēs* used in Exod 28:4 LXX for the robe of the high priest. One translator gives "the full-length robe". It is also used in Ezek 9:11 LXX of the clothing of the man with the ink-horn. This latter scene deals with judgment. The long robe publicly attests the official position of an accredited dignitary. Priestly character is in view but, instead of acting for man, Godward, the priest is acting for God, manward. In fact the Son of man is seen as a Priest-Judge.

The girding of the Son of man at the "breasts" (RV) is unusual. The high priestly girdle had gold interwoven but would seem to have been about the loins. Girding about the loins indicates a readiness to serve (Dan 10:5) but the girdle worn about the breasts, in accepted custom in many eastern lands was an indication of regal dignity. The gold would show that every action of this Priest-Judge will not be governed by human sentiment but will bring glory to God as manifestly righteous. It should be noted that the seven angels in 15:6 are girded in the same way. The idea of judicial action is the same in both passages but while the Lord deals with the churches Himself, He uses accredited agents for the execution of judgments upon men generally.

14 Seven features of this Majestic One are described, "His head and his hair were white like wool, as white as snow". On His head rests neither mitre nor crown as this royal Priest fills His role for God as Priest-Judge. Neither priestly intercession nor kingly rule is in view. As a Man acting for God He requires infinite wisdom based on maturity and experience. What was seen in the Ancient of Days (Dan 7:9) is now seen in the Son of man. It is true that the "hoary head" is honourable (Prov 16:31), yet we are inclined to associate it with age and decay. No such thought is implied here. The word "white" (*leukos*) has often associated with it the idea of "bright" as in Matt 17:2. This brightness is emphasised in the two similes: "white as wool" and "white as snow". This judge makes no mistakes; He is the infallible One.

"His eyes were as a flame of fire". In Dan 10:6 the eyes of the man by the river in Daniel's vision are described as "lamps of fire". Here it is not merely the luminosity of the eyes that arrests John but their penetrating power. This searing beam cuts through all sham and hypocrisy; it will not only reveal but destroy. The Lord Himself draws attention to this feature when He speaks to the church in Thyatira (2:18). The look that sought out a Nathaniel (John 1:48) or arrested a Peter (Luke 22:61) can still search every heart. He is the undeceivable One.

15 “His feet were like unto fine brass as if they burned in a furnace. The word *chalkolibanos*, translated “fine brass” or, as in the RV “burnished brass”, is unknown outside the two occurrences in this book (see 2:18). It would seem to indicate (see W. Kelly), a specially purified brass alloy, almost white, used in the making of military armour and weapons. The participle “burned” allows us to see the metal glowing in the furnace. It stresses its purity. These are the feet that were weary with the journey through Samaria (John 4:6), that were washed with the tears of a sinner (Luke 7:38) and were wounded on the cross (Luke 24:39). Now they tread majestically in the midst of the lampstands. The thought seems to be that He is the implacable One, nothing can deter Him as He moves to deal with all that is opposed to divine righteousness. The corrupt in Thyatira may well take note (2:18).

“His voice was as the sound of many waters”. This descriptive note is virtually a quotation from Ezek 43:2 where the voice of the God of Israel “was like the noise of many waters”. To stand near to many waters, as in a waterfall, is to be overwhelmed by the sheer power of the sound as it covers the whole range of audible frequencies, it is impossible to speak above it or against it. The voice of the Son of man is overwhelming; it drowns all others. When he speaks He is the unanswerable One.

16 “And he had in his right hand seven stars”. The hand in scripture denotes activity (Acts 11:21). The right hand generally speaks of authority, the right to act. When something is “in” the hand there is the added thought of possession. The Son of man possesses, controls and has the right to act in respect of these seven stars. The absence of the article before “stars” rules out any thought of the identification of any astronomical star group. Fanciful ideas have been suggested by some commentators with regard to the seven planets known at this period or the constellation of the Pleiades (the seven sisters). It is not astronomy that is being presented in this feature but a spiritual reality. The symbol of the stars will be explained by the Son of man Himself (v.20) but it is useful to see that the stars are quite distinct from the lampstands. Having these stars in His right hand shows His absolute control. They are safe with Him, no one can take the stars out of His Hand. He is the unassailable One.

“Out of his mouth went a sharp two-edged sword”. The word used for sword (*romphaia*) is peculiar to this book (apart from a figurative use in Luke 2:35). It is the large, broad, tongue shaped sword of Thracian origin (Swete) used by the Greek hoplites and distinct from the shorter bayonet-like sword of the Roman legions. It is a very appropriate symbol for the word of God. That sword can be used with equal effect against the compromising elements in Pergamum (2:12,16) or against the gathered armies of a rebel earth (19:15,21). He is the invincible One.

"His countenance was as the sun shineth in his strength". As men cannot gaze upon the sun so John found the dazzling radiance of the Son of man overwhelming. The word "countenance" (*opsis*) can be translated "face", as it is in John 11:44, one of only two other NT occurrences of the word, but it stresses the impact that the face makes on another. It appeared to John like the sun, not at sunrise nor sunset, but blazing in the fulness of its noon-day strength. There is an echo of the song of Deborah and Barak (Judges 5:31) in the metaphorical language. The very face that was stained with tears, from which the hair was plucked, that felt the spittle of men, is now resplendent with glory. John cannot look upon Him; he must fall at His feet. When acting in judgment He is the unapproachable One.

17-18 The disciple who leaned on the breast of the Savour (John 13:23) now falls at His feet. Deity revealed has ever had this effect on men: Abraham (Gen 17:3), Manoah (Judges 13:20), Ezekiel (Ezek 3:23) and Daniel (Dan 8:17). John's reaction indicates that being "in the spirit" does not suspend, but rather intensifies, the normal human faculties. Later in the visions John will be seen weeping (5:4), wondering (17:6) and worshipping (19:10). The simile "as dead" describes the total prostration and lifeless appearance (as Mark 9:26) as one from whom life had gone. A similar experience on the mount of transfiguration (Matt 17:6-7) brought a similar tender response from the Lord. The Lord put His hand upon John. On this occasion John, with heightened faculties, notes that it was the right hand of the Son of man. The hand that, symbolically, had held the seven stars is laid upon the trembling seer. The vision thus readily moves from symbolic picture to physical touch, from care of the churches to comfort for His prostrate servant. John would recall that earlier touch and know it was the same Son of man. The voice, too, conveying the same message would banish all fear. The imperative with the negative in the words "fear not" can be translated "Stop being afraid" (Rienecker).

The banishment of fear involves not only the touch and the voice of the Son of man but the recognition of His Person. In four statements He introduces Himself to John that he, and through him the readers of this book, would fully grasp who it is that acts as Priest-Judge in the midst of the churches.

"I am the First and the Last". The Son of man is the eternal One. The God of Israel bears this title in the ministry of Isaiah. Comfort to a people trembling before the impending judgment announced by the prophet is ministered through occupation with One who is "the First and the Last". This One, who stands outside history (Isa 41:4), stands outside the history of redemption (Isa 44:6), stands also outside the history of creation (Isa 48:12). In fact, time is but an interlude in His eternity. The Son of man is untouched by time.

"I am he that liveth and was dead". The Son of man is the living One. The God of Israel bears this title in the prophecies of Daniel (Dan 4:34;12:7). It is repeated in this book at 4:9, 10; 5:14; 10:6; 15:7 and reflects the essential life inherent in deity. Yet through taking humanity He did what would otherwise have been impossible: He died upon a cross. The graphic translation of JND, "I became dead", is to be preferred to the AV "was dead". This points to the moment of His death on the cross. The Son of man was not the victim of circumstances; He took positive action for the redemption of men.

"Behold I am alive for evermore". The Son of man is the risen One. Dramatically (note the exclamation "behold") this One is still the living One as a Man in glory who will never die. The attributes of deity are seen in His humanity. "For evermore" translates the same expression "forever and ever" found in v.6, the strongest expression in the language to express time unending. There will always be this Man in glory. While textual criticism may dispute the authenticity of the "Amen" there is no doubt it is a very appropriate response as the heart is taken up with Christ.

"I have the keys of hell and of death". The Son of man who thus links deity and humanity has "the keys of death and of hell". The very things which have caused men the bitterest tears down the ages are now under the authority of this risen One. The "key" is the recognised scriptural and cultural symbol of authority. Used as the scriptural symbol of the steward (Isa 22:22) it indicated the authority he had to disburse the resources of the master. The Lord used the symbol of the "keys" in this way when He spoke of "the keys of the kingdom of heaven" (Matt 16:19). Absolute authority in the realm of "death and hell" (see RV order on manuscript evidence) belong only to Christ. What was claimed by a usurper because of sin (Heb 2:14-15) is no longer in dispute. Through His death and resurrection Christ has triumphed over Satan and won the right to hold absolute authority over death, the state related to the body, and over hell (*hades*) the realm related to the soul. W. Kelly has a useful note: "When the Lord says He has the keys of death and of Hades, He intimates that He is the absolute master of all that might threaten man whether for the body or the soul. Satan's power in this respect is annulled; Christ has it all". For discussion of "hell" see Note.

The truth has, of course, vital implications for believers in this age. It must have brought tremendous comfort to believers when the blazing stake and the raging beasts told of Caesar's authority over life and death. It still brings its comfort to believers through the dark experiences of life. However, it will be particularly comforting to saints in tribulation days, when under the persecution of the Beast and the physical calamities of divine judgment, death will be sweeping millions from earth. This truth is symbolised under the fourth seal (6:7-8), "And I looked and behold a pale horse: and his name that sat on him was Death, and Hell (*hades*) followed with him". Whatever the appearance to the contrary Christ will still hold the keys. *Hades* will continue to hold the souls of those consigned to it until, body and soul reunited, sinners stand for final judgment before the great white throne (20:11-15). After this, their function fulfilled and no longer needed, God deals with both in summary fashion and their final mention in scripture is terse, "death and hades were cast into the lake of fire" (20:14).

19 John, prostrate at the feet of the Christ, feels the touch of His hand, and hears His voice in direct command. The instruction is simple; Write! The best texts include another word that heightens the impact and gives the connection: "write therefore" (RV). Deity in humanity belongs to eternity and has all authority. John is required to write. It is to be observed that the command to write in v.11 embraces "what thou seest" which must be interpreted to include this whole book, now, more detail is given. The contents of the book are divided by the Lord Himself into three sections; the three sections come after the imperative "write" and are clearly marked by the repetition of the word "things".

(1) "The things that thou hast seen" points back to what therefore John had already seen. This of course embraces vv.10-16 and echoes the verb "I saw" of vv.12, 17. Their subject is: Christ communicating with his servant.

(2) "And the things which are" distinguishes a second group of "things" and the present tense of the verb shows that they are presently existing. These "things" will be detailed in chs. 2-3 which deal with existing churches and unfold: Christ examining the seven churches.

(3) There are also "things which shall be hereafter". The RV is possibly the most literal "the things which shall come to pass hereafter". In other words there is a third group of "things" to be distinguished in the book. Clearly they will follow the first two groups in time. The words "after these things" occur ten times in this book and always denote a sequence. The next occurrence of the phrase is at 4:1 and marks the beginning of the third section of the book. Its subject is: Christ acting in the cosmos (chs. 4:1-19:10).

The Lord Himself thus gives the key for the understanding and interpretation of this book. It will be shown in the exposition that any scheme that ignores this key is doomed to chaos and confusion. When the key is used, the secrets of this great book lie open for the encouragement of the Lord's people in this age of grace and in the tribulation to follow. Not only does it yield a self-consistent scheme of interpretation without manipulation and special pleading, but the interpretation is in perfect harmony with other prophetic scriptures. It has been argued in the introduction that this can be said of none of the other methods of interpreting the book. This approach to the book is often spoken of as "futurist", because it places the major portion of the book (chs. 4-22) in the period after the rapture of the church. Since this is exactly what the Lord has done there can be no disgrace in using the term. Any argument that the book then loses its immediate value for suffering saints in John's day, or that it becomes irrelevant for saints of our day, is patently false and shows lack of understanding of the book. This revelation is given to show the triumph of Christ on earth. The truths associated with it are vital and stimulating for saints of all the ages. If this book had been a study of the Roman Empire in the first century the (preterist view) or a telescopic prophecy of events throughout the history of the church (the historicist view) its interest for us would be minimal and mainly antiquarian. On the other hand, on the futurist view the triumph of Christ lies ahead and in it saints of this dispensation will share. What comfort and challenge this has brought to saints down the ages and still brings to our hearts in this latter day. The message of Revelation has always been timeless.

20 The Lord Himself interprets the symbols with respect to the seven churches. He does it in parallel statements as follows:

"The seven stars are the angels of the seven churches"

"The seven lampstands are the seven churches".

It is clear that this is the description of a night scene with stars in the heavens and lampstands upon earth. The difference in symbols is to indicate a view as seen against the heavens (stars) and a view as seen against the earth (lampstands). The Lord explains the lampstands as the seven churches, clearly their physical reality in the gathering of believers in each district is in view. It would then be expected that the Lord would emphasise some spiritual dimension of the churches. Surprisingly the Lord interprets the stars as angels.

The understanding of the "angel" related to each church has been a major point of controversy over many years and a variety of views have been expressed. These are discussed in the Appendix to this chapter: The Angels of the Churches.

The present author's view is that the stars represent the same companies but in their moral and spiritual condition against a heavenly background. The Lord uses the word "angel" representatively to focus the thoughts upon the true "spirit" or "essence" of the assembly. In the representative angel the company is seen against a heavenly background and hence there can be no deceit; all is real; the actual state of the assembly in question. For this reason it is the angel, the church viewed in its actual spiritual state, which is variously commended, condemned, charged and challenged.

The question might well be asked why the Lord should use the word "mystery" in connection with the seven stars and the seven lampstands. Since He Himself explains the symbols the mystery cannot lie in this. In addressing this question it is important to note first that there were other assemblies in the province. Although Ephesus is the only one of the seven for which we have NT information as to its founding and something of its subsequent history, nevertheless it is clear that there was an assembly at Troas (Acts 20:6-12) as well as one at Colosse (Col 1:2). Reliable traditions place a large assembly at Hierapolis as well as assemblies in several other cities. It can be said that, on a very conservative estimate, at least ten assemblies existed in this province and possibly many more. Given that the number seven speaks in Scripture of completeness, the fact that seven and only seven churches were selected by Christ must have significance.

A second matter of importance is that, while these seven cities lay on the main highway through the province, it is quite wrong to assume that Christ had to follow this order when addressing them. There is no need to assume that one messenger would deliver the book to all the churches, and even if he had there were many subsidiary routes joining the cities. The traveller from Ephesus to Philadelphia, for example, did not have to travel via Sardis. The order in which the churches are addressed was not dictated by geography but chosen by Christ. With the above points in mind it is justifiable to conclude that the Lord used the word mystery to indicate that there is more involved than just seven messages to seven churches. That secret lies in His selection of the particular churches addressed, and in the order in which He addressed them.

Notes

18 Death (*thanatos*) is a state describing what happens to the body, the material part of man; hell (*hades*) is a realm that embraces the soul, the immaterial part of man, when the body dies. *Hades* is the Greek word answering to the Hebrew *sheol*. While there is some disagreement as to the derivation of the word it is generally conceded to be linked to the verb *eidō* ("to see") with the negative particle prefixed. It is a term descriptive of the unseen realm. The translation of *hades* in the AV as "hell" has focused on one region of that realm unseen by man. That region, as seen in Luke 16:23-31, is where the souls of the lost are detained. It is not the permanent abode of the lost for which the Gospels have the word *gehenna* (also translated "hell" in Mark 9:43-48) which is used on eleven occasions by the Lord Himself. *Gehenna* is used on only one other occasion in the NT in James 3:6). Revelation will show that *gehenna* has its fulfilment in the lake of fire (19:20; 20:10, 14, 15; 21:8).

Light is shed on the realm called *hades* by Peter's quotation of Ps 16:8-11 with reference to Christ in his preaching in Acts 2:27. Notice the parallelism based on the underlying Hebrew:

"Because thou wilt not leave my soul in hell (*hades*),
Neither wilt thou suffer thine Holy One to see corruption".

This first statement refers to the soul; the second statement refers to the body. The risen and ascended Christ is the assurance to believers that neither hades (that unseen realm) nor death (that dreaded state) can now have any claim over them. The soul of the saint who dies is immediately where Christ is in the Father's presence (Phil 1:23). The believer may be "put to sleep" and the body may be consigned to a grave (1 Cor 15:18) but this is but to await the summons of the Lord to "put on incorruption" (1 Cor 15:54). Christ has absolute authority both in the seen world where death operates and in the realm that, as yet, we cannot see. He alone has the keys.

19 This verse has always been a problem to those commentators who, on other grounds, refuse to accept the futurist view of the book. G.B. Caird in *Black's New Testament Commentaries* describes the analysis given here as "a grotesque over simplification", but the only way in which he can avoid the implication of the three statements is to change the tense of the first statement from the past to the present so that it reads, "what you see" thus making it cover the whole of the book. He makes the textual change without any manuscript support whatever and offers no justification. If the scripture can be treated in this cavalier fashion then sensible interpretation must end. Many others follow this pattern of either tampering with the text or forcing another interpretation of the accepted text. Against all grammarians (including Alford who speaks strongly against it) E.W. Bullinger sees only one aspect of things in this verse - the future. To support this view he makes the verse read, "Write therefore the things that thou sawest, and what they are (i.e. what they signify) even the things which shall come to pass (i.e. happen as in Acts 26:22) hereafter". This faulty translation allows scope for faulty exegesis to fit Bullinger's own idea that the whole of the book lies in the future and has nothing to do with the church. The seven churches, on this view, become seven synagogues in the tribulation period. Using the key provided by the Lord Himself preserves from many such misinterpretations.

Appendix: The Angels of the Churches

The understanding of the "angel" related to each church has been a major point of controversy over many years and a variety of views have been expressed. Some commentators insist that the difficulty arises because the word *angeloi* has been transliterated instead of translated. Instead of its usual meaning of "spirit being" those who hold this view would translate it as "messenger". It must be conceded that it is so translated in Matt 11:10; Mark 1:2; Luke 7:24, 27; 9:52; 2 Cor 12:7; James 2:25 – in fact, seven times out of a total of 186 occurrences of the word. This makes the angel simply the human messenger who would carry (as a postman) the relevant epistle to the named church. The commentator advancing the clearest arguments for this view is possibly G.A. Hadjiantoniou in his book *The Postman of Patmos*. While attractively simple the arguments against this view are weighty:

1. Why "angel" should be translated "messenger" in these first three chapters and all the other 67 occurrences of the word in this book as "angel" has never been satisfactorily explained.
2. It is very difficult to see how a "messenger" or, even as some would suggest a "secretary" or "correspondent", would be held responsible for the failures within the church. The angel is charged or commanded by the Lord as if he were the church.

Many commentators, perhaps a majority, would make the angel a symbol of "the bishop", "the pastor" or "the minister" of the church. The term varies in accordance with the ecclesiastical background of the commentator but, generally, the angel is seen as the man responsible for the church. Those who would see such terms as unscriptural as well as anachronistic would see the angel as symbolising "the responsible elder", "the responsible element" or simply "the oversight" in the assembly. These explanations are again attractively simple but do face the following difficulties:

1. The angel is clearly not a part of the church physically since the stars are in the hand of the Lord as He is in the midst of the lampstands.
2. The angel is addressed and charged as if he is the church. The Lord never hints that the angel should take action independently of the church.
3. The stars are symbols; the Lord has explained the symbols as angels. To go a step further does seem to make a symbol of a symbol and add a personal explanation. While admitting that a double symbol is used in 17:9-10, it is explained there. No explanation is given here and it seems, at least, as if care would be needed in the acceptance of this interpretation. There is always a danger of imagination in this method of interpretation. Such a step of double symbolic interpretation would need some clear indication

> which is not present in this case. W. Hoste in reference to this interpretation of the angel puts the matter very plainly: "Others again, with more scriptural authority perhaps, see in the angels those gifted to rule and edify in the churches – the under-shepherds responsible to the Great Shepherd. The objection to this, which I judge insuperable, is that a symbol cannot be interpreted by a symbol. The lampstands are symbolic of literal churches, and the stars can only represent literal angelic beings."

To see the angel of each church as a literal angel is perhaps the view with the most scriptural support. There can be no question that literal angels have an undoubted interest in the church dispensationally (Eph 3:10) and locally (1 Cor 11:10); yet, to assume that a literal angel is associated with a local assembly is to raise a number of questions very difficult to answer. The idea of a guardian angel of an assembly may appeal to a religious inclination of mind but has little scriptural support. It also seems rather more than strange that angels, which are called "holy" and "elect" can be charged with failure and sin and called upon to repent. To say that the special features of this book demand this method of presentation seems simply to avoid the issue, and to raise difficult questions as to how communication between angel and church is to be achieved. The literal view will need some modification.

While taking the angel literally there is a scriptural way of understanding what the Lord means by its use. There is a line of teaching in scripture that shows a correspondence between heavenly things and their earthly counterparts (see Heb 8:2, 5; 9:23-24). When it is a matter of persons it would seem that the word "angel" is used representatively. This is how the Lord used the word in Matt 18:10 in respect to those whom He called "little ones". "For I say unto you that in heaven their angels do always behold the face of my Father which is in heaven". This is not to be misinterpreted in terms of guardian angels - rather the idea is that the little ones are represented by angels in heaven. The answer of the assembled saints, "It is his angel" (Acts 12:15) to Rhoda's announcement of Peter's arrival falls into the same class – they did not mean "his ghost" or "his guardian angel" they meant "his representative". The word of reassurance to Joshua, the high priest of the nation of Israel restored from Babylon in Zech 3:7 is very relevant. "I will give thee places to walk among those that stand by". The interest of heaven was such that they were represented in heaven. The idea is representation before God.

Thus if the lampstands represent literal physical congregations viewed against an earth background, then the stars must represent the same company but in their moral and spiritual condition against a heavenly background. The term that the Lord uses to represent their true condition is "angel". If the argument is raised that this seems to be repeating the double symbol mistake this is not so; it is simply taking the word "angel" in one of the authorised meanings presented in scripture. The Lord's use of the term "angel" representatively focuses the thought of the true "spirit" or "essence" of the assembly. In the representative "angel" the company is seen against a heavenly background and hence there can be no deceit - all is real, the actual state of the assembly in view. For this reason it is the angel, the church viewed in its actual spiritual state, which is variously commended, condemned, charged and challenged.

It might well be asked why the Lord uses the word "mystery" (*mustērion*) with regard to the seven stars and the seven lampstands. The word must carry its normal NT meaning as that which cannot be known by the processes of human deduction but is *revealed by God* in His own time. The mystery must lie, rather, in the reason or reasons, why the Lord chose these seven particular churches to receive the messages. In other words the Lord is indicating that there is more involved than just seven messages to seven churches. That mystery will be unfolded in the Lord's own time.

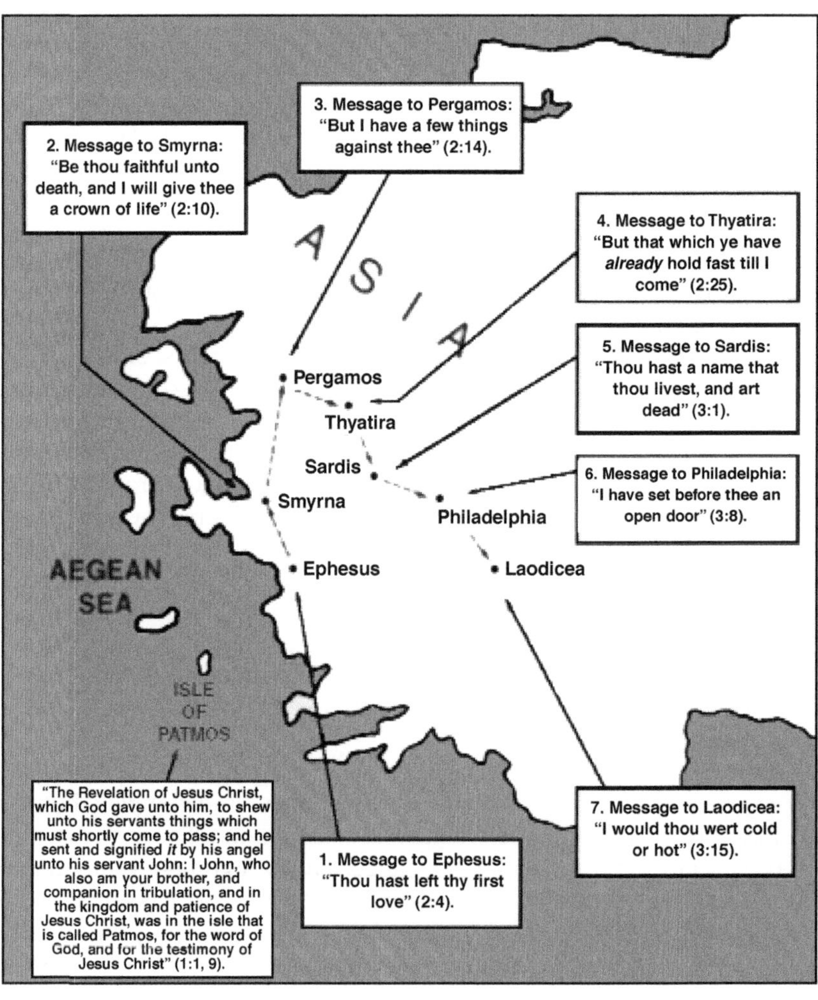

CHAPTER 2

3. *The Messages to the Churches* 2:1-3:22

In the previous chapter John has been commissioned (v.11) on divine authority to send the completed revelation to seven churches in the Roman province of Asia. The churches are named as Ephesus, Smyrna, Pergamum, Thyatira, Sardis, Philadelphia and Laodicea. It has been observed that they form a rough crescent following the main highway from the seaport of Ephesus and, moving clockwise through the province to end at Laodicea directly inland from Ephesus. It has been further noted that the lampstand represents the literal congregation of the saints bearing light on earth, while the actual spiritual state of the church is seen representatively in the angel. It is for this reason that the angel is addressed by Christ in each church.

The lessons to be derived from these letters may be summarised by considering the churches as follows:

1. They are seven literal churches made up of living saints facing their own problems in their local circumstances. Christ shows Himself to be very much aware of their individual circumstances, their dangers, their strengths and their weaknesses. This is the primary lesson.
2. They are seven representative assemblies reflecting spiritual conditions that would affect churches throughout the dispensation. Like the seven colours of the rainbow, from which any other colour can be formed by a suitable combination of two or more colours, so these seven basic spiritual conditions reflect a full spectrum of spiritual experience. Any assembly in any age can find that which answers to its own condition in these letters, can read the Lord's assessment of it, and find the appropriate remedy for it.
3. Many expositors believe that there are also foreshadowed in the seven churches seven stages of history that would mark the testimony of local assemblies as the age progressed. The evidence for looking for such a prophetic foreshadowing is discussed in the Appendix on page 136: Prophetic Foreshadowings in the Seven Churches.

There is, in addition, a fourth application which must never be overlooked. That is the personal message for every believer, emphasised by Christ Himself, when seven times He repeats, "He that hath an ear, let him hear what the Spirit saith unto the churches".

It will be noted that Christ followed a set pattern in addressing each assembly as if He deliberately wished to emphasise His impartiality. In each message there are seven general matters upon which Christ touches. These may be illustrated with respect to Ephesus (Quoted from R.V.):

1. Commission from the Christ	"To the angel of the church in Ephesus ... write"
2. Character of the Christ	"These things saith he that holdeth the seven stars ..."
3. Commendation from the Christ	"I know thy works, and thy toil and patience ..."
4. Criticism of the Church	"But I have this against thee ..."
5. Counsel to the Church	"Remember, therefore ... and repent ..."
6. Call from the Christ	"He that hath an ear let him hear ..."
7. Challenge from the Christ	"To him that overcometh ..."

This pattern is repeated in all the seven and where there is any variation in the pattern it is a matter to be noted and there is a reason for it. It will be observed, for example, that:
(a) in Smyrna and in Philadelphia there is no word of criticism;
(b) in Sardis and Laodicea there is no word of commendation;
(c) in the last four churches the call from the Christ is moved from sixth to seventh place.

The lessons to be drawn from these messages to the seven specific churches are practical. They are similar to the lessons drawn from any NT epistle with the added weight that these letters come directly from Christ Himself.

(a) *The message to Ephesus (vv.1-7)*

v.1 "Unto the angel of the church of Ephesus write; These things saith he that holdeth the seven stars in his right hand, who walketh in the midst of the seven golden candlesticks;

v.2 I know thy works, and thy labour, and thy patience, and how thou canst not bear them which are evil: and thou has tried them which say they are apostles, and are not, and hast found them liars:

v.3 And hast borne, and hast patience, and for my name's sake hast laboured, and hast not fainted.

v.4 Nevertheless I have somewhat against thee, because thou hast left thy first love.

v.5 Remember therefore from whence thou art fallen, and repent, and do the first works; or else I will come unto thee quickly, and will remove thy candlestick out of his place, except thou repent.

v.6 But this thou hast, that thou hatest the deeds of the Nicolaitans, which I also hate.

v.7 He that hath an ear, let him hear what the Spirit saith unto the churches; To him that overcometh will I give to eat of the tree of life, which is in the midst of the paradise of God."

The first of the seven churches to be addressed by Christ is Ephesus. Citizens of this city would, doubtless, have found His choice very appropriate since they liked to talk about the city as the "first city of Asia". While it was not the capital of the Roman province of Asia – that honour belonged to Pergamum – Ephesus had many claims to that title. Sixty miles of sailing directly eastwards from Patmos brought the traveller to this vibrant port at the mouth of the Cayster river. It was the city of "first landing" where the great galleys from Rome brought officials of the Empire en route for their posts throughout the East. These same galleys took back produce of the whole area so that Ephesus was the trading port through which trade of the continent was processed. The huge warehouses were but a symbol of the greatness of the trade. This was also the city which acted as host to the world-famed Asian games, which made it a serious rival of Olympia and Corinth in the sporting and entertainment sphere. The fact, too that it was "the temple-sweeper", or guardian (Acts 19:35) of one of the most prestigious temples in the pagan world – the Temple of Artemis (the Roman Diana), added to its self-importance. Citizens of Ephesus regarded their city as "the metropolis of Asia".

It was neither the geographical location nor the cultural status of the city that caused Christ to select this assembly for His first message. As explained in the introduction to this chapter Christ had reasons for addressing these particular assemblies that went beyond the immediate and the local. Christ would not only expose spiritual conditions but He would warn of the danger of one condition deteriorating into another more serious departure that would spell spiritual disaster. In Ephesus He selected an assembly that had all the outward form of obedience and truth, but which carried within its present condition the root of all subsequent departure. Having "left thy first love" (v.4) Ephesus had become a fallen church. This is in fact the core issue in all departure from truth and thus the reason why Christ selected Ephesus for His first message.

The assembly at Ephesus was the result of the preaching of the apostle Paul in the period from the Autumn of 52 to the Spring of 55 when the silversmith riot led to his abrupt departure from the city (Acts 19:1-20:1). As with all other NT assemblies we have no information as to its numbers. However we can gather much about its spiritual condition from its subsequent place in NT writings. Paul's address to the Ephesian elders as recorded by Luke in Acts 20:17-38 gives a clear insight as to its formation. From the letter that Paul wrote to it from the first Roman imprisonment (60-63) we can glean something of its spiritual development and progress. After his release he would appear to have visited Ephesus with Timothy with the intention of dealing with certain erroneous teaching and teachers who had emerged in the assembly. Timothy was left there (1 Tim 1:3-4) to continue this work and Paul's letters to Timothy provide valuable information as to the state of the Ephesian assembly.

Tradition places John at this centre of testimony towards the close of the first century until he was exiled to Patmos. Tradition says that he returned to Ephesus after his release from Patmos and died there. So this church had had the benefit of the greatest of evangelists, the best of pastors (in the NT sense of the word) and the finest teachers in the forty years of its testimony. Recognising afresh the rich spiritual heritage of this assembly makes Christ's message very searching indeed.

1 The word "church" must be understood in its NT sense. It describes a company of people called or summoned out. When the summons is divine then the resulting gathering is a NT church and when given a local designation as here "in Ephesus" (RV), or where it is described as church of God (1 Cor 1:1) it always refers to a discrete local company of saints gathered in testimony in (*eis*) the name of the Lord Jesus Christ. The application of the word to describe a building or a world-wide organisation is a development of history and has no NT authority. For this reason the word "assembly" is sometimes preferred when a local congregation is in view. However it may be better to use the word "church" as in the AV.

As suggested in the discussion of the word "angel" in 1:20-21 Christ is addressing here neither a human messenger nor a literal angel. It has been shown that either of these suggestions is a possible and scriptural interpretation of the word *angelos*, but in this context neither adequately explains why the angel should be the object of Christ's commendation or condemnation. A human messenger cannot, in all justice, be held responsible for the state of the assembly. A literal angel too can scarcely be held responsible for an assembly. The idea of a guardian angel appeals to religious minds but lacks scriptural support. These difficulties are resolved when we observe that Christ is using the word "angel" in a special way. He uses it in a representative way (see *Expository Dictionary of NT Words*, Vine, One volume edition, 1952, Oliphants, p. 55 where he quotes Matt 18:10; Acts 12:15 as illustrative). The angel cannot be only a part of the church. That the angel symbolises a pastor or cleric in charge of a church owes more to unscriptural tradition than fair exposition. The same argument shows that it cannot be a symbol for the "oversight" or the "responsible element" in the church (favoured by most non-conformist commentators). In other words it must represent, in some way, the whole local church. If this is so then it stands in apposition to the lampstand – doing in the view of heaven what the lampstand is doing in the view of earth. If thus the lampstand represents the physical gathering of the church on earth then the angel must represent the spiritual condition of that same church. So it is suggested that the angel represents the church in its unseen character – its "spirit" (or angel) visible only to Christ Himself. Thus before Him as He addresses the church for condemnation, criticism and challenge is the true spiritual condition of the particular church addressed. We use somewhat similar language when we speak of a church that displays great energy in the gospel as having a "missionary spirit" or speak of another as having a "poor spirit". We often thus commend or criticise in these very terms; here Christ presents the matter in this concise but graphic pictorial form.

R. L .Thomas points out (page 131) that a peculiarly Koine Greek idiom is used in the expression "These things saith the One" that occurs only in these seven letters and in one other passage in the NT (Acts 21:11) where the Holy Spirit is the speaker. In secular usage it was reserved to introduce authoritative utterances and particularly those of kings. Christ is speaking here with all the authority of deity.

It is clear that when Christ speaks to each individual church He draws frequently upon the description of the Son of man in ch. 1. It is equally clear that the particular feature stressed has special relevance to the need of that church. In light of the serious matter that He will raise with Ephesus it can be seen that the fact that He is the One holding the seven stars in His right hand (see 1:16) and the One walking in the midst of the seven golden lampstands (see1:13) is most appropriate to their need. It emphasises His absorbing interest and care; there could be no "falling" (see v.5) in a spiritual way, nor any "removal" (see v.6) in a physical way, without His knowledge. The present participles show that the activity is characteristic of Christ. In 1:16 Christ "had" (*echō* as in 3:1) the seven stars, while in this verse the word is "holdeth" (*krateō*). Robertson points out that the second word is much stronger (See Robertson *in loc*); J. F. Walvoord points out that the verb from which it is derived means "to hold authoritatively" and the same verb must have this stronger sense in 2:25; 3:11. The fact that the stars are in the hand of Christ speaks of security. The absolute eternal security of saints was shown by Christ in the statement "No man is able to pluck them out of my Father's hand" (John 10:29). The right hand in Scripture symbolises authority and power.

The walking of the Christ in the midst of the lampstands again draws attention to His priestly activity. It is reminiscent of the typical movements of the OT priests in the Holy Place in their attendance upon the lamps in Exod 30:7-8. They carried responsibility for their lighting, the supply of oil, and their trimming. Christ in His High Priestly ministry cares not only for individual saints (Heb 4:14-16) but cares for the assemblies of His saints. This very care demands His critical judgment of their condition.

2-3 For all the churches, except Sardis and Laodicea, Christ has a preliminary word of commendation. His eye fastens first on those areas of their testimony of which He could speak with divine approval. In each case His message is introduced with the words "I know" (2:2, 9, 13, 19, 3:1, 8, 15). He uses in each case the same verb (*oida*) that speaks of full and complete knowledge. The verb is summarised by Robertson (quoting Swete with approval), "It emphasises better the absolute clearness of mental vision which photographs all the facts of life as they pass". The One who walks amidst the lampstands is fully aware of all that concerns each church – their attitudes, associations and activities, the spiritual condition and the circumstances that produced it. That which Christ knows so fully is described as "thy works". This will be repeated to four other churches (following the RV text) and is omitted when Christ addresses Smyrna and Pergamum. The plural word does not normally point specifically to major undertakings but covers the whole course and conduct of life.

The whole pattern of the lives of the Ephesian believers is covered by Christ in three couplets which show both the active and the passive sides of testimony. The first couplet shows that the assembly was *instructed in foundational truth*.

On the active side of the testimony there is commendation for their "labour" (*kopos*) – "toil resulting in weariness" (Vine). The verb is used in the NT both of physical and mental effort (for the latter see 1 Thess 5:12; 1 Tim 5:17). On the passive side is "patience" (*hupomonē*). This is the NT word for the character developed through the trials of life. It is used thirty times in the NT and the verb is used fifteen times. It still has something of its classical Greek background where it is used of the character of a man who faces up to something that comes uninvited, as for example the sting of grief, the shock of battle or the coming of death. The word is never used of God since deity can never be subject to things against the divine will. Barclay defines this word as "a masculine constancy under trial". It is the believer's triumphant acceptance of all the happenings of life in the will of God. The linking of "works", "labour" and "endurance" echoes the commendation of Paul to the Thessalonian church in 1 Thess 1:3. The assembly in Ephesus evidenced foundational truth in the character of their lives.

The second couplet shows that the assembly was *intolerant of false teachers*. While the first couplet was positive, the second couplet is negative and yet Christ gives His approval. "Thou canst not bear them that are evil". The idea in the verb "bear" (*bastazō*) is that of a burden being carried. The burden may be literal (Matt 3:11) or metaphorical (Gal 6:2). In the latter scripture saints are encouraged to "Bear ye one another's burdens" but Christ commends the intolerance of this church which refused to bear the burden of evil men. The word "evil" (*kakos*) describes "evil in influence" rather that the stronger word (*ponēros*) which describes "evil in essence" (see Vine). The word is used in literature to describe a cowardly soldier or a lazy student; the influence they spread is most damaging. The church here is commended because they were not prepared to put up with the unwholesome influence of those in whom profession and practice did not match. "Thou has tried them which say they are apostles and are not". The second statement hints at a more dangerous situation in which the assembly again showed commendable intolerance. False apostles identified by their teaching had appeared as early as the time of the apostle Paul (2 Cor 11:13). Close to the end of the apostolic age, as Christ is speaking, it is not unexpected that men would arise claiming apostolic authority, perhaps even claiming apostolic succession. The mention of the deeds of the Nicolaitans (RV spelling) offers some support to this suggestion. Such men claiming apostleship had appeared at Ephesus and the church, wisely and commendably, had given them little credence. When tested these men had authority from neither Christ (apostle in the primary sense) nor even derived authority (in the secondary sense of the word as in 2 Cor 8:23). Quite simply they had been shown to be "liars". Christ agrees with the principle of testing such and validates the result. The verb used to describe the test (*peirazō*) has its origins in the picture of the metallurgist analysing the content of an ore. It emphasises the process of putting through the fire to bring out its character, whether good or bad. (This verb is to be contrasted with *dokimazō*, 1 John 4:1, which implies expected approval.) The aorist tenses of both the verbs in this couplet could well point to some major crises in the previous years when false apostles had appeared in Ephesus. Christ valued their intolerance of that which was damaging and dangerous.

The third couplet shows that the assembly was *intelligent in fundamental* testimony. These two statements present again a negative and a positive side: "hast borne and hast patience"; "hast laboured and hast not fainted"

Between the two parts of the statement come the significant words "for my name's sake". This phrase has a double function. It provides an explanation for the first statement and unfolds a motive for the second. In this twofold way the assembly showed their spiritual intelligence in the basics of assembly testimony. On the negative side the church had suffered much from the pressure of men and the pressure of circumstances. The latter would likely be the result of the first. The repetition of the verb "to bear" suggests that the burden was because of the evil men mentioned in the previous verse. The repetition of the word "patience" draws attention to the circumstances through which the character of the saints was being fashioned. The sustaining strength for this burden and for this battle was "for my name's sake"; which phrase echoes the words Christ used in Matt 10:22; 24:9. The phrase includes all that has been revealed in Christ and stresses its completeness and finality. That which is the object of attack from those refusing the truth becomes the inspiration for the propagation of that same truth. This is seen in the positive part of the statement. The perfect tenses in the final two verbs show that the past years of trial and testimony have results that still remain. The omission of the first of these verbs "hast laboured" in JND and the RV accord with the Majority Text but this makes no differences as the verb repeats the statement in the first couplet. Swete has proposed that the perfect tense of the final verb (*kopiaō*) be translated "you are not weary" which seems to catch the thought exactly.

4 Abruptly Christ changes His tone. From commendation He moves to criticism. The AV may present more correct English but weakens the force of the criticism with the inclusion of the word "somewhat". JND and the RV, "but I have against thee" are more accurate and reflect the abruptness of Christ's criticism. This is no minor matter that Christ has against the assembly.

Most commentators are agreed that "thy first love" must be the love of the first days after conversion and equate it with that which was evident in Israel towards Jehovah in the days immediately following their redemption from Egypt. Jeremiah puts it forcefully and picturesquely in unforgettable language, "I remember thee, the kindness of thy youth, the love of thine espousals, when thou wentest after me in the wilderness, in a land that was not sown" (Jer 2:2). All are agreed that responsive love for the Saviour answering to the "love of thine espousals", is characteristic of souls in the days after conversion. All true believers have experienced the warmth of love to Christ in response to the presence of the Holy Spirit within (Rom 5:5). This love to Christ (2 Cor 5:14) overflows in brotherly love to saints (1 John 3:23) and then moves out to embrace sinners (Rom 5:8). Assembly experience often follows the same pattern. A fervent love for Christ gathers the saints and in the glad joy of fellowship saints are blest and sinners reached. This fresh love produces the "first works" of the next verse. These is a freshness about the works that spring from such first love, and such love is the inspiration of all that is vital and valuable in christian testimony. For this love to cool or to be abandoned leaves a mere façade in testimony; there is a formality with little reality, a certain faith without fervour; the vital inspiration and the essential ingredient of true service is missing. That this love has been a feature of earlier days in Ephesus is beyond doubt. Paul was able to write: "Wherefore I also, after I heard of your faith in the Lord Jesus, and love unto all the saints, Cease not to give thanks for you" (Eph 1:15-16) even though he felt constrained to exhort them in a later chapter, "Walk in love" (Eph 5:1) as if he feared the waning of this passion. Now thirty years or so later when a second and third generation of believers have been brought into the testimony Christ's criticism must have sobered the saints, especially when outwardly all was in order.

The use by Christ of this particular verb *aphiēmi* suggests that there may well be another strand in the charge against the assembly. It is often translated "to forsake" or "to abandon". In 1 Cor 7:11-13 it is translated "put away" or "leave" and carries the idea of divorce. Thus the idea may be not simply the abandonment of a passion but the leaving of a person. The aorist may point to the moment when this happened. Thus Christ's charge is not that an emotion had inadvertently faded but that a person had been deliberately forsaken; He Himself as the heart of the assembly had been replaced with another. In the very same passage in which He speaks of the "love of thine espousals" Jehovah makes the same charge against Israel: "My people have committed two evils; they have forsaken me the fountain of living waters, and hewed them out cisterns, broken cisterns, that can hold no water" (Jer 2:13). It would seem that something had happened that had shown Christ that He no longer was loved as formerly in the Ephesian assembly. They had abandoned Him for another. An illustration may be seen in King Solomon. It is recorded, "And Solomon loved the Lord" (1 Kings 3:3). Later the charge is made, "But king Solomon loved many strange women" (1 Kings 11:1). Jehovah had been displaced in the affections of Solomon. This view of the verb is supported by the specific charge of the next verse "thou art fallen". The perfect tense describes not the act of falling, but the condition resulting from the fall. A once-loyal bride (an Ephesian picture where the word Ephesus means "desirable") has allowed her affections to be alienated. Disaster followed.

5 While v.4 identifies the cause and shows the basis of Christ's criticism of the assembly this verse describes the resulting condition and prescribes the only possible corrective. Part of any recovery must be the accurate assessment of the condition. Here Christ simply says "thou art fallen". The perfect tense shows that having fallen the church is still in the fallen condition. The words of Christ carry an echo of Eden and an Eve who, by satanic subtlety fell. Thus even at this early stage in assembly testimony Christ has to speak of another fall. What Paul feared for the Corinthian assembly (2 Cor 11:1-3) has happened in Ephesus. The betrothed of Christ has betrayed her trust.

This condition demands immediate action. In the present imperative "remember" is the suggestion that already the assembly was looking back with longing. Robertson translates "continue mindful". In any recovery whether of an individual or a congregation the memory of what has been lost often provides the first stirrings of genuine repentance. The believers recall the warmth of that affection for Christ of earlier days and they long to get back to the condition enjoyed before the fall. The fact of repentance and its fruit are to be seen in the next two verbs, "repent and do". The imperatives leave no option. Christ is not giving advice but issuing commands. The aorist tense of "repent" points to a crisis that takes the saints back to the point of departure. This retracing of the past is already in the verb "repent" (*metanoeō*) the basic meaning of which is to "change the mind". In spiritual things this means to take God's view of the matter. The decisions that resulted in the forsaking of Christ have to be reversed; the sins that had resulted or were inherent in the decisions had to be confessed. Only thus would that early love be enjoyed that would produce the early works. The aorist "do" probably should be translated "begin to do". The first works are simply the same kind of works that flowed from the same kind of love. Christ had already commented on their works (v. 2) but He desires them to get back to the freshness of their earliest activities. Christ seems to long for the recovery of the fervour to Himself that produces such fruit; affections centred on Himself would produce actions of that early character.

The alternative to repentance is the removal of the lampstand, a special judicial act by Christ Himself. The present tense of "come" as reflected in JND "I am coming" or the RV "I come" (not the future as in the AV) stresses the imminence of the action as if Christ was already on the way to take action. Christ is plainly saying, "Either you act or I will". The verb "to come" (*erchomai*) is used to refer to the Second Coming (see for example 1:7; 3:11; 22:7, 12, 17, 20 where this meaning is clear). However the meaning of words is related to context and the coming here as in v.6, cannot refer to the coming of the Lord to the air for His church. Arguments from commentators who support the interpretation of the Second Coming in this passage ignore the fact that this would make the Lord's coming dependent on the failure of one assembly to repent. This is certainly not in keeping with general scriptural teaching with regard to the coming. Further this interpretation overlooks the fact that when Christ comes every lampstand will be removed. This coming must be interpreted as the personal action of Christ in dealing with the condition of this assembly.

The removal of the lampstand can be no less than the physical dispersion of the company of believers. Some commentators have argued that the lampstand is the testimony as distinct from the physical gathering, in other words that the literal congregation could remain while that which really constitutes the testimony is removed. In support of this view Ezekiel's description of the departure of the Shekinah from the temple at Jerusalem is often quoted (Ezek 10:18). Despite the interesting analogy this is a false parallel and does not fit the situation here. The Shekinah was always distinct from the material building. Here the lampstand is the symbol for the church (1:20); it is not some mystical part of the church. The symbol of the lampstand represents the actual local company. Christ does not threaten the extinguishing of the light but the removal of the lampstand. The company is to be dispersed. In OT history the removal of Israel as the lampstand was the actual removal of the nation to Babylon. When God removed the two witnesses spoken of as lampstands (11:4), He removed them physically. These letters show that in any scriptural assembly there is always room for recovery through repentance. If this is denied it is Christ's prerogative to remove the lampstand.

While the act of removal is Christ's personal discipline there is nothing said about the means He may use to effect His purpose. It is certainly His prerogative to use a special act of judgment. The word "quickly" in the AV has only minimal manuscript support and most textual critics omit it (see JND and RV). Christ may use a variety of means to effect this purpose. To remove an assembly Christ may permit changes in climate or geography, changes in governments or politics, the sweep of military movements, or more frequently, socio-economic factors that alter the character of a district. However these are but His agents, in the final analysis it is His act of judgment. One may well ponder if the very fate of Ephesus as a city depended, not on the silting up of the harbour (the ostensible reason), but on the response of the church in that city to the challenge of her Lord. Today the wind whispers through the reeds on the site where mighty Ephesus once stood; the desolation and the barrenness but emphasise the silence. The solemn "or else" of our Lord may have had implications not only for the church but for the city as well.

6 Before issuing the challenge to the church Christ commends one further matter. From its position, this commendation must be secondary to that which had earlier earned His full approval. His earlier commendation (v.2) was of the positive features that were evidence of some residue of love that inspired them for the task, encouraged them in truth and enabled them to stand up to trials in testimony. Here the negative feature which Christ commends serves only to offer some hope that their condition is not yet beyond recovery. There is still love for His person but shown in a negative way in the hatred of that which He hated. The verb "hate" (*miseō*) is used with full force of "utter detestation". The detestation is not for people, but for certain practices (*erga*) that are identified as belonging to the Nicolaitans. In the OT the hatred of Jehovah for all idolatry and immorality is made abundantly clear (Isa 61:8; Jer 44:4; Amos 5:21; Zech 8:17); for His people to share that hatred, even in the days when they were failing in complete obedience to him, was to evidence a measure of fellowship with Him and provide a basis for recovery. This is the idea here. While love for Christ may have waned, to share in hating what Christ hated was some evidence of the operation of grace and a basis for hope that there might be full recovery.

Much learned discussion has centred upon the Nicolaitans. There have been many suggestions as to the identity of this group but these fall generally under two main views:

VIEW 1. This may be called the *historical view*. This is the oldest view. It has been held from the time of Irenaeus in the last quarter of the second century. This early writer linked the Nicolaitans with a heretical sect taking their name from Nicolas of Antioch one of the seven original deacons (Acts 6:5). This Nicolas was charged with being a Jewish proselyte who apostatised. This view had strong support from many of the early fathers who claimed they were a sect of licentious antinomian heretics who, under the cloak of the professed liberty claimed in Christ, indulged in the most profligate and immoral behaviour. In this perverse way the sect sought to link christianity and paganism. Hymenaeus and Philetus (2 Tim 2:17) have been named as belonging to this sect. Commentators who follow this tradition insist that they parallel, in NT times, the teaching of Balaam in an OT day. Some also insist that there is a parallelism between the Greek etymology of "Nicolaitan" (the conqueror of the people) and the Hebrew etymology of Balaam (the devourer of the people). See comments at vv. 15-16. The argument is that the teaching of Balaam and the Nicolaitans served to break down the separation that God had put between His people and the world around. Thus the social and sexual temptation offered by the Moabitish women at the instigation of Balaam, resulted in an Israel judged by God for idolatry and immorality. A strong element of gnosticism in the teaching of the Nicolaitans would lend intellectual respectability to such libertine teaching. This in turn would encourage believers to be linked again with the pagan practices from which Christ had delivered them. It will be shown, however that Christ distinguishes between two separate groups of people (v. 15) and this, in itself, is a very weighty argument against the identity of the teaching of the Nicolaitans and Balaam.

The real trouble with viewing this sect as libertines owing their existence to the teaching of Nicolas the deacon is very simple. The evidence for it historically is so meagre as to be almost non-existent. Nicolas in the estimation of many competent historians has been maligned sorely without good reason and on the basis of his name alone. The sect itself seems to owe its origins to his name and to be without independent witness. Commentator historians of the calibre of Alford, Hort, Beckwith and Swete find no evidence for such a link with the Nicolas of the NT. The best they can suggest may be summarised in the words of Swete, "On the whole it seems best to fall back upon the supposition that a party bearing this name existed in Asia when the Apocalypse was written, whether it owed its origin to Nicolas of Antioch, which is not improbable, or to some other false teacher of that name". In fact the historical argument for such an identification is entirely negative. W. Lincoln sums the matter up concisely (*Lectures* page 52), "men have assumed this sect's existence then fancied it had its origin from some Nicolas, and then the very Nicolas has been identified – all in imagination."

VIEW 2. This may be called the *etymological view* and has much more to commend it. The identification of this group is derived from the etymology of the word "Nicolaitans". The words making up the name are *nikē* ("victory") and *laos* ("people") which gives the meaning "the conqueror of the people". This view sees the Nicolaitans as the forerunners of the clerical hierarchy which claimed dominion over the believers. NT teaching indicates how spiritually gifted and equipped men are to be recognised as elders, overseers and deacons in the local assemblies. Paul's message to the elders at Ephesus shows how this was to be done (Acts 20:28) and, at the same time warns against those who would rise up to "draw away disciples after themselves" (Acts 20:30). The time of which Paul warned over thirty years before had apparently arrived in Ephesus; men were seeking to build up a personal sphere of influence and establish a clerical hierarchy to dominate the assembly. What is seen here in the Nicolaitans is, in essence, the rise of clericalism and ecclesiasticism. This turning away from scriptural truth is well defined in the words of W. Lincoln in his commentary *The Book of the Revelation*, "As respects God, it is the ceasing to give Christ His own place in the assembly of His saints, together with the ignoring of the Holy Ghost's presence. On the human side there is, instead, the leaning on some gifted individual, and ultimately the ruling of a caste, originally of such individuals, to conduct the worship etc." This explains Christ's special hatred as He Himself is displaced. T.F. La Haye, himself a pastor, writes tellingly, "The greatest single curse in modern christendom is ecclesiasticism. When men get control of the spiritual training of other people and are in a position to dominate the church, their theological position will eventually dominate that church. The history of the church of Jesus Christ is a continuous cycle of autonomous churches amalgamating into great conventions or denominations of ecclesiastical hierarchies that eventually become apostate" (*Revelation – Illustrated and Made Plain*, T.F. La Haye). In Ephesus in the Nicolaitans is seen the emergence of clericalism. The One who holds the seven stars and scrutinises the seven lampstands has absolute authority and will scarcely delegate this to self-appointed, or even church-appointed men. It can also be seen how the deeds calculated to achieve this domination of the laity appear first and then there would be developed the doctrine (v. 15) to justify it.

7 During the earthly ministry of Christ, John must have been familiar with His oft-repeated challenge to the audience, "He that hath ears to hear, let him hear" (Matt 11:15; 13:9, 43: Mark 4:9, 23; Luke 8:8; 14:35). Physical hearing could be the path to spiritual blessing if attention was given to the message. Here a single "ear" could be the path to spiritual blessing provided there is the will to obey.

The aorist imperative in the command "let him hear" leaves no room for trifling; an instant individual response is demanded. While it is Christ speaking, through John as the channel of writing, the Holy Spirit presses the relevant message upon the individual believer, so it becomes "what the Spirit saith". That the Spirit will speak to a wider audience than the assembly in Ephesus is clear by Christ's use of the plural "churches". This plural not only shows that the seven messages were all intended to be part of a whole but also indicates that the messages would speak to churches of all times.

It will immediately be noted that in the first three churches this call precedes the promise to the overcomer, while in the last four churches the call follows the promise to the overcomer. Two reasons may be advanced for this change of position:

1. It is possible that in the first three churches the believer with the hearing ear can be found in the church as a whole. In the last four churches the suggestion is made that the spiritual condition of the churches has deteriorated so seriously that the one with the hearing ear will be found only amongst the overcomers in the church. Hence the call comes after the promise to the overcomer (Hamilton Smith).
2. On the prophetic view of the churches, as spiritual conditions deteriorate, the last four churches reflect conditions existing side by side. Thus, whatever the local conditions, it will require an overcomer with a responsive ear to maintain the local testimony for Christ.

The last word to each of the first three churches and the penultimate word to each of the last four churches is the promise to the overcomer. This is a simple personal promise of Christ Himself to the overcomers in each church.

Different views have been taken of those described as "overcomers". Some commentators, including those holding partial-rapture teaching, see in the overcomers a special group of spiritual believers who respond to Christ's challenge to repent. This assumes that all within the churches are regenerate but that only some qualify for the designation of "overcomer" and thus only some share in the promise. The most serious objection is that it divides believers into two groups. While admitting that believers may be "spiritual" or "carnal" (1 Cor 2:14-3:4) there is no hint in other scriptures of any separation into an "overcoming" class and a "non-overcoming class". Secondly, the promises to the overcomers offer only what is the common heritage of all believers. For example this first promise "to eat of the tree of life" is the scriptural figure for the enjoyment of eternal life (22:2). It is to be carefully noted that all that is promised in the seven promises to the overcomers is detailed in the final three chapters of this book as the Eternal State is described. In that Eternal State there are only two classes – the saved and the lost. This is very clear in 22:7-8 which distinguishes between those who "inherit all things" and those who "have their part in the lake which burneth with fire and brimstone". There is no intermediate class. Thirdly, this view overlooks the fact that use of the term "overcomer" is characteristic of John. Of the twenty seven occasions that the verb "to overcome" (*nikaō*) is used, twenty three are found in John's writings (the exceptions are Luke 11:22; Rom 3:4; 12:21 (2)). "Overcoming" in John's language is synonymous with "believing" in Paul's language. This is evident in 1 John 5:4-5 where faith in Christ is shown in the overcoming of the world in the pattern of the Saviour Himself (John 16:33). With this in mind, it is much more satisfactory to see that the word defines what a true believer is expected to be in the local assembly. This admits that in assemblies on earth, where human failure can be assumed, there will be those whose faith is merely nominal. As failure deepens, in the generally deteriorating spiritual conditions (there are exceptions) from Ephesus to Laodicea, the number of mere professors increases. Against all the variety of those spiritual conditions true believers will stand out locally as marked by an active faith that cannot be hidden. They believe, therefore they overcome. W. Scott makes the right connection: "In all cases the witnessing is individual, and of course the overcomer is one who in the energy of faith surmounts those special difficulties in which he finds himself. The overcomer in Laodicea has a more serious task before him than the overcomer in Ephesus. The position, circumstances, and character of the conflict are different in each church".

The first promise speaks of the "tree of life" which recalls Genesis and the Garden of Eden. There came the fall of man and, as a consequence, his exclusion from that garden. One act of disobedience (Rom 5:19) brought man to a distance where he could not enjoy the tree of life. Now through grace one act of obedience by Christ (Rom 5:19) has allowed Him to be the dispenser of eternal life (1 John 5:11-12) but only, of course, to believers (John 3:16, 36). Note the personal emphasis by Christ in the expression "I will give". This enjoyment of the fruit of Christ's work is open to every believer now in their overcoming; this is their portion in fellowship with Christ. It will, however, also embrace a full enjoyment in a day to come (see 22:2,14). Those who refuse to allow the fallen condition of a church to rob them of giving Christ the full devotion of heart have a portion now and forever. This anticipation of future enjoyment is stressed by Christ pointing out the location of the tree of life. It is in the midst of the paradise of God.

The word "paradise" is a Persian loan word meaning "enclosure" or "park" (Kittel and Friedrich) and carries the idea of a "pleasure garden". It comes into the OT through the LXX in Gen 2-3 and is used for "forest" (Neh 2:8), "orchard" (Eccl 2:5; Song of Songs 4:13). While drawing upon the garden background of the word the NT raises it to a far higher level as descriptive of the abode of the redeemed. This is clear from Christ's words of assurance to the dying thief on Calvary (Luke 23:43). In the world, unseen by mortal eye, the dying thief was to join Christ in Paradise. It was to this same Paradise that Paul was caught up and which is identified with the third heaven (2 Cor 12:2-4), the abode of deity. It is here that eternal life is to be enjoyed in all its fulness and, to use the symbolic language of this promise, where the tree of life is located. In a day when the real becomes visible to the eye then this paradisaical state of blessedness will be seen in an actual city (22:2). This will be where the saints enjoy the very presence of God and the very fulness of eternal life (22:2). The overcomer has a delectable portion now and it will be fully enjoyed in a day to come.

The Genesis period

In studying the history of the church throughout the dispensation, as it is foreshadowed in these letters from Christ Himself, it is not surprising that there will be found pictures drawn from the history of the saints of a past dispensation. Christ's letter to Ephesus may, from the references found in it, be called the Genesis period.

In this period are found the beginnings of testimony. In Genesis God is spoken of as the One "walking in the garden in the cool of the day" (Gen 3:8); here Christ is identified as the One "who walketh in the midst of the seven golden lampstands". God in Genesis had to deal with a fallen man; here Christ has to deal with a fallen Church. In Genesis God had to remove man from the garden; here Christ may have to remove the lampstand from the place of testimony. Paradise in Genesis is closed to man through sin, here paradisal conditions may be enjoyed through personal repentance as a believer overcomes in the prevailing circumstances.

Notes

5 It should, of course, be perfectly clear that the movement of an assembly from one location to another through the exercise of the believers is a totally different matter. In certain circumstances the Lord closes one door to open another. The matter under consideration here is the removal of the assembly by an act of divine judgment.

(b) *The message to Smyrna (vv. 8-11)*

v.8 "And unto the angel of the church in Smyrna write; These things saith the first and the last, which was dead, and is alive;
v.9 I know thy works, and tribulation, and poverty, (but thou art rich) and I know the blasphemy of them which say they are Jews, and are not, but are the synagogue of Satan.
v.10 Fear none of those things which thou shalt suffer: behold, the devil shall cast some of you into prison, that ye may be tried; and ye shall have tribulation ten days: be thou faithful unto death, and I will give thee a crown of life.
v.11 He that hath an ear, let him hear what the Spirit saith unto the churches; He that overcometh shall not be hurt of the second death."

35 miles almost due north of Ephesus on a bay of the Aegean Sea was the city of Smyrna. The city occupied a most attractive site. At its feet the blue waters of the Aegean Sea were ringed with golden sand and inland it was encircled by the dark green of the cypress-clad hills. The city itself was known as "The Lovely – The Crown of Ionia", "The Ornament of Asia" (Unger). Yet behind the physical beauty lurked a wickedness that rivalled and was, in fact, more deadly than that of Ephesus; the city was the spearhead of satanic opposition to Christ in Asia. No other of these seven cities was so stained with the blood of the martyrs of Christ. It was here that the aged Polycarp was to die at the stake in 169 (Unger's date).

Smyrna rivalled Ephesus not alone in wickedness but also in wealth. The trade centre for the export of wine and myrrh (an aromatic gum used in the embalming of the dead) this bustling city, at the beginning of the new century, would replace Ephesus as the first trading city of Asia. While Ephesus waned in importance, largely due to the silting of the harbour, Smyrna prospered so that one historian noted, "Everything in Smyrna is measured by the standard of wealth". The ideal climate, the beautiful situation and the material prosperity might lead the historian to expect a broad-minded approach to religion. In some respects this was true for almost all the pagan gods were given credence in Smyrna. However, this was balanced by unhesitating, even fanatical allegiance to Rome. This was not only political expediency but it brought an uncharacteristically uncompromising element into the religious observances of the city and was to lead to the putting to death of many Christians. Beyond the nominal adherence to the usual deities of paganism the city subscribed enthusiastically to the cult of Emperor worship. As early as 196 BC an altar had been erected to *Dea Roma*. This goddess was the deification of the spirit of Rome. Over a century later an altar was built to Tiberius Caesar (See F. A. Tatford in his book *The Patmos Letters*. p.49) As Tatford points out, "The worship of the Emperor was compulsory. Each year a Roman citizen had to burn a pinch of incense on the altar and to acknowledge publicly that Caesar was supreme lord". Under Domitian (81-96AD) in the time of this letter, emperor worship was compulsory for every Roman citizen. The burning of the pinch of incense was rewarded by a certificate which had to be renewed annually. Failure to produce a certificate meant being branded as a Christian and this opened the way, if the magistrates so decided, for the death penalty on the ground of treason. Admittedly the burning of the incense was more an act of political loyalty than a religious observance, since the citizen was then free to worship whatever other god or gods he chose. Nevertheless no believer loyal to Christ could do this (see Luke 14:26). Many, like Polycarp, perished at the stake or were torn apart by the beasts in the arena because they refused this test of allegiance to Caesar. The cypress-clad hills around Smyrna were both crowned and crowded with pagan temples. The whole religious pantheon was represented there: temples existed to Zeus, Apollo, Aphrodite, Asclepius, Demeter and Cybele. Cybele the Mother was the particular pride of Smyrna. Her magnificent temple stood at the eastern end of the curving Street of Gold with the great temple of

Zeus at the other end. This ring of temples around the city was called the "Crown of Ionia". Saints, faithful to Christ, dying at the stake would lift their eyes from this earthly crown to the one that Christ held out, "the crown of life" (v. 10).

In this beautiful situation, surrounded by an unashamedly-materialistic society and under the shadow of Caesar-worship existed a collective testimony for Christ. Christ owns it as faithful and offers no word of criticism. Of the assembly itself we have no other information than is contained in this letter. Neither the NT nor verifiable history offers any further details. While Smyrna is not mentioned directly in the Acts or Epistles it is possible that it is included in the general statement of Acts 19:10 concerning Paul's stay at Ephesus, "So that all they that dwelt in Asia heard the word of the Lord Jesus, both Jews and Greeks". An early tradition does claim that Paul visited the town on his way to Ephesus at the beginning of the third missionary journey but there is no historical confirmation of this visit. The city on this site today is called Izmir and is the provincial capital of Anatolia in Turkey with a population of around 200,000 people one third of whom profess christianity.

8 Christ addresses the angel of this church in words identical with those used to Ephesus. Again, it is the spiritual condition represented in the term "angel" that is addressed in Smyrna. Against the backdrop of this beautiful, wealthy, fanatical city there was a called-out company of saints giving Christ His place in their life and testimony.

The character in which Christ introduces Himself is most suited to the condition and circumstances of the assembly. When he speaks of Himself as "the first and the last", Christ is claiming absolute deity. As "the first" He predates all created things and as "the last" He remains when all else has passed away; to Him alone belongs unconditional, inherent and underived immortality. This belongs to deity as by right (1 Tim 6:16). Untouched by all that may occur in time the title throws into true perspective the storms that engulf believers on earth. Like a storm sweeping round a mighty rock bastion none of the vicissitudes of earth can touch Him. Thus the sorely persecuted believers in Smyrna could take refuge in Him. The title is descriptive of Jehovah in the OT (Isa 44:6) and shows that He is the same Lord in respect of the present testimony. From the first chapter of the book (1:17) until the last (22:13) He remains the same, unchangeable and unchanging. He is God.

The second part of Christ's introduction stresses His humanity. This One who is inherently transcendent and above time is the One who stepped into time. This One has become so identified with suffering humanity that He "became dead" – a more literal and exact translation (see JND). The aorist tense points to the cross and the deliberate action of Christ in willingly subjecting Himself to death. Implicit is the thought of the opposition and persecution that led to such a death. Human understanding is superseded. He belongs to eternity and yet in time He allowed Himself to be put to death. The final note is triumphant. It could be missed in the weak AV translation "is alive". To clarify the point the JND marginal note is useful, "that is after having died". It is the victory of the resurrection that is in view. The aorist points back to the fact of resurrection and stands in contrast to the present participle in 1:18 which stresses the fact that He is now living. The believers in Smyrna themselves faced with death would see immediately that the fact of Christ's death and resurrection robs death of its terror. The patron goddess of Smyrna was Cybele the nature-goddess whose worship was based on her descent into death in the winter and her supposed glorious resurrection in the spring. Believers would turn with confidence from the mythology of their past and the shadows of imagination to worship One who died and burst from the grave in resurrection power. The shadows all disappear in the sunlight of His resurrection.

In this connection F.A. Tatford points out that Smyrna itself was known as the city that "became dead and lived again" (*Prophecy's Last Word*) p.43. He writes, "In 600 BC Smyrna was captured and destroyed by the Lydians, and Strabo states that for four centuries its name was obliterated from the roll of cities but it was restored once more and again became an autonomous Greek city". Thus the myths of heathendom and memories of history all fade as believers are presented with the risen Saviour.

That the fanaticism of a city devoted to Emperor worship is already, at this early date, causing severe persecution for believers in Smyrna becomes apparent as we listen to Christ's words to this church. It is useful to note that the word *smurna* (the origin of the name of the city) means "myrrh". It is so translated in Matt 2:11; John 19:39. The city was traditionally associated with the trade of this aromatic arabic gum from the *Balsamodendron Myrrha* tree (Unger). Used in embalming the dead it was associated with death and suffering. The etymology of the word *smurna* points to the meaning "bitter" yet, when crushed or burned, myrrh gave off a delightful perfume. It is not without significance that myrrh is linked with the Christ at His birth (Matt 2:11) and at His death (John 19:39). Its OT usage in connection with the holy anointing oil (Exod 30:23), with the bride in the Song of Solomon (*Song of Songs* 3:6) and with the King-bridegroom in the Psalms (45:8), all carry a typical significance.

9 The omission of the words "thy works" in the majority of the older manuscripts suggest that the words may have been interpolated by scribal addition to conform with the other letters. There is no doubt that their omission shows that Christ is concerned with their suffering rather than their service. That believers serve while they suffer is certainly true but, when persecution rages, service as such may be very restricted.

In detailing three particular matters Christ shows He is perfectly aware of all the circumstance of their testimony.

1. "Thy tribulation" (*thlipsis*) speaks of the pressures under which they lived.

The circumstances were being used to attempt to crush the testimony for Christ. The local civil magistracy in Smyrna was placing every possible social and commercial pressure on believers.

2. To the pressures of unsympathetic civil authorities were added the everyday problems of "(thy) poverty" (*ptōcheia*). For the Christians to earn a living would be very difficult since it was impossible to join the trade guilds because of their pagan associations. The refusal of the token allegiance to Caesar would make them politically suspect and liable for accusation on any issue of the day. Suffering confiscation of goods on the same grounds, these Christians were not merely poor (the word, in this case would have been *penēs*), but they were actually destitute, stripped of all material resources (*ptōchos*). Starving and homeless they shared in the poverty of the Saviour (2 Cor 8:9). It is against this background of material poverty that Christ pointed to their spiritual heritage in the parenthetical words, "but thou art rich". This was wealth that the enemy could not touch. How different in Laodicea (3:17) where the material wealth of the Christians but highlighted their spiritual poverty!
3. Social pressures and material poverty were made worse by the calumnies and insults of neighbours. The word "blasphemy" (*blasphēmia*) is better translated "railing" when directed against men (see JND). However the AV translators may quite correctly have concluded that the words went beyond the Christians as the immediate targets and the insults were aimed at Christ. Hence the translation "blasphemy".

Paganism in general and the magistrates in particular were often remarkably tolerant of the Christians provided that the security of the Empire was not in jeopardy. In the earliest days the Christians were regarded as simply a sect within the permitted religion of Judaism. However many Jews were very unhappy about this and their bitter antagonism led them to stir up civil and social unrest against believers. Charges and slanders of the most despicable character were circulated. The very language that Christians used about the Lord's supper was twisted to raise charges of cannibalism. Civil disturbances fomented by the Jews drew in the Roman magistracy and the whole might of Rome would be directed against these "tumultuous" Christians. This is the background to Christ's identification of these blasphemers. They were those who say "they are Jews and are not". The interpretation of this phrase depends on the understanding of the word "Jews". To suggest these are Greeks calling themselves Jews to stir up trouble so that the Roman magistrates would press for the ban on all Judaism in neither feasible nor possible in the clear-cut world of the Roman Empire. Christ is describing those who, while Jews by birth nationally, show that they are not so in spiritual reality. The word is used like this in Rom 2:28; 9:6-7. The Jewish community at Smyrna belonging to the synagogue in the city had clearly rejected Christ and were heaping false accusations on those who had believed in Him. This was stirring up and using the magisterial arm of Roman Law against the followers of Christ. Historically it is a well established fact that the Jews took a very active part in the martyrdom of Polycarp. Christ in this terse statement identifies the kind of persecution and the personage behind it.

10 The negative with the verb in the imperative may be translated "stop fearing" (Robertson) – an almost sharp rebuke bidding a cessation of a fear that was already gripping their hearts. The storm clouds of persecution were gathering but Christ is anxious that the Christians should not live in constant dread. For their comfort, contrary to the thinking in man's psychology, Christ does not promise them immediate relief or that the worst will not happen. Nor, perhaps surprisingly, does He suggest relief in the consciousness of His imminent return. He tells them plainly that things will get worse. The dark thunderclouds of the gathering storm will break upon them. He speaks of "those things which thou shalt suffer". The words "shalt suffer" include the verb *melleis*. This would be better translated "about to", a translation that would be consistent with the other times it is used in these letters (Sardis 3:2; Philadelphia 3:10; Laodicea 3:16). It suggests the imminent bursting of the storm.

The comfort that Christ gives is set out in four matters:

1. The identification of the person behind the persecution: The previous verse has identified Satan as the implacable adversary of Christ and His people. This verse speaks of that same one under the title of "the devil" (*diabolos*) the name that identifies him as the accuser. The opponent of the purpose of God and the accuser of the people of God is about to use all his considerable power to stamp out the testimony for Christ. His agents would be the religious dupes of Judaism stirring up the civil authorities to stamp out this subversive teaching of Christianity, but the devil is the ultimate source of the opposition. The result would be both loss of liberty and loss of life for many a believer. While religious fanaticism or political expediency may have served as an excuse it would comfort believers to know that Christ recognised that they were the objects of infernal attack.
2. The indication of a purpose in the persecution: Grasping that behind the most unpleasant circumstances of life there is a purpose brings divine strength into the trial. The very verb used in the expression "that ye may be tried", (*peirazō*), has its background in the art of the metallurgist in the fire treatment of metallic ore. (The related verb *dokimazō* implies that the testing will bring approval). This verb leaves the outcome of the test in doubt and is better translated "tempt" as it is in thirty-three of its thirty nine occurrences in the NT. The noun is "the tempter" (Matt 4:3). It would be a matter of great comfort to tempted saints to know that Christ endured the same assault as they were to face and from the very same enemy. The devil's activity in Smyrna through his agents would be a severe test of the

faith of all the believers. The picture presented is that one believer after another is being led off to prison amidst mounting tension. By the pressure of false accusations and civil charges, with death as the ultimate weapon, the devil hopes to cause them to renounce their faith in Christ. It makes little difference to the understanding of the passage whether it is the ones who are cast into prison ("some of you") or the whole assembly who were being tempted. A weighty point is made by H.B. Swete who points out that where the verb *mellei* ("about to") is used in the NT there are always overtones of divine purpose involved (notice the thirteen references in this book 1:19; 2:10 (twice); 3:2,10,16; 6:11; 8:13; 10:4,7; 12:4,5; 17:8). When the prospect of the crown of life is taken into account there is a definite suggestion that Christ is glorified through the very pain that the devil means for ill. Viewing their suffering in this light would bring new strength to believers.

3. The limitation of the period of persecution: There is no reason to take the mention of prison here in any other than a literal sense. This argument applies with equal force to the ten-day tribulation (*thlipsis*). Christ is warning the believers that there is a particular period of intense pressure that they will face in the future but it will be limited in duration to ten days. If there is a symbolic meaning in the number it may simply suggest, as "ten" often does in scripture, that human responsibility is involved. The faith of believers will be tested to the limit. There is no particular need to search historical records for this period of persecution. If this letter reached Smyrna in the year 96 AD then these ten days could well have occurred in Smyrna in the bitter periodic persecutions of the closing years of the reign of Domitian (81-96 AD). When the storm did burst in its fury this assembly would be able to count the days fortified by knowing that Christ had set a limit upon the period of their trial. Many and various are the arguments that have been advanced to evade this most natural interpretation. Some commentators would take the days symbolic of years or longer periods of time. In the simple message to the church there is no need for this. As noted previously there are prophetic foreshadowings in Christ's messages to the churches but these can be seen only in the light of history. Within the context of this letter Christ warns the saints in Smyrna that a ten-day period of intense pressure would come within their generation to test their faith in Christ.

4. The promise to the persecuted: The first imperative in the verse as shown could be translated "stop fearing": the saints were not to be dismayed by the gathering stormclouds of tribulation; this last imperative could be translated "keep on proving yourselves faithful" (Alford). While *pistos* can have the active meaning of "believing" (Gal 3:9; 2 Cor 6:15) the more usual idea is "faithful" or "one to be trusted": a believer whom Christ could trust to maintain confidence in Him until

death itself. "Until death" (Newberry margin) expresses not duration but the degree of faithfulness that Christ expects: faithfulness right up to the point of death. The implication is that the death expected is a violent one. Christ is not, of course, anticipating that all would die as martyrs, but He is showing that the degree of faithfulness He expects is measured by willingness to die for Him. For the faithful He holds out the promise of "the crown of life". The NT frequently draws upon the Greek-Roman background of the great athletic contests for metaphors and pictures of the christian life (cf. 1 Cor 9:24-25; 2 Tim 2:5). The major centres for these games were Olympia, Delos and Corinth but many other cities held their own games, not least of which was Smyrna. Inherent in the idea of the crown (*stephanos*) in Smyrna is not only recognition and reward but also victory. This is the emphasis when Paul in light of his own martyrdom uses the same imagery in 2 Tim 4:8. There is no loss, only recompense, full and complete; there is no defeat, only victory enjoyed with the risen One already crowned with honour and glory. The same crown is promised to the tried saints in James 1:12. In both cases the question arises whether the "crown of life" is to be understood as "life's crown"; that would mean that it is a special reward above the eternal life enjoyed by other saints. Some commentators (see W. Scott p.69) suggest that this is the thought intended. On this view this is therefore the martyr's crown to be won by those who seal their testimony in blood. The alternative is to render the phrase "a crown which is life". Since faithfulness (and not death) was Christ's requirement for such recognition, this best suits the context. Not all believers, even in Smyrna, would die a martyr's death but all the faithful ones would share the victory of Christ. Eternal life cannot be earned by faithfulness; such a thought would be contrary to all NT teaching that presents life as "the gift of God...through Jesus Christ our Lord" (Rom 6:23). Faithful testimony would evidence the reality of the divine life they already possessed and the crown would reflect their faithfulness to Christ whether in life or death. Beyond the prison cell and the burning stake there shone a crown: life in its fulness.

11 Christ now repeats the call He made to the believers in Ephesus (see comments on v.7). It is not merely a call but a command. Note the singular "ear" which emphasises both the metaphoric nature of the language and the individual responsibility of the saint to respond to the Spirit appealing through the written word. The widening of the scope of the message "to the churches" implies both the oneness of this book and also that Christ knew that similar conditions would exist in a multiplicity of churches. Where persecution would arise the churches would need the same comfort as given to this church whatever the time period.

Christ knew that the Spirit of God would have ample opportunity to apply this message in all ages.

The one who lends an ear to the Spirit (v.11a) in these circumstances, could find himself tested (v.10b) to the very point of death. That death could include torture; the rack would be followed by the stake or being thrown to the beasts in the arena. Fiendish cruelty and devilish maltreatment awaited the faithful believer under Smyrnan conditions but Christ's promise shines through the pain. Death, physical and painful, may be meted out by men, but the believer cannot be touched by that which is unimaginably worse: "the second death". This term awaits the full explanation of 21:8 where it is shown to be the portion of the unbeliever. In this light it is clear that every believer is an overcomer, a truth made abundantly clear in 20:6 since every believer has a part in the first resurrection. That the "second death" involves conscious physical pain is demanded by the verb "hurt" (*adikeō*) which in every other occurrence in this book implies physical harm or injury (6:6; 7:2,3; 9:4,10,19; 11:5). In its participle form in 22:11 it may carry the same thought. The identification of "the second death" as "the lake of fire" in 20:14 adds a terrible explanation to a death from which there can be no resurrection. It has to be seen as involving conscious, unending pain. What man inflicts on his fellow makes a terrible record but the righteous judgment of a holy God against sin makes the soul to tremble.

The comfort for the overcomer is couched in the strongest negative of which the Greek language is capable. It may be translated "in no wise" as in the Newberry margin; there is no way in which the overcomer can be harmed by the second death.

The Exodus period

After the age of promise to the patriachs (Abraham, Isaac and Jacob) the children of Israel for a period of 400 years knew what it was to live in Egypt (Gen 15: 12-21). They knew the tribulation, the poverty and eventually the persecution of such a dwelling place. Egypt has ever been associated with death; the famous "Book of the Dead" originated there, the rites for the dead were faithfully observed there, the pyramids as the tombs of the dead still bear witness to their obsession with death.

God had revealed Himself to each of the patriarchs as Jehovah (Exod 6:3 should end with a question mark) the living One. Each patriarch had known something of resurrection or the "one who became dead and is alive" (Heb 11:12. This living One preserved His people and delivered them so that Joseph could anticipate the crown after the prison (Gen 49:26); after the pit came the palace.

Now in the Smyrnan period of testimony for Christ, the One "who became dead and is alive" holds out to the faithful the "crown of life". That death that hangs over sinners cannot touch the saints. They cannot be hurt of "the second death". Even today where believers suffer for their faith this word of comfort is still available. There is still a "crown of life" to be won.

(c) *The message to Pergamum (vv. 12-17)*

v.12 "And to the angel of the church in Pergamos write; These things saith he which hath the sharp sword with two edges;
v.13 I know thy works, and where thou dwellest, even where Satan's seat is: and thou holdest fast my name, and hast not denied my faith, even in those days wherein Antipas was my faithful martyr, who was slain among you, where Satan dwelleth.
v.14 But I have a few things against thee, because thou hast there them that hold the doctrine of Balaam, who taught Balac to cast a stumblingblock before the children of Israel, to eat things sacrificed unto idols and to commit fornication.
v.15 So hast thou also them that hold the doctrine of the Nicolaitans, which thing I hate.
v.16 Repent; or else I will come unto thee quickly, and will fight against them with the sword of my mouth.
v.17 He that hath an ear, let him hear what the Spirit saith unto the churches; To him that overcometh will I give to eat of the hidden manna, and will give him a white stone, and in the stone a new name written, which no man knoweth saving he that receiveth it."

From the physical beauty of attractive Smyma to the intellectual challenge of academic Pergamum involved a journey of 55 miles due north from Smyrna. The traveller would then be in "a city, a university town, and a royal residence" (F.A. Tatford *The Patmos Letters* p.73). Nevertheless the outward calm of academia held no less a challenge to the Christians there than the fanaticism of Smyrna. Three couplets sum up the claims of Pergamum:

1. Roman Imperialism: Until the end of the first century Pergamum was the capital of the Province of Asia. From 133BC when King Attalus III ceded his kingdom to Rome in exchange for military aid against the encroaching Syrians this city was the centre of administration for the whole province. The symbol of this rule was a sword. The proconsul, as the chief magistrate, had the right of passing the death penalty without recourse to any higher authority (this was called throughout the Roman Empire "the right of the sword" (*ius gladii*). It is not without significance that Christ presents Himself to this church as the One who "hath the sharp sword". Magistrates have a delegated authority from God (Rom 13:1-4) for the maintenance of justice upon earth, but absolute authority belongs to Christ. For the believer there can be no question to whom he owes primary allegiance. In any conflict of loyalty Christ must take precedence.
2. Proud Intellectualism: Of all the religions that were acknowledged in Pergamum the one with the greatest following was the worship of Asclepius. This was the god of medicine, locally known as the god of healing, and given the titles of "saviour" and "preserver". Filling the avenues and streets of the city were a multitude of statues, altars and sacred groves dedicated to Zeus, Apollo and the whole pantheon of pagan gods, but the most magnificent temple in Pergamum was that of Asclepius. His symbol was the *caduceus* – the entwined

serpent on a pole; a symbol that appears on the coins used in the city. According to the legend (Vincent) Asclepius was worshipped in the feeding of a serpent kept in this temple. Inscriptions honour Pergamum as "temple sweeper" of this god (cf. Acts 19:35 Newberry margin where *neōkoron* is translated "Temple-Keeper". The terms are virtually synonymous. As well as "the city of the sword", this was also "the city of the serpent". Associated with the worship of Asclepius, and indeed part of it, was a medical school which drew students from over the world. The magnificent library of over 200,000 parchments was rivalled only by the library at Alexandria. The reproduction of parchment copies of these books was a major industry. It was in Pergamum that the art of treating animal skins to make parchment for writing purposes was perfected; though little used now outside technical journals there is still a word "pergameneous" (of the nature of parchment) in English.

3. Religious Syncretism: Imperial Rome, while tolerant of religion in general and prepared to accept even the most debased practices provided they did not pose any danger to the state, found the variety of religions in Pergamum too perplexing and demanded a unifying religious principle. This they found in Caesar worship. Pergamum was the first city in Asia to erect a temple and establish a great altar in honour of Augustus Caesar. This happened as early as 27BC. So this city as well as "the city of the sword" and "the city of the serpent" became historically "the city of the altar". The worship of Caesar as a god, crossing all religious boundaries, was expected to be the religion that would be the uniting bond of Empire. So long as Caesar was acknowledged then any other god could be worshipped at will. R. L. Thomas writes, "Compared to all the surrounding cities, Caesar worship was the most intense here. In other cities a Christian might be in danger on only one day in the year when a pinch of incense had to be burned in worship of the emperor. In Pergamum, however, Christians were in danger every day of the year for the same reason".

12 In language identical to that which He used to Ephesus and Symrna Christ begins His message to the church in Pergamum. Over against the background of Roman Imperialism, proud intellectualism and religious syncretism in this city there was a company of believers gathered to bear testimony to Christ. Of their origin or history we know nothing beyond this letter, the NT and history are both silent about them. It is enough to know that Christ valued their witness under such conditions.

Christ introduces Himself as the One "having the sharp two edged sword". The description is taken from 1:16. On the three occasions of the mention of this sword (1:16; 19:15, 21) it is associated with His mouth to indicate that it is a symbol of the penetrative, executive power of His word. While believers in Pergamum may die under the misused sword of Roman judicial authority there is another, far mightier than the Roman magistrate, who wields the sword for God. It is this One whom they ought to fear.

13 As He does to each of the churches, Christ draws attention to His intimate knowledge of them. Note His reference to:

1. Their situation – they lived in a dangerous place. Christ fastens upon the vital point that has a major bearing on their testimony, "I know where thou dwellest". The omission of "thy works" in the RV, on good manuscript authority, serves to heighten the impression that Christ is deeply concerned about where they live. Christians in Pergamum were at the very centre of the conflict between Christ and Satan. This very city was the place "where Satan's seat is", "where Satan dwelleth". This was a place above others on earth where Satanic authority was to be seen and Satanic presence to be felt. This was "the city of the serpent" and the very atmosphere was infused with such worship. Believers had their homes here; the verb "to dwell" (*katoikeō*) means "to settle down" or "to make a home". In this context, it carries no moral implication; this was simply their home town, they had no other country of residence. Satan had invaded it and made it his permanent dwelling too.

   The word "seat" (*thronos*) of the AV should be translated "throne". This word demands a centralisation of the power of Satan in this earthly centre. The same verb as used of the citizens, *katoikeō*, indicates that Satan physically and personally had taken up his residence here. While a mighty personage, Satan does not have attributes of deity and can be only in one place at a time. Christ shows that at this time Satan had taken up residence in Pergamum.

   Most commentators are agreed that the language regarding Satan goes beyond the metaphorical and indicates a physical location for the throne. At this point unanimity ends and many suggestions have been offered as to the identification of the throne of Satan

   a. Some commentators insist that it was the great temple of Asclepius which rivalled the temple of Artemis at Ephesus and the temple of Apollo at Delphi. Believers would readily identify the serpent with Satan (Gen 3: 1-5). The healing ministry of Asclepius the "saviour" allied with medical practice could readily deceive men, as Eve had been deceived, as to the true nature of the enemy. When this is linked with the Babylonian background of the worship of Asclepius, much can be said for this suggestion. However, the weighty argument against this identification is that, after all, this god was but one god amongst the whole range of gods worshipped in paganism. Why Satan should take up residence in this particular temple has not been satisfactorily answered.
   b. Other commentators are equally sure that the throne of Satan must refer to the great altar to *Zeus Sōtēr* (Jupiter the saviour) which archaeologists now agree, because of its very size and magnificence,

must have dominated the city. They argue that this depicted a throne. Nevertheless, many of the other cities had altars that dominated the skyline, and the same doubts arise about why Satan chose to dwell in this altar.

c. A worthwhile suggestion is to note the one feature that made Pergamum unique at this period, which could well be the reason why Christ designated it the place where Satan had established his throne. This city was the centre of the cult of emperor worship; it was the city that spear-headed Caesar-worship in Asia. It was this worship that was beginning to pervade the empire and, in large measure if not displace, at least supersede the pagan deities. As pointed out Pergamum was the first city in Asia to build a great temple to Augustus as early as 27BC and gave him divine honours even before the Senate voted to do so. With him in deification they linked Roma the deified state of Rome. Before this temple stood the great altar where citizens were expected to pay their tribute of incense and where, very possibly, Antipas died. The multifaceted idolatry of the Roman and Greek pantheon was widespread and powerful but was of little help in unifying the diverse peoples of the empire. This new cult of Emperor worship, stemming from the time of Augustus, was seen as the binding agent that was expected to link the various races within the empire whatever their religion. It would thus be in keeping with this historical fact if Satan had taken up residence here to promote that which, in fact, would be the ecumenical movement of the day uniting all religions. Emperor worship became the agent of satanic power to destroy any witness for Christ. The challenge was clear: it must be either Caesar or Christ. Here Christ is identifying the very source of that power and showing that it is the result, not of human planning or political expediency, but of the direct and personal action of Satan. That they had already identified it as such and taken their stand is seen in the faithfulness of the believers living even in such a dangerous place. While the language of "throne" may refer to a literal location in the temple of Augustus, it really became symbolic of the satanic power enshrined in the cult of emperor worship.

2. Their condition – a faithful testimony. The present tense "holdest fast" (*krateō*) shows that the Christians were maintaining a faithful testimony despite the pressures upon them. In some contexts (see 3:8) "my name" refers to the scriptural revelation into which believers have been brought through confession of Christ. Here it describes loyalty to Christ personally. The two meanings are closely allied (as in Matt 18:20) but the emphasis here must fall on personal devotion to Christ.

In His second statement Christ assures the assembly that He has not been unobservant of the crisis through which they had just passed. The aorist "denied" suggests that their allegiance had just been severely tested in some specific incident. The presence of the article before "faith" would allow it to be interpreted as the body of truth (see Walvoord). Nevertheless it is more in keeping with the crisis context to see it as pointing to personal trust in Christ. The believers had remained unshaken under attack; they never doubted. This is in keeping with how the word "faith" is used in this book. Whether it has the article or not, it generally seems to demand the idea of "believing" (see 14:12). These Christians retained personal loyalty to Christ ("my name") and personal trust ("my faith") in Him. These are the vital aspects of testimony.

3. Their crisis – a dangerous time. This personal loyalty and faith in Christ was no academic exercise but a living reality. This was shown by the way they had stood for Christ during a crisis situation, even during a time when one of their number had died for his faith. Antipas had just paid the highest price for his faithfulness: "slain among you". The "among you" makes the slaying graphic. Robertson would translate "at (or by) your side". It would appear as if the other Christians were present at the martyrdom, possibly by magisterial order. Antipas had an honoured name amongst the believers and Christ gives him the highest accolade to be won on earth when He calls him "my faithful martyr". Christ Himself bears this title in 1:5, so Antipas faithfully represented Christ in Pergamum. The word *martus* originally meant a "witness of" some event, as in 1 Pet 5:1, but came to mean a "witness to" in the sense of "bearing testimony to" (Acts 1:8). This book clearly shows a further shift of meaning to "witness for" with the added dimension of a "witness for" Christ even to death. This may be one of the first occasions when the word is used like this, a usage that was to become common in the second century. Little is known of Antipas beyond this passage. Historians have uncovered traditions (one quoted by Swete) which identify him as a dentist who, when challenged by the magistrate to burn incense to Caesar, refused. He was enclosed in a brazen bull which was then made red-hot over a fire. This was said to be early in the reign of Domitian (81-96) so it could not have been many years before this message from Christ. In retrospect his name must carry some significance. *Antipas* may be taken as composed of *anti* (meaning "against") and *pas* (meaning "all"). Christ's words show a man willing to stand alone for Him.

14-16 The warmth of the commendation shows how Christ valued the testimony of the assembly in a dangerous place and at a very dangerous time. Nevertheless, in faithfulness to them, Christ had now to present a very serious criticism. The strong adversative "but" (*alla*) highlights the contrast with what He has just said. The expression "a few things" does not indicate that these matters were unimportant but that they were few in number. There are but two matters, but so vitally important that if they are not dealt with immediately by repentance Christ Himself would have to act (v.16).

The particular criticism of Christ has to do with an unacceptable toleration that was being shown in the assembly. They tolerated some who were holding doctrines subversive by the very principle of divine testimony. They did not seem to recognise the danger of what was being taught. The assembly would have to act in discipline lest this weakness should destroy the testimony. There are two groups identified by their doctrines:

1. "Them that hold the doctrine of Balaam". The criticism of Christ is not the doctrine of Balaam, which stands totally condemned in scripture, but of the assembly who would permit those who held such doctrine to be associated with its fellowship. The use of the same verb *krateō* draws attention to the ambiguity of the assembly "holding fast" the name of Christ (v.13) while at the same time having within it some who were "holding fast" this evil teaching.

   Christ's reference to Balaam looks back to the incident in the wilderness concerning Israel (Num 22-24). Balaam's "way" (2 Pet 2:15) and Balaam's "error" (Jude 11) were personal miscalculations that doomed this false prophet to divine judgment. Balaam's way was to sell the prophetic gift for money; Balaam's error was to imagine that God would change His mind and curse Israel. Here Christ draws attention to Balaam's "teaching" that brought such terrible disaster upon Israel. Prevented by divine action from cursing the people of God Balaam had set his covetous heart on the reward offered by Balak king of Moab. Secretly he whispered into the ear of Balak a method of accomplishing what cursing could not do: destroy this testimony for God. While Num 25 makes no specific mention of Balaam in the breakdown of separation between Israel and the people of Moab, and places the responsibility totally on Israel, nevertheless Num 31:16 shows whose whisper had directed the whole attack. Whether Balaam had used his influence as a prophet (albeit false), to whisper also to Israelities that there would be no harm in such an association with Moabite women, may be implied in the story. Baal-Peor was a lesson Israel would never forget. The counsel of Balaam cast a "stumbling block" in the way of the people of God. The word "stumbling block" (*skandalon*) presents a dramatic picture! It originally meant a "trap" or a "snare" laid with a tempting bait to entice an unwary animal. Once the bait was taken the trap was sprung and the animal was caught. Clearly Balaam had advised Barak that a direct curse being impossible, the only way to destroy this people was to offer the Israelites a "bait" in the lovely women of Moab. Num 25:1-2 shows how immorality and idolatry were closely intertwined as divine separation was broken down. Balaam knew enough of the character of the God of Israel to reason that once their separation was compromised then God would be compelled to judge His own people. Scripture records with terrifying simplicity the success of the trap set for Israel. 24,000 graves testify to its success (Num 25:1-9). Only the javelin of Phineas stayed the plague that would have wiped out the nation. The subtlety of this teaching was that Balaam used what he knew of the character of God to lay a trap for His own people. The false teachers at Pergamum were apt students in the Balaam school. They would teach that separation to Christ in such strict social terms was not necessary. Loyalty to Christ personally, a feature of Pergamum, could be relaxed. Their arguments seemed plausible. Such rigid separation in social and religious matters would alienate the pagan population! Compromise on social lines would enable a wider audience to be reached, this is Baalamite teaching!

The effect of Balaam's teaching in Israel is summarised in two aorist infinitives: to eat things sacrificed to idols; to commit fornication.

The idolatry and immorality of the children of Israel were, of course, literal. Loyalty to Jehovah was betrayed in this literal way. Here the context demands an equally-literal understanding of the teaching. What Balaam did of old, these false teachers were doing again within the very same heathen context. The social and commercial life of Pergamum centred on social gatherings where food offered to idols was eaten. These feasts frequently ended in immoral orgies when libations were poured out to the gods of paganism. Loyalty to Christ demanded total abstention from such gatherings whatever the cost. These teachers were obviously offering reasons why believers could still retain their loyalty to Christ and be a part of this social life. Christ is alerting every responsive saint to the hiss of the serpent in such teaching. A generation before, the apostles and elders had given plain instruction about such matters (Acts 15:29). Now Christ has to rebuke the assembly for the toleration of those who taught such things.

2. "Them that hold the doctrine of the Nicolaitans". Many able expositors would make this group of false teachers the same as the previous group under a different name. They do this by:

a. stressing the "'so" (*houtōs*) which introduces the verse and the inclusion in the RV of "likewise" (*homoiōs*);
b. Linking the Greek etymology of the word "Nicolaitan" as "conqueror of the people" with the Hebrew derivation of "Balaam" as "devourer of the people". It should be noted that John does, on occasion, link the Greek and Hebrew for the same object (see 9:11 for *Apollyon* and *Abaddon*),
c. Taking the view that the Nicolaitan teaching was the libertine doctrine of some poorly identified Nicolas (see comments on v.6). This would be the same "anti-separation" teaching of Balaam under a NT name. In this way Christ would be illustrating this dangerous teaching from the past (in Balaam) and identifying it in the present (in the Nicolaitans).

It must be said, however, that this case for one group of false teachers is very weak: the "so"' is balanced by an "also" with the "likewise" coming at the end of the sentence. On the simplest reading grammatically this sentence structure demands a distinct group, the effect of whose teaching would "likewise" bring disaster on the assembly. It is more in keeping with the context and, in accord with the former identification of the Nicolaitans in v.6, to see these two groups of false teachers as totally distinct.

This second group has already been identified at Ephesus by their "deeds". It has been shown that Nicolaitanism is the emergence of a strong ecclesiastical hierarchy usurping rule over the laity. In Ephesus it was their deeds which were repudiated by that church. Here the doctrine has emerged to justify the deeds and is being propagated by a group within the church. This group has an identifiable "teaching" (*didachē*), which doubtless included scripture wrested out of context (2 Pet 3:16), to justify their practices. The tragedy was that the assembly, instead of rejecting both teaching and teachers, was tolerating the teachers. While the Balaamite teaching turned the spiritual liberty of believers into licence, the Nicolaitan teaching turned the scriptural leadership of believers into clericalism. While the first group of teachers would demand relaxation of loyalty to Christ, this second group would demand restriction in the leadership to those whom they judged qualified. Disdaining the scriptural principles and pattern of NT teaching with respect to the plurality of elders, overseers or shepherds within the local church, seeds were being sown that would develop into the hierarchical system of ecclesiasticism. Christ has already expressed His absolute detestation of their deeds in v.6 and He repeats that abhorrence in the words "which thing I hate".

16 The challenge that Christ brings to the church is abrupt and clear. There is a connecting "therefore", omitted in the AV, that shows that this matter has to be faced immediately. There is a sting with Christ's words "repent therefore...or else". The singular number in the verb "repent" (*metanoeō*) indicates that the assembly as a whole must change its mind on the issue of toleration of the evil teachers. The context demands not only a repudiation of the teaching but of the teachers. This can mean nothing less than the excommunication of these teachers from the assembly.

Should the assembly not act the alternative is solemn indeed. Christ Himself will take action. This action would be in the form of a disciplinary visitation. The present tense would be better translated "I am coming" and the "quickly" but stresses the urgency with which action has to be taken. The action must be interpreted as deliberate governmental action such as that seen earlier in Ananias and Sapphira (Acts 5:1-11)) or that which had taken place at Corinth (1 Cor 11:30). Christ would use the sword of His mouth, His spoken word, in judicial action against these subversive teachers. It is the same sword that will later destroy opposition on a world scale (19:21). Christ would not allow such evil to go unjudged in a local assembly since it threatened the very nature of testimony for Him. This interpretation is strengthened by the contrast between the pronouns "thee" and "them" distinguishing between the assembly as a unit and the evil teachers. It is the evil teachers who are to be dealt with by the sword.

Some expositors (notably R.L. Thomas) have sought to show that the language of this verse demands the coming of Christ at the rapture. It is certainly true that the same verb and adverb (*erchomai tachu*) are used of that coming in 3:11; 22:7, 12, 20. The judgment, on this interpretation, would therefore be the Judgment Seat following the rapture. However this poses insuperable difficulties. Not only does it make the coming of the Christ depend upon the non-repentance of a church but it ignores the whole immediate context of the false teachers. The coming here is to be seen as a threat to the assembly ("thee") while the judgment action is against the false teachers ("them"). It is much more satisfactory and convincing to see this as assembly discipline wielded by the assembly (in repentance) or, if this is not carried out, by the direct intervention of Christ Himself. It is a very solemn warning against the toleration of evil teachers.

17a With words identical to those used to Ephesus (v.7) and to Smyrna (v.11) Christ calls for the attention of each spiritual saint that He might disclose the special promise to the overcomer. A believer loyal to Christ would be resistant to the false teaching which, very possibly, was being whispered surreptitiously behind closed doors. Overcomers would be marked by separation from the social banquets, trade guild dinners and political and religious festivities in Pergamum. Their very overcoming would mean ostracism and loneliness in their testimony for Christ. It would likely mean poverty and persecution. The believers would know in real experience the path of the stranger through the wilderness.

17b Two things are promised by Christ to the overcomer:

1. The hidden manna. Manna was the special wilderness food for the people of God. As the bread which came down from heaven it was a unique type of Christ in incarnation. The fact that it was small, round and white is clearly indicative of His lowliness, perfection and purity. It is called "'spiritual meat" (1 Cor 10:3) and sustained Israel for the forty years in the wilderness. The hidden manna is a reference to the manna stored in the golden pot within the ark of the covenant (Exod 16:31-35). This manna was for the eye of God, and doubtless unfolds aspects of the life of Christ that were known only to God. Believers in Pergamum faithful to Christ would be denied access to many of the physical delicacies of the feasts in the social life in Pergamum, but they would enjoy a special spiritual provision that had already delighted God. They would enjoy a very special spiritual food.

2. The white stone. Commentators have varied widely in their interpretation of the white stone. Some relevant suggestions have been as follows:

a. A suggestion that finds wide acceptance is to see it as the "voting pebble". When the evidence had been presented in a criminal trial then the jury was often called to decide the case by majority vote. Each jury member cast a stone into an urn. A white stone signified an acquittal while a black stone signified condemnation. It is this word (*psēphos*) that is used by Paul in Acts 26:10 and translated in the AV "I gave my voice (*psēphos*) against them". On this interpretation the message is that while pagan Pergamum may condemn a believer to death Christ absolves him from every false charge. The difficulty with this interpretation is that it offers no explanation of the name on the stone. The voting pebble did not have a name on it.

b. Other commentators have suggested that the stone may refer to the "white stone" given to the victor in the Olympic games. This stone did have the victor's name inscribed on it. R.L. Thomas writes of this view, "'It was also a well-established custom to reward victors at the games with such a token enabling them to gain admission to a special feast". This explains the name but does not explain the new name of the Christ's promise.

c. F.A. Tatford quotes an old commentator (Ewald) to show it could refer to the *tessera hospitalis* which wealthy families gave to close friends with the donor's name on it (F.A. Tatford in *Prophecy's Last Word* p.50. The person who had this stone could always claim a warm welcome and ready hospitality from the donor. Recent archaeology has shown that this practice also operated with regard to some temples when a white stone was given to devoted worshippers to guarantee them access to the feasts in honour of the god. This could be the background here where Christ would be assuring believers, despite ostracism in Pergamene society, of their access to a feast in which no unbeliever would share.

Thus in these two promises the overcomer would enjoy a very special spiritual food and favoured access to a sacred fellowship where the festivities would be eternal. This latter promise could well embrace foreshadowings of kingdom festivities (Matt 7:21-23).

On the stone is a "new name". This inscription can scarcely be linked with "my new name" (3:12) since the name there is public; here it is private. Again there is no obvious link with "a name written which no man knoweth but he himself" (19:12) since there no one knows the name but Christ Himself; here the overcomer knows the name. The adjective "new" (*kainos*) would suggest, not a name recently acquired but a name different from that previously borne. It thus strongly suggests that Christ Himself has changed the name of the believer. The name is personal to each believer and reflects Christ's estimate of the character formed in the dangerous days of testimony in Pergamum.

The name being "written" (perfect passive participle) shows the permanence of the character formed. The fact that it is secret – "no man knoweth saving he that receiveth it" – shows it is both personal and inviolate, no one else can take it. Scripture shows that new names were given to mark new relationships. A look back at Abram (Gen 17:5), at Sarai (Gen 17:15), at Jacob (Gen 32:28) will show how a relationship was reflected in a new name. To the church in Pergamum where loyalty was so costly, Christ shows how much He values those of such a character.

Notes

12 Pergamos: the name of this city occurs only twice in scripture. In 1:11 it is in the accusative case (*Pergamon*) and here it is in the dative case (*Pergamo*) and thus it is impossible to tell directly whether it is feminine or neuter. This has led to a certain confusion as to whether the name should be "Pergamos" or "Pergamum". This confusion exists in secular writings but the weight of academic opinion is that the name should be "Pergamum" as in the RV. This name will therefore be used throughout the commentary.

17 The White Stone: Objections have been made to this interpretation on the general grounds that Christ would not draw lessons from heathendom. This criticism is invalid on the following grounds:

a. the picture is drawn, not from heathendom as such, but, simply from the culture with which the believers were familiar;
b. use of a picture from the background culture of the day does not give approval to the custom. This can be seen in Paul's frequent use of the "games" to illustrate christian life. It would be most unlikely that Paul, either in his days before conversion as a Pharisee (Phil 3:5), or later in his christian life, would ever have attended any of the games, yet he uses the language of the games because it was simply part of everyday language. Pictures are imbedded in words;
c. the picture is used not to compare but to contrast, to show that no matter what the loss for Christ may be, there is a compensation far beyond what is sacrificed. Refusal to be associated with the idolatry and immorality of Pergamum shut out believers from social intercourse in terms of food and fellowship. Christ promises them corresponding compensation.

The New Name: some see in this a special revelation of Christ personal to the overcomer. In the cultural thought of Roman times "to know the name" of a god was equivalent to "have power over" the god. The one who knew such a name was thought to have all the power of the god at their disposal. F.A. Tatford sees his background here and writes, "What the mysteries promised to give, Christ actually bestows. He gives His own new name – the source of power and wisdom – to His own people". It is clear that such an interpretation, while attractive in some aspects, does not meet the requirement of the text. This name is personal to each recipient reflecting Christ's appreciation of the person receiving it.

(d) *The Message to Thyatira (vv.18-29)*

v.18 "And unto the angel of the church in Thyatira write; These things saith the Son of God, who hath his eyes like unto a flame of fire, and his feet are like fine brass;
v.19 I know thy works, and charity, and service, and faith, and thy patience, and thy works; and the last to be more than the first.
v.20 Notwithstanding I have a few things against thee, because thou sufferest that woman Jezebel, which calleth herself a prophetess, to teach and to seduce my servants to commit fornication, and to eat things sacrificed unto idols.
v.21 And I gave her space to repent of her fornication; and she repented not.
v.22 Behold, I will cast her into a bed, and them that commit adultery with her into great tribulation, except they repent of their deeds.
v.23 And I will kill her children with death; and all the churches shall know that I am he which searcheth the reins and hearts: and I will give unto every one of you according to your works.
v.24 But unto you I say, and unto the rest in Thyatira, as many as have not this doctrine, and which have not known the depths of Satan, as they speak; I will put upon you none other burden.
v.25 But that which ye have already hold fast till I come.
v.26 And he that overcometh, and keepeth my works unto the end, to him will I give power over the nations:
v.27 And he shall rule them with a rod of iron: as the vessels of a potter shall they be broken to shivers: even as I received of my Father.
v.28 And I will give him the morning star.
v.29 He that hath an ear, let him hear what the Spirit saith unto the churches."

About 40 miles south-east of Pergamum situated in a long north-south valley connecting the Hermus and Caicus river valleys was the town of Thyatira. Surrounded by a rich agricultural area around the river Lycus it stood at the junction of three major highways connecting Pergamum, Smyrna and Sardis. While Thyatira had not the look of a natural fortress, being surrounded by gently sloping hills, it nevertheless had had a strategic importance in the days of the Seleucid dynasty. It was founded as a Greek colony by Seleucus Nicator one of Alexander's generals who upon his death (323BC), divided up the empire. He named it "Thyatira" in honour of his daughter's birth. It was meant to be a frontier town of the Seleucid Empire guarding against the incursions of the Pergamenes who were backed by Roman power. With the defeat of Seleucus by the Romans at the battle of Magnesia (190BC) and the subsequent incorporation of Thyatira into the Roman province of Asia, the city lost all strategic importance. Its military significance was only a memory, a cherished memory, it could be said, for the coinage of the city carried a representation of the sun-god Tyrimnus (one of the many forms under which Apollo was worshipped) as a warrior riding forth to battle, armed with a double-edged battle axe, the symbol of smashing military power. It is against this background that Christ introduces Himself to the church as the Son of God in warrior dress. The promise to the overcomer significantly fastens on the very thing Thyatira had lost: "power over the nations". Their battle-axe-wielding god was only a memory in mythology. Christ to the hearts of His own was a glorious reality.

Thyatira acknowledged the full pantheon of heathen gods and goddesses and included the state religion of Emperor worship. None of these religions seems to have posed any direct problem to the church in Thyatira. While archaeological investigation has shown that there was also a large colony of Jews located here, as would be expected in such a rich trading centre, they too do not seem to have shown the same bitter hostility to Christians as was shown by their fellow-Jews in Smyrna. There would appear to have been little persecution of Christians. The fact that on many Thyatiran coins the city is depicted as a woman crowned with battlements offers a clue as to the pride and power of the city. It suggests weakness in womanhood, but a weakness fortified with victory. Some authorities suggest that behind the woman honoured in the founding of the city is a hint that the origin of Thyatiran strength went back to another woman – Semiramis queen of Babylon.

The most important thing however about Thyatira at this period, was neither her military power nor her religious superstitions but her wealth and prosperity. Her agricultural hinterland gave her a wealth of exportable produce as well as the raw materials for many manufacturing industries. Her location at the intersection of several important highways made her a strategic trading centre through which a vast trade passed daily. One of the most celebrated of her trades was the production of a purple dye (possibly closer to scarlet) that was obtained from the madder root, a plant grown in the area. Some authorities speak of the same dye as extracted from the crushing of the murex, a shell-fish from the Lycus river that flowed through the town. Lydia is referred to in Acts 16:14-15 as a "seller of purple" and it is apparent that she was the representative of a well-established Thyatiran trading-house marketing its products in Europe.

The manufacturing industries were the base of what was recognised as the most noted feature of the city, the existence of workers' trade guilds associated with the various industries. While similar guilds existed in most other cities, they were most in evidence in Thyatira. Potters, dyers, tanners, bakers, metalworkers, textile-makers, bronze-smiths, slave-dealers, leather workers etc., all had their own guilds. Membership for all who would practise these trades was compulsory. Refusal to join meant that essential recognition was denied and it was not possible to obtain a job in that trade. These guilds were well-organised corporate bodies with a tightly-controlled membership and disciplinary procedures for action against those who infringed their rules. Membership fees were high and the guilds were able to buy property, lend money and promote the interests of their members. They were the trade unions of the day.

Apart from an unequal yoke the particular feature that put these guilds in direct conflict with Christianity was the fact that each guild was under the patronage of a particular pagan god. Their buildings were dedicated to this god; all their gatherings commenced with homage to this god; their frequent festivities commenced or ended with a libation of wine to this deity; certain foods were owned as dedicated to the god. The feasts ended frequently in orgies; idolatry was closely linked with immorality. Sexual freedom was not only permitted it was deliberately encouraged, and in some cases demanded, as part of the idolatrous worship of such debased deities. Since attendance at these gatherings was not optional, but obligatory for all members, a confrontation between faithful followers of Christ and the power of the trade guilds was inevitable. Christ's message to this church envisages just such a clash.

The NT gives no information as to the establishment of the church in this city. Tradition is equally silent. Whether the citizens first heard the gospel during the extended stay of Paul in Asia (Acts 19:10) or whether Epaphras (Col 4:12) or Archippus (Col 4:17) preached here is not known. It is certainly a reasonable deduction, even if it lacks spiritual evidence, that Lydia after her conversion returned to her native city and brought the gospel with her. It will be noted how women have played a part in the history of Thyatira: in the founding of the city (the daughter of Seleucid Nicator), in the possible introduction of the gospel (Lydia) and sadly, in the corruption of the testimony (Jezebel).

18 With words identical to those He has used to Ephesus, Smyrna and Pergamum Christ addresses the church within the local setting of this busy commercial city.

A three-fold self-identification sets Him apart from all that in pre-conversion days would have claimed the allegiance of citizens. In each term is a claim to deity. He shows Himself to be omnipresent, omniscient and omnipotent:

1. The Son of God. The sun-god deity worshipped in Thyatira may dazzle men but Christ reveals Himself as the Son of God. For the only time in these letters Christ uses the title that recalls the confession of Peter (Matt 16:16-17), the confrontation with the national leaders of Israel (Matt 26:63) and the direct confirmation of heaven in His resurrection (Rom 1:4). The title is a clear reference to Ps 2:7 and the authentication by heaven of Christ's sonship. A further reference to this psalm is to be seen in v.26 where the overcomer is promised a share in the reign of the Son of God upon earth. As God he is *omnipresent.*
2. The words "who hath eyes like unto a flame of fire" are taken from John's description of Christ in 1:14. They will be used again in 19:12 to describe the mighty Victor when He returns to earth. They describe a penetrative incandescence, from which there is no hiding; He cannot be deceived. All is searched out by these probing eyes, an anticipative warning most appropriate for Thyatiran conditions. He is *omniscient.*
3. "His feet are like fine brass". The words are taken again from John's description in 1:15. As shown there the words "fine brass" are descriptive of the highly purified metal, burnished and shining with dazzling brilliance. H.B. Swete describes His feet as "shining as if the metal was still molten in

the furnace". The fine brass was used to make durable weapons for the Roman legions. There was in fact a weapons-manufacturing industry in this city so the citizens were familiar with this material. Purity is the idea, a purity that gives durability. Used in the feet it introduces the idea of implacability. His eyes would discern; His feet would trample every opposing force and ruthlessly crush every evil thing. He is *omnipotent.*

19 The penetrative power of those eyes is seen in the disclosure of the activities of the Thyatiran church "I know thy works". It is possible to take the six things that Christ mentions as members of an ascending series that returns to the first item, thus mounting to a climax. Each item has the article that may be translated for emphasis thus: "thy works, and thy charity, and thy faith, and thy service, and thy patience and thy works". On the other hand it is better to translate the first "and" as "even" (as to Ephesus in 2:2), so that the four following items are explanatory. The works are then identified as "thy love, thy faith, thy ministry, thy endurance". The repetition of works at the end and its qualifying statement thus emphasise the fact that instead of fading with time, as would be natural, their works were actually increasing evidence of the Holy Spirit at work.

The more correct order of the RV quoted above (love, faith, ministry, endurance) may possibly unfold the links between the different items. When God works by His Spirit and His word within the believer the result is love and faith. The outward result of service and endurance follow in the life of the saint. Love both toward God and men is the result of the presence of the indwelling Holy Spirit (Rom 5:5). Faith is best understood here to be the willingness to believe, and hence to obey, the word of God. The outflowing of their love and the inspiration afforded by their faith resulted in service. The word carries all the dignity of voluntary service which has the good of others in view. Its usage in the NT covers service in both the material and the spiritual realms. Christ is the pattern minister who always acted for the good of others (see Rom 15:8; Gal 2:17). In the spiritual realm Paul served in a deacon ministry for others. The more mundane use of the word covers the giving of the physical necessities of life, food and clothing (Acts 6:2; Rom 15:25, 31; 1 Cor 16:15; 2 Cor 8:4; 9:1; Heb 6:10). Within the context Christ is commending the sacrifice shown in ministering to the needs of others; faith based on the promises of the word of God would inspire their endurance in the trying conditions in Thyatira. The word reflects the steadfastness of christian character that enables believers to hold the head high whatever troubles assail them.

"Thy last works are more than the first" (RV) shows the assessment of Christ over the period of their testimony. In contrast to what is often regarded as normal christian experience this church seemed to be making spiritual progress. Their exercise and energy as inspired by love and faith were on the increase. The phrase "more than" is somewhat ambiguous as to whether quantity or quality is being compared. Whichever way it is viewed there was a positive, measurable development in their testimony. This is a delightful commendation from Christ.

20 The warm commendation of Christ gives way to sobering censure. The "but" translated "notwithstanding" in the AV, is strongly adversative. Conservative textual criticism on strong manuscript evidence omits "a few things" as having been copied from v.14. The omission makes the censure even more direct. That which Christ has against this church is but one matter alone: "thou sufferest that woman Jezebel". The verb "to suffer" in this context, would be better translated "dost tolerate". It is the presence of this woman in the church, the fact that she is allowed to continue in the fellowship, that is the point of Christ's criticism. The grammar and word order demand that it is not merely the teaching of Jezebel to which Christ objects but her very presence. Both her teaching (and she does teach) and her practices (for she seduces) would be brought to an abrupt close if her presence in the assembly was to be judged. This is more serious even than the situation at Pergamum where "thou hast" describes the mere presence of the false teachers; "thou sufferest" indicates not only toleration but accommodation. The assembly would seem even to welcome her presence. Could it be that they were proud to have such an able and gifted woman in their gathering? There is a sting in the words of Christ that would allow this thought.

That a particular and identifiable woman falls under this terrible censure from Christ Himself is scarcely to be doubted. This is demanded by the terms used. The claim to be a prophetess and the distinction between Jezebel and her partners (v.22) and her children (v.23) are better explained in terms of a real person. The language itself gives no hint of symbolism. Some of the nineteenth century commentators (see Beckwith in loc), already wedded to the idea of the angel being the pastor or elder in the church, point to the disputed inclusion in some manuscripts of the personal pronoun "thee" in v.20 and translate "thy wife Jezebel". This is to be rejected both on textual grounds, since manuscript support is very weak (in spite of the special pleading of Alford), and on exegetical grounds as not making sense on any scriptural interpretation of the angel.

The simplest interpretation is to see Christ speaking of an actual woman in Thyatira, a woman of intellect and ability who, with dominant personality and forcefulness of character, has found her scriptural place too restrictive and has taken the place of a teacher in the church. To lend credibility to her pretensions she claimed to be a prophetess. The NT sense of the word would allow that she told out "truth for the times", patterned possibly on the daughters of Philip (Acts 21:9). The character of that teaching and its results in practice are identified by Christ in the use of the name Jezebel. While it is unlikely that this is the actual name of the woman the believers would be able to identify her immediately. The name that Christ gives her is designed to show His judgment of her person and influence. She is fulfilling the role of her namesake from a previous era.

The OT Jezebel was the worthy daughter of Ethbaal, king of the Sidonians. He had seized his throne with murder and maintained it with blood. His daughter had learned the lessons well and, becoming the wife of Ahab king of Israel (1 Kings 16:31), she carried murder and bloodshed into Israel. Baal worship was already constantly recurring in Israel but she introduced a new compromise that combined the worship of Jehovah and the worship of Baal. She also introduced the worship of Astarte (Semiramis of Babylon) and with it all the degraded immorality that was part of such worship. The divine judgment upon Israel was the three and a half years of famine on account of this idolatry. The emergence of Elijah showed how God would seek to recover His people. A weak king in Israel gave room for this wicked woman, who with painted face and persecuting ferocity put to death all who would be faithful to Jehovah. The story of Naboth and his vineyard (1 Kings 21) is typical of her intrigues. False accusation, corruption and murder based on greed were simply part of her armoury. In the matter of Naboth she schemed to use scriptural principles and godless men to put to death, on false charges, one who refused to sell or barter his heritage. She put to death the prophets of Christ and sought to slay Elijah. She stands on the pages of scripture as the symbol of immorality and idolatry backed up by scheming subtlety. The prophecy of Elijah concerning her, "In the portion of Jezreel shall dogs eat the flesh of Jezebel" (2 Kings 9:36), was fulfilled under Jehu (2 Kings 9: 30-37). Her end was entirely fitting, no grave or monument was ever to be raised to the memory of this evil woman.

An influential woman in Thyatira, whatever her name, had the same influence on the assembly as the historic Jezebel had on Israel in the past. To support her claims to speak with authority she claimed to be a prophetess. The only other person bearing this title in the NT is Anna (Luke 2:36) whose gift enabled her to point out the Christ. Anna belonged to an OT order of prophets. Jezebel would have claimed to be a NT prophet after the pattern of those whom God used locally (Eph 4:11) and for a limited period (1 Cor 13:8) to build up the church. She would doubtless have claimed to follow the pattern set by Philip's daughters (Acts 21:9). However, the words "calleth herself" indicate that she was self-proclaimed. She was both a false prophet and a false teacher (2 Pet 2:1). Alleging special revelation from God she was exercising a ministry both defiling and destructive. The terrible thing to the eye of Christ was that the assembly was tolerating the presence of this woman.

It would seem from the present tense of the verbs that even as Christ was dictating this message she was actively doing her evil work. Weak leadership (as in Ahab of old) was permitting a woman to do what apostolic teaching directly forbade (1 Tim 2:12). The place of women in local testimony would have been well known in the Asian churches only a generation after Paul and Timothy. The evil of toleration was aggravated by the evil of her teaching. This teaching was leading saints astray. The verb *plana* translated in the AV "seduces" is better translated "deceives". It is the same verb as is used of the activity of the false prophet (13:14) and of Babylon itself (18:23). The root idea in the verb is to "lead away", and, in its participle form, is used to describe Satan himself (12:9). Jezebel was a useful agent of Satan.

Christ speaks of those attacked as "my servants" (*doulos*). The choice of the word, with slave background, indicates just how seriously Christ viewed any interference with those who were His own property. Recalling the background of this city with its trade guilds and their inherent link with idolatry and immorality it is a reasonable assumption that the teaching of Jezebel was designed to break down separation. She would argue very plausibly that, since there was nothing in the idol itself (1 Cor 8:4), and, since the god had no real existence, enlightened Christians need not hesitate to belong to a trade guild. Partaking of the food offered to the idol and sharing in the libation were, after all, only social activities. The sexual licence of such gatherings would be classed as merely physical (1 Cor 6: 12-14) and irrelevant for spiritual Christians! With plausibility and subtlety the clear separation expected of followers of Christ would be undermined. For believers suffering for their separation in refusing to join the trade guilds this line of teaching, with the support of a seemingly Spirit-filled prophetess would offer a tempting compromise. This plausible reasoning, offering an easy solution to their problems was clearly winning a following in the church. Some were already being led "to commit fornication" and "to eat things offered to idols". The testimony for Christ was in dire danger.

21 Christ had already warned Jezebel. How He had done this we are not told, but He may have used John as He did in the case of Diotrephes (3 John 10). This is the implication in the mention of the period (*chronos*) that Christ gave Jezebel to repent and repudiate her teaching. This she had refused to do and, as Christ speaks, is still refusing. JND translates "and she will not repent of her fornication". As R.L. Thomas points out "The durative force of the present tense of *thelei* conveys the sense, 'she still does not wish to repent' ". She shows no inclination to change her mind.

While the fornication in this verse may well be the physical immorality of this woman personally, it is more probable that the word is now used by Christ, with the added dimension of spiritual fornication (the misuse of things sacred), to describe the effects of her teaching and activities. The term is used in this wider sense in connection with the OT Jezebel (2 Kings 9:22), and is a familiar OT figure for spiritual and religious infidelity (Jer 3:6; Ezek 23:19; Hos 9:1). This is not to deny the literal sin of fornication in connection with Jezebel but to suggest that, in this verse, it goes beyond the physical and includes the further spiritual element.

22-23 Christ threatens immediate action. That the action will be spectacular is seen in the use of the demonstrative "behold": all should stop and examine it closely. The judgment will be in three parts; it will be against her person, her partners and her progeny. Such will be the effect that "all the churches" will know that Christ has personally intervened.

1. Against her person: The present tense of the verb "cast" is a dramatic way of expressing something so certain that it is as if it were already happening. What has been for this woman a bed of pleasure and sin becomes a bed of pain. Hebrew parallelism which seems to underlie the statements would suggest that the end results of the three judgments visualised in the words "bed", "great tribulation" and "death" are all of the same genus. For her there is the added trauma that from this dying bed she may witness the judgment upon those linked with her.
2. Against her partners: Those who were having (the present participle is again dramatic) illicit intercourse with her would not escape judgment. They would find themselves cast (the verb is to be understood) into great tribulation. There is, however, one note of hope in this case. Since they have been deceived by the wiles of the woman Christ keeps open the possibility of repentance. Good manuscript evidence would make the reading "her deeds" (*ergōn autēs*) rather than "their deeds" (*ergōn autōn*). This more difficult reading, while it makes little difference to the sense, emphasises the repudiation of their teacher. Nevertheless their need of personal repentance shows they are responsible for their own behaviour. They cannot pass the blame to Jezebel. Failure to repent brings tribulation. The word "adultery" is here used for the only time in the book as the species of which fornication, the all embracive word, is the genus. Adultery fastens on the violation of the marriage vow. The fact that Jezebel was a married woman explains the use of the word in the physical sense. In the spiritual sense the commitment of the believer to the person of Christ illuminates the use of the word (see James 4:4). Christ is clearly using the words fornication and adultery here to embrace both literal and spiritual infidelity. "Great tribulation" without the article is to be distinguished from the expression "*the* great tribulation" (*tēs thlipseōs tēs megalēs*) of 7:14. In context it must refer to a time of pressure and pain ahead for this woman personally; it has nothing directly to do with the seven-year period of tribulation that precedes the coming of Christ to earth. (See *The Thyatiran Period of Church History* p.152).
3. Against her progeny. The simplest interpretation is to take these children as the actual children of Jezebel born possibly as a result of her adultery. They clearly shared her character having been brought up in her teaching and influenced by her behaviour. Any objection that their punishment was more severe than that of their mother fails to take account of the Hebrew parallelism which makes the three judgments the same. It will be remembered that David's son from an adulterous relationship died physically (2 Sam 12:14) as did all the sons of Ahab (2 Kings 10:7).

Many commentators interpret the children here rather as spiritual children who have been nurtured on her teachings and reproduce features of their mother. Christ used the father figure to identify the men of His day (John 8:44); Paul and John use the father figure in their epistles in a good sense (Gal 4:19; 1 John 2:1) and Paul used the mother figure of the Thessalonian believers (1 Thess 2:7). There is quite a lot to be said for this view. Any difficulty in distinguishing them from the previous group may be overcome by seeing the partners of Jezebel as willingly participating in her sins, while her children simply embrace her teachings and ways.

The judgment on Jezebel's children uses an unusual expression which on literal translation would read "I will kill with death" (*apoktenō en thanatō*). Because *thanatos* on 35 occasions is used by the LXX to translate the Hebrew word for "pestilence" the word came to mean death by plague (see 6:8). Christ promises to deal with the offspring of this wicked woman, whether they are literal or spiritual offspring makes no difference. They are visited with a real plague that is readily indentifiable as a divine judgment. Lacking spiritual life the ultimate end of these children is eternal death.

These acts of judgment are a witness to the omnipotence and omniscience of Christ, the One who has already identified Himself as the Son of God. The phrase "all the churches" in the immediate context must be all churches in the Roman province of Asia where Jezebel was known. The single act of divine judgment would make every church tremble. The emphatic "I" in "I am" echoes 1:17. Only the omniscient One could search "reins and heart". The expression is an OT one belonging to deity and quoted from Jer 17:10. "Reins" is literally "kidneys" and in scripture denotes the inward affections. The word "heart" speaks of the thoughts that motivate the will from which the actions spring. Christ can appraise more than the actions; He can look behind them to the motivating affections and thoughts. Jezebel, her lovers and her children cannot hide from the "eyes like unto a flame of fire". This brings a measure of godly fear to every considering heart. There is a threat but also a note of reassurance in the following promise, "I will give to every one of you according to your works". The plural "you" embraces every believer, while the "every one" points to personal responsibility and reward. Each person will receive from Christ what they have earned either in judgment now or reward in a coming day. The choice is very clear; the "works" describe a lifestyle either in conformity to, or in separation from, the teachings of Jezebel. Separation from her principles and practices would carry its reward from Christ. The judgment seat of Christ is where the final rewards for the believers of the church age are given (2 Cor 5:10). Behaviour now has results then.

24-25 The "but" marks the point where Christ turns from the church as a whole to address a group within it. For the first time in these letters it would appear that a majority were going to ignore the appeal of Christ. To those faithful to Himself Christ addresses words of instruction and comfort. These are identified as "the rest" and "as many as have not this doctrine" The second statement enlarges on the first, there is just one remnant company. The omission (on good authority) of the "and" by the RV confirms this. The word "rest" could be translated as "remnant" and the second statement describes their separation from the false teaching of Jezebel. The idea of the remnant does not in itself demand a minority (see 1 Thess 4:13 RV where it cannot be a minority), but it does suggest that the tide of opinion is flowing against these faithful saints. The danger of the teaching of Jezebel is described in the expression "the depths of Satan". This expression must be understood on the same pattern as "the synagogue of Satan" (v.9) in Smyrna and the "throne of Satan" (v. 13) in Pergamum. In Smyrna Satan stirred up persecution against the Christians using national Jewish antagonism; in Pergamum compromise was clearly worldly wisdom in view of the power of Satan; in Thyatira it is corruption and contamination of holy things that are being used to destroy the local testimony. The more literal rendering of the RV "the deep things of Satan" puts this teaching in sharp contrast with "the deep things of God" (1 Cor 2:10) which have been made accessible to believers by the Holy Spirit. In this church Satan, through Jezebel, was holding out a secret knowledge accessible only to a few. The teaching may even have included a superior morality that claimed to keep a higher law than that of Christ. That ecstatic experiences were associated with this teaching may be shown by the loaded use of the verb "know" (*ginōskō*), – a favourite verb of gnostic teachers. The aorist tense indicates the complete rejection of such supernatural experiences by the believers; they would have nothing to do with such thrills. Christ shows in these words the Satanic power behind such a seemingly-simple action as participating in a trade-guild banquet; it opened a whole realm of power to those prepared to be initiated. There was a close parallel with the sacred meals of Babylon and initiation into the mysteries.

The next phrase "as they speak" poses the problem of its connection. Alford with considerable weight divorces it from the preceding passage and suggests it must stand as the opening words of the Christ's following words. The "they" on this interpretation becomes apostolic testimony, a testimony now reinforced by Christ Himself. Alford finds the original parallel in the words of Acts 15:28 where the council of Jerusalem sent out the message: "It seemed good to the Holy Ghost, and to us, to lay upon you no greater burden than these necessary things". This interpretation explains Christ's use of the word "burden" in this context. Attractive though this explanation is, and while it could possibly be assumed that the church would be familiar with the council's letter, it is more than strange that Christ, in such a solemn matter, should simply endorse an earlier apostolic word.

An alternative interpretation is that this may have been a way in which the false teachers themselves identified their teaching. They would thus unashamedly be claiming that their teaching was the only way in which the believer in Christ could demonstrate his superiority and spirituality. In attending the trade-guild feasts he would show his conquest of idolatry and his indifference to immorality.

They would argue that to remain separate from these social and commercial obligations would be to display weakness and not strength. While this inverted reasoning was somewhat typical of gnosticism it is difficult to believe that professedly-christian teachers would designate their teaching in this way. The subtlety is a little too subtle. The soundest interpretation is to see in this statement an acknowledgement by Christ that the faithful in Thyatira had already identified the evil teaching in their midst as offering a satanic counterpart to spiritual realities. They had put their own label upon it and Christ endorses their view. This would be an added incentive to keep apart from it.

While Christ acts in judgment towards Jezebel – "I do cast her into a bed" (RV), He acts with grace towards the faithful – "I will cast upon you none other burden" (RV). The same verb in the same tense (present) is used in the contrast. They already have a "burden" in the sense of a weighty responsibility already accepted. Christ will not add to that. The RV omits "already" and reads, "Howbeit that which ye have, hold fast till I come". The important matter is that the Christians keep doing what they already are doing – standing apart from the satanically deceptive teaching. The clause "what ye have" refers to the things Christ has already commended. It must include both service to others (v.19) and the insight (v.24) they have into the nature of the false teaching. Christ asks for nothing more; continuing like this will preserve them. The aorist imperative of the verb "hold fast" may be translated "start holding fast". Hort translates "once and for all, take a firm hold upon what you have been taught". This may imply some weakness in their present condition, so it is perhaps better to see it as describing a lifestyle lived in the light of His arrival.

It is here that Christ introduces to the churches for the first time the promise of His coming for His church. The coming mentioned earlier in the chapter, to the churches in Ephesus (v.5) and Pergamum (v.16) has been shown to be a personal visitation for investigation and discipline. In those earlier verses the verb is *erchomai* which stresses the action itself (see Vine). The verb here is *hēkō* which lays stress upon the person who is coming. Newberry translates it "till I arrive". Facing the pressure of the false teaching faithful believers would be much encouraged by the imminence of the Saviour's arrival.

26-28 It is in the message to this fourth church that the challenge to the overcomer and the call to the responsive hearer are first interchanged in position. In the last four churches the call to the believer with the spiritual ear is the final word from Christ. Keeping in mind also that it is in this message that the remnant is first mentioned it is tempting to see the reversal of the order as a hint of the deteriorating spiritual condition of the assembly generally. Christ seems to expect that responsive hearers will be fewer in number.

The exhortation to hold fast is followed closely by the promise of Christ to the overcomer. It seems as if the incentive belongs to the encouragement, a deduction reinforced by the fact that this is the only time in the seven letters that the promise is joined to the preceding statement by the word "and". The overcomer is identified as the one "keeping my works unto the end". As already pointed out (v.7) the term "overcomer" describes what every believer is expected to be – and will be when faithful to Christ. The faithful believer in Thyatiran conditions would keep what Christ describes as "my works" (v.23). To "keep my words" (John 14:23) is Christ's metaphor for obedience; to "keep my works" is more unusual, but there is no doubt that the one keeping the words will certainly be doing the works of Christ. The works are those belonging to Christ, so that the believer is simply His agent in the circumstances. In the believer's life evident obedience to Christ leads to separation and then service of which Christ is not ashamed. "Until the end" is the goal of testimony for this age; a goal reached when Christ arrives.

The two-part identification of the overcomer is followed by the double promise of Christ seen in the repetition of the words "I will give":

1. "To him will I give power over the nations" (v.26). The word "power" (*exousia*) shows that the overcomer will reign with Christ in the messianic kingdom. The previous expressions "till I arrive" and "unto the end" have pointed the saints to His coming. This promise goes beyond the coming to show that the reward of faithfulness will be rule with Christ in that millennial reign (2 Tim 2:12). It is this kingdom that is in view in the reference to Ps 2:8-9. The Hebrew of Ps 2:9 reads, "Thou shalt break them with a rod of iron; thou shalt dash them in pieces like a potter's vessel". Hebrew parallelism suggests that the second verb emphasises the nature of the first; thus the "breaking" and the "dashing in pieces" are different verbs to describe the same action. This action anticipates 19:15 where Christ comes to establish His kingdom. The nations are "broken" and "dashed in pieces" at the battle of "that great day of God Almighty" (16:14). The Greek verb *poimainō* ("rule") is often translated as "to tend as a shepherd". This meaning is very suitable in Matt 2:6 referring to Judah, "for out of thee shall come a Governor, that shall rule (*poimainō*) my people Israel" a reference to the administrative rule of Christ over Israel. It also suits admirably the figurative description of the character of leadership in a NT assembly (Acts 20:28; 1 Pet 5:2). In light however of Hebrew parallelism from the Psalm and the violence in the second verb, it is most likely that in this present context the verb should have its extended meaning of "destroy". Both verbs would thus refer to the smashing of all earthly national power as Christ comes to take the kingdom. Saints, including the overcomers of the church age (19:14), share that moment when Christ is seen as "King of kings and Lord of lords". The "rod of iron" is descriptive of the royal sceptre when used against His enemies. The smashing of brittle clay vessels is an apt metaphor for this climax

of history. So all opposing nations will be shattered when Christ sets up His kingdom. Christ links with Himself the overcomers under Thyatiran conditions.

In the past history of nations this authority has been usurped or imposed by force. It is not so with Christ. The perfect tense of the verb "received" points back to the receiving by Christ of the legal entitlement to His kingdom direct from the Father at the time of His resurrection and ascension. Christ has this entitlement now (Ps 2:6-9) but as He takes the kingdom will act to deal with His enemies and establish His rule. The overcomers will share that reign.

2. "I will give him the morning star" (v.28). It is possible to see this as a symbolic way of repeating the first promise. The star becomes a symbol of sovereignty. Scriptural support could be drawn from the prophecy of Balaam, "There shall come a star out of Jacob" (Num 24:17). This would also fit in with the messianic promise associated with the kingdom when "they that turn many to righteousness shall shine as the stars" (Dan 12:3). It is, however, more in keeping with the imagery of this book, as well as more satisfying, to see here a reference to Christ Himself. He identifies Himself in this way in 22:16, "I am the bright and morning star". Christ thus promises to the overcomer, not Himself personally, but an aspect of Himself that would strengthen faith under the pressure of Thyatiran testimony. The morning star is the harbinger of the dawn as its shining precedes the sunrise. Tried believers are encouraged by Christ to look ahead to the establishment of the kingdom (as in v.27) and the sharing with Him in rule. Christ would then be seen as "the Sun of righteousness" (Mal 4:2). Believers with eyes fixed on the horizon awaiting the dawn would see first the dazzling splendour of the morning star. Only believers would appreciate this aspect of Christ, coming to catch away His church at the rapture just before the dawn breaks upon earth in the establishment of His kingdom.

29 The call of Christ for a hearing ear is the same summons as that directed to the churches in Ephesus (v. 7), Smyrna (v.11) and Pergamum (v.17) except that this time it is His final word to the church. The change of position, now placed after the promise to the overcomer, may suggest that faithful and responsive saints are in the minority. They may need as an added incentive the promise to the overcomer to allow them to give ear amidst all the clamour of their surroundings.

The Kingdom period

The imagery in this letter is taken from the kingdom period in the history of Israel. The mention of Jezebel (1 Kings 16:29-34) takes us back to that period when the people of Israel should have been enjoying the possession of the land under a king of the Davidic line. Instead they lived under an apostate king, Ahab, whose wife was a murderess and the patroness of the worst form of immorality and idolatry. Even the ministry of Elijah and the three and a half years of drought could only stay the evil, not eradicate it. There was no national repentance; there was only a remnant of seven thousand. What happened to Jezebel and her children historically (2 Kings 9:22-37) is only a portrayal of what will be experienced by this new Jezebel and her children when Christ deals with her (see ch. 17).

That for which Roman Catholicism has plotted and planned, manoeuvred and murdered throughout the ages, is "power over the nations" (v.26). It will belong to her for three and a half years at the beginning of the tribulation period as she will "sit on a scarlet-coloured beast" (17:3). Then, under the judgment of God, through the agency of the very nations she thought she controlled, she will be destroyed (17:16-17). It is to be noted that the very thing to which this satanic system aspired will be the portion of overcomers in association with Christ as the King of the Davidic line.

CHAPTER 3

(e) *The message to Sardis (vv.1-6)*

v.1 "And unto the angel of the church in Sardis write; These things saith he that hath the seven Spirits of God, and the seven stars; I know thy works, that thou hast a name that thou livest, and art dead.
v.2 Be watchful, and strengthen the things which remain, that are ready to die: for I have not found thy works perfect before God.
v.3 Remember therefore how thou hast received and heard, and hold fast, and repent. If therefore thou shalt not watch, I will come on thee as a thief, and thou shalt not know what hour I will come upon thee.
v.4 Thou hast a few names even in Sardis which have not defiled their garments; and they shall walk with me in white: for they are worthy.
v.5 He that overcometh, the same shall be clothed in white raiment; and I will not blot out his name out of the book of life, but I will confess his name before my Father, and before his angels.
v.6 He that hath an ear, let him hear what the Spirit saith unto the churches."

A traveller from Thyatira would cover 33 miles in a generally-southward direction along the main Roman highway before reaching Sardis. From this northern approach Sardis was a most imposing sight. A fortress-like city set on a commanding escarpment about 1500 feet high, it looked totally impregnable, dominating the broad Hermus valley and backing on to the foothills of Mount Tmolus (5900 feet). The almost-perpendicular cliffs looked unscalable and the only possible approach was a gentle sloping neck of land to the south. This single approach road could easily be fortified and defended.

Sardis was one of the oldest cities in Asia with a history dating back to the establishment of the Lydian kingdom c.1200 BC. Names like King Midas of Phyrgia (of the famous golden-touch legend) and King Croesus (reputedly the wealthiest king of all time) were associated with Sardis. In a strange way the very appearance of impregnability given by Sardis had a crucial and somewhat disastrous part to play in the history of the city. The fact was that the Sardians believed their own propaganda. They never seemed to realise that their defences had a fatal flaw. Resting in the false security of their fortress-like situation they were apt to become careless and unwatchful at critical times. This opened the way for several major disasters. W. Ramsay, the archaeologist, describes their situation exactly: "But, close at hand, the hill is seen to be but mud, slightly compacted, never trustworthy or lasting, crumbling under the influence of the weather, ready to yield even to the blow of a spade. It was an appearance without reality, promise without performance, outward show of strength, betrayed by want of watchfulness and careless confidence." Cyrus the Persian captured the city in 549 BC by sending a cohort of soldier-mountaineers up the cliffs that King Croesus had left unguarded imagining them unclimbable. The city was captured and looted. The Sardians never seemed to learn the lesson and, in the changing politics of the pre-Roman era it was captured by Alexander the Great (334 BC) and somewhat later by Seleucid Antiochus (214 BC) using the same tactics. Trusting in a false impregnability Sardis was an easy prey to a determined enemy.

In the period of this letter most of the greatness of Sardis lay in the past. The city was inclined to look back to glories that had gone. Recent scholarship (C. J. Hemer *The Letters to the Seven Churches of Asia in their local Setting*) has modified this view somewhat, pointing out that it was still the main strategic centre from which roads radiated to Thyatira, Pergamum, Smyrna, Philadelphia and Hierapolis. The trade of earlier days still passed through Sardis. The coinage system that led to the production of "Lydian staters" in the sixth century BC was the product of a simplified barter system. This trade seems to have flourished under Rome so that Sardis was, perhaps, the wealthiest city in the whole province. Agricultural produce from the wide Hermus valley was brought to Sardis as the market centre. Sheep-rearing on the Phyrgian plain led to a wool trade which was the basis of industries like textile manufacture, carpet weaving and cloth-dyeing. There seems also to have been considerable gold-refining and jewellery-making. Tradition says the gold came from the sand of the Pactolus river. Wherever this gold came from it is a well-established fact that in recent years no trace of gold can be found either in the river or in the neighbourhood of Sardis. Again it seems to be largely a matter of reputation.

Recent archaeological evidence tends to confirm the statement of Josephus that Sardis was a centre of the Jewish diaspora, yet the Jewish community does not seem to have played a big part in the life of the city. The emperor cult took on an added impetus when, after the devastating earthquake of 17 AD, Tiberius Caesar remitted all taxes for five years and granted the city ten million sesterces towards its rebuilding (F. A. Tatford *The Patmos Letters* p.104). Nevertheless even this political cult does not seem to have stirred much enthusiasm. The patron deity of the city was Cybele, the mother goddess. W. Ramsay identifies her with Artemis. Her temple, of which two pillars still stand today, dominated the city. Her worship was perhaps the most degraded in paganism. Orgies embracing the most debased of sexual sins were celebrated in her honour. The drunken orgies of Dionysus were but an introduction to the depravity expressed in the worship of this pagan goddess. Her priests and priestesses clothed in the whitest of robes prostituted themselves in acts of devotion that show to what depths human nature can sink.

The citizens of Sardis were proud of their history, their traditions and their myths. While admitting that their greatness belonged to the past, they tried to recall it and sought to maintain it with ceremonies and processions. Their famed civic register enshrined the famous names of their history. Civic receptions were linked with religious processions and ceremonies to recall a proud history. These debauched festivities led by white-robed priests and priestesses were the occasions that gave the city the name of decadence. History records them as effeminate, pleasure-loving voluptuaries (F. A. Tatford). Pride, wealth and immorality under the guise of religion was not a congenial environment for Christians; yet in this opulent and decadent city there was a testimony to Christ.

Of the founding of the church in Sardis we have no NT information. History and tradition are equally silent. It could be reasonably deduced that the gospel reached here from Ephesus either during or after the three years (Autumn 52-Spring 55) that Paul was in Ephesus fifty miles to the southwest. If this is so then in the short space of a generation this church had seen very sad changes. In fact it shares with the church in Laodicea the dubious distinction of being the only church of the seven to which the Lord offers not a single word of commendation.

1 In words identical to those used to the four churches already addressed (2:1, 8, 12, 18) John is commanded to pen the Lord's solemn message to the church in Sardis. To Ephesus Christ presents Himself as the vigilant priest who examines the lampstands; to Smyrna He shows Himself as the faithful witness who suffered and died; to Pergamum He is the righteous judge with absolute authority, and to Thyatira the militant Son of God treading down all that is in opposition to God. To this church, with the background of the busy markets of Sardis, Christ shows Himself to be the divine trader in whom are the resources to meet every market exigency. Since Christ holds the seven stars in His right hand (1:20) it is a fair inference that the seven spirits of God are held in His other hand. The picture presents Christ weighing resources against conditions. Whatever deficiencies exist in the actual spiritual condition of the church can be matched by that which Christ can supply out of the divine fulness in the Spirit. As already discussed (see under 1:4) it is clear that the seven Spirits display the person of the Holy Spirit seen in the plenitude of His power. That Christ "has" the Holy Spirit indicates that He is the One who in the church age, supplies the Holy Spirit (Acts 2:1; John 14:25). He incorporated the church and introduced the age with the baptism in the Holy Spirit at Pentecost. In the careful guarding of divine relationships it may be noted that the strong word "holdeth" (*krateō*), used of the seven angels in 2:1, is replaced by the simple verb "hath" (*echō*). Christ personally knew this divine fulness in His service on earth (Isa 11:2). Now through the agency of this same Spirit He is able to meet the need even of the saints in Sardis.

Without one single word of commendation to this church Christ passes directly to criticism. His scrutiny of their works leads to the chilling message, "Thou has a name that thou livest and art dead". The use of "name" is best taken, not in the Hebrew sense of the revelation of the person, but rather in the Greek sense of the reputation of the person. Here it is applied corporately. The church had the reputation of a living, vital, energetic body of saints. External observation confirmed this. They could show a real spectrum of seemingly-vibrant christian activity; there would be much that would appear spiritual in their praying and their preaching. The words "thou livest" (*zaō*) speak of more than merely physical life (*bioō*); reputedly there was divine life in this church and they would have been deeply insulted if any had questioned the reality of this life. In one brief word Christ shatters that complacency. This is more than criticism; it is condemnation – "and art dead" – the present tense simply describing the existing condition. The contrast (even using the "and") is clearly between the many activities still maintained that would normally evidence divine life and their real condition. The assembly may maintain the activities but they are living on a past reputation. The life is gone. There is profession without possession.

A parallel with the city is inescapable; fortress-like with a proud history, if the defeats due to a lack of watchfulness are ignored. Proud of the great names in its past recorded in the civic register, the civic authorities sought to recapture with ceremonies and processions the greatness of that past. They tended to ignore the present decay. These city features in a spiritual way were in measure reflected in the church. It would seem to be a fair deduction that what had begun as a vibrant testimony for Christ had become a gathering where the majority were only lifeless professors. Satisfied with externals and the outward show of spiritual life, true spiritual life was missing. Death reigned in Sardis.

2-3 While the general picture is dark the next words show that the death of which Christ spoke was general but not absolute. There were yet those in the church to whom Christ could appeal. If there was a response to that appeal there was yet hope. The response demanded by Christ may be set out in the two double imperatives.:

1 "Be watchful and...strengthen"

2 "Remember therefore...and repent".

In each case a verb in the present imperative is followed by one in the aorist imperative. The first action demanded by Christ "Be watchful" may be more accurately translated "become awake and on the watch" (Vincent) or "prove yourselves to be watchful" (R. L. Thomas). Obedience would demand that they run to "strengthen the things which remain". This dramatically pictures the awakened sentry rushing to the weak point in the defences, a picture that recalls the rebuilding of the wall of Jerusalem in Nehemiah's day (Neh 4:20). The believers in Sardis must be like awakened sentries rushing to the preservation of the testimony. In non-figurative language the believers must be prepared to see that scriptural teaching was applied in a practical way to maintain separation for Christ. It is possible that the most fundamental principles of reception and discipline that are the basis of church testimony were about to be lost in Sardis. If saints did not wake up to this, then civic history was about to be repeated in church life. The unbelievable carelessness and complacency that had failed to put a man on guard over the seemingly-unscalable cliffs had resulted in the past in the fall of the city. The spiritual complacency and lethargy of the Sardis church would carry a like penalty in spiritual terms.

The "things that remain" as a neuter noun must embrace principles and practices. However Alford insists, from a detailed examination of the usage of the expression, that it must include the persons who held the principles and carried out the practices. Thus the remnant principle, which first appeared in Thyatira, is clearly visible here. The emergency situation is emphasised in the statement that they were "ready to die", which may be paraphrased "on the point of expiring". The last spark of life was about to go out. The past tense in the expression (see RV) does not need emphasis but is to be explained by seeing that the matter is viewed from the point of view of the church receiving the letter (R. L. Thomas).

The explanation for this vigilance is that Christ has not found the works of this church "perfect before God". The idea in "perfect" is that the works have been begun but not satisfactorily completed. Incomplete fortifications are not of any real value to a besieged city, neither do fortifications without a watchful sentry constitute a complete defence. The history of the city was proof of this. Lest the history of the church duplicate the history of the city Christ sought to awaken the saints to the danger. The inclusion in many manuscripts of "my" and the translation "my God" (RV) show that Christ is acting as a priest for God. The use of the verb "found" implies a search, a search that so far had proved disappointing.

As He did in His message to Ephesus (2:5) Christ calls on the church to "remember". These memories would be a major factor leading the believers to a decisive step of repentance. Complacency is sin and immediate remedial action must be taken. Christ challenges them to recall the spiritual blessings they have already received. "How thou hast received" not only looks back to the actual blessings but to the joy and gladness that came with them. Those had been happy days. The tense of "hast received" indicates that the blessings were still there; the blessings had not changed but the saints had changed. Their response in the past is recalled in the verb "heard"; the tense may point first to the moment of conversion but it must also include their response to the teaching that established the assembly. Christ desires that they continue to hold fast these truths. The object of "hold fast" may be understood as "the things remaining" from v.2. Keeping a firm grip on what they had of the original principles of testimony would provide a good basis for the spiritual recovery expected in the command "repent". Repentance not only involves regret for the past but calls for a change of mind about what has been done. Doubt as to the response of the saints led Christ to spell out the consequences. Robertson translates the verb "watch" most dramatically: "if you do not wake up". The failure to heed the voice of the Lord would show that their trouble was not sleep but death (v.1).

The first "therefore" in the verse opens the way for recovery through repentance; the second "therefore" spells out the result of the refusal to repent. The result would be that the coming of Christ would take them completely by surprise. With the church in Ephesus (2:5) and in Pergamum (2:16) Christ would deal governmentally. Here to the church in Sardis as to the church in Thyatira (2:25) the judgment would take place at His coming for the church at the rapture. The same verb *echō* as used to Thyatira should be translated "I will arrive". The failure of the church to "wake up" would mean that Christ would arrive "as a thief". The unexpected and unheralded arrival of a thief takes the sleeping householder by surprise: so Christ would come to this sleeping church. It is important to see that where the figure of the thief is used in connection with Christ's coming it always has unbelievers in view, as a study of the passages where Christ Himself uses the figure will make plain (Matt 24:43; Luke 12:39). The apostolic warnings in 1 Thess 5:2; 2 Peter 3:10, as well as the only other occurrence of the simile in 16:15, all make this point abundantly clear. For true believers the Lord is never seen coming as a thief. To the church He has already pronounced "dead" (v.1), composed largely of empty professors, Christ's coming at the rapture would take them completely by surprise. Their failure to respond to His counsel would but show the absence of spiritual life. The word "thief" (*kleptēs*) is the word that describes the night prowler who uses silence and stealth. The unexpectedness of Christ's coming to this church is emphasised in the final statement of the verse. The double negative is said by grammarians (see Robertson) to be the strongest negation in the language and should be translated colloquially "by no means will you know". This is a further indication that the second coming of Christ is in view echoing His own words of Matt 24:36. The rapture of the church is the first stage of that coming. Date-setting for His coming is totally unscriptural and believers are expected to live in the anticipation that He may come at any moment. The complacency and carelessness in Sardis showed that many in the congregation, perhaps the majority, had no spiritual life. Thus the coming of Christ would be as unexpected as the coming of a thief and would rob them of all hope for the future.

4 As pointed out there is no commendation for the church as a whole but there is a note of commendation for individuals. Even in Sardis, with perhaps a majority of mere professors, there were a number upon whom the eye of Christ rested with favour. The implied contrast with the major part of the company is seen in the strong adversative "but" (*alla*), omitted in the AV, which shows that even amidst the prevailing profession there were a few who had divine life. This minority, perhaps even smaller than the remnant in Thyatira, is seen in the expression "a few names". "Names" is used in the colloquial sense as describing individuals; it is used in a similar way in Acts 1:15 and in 11:13 (RV margin). Christ is not counting members but identifying individuals whose lives show a holy distinction from the prevailing death around them. The character of these saints is described figuratively as those who "have not defiled their garments". Garments are used in scripture to speak of what can be observed in the conduct and character of the individual. The metaphor shows a life-style unstained by defilement. Garments washed (7:14) at conversion have remained undefiled by subsequent conduct. Vine gives the literal meaning of the verb "defile" as "to besmear, as with mud or filth, to befoul". Used figuratively, as here, it would be better translated "did not defile". It points back to occasions when these believers refused to be associated with the defiling practices of paganism. They showed the same character as Daniel did in Babylonish conditions: "he would not defile himself with the portion of the king's meat" (Dan 1:8).

The procession of the white-clothed priests to the temple of the mother-goddess Cybele in Sardis was a familiar sight to the citizens. On the day of a triumph granted by the Roman Senate, citizens donned the white toga, while specially-honoured dignitaries walked with the honoured one in ceremonial procession to the civic reception. Believers faithful to Christ in Sardis would never share in any of these religious or political processions of earth but, in contrast, they would share in a far greater ceremonial procession to the greatest civic reception of all time and they would have the personal companionship of Christ Himself. What God had expected to enjoy with Adam (Gen 3:8) and did enjoy with Enoch (Gen 5:22) will be realised in Christ with His faithful ones. Uninterrupted companionship and unimpeded fellowship are promised. Christ continues the metaphor of garments; the undefiled garments of earth will be replaced by the "white" garments that are not only suitable to glory but reflect the character of Christ's own apparel.

There could be no higher commendation for any saints than for Christ to pronounce them "worthy". This is the word used of God in 4:11 and of Christ in 5:9. It is understandable that in light of creation and the cross all creatures should acknowledge the worth of deity. It is startling grace that Christ should speak thus of His own, even the faithful ones, who in the midst of weakness maintained a true testimony to His name. It shows how He values faithfulness to Himself. This word is used of only one other company in this book and what a contrast there is in 16:6. In this passage saints show themselves fit for Christ's commendation; in that later passage sinners show themselves fit for divine retribution.

5 Christ makes three promises to the overcomer. There is no doubt that they are designed to stand in contrast to the civic honours available to citizens in the city of Sardis. He promises:

1. A Civic Investiture: "shall be clothed in white raiment". The scriptural background is found in Zech 3:1-7 showing the action of Jehovah in dealing with the defiled garments of saints who had come out of Babylonish conditions. While in that passage the priesthood is primarily in view it is clear that Joshua represents the whole nation of Israel. Christ is implying that the overcomer will be involved in priestly functions in the Messianic kingdom (1:6). The future tense in the verb "shall be clothed" indicates that the moment of investiture is still ahead. Purity that the saints manifest in their lives on earth will be reflected in garments that will show the purity of heaven itself (7:9, 13). The correspondence in the language shows that the believers of v.4 have become the overcomers of v.5
2. A Civic Recognition: "I will not blot his name out of the book of life". The verb "blot out" is used in the NT in the metaphorical sense of remove, wipe off, obliterate (Vine). It is used of sins (Acts 3:19), of the handwriting of ordinances (Col 2:14) and of tears (7:17; 21:4). Here it is the complete removal of the name. Amidst all the conflicting opinions that have centred around the understanding of this second part of the promise to the overcomer, two matters must be kept in mind.

a. There does not seem to be any valid reason for making a difference between this reference to the "book of life" and the other seven references in this book (13:8; 17:8; 20:12, 15; 21:27; 22:19 (twice)) nor the other NT reference in Phil 4:3. (In Luke 10:20 there is no specific reference to the book.) There would also seem to be no valid reason for making a difference between the book of life and the Lamb's book of life. Some do make a difference as W. Scott writes: "In chapter 3:5 the 'book of life' is the record of christian profession; in chapter 13:8 the 'book of life' is the record of reality. In the former the true and false are found; in the latter the true only". This seems a somewhat arbitrary conclusion without any clear support from Scripture. It is much more consistent to accept that the book is the same in all the NT passages quoted. This is the heavenly register of all believers in Christ.

b. The blotting out of names is certainly an OT truth. However the idea must be physical death in the two passages where the expression occurs: Exod 32:32 with respect to Moses and Ps 69:28 with regard to the wicked. Thus in the OT to "blot out a name" is a metaphorical way of speaking of physical death.

Scripture is perfectly clear on the eternal security of a NT believer so that there is no possibility of a name being blotted out of the register of heaven. Christ is not threatening the removal of a name but is encouraging the overcomer. The same strong negative used in v.3 is repeated here; Newberry translates "by no means". The expression involves a figure of speech, litotes, where a very strong negative is used to emphasise the opposite (see Heb 4:15 for a good example). The positive truth, however, must be something more than the simple fact that the name is in the book. Perhaps the civic background of Sardis completes the picture. As F. A. Tatford writes lucidly, "Practically every city of that day kept a roll or register of its citizens. In that record was entered the name of every child born in the city. If one of the citizens proved guilty of treachery or disloyalty, public dishonour was heaped upon him by the expunging of his name from the register. On the other hand, one who performed some great exploit deserving of special distinction, was honoured by having his name inscribed in golden letters in the citizen's roll. Our Lord's emphatic statement, therefore, implies not merely that the name of the overcomer shall not be expunged but *per contra* that it shall be inscribed in golden letters in the heavenly roll" (*Prophecy's Last Word* p.62). In this graphic way the Lord fastens upon a feature of their civic background to stress the honour to be gained by the overcomer in such difficult circumstances.

3 A Civic Presentation: "but I will confess his name before my Father and before his angels". The confession of the name of Christ in Sardis may

have cost the overcomers friends and family on earth. Under such pressure it would soon be clear who were true believers; such would have no civic recognition in their home city. To these saints Christ promises the civic investiture of the white garments and the civic recognition of having their names shine forth from the book of life. He goes a step further and climaxes the promises with the assurance of a civic presentation. There in a moment when He will present His faithful ones by name before the Father and before His angels. David when he came into his kingdom recalled the years of his rejection in the naming and acknowledgement of his mighty men (2 Sam 23). In far grander fashion before the august court of heaven, before the Father and His holy angels, saints of the church age will be presented. Names unknown and unrecognised on earth will then resound through thc heavenly court and recall for Christ the days of His rejection. These saints confessed His name on earth; He will confess their names in heaven. What higher honour could there be or what greater encouragement for the overcomer?

6 In the same words as to each previous church Christ appeals to the individual to respond to His warnings and entreaties. Originating with Christ but carried by the Spirit of God it summons each responsive saint. The plural "churches" indicates that a wider audience even than the seven churches of Asia is anticipated. Churches with much false profession could learn solemn lessons from the message of Christ to Sardis. The position of this call at the very end of the message suggests, as it did in Thyatira, that Christ anticipates that while the majority may reject His call there would still be individuals who would respond to His word.

(f) *The message to Philadelphia (vv.7-13)*

v.7 "And to the angel of the church in Philadelphia write; These things saith he that is holy, he that is true, he that hath the key of David, he that openeth, and no man shutteth; and shutteth, and no man openeth;

v.8 I know thy works: behold, I have set before thee an open door, and no man can shut it: for thou hast a little strength, and hast kept my word, and hast not denied my name.

v.9 Behold, I will make them of the synagogue of Satan, which say they are Jews, and are not, but do lie; behold, I will make them to come and worship before thy feet, and to know that I have loved thee.

v.10 Because thou hast kept the word of my patience, I also will keep thee from the hour of temptation, which shall come upon all the world, to try them that dwell upon the earth.

v.11 Behold, I come quickly: hold that fast which thou hast, that no man take thy crown.

v.12 Him that overcometh will I make a pillar in the temple of my God, and he shall go no more out: and I write upon him the name of my God, and the name of the city of my God, which is new Jerusalem, which cometh down out of heaven from my God; and I will write upon him my new name.
v.13 He that hath an ear, let him hear what the Spirit saith unto the churches."

Philadelphia was the most modern of the cities addressed in these letters. It had been built c 189BC by Attalus II the king of Pergamum as a tribute of loyalty to his older brother Eumenes II. The name, derived from *phileō* ("to love") and *adelphō* ("a brother"), reflects this brotherly devotion. Despite attempts at various times to change the name the citizens of Philadelphia remained unusually faithful to the old name. W. Ramsay points out that after the devastating earthquake of 17AD so grateful were the civic authorities for imperial help that they renamed the city Neocaesarea. However within thirty years the new name had gone and the old name was in place again. It was under its own ancient name that this city became the last city of the Roman province to capitulate to Ottoman forces as late as 1392AD. Its reputation for faithfulness was retained to the end of its history.

The site of the city had been chosen with deliberation. About twenty-five miles southeast of Sardis the road ran along the course of a tributary of the Hermus and then began to climb into a beautiful valley. The city was built at the eastern mouth of the valley where it entered the great central plateau of Phyrgia. The road was somewhat steep as the city was a thousand feet above Sardis, but it was the main route from Smyrna with its fine harbour, through Sardis and onwards to Phyrgia and the east. This road was a serious rival to the great Ephesus highway and became an imperial postal and trade route.

Archaeologists, notably W. Ramsay and in more recent times C. J. Hemer, have pointed out that the primary purpose for the establishment of this city was neither military occupation nor territorial domination. It was not designed to be a fortress even though its location on a wide hill, with Mount Tmolus behind it and open to the plateau on one side only, did mean that it could be defended with a minimum of fortifications. Ramsay's comments are worth recording: "The intention of the founder was to make it a centre of Greco-Asiatic civilisation, and a means of spreading the Greek language and manners in the eastern parts of Lydia and Phyrgia. It was a missionary city, founded to promote a unity of spirit, custom, and loyalty within the realm, the apostle of Hellenism in an oriental land. It was a successful teacher. Before 19AD, the Lydian tongue had ceased to be spoken in Lydia and Greek was the only language of the country" (W. Ramsay *Letters to the Seven Churches of Asia* (p.391).

Philadelphia had one major drawback. It was situated in an area where volcanoes were active and earthquakes were frequent. On the plus side, the volcanic ash on the Phyrgian plain gave it a rich fertility that made the plain a centre for the cultivation of vines. But earthquakes were sometimes devastating. The great earthquake of 17AD which shook the whole province brought greater initial damage to Sardis (R. L. Thomas) but Philadelphia, nearer the epicentre of the earthquake, suffered more damage in the aftershocks. Strabo, the Greek writer, records that after the initial earthquake, so continuous and violent were these aftershocks that the whole population moved outside the city for a time. They built temporary huts rather than attempt to rebuild their homes.

Since vine-growing prospered in the rich soil of the Phyrgian plain it was inevitable that the wine trade should centre there. It was equally inevitable that the patron god of the city would be Dionysus, the god of wine (the Roman Bacchus). Associated with this pagan worship were orgies of the most licentious kind in honour of Bacchus. Emperor-worship in the last decades of the first century was not locally encouraged and, in fact, seems to have been actively discouraged. The reason was very simple: a change of imperial policy under Domitian had demanded the replacement of vineyards by cornfields. This was designed to meet the chronic shortage of corn for the imperial capital, a problem that had already caused riots among the slave population of Rome. Philadelphia's prosperity suffered severely as a result. Archaeology has not yet unearthed any evidence of a Jewish community but it is clear from this letter (v.9) that there must have been quite a substantial one in the city.

7 In the words identical to those used to the previous five churches Christ addresses the church in Philadelphia. Of how or when this church was established we have no NT record. With the other churches it could have been the result of the apostolic labours of Paul and his fellow-preachers in the years when he was based in Ephesus (Autumn 52-Spring 55). Another possibility is that the gospel reached here from Colosse. About 62 or 63 AD Paul could write to the church in Colosse: "the word of the truth of the gospel; which is come unto you as it is in all the world; and bringeth forth fruit" (Col 1:5-6). Colosse was less than fifty miles from Philadelphia. The fruit in Philadelphia was sinners converted and gathered in the name of the Lord Jesus Christ. Philadelphia is linked with Smyrna as the two churches for whom Christ had not a single word of criticism.

Christ presents Himself to this church, not in His official capacity of priest-judge but in His essential character, what He is in Himself. The faithfulness of believers in this church is the ground of an intimate revelation of His person, yet their allied weakness draws forth His tenderness. Thus the descriptive terms are not taken from 1:14-16 but are fresh unfoldings of Himself. Four descriptive notes may be observed in His revelation of Himself.

1. "He that is holy". "Holy" describes what is free from sin; it is an attribute of deity (4:8; 6:10). In wider NT usage it includes the thought of what is set apart for God. It is used in this way of Christ Himself (Mark 1:24;

Luke 1:35; 4:34; John 6:69; Acts 4:27, 30; 1 John 2:20). While saints are set apart by the action of God, Christ is the One in whom absolute purity is personally displayed. Any believer with a Jewish background would be immediately reminded of such scriptures as Ps 16:10; Isa 6:3; 49:7. Christ in this title stresses His deity.

2. "He that is true". "True" is a particularly Johannine word. It occurs ten times in this book and twelve times in his other writings. Sometimes it is coupled with "faithful" as in 3:14; 19:11; 21:5; 22:6, and sometimes with "righteous" as in 15:3; 16:7; 19:2. Here it stands alone and speaks of absolute reality. The other word for "true" is *alēthōs* emphasises what is true as distinct from false. *Alēthinos* means "genuine" (Vine). When the Lord spoke of Himself as the "true bread" (John 6:32) He did not mean that every other bread was false, but rather that if bread in its "essence" was desired He was bread in "reality". Israel had the typical and the imperfect enshrined in type and ceremony. Valuable in their own place Christ shows Himself to be the reality behind the type. Any believers of Jewish background must learn that they cannot stay with the imperfections and the shadows of Judaism (Heb 10:1). Reality is to be found in Christ.

3. "He that hath the key of David". The idea in "the key" is absolute authority. This is a quotation from Isa 22:22 with the words "the house of" omitted by Christ. Shebna was the steward of Hezekiah's house but because of pride and arrogance had to be removed from office. He was replaced by the faithful steward Eliakim of whom it was said, "And the key of the house of David will I lay upon his shoulder". The key was a symbol of the trust and confidence vested in him. That OT drama finds complete fulfilment in Christ. All other stewards for God have proved unfaithful, but God has now invested His faithful Steward with the symbol of authority. Any Jew would recognise immediately that Christ was claiming the right of the Messiah. Kingdom authority (note the mention of David) was entrusted to Him. Christ is showing that He holds the key to the messianic promises: He would open the treasure house of David. The omission of the words "the house of" would be a clear indication that the messianic promises are not to be limited to Israel. Jew and Gentile would be provided for as Christ fulfils messianic expectation.

Believers from a pagan background may not have known much about messianic promises; for them the meaning of the key held a different implication. In pagan minds the god Janus was the key-bearer. He had power:

a. to open the year (hence our name for the first month of the year).
b. to open or shut the gates of heaven
c. to open or shut the gates of war and peace on earth. Colloquially he is spoken of as "the opener and shutter" (F. A. Tatford)

Christ thus presents Himself as the One with absolute authority; no pagan deity can claim power amongst His people.

4 "He that openeth and no man shutteth and shutteth and no man openeth" is a quotation from the same passage in Isa 22:22. The point here is not the possession of the key but the use of it. Doors are to be opened or closed and no other may interfere with the key-bearer's judgment. The metaphorical doors may be those of the store cupboards from which food is dispensed and the need of a household met. Alternatively, they could well be the doors to the outside world through which the persons and the supplies of the household must pass. As the faithful steward Christ oversees all that pertains to the well-being and prosperity of the testimony. He has the final word in all necessary activity.

8 Christ uses the same searching word that He has used to Ephesus, to Thyatira and to Sardis: "I know thy works". It reflects the same perfect acquaintance with the state and activity of this church as it did of the others. In contrast to the previous church Sardis (v.1), where this statement is followed by unqualified condemnation, here it will be followed by qualified commendation. However before the commendation Christ gives a needed word of reassurance. This word is required because the saints seem to have had some measure of apprehension, possibly arising from their weakness, about their ability to maintain the testimony. To deal with this concern Christ assures them that that door of opportunity opened by Him cannot be closed by another. The verb "set before thee" is the perfect tense of the verb "to give". The action that Christ has taken in the past still stands; I. T. Beckwith translates, "I have given and it remains given". The word "open" qualifying door would be better rendered "opened". The door has been opened and it remains open. The next statement restates the same truth more explicitly and emphatically. No man has the strength (*dunatai*) to shut it. The saints need not fear; the Lord has acted for them and the opportunity will remain open to them.

That this is not the door of admission to either the kingdom or the church is perfectly clear from the context. "Door" is used figuratively, as it is in Acts 14:27; 1 Cor 16:9; 2 Cor 2:12, of the opportunity for missionary service. A cultural background picture is available in that the city was widely known as a missionary city, the city from which Greek culture spread into lands to the east. Christ shows that the local church had a far more vital missionary role in carrying the gospel into the hinterland of Asia. For the consciously-weak church of Philadelphia this was an awesome responsibility and Christ puts in the word of reassurance for their encouragement.

After this aside Christ recognises that the works of the Philadelphian church were the evidence of but "a little strength". The present tense of the verb "hast" describes a continuing condition that gives meaning to the two past tenses to follow. That strength has been manifest in a positive way ("hast kept my word") and in a negative way ("hast not denied my name"). While this clearly falls short of unreserved commendation it is just as clearly a note of warm appreciation from the Lord. They had a spiritual vitality that was unrelated to their actual numbers or wealth. Even if it is assumed that the church was weak numerically with little material assets Christ identified and commends a spiritual strength. This is the very reason why He had opened the door of opportunity for them, "for" should be rendered "because". Their strength might be measured by Christ and described as "little", but it is both vital and valuable. Two crises had shown the reality of this power, "little" though it was. Christ summarises the crises thus:

1. Loyalty to the Scriptures: "Thou hast kept my word". The tense points to an occasion (or occasions), when, under attack, the assembly had shown their adherence to the teachings of the Word. To "keep the word" is a normal scriptural metaphor for obeying the Word. They had decisively and deliberately decided not to disobey.
2. Loyalty to the Saviour: "Thou has not denied my name". The second verb points back to a time or times when they had been under pressure to renounce the claims of Christ and had stood firm. Loyalty to the "name" (as pointed out in 2:13) means nothing less than loyalty to the person. This assembly when under pressure to renounce the claims of Christ had maintained their testimony. Loyal to His person they would accept no other name. Just as the city had refused to accept any change of name so the church was adamant in adhering loyally to the name of Christ.

9 In response to the faithfulness of the believers in the midst of conscious weakness Christ gives them three promises. The repetition of the word "behold" in the verse indicates just how remarkable this happening will be, especially in light of Christ's assessment of the weakness. It is nothing less than the vindication of their testimony and the complete answer to the sneers of their enemies. Christ would publicly give them converts from the Satan-inspired opponents ranged against them. These erstwhile-satanic agents would be humbled and their repentance would be seen in their change of attitude to the church they had previously so despised.

The first verb "I will make" (*didōmi*) rendered by Newberry "I will give" has no expressed direct object. To clarify the meaning the AV supplies "them" – taken from the second verb. The meaning may be shown thus – "I will give ...I will make them...". The "them", the direct object of both verbs, are clearly the local enemies of the believers. These enemies are the same kind as those troubling the church in Smyrna (2:9). Jews by nationality, they showed by their actions that they did not belong to the people of God (Rom 2:28; Matt 3:9; John 8:33; 2 Cor 11:22; Phil 3:4). Their actions in stirring up the civil authorities against the believers showed that their spiritual home was not merely "the synagogue of the Jews" but "the synagogue of Satan". Whether there was a literal synagogue in Philadelphia may be an interesting archaeological study but it makes no difference to the understanding of this verse. These Jews were showing their spiritual identification with Satan as the adversary of Christ. The clarifying remark "but do lie" links them the more closely with the "father of lies" (John 8:44; 1 John 2:22). These followers of Satan, by a miracle of divine power, will be made to come and worship before the feet of the saints. Isa 60:14 gives the background picture for this promise: "The sons also of them that afflicted thee shall come bending unto thee; and all they that despised thee shall bow themselves down at the soles of thy feet; and they shall call thee the city of the Lord, the Zion of the Holy One of Israel". This millennial promise relating to the nation of Israel still awaits fulfilment but Christ uses the picture to show how He will work with similar enemies of the church in Philadelphia. Bitterly-antagonistic Jews will acknowledge God's blessing on Gentiles. The verbs "to come", "to worship" and "to know" dramatically define what a change has been wrought by Christ in these one-time enemies. This action is a public repudiation of their previous attitude. Some would argue that this is the result of divine compulsion as envisaged on a worldwide scale when every knee will bow to Christ (Phil 2:10). They would see this as happening when Christ comes to earth and the verb "worship" (*proskuneō*) should then be rendered "do homage" as in JND. While this interpretation is possible it does not fit the context. It is difficult to see how the Philadelphian church can thus be singled out in this eschatological happening that will bring earth to the feet of Christ. It is better to see the promise as describing a divine work of grace in the conversion of the one-time adversaries in Philadelphia who will thus demonstrate in a public way their change of heart. It must be pointed out that the worship is not directed to the assembly but to God in the presence of the saints. The mention of the feet stresses the real humbling of heart that has taken place; they cannot get any lower. The emphatic position of the singular "thee" as the last word in the promise highlights how the thinking of the enemies has been reversed. They will be brought to see that this gathering of saints, both Jew and Gentile, is the object of the divine love. By implication they understand for the first time the operations of divine grace.

10 Because of their past endurance Christ gives them a further promise. He promises to keep the saints out of the tribulation period about to come on the earth. The tense of the verb "kept" summarises the whole lifetime of the believers. They have shown throughout their lives the same endurance that Christ showed when He was here on earth (2 Thess 3:5; Heb 12:3). Some commentators (F.A. Tatford, W. Scott) suggest that the endurance is that shown by Christ as He awaits in glory the moment of His coming, and the implication is that believers show the same patience as they await His coming. This interpretation does not suit the context nor does it give the word "endurance" its usual meaning. Rather the idea is that since believers have proved the reality of their faithfulness in times of stress, Christ promises to keep them from the most severe trial of all. Note also the emphatic "I"; Christ will act personally to do this. Three things are to be noted in connection with this promise.

1. The Period of the Tribulation: "The hour of temptation" (*tēs hōras tou peirasmou*). The presence of the article with "tribulation" indicates the "well-known" period of trial of which the Lord Himself had spoken in the Olivet discourse (Matt 24:21): "For then shall be great tribulation, such as was not since the beginning of the world to this time, no nor ever shall be". The word "hour" in normal speech is often used to describe a relatively short period of time; the tribulation may be actually seven years (Dan 9:27) but measured against the span of earth history it is only an "hour". The expression "the great tribulation" (in 7:14) will be shown to refer specifically to the last three and a half years of the period.
2. The Place of the Tribulation: "Upon all the world". The word "world", which would be better translated "inhabited earth", cannot be of narrower compass than the whole of earth. There is no justification in the passage for limiting it to either the land of Israel or to the Roman Empire. The inclusion of the word "all" leaves no doubt on the matter. The term embraces the inhabitants of the earth who are described as "earth dwellers". This is the first occurrence of a term that will be repeated some twelve times (6:10; 8:13; 11:10 twice; 12:2; 13:8, 12, 14 twice; 14:6; 17:2, 8). A study of these occurrences will show that the term does not describe simply the fact that these folk live on earth but it takes on a disparaging meaning to indicate a moral connection between the people and the earth on which they live. They are those who have made their dwelling on earth; they are at home on earth; they belong to earth. It will be shown in this book that their moral and spiritual choice has been made in rejecting the call of the Lamb (15:3-4) and accepting the claims of the Beast (13:15-17).
3. The Purpose of the Tribulation: "To try them that dwell on the earth". This period of trial has a purpose that is described by the related verb "to try". To use the figure in the verb – for a period, men who belong to earth, will be put through the furnace. This will show what they are and, as trial follows trial through the climaxing judgments of the seals, the trumpets and the bowls, the hearts of all men will be fully displayed.

> With the crash of the final judgment the record is given, "And men blasphemed God" (16:21).

In light of this coming tribulation period upon earth the promise to the believers is expressed in unequivocal language. They are to be kept from the hour of temptation. There is a deliberate action and reaction in the repetition of the same verb by Christ: "because thou didst keep ... I will k eep". The preposition ek with the verb *tēreō* allows no other idea than "preserve from", "protect from", or "keep out of". The expression is also suggestive of the imminence of the danger. Christ could have used other prepositions with the verb to define either "preservation in", or "preservation through" the time of trial. While it is true that with certain verbs *ek* can retain its primary idea of "motion from within" (as it does in 7:14 with the verb "to come") with the verb "to keep" it always has its secondary meaning of "complete preservation from". The apparent exception of John 17:15 is no real exception to this rule. When the Lord prayed "that thou shouldest keep them from the evil" (*tērēsēs autous ek tou ponērou*), He was speaking of "the evil" already round the disciples; in this passage it is "the hour" that is coming from which the saints are to be kept. In either case the idea is "complete preservation from". The only legitimate deduction from the promise here is that Christ is assuring the saints of complete physical preservation from the tribulation period coming on the earth. There would be little of comfort for faithful believers of Philadelphia to know that they would be preserved through further terrible trials, but there would be real comfort to know they would not be here when earth's tribulation days arrived.

In this promise Christ takes His teaching about the rapture a step further. To Thyatira Christ has revealed Himself as "the morning star". He will come before the millennial reign anticipated in the sunrise upon earth. To the major part of the church in Sardis, the merely nominal professors, He would arrive "as a thief". The truly-converted would be caught up and the unsaved professors left behind in their loss. Now, in this message to Philadelphia, Christ makes plain that He comes to take home His saints before the tribulation begins on earth.

11 Christ now explains how this promise He has just made will be kept. The believers, unlike the citizens of earthquake-prone Philadelphia, had no need whatever to view the future with fear. Earth will be shaken by greater convulsions than ever engulfed the city of Philadelphia but the saints will not experience these shocks. Christ is coming and He adds the word "quickly" (*tachu*) that the Philadelphian saints may know He could come in their lifetime. This is the positive implication of imminence that is made here and re-echoed in the promises of Christ in 22:7, 12, 20, "Behold I come quickly". There is nothing in the prophetic calendar that must take place before He comes for the church. That this cannot be a disciplinary visitation as His coming to Ephesus (2:4) or Pergamum (2:16) is made clear by the omission of the words "unto thee". This is the coming of Christ to the air for the church as promised in John 14:3; 1 Cor 15:51-53; 1 Thess 4:13-18. This is to be the positive expectation of the Philadelphian saints. It is not to be limited to them alone but is the common heritage of all saints of this dispensation.

This promise forms the basis of a plea from the Lord Himself. They are to "hold fast" (*krateō*) what "they have" (*echō*). This echoes what the Lord has identified in the assembly already in v.8, "thou hast (*echeis*) a little strength". Christ warns that failure to hold fast would mean the loss of "thy crown". The singular "crown" (*stephanos*) shows that individual crowns are not in view. The present tense of the verb "take", and even the use of this transitive verb *lambanō* itself, shows that the loss is now in the present age as distinct from a day to come. Christ is clearly using the idea of the crown figuratively in the way it is used sometimes in the OT. In Lev 21:12 the explanation of the high standard of sanctification of the high priest is explained in terms of a crown "for the crown of the anointing oil of His God is upon his head". In Num 6:7 the same word for crown (*neezer*) is translated "consecration" and explains the separation of the Nazarite. The high priest and the Nazarite would have lost their crowns, if someone or some act had infringed their separation. That symbolic "crown" was the key to their service; to lose it was to lose that which set them apart from others in service for God. Here Christ appeals to the assembly to allow no one to act in such a way as to rob the church of that distinctive mark of separation to God, their "crown".

12 While the holding fast of the previous verse is clearly an assembly responsibility the challenge to the overcomer is personal. Two matters must mark the life of an exercised saint. The first is the worship of God; the second is the work of God. Absorbing as these matters must be for a saint now, they will find their fulness in a day that is coming. In that day faithfulness under Philadelphian conditions will have its full reward. These rewards will fittingly centre on:

1. The Temple of My God – Worship
   The worship of the cosmos finds its fulfilment in the new Jerusalem, "And I saw no temple therein: for the Lord God Almighty and the Lamb are the temple of it" (21:22). The overcomer is promised the status of a "pillar" in this temple. Heathen temples were resplendent with pillars often bearing the names of wealthy benefactors. Some of these pillars are still standing in Philadelphia today in spite of the earthquakes. In the temple of Solomon two special pillars are named as Jachin ("establishment") and Boaz ("strength"). In this coming day those who have shown their reliability in testimony on earth will be honoured as

"pillars" in the temple of God and the Lamb. A note of security is added by Christ. Temple worshippers in Philadelphia were accustomed to vacate temple and city when earthquakes rumbled. In this temple of God will be no such earthquakes and Christ promises uninterrupted security, "he shall go no more out". In the worship of this sanctuary the identification mark will be clear. As the Aaronic high priest had the golden plate with the engraven words "Holiness to Jehovah" (Exod 28:36-38), so in this coming day worshippers can bear no greater name than that which the promise of Christ mentions, "the name of my God".

2. The City of My God – Work
The terms in which this city is described by Christ identify it as "the holy city, the new Jerusalem" of 21:2. The administrative capital of the cosmos is now the eternal home of the saints. Faithful saints will be entrusted with service throughout the cosmos and they are identified with their city-centre. Christ promises to "write upon him the name of the city of my God", which could possibly be their initial commissioning in this holy service. The title "the new Jerusalem" sets it in contrast to the old sin-stained, blood-stained, earthly capital of the nation of Israel. New (*kainos*) in character, its creator is "my God" and its sphere (out of heaven) shows that it belongs to "the new heavens and the new earth" (21:1). To bear the name of this city implies not only to have citizenship within it, but to have the "freedom" of it; this is defined as the right to come and go at all times (R.C. Trench *The Seven Churches of Asia*). Made strangers on earth by identification with Christ in the church age, now their citizenship of this administrative capital of the cosmos will be publicly displayed.

The final word is a promise by Christ to write on the overcomer "my new name". The Philadelphian overcomer who refused to "deny" the name of Christ in this dispensation (v.8) will then be honoured by receiving upon his person Christ's new name, a name not as yet communicated to man (19:12). There is a depth to the person of Christ not yet possible of human apprehension. In this coming day the overcomer will be permitted to display the fact that he is highly honoured by Christ.

13 The final call to the church is identical with that given to the other churches. It anticipates that the particular challenge in the circumstances in Philadelphia will be needed by saints in churches not only in the province of Asia but throughout the whole age of church testimony.

Notes

7 This key should be clearly distinguished from other keys in the NT. There is no scriptural warrant for linking this passage with either:

1. the keys of Hell and of death (1:18); where the authority is cosmic. Christ is shown to

hold the authority over all mankind whether in the body or not. In this passage the authority is within the church and, eventually, within the millennial kingdom on earth. They are different keys.

2. The keys given to Peter (Matt 16:19). These are called the "keys of the kingdom". By this expression the Lord was indicating the authority given personally to Peter to open the door of the kingdom in the church age. He used these keys to open the door to believing Jews in Acts 2 and to believing Gentiles in Acts 10. As W. Scott writes: "The keys having been used, and the doors opened, a successional and vested right in 'St. Peter's keys' is absurd. Peter left the door open; hence they are of no further use".

It is useful also to recall that in its geographical setting Philadelphia was a "key" city. All persons and trade passing into the eastern uplands did so with the permission of Philadelphia. Christ shows that it is not the church that has the "key" but that ultimate authority rests with Him.

(g) *The message to Laodicea (vv.14-22)*

v.14 "And unto the angel of the church of the Laodiceans write; These things saith the Amen, the faithful and true witness, the beginning of the creation of God;
v.15 I know thy works, that thou art neither cold nor hot: I would thou wert cold or hot.
v.16 So then because thou art lukewarm, and neither cold nor hot, I will spue thee out of my mouth.
v.17 Because thou sayest, I am rich, and increased with goods, and have need of nothing; and knowest not that thou art wretched, and miserable, and poor, and blind, and naked:
v.18 I counsel thee to buy of me gold tried in the fire, that thou mayest be rich; and white raiment, that thou mayest be clothed, and that the shame of thy nakedness do not appear; and anoint thine eyes with eyesalve, that thou mayest see.
v.19 As many as I love, I rebuke and chasten: be zealous therefore, and repent.
v.20 Behold, I stand at the door, and knock: if any man hear my voice, and open the door, I will come in to him, and will sup with him, and he with me.
v.21 To him that overcometh will I grant to sit with me in my throne, even as I also overcame, and am set down with my Father in his throne.
v.22 He that hath an ear, let him hear what the Spirit saith unto the churches."

Situated forty miles south-east of Philadelphia and almost due east of Ephesus, Laodicea was at an important highway junction. Along the Meander valley lay the route of the west-east highway from Ephesus through Laodicea to the centre of Asia. At Laodicea too the highway from the south turned north-eastwards up the Lycus valley towards Philadelphia. Colosse lay ten miles eastwards along this highway and occupied a higher level on the side of the valley. Hierapolis lay six miles to the north between the river valleys. Laodicea formed the third point of this triangle of cities.

It might have been expected that this strategic position between the valleys would give Laodicea great military significance. That this was not so was due to a geological irregularity that made the city indefensible. Laodicea, despite the streams all around it, had no internal water supply. In the early days of its history water was drawn from the streams nearby but, as the city developed, these soon became inadequate. Water had to be piped in from springs six miles south of the city. Stone piping and large aqueducts required major engineering works. The pipes, though covered or sunk underground for long distances were still a source of weakness. Laodicea could never sustain a siege. As a direct consequence Laodicea could never afford to take sides in the changing political allegiances of the times. Its policies had to be based on compromise and conciliation. It could not afford to be too independent in its actions.

In the swirl of politics after Alexander the Great, the Syrians captured the site, destroyed the buildings and rebuilt it. Antiochus II named it after his beautiful wife Laodice (250 BC). Although Antiochus divorced his wife a few years after the founding of the city he allowed it to retain the name. The very name of the city stirred the memory of a lost love.

Three matters about the city are relevant for the understanding of the message of Christ to the church. These are:

1. The city was famed for its *wealth*. Gold, imported from the interior of Asia, was refined here and stamped for purity. This particular trade encouraged the establishment of banking centres that financed trade growth and became "exchange centres" for the multitude of currencies flowing through the city from the surrounding provinces. The bankers boasted of being able to meet any exigency. When the city was virtually destroyed in 17AD, and again in 61AD, by major earthquakes, the municipal authorities refused imperial aid and financed their own reconstruction.
2. The city was noted for its *wool*. The Lycus valley was ideal for sheep. A particular breed of black sheep giving rich glossy wool was specially suited to the area. In Laodicea cloth and carpet were manufactured from this superior wool. These were treasured articles across the Roman world (Ramsay) and became symbols of wealth and status.
3. The city was famous for its *eyesalve*. A school of medicine flourished in Laodicea dedicated to Asclepius (see comments under Pergamum) and it was particularly successful in the treatment of eye and ear problems. Sufferers travelled from all over the Empire to Laodicea to secure this special eye-salve.

Laodicea was a city sure of its own resources and proud of its wealth. It felt no need of anything beyond the material goods it possessed. It is interesting that in contrast to the other cities in the province, archaeology yields little evidence of any religious conviction in Laodicea. While heathen gods there must have been, and a Jewish synagogue there should have been because of the size of the Jewish community, yet religion was clearly a minor matter in Laodicea. Business was business in this city.

14 In the midst of the materialism of this wealthy city there was a local church gathered to the name of the Lord Jesus Christ. It is a reasonable assumption that the gospel reached here from Colosse, possibly through Epaphras (Col 1:7), in the mid-fifties of the first century. The church is linked with Ephesus and Colosse in the letters of the apostle Paul (Col 4:16). Beyond this we have no NT information and the only item that extant history records is the mention of a church council held here in 367 (F. A. Tatford). Christ addresses this church with the same words He has used to the previous churches. The AV reading "to the angel of the church of the Laodiceans" is based on inferior manuscript evidence and the RV is to be preferred, "to the angel of the church in Laodicea". This makes the introduction the same as to the other churches.

In three distinctive titles Christ refers to His deity, His humanity and His eternity:

1. He is "the Amen" – His deity
   This title of deity is taken from the Hebrew text of Isa 65:16. The AV, following the LXX, reads "God of truth" instead of "God of [the] Amen". The word itself describes what is "fixed", "true", "unchangeable". Understood in this way Christ is the final truth (John 14:6). Used as the last word in a prayer on the lips of men it is supplicatory and means "may it be so". When the statement is from God it indicates the final word and means "it shall be so". Christ is God's final word to men; He has nothing more to say beyond His statement in Christ.
2. He is the faithful and true witness – His humanity
   Deity is implied in the Amen, a title that points to the incarnation that brought Christ into time. This second title points to the life and testimony of Christ while on earth. From the manger to the cross He was both "faithful" and "true" (*alēthinos*). As shown in comments on 2:13 the word "witness" had come to mean a "witness for" and can be translated as "martyr". Christ, absolutely trustworthy and genuine as a witness for God, died for that testimony. This title covers His life on earth and includes the cross.
3. He is "The beginning of the creation of God" – His eternity
   This title is a clear statement of the fact that Christ stands outside of time. Nevertheless it sets forth a truth constantly denied by false teaching. Understanding "beginning" in a passive sense as "one begun", heretical teachers at various times in church history insisted that Christ was the first created being, that He was simply a creature. This heresy became the foundation stone of the Arian heresy of the fourth century but the seeds of the teaching were already in the neighbouring church of Colosse (Col 1:18). Such teaching contradicts a whole body of NT teaching (see also 1:18; 21:6) concerning the person of Christ. The word *archē* must be taken in the active sense, meaning "source" or

"origin". It could be rightly translated "the beginner of creation", the One from whom all created things originate. This is clearly the meaning of Prov 8:22 LXX upon which this title is based (see 22:13). In Col 1:15-17 Christ is the source of all creation, a truth stated by John in his Gospel (John 1:1-3). As such, eternity, not time, is His realm. While the creation of Gen 1-2 is necessarily in view, the new creation must also be embraced in the title. In resurrection Christ is the head of the new creation and all is founded upon Him. Spiritually the new creation is seen in the regeneration of sinners (2 Cor 5:17); physically it will be manifest in the redemption of the bodies of believers (Rom 8:23); and finally, the material cosmos will be changed (21:1; 2 Pet 3:13) and there will be "a new heaven and a new earth" (21:1). Christ is and ever will be the "beginning" (originator) of the creation of God.

15 For the seventh time in these letters Christ uses the word "I know" (*oida*); a word that shows complete comprehension based on omniscience. For the fifth time in the letters He speaks of "thy works" (omitted to Smyrna and Pergamum on good manuscript authority). As He does when speaking to Sardis, Christ mentions their works, but passes immediately to condemnation as if He could find nothing to commend. This must have come as the first shock to the Laodicean church. They seem to have been constantly reviewing their own state (note the present tense of the verb "thou sayest" in v.17), and possibly awaited with some complacency the verdict of Christ on their full programme of meetings and their healthy bank account.

Laodiceans would judge Christ's approval was inevitable since they could not be charged with the liberal toleration of Pergamum, the licentious teaching of Thyatira, the lifeless profession of Sardis or the evident weakness of Philadelphia. In their own judgment they were the ideal assembly. It is worth noting that the name "Laodicea" is a compound of two words *laos* ("people") and the noun *dikē* ("judgment"). A good interpretation would be "the judgment of the people". Having reached such a favourable judgment they doubtless expected Christ to confirm it.

The sobering words of Christ's first statement must therefore have come to the church almost with the impact of a physical shock, "thou art neither cold nor hot". The metaphor and its implications would have been immediately apparent to every believer with a Laodicean background. They knew that in Hierapolis, six miles away, the water from the hot springs had a real medicinal value. They knew too that in Colosse, ten miles away, the pure cold water was most refreshing. They knew their own water in Laodicea was notorious throughout the province. Ducted in through closed conduits and over aqueducts from six miles south it was lukewarm and totally unpalatable, even nauseous, to drink. A normal reaction was to spit it out as repulsive. For Christ to use such a metaphor must have shocked the church.

It should be kept in mind that the metaphor depicts the church state towards Himself as found by Christ. It is easy to understand "cold" as being totally without affection for Christ. This word would most naturally describe individuals from the pagan society around. The Apollo worshippers of Hierapolis would be good examples of this state. By contrast "hot" is readily understood as that condition where love to Christ sets the individual soul on the boil. The word *zestos* is a derivative of the verb "to boil" (*zeō*); it is translated "fervent" in Acts 18:25; Rom 12:11. This is the normal spiritual condition Christ expects in His own. Perhaps examples could be found in the church in Colosse.

Difficulty has been expressed with this interpretation in view of the further word that Christ adds to is condemnation, "I would that thou wert cold or hot". The objection, which at first sight seems reasonable, is that Christ would scarcely be desiring them to be still unbelievers. To raise this objection is to fail to understand at least part of what Christ is saying. Two things are involved. First, their present state is nauseous to Him, as the last statement in the verse will show; but the second point is that in this condition He finds it impossible to do anything with them. In the case of unbelievers He can do something with them; hostile bigots like Saul of Tarsus may be reached and won to Him. He can do something with devoted, fervent-spirited believers. The in-between state of complacent indifference is not only tasteless but hopeless. The "would" (*ophelon*) expressed the longing in the heart of Christ; a longing for the basis on which He could do something with them.

Some have sought to avoid this problem by insisting that the language demands that both conditions of "cold" and "hot" are equally acceptable to Christ. The analogy of food has been used to support this argument. Cold food and hot food are both food, and both are equally-acceptable under different conditions; it is the lukewarm food that is repulsive. This would mean that "cold" and "hot" must describe believers in two equally acceptable states. It must be pointed out that the use of this kind of analogy is very misleading since food is not mentioned in this passage where "cold" and "hot" are metaphorical. It is also very difficult to offer any reasonable explanation of how "cold" believers could be equally acceptable to Christ as "hot" believers. The interpretation suggested above is much to be preferred.

16 Having defined the two states upon which He could work Christ identifies the in-between state of Laodicea that makes them so repulsive to Him. Christ uses a word not used elsewhere in Scripture but which takes vivid meaning from the Laodicean background. The word accurately describes their water-supply. "Lukewarm" is a very accurate description of the tepid drinking water of Laodicea. Unpalatable and sickening as the water was, Christ's reaction in a spiritual way re-echoes what Laodiceans did physically with their water every day: they spat it out. The statement of Christ with the inclusion of the verb "about to" (*mellō*) indicates an action about to be taken. In this there must be a note of grace in addition to the solemn warning. "I am about to spue you out of my mouth" (JND) is the sentence from Christ. The word "spue" is the normal verb "to vomit" (*emeō*) from which the English word "emetic" is derived. See Lev 18:28 for an OT warning in similar terms to Israel in view of their entry to the land of Canaan.

How Laodicea had become lukewarm has been the subject of much discussion. Omitting irrelevant suggestions imported from the prophetic view, such as a revival in Sardis or a cooling down in Philadelphia there is only one possible explanation. Since Christ introduces the two opposed conditions of "cold" and "hot" it is clear that a "mixing" has taken place with the resulting temperature measured as "lukewarm". The spiritual implication is that the Laodicean church has in it many individuals who were not truly born again. If perhaps, over the preceding generation there had been a relaxation or abandonment of truths regarding reception to the church the present state is readily explained. Mere nominal professors without divine life received into the fellowship would provide a "mixing" that would quickly lower the spiritual temperature in the church. In such a mixed company it is easy to see how, instead of scriptural conviction and spiritual communion, there had arisen compromise and concession for the sake of peace. Empty professors without real faith demanded ritual on the one hand and entertainment on the other. A variety of programmes, committees, activities without spiritual power (2 Tim 3:5) took the place of obedience and devotion to Christ. Free from imperial prosecution and untroubled by false teaching, orthodoxy became linked with a worldliness that Christ found revolting. This lukewarm condition of nominal christianity invited the repudiation of Christ Himself.

Within the context of the interpretation given of "cold" and "hot" it is clear that this threat of "spewing out" must be a public action by Christ Himself. It has been observed that the coming of Christ to the church in Ephesus (2:5) and to the church in Pergamum (2:16) were judgments that could be carried out locally and presently. This judgment of Laodicea must be viewed in the same way as the threat of Christ to Sardis (v.3) and the promise to Philadelphia (v.11) as pointing directly to the coming of Christ at the rapture. The use of the verb *mellō*, translated by the Newberry margin as "am about to", confirms this conclusion. The use of the same verb in 1:19; 2:10 shows that the idea is not immediacy but imminency. The coming of Christ overhangs this church. There was nothing, even as Christ spoke to Laodicea, that had necessarily to intervene before His coming. When He did come the church in Laodicea the majority of its members merely nominal believers, would be left on earth. This would be the "spewing out" of which Christ warns. The metaphor demands the repudiation of the company in this public way. There could scarcely be a more public repudiation of a church than this; all the world would see that Christ rejected the testimony of this church.

It is not a valid argument against this interpretation to point out that Christ has not yet come and the local church in Laodicea has long gone from the scene. Christ's coming has always been imminent and is still imminent. The coming of Christ could have taken place in their day and this threat would have been demonstrably fulfilled. That other events have come in does not affect the imminence of the coming. Doubtless when Christ does come the threat He made to Laodicea will be fulfilled to many a Laodicean-type church. The very delay in His coming gives a period of grace to mere professors but Christ's solemn warning still stands.

17a The judgment that the Laodiceans had reached of their own spiritual condition is couched in terms familiar in their city. Laodicean banks were both famous and were viewed with pride by the citizens. Their currency was gold. To have gold in the bank was the object of every businessman in the city. When they had this the believers could say "I am rich". The ostentation of wealth is in the next statement. "Increased with goods" rightly surveys the lifestyle financed by the gold. To translate the perfect tense literally allows the complacency in their own efforts to be heard: "I have become rich". It is possible that the rich glossy cloaks manufactured in the city were the status symbol of the wealth. Now that they were able to purchase these, their very garments displayed their prosperity. To "have need of nothing" stresses the self-sufficiency of Laodicea. The medical faculty of the Asclepius University producing the famous eyesalve doubtless made them feel independent in every area. There was nothing they needed. They would claim that the Lord had indeed blessed them.

These terms of Laodicean self-complacency must not be restricted to the material. It is certainly true that the materialism of the city had invaded the church but their material wealth and their pride in it were but the ground of a deeper malaise. It is clear that their self-complacency extended to the spiritual realm. In this realm they felt no deficiencies whatever and were obviously proud of their spiritual possessions. It is possible that Christ allows the material to symbolise the spiritual. They would seem to be boasting in the riches of their spiritual gift; what spiritual revenue they handled! They possibly boasted of the spiritual graces manifest in them; how fine Christians they were! They possibly boasted in spiritual remedies they possessed; how adept they were in handling the Word and reaching others! Material wealth and spiritual pride go together. It was all a facade and a sham and Christ moved swiftly to deal with it.

17 The ignorance in the church of its true spiritual condition is exposed by Christ. The verb *oida* that Christ uses in v.15 to show His knowledge of their condition is used again to show what they did not know. His exposure is given in five devastating and sobering terms. The first two terms describe their condition generally; the final three add graphic detail. The emphatic "thou" must have made the believers cringe under Christ's accusing finger. The word "wretched" is used by Paul of himself (Rom 7:24). It describes an emergency situation, a person who needs urgent help; in secular writing it is used to describe patients in a hospital ward. The word "miserable" is better rendered "pitiable" (Newberry margin). The only other time it is used in the NT is in 1 Cor 15:19 where it describes those whose hopes have been completely smashed. If Christ has not been raised from the dead, Paul argues, then believers are left hopeless and they should be looked upon with pity. It is a fitting word to describe those abandoned to a "workhouse" or a "debtor's prison" in eighteenth century England. Such persons had no real future. In spiritual terms, in spite of their self-satisfied complacency the Laodiceans needed help urgently. These are two graphic pictures of the Laodicean state: they were both "dying" and "destitute".

The three objective terms that follow are Christ's answer to the false assessments in the minds of the Laodiceans. In real terms they were "poor". The word that Christ uses, *ptōchos*, defines real destitution, a totally-penniless condition when begging is the only answer to the need. It must have been a shock to Laodiceans, with all their wealth in the bank, to think of themselves as beggars. Their sense of values was clearly wrong! Smyrna stands in obvious contrast where material poverty was seen against the background of spiritual wealth (2:9). Here professed saints were rich in the wrong way. The second term "blind" is the normal term for physical blindness but it is frequently used in the NT figuratively for spiritual blindness (Matt 23:17; Rom 2:19; 2 Pet 1:9). In a city famous for its eyesalve Christ's words had an added sting. Perfect vision for earth does not guarantee spiritual vision! The third term is equally devastating to Laodicean pride. Christ speaks of them as "naked". In a city famed for the rich glossy cloaks made there, this must have been the final blow to Laodicean complacency. Garments in NT imagery speak of works that manifest character (see 3:4; 19:8); the outward and the visible reflect the inward and the hidden. For the believer this kind of "garment" is produced by the life of Christ within (Gal 2:19-20). Nakedness here means there was no real evidence of life in Christ. Virtues flowing from divine life were absent; no spiritual garments were being woven in Laodicea (19:8). In summary Christ shows in these picture-words their basic values were wrong, their spiritual vision was missing and the vital virtues of Christ were absent from their lives.

18 In terms with which the wealthy merchants of Laodicea would be familiar, Christ speaks as a market counsellor acting for heaven. His counsel would not make them wealthy in Laodicea but it would enable them to lay up treasure in heaven. Caiphas was national counsellor for Israel, for earth and for time (John 18:14) but Christ counsels His own for heaven and for eternity. The Laodiceans sorely needed this counsel.

Christ points out in explicit terms that there were three things the Laodiceans needed. Of each of these commodities Christ is the sole supplier; from Him alone they may be bought. The aorist of the verb "to buy" (*agorazō*) summarises a lifetime of trading with Christ. This is not just one transaction. The object of the trading is to obtain gold. The qualifying participle "tried in the fire" stresses the purity and hence the value of this gold. Laodicean merchants were proud of their ability to judge all kinds of gold; they were renowned for their ability to detect false gold at a glance. They, and all the bankers, knew that gold that had been through the fire was absolutely pure, did not corrode and was highly priced; such gold carried a special stamp put upon it. In metaphoric terms Christ was offering the very currency of heaven. Gold in scripture speaks of the glory of God. But the glory of God is the doing of the will of God (see John 17:4). This is where men had failed and come short of His glory (Rom 3:23). Now men on earth, through faith in Christ, can do the will of God and as a consequence reflect that glory (see 1 Pet 1:7; James 1:3). For the worldly-wise materialistic Laodiceans to do the will of God would cost them much in the currency of Laodicea. Time and talent, formerly given to the world, would now have to be used to do the will of God in their lives through obedience to Christ. This is the metaphor in the imperative of Christ "buy from me". This transaction would bring them real wealth which Christ holds out to them in the expression "that thou mayest be rich" which is literally "that you may become rich" (Alford). In the context this must point onwards to the judgment seat when the true wealth will be revealed (1 Cor 3:12-13).

Christ would also have His people purchase "white garments". The contrast between the white garments offered by Christ and those made of the glossy black wool manufactured in the city could hardly have been missed by the first readers. In the clear symbolism of this book the white garments speak of the righteous acts of believers arising out of their faith in Christ. The garments speak therefore of the witness for God borne as saints doing the will of God. Faith would issue in the virtues of christian living that would reflect Christ. "That thou mayest be clothed" points forward to the outcome of the judgment seat of Christ and the robing of the bride described. "And to her was granted that she should be arrayed in fine linen, clean and white, for the fine linen is the righteousness of saints" (19:8). To use the language of this passage, the robes of heaven are "bought" from Christ while on earth. What has been "bought" in a lifetime of service will be suitable attire for the saints in glory. That "the shame of thy nakedness do not appear" is the consequence of having these white garments. The verb "appear" or its alternative translation "make manifest" is a familiar verb in connection with the judgment seat. It is used positively with respect to believers (1 Cor 3:13; 4:5; 2 Cor 5:10). Here it is used negatively and would be better translated, "may not be manifested". Any believer, even a Laodicean believer with materialistic values, must shrink from the very possibility of nakedness at the judgment seat. The figurative language has nothing to do with salvation but refers to service done on earth for Christ.

In spiritual terms bankrupt saints may buy gold; naked saints may buy white robes and blind saints may buy eyesalve. All are available from Christ. The famous local eyesalve could not deal with spiritual myopia. Far-sighted physically, or even metaphorically in business dealings, Laodicean saints were spiritually blind. They would require something more than the local "eye-salve", the Phyrgian powder used in the Asclepian Medical School for eye troubles, but Christ uses this to illustrate what the saints would need to see spiritually. The anointing required (and the word "anoint" is the normal technical word for the anointing of eyes) would give believers a new corrected vision. Anointing in scripture is always a ministry of the Holy Spirit (1 John 2:20, 27). The yielded believer finds his view of things changed by the Holy Spirit. The aorist tense of the previous verbs ("mayest be rich", "do not appear") is changed to the present tense in the verb "mayest see" indicating that it is not the judgment seat but present experience that is in view. New spiritual vision would be the result for saints now; it would be too late at the judgment seat.

19 Abruptly and without introduction Christ introduces two startling statements. First He gives a word of explanation. The absence of any conjunction indicates urgency. Even in Laodicea there were those in whom Christ is finding pleasure. That is indicated by the use of the verb "love" (*phileō*) which indicates personal affection and the pleasure taken in a loved one. Now Christ explains that this love is not something to be seen in preferential treatment or special preservation from the ills and cares of life. This is how the human heart interprets love. The love of Christ is displayed in a very different way. Even in the midst of the materialistic atmosphere of Laodicea Christ dare not allow His loved ones to behave as they like. Divine love demands that He rebuke and chasten them when they require it. "Rebuke" is verbal remonstrance, as Christ speaking through His word seeks to bring the believer to face his sin. When this is ineffective chastening follows. The word *paideuō* is used in Heb 12:3-15 of the educational and disciplinary process in any family where the father has the interests of the children at heart. Family love demands discipline. Christ would have true believers in Laodicea know that the trials they were going through were neither fortuitous nor accidental; they were being dealt with by Him for their own blessing.

Christ adds to this explanation a word of exhortation. The singular verbs show that the word is addressed to the assembly as a unit. Christ deals with individuals but expects the effects to spread to the assembly. This is the force of the "therefore". Two verbs show the urgent action to be taken. "Be zealous" (*zēleuō*) related to the adjective "hot" (*zestos*) in v.15. It shows that Christ found nothing commendable in either the cold or lukewarm state; He desired them "hot". The obstacle to this is nothing other than sin and demands repentance. "Repent" demands a decisive repudiation of sin that has brought about the lukewarm condition.

20 Rebuke and chastening show Christ's love for His own. This is further developed by this picture drawn by Christ Himself. For the final time in these letters the word "behold" points to a startling truth. Christ has taken His stand outside a door and, knocking and speaking, awaits entrance. There have been many suggestions as to the interpretation of this metaphorical door. Quite a few commentators see it as the eschatological door through which Christ will come at His return. J. A. Seiss and R.L. Thomas insist that this is in keeping with the imagery used by first century believers as they looked forward to Christ's coming. Scriptures cited in support are Matt 24:33; Mark 13:29; Luke 12:36; James 5:9. The insuperable objection to this view is that it makes the timing of Christ's coming dependent upon the response of an assembly. Also the verb used is not "come" (*erchomai*) as in the other letters but "come in" (*eiserchomai*) which is never used of Christ's coming. Scripture teaches that the timing of the Christ's coming is firmly in the will of the Father (Matt 24:36). Other commentators insist that this must be the door of the Laodicean assembly. In support they would argue that Christ's place in the assembly is "in the midst" (Matt 18:20), but in the Laodicean condition Christ is seen outside and seeking admission from an exercised believer. There are two major problems with this view. The first is one of logic. The very existence of a local church presupposes Christ in the midst; with Christ outside the question arises could Christ address it as a church? Christ has already addressed it as such. The other problem is a scriptural one, there is no scriptural support for Christ outside an assembly. There is no suggestion of Christ displaced even in churches where there was moral failure (Corinth) or doctrinal failure (churches of Galatia). This view cannot be scripturally sustained.

The simple view that fits the context admirably is that Christ is dealing with an individual believer. The door is the door of the believer's heart. It should be understood that this is not the door of the intelligence; the individual knows who is standing and knocking and speaking. It should also be recognised that the heart does not represent the emotions as in contemporary culture. The heart in scripture is the citadel of the personality where decisions are made, in fact it may be referred to as the door of the will. (Rom 10:10 puts it clearly, "For with the heart man believeth unto righteousness".) Whether the individual here is a believer or an unbeliever is not indicated. While arguments can be presented on either side it does not make a vital difference, the truth is the same in either case. Christ has been excluded from the throne-room of this human personality and now He seeks entry. Graciously He has taken His stand outside the door and, speaking ("my voice") and knocking awaits the response of the individual. The speaking and knocking within the context could be seen as the rebuking and chastening of the previous verse if a believer is in view. The objection that a believer already possesses Christ as Saviour is answered by the fact that not always is Christ given His place of authority in the life. This is what Christ is here demanding. In the previous verse this was called repentance. It should also be clear that in a company like Laodicea, where there is the probability of many mere professors, the way is open for true conversion as the interpretation of the picture.

Two verbs show the positive action for which Christ waits. "Hear" is what Christ expects and "open the door" will be the response to the hearing. The arresting of attention, the identification by the voice followed by the opening of the door are normal parts of the metaphor (seen literally in Acts 12:13-14). To "open the door" describes figuratively the individual response of faith. The same figure is used poetically in the Song of Songs 5:2 where the bride hesitates to open the door to the bridegroom and missed the fellowship that could have been enjoyed. The promise "I will come in to him" is a prelude to the fellowship "I will sup with him". The evening meal, the main meal of the day, is in view in the verb "sup". At that meal mutual fellowship is enjoyed and Christ seems to move from the role of guest to that of host: "I will sup with him and he with me". This promise must be kept in context and seen as the fellowship enjoyed as the result of repentance. The supper has nothing whatever to do with the Lord's supper (1 Cor 11:20) or with the kingdom supper (19:9). To link it with either is to miss the whole point of the passage, the personal appeal and the personal promise of Christ to the individual saint.

21 The overcomer in Laodicea merits very special recognition from Christ. On the great occasions of state eastern kings did not occupy a single-seat throne but a broad-based dais. Honoured guests would be invited to sit alongside the monarch and share his glory. Christ shows His appreciation of the faithful believer by inviting him to share the throne with Him. This is called "the throne of his glory" (Matt 25:31) to which He is heir prophetically (Acts 2:30; Ezek43:7); and is the throne of Christ in the millennial kingdom. The promise to the overcomer in Thyatira emphasises the rule that saints will share; here the emphasis is upon the royalty that Christ will share with them. Christ the mighty Overcomer now shares the Father's throne, in the day of millennial glory He will share His throne with His saints.

22 For the seventh and final time in these letters the Christ issues His call for the responsive ear. Particularly addressed to the Laodiceans it is still relevant to the other assemblies and throughout all ages. To every believer it becomes a personal responsibility to catch His voice and respond to it. The imperative "let him hear" shows this is not an option but an obligation for each believer.

Appendix – Prophetic Foreshadowings in the Seven Churches

Many expositors believe that there are foreshadowed in the seven selected churches stages of history that would mark the testimony of local assemblies as the age progressed. The evidence for looking for such prophetic foreshadowing lies in three considerations:

a. The description of the book as "this prophecy" (1:3). While admitting that prophecy need not always involve prediction it is suggested that, in the context, to omit the idea of prediction in this book would be ludicrous. The question then arises whether chs. 2 and 3 are to be omitted from the prophetic aspect of the book. Some commentators (of whom R.L. Thomas is a representative) deny this aspect of teaching in these churches and insist that the prophetic section of Revelation commences only at ch. 4. This, however, is hardly a valid viewpoint since it has been pointed out already that the book is a unit (1:10). There is thus sufficient evidence to warrant looking for some note of prophecy in the messages.
b. The use of the word "mystery" (1:20) cannot be limited to the use of symbols in the vision, for they are explained. There seems little mystery about letters to seven churches even if they do come directly from Christ Himself. Is not Christ indicating that behind and beyond the direct messages to literal churches, there is a significance which will become apparent in the Spirit's own time as the church progresses?
c. The third argument for looking for a prophetic panorama in these churches depends upon an analogy with other aspects of truth. It is recognised that an analogy in itself does not carry much weight, but when it supports other arguments there can be substance to it. In Lev 23 there is a prophetic unfolding of the spiritual history of the nation of Israel in the annual feasts; it was hidden then but obvious now in the light of history. In Matt 13 there is a prophetic unfolding in parabolic form of the spiritual history of the kingdom of God; hidden then, but becoming clear in the light of history. Thus, there does not seem to be any logical reason why, in these messages, Christ may not be giving a spiritual outline of the history of that which is so dear to His heart – the local assembly gathered to His name. It should really be no surprise that in this prophetic book there should be found foreshadowings of church history.

It must be clearly stated that these messages are not direct prophecy. Direct prophecy for the church age would not be in keeping with the truth of the imminence of Christ's coming. If the imminence of Christ's coming and divine foreknowledge are to be kept in perfect balance then any prophetic outline must be set forth in such a way that two criteria are fulfilled:

a. The truth must be revealed in such a way that at no time could believers on earth during the church age say that Christ cannot come yet since certain things have to happen in church testimony.

b. At the same time, lest believers should be taken unawares by departure, it is necessary to impart certain information that, on looking back, they can grasp with Spirit-given insight the fact that Christ knew exactly what would develop. This kind of prophecy is illustrated in the betrayal of Christ by Judas. Christ Himself made this very plain when He said, "Now I tell you before it come, that when it is come to pass, ye may believe that I am he" (John 13:18-20). This was essential lest the betrayal of Judas should shake the faith of the disciples. In the way that Christ dealt with the matter He neither overruled the free-will of Judas, nor gave approval to his action. What He did do was steady the faith of the disciples after the betrayal. It was a comfort to them to know that Christ had foreseen the action of Judas. There is exactly that kind of value in these messages to the seven churches.

Most beautifully and completely do these messages answer the prophetic criteria. The truths are presented in such a way that they neither cast the slightest doubt on the imminence of Christ's coming, nor suggest any long delay. Yet, at the same time they warn of the danger and departure in the history of local assemblies. Those very matters that were to cause saints the greatest grief are shown in their origin and nature. The remedy in each case, outlined by Christ Himself, has also stood as an encouragement to responsive believers throughout the ages of assembly testimony who have had an "ear to hear".

Some commentators, objecting to this line of interpretation, point out that none of the commentators of the early centuries whose writings have come down to us make any reference to such a line of thought. Victorinus (died c.303) generally reckoned to be the earliest writer on this book, is often quoted in this connection. A little consideration, however, will show that this is exactly what should be expected. The prophetic truths foreshadowed in these messages could come to light only as the centuries passed. It is only looking back over the history of church testimony that we can see that the trends and troubles were foreseen by Christ from the beginning. From this point of view believers in this age have a distinct advantage over earlier saints. While this brings an added measure of responsibility, it also brings an added confidence in Christ. The difficulties and departures of the church age did not take Him by surprise. Alva J. McClain in his book *The Greatness of the Kingdom* sums up the matter concisely, "For the true explanation may be that in the seven churches of the Apocalypse the Holy Spirit did give a *latent* revelation of the Church's career on earth, but so obscure that it could not be clearly discerned until the last or Laodicean era had been reached. If so, it would be significant that only in modern times have many devout Bible students come to agree that there was such a revelation and that we are now living in the final era of the church on earth. Such a method of revelation is not novel in scripture: for the Second Advent of the Lord could not be certainly identified in OT prophecy until the first advent had been realised in history".

Viewed in this way the seven churches present a chronological development of assembly testimony spanning the age of local testimony for Christ between Pentecost and the rapture. Beginning with the immediate post-apostolic period, reflected in the fading devotion of Ephesus, the different stages of the church history are presented in general terms in the messages to the seven churches, closing with the hidden poverty of Laodicea. As the letters are studied it will become clear that:

a. Christ touches upon the origin of serious disorders that, if not arrested by repentance, will develop to greater evils. This proviso of repentance is important as Christ leaves the way open for assembly recovery at each stage. The only two churches where repentance is not demanded (Smyrna and Philadelphia) are those where there is displayed an evident faithfulness to Christ.
b. As each prophetic period is examined within the time marks suggested, it is not demanded that every local assembly conform to the features of the period. The trends that Christ highlights can be only general features of perhaps a majority of assemblies. The fact that, historically, the gospel moved westwards first does give western lands a start in spiritual declension, so that it is evident that they have reached a Laodicean stage ahead of assemblies in lands where the gospel has more recently been preached.
c. Saints are not expected to become church historians to grasp the prophetic message. The attempt to explain every reference in each message in terms of prophetic content has led to the strangest interpretations and brought this very principle of prophetic interpretation into disrepute. Christ was giving indications and trends, coupled with warnings, to alert the spiritual mind during the church age. When this is grasped the general teaching is clear and the progression through the ages is too obvious to be missed.

This last point is vitally important. Those who ignore this prophetic foreshadowing are closing the mind to a series of historical correspondences that cannot be merely coincidental. Such correspondences are far too numerous and far too clear to be dismissed in this way. There can be little doubt that in addition to the other purposes already mentioned Christ was desirous of giving in broad outline the spiritual trends in local testimony throughout the age. One argument often used by opponents of this line of thought is that there is frequently a wide divergence of opinion in the prophetic references intended. They demand that such references should be unequivocal and explicit, capable of only one interpretation. They fail to see that this is going beyond what Christ intended; He was not prophesying concerning events, He was foreshadowing trends. While admitting that sometimes prophetic interpretations can be pressed too far and owe much to the imagination of the commentator, we submit that to deny its existence here is to exclude a line of thought that Christ meant to become clearer as the age moves to its climax: His coming for the church.

While there is no absolute unanimity amongst commentators on the details, the following are generally acceptable as presenting the main lines of prophetic foreshadowing in the seven churches:

PERIOD REPRESENTED	DATES SUGGESTED	CHURCH CHARACTER FORESHADOWED
1. EPHESIAN	70-170	THE POST APOSTOLIC CHURCH

By 70 all the apostles except John had sealed their testimony in blood.
169 is a generally accepted date (Unger) for the martyrdom of Polycarp in Smyrna.
Early devotion to Christ begins to fade.

2. SMYRNAN	170-312	THE PERSECUTED CHURCH

These dates embrace the great general persecutions of the Roman Emperors. See note in exposition for the dates of the ten major pagan persecutions during this period.
312 is the date of the professed conversion of Constantine.

3. PERGAMENE	312-606	THE PATRONISED CHURCH

312 and the conversion of Constantine marked the beginning of the period when to become a Christian was the popular thing and became the path to promotion and power within the Empire. 606 is the year when Boniface, Bishop of Rome was acknowledged "Universal Bishop" in fact the first pope.

4. THYATIRAN	606-RAPTURE	THE PAGAN CHURCH

The development of Roman Catholicism proceeded apace during the Dark Ages until it had become the institutionalised system which it is today. While shaken by the Reformation it has continued virtually unchanged and will continue until the rapture. The removal of believers at the rapture will leave Roman Catholic congregations virtually untouched so that the harlot features of "Mystery, Babylon the Great" will be developed (ch. 17). This broad outline cannot deal with the multitude of believers who maintained a local testimony in their area and were persecuted for their faithfulness to Christ during the Dark Ages right through the Middle Ages.

5. SARDIAN	1517-RAPTURE	THE PROFESSING CHURCH

On 31st October 1517 Martin Luther nailed his famous 95 theses to the Church door in Wittenberg, Germany. This is generally accepted as a convenient date to mark the beginning of the Reformation. Denominationalism developing from the reformation period will continue until the rapture of the church. Again the broad outline does not take account of non-conformity which led to the establishment of many testimonies apart from the great denominations when saints sought to be faithful to Christ.

6. PHILADELPHIAN 1750-RAPTURE THE FEEBLE CHURCH
The evangelical preaching of John Wesley (1703-1791) and George Whitefield (1714-1770) was followed by the recovery of missionary zeal under William Carey (1761-1834) "the father of modern missions", and a world-wide exercise about ecclesiastical truth that led to recovery of scriptural principles of gathering under J. N. Darby (1800-1882) and many others; all marked an evangelistic revival. In many parts of the world the fruit of this recovery will be felt until the rapture.

7. LAODICEAN 1900-RAPTURE THE LUKEWARM CHURCH
Many assemblies today would admit a lukewarm condition. The very existence of this in some assemblies is a witness that the rapture of the church cannot be very distant. The widespread embrace of charismatic teaching has also led to a spiritual complacency that hides a poverty in many congregations which, in spiritual terms, is very similar to what existed in Laodicea. Churches of this kind often have large numbers, great profession and great activity but with little fidelity to either scripture or Christ. Some even boast that they "have need of nothing".

The four conditions represented by the last four churches are, in fact the main components of that which is called "Christendom" today – if the word is taken in its usual meaning to describe all that professes to belong to Christ.

As noted earlier it would be impossible and inappropriate to draw rigid date lines across history. The above dates are suggested as marking suitable points when the trends in the various periods become obvious as we look back. At the present moment across earth there are doubtless assemblies exhibiting the various conditions; some in the Ephesian condition, some in the Smyrnan condition and so on. Few would dispute that, in the highly favoured western lands where the gospel has been known for many centuries, there are many assemblies in the Laodicean condition. This reminds each believer that the Lord's messages to the Philadelphian assembly is relevant, "Behold I come quickly".

The Ephesian Period of Church History 70-170AD

In the Acts of the Apostles, from the pen of Luke the historian, there is the divinely-given record of the first thirty years of local testimony on earth (from 32-c.63).

Assemblies were established across the Roman Empire from Jerusalem to Rome. From these centres the gospel sounded out and further autonomous assembles were established throughout the provinces of the Empire. Several scriptures suggest that even before the canon of scripture was completed and before the last apostle died the gospel had spread across the world (Rom 10:18; 16:26; Col 1:6, 23).

Ephesus was one of the assemblies established in those early years and Christ's commendation of their activities and His approval of their faithfulness is very evident. The evangelisation of the Roman Province of Asia had resulted from their exercise in the gospel. There can be no doubt that their early love to Christ was the source of their spiritual energy. But the fact that they had left their "first love" would be to open the way to spiritual disaster. It is at this point that the prophetic lesson begins to come into focus.

There are four particular ways in which Christ's message to Ephesus conveys foreshadowings of the Ephesian Period of church history (70-170). These are:

1 Gospel Preaching

That which began in the Acts continued throughout the first century and paganism was in retreat. Despite pagan-inspired lies as to the practices of the believers the gospel swept through the Empire and, if traditions have some measure of truth, even far beyond. It would seem that the gospel reached to India and to China. Christ's words were a divine summary of the activity of these years – "For my name's sake hast laboured".

2 Fading Passion

It is clear, even from the pastoral epistles of Paul, that the devotion of earlier days was waning and love to the person of Christ had begun to fade. Second and third generation believers were holding to the form of teaching without the accompanying fervour characteristic of an earlier day. When the earliest "apologies" written in defence of Christianity are read there is a distinct impression that faithfulness to certain forms and traditions had begun to replace the warmth of real devotion to Christ. Formality seems to replace faith, a certain kind of legalism replaces love. Thus, while the outward testimony was maintained something vital had gone. Christ's charge against Ephesus was true on a much wider scale, "thou hast left thy first love".

3 Apostolic Deception

Even in days when the original apostles were still alive there were those who would have claimed apostleship. Paul speaks of such as "false apostles, deceitful workers" (2 Cor 11:13). John recognised the danger of "false prophets" (1 John 4:1) while Peter warned of "false teachers" (2 Pet 2:1). Historically it is evident that this was the time when, as one by one the true apostles laid down their lives for Christ, other men arose claiming apostolic authority and even apostolic succession. Ephesus was commended by Christ for the way they treated such impostors. He clearly expected succeeding generations to follow that pattern: "Thou hast tried them that say they are apostles and are not".

4 Hierarchical Pretension

Even in apostolic days there were those who after the pattern of Diotrephes (3 John 9-10) claimed lordship over the people of God. It is of this class that Peter warned in 1 Pet 5:3 when he wrote of some "as being lords over God's heritage". It is from this class that clericalism would develop; the English word "cleric" is derived from the word for "heritage" (*klēros*). A class of men would make their own that which belonged to God. This is the same class identified by Christ in this letter as the Nicolaitans (see comments at v.6). Thus Christ in this first church is indicating that the fading love would open the way for the emergence of a clerical system that He abhorred. Men would arise to claim priestly function not merely in, but over, the assembly. On this a system would be built until men would claim the episcopal mitre and the bishop's throne. They would interpose a priestly hierarchy between Christ and His people. The evidence of this development lies in the history of the post-apostolic fathers in this "Ephesian" century between 70-170AD.

The Smyrna Period of Church History (170-312)

The early days of church testimony were marked by persecution. In Jerusalem there was the Sadducean persecution (Acts 3-5), followed by the Pharisaic persecution (Acts 8-9), followed in its turn by the Herodian persecution (Acts 12). Men died for their faith. The fact that the gospel delivered men from idolatry throughout the Roman Empire soon caused the believers to be regarded as atheists since they rejected the whole pantheon of pagan gods. This led to suspicion and the wildest accusations. Local commercial interests too, as happened at Ephesus (Acts 19: 23-41) where trouble was stirred up by the guild of silversmiths, often led to local disturbances centred on the Christians. Judaism, becoming apostate as it rejected Christ when the gospel was locally preached, became the bitter opponent of Christ, and increasingly, the very tool of Satan. In many places the local synagogue became the centre of opposition to Christ and took every opportunity to stir up hatred against Christians. Repudiated and denounced by Judaism it was no longer possible to regard christianity as a branch of Judaism and thus a "permitted religion" in the Empire. Thus Christians found themselves the object of magisterial suspicion throughout the Empire.

The first direct persecution of believers from the Roman Empire may well be the edict of Claudius in 49AD by which all Christians, along with the Jews, were expelled from Rome. The biographer of the Caesars, Suetonius, says that Claudius "expelled the Jews from Rome because they were indulging in constant riots at the instigation of Chrestus". The name *Chrestus* is generally regarded by historians as a variant spelling of *Christos* in Greek. It is likely that the preaching of Christ had stirred up bitter animosity amongst the Jews in Rome and that spilled over into civil disorder. Aquila and Priscilla suffered under this edict and moved from

Rome to Corinth. The second direct persecution was in 64AD when debauched Nero, knowing that various plots were afoot to overthrow him and seeking to divert criticism of his depravity, seized on popular superstition to malign the character of Christians and, finally, to blame them for the fire of Rome. This gave the excuse for the martyrdom of many thousands of believers. This period lasted for several years and it was during this period that Paul was put to death.

There are three special features that mark out this Smyrnan Period of Persecution:

1. While many believers and the apostles themselves had suffered under the Roman Empire up to 70AD this Smyrnan period of suffering is characterised by the fact that the persecution became the imperial policy of the Empire. The actions of Claudius and Nero stemmed mainly from their own situations and were responses to a local condition. Now, however, as Christianity made serious inroads into the religious life of the Empire action was taken to prescribe such an "atheistic" religion and persecute the believers who, by definition, were treated as seditious.

   It became policy to deny the believers in Christ any civil rights, any property rights and even the right to life itself. Christians as a matter of imperial policy were to be dispossessed, tortured, banished, burned or thrown to the wild beasts in the circus as entertainment for the people. Reasons behind these waves of persecution varied. Some of the Caesars, as Nero had done, used them as a kind of safety valve to divert attention from the maladministration of government, the corruption of officials and the everyday hardness of life in the Roman Empire. By stirring up the hordes of slaves to attack the Christians Caesar diverted attention from his own failures and the failures of government. Lies and calumny were the agents of the enemy. Rumours were circulated charging that the "breaking of bread" practised by believers was an excuse for human sacrifice and blood drinking. The refusal of Christians to be associated with the idol temples, sacred sacrifices and all the penetration of paganism into everyday life caused them to be branded as atheists. Since no Christian who gave Christ His place as Lord could burn the pinch of incense to Caesar, this was used as the basis of a charge of sedition which carried the death penalty.

2. As a matter of historical fact the persecution during these centuries was often stirred up by apostate Judaism. Refusing to allow those associated with the hated Nazarene to be sheltered by the "permitted religion" (*religio licita*) law that embraced Judaism, they denounced Christians to the magistrates. The reaction of the local magistrate was critical (see the attitude of Gallio in Acts 18:12-17); if he did not judge that the matter was seditious he had the right to act on his own authority and dismiss the case. If he did so he had to be ready to answer any charge against him that might be conveyed to Caesar or to the Roman Senate from the Jewish community. He could demand that the accused take the loyalty test (the offering of

the pinch of incense to Caesar) and put to death, on the ground of treason, those who refused to worship Caesar. The only other alternative was for the magistrate to refer the matter to Caesar. The increasing number of these appeals to Rome led, under various emperors, to edicts of persecution. Hence in this letter the reference to the "synagogue of Satan" refers to the Jews stirring up trouble and calling upon the civil power (the Roman Empire) to destroy those who would not conform to the state religion. Laws to encourage the denunciation of Christians by their fellow citizens allowed the informers to claim the property of believers. No one would take the risk of employing such suspect persons. Thus Christ makes special reference in this letter to the poverty of the suffering saints. Poverty, prison and death were all that those who trusted Christ could expect at this period.

3. For the better part of two centuries sporadic and then general persecution was endured by Christians. There were, no doubt, political, commercial and religious reasons that for the Roman Empire seemed sufficient cause to introduce pogroms against Christians. Christ in this letter shows that behind all this persecution there lay the infernal adversary (Satan), the inveterate accuser (the devil) of the people of God. Satan stirred up the storm that he judged would sweep testimony for Christ from the earth. Never again on such a world-wide scale would such an attempt be made to wipe out Christians. As so often in his opposition to God, Satan had miscalculated and, as Tertullian (c.200) was to write, "the blood of the martyrs became the seed of the church". The patience of believers under the most cruel torture and their faithfulness unto death led to the spread of the gospel. Paganism was powerless to inspire such devotion.

Yet behind this fury of Satan against Christians there can be discerned quite clearly another reason. Divine permission is evident. The fading devotion of Ephesus would be fanned into a flame of passion in the storm-winds of persecution. Like the metallurgist putting the ore into the flame of the furnace, Christ would use these conditions to test faithfulness and to purify the testimony. The witness of the martyrs in the second and third centuries makes tragic reading and yet, at the same time, the record of their faith and faithfulness strikes a tremendously triumphant note. Despite many failures and, strange as it may seem, even at times a tendency to be in love with martyrdom itself, there was displayed a burning love for Christ, a love that was prepared to go even "unto death". A litany of names has come down through history that carries a fragrance of Christ; a noble army of noble men and noble women from all strata of society marched toward the stake and the cross and the wild beasts. Names that stand out are Ignatius (burned at Rome 117), Justin (beheaded at Rome c.156), Polycarp (burned at Smyrna c.169), Blandina (the slave girl in France), Perpetua and her companions in N. Africa. They are in the vanguard of a mighty army that some historians estimate to have been in the region of five million martyrs. In the reign of Diocletian this persecution was to reach a terrible climax. The ageing Emperor introduced a new imperial system of government that brought his son-in-law Galerius on to the world stage. The mother of Galerius was a bitter pagan who hated Christians and used all her new-found power and authority, at the instigation of the pagan priests, to destroy Christians. Edict after edict was issued at the insistence of Galerius and his mother to root out every Christian and burn the scriptures. One historian has written: "Historically, it was the final and fearful struggle between paganism and christianity; the contest was now at its height and drawing to a crisis. Public proclamation was made through the streets of the cities, that men, women, and children, were all to repair to the temples of the gods. All must undergo the fiery ordeal-sacrifice or die. Every individual was summoned by name from lists previously made out. At the city gates all were subjected to rigid examination, and such as were found to be Christians were immediately secured". (*The First Five Hundred Years*, A. Miller). Miller continues "in almost every part of the Roman world such scenes of pitiless barbarity continued with more or less severity for the long period of ten years". Another historian has written, "During the second and third centuries this persecution age saw hundreds of Christians brought into the amphitheatres of Rome to be fed to hungry lions while thousands of spectators cheered. Many were crucified; others were covered with animal skins and tortured to death by wild dogs. They were covered with tar and set on fire to serve as torches. They were boiled in oil and burned at the stake, as was Polycarp in the city of Smyrna itself in 169AD. One church historian has estimated that during this period, five million Christians were martyred for the testimony of Jesus Christ" (T.F. La Haye). There is no doubt that the emergence of Constantine and his professed conversion to Christ (or Christianity) in 312 marked one of the most dramatic, and for the suffering saints in his day, one of the most welcome, changes in church history.

The mention of "ten days" in v.10 in this letter in its original setting and interpretation, must refer to a local persecution of this duration in Smyrna. Some commentators will argue that it refers, in this prophetic context, to this last persecution under Diocletian which spanned ten years. This may be so but, it should be pointed out, that such an interference can, of course, only be drawn in the light of history. There is nothing in the text to suggest that a day is to be equated with a year. Other commentators have pointed out that the reference to ten may refer to the ten specific periods, when, they insist, persecution was general throughout the Empire. While there is some variation amongst historians as to the Emperors selected those generally listed as persecuting emperors are (with the date of their reigns):

Nero	54-68 AD
Domitian	81-96 AD
Trajan	98-117 AD
Marcus Aurelius	161-180 AD

Severus	193-211 AD
Maximinius	235-238 AD
Decius	249-251 AD
Valerian	253-260 AD
Aurelian	270-275 AD
Diocletian	284-305 AD

Whether this is accepted or not there is no doubt that the period from the death of Polycarp (169) to the conversion of Constantine (312) saw a period when bitter Empire-wide persecutions raged against believers. Those faithful to Christ were passing through the furnace.

The Pergamum Period of Church History (312-606)

Meaning of Pergamum – From its etymology the word "Pergamum" can be understood in two different ways. J. Ritchie gives "height"; Newberry as his first meaning "elevation", and as his second "actual marriage", derived from *gamos* ("marriage") and the suffix *per* which generally means something "carried to the fullest extent". This becomes of significance when it is recognised that the prophetic period covered will see unfolding an unholy alliance between the church, and the world. The elevation of christianity to the state religion was indeed an "elevation" and it led to a "marriage" – but a marriage with the world.

Satan learned from his attack on the testimony for Christ over two centuries that persecution seemed only to cause the churches to flourish and multiply. In fact it seemed to keep them in a perpetual state of revival. After putting believers through a fiery trial (1 Pet 4:12) under the persecuting emperors, Satan now changed tactics. Instead of the roaring of the lion the saints were now to meet the subtlety of the serpent.

After the death of Galerius, the son-in-law of Domitian who had been the spearhead of attacks on the Christians, Maxentius and Constantine contended for the throne of the Empire. There is no doubt that the "conversion" of Constantine when on his way to do battle with Maxentius, however it is regarded, marked a major turning-point in history. Whether policy or superstition played a part in this conversion is almost impossible to say at this late stage. The account of his vision of the cross with the sign inscribed "By this conquer" (*in hoc signo vinces*), and the account of the night vision of Christ that followed, savour much of fable and elaboration by his historian Eusebius. The historical fact is that at the Battle of Milvium Bridge that followed the vision, Constantine defeated Maxentius, went on to defeat Licinius and established himself as a sole master of the Roman Empire.

Secular historians, anxious to play down any divine intervention and explain the actions of Constantine in terms of politics, point to many factors that must have weighed with such a skilful strategist viewing his options as he neared the fateful encounter with Maxentius. As sole ruler of the Roman Empire his background of christian influence must have played some part in his policy decisions. Factors that might have weighed with him may be noted:

1 Paganism in its multitudinous variations was largely a spent force in the minds of thoughtful men. Reasonable people, who would not have regarded themselves as philosophers, were disillusioned with the multiplicity of gods. The slave masses had been satiated with the bloodbath of circus and arena. Misgovernment and debauchery had robbed even emperor-worship of this appeal. There was little cohesive force left in paganism to bind the empire together.
2. Amongst all the recent leaders of the empire the only one who had gone to a peaceful grave was his own father (Constantius) who had protected and favoured christianity.
3. The demeanour and behaviour of the Christians under the most appalling torture, and the amazing vitality of the gospel under the most dreadful persecution.
4. Licinius, his defeated rival, had favoured the pagan priests and put the Christians to death.

There is no doubt that Constantine was an astute politician, an able prince, and, on the whole, an honourable man. Whether he was truly born again must be left with God. Many of his actions suggest the clever strategist making use of christianity as a uniting bond of Empire rather than a true believer. It is the effect of his twenty five years of rule (312-337) that left such a mark on church testimony.

The special features of the letter to Pergamum that carry a prophetic foreshadowing are as follows:

1. The spirit of compromise. There is no doubt that while the Christians had borne good testimony for Christ during the persecution period covering two centuries, they had grown weary of the trials and the tears. Immediately then after the conversion of Constantine, the relaxation of persecution under the edict of toleration, the famous Edict of Milan (313), came as a tremendous relief to sorely tried Christians. As the self-styled "protector of the christian faith" he showered favours on Christians and wealth on the churches.

   It was somewhat to be expected then that the love of Christ, already cooling under Ephesian conditions and no longer stirred to a white heat by persecution should permit a toleration and compromise that promoted worldliness in the church generally. There is no doubt that Constantine did all in his power to further christianity. The Edict of Milan conferred toleration on Christians throughout the empire and was the basis of the legal establishment of christianity. This was symbolised in the selection of a new Imperial standard (see Miller *in loc*). This banner (the labarum) comprised the initials of Christ, the cross and a picture of the Emperor. The union of christianity and paganism was thus publicly declared; church and state were united for the first time. It would require "the sharp sword with the two edges" (v.12) to separate this unholy alliance. As Walter Scott points out (page 73), "Pagans were banished from the court, and Christians advanced to positions of honour. Constantine offered his gold and patronage to the church, and it eagerly swallowed the bait, sacrificed its conscience and allegiance to its Lord, and the church and the world which had hitherto walked apart...were soon locked in each other's arms".

2. The source of compromise. To see in the mention of Satan's throne and dwelling a clear reference to the ecumenical syncretism of Emperor worship has support from history. The religion of Babylon established under Semiramis was the first world-wide religion. Under all the different disguises of idolatry it covered the world. When Cyrus captured Babylon in October 539 BC the priests of the Babylonish mystery religion fled the city and established themselves in Pergamum. Under the guise of the healing ministry of Asclepius they established what was to become a satanic centre. When this kingdom was ceded to Rome (133BC) these priests carried their mystery cult to Rome and established themselves on the Etruscan plain. From this base they controlled the Caesars and the Empire. Julius Caesar wore the ring bearing the title *pontifax maximus* thus indicating his high priesthood of the Mysteries that had their origin in Babylon. Emperor worship thus became the latest manifestation of a religion by which satanic power imposed itself on the minds of men on a world-wide scale. With the great temple and altar to Caesar the Pergamum assembly felt the very nearness of Satanic residence. Loyalty to Christ demanded complete separation from the ecumenism. As the years passed the paganism that had been so stoutly resisted in the Smyrna period was now embraced step by step under christianised names. The spirit of toleration condemned by Christ in Pergamum contributed to this change. To please the emperor, customs were adopted that were parallel to pagan practices, and by the close of the period, the church had lost its distinctive character.

One matter on which there could be no compromise may well be foreshadowed in Christ's commendation "thou has not denied my name". At the council of Nicea in 325, called by Constantine and presided over by him, the great orator Arius had virtually carried the council with him in his heresy. Arius refused full deity to Christ, seeing Him only as a man and claiming that while Christ was the greatest of all created beings He was not one with the Father. Nevertheless many of the representatives of the churches, by now calling themselves bishops, rejected the false teaching completely and, led by Athanasius, framed a confession that virtually settled this fundamental issue for the span of many centuries. In the Nicean creed the Lord Jesus Christ was declared to the "very God of very God," "perfection of perfection" and "God and Man in one person". Arianism has re-appeared in various guises over the years and currently is virtually the heretical view of Christ presented by the modern Jehovah's Witnesses. Christ's commendation has thus relevance to Pergamum conditions "thou hast not denied my name". Viewing matters from the human standpoint, even in these dark days, there was a true confession to Christ.

3. The success of compromise. The patronisation of the Emperor altered the whole status of christianity. Wealth that formerly had flowed to pagan temples was now showered upon the churches. The believers who had been sorely persecuted were now promoted. Pagan counsellors were replaced by christian "bishops" so that now the path to favour and promotion lay by way of christian profession. Heathen temples were now consecrated as christian "places of worship"; heathen priests could now confess Christ and be accepted as the new hierarcy.

The two evils seen by Christ as being tolerated in Pergamum are reproduced in this very period of church history:

1. The Doctrine of Balaam. This pagan influence did not come in overnight. Yet over the three centuries of the period there were introduced step-by-step, as one compromise led to another, all the pagan practices that had originally come from Babylon. To the natural mind such accommodation was essential that the world should be christianised, but the result was inevitable: the testimony for Christ in these centuries gradually lost its distinctive character and clear gospel preaching was replaced by a mysticism that was reminiscent of Babylon. Amongst the unscriptural practices introduced were the following:
   a. From the date of the conversion of Constantine it was common to alter the Hebrew letter *tau* (t) for Tammuz, the son of Semiramis, into the sign of the cross. There are records of the sign of the cross being used as early as 300 (it is relevant to recall the conversion of Constantine) but in this period the use of it became universal.
   b. Idolatry was surreptitiously introduced in the form of adulation, and eventually worship, given to saints and angels (375) and particularly Mary (431). These practices were simply Babylonish practices under new names.
   c. Baptism was now preached as entry to the church. This was taken as synonymous with new birth and conversion. It was soon accepted that immersion was not required but sprinkling took its place. With the second generation it became routine to sprinkle infants. Thus, under christian names, the practices of Babylon were perpetuated. Miller writes, "The words in the Book of Common Prayer 'Baptism, wherein I was made a member of Christ, a child of God, and an inheritor of the Kingdom of Heaven). These words are taken, not

from scripture but from Chrysostom". John Chrysostom (347-407) was Bishop of Constantinople from 398-403. NT baptism was never entry to anything; it was a testimony to an adult confession of faith in Christ.

2. The Doctrine of the Nicolaitans. The emergence and development of a hierarchical clerical structure in the church: bishop, archbishop, metropolitan bishop and finally "universal bishop" all emerged at this point. While the origin of the papal period is often linked with Gregory the Great (590) an historical landmark for the commencement of the papal period can be found in the election of Boniface, the Bishop of Rome, to be "universal bishop" in 606. Associated with this were the splendid buildings patterned on pagan temples instead of the unpretentious meeting rooms and private houses of the persecution centuries. This necessitated the gorgeous robes and golden ornaments of priestly array copied from Judaism and paganism. It was c.500 that a distinctive dress for the officiating priests became common practice. Such priestly distinction was typical of Babylon. The domination of this class meant that no baptism was recognised, no wedding could be carried out, no breaking of bread could proceed without the presence of such officials. To put further power into the hands of these priests, doctrines like Extreme Unction (526) and Purgatorial Cleansing (593) were preached. Through this kind of unscriptural priestly ministry the churches lost the pilgrim character. Grand buildings and gorgeous robes demanded glorious music for the ceremonies that replaced the simple NT gatherings of the believers. The burning of ritualistic candles, incense, images, processions and innumerable other things were to be introduced over the fourth and fifth centuries.

The hierarchical structure led inevitably to the calling of church councils and the union of all the churches into one "catholic" (in its original meaning of "universal") church. It was then easy to draw up creeds and demand conformity to doctrinal statements. Those who did not conform were subject to banishment and even death. Things changed remarkably in a short time. The persecuted had become the persecutors. Now it was professing Christians who were putting to death faithful believers who would not conform. Faithful Antipas became the pattern of many who would die as they stood by their scriptural convictions.

The emergence of ascetic practices developed into monasticism. On the pattern of paganism such ascetics were regarded as "saints" and "holy men". The NT teaching on salvation and sanctification were lost amidst fleshly ritualism and asceticism.

Many will argue that the conversion of Constantine and the elevation of christianity to the religion of the state allowed the gospel to spread over the whole world. This is certainly true; what had been a minority teaching, heard and examined by few, was now preached across the world. For this, thanks is to be given to God. Eternity alone will reveal how many heard the gospel as it swept the Empire; doubtless many were truly born again. History takes little account of the many who heard and were brought to know Christ. Nevertheless as the records are studied of the church leaders, their unscriptural teaching, their jealousies, their intrigues, even their murders, it might well be asked how much was real. The picture seems very dark. Yet E.H. Broadbent has shown in his history *The Pilgrim Church* that even in these days of compromise and corruption there were many assemblies and a multitude of saints who resisted these trends. In their own circumstances, out of faithfulness to the word of God and their Lord, they stood apart from the corruption to become overcomers. Nevertheless in general terms, true testimony for Christ, borne out of love to His person, was almost overwhelmed by an externalism, a formalism and a ritualism that was essentially paganism coloured by Judaism.

Christ in this message to the church in Pergamum identifies the compromise tendencies that would characterise this period in church history. There was always an answer to the condition but it involved repentance that became increasingly difficult as the years ran into centuries. Traditions became entrenched and the word of God was dismissed as irrelevant. In this way the effect of the compromises of these centuries is still being felt today.

Amongst the doctrines of the NT that were either surrendered to paganism or altered considerably was the teaching of the imminent, pre-tribulational return of Christ and the establishment of His literal millennial kingdom. The blessed hope of the rapture, espoused by the church in the first three centuries, had been the inspiration for evangelistic fervour and godly consecration in the midst of persecution. Now, with christianity the state religion, the expectation was that the world would get better and better, and the social gospel, to become so prominent in the 19th century, appeared for the first time. It was taught, notably by Augustine in this book *The City of God*, that the kingdom was already ushered in and that Christ would come at the end of the thousand year period. All the characteristic doctrines of post-tribulationism appeared now for the first time. Once the literal interpretation of prophetic scriptures was abandoned the only alternative was the allegorical spiritualising method of interpretation which, coming into vogue at this period, has remained a favoured way of escaping from the truth of the clear statements of scripture.

As a consequence of this line of kingdom teaching the status of Israel had to be reinterpreted. Israel had now to be seen as cast off forever; all the promises had to be transferred to the church as the "new Israel". Of course all the curses must be left with national Israel. As a direct consequence anti-semitic teaching appeared for the first time.

A study of the written works of this time make it quite clear that the apostolic teaching with respect to the coming of Christ and the rapture of the church was gradually banished from the platforms and pulpits of the state church. With this were lost many of the characteristic truths that were meant to keep the church and the world separate. The church and the world were now hand in hand. Not for many centuries would the truth of the imminence of the rapture be recovered and with it the return of the evangelistic fervour that the church had lost in this Pergamum period.

The Thyatiran Period of Church History (606-Rapture)

Most grammarians derive the name "Thyatira" from *thuō* ("to sacrifice") and the verb *ateirō* ("not to become weary"); hence the meaning "unweary of sacrifice" or "continual sacrifice" (Newberry)

The seeds sown in the Pergamum period bore fruit in the next period of church history. Like the grain of mustard seed of which Christ spoke in the third kingdom parable (Matt 13:31-32) an unnatural growth resulted in something never intended or expected. The Pergamum period saw the church, heavenly in origin and destiny, become a world power, through its union with the state. In terms of the parable the grain of mustard seed became a great tree. The Thyatiran period that followed continued this transformation so that the church, losing all its heavenly features became, in the eyes of men, a mighty organisation. Its pope and its prelates became the mighty of earth. The pope controlled kingdoms and claimed authority to crown and depose monarchs at will. Claiming a monopoly of the means of salvation, denying that any could be saved without its ministrations, the church professed to decide the destiny of men. Through the doctrine of purgatory (593) and the sale of indulgences (1190) wealth flowed into its coffers. In pomp and arrogance its bishops far outshone the princes of earth. All this was done in the name of Christ. The special feature of the Thyatira period is reflected in the fourth kingdom parable (Matt 13:33). There a woman is seen hiding leaven in three measures of meal. The silent propagation and all-pervading permeation of the leaven reflects the spread of evil doctrine in this period of church history. The gospel light, already threatened by paganism in the Pergamum period, would be well-nigh extinguished, in this succeeding period. It is to be noted that, even in secular history, this period is known as the Dark Ages. These ages when spiritual darkness reigned would continue until the gospel light broke forth anew in the Reformation period (1519).

The election of the bishop of Rome Boniface III as the universal bishop in 606, was the result of a long battle for supremacy within the church. It is also a convenient historical landmark for the emergence of what is now known as the Roman Catholic Church. While many of the distinctive doctrines of Roman Catholicism had already been introduced before this date the crowning of this universal bishop set the stage for the "catholic" claim of universal control over all churches. This claim while challenged on occasions through the following decades has never been abandoned by Rome. Not all the features of this system were developed at once, but step by step as the centuries moved on spiritual darkness deepened. Darkness reigned where there should have been light, death ruled where there should have been life, and where there ought to have been liberty men were brought into a bondage more terrible than they had known under paganism. Yet it is most encouraging to know that there were still many saints, even in this period, who had not known the "depths of Satan", so that Christ preserved a faithful testimony even through the darkest centuries. The main features of this dark system of Roman Catholicism as developed in the Thyatiran period may be summarised as follows:

1. Pre-Eminence of the Church of Rome

The bishop of Rome claimed, intrigued to get and fought to preserve the pre-eminence of the Roman See over the other three metropolitan bishoprics established by Constantine: Antioch, Alexandria and Constantinople. The bishop of Constantinople refused to grant this primacy to Rome and, aided by the Arian controversy, broke away to form the Eastern Orthodox Church. The domination by Rome was absolute in all matters of faith and practice. All other churches throughout the world, on threat of excommunication, had to submit to Rome. Outside communion with Rome, no national or local church was allowed to exist and no individual could enjoy salvation. In later developments the pope would claim power over the kingdoms of earth and not only become the arbiter of world empire but claim the right to dispossess princes and appoint or depose kings. From the 9th century the term "vicar of Christ" was claimed by the pope. It is to be noted that the promise to the overcomer (v.26) in this church envisages just such powers but it is in association with Christ in His kingdom. At the instigation of popes wars were started, crusades were launched, kingdoms were ravaged, and millions perished to satisfy these power-crazed prelates. The blasphemy lies in the fact that it was all done in the name of Christ.

2. Pronouncements of the Church of Rome

To maintain this position of power which Scriptures would never allow, the word of God had to be devalued and kept from men. In place of the word of God the word of the church emanating from the pope was first added to, then substituted for the inspired Word. It was in 1129 that the Bible was forbidden to laymen on the argument that priests alone were equipped to interpret it. The claim of apostolic succession from Peter was a convenient doctrine and allowed the pope to speak with the voice of absolute authority. It is to be noted that, in this fourth church, as in the fourth parable (Matt 13:33) a woman takes prominence. It is Jezebel, claiming to be a prophetess who promotes the teaching that corrupted. Under this OT name Christ pictures corruption stemming from the teaching of the Roman Catholic church. When the church spoke men had to heed; what the church introduced into doctrine was calculated to corrupt. In every *ex-cathedra* utterance of papal authority can be heard the teaching of the prophetess Jezebel.

3. Practices of the Church of Rome

Using the power it had usurped and the spurious claim to apostolic succession the Roman Catholic church introduced doctrines and practices that belonged to paganism. Every one of these can be traced back to Babylon (see *The Two Babylons* by A. Hislop). In this way there were introduced:

The sacrifice of the mass. The characteristic feature of Roman Catholicism has ever been the denial of the finished work of Christ. This opened the way for the blasphemy of the mass and the power put into the hands of priests to re-enact the work of the cross;

The sprinkling of infants. "Holy water" was introduced c. 850;

The worship of Mary and prayers to saints. Associated with these ideas was the canonisation of dead saints (995), fasting on Fridays and during Lent (998);

The worship of images and relics (786);

The celibacy of priests (1079);

The practice of monasticism (4th century);

Auricular confession.

Images, relics, candles, incense and many other features of paganism found new life under christianised names. The word of the church replaced the word of God and few were the voices raised in protest. As each new departure was introduced into the church there was doubtless a "space to repent" (v.21), but the voices were few; the religious system had virtual control. Not until God raised up a man for the hour in Martin Luther (1483-1546), was this worldwide edifice shaken to its foundation.

4. Persecution by the Church of Rome

Since the authority of the Roman bishop became absolute in these centuries, it was inevitable that any who differed from the system would have to be persecuted. From the earliest days those who refused allegiance to the dictates of Rome were first excommunicated, then dispossessed, tortured and finally, put to death. The Dark and Middle Ages unfold a terrible catalogue of persecutions of all dissenters. The history of the Albigenses and the Waldenses makes sad reading. The bigotry and blasphemy of the crusades and the inquisition (established 1184) form a terrible indictment of a satanic system. The "depths of Satan" are there exposed.

The foreshadowings of the thousand years until the Reformation are seen in Christ's remarks to the church in Thyatira and may be summarised:

a. the active propagation of evil: "thou sufferest that woman Jezebel to teach" (2:20). What had been tolerated is now actively taught. Identifying Himself as

Son of God for the only time in these letters sets Christ in contrast to this false prophetess. In developing Romanism the voice of the church takes precedence over the voice of Christ through His word.

b. For the first time a remnant is recognised (v.24). Christ shows that the majority of those under Jezebel's teaching would not be recovered. While various local recoveries brought blessing to many individuals and in the Reformation itself a multitude of souls were blessed, these were still only a minority.

c. The call to "hear" coming after the promise to the overcomer for the first time shows that the majority would pay little heed to the call of Christ.

d. For the first time the rapture is specifically mentioned. Christ is seen as the "morning star". The kingdom age was coming on earth but the herald of the dawn would be Christ coming for the rapture of the church. Thus Christ indicates that when He comes there will still be a Roman Catholic system on earth; Jezebel will still be doing her deadly work. It is to the remnant that He says, "Hold fast till I come". It is clear that the multitudes deceived by Romanism will remain on earth after the rapture to become the world-wide ecclesiastical system symbolised in the harlot of ch.17. The name on her forehead, "BABYLON THE GREAT, THE MOTHER OF HARLOTS", is sufficient to identify the origin of the practices, the principles and the persecution of Roman Catholicism.

The Sardis Period of Church History (1517 to the Rapture)

When on 31 October 1517 Martin Luther, a Roman Catholic monk, nailed his famous ninety-five theses attacking the teachings of the Roman Catholic church to the church door in Wittenberg, Germany he was expressing a protest that was to shake that church to its very foundations. Paganism enshrined in the rituals of Romanism had reigned supreme for centuries. The sale of indulgences by Tetzel, the emissary of the pope, for the rebuilding of St. Peter's church in Rome, was but the spark that ignited the sweeping blaze of Protestantism. Luther turned men's minds from ritualism and formalism to the Scriptures; the rallying cry that challenged the might of Rome was the word that had brought salvation to Luther personally, "The just shall live by faith". Suddenly men wanted to know, "What saith the Scripture?"; a question not readily answered since the Scriptures had been forbidden to laymen since 1129. Nevertheless, God raised up men equipped to preach the Word, to translate the Word and to print the Word. The printing press had been used by Caxton in 1487 and the first book printed was the Bible. Men of God followed Luther and the history of the church is ennobled by the names of Melancthon, Erasmus, Zwingli, Calvin, Wycliffe, Tyndale, Farel and a host of others. Life through Christ alone was preached and multitudes were saved by grace. There was tremendous promise in the power of the Spirit of God seen in the early days of the Reformation period. Across many lands the message spread despite the efforts of the Roman Catholic church and the counter-Reformation.

It soon became clear, however, that that early promise would not be fulfilled, and it is in the subsequent developments that the prophetic foreshadowings given by Christ in the message to Sardis become very evident. The foreshadowings in this message of this period of church history may be listed as follows:

1. The Scriptures

While the early Reformers insisted on the authority of Scriptures with respect to salvation, many did not see that the same Scripture gave clear instructions for the believers on church order and practice. Few of them saw the autonomy of local churches as a vital matter. One who did was W. Farel who laboured in France and French-speaking Switzerland (see *Life of William Farel* by Bevan), but his was a lonely voice. When faced with opposition of the papacy the natural reaction was to unite churches into a nationwide organisation patterned largely on the Roman Church. When threatened by the armies put in array against them by papal decree, Luther sought assistance of the German princes and opened the way for state churches supported by political and military power. Men found it easier to depend on men than upon the might of the Spirit of God. They preferred to rely on human intrigue and physical force. Despite their claim of *sola scriptura*, the scripture was not enough. As a result the work remained incomplete.

2. The Works Unfulfilled

With the Scriptures not obeyed and the Spirit of God not given full authority it was clear that the result would be the establishment of hierarchical structures based on the pattern of Roman Catholicism. While Protestant preaching presented the gospel and salvation by faith though grace, church organisation and administration was patterned largely on what had been known in Romanism. The priests of Rome were replaced by new clerics. It is true that in the early days most of these would be genuinely-converted men, but with the passing years academic qualifications became more important than the new birth and pulpits in denominational systems were filled with unconverted men. This promoted nominal profession without genuine possession of life. Accommodation became the important principle not the truth of Scripture. To accommodate the susceptibilities of a people coming out of the darkness of Romanism clear NT teaching was rarely preached, but familiar Romish practices were continued under different guises. Infant sprinkling, the sacramental eucharist and the ordination of clergy were retained. The promise of the early Reformation years was not fulfilled. Denominational organisations based on national boundaries where whole populations "belonged" to the church were established. Christianity became merely a matter of profession. There was little evidence of divine life in many a church. "A name to live" in Protestantism soon developed in such a way that Christ could have addressed many a church as He did Sardis with the solemn condemnation, "Thou art dead".

3. Great Names

At no other stage in church history did great names play so major a part in the history of the church. Some of these men were mighty servants of God in their day. Yet sadly the record is that their names were used to divide Christians from Christians and the result was inevitable - denomination came out of denomination. Luther left behind him Lutheranism, Calvin gave to history Calvinism and Wesley founded Methodism. Each organisation developed in its own structure, built its own magnificent cathedrals and churches, arranged its own liturgy, with minimum reference to Scripture. Different from Romanism but having its roots in it, this great Protestant structure looked most imposing but, like Sardis of old, it carried within each denomination an inherent weakness that has proven fatal. Church organisation depended on the training and education of suitable clergy. These had to be graduates of universities and training colleges where the faculty in the early years were converted men. As the years passed the original teachers were replaced by others who had not the same convictions. Within a generation that which had begun as an evangelical and conservative training school became liberal in outlook, the Scriptures were questioned then denied. With unconverted men filling the pulpits agnosticism and atheism invaded the church and mere professors filled the pews. It is no wonder that the Lord will come to denominationalism as a thief. The major part have never known divine life. The book of church membership bears little relation to the book of life.

4. A Remnant

Yet amidst much nominal profession Christ still has "a few names" known to Him personally who walk apart from all the deadness around. Ritualism and rationalism may be the prevalent climate in many a denomination, but Christ, in the Sardian age, has had those who have walked with Him. These overcomers He will gladly own before His Father in a day that lies ahead.

The Philadelphian Period of Church History (1750-Rapture)

The bright early years of the Reformation, when the gospel was preached with power and souls were saved, soon gave way to the acceptance of a nominal profession of Christianity that became the characteristic mark of Protestant denominationalism. Submission to the ceremonies of infant sprinkling and church confirmation produced nominal Christians with little evidence of divine life. This is the kind of "death" reflected in the Sardian period, a deadness that was soon to be evidenced by the wave of infidelity that swept through Europe in the aftermath of the French Revolution (1793). With Protestantism the groundwork for agnosticism had been laid in the emergence of the school of Higher Criticism in the theological departments of the European universities. When J.G. Eichorn (1752-1827) published his major work *Old Testament Introduction* (1787) it became a text book for those who wished to throw doubt upon the divine inspiration of the Scriptures. A major assistance to the spread of unbelief in England was provided by the publication in 1830-1833 of Charles (later Sir Charles) Lyell's book *Principles of Geology* which, with its interpretation of the geological record in the rocks of earth, laid the groundwork for the theory of evolution by Charles Darwin. Publication of Charles Darwin's *Origin of Species* in 1859 carried infidelity into schools and colleges and gave it respectability. Men now had scientific support for their infidelity.

Against this background of infidelity there was a real work of God in the recovery of certain scriptural truths that were to bring much blessing in their train. These truths are foreshadowed in the Lord's message to the church in Philadelphia. They may be summarised thus:

1. Evangelistic Truth: In the English-speaking world the period from c. 1730 to 1800 is known as the Great Awakening, when through the preaching of George Whitefield (1714-1770) and John Wesley (1703-1791) great companies throughout the British Isles were saved. A Second Awakening followed in the nineteenth century when God raised up another generation of gospel preachers of whom the best known are D.L. Moody (1837-1899) and C.H. Spurgeon (1832-1892). True conversion led to a true concern for souls and it was in these years that the worldwide missionary movement carried the gospel to the ends of the earth. Names of men and women stand out in the records that tell of sacrifice and service for Christ. W. Carey (1761-1834) of India, Hudson Taylor (1832-1905) of China, David Livingstone (1813-1873) and F.S. Arnot (1858-1914) of Africa are but a few names that represent a missionary zeal over the world. Truly a "little strength" but yet the Lord said "I have set before thee an open door". It is remarkable that this is the very period when missionary enterprise was rediscovered.

2. Ecclesiastical Truth: It should not be a matter of surprise that when true conversion encourages men and women to study and search the Scriptures, new truths should emerge that had been buried under tradition and lifeless profession. It was in these years that loyalty to the Scriptures ("thou hast kept my word") and loyalty to the Saviour ("thou hast not denied my name") led many to question their association with denominationalism. This new exercise led many saints to seek to return to the simple NT pattern of gathering to the name of the Lord Jesus Christ in testimony. The result was the establishment of gatherings without

denominational ties in many places round the world at about the same period. The better known of these places, because of their subsequent history, were Dublin and Plymouth but these were but representative of a movement that spread worldwide. Men like J.N. Darby (1800-1882), George Muller (1805-1898) and W. Kelly (1821-1906) were but representatives of a multitude of godly men that God raised up to teach these principles of gathering based on the Scriptures without all the additions of tradition. In these gatherings a shared life in Christ, a shared liberty in the Spirit and the shared light from the Scriptures led to a special appreciation of "brotherly love" enjoyed in Christ. Truly a Philadelphian experience. Many an objector, on the pattern of v.9, was brought to acknowledge that the Lord had loved that simple gathering of believers who honoured Him in their mode of gathering. Assemblies commenced on this NT pattern have resulted from the exercise of these years and are to be found all over the world. The characteristic word of Christ describes this movement exactly "a little strength".

3. Eschatological Truth: It is to be observed that Christ makes direct reference in His message to the church in Philadelphia that the saints were to be kept out of "the hour of temptation" which the exposition has shown to be the tribulation period. It must not be forgotten that it is in this Philadelphian period of church testimony that, following the evangelistic preaching and the re-emphasis on the scriptural mode of gathering, the truth of the Lord's coming for the church at the rapture was rediscovered. Associated with this recovery of truth was a whole new appreciation of the teaching concerning the end-time events centred around the pre-tribulation rapture. These truths had for many centuries of church history been not altogether unknown, but largely misunderstood and ignored. In this Philadelphian period they have been brought to light again by the Spirit of God. The Lord has foreseen this very fact in this message to the church in Philadelphia.

The Laodicean Period of Church History (1900-Rapture)

It has been pointed out that in the prophetic aspect of Christ's messages to the churches the last four church conditions emerge one from the other so that when the Lord comes the four conditions will exist side by side. These four conditions when viewed together present a full picture of christendom if it is defined as all that professes Christ in the days prior to His coming. There will be thus:

the Thyatiran condition	seen in Roman Catholicism and Eastern Orthodoxy
the Sardian condition	seen in Protestant denominationalism
the Philadelphian condition	seen in scriptural testimony and evangelical witness.

The fourth condition must be Laodicean and it comes out of the evangelicism and fundamentalism of Philadelphia. The very emergence of this condition signals that the coming of the Christ cannot be far distant. To the remnant in Thyatiran conditions Christ is seen coming as "the morning star"; He is the herald of the dawn and comes before the sun rises in millennial splendour. To the majority in Sardian conditions Christ will come unexpectedly as the thief; all the lifeless professors of nominal Protestantism will be taken unawares. To the expectant saints under Philadelphian conditions the promise of Christ is very real, "Behold I come quickly". The actual coming is not mentioned in connection with Laodicea; clearly they have no appreciation of it but a judgmental aspect is implied in the statement of Christ, "I will spew thee out of my mouth", which, as shown in the comments, must mean public repudiation as the majority of the company are left behind when Christ comes. The individuals taken will clearly be those who have responded to His appeal to "open the door".

The special features in Laodicea which make it a very fitting picture of the closing stage of church history may be summarised thus:

Complacency: Having passed their own judgment on their condition the note of self-complacency is very evident: "I am rich and increased with goods and have need of nothing". As shown in the comments while this speaks of the material wealth that they possess it cannot be limited to this but reflects the spiritual complacency of this fashionable church. With neither doctrinal heresy within, nor satanic persecution without, this church feels itself enjoying all material and spiritual enrichment. With fine buildings, a large bank account, well-educated preachers, a full programme of meetings and an active missionary outreach they feel that no church is quite in their class. This proud self-satisfaction is certainly symptomatic of many a church in these closing decades of the twentieth century. Fearfulness of the future that characterised Philadelphia is noticeably missing in Laodicea. They have not the slightest doubt that Christ will give them divine approval.

Lukewarmness: With all the activity there is a noticeable lack of real devotion to Christ. This condition has been the result of a mixing of the hot (believers) and the cold (unbelievers). This of course, could only arise when the scriptural teaching on church reception and discipline has been ignored and relaxed. With such a mixed company it is clear that democratic rights would be demanded and the result would be that all judgments would be settled by majority rule. This was the cause of the exposure by Christ of the church as "poor" and "blind" and "naked" in spiritual terms despite large profession. It is clear that in the departure from the simplicity of Philadelphia - in obedience to Scripture ("thou has kept my word") and devotion to the person of Christ ("thou hast not denied my name") - a Laodicean condition has emerged in these last decades. Profession without power, many high claims with little reality as seen in many "house churches" and "fellowships" and a variety of gatherings, many claiming charismatic endowment, have hidden a spiritual poverty truly Laodicean in character.

CHAPTER 4

III. Vision 2: Christ and the Cosmos (4:1-19:10) Christ Acts – the Lamb

Chs.4, 5 describe an awesome scene, a scene that provides the introduction and then furnishes the background to the rest of the book. Invited to enter heaven John is permitted to view the throne of God and witness one of the most dramatic actions in the whole history of creation. Deity enthroned is served by four living creatures, surrounded by twenty-four elder-filled thrones and attended by myriads of angels. When Christ as the Lamb takes the book from the hand of God worship begins and swelling notes of praise rise from rank upon rank of created beings until, as new voices join the chorus, the whole creation is bowed in worship around the throne.

In view of the important place this scene fills in the book three key matters need to be addressed:

1. the relationship between this throne scene and the rapture of the church;
2. the relationship of this throne scene to the tribulation;
3. the relationship between chs. 4, 5.

That this throne scene forms the introduction to the third section of this book follows from the outline given by Christ Himself in 1:19. The "things which thou hast seen" have been shown to refer to the vision of Christ in 1:9-19. The "things which are" have been dealt with by Christ in the letters to the seven churches in chs. 2 and 3. The remaining part of the book from chs. 4 to 22 falls into the third section under the heading "the things which shall be hereafter". While some may argue that the expression "after this", with which this chapter opens, simply describes the fact that John received this vision after the earlier visions, the repetition of the same words at the end of the verse makes it abundantly clear that the events themselves must come after the history of the church age has closed. The length of the period on earth between the rapture of the church and the opening of the seven-year tribulation period is not given in scripture. However long or short it must come between ch. 3 and ch. 4 of this revelation to John.

It should be further observed that the fact of John being introduced to heaven at this point cannot be without significance. Commentators who hold the futurist view of the book have no difficulty in seeing in the removal of John from earth to heaven a picture of the rapture of the church. While absolute proof is lacking the strong coincidental element in John's removal to heaven just after the close of the messages to the churches is to be noted. Interlinked with this chronological question is the identification of the twenty-four elders around the throne. It will be argued in the comments to follow that these elders represent the church seen in heaven acting in priestly capacity. It will be shown that they are redeemed ones, in resurrection bodies, judged and crowned. It will be further argued that, since the church is the only complete company of saints of which these things can be said before the tribulation commences, these elders must represent the church of this dispensation.

Support for the analysis that the church is removed from earth before this throne scene takes place lies in the following facts:

(a) The church is not mentioned nor even referred to on any occasion in the tribulation scenes between chs. 5-16 but reappears as "the wife of the Lamb" just before Christ's return to earth (19:7). It may be noted that the last mention of the twenty-four elders (19:4) occurs just before the bride is introduced. That is also the last mention of the four living creatures, but, as will be shown in the comments, their disappearance may be interpreted differently.

(b) In chs. 2 and 3 the familiar challenge from Christ, "He that hath an ear let him hear what the Spirit saith unto the churches", occurs seven times. In 13:9 when the challenge is repeated there is the significant omission of "what the Spirit saith unto the churches".

(c) The words used for deity in this section of the book, "God", "Lord God", "Almighty" are more reminiscent of OT times than the intimacy of the church-age language of the epistles. It seems strange if the church is on earth at this period that the word "Father" is never used with respect to believers on earth (in 14:1 it is the relationship between God and Christ that is in view). Thus there is at the very least, a very clear inference, that the church has gone from earth before this period of tribulation begins. Thus the rapture must take place between the end of ch. 3 and the opening of ch. 4, and it is perfectly feasible that John's introduction to heaven pictures this event.

Those commentators who insist that the church remains on earth throughout all or part of the tribulation period will quarrel with this interpretation as being based on inference. They will point to the fact that the rapture is not mentioned. This is true but it should be recognised that the Revelation is not giving a programme of events linked to the church, a subject covered in the epistles, but, as is stressed in the title of the book, it is the unveiling of Christ in His relationships – first with John (ch. 1), then with the churches (chs. 2 and 3) and now with the universe (chs. 4-22) that is in view. The rapture of the church, clearly taught in other scriptures (John 14:1-3; 1 Cor 15:51-52; 1 Thess 4:13-17), is incidental to the main purpose of this book and thus becomes merely the chronological link between two aspects of the revelation of Christ. In the removal of the church from earth (pictured in John) the way is opened for the tribulation to begin.

The fact that Christ is introduced as the Lamb in this throne scene makes it very clear that this scene takes place after the cross, after His resurrection and after His ascension. His work of the cross is the very basis for His taking of the book. The words of Christ in 3:21 show that in this church age He is seated with the Father on His throne. In this scene this is no longer the picture, Christ is here presented as a Lamb before the throne of God. This suggests that the church age is closed and Christ is seen in a different relationship. Equally clear is the fact that the opening of the first seal of the seven-sealed book by the Lamb introduces the tribulation period, a period very different from the age of gospel preaching. In contrast to the present age the tribulation period is described as "the wrath of the Lamb" (6:16) and later, as "the wrath of God" (16:1). Thus it may be fairly deduced that this throne scene takes place after the rapture of the church and is the prelude to the opening of the seven-year tribulation upon earth.

Chs. 4 and 5 therefore provide the introduction and furnish the background to the remaining chapters of the book. When in this throne scene the Lamb takes the book from the hand of God the stage is set for the dramatic events on earth that, covering the tribulation period, will climax in the return of Christ to earth as "King of kings and Lord of lords" (19:11-16).

The chapter division interrupts the unity of the scene. Ch. 4 is but the background for the action of ch. 5 when the Lamb takes the book from the hand of the Throne-sitter. Since the book is sealed with seven seals the opening of these seals is the action in heaven that precipitates dramatic events on earth. It is a mistake to see the two chapters as being in contrast (setting creation over against redemption) or even as being complementary, as two sides of the matter. Rather it is important to see that they present a single scene with one dramatic action described in the two chapters of the text.

1. *The Throne Scene in Heaven* 4:1-5:14

Three things catch the eye of John as he views this heavenly scene:

(a) *The Throne – Service in the Cosmos (vv. 1-11)*

v.1 "After this I looked, and, behold, a door was opened in heaven: and the first voice which I heard was as it were of a trumpet talking with me; which said, Come up hither, and I will shew thee things which must be hereafter.
v.2 And immediately I was in the spirit: and, behold, a throne was set in heaven, and one sat on the throne.
v.3 And he that sat was to look upon like a jasper and a sardine stone: and there was a rainbow round about the throne, in sight like unto an emerald.
v.4 And round about the throne were four and twenty seats: and upon the seats I saw four and twenty elders sitting, clothed in white raiment; and they had on their heads crowns of gold.
v.5 And out of the throne proceeded lightnings and thunderings and voices: and

there were seven lamps of fire burning before the throne, which are the seven Spirits of God.

v.6 And before the throne there was a sea of glass like unto crystal: and in the midst of the throne, and round about the throne, were four beasts full of eyes before and behind.

v.7 And the first beast was like a lion, and the second beast like a calf, and the third beast had a face as a man, and the fourth beast was like a flying eagle.

v.8 And the four beasts had each of them six wings about him; and they were full of eyes within: and they rest not day and night, saying, Holy, holy, holy, Lord God Almighty, which was, and is, and is to come.

v.9 And when those beasts give glory and honour and thanks to him that sat on the throne, who liveth for ever and ever,

v.10 The four and twenty elders fall down before him that sat on the throne, and worship him that liveth for ever and ever, and cast their crowns before the throne, saying,

v.11 Thou art worthy, O Lord, to receive glory and honour and power: for thou hast created all things, and for thy pleasure they are and were created."

1 The first words, "after this", identify the time sequence of the vision as subsequent to that of the messages to the seven churches. That aspect of prophecy is closed and John is now introduced into heaven for this new revelation of future events. The eye of John is arrested by a startling sight that draws from him that exclamation of wonder "behold". It is not simply that "the heavens were opened" (an expression used in Ezek 1:1; Matt 3:16; Acts 7:56) to allow John to look into heaven but something far more personal. A door "was opened" in heaven: as if John was invited to enter there: a welcome is implied. The perfect participle may be better translated "set open". Heaven here is neither the aerial heaven nor the astral heaven but "heaven itself" (Heb 9:24), described in Scripture as "the third heaven" (2 Cor 12:2). Here Deity dwells. The welcome implicit in the opened door is audibly expressed in the summons to John to "come up hither". "The first voice which I heard" Alford translates as "the former voice". This is clearly a reference back to 1:10 where the same trumpet-like voice was identified as that of the conducting angel. Such a trumpet-like summons could not be ignored.

The purpose of the invitation to John is given in the promise, "I will show thee things which *must* be hereafter". This statement must be compared with 1:19, "the things which *shall* be hereafter," to see that John is to be shown events that follow the church age. The things revealed will comprise the next section of the book (4:1-19:21). The change from "shall" (1:19) to "must" indicates that the events are not merely to be expected but are part of God's intended programme; so they are both irrevocable and inescapable. That the "opened" heaven is a keynote in the unfolding revelation may be observed in the following sequence:

4:1	and, behold, a door *was opened* in heaven,
11:19	and the temple of God *was opened* in heaven,
15:5	and, behold the temple of the tabernacle of the testimony in heaven *was opened*,
19:11	and, I saw heaven *opened*.

With the final opening of heaven Christ comes forth in majestic splendour to claim sovereign rights over earth. It is to this climax that the book of Revelation moves.

2 Heaven's command allows no delay. The omission of "and" (as in the RV) and the inclusion of the adverb "immediately" indicates an instant response to this order. "In spirit" repeats John's experience of 1:10 (see also 17:3; 21:10) and indicates his ecstatic elevation beyond the natural. The action involves the human spirit but the agent must be the Holy Spirit since deity is involved. While his body remains on earth John is introduced to heavenly scenes "in spirit". John's vision is filled by a throne. The repetition of "behold" gives the sense of awe in the presence of the throne (mentioned seventeen times in these two chapters). The imperfect tense of the verb is correctly translated "was set" (see John 2:6) and draws attention, not to the placing of the throne but to its permanent location: it was set "in heaven". The very absence of any further description heightens the sense of awesome majesty. Human language is inadequate.

John's eye moves to the "Throne-sitter". The familiar imagery of sovereignty in OT scriptures is to see one seated on a throne (1 Kings 2:19; Isa 6:1; Ezek 1:26-28; Dan 7:9) and this finds majestic expression in this scene. There is no description of the throne; neither is there any description of the One sitting on the throne. The Scriptures never describe deity and since "God is Spirit" (John 4:24 R.V. margin) any description in human term would be totally out of character. There is no question that the One who fills the throne is God. If any question is raised then the explicit statement of 7:10 puts the matter beyond doubt: "Salvation to our God which sitteth on the throne"; and the statement of 19:4 is confirmatory: "And the four and twenty elders and the four beasts fell down and worshipped God that sat on the throne". This is the throne of the Eternal God. Some have wondered whether Christ fills this throne since He is eternally the image of God (Col 1:15) in representation and manifestation. While there may be something to be said for this view in general terms, the fact that Christ comes into view as the Lamb in ch. 5 (which, of course, is part of the same scene), would argue convincingly against it. It is better to see absolute deity as filling the throne in ch. 4 where the worship on the ground of creation is involved. The rest of the scene (ch. 5) will bring Christ into view as the Lamb.

3 The impression of the throne conveyed to the human eye is the blaze of light that emanates from the Throne-sitter. Truly God is light (1 John 1:5) and appears to John "like a jasper and a sardine stone". These two precious stones are mentioned again in 21:19-20 in connection with the foundation of the city. The word jasper comes from a Hebrew root meaning "to be bright" and describes a clear stone like a diamond that, sparkling, reflects light unrefracted. The overwhelming impression is of crystal purity. This is the colour that represents the glory of God in the Holy Jerusalem (21:11). The sardine is a beautiful ruby red stone. The fiery red appearance of this stone has often been linked with the symbolism of "divine anger and punitive righteousness" (F. A. Tatford) *Prophecy's Last Word* (p.76), yet the colour itself may suggest that that righteous anger of God has found satisfaction in the blood and there seems to be in this stone more than a hint of redemption. It should also be noted that these particular stones in the reverse order were the first and last on the breastplate of the high priest of Israel (Exod 28:17-21); the jasper stone was linked with Reuben (meaning "behold a son") and the sardine stone with Benjamin (meaning "son of my right hand"). When "unveiled" on earth (19:12) Christ the Son will display in His person all that belongs essentially to deity.

The rainbow encircling the throne in the vertical plane links both creation and redemption. After the cataclysm of the flood God placed His "bow in the clouds" (Gen 9:13) as the token of a covenant of divine preservation. The fear of a holy God seen in a storm is to be tempered by His faithfulness to His covenant with regard to earth. It should not be forgotten that, when God was about to intervene dramatically in earth affairs in judgment in the destruction of Jerusalem by the might of Babylon, Ezekiel saw the same rainbow around the throne (Ezek 1:28). So in this vision, before this terrible tribulation storm reproducing physically many of the seismic upheavals of the Noahic deluge, breaks over earth the emerald rainbow speaks eloquently of God's unbreakable covenant with His creation. Man from earth can only see segments of the rainbow but from heaven John can see it complete. That it is described as being "round about the throne" shows that the very throne of God is engaged with the fulfilment of His purposes. Under normal circumstances as light is refracted, a rainbow comprises all seven colours of the visible spectrum - red, orange, yellow, green, blue, indigo, violet. Here the colour is confined to the green of the emerald stone. There is likely a symbolic suggestion that green links both earth (physically) and grace (metaphorically). Dreadful judgment is about to fall upon earth in keeping with divine righteousness but God's covenant promise to Noah would never be forgotten, and in the midst of wrath, grace would still be evident.

That the throne is the very centre of this scene is emphasised by the use of four spatial prepositions that are used in the description of the scene.

1. Round about (*kuklothen*) the throne – "four and twenty seats"

While the rainbow is in the vertical plane it would appear that these "seats", or better, "thrones" (see RV and JND), are in the horizontal plane. The word "seat" ("*thronos*") is exactly the same word as is used for the central throne. On these thrones were seated "four and twenty elders". Any scriptural identification of these elders will have to take into account

(a) the word used to describe them – *presbuteroi*
(b) their number – twenty-four
(c) their dress – white garments (*himatiois leukios*)
(d) their golden crowns (*stephanous chrusous*).

They are mentioned as a group on twelve occasions in the book: 4:4, 10; 5:5, 6, 8, 11, 14; 7:11, 13; 11:16; 14:3; 19:4.

Many and varied have been the suggested interpretations of these twenty-four elders. That there has been so wide a range of interpretation is somewhat strange when the facts as given seem to point in one direction. Four facts settle the matter.

(a) the word "elders" is used in Scripture only of men. The very word *presbuteros* in the comparative degree (an older man) rules out "angels" of any order whatever since there is no suggestion in Scripture that they age as men do. The word is used to describe men as representatives of the local synagogues in Israel (Matt 15:2; 16:21) or as representatives of local assemblies (Acts 20:17; 21:18; James 5:14)

(b) The number twenty-four is clearly based on the representative priesthood in Israel at the time of the kings (1 Chron 24:3-5). What was national and typical is now seen as universal and real. It is to the sharers in the first resurrection that priesthood is promised (1:6; 20:6) and since only the believers of the church age (the "dead in Christ" of 1 Thess 4:16) have been resurrected at this point the strong inference is that these elders represent the church in priestly character. The argument that these elders cannot be representatives since they speak as individuals (7:13) is very weak; the representatives of the OT priesthood did just this in Isa 37:2: Jer 19:1; in these passages men acted as individuals and representatives at the same time.

(c) The "white garments" are characteristic of redeemed men (3:5, 18; 6:11; 7:9). Note that the word in 15:6 with respect to the clothing of angels is "bright" (JND) and not "white".

(d) The "golden crowns" (*stephanos*) are most naturally interpreted as the crowns promised to believers of the church age (2:10; 3:11; 2 Tim 4:8; James 1:12; 1 Pet 5:4). The fact that they are wearing the crowns is a clear indication that the assessment of their service is over and they have been rewarded.

Putting these facts together there can be little doubt that these twenty-four elders are redeemed ones from earth, already in resurrection bodies and bearing the evidence of divine assessment of their service in the fact that they are crowned. With reference to their function, it is clear that they must be both kings (note the thrones) and priests (note the white garments and their ministry). Thus as king-priests there is a reference back to 1:6 "And hath made us kings and priests unto God and his Father". Dr. H. Ironside (p.82) puts the case concisely: "When the twenty-four elders met in the temple precincts in Jerusalem, the whole priestly house was represented. The elders in heaven represent the whole heavenly priesthood. In vision they are seen – not as a multitudinous host of millions of saved worshippers, but just twenty-four elders, symbolising the entire company". Thus these twenty-four elders represent the church in priestly ministry before the throne of God.

While agreeing that the twenty-four elders are representative of redeemed men many commentators insist that they represent both Israel, a nation originating with the twelve patriarchs, and the church of this dispensation founded by the twelve apostles. Alford in a long discussion insists that OT saints must be included. Ironside, in the sentence following the quotation given above, states, "The church of the present age and the OT saints are alike included". Many more recent commentators take his view. While there is an appealing logical completeness in this suggestion it has no firm scriptural basis and, in fact, conflicts with the distinction that Scripture makes between Israel and the church. Further, since the saints of the nation of Israel are not resurrected until the end of the tribulation (Dan 12:1-2) and they are judged and rewarded as they go into the millennium (11:18) they are not seen in this picture. Their history and destiny are linked with the nation of Israel passing through the tribulation period on earth. The church raptured and judged is the only body of believers complete in heaven at this stage and is represented by these twenty-four elders acting as king-priests before the throne. The fact that they disappear from the record in 19:4 just before the bride comes forth to her marriage may be significant. The church will be associated with Christ in the manifestation as His kingdom is established on earth.

2. Out of (*ek*) the throne – "lightnings and thunderings and voices"

That this scene does not belong to the church age of gospel preaching is now made abundantly clear to John. The throne of grace (Heb 4:16) has become a throne of judgment. The echoes are of Mount Sinai (Exod 19:16) but much more terrifying, as God is about to act in divine judgment upon earth. The word "voices" (*phōnai*) is not meant to describe individual human voices but in this context would be better rendered "sounds" or "noises". It will be noted that they always occur in the record between what is visible (lightnings) and what is audible (thunders). These storm scenes form a background for judgment as follows:

4:5 out of the throne	"Lightnings and sounds and thunders" (RV order)
8.5 after the seventh seal	"Thunders and sounds and lightnings and an earthquake" (RV order)
11:19 after the seventh trumpet	"Lightnings and sounds and thunders and an earthquake and a great hail"
16:18 after the seventh bowl	"Lightnings and sounds and thunder and a great earthquake .... and great hail"

The intensification of divine judgment upon earth in this period is reflected in the added storm features (earthquake, hail) as the tribulation moves to its climax in the seventh bowl just before the coming of Christ to earth.

3. Before (*enōpion*) the throne

Immediately before the throne, and thus in closest association with it, are the seven lamps of fire divinely interpreted as the "seven Spirits of God". In the first occurrence of this term (1:4) it was shown that this term defines the fulness and completeness of the sevenfold ministry of the Holy Spirit of God. The particular symbol of "seven lamps of fire burning" shows self-sustaining illumination. As the Holy Spirit in this church age acts in keeping with God's purposes of grace, He will act in the tribulation age in keeping with God's purposes of judgment. This holy One, not normally visible to human view, in the days of the Lord's ministry took the form of a dove (Luke 3:22), and when introduced in the age of grace is seen as cloven tongues of fire (Acts 2:3). This new symbol reflects this new ministry in the tribulation days. The lampstands (*luchnia*), which are oil-dependent, have been used of the churches (1:12). The word used here for "lamps" (*lampades*) would be more accurately translated "torches" and shows the self-sustaining testimony of the Holy Spirit as a divine person. The fourfold mention of "the seven spirits of God" in 1:4; 3:1; 4:5 and 5:6 furnish a comprehensive statement as to the work and function of the Holy Spirit in fulfilment of divine purpose on earth. It is for this reason that they are seen "before the throne". The Holy Spirit in the completeness of His ministry is the readily-available and responsive Executor of the throne.

Stretching out from the throne was a pavement that is described by John as a "sea of glass". The constantly moving sea is used in Isa 57:20 as the symbol of restlessness. Here all is at rest. No waves or storm can disturb the tranquillity of this sea. If the normal sea pictures the natural restlessness in the minds of men then this "sea of glass" must symbolise the purposes in the mind of God, which, fixed and eternal, form a secure base and solid foundation for all resting upon it. The common glass in John's day was generally cloudy and opaque so he adds a descriptive simile: "like unto crystal". This word describes rock crystal of perfect transparency and beauty; the throne would be reflected in this perfect transparent pavement. Some commentators relate this sea of glass with the "sea" in which the priests washed in the temple of Solomon (1 Kings 7:23). The comparison is more apparent than real. In that former "sea" the water reminded of needed cleansing as men approached God; here the "sea of glass" reminds men of the available security and rest in the presence of God. Moses as he approached deity saw "under his feet a paved work of sapphire stone and as it were the body of heaven in its clearness" (Exod 24:10). Ezekiel had a similar experience: "And the likeness of the firmament upon the heads of the living creature was as the colour of the terrible crystal, stretched forth over their heads above" (Ezek 1:22). In the OT visions no one was permitted to share the crystal pavement with deity, the persons of the Trinity were not as yet clearly distinguished; in this picture the Holy Spirit rests there. While the sea has no other occupants as yet, this book will show that before the end of the tribulation period this sea of glass will be filled with a host of redeemed ones (15:2). Their song will be reminiscent of that which rose on the further bank of the Red Sea as Israel came out of Egypt. The sob and sigh of a tyranny greater than that of Egypt, by that stage will have given way to the song of victory.

4. In the midst (*en mesō*) of the throne (vv. 6-8)

6-8 The final spatial remark centred on the throne is a double one: "in the midst of the throne and round about the throne". The idea seems to be a three-dimensional view with the four living creatures moving around the throne symmetrically. Alford has this idea when he shows that to John's eye they are so closely related to the throne that in their movements "They partly hide it, partly overlap it, being symmetrically arranged with regard to it – one in the middle of each side". The word "beasts" is a misleading translation of the word *zoa*. A better translation would be either "living creatures" (JND, RV) or "living ones" (Newberry). Possibly the clearest idea is conveyed by the translation "life forms" (F.C. Jennings). The word "beast" is better reserved for the translation of *thērion* (wild beast) as in 13:1.

These "living creatures" are often linked with the seraphim of Isa 6:1-6. Their attendance upon the throne, the fact that they have six wings and they cry, "Holy, holy, holy", lends some support to this identification. While there is seraphic character about the service of these living creatures the further descriptive terms make them more than simply seraphic guardians of the throne. The passage will also show that while they have features of angels they are to be distinguished from the angels (see 5:11). A better case can be made for identifying these living creatures with the "four living creatures" of Ezek 1:5-28 who bear the firmament upon which the throne of God rests. In Ezekiel's vision each living creature had four faces: the face of a man, the face of a lion, the face of an ox and the face of an eagle. In Ezekiel's vision the subject is the "glory of the Lord" (Ezek 1:28) seen in the providential control of events on earth. The cherubim there are symbolic representations of the agencies of the throne that bring to pass the purposes of God on earth. Here the living creatures are not seen as agents of the throne, but rather are worshippers who give "glory and honour and thanks to him that sat on the throne".

A further fact to be noted is that in three references (5:8, 11, 14) they are distinguished from the twenty-four elders. So they are neither angels, cherubim nor men. Some insist that because they speak and act and worship they must be men. This can hardly be so for the seraphim in Isa 6:1-6 also speak and act and worship. They have, in fact, none of the features indicative of resurrection or reward seen in the twenty-four elders.

Recalling the symbolic nature of this vision helps in the interpretation of the four living creatures. The redeemed of this dispensation are represented by the twenty-four elders, the Holy Spirit is symbolised by the seven lamps. The four living creatures must represent something seen universally (the meaning of the number four) on earth. The lion, the calf, the man and the eagle are the representatives of the wild animals, the domesticated animals, man and the birds. The living creatures thus must be actual living creatures who symbolise attributes of deity that are manifest in a living creation. The lion, as king of beasts unfolds majesty and strength; the calf or the ox manifests patience and submission; man reflects intelligence and service; the eagle shows keenness of sight and rapidity of action. Divinely-imparted life given to creatures manifests itself in different ways in the different life forms. These living creatures are therefore real creatures, but distinct from angels and seraphim, they symbolise the variety in creation that brings glory to God. The twenty-four elders are real men but they represent creation as created by God. All join in a symphony of praise.

If the living creatures use their wings as do the seraphim, then the service of God as anticipated in creation ideally is executed reverently (the face covered), with humility (the feet covered) and with celerity (they did fly). The expression "full of eyes" represents perfection of vision; "before and behind" indicates that nothing escapes their vigilance. The "within" of v.8 indicates perspicacity - they know all that goes on in the cosmos.

These living creatures who in their persons represent the living creation, worship unceasingly. "Day and night" is metaphorical language denoting continuation without interruption (Luke 2:37). It can scarcely be taken literally since in the presence of God there is "no night there" (22:5). Unwearying in their worship they ascribe to God absolute holiness (*hagios*): "Holy, holy, holy". They further ascribe to Him unqualified deity, "Lord God Almighty", and acknowledge His eternity, "which was, and is, and is to come". The cry echoes the seraphic adoration (Isa 6:3) touching the very personality of deity and acknowledges the absolute supremacy of One before whom all must bow: the Almighty. The title "which was, and is and is to come" echoes 1:8 and stresses the permanence of deity as compared to time-related creation. Time is simply an interlude that has been introduced into an eternity that belongs to this supreme One. The particular titles and terms used in the worship show that creation is particularly in view and these living creatures recognise the purity, the supremacy and the eternity of the One who fills the throne.

9-10 While worship is uninterrupted and unceasing it is clear that there are occasions when a crescendo is reached. When the living creatures give "glory" and honour and thanks – the repetition of the "and" builds to a climax. The living creatures worship the Throne-sitter as the supreme One; they recognise too that unlike them His life is underived. He is the living One – the self-existing One. This fitting tribute from worshipping representatives of dependent creation moves the twenty-four elders to a striking act of homage. The future tenses are dependent upon "when" and show that here the living creatures take the lead. The worship of God by His creatures is the subject, yet redeemed men necessarily share in this. The fuller worship in 5:9-10 is a result of redemption. Because of sin God's creatorial rights have been denied but they still exist and redeemed men acknowledge this in fellowship with creation itself. In the casting of the crowns before the throne there is an admission that they owe their victory and their consequent sovereignty to the One who sits on the throne. In the unfolding drama of the book they will be seen again to fall before the throne and worship at climactic points (11:16; 19:4) as they lead the praise rising to the Throne-sitter. Since no further mention is made of the crowns it would seem that they remain before the throne as a witness to its absolute sovereignty and to their adoring submission.

11 The textual emendation that allows the RV and JND to translate, "Worthy art thou, our Lord and our God" is worthy of note for it introduces a much more personal note from redeemed men than is heard from the living creatures. Their praise begins with "worthy" (see 5:9) and shows their appreciation of His person as the Source and the Sustainer of the whole cosmos. They repeat the worship of the living creatures (v.9) with one change of word from "thanks" to "power". The word "power" (*dunamis*) used here refers to the creatorial right of deity to act within history and bring it to its designed goal. In contrast the word power (*kratos*) in the doxology in 5:13 (JND translates "might" and the RV "dominion") defines the power of God to accomplish His sovereign will on earth. Creation is the work of God – "Thou hast created all things". The past tense points back to the moment when God spoke and brought the creation into existence. The "all things" is a scriptural term for the universe (Col 1:16-17) and embraces all the things created within the six literal days of Gen 1-2. This is the only creation period of which Scripture speaks. The reason for the very existence of a creation lies in the will of God. The RV makes this point clear: "because of thy will they were". The imperfect tense "were" defines present existence. Worship rises from creation to the Creator.

Notes

3 Some able commentators suggest that the twenty-four elders are "angelic administrators of the cosmos" (see particularly *Paul before the Aeropagus* by N.B. Stonehouse). This is argued on the basis that:

(1) the personal communication with John (5:5) suggests individuals and not representatives;

(2) their number is the pattern for the earthly national priesthood of Israel (1 Chron 24:3-5);

(3) the golden crowns show that they share divine glory; the use of the word *stephanos* (a victor's crown) and not *diadēma* (a royal crown) is explained by suggesting they belong to the group of "elect angels" (1 Tim 5:21);

(4) the casting down of their crowns before the throne (4:10) is the symbolic abdication of their authority in favour of the Lamb who is now God's administrator on earth;

(5) the critical text of 5:9-10 leaves out the personal note so that the inference is that these angelic administrators sing of redemption but do not share in it.

While the case appears formidable it is in fact very weak. The first four points have been answered fully in the comments on the text which show that the twenty-four elders must be redeemed men.

On the textual argument, even if the RV text of 5:9-10 is accepted, it still does not prove that these elders are angelic beings. There is, however, considerable scholarly doubt as to the reality of the textual variants accepted in the RV. For full discussion see comments *in loc*.

Of other possible interpretations of the twenty-four elders the only one worth consideration is a suggestion by H.M. Morris presented in his book *The Revelation Record* p.87. He proposes that since creation is in view in ch. 4 then the twenty-four elders are twenty-four heads of the human race beginning with Adam. He would take twenty-four of the leading names in Genesis. While this is interesting it makes an unnecessary division between ch. 4 and ch. 5; it fails to see the weight of evidence in connection with resurrection and reward and more fundamentally lacks any definitive scriptural support.

6-8 Rabbinical writers linked the four leading tribes of Israel as stationed round the tabernacle (Num 2:2) with the lion (Judah) , calf (Ephraim), man (Reuben) and the eagle (Dan). Other commentators link the four living creatures with Christ as presented in the four Gospels. F. C. Jennings p.178 writes, "Each of the four pictures we have of Him in the four Gospels portrays Him as one of these life-forms. In Matthew He expresses that royal majesty so perfectly figured in the king of beasts. In Mark we love to trace the patient path of the perfect servant, to picture whom God has made the young ox, ready alike for labour or sacrifice. Closer, and still dearer, does He come to us in Luke, looking into our faces with human eyes filled with compassion and sympathy; it is the face of a man. Till, finally, we fall in adoring worship at His feet as we follow Him in John's Gospel, where He, as it were, soars far out of sight of the merely natural eyes, and is indeed as a flying eagle!" It is not inconsistent with the interpretation of the living creatures given in the comments above to see these same features reproduced in Israel, the head of the nations, imperfectly reflected it is true, but reflected perfectly in Christ the "head of all things" (Eph 1:22). Glory is brought to the Creator.

CHAPTER 5

The chapter division disrupts the unity of this majestic throne-scene that provides the background in heaven for the unfolding drama of the happenings on earth during the tribulation period. The creatorial worship to God in ch. 4 and the redemptive worship of ch. 5 are both essential elements and each contributes to the understanding of this dramatic moment when the Lamb takes the book from the hand of God. Ch. 4 sets the scene while ch. 5 fastens on the action.

(b) *The Book - Search through the Cosmos (vv.1-4)*

v.1 "And I saw in the right hand of him that sat on the throne a book written within and on the backside, sealed with seven seals.
v.2 And I saw a strong angel proclaiming with a loud voice, Who is worthy to open the book, and to loose the seals thereof?
v.3 And no man in heaven, nor in earth, neither under the earth, was able to open the book, neither to look thereon.
v.4 And I wept much, because no man was found worthy to open and to read the book, neither to look thereon."

1 The scene is set for the action when John's eye is drawn to the book "in the right hand of him that sat on the throne". The use of the word "book" is an anachronism since books with individual leaves did not appear until early in the second century AD. The strict translation would be "scroll". The preposition "on" (epi) suggests that the scroll is not simply being held in the hand of the One on the throne but is lying upon the outstretched hand as if offered to one fitted to take it. It has been shown that this One who sits on the throne is God (see comments at 4:2).

The offering of this scroll by the One on the throne and its acceptance by the only One in the whole of the cosmos qualified to take it makes this action the key to the remainder of the book. It will be the opening of the seven seals of the book that will precipitate action on earth. As the seven seals are opened events occur on earth that show that heaven is interfering dramatically in earth's affairs. Then from the seventh seal come the seven trumpets and from the seventh trumpet come the seven bowls that bring the tribulation to a close and open the way for the millennial kingdom and the events to follow. It is therefore essential to understand clearly the meaning of this scroll.

Many commentators understand it as symbolising the revelation of God's purposes regarding earth. In other words they see it as a symbolic embodiment of "the things which must be hereafter" (4: 1) which John had been summoned to heaven to receive. F. A. Tatford writes, "The ensuing chapters make it clear that the book contained the record of the divine counsels concerning the world, the principles of divine government, and the judicial decrees which were about to be put into operation". On this view the tears of John (v.4) are to be understood as tears of regret that he is unable to view God's programme for earth. Advocates of this view contrast the sealed book of Dan 12:4 with this book now to be opened. As Christ opens the seals prophetic events are revealed.

A number of reasons make this view at least very unlikely. It does not explain:

1. why the book is sealed; the only sealed book in this context is the book of Dan 12:4 and it is not suggested that this is the same book.
2. why it is Christ alone who can open the seals on the divine programme since God has used men in the past to speak prophetically.

A more relevant point is that when the Lamb does take the book and the song breaks out, it is not a song celebrating revelation but a song celebrating redemption. Clearly the taking of the book is related to the redeeming action of the Lamb. This is why John weeps so bitterly, not because he is in danger of being denied details of things to come, but because he knows that should this book remain unopened the results of Christ's redemptive work cannot be realised on earth.

In the positive identification of this book two points need to be considered. The first is a somewhat unusual feature in that the scroll was "written within and on the backside".

It certainly does not suggest that the scroll was inadequate for all the writing and the extra material was written on the outside. Such a suggestion is unworthy of the dignity of a book in the hand of God. Some grammarians (see Zahn) have argued that the expression "on the backside" should be construed with the following verb to give the meaning "on the backside sealed with seven seals". While tempting and grammatically possible it has to be pointed out that this adverb in its seven occurrences in the NT invariably modifies the verb that precedes it which, in this case, is the verb "written". This fact gives a strong indication of the correct interpretation, for the writing "within and without" was characteristic of scrolls used in Israel's land-purchase system. The outer writing indicated the contents, very much like the descriptive title of a book in our time. R. Showers has written, "The fact that the sealed roll of Rev 5 had writing both on the inside and outside (v.1), in the same manner as Jeremiah's and other deeds of purchase in Israel's land redemption system, indicates that it is a deed of purchase". Of this same feature J.A. Seiss writes p.112, "This again tends to identify it with these books of forfeited inheritances. Within were the specifications of forfeiture; without were the names and attestations of the witnesses; for this is the manner in which these documents were attested".

The second point about the book is that it was "sealed with seven seals". Sealing was ordered for Daniel's book (12:4) but no mention is made of any specific number of seals. A more relevant passage concerns a land transaction by Jeremiah (Jer 32:6-25) where one copy of the deeds was sealed and one left open. Again no mention is made of the number of seals. E. Stauffer in his book *Christ and The Caesars* points out that Roman Law demanded that a will be sealed with seven seals. Two emperors, Augustus and Vespasian, left wills sealed in this way to be opened by their successors. The idea in the sealing is, to ensure that there has been no tampering with the contents since originally written. Alan F. Johnston in *The Expositor's Bible Commentary* provides an interesting cultural note: "Scrolls..... were sealed with wax blobs impressed with a signet ring to protect the contents or guarantee the integrity of the writing. Only the owner could open the seals and disclose the contents. Original documents were usually sealed, copies were not. Sealed documents were kept hidden while unsealed copies were made public".

There is no reference to the way in which the seven seals were attached to the scroll. The common inference that the seals were attached to the edge of the scroll in such a way that the scroll could be opened stage by stage as the seals were successively broken has neither contextual nor cultural support. The idea seems to have arisen to accommodate the principle of an unfolding revelation. Most authorities agree that a sealed scroll could not be opened until all the seals were broken. This has implications for the seal judgments. They would then be preliminary to the actual opening of the scroll. Perhaps the unrolling of that scroll and the scrutiny of its contents is implied in the silence of half an hour in heaven in 8:1; a silence perhaps linked to the fact that while the seal judgments have a providential character the trumpet and bowl judgments, which follow the unrolling of the scroll, display direct divine intervention on earth.

These identifying marks point clearly to the OT passage in Jer 32:6-25 as providing the background to this book. Jeremiah as the kinsman-redeemer to his cousin, in view of the impending Chaldean invasion, purchased a field. Two copies of the transaction were made and both were witnessed by trustworthy persons. One copy was sealed and the other left open. Both were carefully buried in an earthen vessel awaiting the day when evidence would be required to establish the rightful ownership of the land. The open copy would declare the rightful ownership but only an authorised hand could open the sealed copy and allow Jeremiah to enjoy the inheritance for which he had paid the price so long before.

It is clear that the principles operative with regard to land redemption in Jeremiah's day are but typical of a much wider fulfilment with regard to Christ and the earth. A kinsman redeemer in Israel and his portion of land pictured Christ and His portion – the whole of earth. Earth belongs to God by right of creation but He gave the tenancy to man (Ps 115:16) to be held for Him. Through sin man has lost his possession to a usurper (Satan) who has provided his own tenants. Now, through a Kinsman-Redeemer (Job 19:25), God has purchased this earth for Himself, a transaction completed at the cross in the price of blood (Eph 1: 7; Col 1: 14; 1 Pet 1:18-19). For all who wish to see the real ownership of the earth the evidence is in the open word of God. However the time has arrived for the sealed copy to be opened by the rightful Owner and the inheritance claimed. It is at this juncture that John sees the Lamb, as the only entitled One, move to take the sealed scroll from the hand of God. In the opening of the seals the Lamb will demonstrate His right to the possession of earth. That this will mean the dispossession of all the satanically-controlled usurpers will become clear as the further judgments fall upon earth. The book must, therefore, be understood to be the title deed of earth. W. Hoste writes concisely concerning this scroll, "It is the title-deeds of the purchased possession-the earth."

2 That the book is central to this drama is seen in the proclamation of the strong angel. The word "strong" would be better translated "mighty". Only on two other occasions is an angel so described and it indicates both the importance of the mission and the importance of the moment. The mighty angel appears here at the commencement of the tribulation period; in 10:1 one will re-appear at the midpoint of the tribulation, while in 18:1 another mighty angel will announce the crash of Babylon at the close of the tribulation. J.B. Smith identifies this angel as Michael who ordered the sealing of the book of Daniel. While interesting and possible there is nothing in the text to support this. The proclamation heralded (*kērussō*) by the angel echoes through the cosmos calling for someone worthy to open the book and to loose its seals. The verb "loose" is explanatory and shows the action necessary to open the book. The word "worthy" has just echoed in the praise of the beasts and elders around the throne as they worshipped God, "Thou art worthy"; now the cry is for one who shares that worth to step forward and take action as the agent of the throne.

3 As the echoes of this proclamation die away there is clearly a pause while the whole realm of the cosmos is scanned for one able to open the book. In heaven where John is, no one is found; on (*epi*) the earth, no one; under (*hupokatō*) the earth, not one. The verb "was able" describes the inherent weakness of all; they did not have the "power" to open the book. "Power" has been ascribed to the One on the throne. It is clear that only one who shares both the worth and the power of the Throne-sitter will be able to do this. Throughout the whole cosmos no one is found. The manifest weakness of all is developed by the second verb, neither "to look thereon". JND's translation of this latter verb is more pointed: "or to regard it". The idea seems to be that, disqualified from handling the book (take it), all are legally barred from scrutinising it.

4 There is now very clearly a dramatic pause, even a silence, in heaven as it becomes obvious that there is no one in the whole of the cosmos qualified to open this scroll. As the meaning of this lengthy pause dawns upon John he begins to weep. The imperfect tense would suggest that the tears flowed for some time. The verb "weep" (*klaiō*) implies an audible weeping, the sobbing of a broken spirit. This same verb describes the weeping of Christ over Jerusalem (Luke 19:4). Tears are peculiar to earth; to see a man weep in heaven is startling. The "much" tells something of the unhurried nature of the drama, the lengthening silence and the heartbreaking sobs. The cause of the tears, John explains, is the failure to find anyone to open the seals and unroll the scroll. A wider and more intensive search than that for Enoch (Heb 11:5) failed to find one worthy to take the scroll. All regions of the cosmos, terrestrial, celestial or infernal have failed to produce one with the moral fitness to claim the inheritance for God. The failure to find such a worthy one causes John to burst into tears. These tears show the inadequacy of the interpretation that sees this scroll as the record of future events. John is not weeping because he is denied an insight into the future. John "in the Spirit" (4:2) recognises that this scroll symbolises the title-deeds of earth. The one entitled to take and open the scroll must be the kinsman-redeemer (Hebrew goel) who had paid the purchase price. This legal document must be opened and read and acted upon if the inheritance of earth is to be reclaimed. John knew full well that if no kinsman-redeemer came forward then all that was in the "open" record (the Scriptures) must fail; the prophecies would remain unfulfilled, the promises would remain unrealised, the hope of the ages would never be enjoyed. It is no wonder he was moved to the very depths of his being as he saw that the usurper would remain in possession of earth and Satan would triumph. John's tears are an evidence that he grasped the solemnity of the scene.

(c) *The Lamb - Song in the Cosmos (vv.5-14)*

v.5 "And one of the elders saith unto me, Weep not: behold, the Lion of the tribe of Juda, the Root of David, hath prevailed to open the book, and to loose the seven seals thereof.
v.6 And I beheld, and, lo, in the midst of the throne and of the four beasts, and in the midst of the elders, stood a Lamb as it had been slain, having seven horns and seven eyes, which are the seven Spirits of God sent forth into all the earth.
v.7 And he came and took the book out of the right hand of him that sat upon the throne.
v.8 And when he had taken the book, the four beasts and four and twenty elders fell down before the Lamb, having every one of them harps, and golden vials full of odours, which are the prayers of saints.
v.9 And they sung a new song, saying, Thou art worthy to take the book, and to open the seals thereof: for thou wast slain, and hast redeemed us to God by thy blood out of every kindred, and tongue, and people, and nation;
v.10 And hast made us unto our God kings and priests: and we shall reign on the earth.
v.11 And I beheld, and I heard the voice of many angels round about the throne and the beasts and the elders: and the number of them was ten thousand times ten thousand, and thousands of thousands;
v.12 Saying with a loud voice, Worthy is the Lamb that was slain to receive power, and riches, and wisdom, and strength, and honour, and glory, and blessing.
v.13 And every creature which is in heaven, on the earth, and under the earth, and such as are in the sea, and all that are in them, heard I saying, Blessing, and honour, and glory, and power, be unto him that sitteth upon the throne, and unto the Lamb for ever and ever.
v.14 And the four beasts said, Amen. And the four and twenty elders fell down and worshipped him that liveth for ever and ever".

5-7 The weeping of John may be entirely natural and it is certainly in sympathy with the weakness of all creation when faced with the problem of redemption (Ps 49:7), nevertheless it stems from imperfect knowledge of what God has done and merits a rebuke from the elder. The imperative with the negative may be translated "stop weeping". The natural reactions of John amid supernatural scenes are interesting. Here he weeps, in 17:6 he wonders "with great admiration" after the woman on the beast and in 19:10 he would worship the angel. In each case he merits the implied rebuke of heaven as natural emotions cloud his spiritual judgment. It is significant that it is one of the twenty-four elders, and not an angel, who brings both rebuke and comfort to John at this point. As belonging to the church age (see 4:4) the elder is more capable than any angel of entering into John's feelings. Seen as raptured and changed he has also a much more complete knowledge than John at this point. His words of comfort point to the person of Christ and the work that He has done. Christ's person is set forth in two titles that link Him with the past and establish in Christ the messianic hopes of the ages. He is first "the Lion of the tribe of Judah'. This title is taken from the words of Jacob on his deathbed: "Judah is a lion's whelp: from the prey my son thou art gone up: he stooped down, he couched as a lion, as an old lion; who shall rouse him up?" (Gen 49:8-12). The mention of the lion in three stages of maturity makes clear two matters about the future ruler of Israel, the Messiah. First that this ruler would come from Judah - the lion tribe. Second - that He would be a man growing up to reach full maturity and the implied sovereignty in Israel. While stressing Christ's true humanity the emphasis lies in the majestic sovereignty invested in this One from the tribe of Judah. The second title, "The Root of David", is taken from Isa 11:1, "And there shall come forth a rod out of the stem of Jesse, and a branch shall grow out of his roots". The emphasis here is that His sovereignty over Israel is absolutely authentic. The wider application of this same title may be seen in Rom 15:12. Christ has human links with the royal house of David (Rom 1:3) so that in human terms David is His ancestor and He belongs to this royal line. While root (*rhiza*) may be taken in the sense of that from which David sprang the general usage of the word (see Thayer) rather demands that Christ came of his line as "the seed of David" (Rom 1:3).

The word in the AV order of the elder's announcement would allow a note of wonder (note "behold") at the uniqueness of the person of Christ; in Christ alone there is absolute sovereignty vested in a man; prophecy and history are joined in His person. However the word order in the Greek is more striking still; the first word after "behold" is "overcame" the aorist tense of the verb *nikaō*. It reads literally: "Behold, triumphed! conquered! the Lion of the tribe of Judah, the Root of David". The triumph must be the triumph of the cross which includes the resurrection and ascension. There can be no question that the only One in the whole cosmos fitted to take this scroll and open the seals is the mighty victor of Calvary. From this introduction it would be expected that John would now see Christ presented in all the glory of messianic sovereignty. As he did look ("I beheld") there is every reason for the repetition of the "behold" of startled surprise. It is true that the RV and JND omit the "lo" of the AV (omitted also in the Majority Text) but the context almost seems to require the exclamation of surprise. Instead of the expected lion John sees a lamb; instead of the evidence of conquest there are the marks of seeming defeat. He sees " a lamb as it had been slain".

6 Suddenly it would seem John's vision comes into focus. For the third time in the chapter he uses the verb "I saw" (RV), but that which fills his gaze is no longer the scroll (v.1), nor the mighty angel (v. 2), but a "little lamb" (*arnion*). The contrast with the lion could not be more dramatic. The word for "lamb" is used twenty-nine times in this book and only once (John 21:15) in the rest of the NT. The word in other NT passages (John 1:29, 36; Acts 8:32; 1 Pet 1:19) is *amnos* and denotes a "sacrificial lamb". Here it is clear that the sacrifice is over and this same lamb is now the executive of the throne. Expecting the lordly lion John sees the little lamb.

Throughout Scripture the lamb has been a recurring theme. From the sacrifice of Abel in Gen 4:4; through the inquiring question of Isaac, "Where is the lamb?" (Gen 22:7-8) and the experience of the Passover night in Egypt (Exod 12:2) to the clear statements of the prophet Isaiah (53:7): in picture, in promise and in prophecy the lamb has been central. Now the Lamb is standing in the midst of the throne, in the midst of the living creatures, in the midst of the twenty-four elders. The Lamb is central in this throne scene.

Three remarkable features set this Lamb apart from all others:-

1. "As it had been slain" describes an animal with the mark of its slaughter upon it; literally it would be possible to translate "with its throat cut". The LXX uses the same word in Isa 53:7. The word points to the wound left by the knife, that knife-wound familiar to all who had stood at an Israelitish altar and seen a lamb die. Yet this Lamb is standing; the sacrificial death is over and yet the victim lives! It presents in one picture the completeness and the value of the death of Christ. This living Lamb, while still bearing the evidence of death, will now be seen as the Kinsman-Redeemer acting to recover the inheritance for God and for man. The price has been paid and Christ as the Lamb is the only one in the cosmos fitted for this responsibility. The foundation of all that is to follow is the sacrifice and subsequent resurrection of the Lamb.
2. A horn in Scripture speaks of power but even more specifically of the power of a king (Zech 1:18). That this Lamb has seven horns stresses the perfection of the power of kingship vested in Him. The fact that the beast from the sea of 13:1 has ten horns speaks of the complete earthly dominion exercised for a time by this usurper. This Lamb with perfection of power will act for the throne of God. Symbolised in the horns are the sovereignty and the power to rule that belong to Him as the Lamb.
3. If the horns speak of divine omnipotence shown in the Lamb-King, then the seven eyes speak of divine omniscience inherent in Him. The "eyes" are more explicitly identified as "the seven Spirits of God sent forth into all the earth". This language is reminiscent of Zech 3:9 and more specifically of Zech 4:10, "They are the eyes of the Lord, which run to and fro through the whole earth". There is no further mention of the "seven lamps" of 4:5 which

have been seen (see comments *in loc*) as symbolic of the Holy Spirit in the fulness of His ministry. In this dispensation the risen Lord sent the Holy Spirit at Pentecost and that same Holy Spirit will conduct the church to meet her Lord in the air (1 Thess 4:17) at the rapture. Here it is indicated symbolically that in this tribulation period on earth after the rapture the Lamb will send forth the Holy Spirit again in the furtherance of His redemptive work.

7-8 The deliberate calm language of John but highlights the drama of the moment. The scene has been set and amid the silence of heaven the Lamb "came and took the book out of the right hand of him that sat upon the throne". This act governs all that follows in this book. The tense has been called by grammarian A. F. Johnston a "dramatic perfect" and explained as "He went up and took it and now has it". The symbolic implication is that the once-slain Lamb is now authorised by the throne to reclaim the alienated inheritance. The usurper is about to be dispossessed. When this book has been opened and the symbolic picture has been translated into reality the earth will be free from Satan and the programme of heaven will be complete.

The significance of this dramatic moment is recognised first by those closest to the throne, the four beasts and the twenty-four elders, who fall down in worship. As the song rises from the twenty-four elders, other voices join in the heavenly symphony. Many angels whose number is given as "myriads of myriads" (v.11) and "thousands of thousands" join the praise, until the swelling chorus rises from "every creature" (v.13) throughout the cosmos.

There are clearly three stages in this heavenly symphony of which only the first is directly called a song. The other companies seem to swell the worship with responsive harmonious chantings.

At the moment when the Lamb takes the book the four living creatures and the twenty-four elders prostrate themselves before the Lamb and give Him worship. That which in the previous chapter was given to God is now given to the Lamb; an incidental confirmation of the unity in deity of God and the Lamb. It has already been shown that the four living creatures have a dual role; they are actual creatures but represent symbolically the attributes of deity reflected in creation (see comments on 4:6-8). It has also been suggested that the twenty-four elders have a dual role too for they are individuals, yet they represent the church in its priestly office in heaven. The clear distinction between these two groups around the throne is seen in the fact that the living creatures have no thrones, they do not sit ("they rest not") and they are not crowned. The twenty-four elders are crowned, they have seats around the throne and their priestly character is seen in that they alone have each a harp and golden bowls. The twenty-four elders are described as "having every one of them harps and golden vials". "Harp" is singular and "bowls" are plural. The grammar is most readily taken as limiting the harp and the bowls to the elders only. JND's footnote is concise when he writes:

"'having' refers strictly only to elders". The word "harp" would be better translated as "lyre", the musical instrument familiar from OT scenes (Ps 33:2; 98:5) but now to be used for the "new song". There is no scriptural record of the lyre being used by spirit-beings either living creatures or angels. It is clear that redeemed men lead the praise. The "vials" find their origin in the familiar "bowls" of tabernacle days. As gold they were linked to the golden altar and hence the immediate presence of God. The implication of the bowls is not praise but petition. The word "odours" is the plural of the word "incense" (*thumiama* LXX). The heart of God is delighted with the "prayers of saints". The word for "prayer" (*proseuche-*) is the normal word for petitions directed to God. The prayers of NT saints have at this stage been answered in a general way; Christ has come and taken them home. Nevertheless there is still a large volume of unanswered prayer with regard to the establishment of the kingdom. The prayer "Thy kingdom come" (Matt 6:9) of saints in all the ages, and the urgent cries of tribulation saints, are presented now before the throne by the twenty-four elders. All these aspirations, cries and prayers are about to have their answer in the coming King. Mediatorial intercession in not in view in this action of the elders but sympathetic priestly presentation of the prayers of saints.

9-10 John has been occupied with the sight of the Lamb, and the smell of the incense; now the sound of the lyre conveys to his ear a song never before heard in courts above. Rising from the twenty-four elders the note swells until all creation is embraced:

v. 9	the twenty-four elders	singing (see RV)
v.11-12	many angels and the beasts and the elders	saying
v.13	and every creature	saying.

The "new song" presents two thoughts:

1. There was an old song linked to the physical creation referred to in Job 38:7, "When the morning stars sang together, and all the sons of God shouted for joy". The Hebrew poetic parallelism describes the creation of angels and the primal joy of creation. This would seem to be the first and last reference in Scripture to angels singing. Sin has robbed earth of its song. Now, in the consciousness of a redeemed creation, the new song rises from those enjoying the benefits of this great work; praise is directed to the Lamb.
2. In the Psalms a "new song" always denotes a fresh deliverance (Ps 33:3; 96:1; 98:1; 144:9; 149:1). New grounds for praise provide new notes of praise, something that may be seen particularly in Ps 40:3, "he hath put a new song in my mouth, even praise unto our God". There can be no

doubt that this new song is the fitting response to the mightiest deliverance ever wrought. The word for "new" (*kainos*) indicates that the song is not merely new in time but the very character of the song is different from all that has gone before. This song, of course, could not be sung prior to the cross but the point made here is that the taking of the scroll, signifying the completion of the redemptive work towards earth, is the signal for the singing of the new song. The song celebrates, not the power revealed in creation, but the person revealed through the cross. Through His blood the Lamb has won the right to take the book and act for God in redemptive power.

It is the Lamb who is celebrated in this new song. To Him the word "worthy", formerly addressed to the "Lord God Almighty" (4:11), is now applied. His "worth" in defined in terms of the sacrificial death that has fitted Him to take the book and open the seals. The results of the cross are seen in two verbs.

1. Thou "hast redeemed us" where the verb is not *lutroō* the usual word for "redeem" (1 Pet 1:18; Titus 2:14; Heb 9:12), but *agorazō* which lays emphasis on the purchase price to be paid in the slave market and is usually translated "buy" (RV "purchase"). Not only did Christ come down into the slave market but the price was high. The expression "by thy blood" shows the cost of redemption and points to the judicial value of the violent death of the cross. The preposition *en* is rightly translated as the instrumental "by". It was "by the means of", or "by the price of the blood". The purchase had the interests of God in view; from the unpromising "slaves of sin" men have been redeemed to God. The scope of this redemption is noticed in the all-embracive quartet covering the population of earth; this redemption brought men from "every kindred, and tongue, and people, and nation". While redemption was on behalf of all, the preposition "out of" (*ek*) indicates that not all men will enjoy the blessing of it. Nevertheless, there is not a culture, nor a country, nor a class of men where the value of this redemptive work will not be effective. The great host of the redeemed will include men from every nation and culture.
2. "And hast made us unto our God kings and priests". The RV is more accurate, "a kingdom and priests". A similar phrase is used on two other occasions in this book (1:6; 20:6). In 1:6 the emphasis in the context falls upon the persons redeemed, as objects of divine love they have been cleansed and fitted for the role of priests unto God. In 20:6 the emphasis falls upon the period that is particularly in view: "they shall reign with him a thousand years". Here the emphasis falls on the place where they reign: "and we shall reign on the earth". The redemptive purpose of God includes the transformation of men to share the

mediatorial reign of Christ in the millennial kingdom. The future tense in the verb "shall reign" supports this interpretation.

Some who have difficulty believing that Christ will reign literally with His saints on earth would translate the expression "over the earth" (see JND) perhaps linking this expression to the home of the bride in the New Jerusalem above the earth (21:2,10). The preposition is *epi* and this is certainly a possible translation. However it should be noted that every other time that *epi* is used in the chapter it must be translated "on" (as it is in v.1). The exact expression (*epi tēs gēs*) occurs fifteen times in the book and each time must be translated "on the earth"; to translate it "over the earth" would be either meaningless or absurd. Grammarians point out that when *epi* is used with the genitive case it always implies contact with the object named in the noun (see v.3 as an example). While admitting that grammar cannot always fix an interpretation it may be fairly deduced from this verse that Christ in His millennial reign on the earth will share that rule with His saints. While the home of the saints will be the city there is every possibility that in association with Christ they will have administrative duties on earth.

In reading the AV it is quite clear that the twenty-four elders share in the redemption of which they sing. This is sometimes used to sustain the interpretation that the twenty-four elders cannot be angels. A more difficult question is whether the expression "they sing" includes the four living creatures. Since the grammar is not decisive this must be decided on other grounds. In can be argued that as representatives of creation sharing the benefits of the redemptive work of Christ there is no reason why they should not sing this personal song. However some of the older manuscripts support the RV translation (also in substance that of JND), "Worthy art thou to take the book, and to open the seals thereof: for thou wast slain, and didst purchase unto God with thy blood men of every tribe, and tongue, and people, and nation, and madest them to be unto our God a kingdom and priests; and they reign upon the earth". It will be observed that the personal note of "us" and "we" is omitted; with this reading the four living creatures and the twenty-four elders therefore simply celebrate the fact of redemption without claiming a personal share in it. Most reliable textual scholars are quite sure that the insertion of "us" was a scribal amendment to give the verb "redeem" or "purchase" a definite object (see Bruce M. Metzger in *A Textual Commentary on the New Testament*). While there is weighty scholarship on either side it would seem that JND has some justification when he adds a footnote to his translation, "Many insert 'us' here .... I have ventured to leave it out". The textual argument has no bearing on the identification of either the four living creatures or the twenty-four elders. As shown above this has been established on other grounds.

11-12 Angels, who are distinguished from the four living creatures and distinct from the elders, now join in the chorus of praise. John's eye "I beheld" rises to the serried ranks of angelic hosts "round-about" the throne and his ear catches the swelling notes of praise. The preposition "round about" could be translated "encircling" to show the rising ranks of angelic beings. The expressions "ten thousands times ten thousand" and "thousand of thousands" are the normal Greek phrases used to describe an innumerable company. It would seem that the action of the Lamb in taking the book, followed by the prostration of living creatures and the song of the redeemed, triggers this note of exultation in a symphony of praise throughout angelic hosts. Thus the living creatures symbolising the attributes of deity seen in creation, the twenty-four elders representing redeemed men and angels, for the first time since the fall of Adam, are all harmoniously united in praise to the Lamb. The threefold acclamation of 4:11 based on creation is expanded to a sevenfold one (note "with a loud voice") based on redemption. The single article with seven nouns joined by the repeated "and" form a crescendo of praise. Power, riches, wisdom, strength, honour, glory and blessing are enduements suitable for One who has triumphed through the cross. For the third time in the chapter (vv.6, 9, 12) the ground of the triumph of the Lamb is emphasised. The One "that was slain" and as the Lamb, still with the marks of sacrifice upon Him, is the One entitled to receive those things that belong to deity.

13-14 This dramatic scene closes with another circle joining in the symphony of praise from all creation. Anticipative as it is, this scene is most moving as "every creature " from all regions of the cosmos joins in the accolade of praise to "him that sitteth upon the throne and unto the Lamb". Both creation and redemption are the manifestation of the greatness of God and the Lamb. The fourfold ascription of praise is the voice of all creation redeemed and restored responding to the acclamation of heaven. The repetition of the article with each note of praise points back to the former chants (4:11; 5:12); *the* blessing, *the* honour, *the* glory, and *the* might are ascribed to both God and the Lamb. In this universal chant of praise every creature joins anticipating the moment when every dissenting voice will have been silenced forever in this redeemed universe. Creation's groan is hushed forever; its travail forever gone (Rom 8:22-23). In anticipation every creature that has breath joins the heavenly anthem. That the cosmos is united is clear from the sweeping statement "every creature which is in the heaven and on the earth and under the earth and in the sea". This scene echoes ascriptions of praise rising from all creation in Ps 148:1-14, the middle psalm of the last five in the psalter, all describing a worshipping universe. When the last seal of this book is opened and the last judgment poured out on earth these psalms will express the worship to God and the Lamb.

The mighty anthem closes and the "amen" of the four living creatures is the response of a creation where God is now honoured through the Lamb. This is not only a prayer-wish, "may it be so"; faith knows that when God acts the cry is "it is so". The final note is fittingly the act of worship of the twenty-four elders. The majestic creatorial anthem, the ringing "amen" and the prostrate elders form a fitting background to the opening of the seals of the book and the unleashing of the apocalyptic judgments upon a rebel earth.

Notes

8-10 Some commentators have argued that when the RV reading on vv.9-10 is accepted this leaves open the identity of the elders so that they could be angelic beings. However, it has already been shown, on other grounds, that the elders must be redeemed men, they are clothed with white robes, they are crowned and they are seated around the throne - all facts that speak of redemption completed. Since their identity is established on other grounds the textual question has little bearing on the point. However some writers like Alexander Reese, who reject the pre-tribulation rapture, have seized upon the RV reading to deny that the church is in heaven at this point and to establish that the song is that of angelic beings celebrating the fact of redemption. His arguments are presented in his book *The Approaching Advent of Christ*. The certainty of a pre-tribulation rapture is fully established in many NT Scriptures and to introduce the textual argument here is irrelevant.

INTRODUCTION TO CHAPTERS 6-16

The dramatic throne scene of the two previous chapters has set the stage for the action in this section of the book. Christ as the glorified man (ch.1) walked in the midst of the lampstands which became the background for the messages to the seven churches (chs.2-3). Now Christ, as the once-slain Lamb, having taken the book from the hand of God, acts for the throne in the release of judgment upon earth. Christ is presented as about to deal with the usurper and claim His inheritance. In this section He will set in motion events leading up to the culmination of earth history. As already noted the scroll is not actually opened until the seven seals are removed. Thus the seal judgments are preliminary and largely providential. In general terms they involve matters like war, famine and death that have been operative throughout history but which will now be seen in more widespread and intense form. When the seventh seal is opened, the scroll is opened and the seven trumpets are blown; from the seventh trumpet come the seven bowls. This telescopic unfolding of these judgments climaxes when, after the seventh bowl has been poured out, the voice from heaven acknowledges, "It is done" (16:17), and the way is opened for the return of Christ to claim publicly His kingdom (19:11). History records how God has acted in literal judgments in past ages, the first cosmos was destroyed by the flood (2 Pet 3:5-6), Sodom and Gomorrah perished under fire and earthquake (Jude 7) and Egypt shuddered under the plagues. In this tribulation period the providential judgments of the seals but open the way for the out-poured wrath of heaven until earth reels under the blows.

For clarity of understanding a number of preliminary matters need to be addressed:

1. *The Ecclesiastical Question – The Place of the Church*

It has already been shown that John's introduction to heaven at the beginning of ch.4 opens the third section of the book, as outlined by Christ Himself, "the things which shall be hereafter" (1:19). It has further been shown that the expression "hereafter" of 4:1, must be interpreted as meaning "after the church age". Thus, while not explicitly stated, the rapture of the church at the close of ch. 3 is clearly implied and the "catching up" of John to heaven could well foreshadow this event. Other scriptures testify independently to the fact that the coming of the Lord to the air closes the age of church testimony on earth (John 14:1-2; 1 Thess 4:13-18; 1 Cor 15:51-53) and the twenty-four elders have been shown to represent the church in heaven.

In complete harmony with this interpretation is the fact that the church is not mentioned throughout this whole section. When Christ speaks to the churches in chs. 2-3 on seven occasions we have the appeal, "He that hath an ear, let him hear what the Spirit saith unto the churches". In 13:9 an identical appeal omits any reference to the churches: "If any man hath an ear let him hear". The church is not seen nor heard throughout the judgment scenes and reappears only under the figure of the bride of the Lamb in 19:4 just before Christ comes to earth. The only mention of "the churches" in the remaining part of the book is in 22:16 as those who will receive this completed revelation through John. Never once is it hinted that the church shares the troubles or the tears of earth throughout this period. Israel as a national entity is taken up again as the testimony for God on earth (7:1-8); the distinction between Jew and Gentile, no longer operative throughout the church age, is re-established and the characteristic word for saved ones is "saints" rather than "believers". The name used for deity is no longer "God and Father of our Lord Jesus Christ" but "God of the earth" (11:4), "Lord God Almighty" (15:3), "God of heaven" (16:11), terms reminiscent of OT days. While not conclusive in themselves, yet these facts are in keeping with the recognition that the church, with its special relationship to Christ, has been removed from the earth. An earthly nation and an earthly city are again at the centre of world affairs.

2. *The Prophetic Question – The Relevance of Other Prophecy*

Three related prophetic matters need to be considered in their relationship with this section of the book –

a. The relationship of this section with the day of the Lord.

The day of the Lord is an OT expression that refers, in a general way, to God's special interventions in the course of world history. In such a day in the past He delivered His people, judged His enemies and accomplished divine purpose in history, demonstrating that He is the sovereign God of the cosmos (Isa 2:10-22). His interventions in this way can be seen in the history of Israel when He acted in judgment on both Israel and the nations. He raised up Assyria to judge the northern kingdom of Israel in 722BC (Amos 5: 18-20), Babylon to judge Judah in 606BC (Lam 2:22; Ezek 13:1-5; Zeph 2:2-3), and Babylon to judge Egypt in the 6th century BC (Jer 46:10; Ezek 30:3). In these divine interventions on earth God did not act openly but used national and human instruments for His purposes.

It is clear from the OT that these divine interventions were seen by the prophets as but the foreshadowing of a future, unique, specific day of the Lord whose terrors and judgments would eclipse all those that had gone before. Thus Isaiah describes a day of the Lord in which God will rise "to shake terribly the earth" (Isa 2:10-21), language that finds an echo in this section (6:12-17) when the Lamb opens the sixth seal. Isaiah and Obadiah both describe a day of the Lord when God will bring widespread judgment upon all nations of earth (Isa 34:1-8; Obad 15) in words that are re-echoed in

9:20-21 when the sixth trumpet is blown. Joel and Zechariah refer to a day of the Lord, which involves gathering all the armies of earth around Jerusalem just before the Lord comes back personally to earth (Joel 3:1-16; Zech 14:1-15). These OT prophecies form the background to the outpouring of the sixth bowl (16:12-16) and the prelude to Christ's appearing in 19:11-21. This day of the Lord, while future to the OT prophets, finds its fulfilment in the judgments of this section of the book. Further study of the OT references also indicates that, as well as the "dark" side of the day of the Lord when God judges Israel and the nations, there is also what might be called a "light" side. After the darkness of Joel 3:1-16 when "The sun and moon shall be darkened, and the stars shall withdraw their shining" there comes a "dawn" illustrating a period of great blessing with the explanation that "The Lord dwelleth in Zion" (v.21). Thus a period of tribulation followed by a period of blessing, or a period of "darkness" followed by a period of "light", recalls that the Hebrew day has first an "evening" followed by a "morning" (Gen 1:4). So it is with the day of the Lord, the tribulation period is followed by the millennial reign and both ideas are included in the expression. In this section the action takes place in the unique and specific "day of the Lord".

R. Showers in this book *Maranatha, Our Lord, Come!* makes a valid distinction between the "broad" day of the Lord as encompassing the whole period from the rapture of the church to the end of the millennium, a period of over a thousand years, and the "narrow" day of the Lord as pointing to one particular day of twenty-four hours called "the great and terrible day of the Lord" (Joel 2:31). It would seem that the judgments poured upon earth, the gathering of the world's armies to Jerusalem and the cosmic disturbances in the heavenly bodies all lead up to the climactic moment when the Lord Himself will be revealed from heaven. This specific twenty-four-hour day is in view in Joel 3:9-16 and Zech 14:1-15; both of the scriptures find their fulfilment in 19:11-12.

This understanding of the day of the Lord, as a day of direct divine action, accords with the NT references to this same day (Acts 2:20; 1 Thess 5:2; 2 Thess 2:2; 2 Pet 3:10). The reference in 2 Thess 2:2 particularly makes it very clear that the day of the Lord does not begin until the church has been removed from earth. A majority of commentators see this day of the Lord as commencing at the signing of the covenant that marks the introduction of Daniel's seventieth week (Dan 9:27). However the wording of 1 Thess 5:2, "For yourselves know perfectly that the day of the Lord cometh as a thief in the night", suggests that the first public, direct divine intervention by God on earth is the rapture of the church, so that this event, and not the signing of the covenant, marks the commencement of the day of the Lord upon earth. The close of the day of the Lord is indicated in 2 Pet 3:10 as the passing away of the heavens and earth after the close of the millennium, and the introduction of the day of God.

b. The relationship of this section and Daniel's seventieth week

While the day of the Lord refers primarily to the nation of Israel the effects of this day touch all nations. This wider scope can be seen in the repeated references to "the earth" in the book of the Revelation, references which cannot be limited to either the land of Israel or the Roman empire. The "seventy weeks" prophecy (Dan 9:24-27) on the other hand is directed to the nation of Israel and describes a special period in their history. In a period of four hundred and ninety years, from a specified starting point, God sets forth a programme for this nation. The sixty-ninth week of Daniel's prophecy, marking four hundred and eighty three years (69 x 7) from its commencement, closed with the presentation of Christ to Israel as their King-Prince-Messiah on the 10th day of Nisan 32 AD when Christ rode on the ass into Jerusalem (Matt 21:6-9). The rejection and "cutting off" of Christ after the sixty-ninth week meant the suspension of the last week of the divine programme. In the interim period, between the sixty-ninth and seventieth weeks, there is the period of grace when the Lord calls out His church. In this way the history of the church falls prophetically between two feasts of Israel: the feast of Pentecost (the sending of the Holy Spirit to earth) and the feast of trumpets (the re-gathering of the nation) in view of the great day of atonement. The sounding of the trumpet at the rapture of the church (1 Thess 4:16; 1 Cor 15:52) heralds the home-gathering of the saints of the church dispensation, the removal of the church from their scene of testimony on earth, and thus opens the way for the recommencement of God's programme for Israel. Only the seventieth week of Daniel's prophecy awaits fulfilment and this must cover the last seven years before Christ's return to earth in glory with all His saints. Thus while there is no direct reference to Daniel's seventieth week it is clear that this section, covering the tribulation, must parallel that period.

Accepting the argument that this section corresponds to the seventieth week of Daniel it is to be noted that the first seal indicates the emergence upon the world stage of a man who will be shown to be the greatest deceiver of all time (6:1-2). This is the NT description of the "prince that shall come" (Dan 9:27), who proves himself to be this very arch-deceiver by the covenant he makes with the national leader of Israel. It may also be noted that the seventh bowl at the close of the section presents the greatest desolation of all time (16:17-21), a fitting tribute to this same deceiver who is called in Daniel's prophecy "the desolator" (Dan 9:27 RV).

This correspondence is further confirmed by the attention given to time-periods that must have as their background the seven-year period of "Daniel's seventieth week". This is seen with reference to the mid-point of the week thus:

11:2	"forty and two months"	three and a half years
11:3	"one thousand two hundred and three score days"	three and a half years
12:6	"one thousand two hundred and three score days"	three and a half years
12:7	"a time, times and half a time"	three and a half years

Whether the specific period refers to the first half of the week or the latter half of the week will have to be determined by the context of the passage. It would be an unjustifiable assumption to state categorically that they all describe the last half of the week. Daniel had already divided the week in this way and spoken of a point in the "midst of the week" when the deceiver would cause "the sacrifice and oblation to cease for the overspreading of abominations" (Dan 9:27). This critical mid-point of the seventieth week is also referred to in Dan 11:31; 12:11 and this last scripture gives a time link: "And from the time that the daily sacrifice shall be taken away, and the abomination that maketh desolate set up, there shall be a thousand two hundred and ninety days". This time period must be read in conjunction with v.7 in the same chapter, where the scattering of the holy people is to be for "a time, times and an half", clearly three and a half years or 1260 days at the end of which period Christ comes. (The additional thirty days marks a further stage in the establishment of the millennial kingdom). The mid-point of the week is thus seen to be at the three and a half year stage.

A further reference to this division of the week by the "abomination of desolation" is made by the Lord Himself in the Olivet discourse: "When therefore ye shall see the abomination of desolation, spoken of by Daniel the prophet, stand in the holy place" (Matt 24:15). This introduces the last half of the seventieth week when the Lord describes the events to take place in the last half of the week:-

Matt 24:16 "*Then* let them which be in Judea flee into the mountains"

Matt 24:21 "For *then* shall be great tribulation such as was not from the beginning of the world unto this time". (See Dan 12:1.)

Matt 24:30 "And *then* shall appear the sign of the Son of man in heaven; and then shall all the tribes of the earth mourn, and they shall see the Son of man coming in the clouds of heaven with power and great glory". This last point corresponds to 19:11-21 and marks the same end-point as the Lord's prophecy in the Olivet discourse and the seventieth week of Daniel.

c. The relationship of this section with the Olivet Discourse

Since the Lord spoke clearly of the great tribulation in the Olivet discourse (Matt 24-25) it would be anticipated that there would be a correspondence between that discourse and events in this section. The Lord spoke of events in the first half of the tribulation period in the Olivet discourse as "the beginning of sorrows" (Matt 24:4-8). That these events do bear a striking resemblance to events precipitated by the opening of the seals is clear from the following correlation of the prophecies:

1. Deception

The Lord, "For many shall come in my name, saying, I am Christ; and shall deceive many" (Matt 24:5).

Seal 1. The White Horse, "And he that sat on him had a bow; and a crown was given unto him: and he went forth conquering and to conquer". It will be shown in the comments on this verse that this picture presents the greatest deceiver and the greatest deception of all time.

2. War

The Lord, "And ye shall hear of wars and rumours of wars" (Matt 24:6).

Seal 2. The Red Horse, "And power was given to him that sat thereon to take peace from the earth"

3. Famine

The Lord, "And there shall be famines" (Matt 24:7).

Seal 3. The Black Horse, "And he that sat on him had a pair of balances in his hand. And I heard a voice in the midst of the four beasts say, A measure of wheat for a penny and three measures of barley for a penny".

4. Death

The Lord "And there shall be ... pestilences and ear thquakes in divers places" (Matt 24:7).

Seal 4. The Pale Horse. "And his name that sat on him was Death, and Hell followed with him".

From a study of these parallels it is evident that the same events are in view. This suggests that, while no time mark is given in the chapter, the action of the Lamb in opening the seals commences the tribulation period and, at the same time, opens the seventieth week of Daniel. The evidence for this latter deduction lies in the fact that while "the prince that shall come" has appeared on the world stage before this point his emergence as the world-leader may date from the signing of the covenant as the great peace-maker. What a deceiver he is! These prophetic comparisons are further strengthened when it is observed that the first half of the tribulation called by the Lord, "the beginning of sorrows ('throes' JND)" (Matt 24:8) also embraces a period of persecution when saints die for their testimony to Christ. The words of the Lord are clear: "Then shall they deliver you up to be afflicted, and shall kill you: and ye shall be hated of all nations for my name's sake" (Matt 24:9). This persecution is clearly in the first half of the tribulation since it precedes the "end" period that is introduced by the setting up of the "abomination of desolation" shown by Daniel to have been the mid-point of the tribulation. The Lord then goes on to speak of a further period of persecution which becomes more intense as the coming of the Son of man approaches (Matt 24:19-22). Thus the Lord clearly envisages a second group of martyrs from this second half of the tribulation.

These two bands of martyrs must be compared with what John saw under the fifth seal. John records, "I saw under the altar the souls of them that were slain for the word of God, and for the testimony which they held". These saints have died for their testimony in the first half of the tribulation. The further group of martyrs from the second half of the tribulation is envisaged in the comfort given to the souls under the altar: "and it was said unto them, that they should rest yet for a little season, until their fellow servants also and their brethren, that should be killed as they were, should be fulfilled" (6:11).

These correspondences show that the opening of the seals heralds the beginning of the tribulation period and, simultaneously, recommences God's programme for the nation of Israel as set forth in the unfulfilled prophecy of the seventieth week of Daniel's prophecy (9:24-27). On earth this period has commenced with the signing of the "covenant" between the two mighty political figures of earth seen later in this book as "the beast from the sea" (13:1-9) and "the beast from the earth" (13:11-18). The false prince and the false prophet as the puppets of Satan do not, of course, realise that in the signing of the covenant they are setting in motion a divine programme. Neither can these men know that the Lamb has just taken the book and judgment is about to burst upon earth.

Thus it is clear that the chs. 6-16 describe events in the seven year tribulation period which is the suspended seventieth week of Daniel's prophecy. The crisis point in the middle of the week, noted by Daniel (9:27) and by the Lord (Matt 24:15), is the moment when the "abomination of desolation" is set up in the holy place in the temple in Jerusalem. This moment will be shown in this section to take place when the image of the Beast is presented for the worship of men (13:15). This divides both the tribulation and the seventieth week into two parts as noted. This seven-year period is described by the Lord in the Olivet discourse (Matt 24-25) and is thus marked by exactly the same features.

3. *The Question of Sequence in the Series*

An over-all view of this section may help to show the sequential nature of the section if the parenthetic passages are set out as follows:-

Commencement	Christ taking the book	chs. 4-5
1. The Seven Seals	6:1-8:1 After the sixth seal is opened and before the seventh thus within the seals	 7:1-17 (Parenthesis 1)
2. The Seven Trumpets	8:2-11:19 After the sixth trumpet And before the seventh thus within the trumpets	 10:1–11:13 (Parenthesis 2) 12:1-14:20 (Parenthesis 3)

3. The Seven Bowls	15:1-16:21	
	after the seventh bowl	17:1-19: 10 (Parenthesis 4)
Consummation	Christ coming to earth	19:11

Having established that this section covers the seven-year tribulation period, corresponds to Daniel's seventieth week and correlates with the Olivet Discourse of the Lord, the major question remaining is the time sequence of the judgments. There is little disagreement amongst expositors that the seals follow one another in sequence and, therefore logically the events precipitated follow each other on earth. Not only do the ordinal numbers used suggest this, but the events themselves are clearly sequential, war leads to famine, famine leads to pestilence and pestilence to death. The same arguments show that the seven trumpets and the seven bowls follow each other in numerical sequence. The main argument has always centred on the relationship between the three groups of judgments, whether they are to be seen as simultaneous or successive.

As in so many questions related to this book the predilection of expositors for a particular method of interpretation often causes them to overlook the obvious inferences of scripture itself. Many expositors of the Topical school of interpretation (see Introduction) insist on the synchronisation of the three sets of judgments so that the seals and the trumpets and the bowls all run simultaneously, the trumpets being simply an intensification of the seals and the bowls an extension of the trumpets. Expositors like Lenski, Hendriksen and Alford favour this view. On the other hand most expositors of the Futurist school, with more logic and much sounder evidence, insist that the three sets of judgments follow each other consecutively.

The acknowledgement from heaven, "It is done" (16:17), closes the period of outpoured wrath upon earth in the tribulation period. The next event in chronological order is the manifestation of Christ and the destruction of the gathered armies of the Beast. The obvious sequential order of the section, while not conclusive, suggests very strongly that the seals, trumpets and bowls follow each other in time.

The order within the section does not suggest that the three sets of judgments are simultaneous. The seven trumpets do not repeat the seal judgments, and while the bowls do, in some respects, intensify the trumpet judgments they are sufficiently distinct to rule out any thought of their occurrence at the same time as the previous judgments. The evidence for simultaneity or mere intensification is totally missing. It is pointed out that:

(i) The seventh seal introduces no distinctive judgment but consists of the seven trumpets. On the opening of the seventh seal there is the silence in heaven for half an hour (8:1) and the very next statement presents the seven angels with the seven trumpets (8:2). Thus the seventh seal consists of the seven trumpets.

(ii) The seventh trumpet introduces no distinctive judgment but the temple in heaven is opened (11:19) from which emerge the seven angels bearing the seven bowls (15:5). Thus the seventh trumpet consists of the seven bowl judgments.

It is submitted that these facts show conclusively that the judgments of the seals, the trumpets and the bowls are meant to be seen as successive. However, a better word that successive may be telescopic. This would indicate that the trumpets open out of the seventh seal and the bowls open out of the seventh trumpet.

An overall picture of the three series of judgments is helpful in grasping the telescopic principle suggested. Thus:

The seven seals

Seal 1.	The White Horse	Person(s) who promote(s)	deception
Seal 2.	The Red Horse	Policies that precipitate	war
Seal 3.	The Black Horse	Prosperity that produces	famine
Seal 4.	The Pale Horse	Pestilence that brings	death

(One fourth of the earth affected)

Seal 5.	The Martyrs' Prayer	Persecution against saints	deliverance promised
Seal 6.	The Cosmic Display	Panic amongst sinners	doom pictured

Seal 7. Since no detail is given of any judgment under this seal, the seven trumpets are seen as the content of the seventh seal thus:

Seven Trumpets

Trumpet 1	Earth smitten	one third affected
Trumpet 2	Sea smitten one	third affected
Trumpet 3	Rivers	one third affected
Trumpet 4	Cosmos	one third affected

(One third of the earth affected)

Trumpet 5	Locusts	five month period
Trumpet 5	Horsemen	one third of men slain
Trumpet 7	Under the seventh trumpet the "temple of God" is opened 11:19) and from this opened temple issue the seven angels with the seven bowls (15:5-8). Since no other judgment is detailed for the seventh trumpet it is clear that the seven bowls are the content of the seventh trumpet. This may be shown thus:	

Seven bowls:

1.	Earth	cancer of the skin
2.	Sea	contamination of the sea
3.	Rivers	corruption of the streams
4.	Cosmos	curse upon the sun
	(All of earth affected)	
5.	Darkness upon the kingdom of the Beast	
6.	Euphrates dried for passage of armies	
7.	Cosmic disturbance and the earthquake	

From the diagram two important chronological matters may be deduced:

(i) that the sixth seal marks the mid-point of the seven-year tribulation and of Daniel's seventieth week. This means that the first trumpet begins the second half of the seventieth week, the period known as "the great tribulation (7:14; Matt 24:21). This chronology is supported by the fact that under the fifth seal John is allowed to see a company of martyrs who are told of another company to join them in a second period of intense persecution. This obviously anticipates the intensification of persecution (Matt 24:9-13) in the second half of the week. After the "abomination of desolation" has been set up in the temple the Lord clearly envisages a second company to die in testimony for Him (Matt 24: 15-23). It is likely that the death and resurrection of the two witnesses (11:7-12) mark this same mid-point of the week.

(ii) that the effects of the sixth seal, while beginning in the middle of the week with its panic-inducing terror, are reinforced by the sixth trumpet and then climaxed by the seventh bowl. This is suggested by the repetition of the earthquake theme in these judgments noted as follows:

Sixth Seal:	"And, lo, there was a great earthquake"	6:12
Sixth Trumpet:	"And the same hour there was a great earthquake	11:13
Seventh Bowl:	"And there was a great earthquake such as was not since men were upon the earth"	16:18

What was first seen under the sixth seal as direct divine intervention in the shaking of the earth, causing men to seek a hiding place from the wrath of the Lamb, is repeated and intensified under the sixth trumpet and finally climaxes in the greatest earthquake ever to shake this earth. This suggests that effectively, the seals, the trumpets and the bowls have all the same terminus in time – the terror of the earthquake under the sixth seal merging into the terror of the great earthquake of the seventh bowl, the movement of the armies under the sixth trumpet climaxing at the gathering to Armageddon under the sixth bowl. The common terminus is the coming of Christ to earth.

4. *The Interpretative Question*

Possibly the most critical issue in this section of the book is the question of whether the interpretation is to be literal or symbolic. Does an "earthquake", for example, mean a literal earthquake or is it to be interpreted as a symbol of some moral or political upheaval on earth.

As discussed in the "Introduction to the Book" all expositors come to the study with certain presuppositions which necessarily colour their interpretation. It has been further shown that the only safe method of interpretation is to use the same principles of interpretation in prophetic scriptures as are applied to all other portions of Scripture. The only sound approach for sensible interpretation is to allow the language of scripture to mean what it says, in fact to recognise that words are used grammatically and with the background culture in which they were first written. In the Gospels and epistles this gives an intelligent understanding of these scriptures and, if allowed, would give an equally intelligent understanding of prophecy. Amillennialism is the sad result of a refusal to treat prophetic scriptures in this straightforward way and apply the same degree of literalness to each statement as is applied to other scriptures. Many otherwise-very-clear expositors show a strange reluctance to allow Scripture to mean exactly what it says. This becomes very relevant in this section. Throughout the study it will be emphasised that, where it is possible, the statements must be interpreted literally. Where symbols are employed to convey the message the context will make this plain. The guiding principle will be that where the literal sense makes good sense no other sense is to be sought lest the result should be nonsense. Applied here, this principle give a very clear and sensible understanding of the judgments.

CHAPTER 6

The taking of the book by the Lamb and the opening of the first seal is the heavenly prelude to the commencement of the divine programme for the seven years of earth's history climaxing in the moment of Christ's return to earth (19:11). As shown in the introduction to this section this period is variously spoken of as "Daniel's seventieth week" (from Dan 9:24-26) or, more generally, as "the tribulation" with the expression "the great tribulation" reserved for the final three and a half years of the period (7:14; Matt 24:21). When this latter period refers to the nation of Israel specifically it is called "the time of Jacob's trouble" (Jer 30:7). The judgments resulting from the opening of the seals, will be shown:

1. to occur in the first half of the seven-year period,
2. to have a providential character, meaning that while war and famine and various pestilences have occurred in history, on this occasion they are distinguished by their scale and intensity, and
3. to be preliminary to the more dreadful judgments to follow in the trumpets and bowls. Only after the seventh seal is opened can the scroll be read (8:1) so that the trumpets and the bowls have a different character from the seals and are to be seen as direct judgments from the throne of God.

The first four seals reveal the well-known "four horsemen of the apocalypse". John offers no explanation of them and it is clear that the vision must be interpreted in keeping with the scriptural use of the symbol. Horses in Scripture speak of the forces in nature available for the benefit of mankind. However a horse always requires the firm hand of the rider for the harnessing of that power, which can be used for good or evil. These four horses therefore become the picture of natural forces which become channels of judgment. The variety in the colour of the horses is reminiscent of those in Zechariah's vision (Zech 1:8-17; 6:1-8), but while the OT horses patrolled the earth these horsemen are used in the punishment of earth. The different colours indicate the different agencies God will use. Worldwide deceptive philosophies (like communism) have ruined nations, terrible wars have ravaged continents throughout history, devastating famines have swept many lands and pestilences of various kinds have decimated populations. These things are not new. Yet at this point in history they are to be repeated on a scale history has never known. Men may call it providence but John is shown that it is the Lamb who, in the working out of the purpose of the throne, precipitates these happenings on earth.

It is possible to interpret the first horseman, on the white horse, as a person and many have done this. However, it is manifestly impossible to interpret the next three horsemen in this way. The fourth horseman on the pale horse is interpreted within the passage as death, this suggests that the horsemen are not to be interpreted as individual persons but rather as personifications – human figures symbolising either principles or powers. The symbol of the horseman (horse and rider) thus presents in symbol form the power of deception (the white horse), the power of war (the red horse), the power of famine (the black horse) and the power of death (the pale horse). These are successively released to wreak havoc as they sweep through the earth.

2. *The First Six Seals Opened*
6:1-17

v.1 "And I saw when the Lamb opened one of the seals, and I heard, as it were the noise of thunder, one of the four beasts saying, Come and see.
v.2 And I saw, and behold a white horse: and he that sat on him had a bow; and a

crown was given unto him: and he went forth conquering, and to conquer.
v.3 And when he had opened the second seal, I heard the second beast say, Come and see.
v.4 And there went out another horse that was red: and power was given to him that sat thereon to take peace from the earth, and that they should kill one another: and there was given unto him a great sword.
v.5 And when he had opened the third seal, I heard the third beast say, Come and see. And I beheld, and lo a black horse; and he that sat on him had a pair of balances in his hand.
v.6 And I heard a voice in the midst of the four beasts say, A measure of wheat for a penny, and three measures of barley for a penny; and see thou hurt not the oil and the wine.
v.7 And when he had opened the fourth seal, I heard the voice of the fourth beast say, Come and see.
v.8 And I looked, and behold a pale horse: and his name that sat on him was Death, and Hell followed with him. And power was given unto them over the fourth part of the earth, to kill with sword, and with hunger, and with death, and with the beasts of the earth.
v.9 And when he had opened the fifth seal, I saw under the altar the souls of them that were slain for the word of God, and for the testimony which they held:
v.10 And they cried with a loud voice, saying, How long, O Lord, holy and true, dost thou not judge and avenge our blood on them that dwell on the earth?
v.11 And white robes were given unto every one of them: and it was said unto them, that they should rest yet for a little season, until their fellow servants also and their brethren, that should be killed as they were, should be fulfilled.
v.12 And I beheld when he had opened the sixth seal, and, lo, there was a great earthquake; and the sun became black as sackcloth of hair, and the moon became as blood;
v.13 And the stars of heaven fell unto the earth, even as a fig tree casteth her untimely figs, when she is shaken of a mighty wind.
v.14 And the heaven departed as a scroll when it is rolled together; and every mountain and island were moved out of their places.
v.15 And the kings of the earth, and the great men, and the rich men, and the chief captains, and the mighty men, and every bondman, and every free man, hid themselves in the dens and in the rocks of the mountains;
v.16 And said to the mountains and rocks, Fall on us, and hide us from the face of him that sitteth on the throne, and from the wrath of the Lamb:
v.17 For the great day of his wrath is come; and who shall be able to stand?"

The First Seal – The White Horse (vv.1-2)

1-2 The drama of the scene is striking. John says "I saw" and, as the Lamb opens the first seal he adds "and I heard", as if the seeing and the hearing were virtually simultaneous. The word order in Greek demands that the thunder describes the voice of the living creature as in the RV "saying as with a voice of thunder". This thunderous voice of the living creature cries, "Come". While a few older manuscripts add the words "and see", the weight of textual evidence suggests they are a scribal interpolation; JND writes, "The words 'and see' here and in vv. 3,5 and 7 are very doubtful". This summons is not to John but to the horseman, as if he had been standing in the wings awaiting the signal to enter the stage. The first century analogy of the stage-manager of the amphitheatre summoning the charioteers may not be irrelevant. While the living creature is not identified and is not of significance the order in which the living creatures are identified in 4:7 might suggest that this first is the one "like a lion". The repetition of the verb "I saw" followed by the exclamation of surprise "behold" shows how startled John was at the sight of the white horse with its bow-carrying rider.

Some commentators insist that this rider must be interpreted as Christ (W. Hendriksen gives seven reasons why this must be so) drawing attention to the white horse at the return of Christ in 19:11. Others see in the rider the progress of the gospel throughout the tribulation period and the references to gospel preaching in the Olivet discourse (Matt 24:14). A little consideration will show that neither of these interpretations is valid. The only point of correspondence between this rider and Christ in 19:11 is the white horse. The white horse is simply a symbol of a victorious warrior but says nothing about the rider. In this passage the rider wears a victor's wreath (*stephanos*) and carries a bow while in the later chapter Christ is crowned "with many crowns" (*diadēma*) and has a sharp sword proceeding from His mouth. These two warriors are not to be compared but contrasted. Since Christ as the Lamb opens the seals, to understand Him as riding forth at the command of the living creature is neither logical nor sensible. F.C. Jennings puts the matter concisely, "The whole context and character of these seals absolutely forbid one thinking of this rider as the Lord Jesus, as so many affirm. His reign will not bring war and strife in its train". Since the four horsemen are clearly meant to be of the same general character this first one cannot represent the victory of the gospel since war, famine and death follow him. Other commentators identify this horseman with the "prince that shall come" (Dan 9:26), the mighty western prince whose covenant with Israel's leader, the false prophet, commences the seventieth week. F.A. Tatford writes p.86, "It is far more probable, however, that the reference is to the rise and career of a mighty imperial ruler after the rapture of the church who brings under his sway a vast territory in an endeavour to maintain peace, order and prosperity". This is a possible interpretation and has much to commend it. Two matters, however, give cause for reconsideration. One is the time factor. If the argument is correct that has linked the opening of the seals with the commencement of Daniel's seventieth week, then the "prince that shall come" is already a world figure able to guarantee a peace covenant with Israel. In this sense his major victories are behind him. This hardly fits with the dramatic appearance here as a result of the action of the Lamb in opening the seal. Further, the description shows that while he has victories behind him (the crown given) greater conquests lie ahead. Since Scripture must be interpreted with consistency a problem arises if this horseman is to be seen as a literal person. It would be consistent, in this case, to interpret the horsemen to follow in the same way and this would be very difficult if not impossible. The answer, as suggested in the introduction, is that the four horsemen be interpreted as personifications of powers or forces released by the Lamb as preparatory judgments on earth.

In light of the above discussion, this horseman should be seen as the personification of the spiritual deception that will engulf mankind as the great peace treaty is signed between the "prince that shall come" (Dan 9:26) and the "many" of the nation of Israel led by the false prophet. The very signing of the peace treaty may well be the satanic stimulus for the deception that sweeps the earth. This mighty leader will be hailed as "the man", "the conqueror", "the victor" for whom mankind has waited; he alone has been able to solve the Middle-East problem where so many have failed in the past. The seven-year covenant is his great triumph in the field of diplomacy. This promotes the greatest deception ever presented to men, this is "the man" for whom the world has waited for centuries. Doubtless this is the basis of the "lie" or "what is false" (2 Thess 2:11 JND) which is a divine judgment upon those who have rejected Christ. Throughout the centuries the multitude of "isms" that have darkened men's minds, such as liberalism, communism and humanism, are all the result of the word of God rejected. This final dark philosophy, personified in the rider on the white horse, is the darkest and deadliest of all satanic philosophies. This understanding of this first horseman is in keeping with the Lord's warning in Matt 24:4-5, "Take heed that no man deceive you. For many shall come in my name, saying, I am Christ; and shall deceive many". The peace treaty, cleverly engineered, gives this deceiver a prominence that opens the way for the worldwide propagation of this satanic deception.

The other details of this horseman fill out the picture of the great deceiver and the worldwide deception centred on his person. In the OT the bow symbolises military power (Hos 1:5; Jer 51:56; Ezek 39:3) and generally power in the hand of an enemy of God. In contrast to the sword the emphasis is on conquest at a distance. Walter Scott writes p.147, "Hand-to-hand conflict demands the use of the sword, a little distance off the spear would be required; while more distant warfare is expressed by the bow. This latter weapon would not do much execution; hence its employment as a symbol of war afar off, and that not of a very deadly character". This agrees with the picture of a philosophy or a belief, which through the news media spreads over and largely conquers the earth. Attention has often been drawn to the absence of any mention of arrows which, some suggest, indicates a bloodless victory. The crown (*stephanos*) is generally a victor's garland but was frequently used in Roman times to depict imperial rule (see R.C. Trench on *stephanos*) and points back to the previous conquests of this deceiver when, step by step, he has subdued nation after nation. Both military conquests and bloodless coups are likely envisaged in Dan 7:8 as this man reaches the upper echelons of world rule. In military might, diplomatic skill and financial wizardry he outranks the greatest figures from world history; here however it is his propaganda machine that brings nations under his sway believing that he is "the man". The fact that a crown "was given" (aorist tense) suggests that this was subsequent to his arrival, with the aorist tense referring to the spectacular signing of the much heralded peace treaty. This promotes his person and his emperor-cult on the world stage. "White" is traditionally associated with peace in every culture and this man is presented as the greatest peacemaker the world has ever seen. The passive voice leaves open the question of who gives the rider the crown. Men will have their explanations but the simple truth is that God permits it for His own purposes. The final statement summarises the further progress of the deception. The confidence placed in this mighty man is seemingly irresistible. JND translates, "he went forth conquering and that he might conquer". While not excluding military conquest it is more in keeping with the symbol and context to see in the statement the conquest of the minds of men. In the later stages of the tribulation this deception crystallises into full-orbed worship of a man as portrayed in 2 Thess 2:3-4.

The Second Seal – The Red Horse (vv.3-4)

3-4 As the second seal is broken by the Lamb the second living creature (the calf-like one, 4:7) issues his command to the second horseman, "Come!" In response another horseman appears on a "red" or "fiery" horse. It is to be noted that the introductory expression used with the other horses "I saw and behold" (vv.2,5,8) is missing, and that the adjective "another" is used only with this horse. These facts suggest that the two horses are closely linked as if they must go together. This is logical when the colours are considered; white in any culture denotes peace while red speaks of war and, as in 2 Kings 3:22-23, can denote slaughter. This is the colour of the dragon (12:3). The same aorist tense "it was given" (RV) as was used of the first horseman, indicates divine permission for providential happenings to take their course. The AV interprets the "it" as "power" which is a reasonable deduction as defining the right granted to this horseman. The repetition of "him" does not demand that the horseman be an individual, it is simply the grammatical way of developing the personification of an abstract power. The purpose of the power granted to him is "to take peace from the earth and that they should slay one another" (JND). "Slay" is a more graphic and more accurate translation of the verb *sphazō* than "kill". What is depicted is worldwide turmoil with state pitted against state and nation against nation. The symbol of authority given to the rider was "a great sword". Used by the Roman legions, this short sword was the symbol of might throughout the empire, and to the conquered a symbol of violence and death.

Hailed as a messianic figure the great peacemaker will be the centre of a worldwide cult of deception, virtually a religion even at this stage. News media controlled by state governments will promote the personality cult of this world-renowned figure. The result will be that nations will admire him or hate him. The inevitable outcome will be that of which the Lord spoke, "For nation shall rise against nation, and kingdom against kingdom" (Matt 24:7).

While some regimes will be prepared to accept this deceptive cult of "emperor-worship" others will not, a fact seen in the cult of emperor-worship in the old Roman empire. It is reasonable to assume that at least Judaism and Islam will resist to death such a claim, while apostate religion alone seen in the harlot (17:3-6) will give whole-hearted support to his claims. Tensions and conflict will give rise to war and bloodshed. International friendship and world tranquillity will soon disappear and strife will set nation against nation; war on an unprecedented scale will ravage the earth

.

The Third Seal – The Black Horse (vv.5-6)

5-6 The opening of the third seal allows the third living creature (according to the order of 4:7 the one "like a man") to summon the third horseman. This time the horse is black, a colour that both scripturally (Lam 5:10; Jer 8:21) and culturally is always associated with mourning. In Lam 4:4-8; 5:10; Jer 14:1-2 this colour is closely linked with dearth and famine. Instead of a bow or a sword this horseman holds a balance in his hand. This symbol was on the official badge of Roman praetors and indicated the administration of justice. When used with food "a balance" (RV) implies a shortage which requires rationing. God warned Ezekiel, "I will break the staff of bread in Jerusalem, and they shall eat bread by weight, and with care; and they shall drink water by measure, and with astonishment" (Ezek 4:16). F.A. Tatford suggests very reasonably that the figure may indicate a general system of rationing. The fact that the voice setting the scale of the rations comes from the midst of the four living creatures (used by metonymy for the throne) suggests that famine conditions are universal and that all nature is involved. A penny was the *denarius*, a small silver coin, generally in the Lord's time a labouring man's wage for the day (Matt 20: 1-16). This would purchase only a "measure" (*choenix*) of wheat, a dry measure equalling about two pints. One person could live on this ration, so the implication is a day's wage for a day's food. Clearly there could be no provision for families or for the support of elderly dependants. For the same price three measures of the cheaper and less sustaining cereal barley could be purchased. At the end of the first century a penny would have purchased about eight measures of wheat and twenty-four measures of barley; what is pictured is an escalation in the cost of living due to shortage of basic food-stuffs. The final note regarding the oil and wine adds a crushing blow on those struggling to survive. At the close of the first century the Roman empire was struggling with a desperate shortage of wheat and other staple foods; the delay of one grain ship from Egypt bound for Rome could spark riots in the capital, but there was no shortage of wine. In fact around Philadelphia on the Phyrgian plain the farmers were ordered by the emperor Domitian (92AD) to replace the vineyards with wheat fields. Olive trees and vines often survived the devastation suffered by the arable crops when an invading army passed through. It is a mistake to regard the oil and the wine as luxuries; they were absolutely essential to normal living. Oil and wine were not regarded as luxuries even in the OT as may be seen in Deut 7:13; Hos 2:8, 22. The oil was for cooking, lighting, washing (equivalent to soap) and healing (ointment) and the wine, in the absence of safe drinkable water, was the normal drink with meals. The blow for men is that, while still available, they had to be sacrificed to maintain life; there was no money to buy them. Inflation had devalued work and wages so that life, under this seal judgment, becomes a struggle to survive. In this symbol is shown not simply famine conditions, for there would seem to be enough food available, but the blighting of a prosperity to which most of the world, and particularly the western world, has become accustomed. With raging inflation and the whole working life devoted to getting a survival wage the prosperous nations are faced with unprecedented economic collapse. The picture is not meant to focus on the drought-ridden lands of third-world countries so familiar today, but inflation-ridden lands where economies have been mismanaged, prices have soared and prosperity vanished. In the search for survival, family life disintegrates and law and order disappear.

It is clear that the order of the horsemen indicates the succession of events that beset the earth as the Lamb opens the seals. First there is the blasphemy that gives to a man the place men refused to Christ. The consequences of this are the conflicts that rage across earth as men accept or reject these claims. These wars, very likely including trade bans and boycotts, result in devastated countries, in destroyed economies and the famine conditions seen under this black horse.

The Fourth Seal – The Pale Horse (vv.7-8)

7-8 With the opening of the fourth seal the fourth living creature (according to the order in 4:7 the one "like a flying eagle") summons the fourth horseman. John introduces what he sees with the exclamations, "And I looked, and behold" (vv.2, 5), indicating startled surprise. This horse is a sickly, pale, greenish hue (*chlōros*) that is generally associated with the pallor of a dead body or the blanched appearance of a person struck with terror. With hardly time to take in this ghastly colour John has no problem in recognising the rider and names him as "Death", confirming that the horsemen are to be seen not as identifiable persons but as personifications. This rider differs from the others in that he has a companion who "followed with him", the preposition "with" (*meta*) suggesting that he accompanied rather than followed the horseman. Wherever Death rides this inseparable stirrup-companion is with him. To this stirrup-companion John gives the name "Hell". Death and hell have been linked in 1:18 as the power (death) and the place (hell) over which, through His resurrection, Christ has absolute authority (the keys), so that for the believer these ancient enemies now hold no terror. The final reference to this unsavoury pair is in 20:13-14 where the lake of fire is shown to be their ultimate destiny. At this period by divine permission they are permitted to ride unrestrained over the earth.

The AV and the RV both translate the next sentence in this verse "power was given unto them", as if Death and Hades both had authority over the fourth part of men. Some commentators have found difficulty in this, pointing out that only death could have authority over living men. W. Scott finds a solution in the reading of JND: "power was given unto him" and writes p.152, "The reading 'him' or 'them' is disputed, but internal evidence would decide. Death acts upon living men. Hades claims the souls of the dead. Death necessarily precedes Hades. Death deals with the living, Hades deals with the dead". However, it should be said that the weight of textual evidence is on the side of the AV. This suggests a possible alternative interpretation favoured by many older commentators, of whom possibly J.H. McIlvaine is the best known. He sets this out in his book *The Wisdom of the Apocalypse* (1886) and suggests that this closing statement should be read by itself as a summary of the result of the activities of the four horsemen seen as a group. The "them" to whom authority is given are the four horsemen together and the sphere of their action covers a fourth part of the earth. Earth must be seen as a whole and there is no justification for limiting it either to the land of Israel or to the boundaries of the Roman Empire; neither of which is even envisaged in the context. The "fourth part" would seem to be descriptive of the area where these horsemen are permitted to ride and, at the same time, implies divine limitation of their actions. The power granted to these horsemen is to kill (*apokteinō*); they do this in four different ways: they do it with the sword, clearly a reference to the *red horse*; they do it with the famine, clearly a reference to the *black horse*; they do it with death, clearly a reference to the *pale horse*. The fourth way in which the horsemen kill is described as "with the beasts of the earth". The word "beasts" (*thērion*) must be translated "wild beasts". The usual explanation is given by F.A. Tatford "A widespread scarcity of food and correlative malnutrition are in their turn, productive of disease and plague. The depopulation caused by war, famine and pestilence ultimately causes the wild beasts to prey upon men". While this is a perfectly feasible explanation it seems a little far-fetched and appears to overlook several relevant points. When the terms used in the whole picture are symbolic, even the horses, there does not seem any weighty reason why literal wild beasts are introduced at the end of the list. The preposition used before the "wild beasts" is not *en* ("by") but *hupo* ("under") which stresses that they are but instruments or agents. It is also important to note the article before "wild beasts". It is suggested in light of this evidence that the "wild beasts" are not literal beasts but men who are to be so described in ch.13: "and saw a beast (*thērion*) rise up out of the sea" (v.1); "And I beheld another beast (*thērion*) coming up out of the earth" (v.11). It is through the agency of these men of beastly character that the fourth horseman on the *pale horse* accomplishes his task of killing men. If it be argued that this anticipates later revelation, it can be pointed out that often in this book matters are introduced as simple statements and left for fuller explanation later. This was pointed out in 2:11 with reference to the "second death". This elliptical reference to "the wild beasts" awaits the fuller details of ch.13.

These four horsemen, called into action at the very beginning of the tribulation period, are never recalled. It would seem that the blasphemous philosophy associated with the worship of a man under the white horse, the belligerent policies that lead nations into war under the red horse, the baneful blight experienced under the black horse, all culminate in the pale horse and his stirrup-rider rampaging over a quarter of earth to the very end of the tribulation. If one fourth part of the earth is directly affected by these judgments the death toll must be very high indeed. While the text does not state that one quarter of the population of earth will die there is no doubt that death will ride triumphantly across earth in these dark days of the tribulation. Earth's population is around six billion (1996) and for a quarter to die would mean that 1500 million souls would perish; in the words of J. F. Walvoord this would "represent the greatest destruction of human life ever recorded in history" p.131. For comparison it might be pointed out that the Second World War claimed over 50 million lives. The Lord's solemn words come to mind: "And except those days should be shortened, there should no flesh be saved" (Matt 24:22). If this is but the "beginning of sorrows" (Matt 24:8) then earth has much to endure in the night of her travail.

The Fifth Seal (vv.9-11)

9 The seven seals are divided into two groups of four and three, a feature that will be repeated in the seven trumpets and the seven bowls. The first four seals have been connected with the four living creatures who, when the seals were opened by the Lamb, summoned the four horsemen to appear. This fifth seal is strikingly different; it reveals to John an altar in heaven beneath which he sees the souls of the martyrs. The idea of heaven being God's temple is a theme of Scripture (Hab 2:20) and will be developed later in the book (11:19; 15:5; 16:17). The altar is not identified as to whether it is the brazen altar or the golden altar of incense, but the mention of "blood" in the cry of the martyrs as well as the expression "under the altar" point to it being the brazen altar. John's eye is drawn to the very place where the blood of the sacrificial victims would have been poured out (Exod 29:12; Lev 4:7), "underneath" (*hupokatō*) the altar. The pouring out of the blood indicated the completion of the sacrifice and signified that a life was poured out (Lev 17:11). Instead of blood John sees souls and the fact that they were underneath the altar is a figurative way of saying that from heaven's viewpoint their untimely deaths are seen as a sacrifice upon God's altar. These saints had died on account of (*dia*) the word of God; in the context this means their adherence to its truth; and on account of (*dia*) their testimony. While this includes the testimony they bore to Christ, the primary emphasis in the verb "held" (*echō*) is the testimony they received from Him (as in 12:17; 20:4); to this they remained faithful. The fact that they were martyrs and had died violent deaths is implied in the verb "slain" (*sphazō*, the participle of the same verb is used of Christ, 5:6). What men had done to Christ they had done to those who had remained faithful to the testimony received from Him.

Two considerations rule out any possibility of these saints belonging to the age of church testimony. First it has been established on other grounds that the church age closed at the end of ch. 3 with the rapture of the saints foreshadowed in the catching up of John to heaven. The twenty-four elders have been shown to represent the church in heaven. These martyrs must therefore have been put to death in the period between the rapture of the church and the mid-point of the tribulation period, specifically in the first three and a half years of the period. It has already been pointed out that the Lord in the Olivet discourse indicated that saints would suffer and die at this very time: "Then shall they deliver you up to be afflicted, and shall kill you: and ye shall be hated of all nations for my name's sake" (Matt 24:9-14). This will be the period when the four horsemen will be rampaging over earth. Individuals who, because of their obedience to the word of God and their faithfulness to Christ, will not accept the creed of the great deceiver, will suffer persecution and death. It is the souls of these martyrs that are seen by John under the altar. How these became believers will be seen in ch. 7.

10 The second consideration that indicates very clearly that these souls do not belong to the church age is the fact that their cry does not rise to the "Father" with the intimacy of family relationship known by believers in the church age, but to God as "Master" (RV) or "Sovereign Ruler" (JND), both of which translate the title *Ho Despotēs*. That title denotes ownership and is used of the owners of slaves in 1 Tim 6:1; 1 Pet 2:18. It is reminiscent of the Psalms and OT days in general (but note its use in Acts 4:24 where believers are being persecuted) and is more suitable to the age in which the everlasting gospel (14:6) will be preached anticipating the coming King. There is no doubt that these martyrs belong to the first half of the tribulation period. Confirmation of this conclusion comes from the content of the prayer. The cry of Stephen, the first martyr of the church, was, "Lord (*kurios*), lay not this sin to their charge" (Acts 7:60); a prayer-cry on the pattern of the Lord Himself who prayed, "Father, forgive them; for they know not what they do" (Luke 23:34). During the church age these very cries have echoed again and again. The cry here is far different. It calls for immediate vengeance. The blood of these martyrs, like the blood of righteous Abel (Gen 4:10), cries in the ear of the One called "holy and true". Holiness and truth found in this Sovereign Lord demand vindication and vengeance. Untainted by evil He will not permit unrighteousness to go unjudged no matter how long His patience with men waits. This language recalls the cries of saints in what are known as the imprecatory Psalms (Pss 74, 79, 89, 94) where tried saints, through their tears, wait for the kinsman-redeemer to act as their vindicator (Job 19:25) in righteous judgment on their persecutors. Heaven's response shows both perfect sympathy with their longings and a readiness to act on their behalf when the moment is ripe. Their blood will be avenged. The cry "how long" (*heōs pote*) would be better translated "until when" (JND marg.), a cry that is the echo of the psalmist, "Lord, how long shall the wicked, how long shall the wicked triumph?" (Ps 94:3) and of the prophet Habakkuk, "O Lord, how long shall I cry, and thou wilt not hear?" (Hab 1:2). These souls have no doubt as to the fact of their vindication and the coming vengeance upon their enemies but the very longing of their soul refuses the thought of any further delay. Judging (*krinō*) and avenging (*ekdikeō*) are the two sides of the vindication that will be the function of Christ on His return and before the kingdom is established on earth (Matt 25:31-46). Note the use of the same verb *ekdikeō* in 19:2, "And hath avenged the blood of thy servants". Thus the guilty are described as "them that dwell on the earth", a phrase (first used in 3:10) which in its twelve occurrences becomes in this book a semi-technical expression for men in hostility to God (R.L. Mounce) and indicates, not merely physical location, but moral identification of a class of people. They are those who, rejecting the truth (Christ), have accepted the lie of the great deceiver (the first seal). As a consequence they have settled down on earth, made this their home and hate intensely all who would confess Christ as Lord. These give wholehearted support to the deceiver, later called "the beast" (13:1), in his desire to stamp out both the name of Christ and all who confess that name. A multitude of martyrs will die under this malevolent hatred. Since there is no middle ground men will be forced to choose between the truth and the lie. The earth-dwellers have identified with earth and its satanic ruler and thus share his guilt for the blood of the saints.

11 In answer to this cry heaven gives two things. The first is a *symbol* of reassurance. The more literal rendering of the RV is to be preferred, "to each one a white robe". "White" when used symbolically of garments, draws attention to two things: the purity acceptable to God (3:4; 7:9; 19:8, 14) and the blessedness enjoyed by the saint. Their bloodstained garments on earth reflected earth's assessment of their testimony, now heaven displays its appreciation; they are acceptable to heaven. This action has given rise to much speculation and discussion. Questions have been raised as to how disembodied spirits, though described as souls, receive a white robe? It is generally agreed that any question of resurrection at this point is not in the passage. An argument has been advanced by some commentators, that this passage supports the idea of a body for the believer in the intermediate state. On this *theory* this body would be different from the body of flesh men have on earth and also different from the resurrection body enjoyed in the future. The following quotation is from J. F. Walvoord (p.135): "It is a temporary body suited "for their presence" in heaven but replaced in turn by their everlasting resurrection body given at the time of Christ's return". Other commentators (such as R.H. Charles) have suggested that resurrection bodies are given to these saints ahead of time as a mark of special honour. Such speculation is both unnecessary and without scriptural support. The symbolic nature of this scene seems to have been forgotten. The scroll, the seals, the horsemen, the altar all convey spiritual truth. The robes are therefore simply the symbolic assurance of heaven as to both the acceptability of the martyrs and their present blessedness.

There is also given to these martyrs a definite *word* of reassurance. The word of reassurance lies in the truth that the delay was almost over. Vindication was sure and the interval was "a little time". In this context the "little time" is the last three and half years of the tribulation until the company of martyrs would be complete.

In the consciousness of this assurance they could enjoy "rest". The verb "that they should rest" is not to silence their cry but speaks of the blessedness they enjoy now and in the interval. Their labours are over, their persecution is in the past and presently there is the peace of heaven and the promise of their vindication. The same verb "rest" (*anapauomai*) is used to bring assurance to the saints who face death in the second half of the tribulation (14:13). In both passages there are echoes of the promise to Daniel, who is in the same line of promised blessing, "For thou shalt rest and stand in thy lot at the end of the days" (Dan 12:13). In this "little time", the final three and a half years of the tribulation called "the great tribulation" (7:14), many saints will die as martyrs; "the beast out of the sea" (13:1) will "make war with the saints and ... overcome them" (13:7); "the beast out of the earth" (13:11) will demand that "as many as would not worship the image of the [first] beast should be killed" (13:15). Persecution will reach a climax and multitudes will die for their faith in Christ. To be identified with Christ or His brethren will mean instant death (Matt 25:34-40), so that martyrdom will become commonplace. These will be the "fellow servants" and the "brethren" for whom this martyr company must wait. Serving the same Sovereign Master and born into the same family, it is only fitting that heaven will avenge them all at the same moment. The last saint put to death in the great tribulation will mark the full quota of those to seal their testimony in blood. The word "fulfilled" (*plēroō*) points on to the completed register of the martyrs. Then heaven acts; Christ returns to earth and righteous judgment is executed on the earth-dwellers. Some expositors think that both companies of martyred saints come from the last three and a half years of the great tribulation. This underestimates the pressures put on saints during the time of the four horsemen and also ignores the two distinct companies of martyrs in the Olivet discourse (Matt 24:9-22).

The Sixth Seal (vv.12-17)

12-14 With the opening of the sixth seal the great cosmic disturbances begin which herald the last days. There are really two scenes – the second arising out of the first:

The repetition of the "and" gives a cumulative effect to this terrifying scene:

> and, lo, there was (*egeneto*) a great earthquake
> and the sun became (*egeneto*) black as sackcloth of hair
> and the moon became (*egeneto*) as blood
> and the stars of heaven fell to the earth …
> and the heaven (singular) departed as a scroll …
> and every mountain and island were moved out of their places

It was a matter of faith to men in general, and Israel in particular, that the ordered movements of the heavenly bodies were a token of God's providential control. A breakdown of this order was a grim reminder that the "end of the world" was at hand. Such is the general consensus in the still-existing non-biblical apocalyptic literature. This had its original basis in Scripture, where physical manifestation of God's interventions on earth are clearly taught as, for example, when God descended at Sinai "the whole mountain quaked greatly" (Exod 19:18). There is no problem whatever with the understanding of the literal terms used; taking the language as it stands it would be difficult to depict a more terrible, or for men, a more terrifying scene. The earth shaking, the sun darkened, the moon as blood, the stars falling, show in the plainest terms the catastrophic judgment of God. When some of these things have occurred on earth in the past, even in a very partial way, men have recognised them as "acts of God".

"And there was a great earthquake". This earthquake which must be just as literal as any in OT history (as in Amos 1:2) is fully in accord with the prophecy of Haggai, "For thus saith the Lord of hosts; Yet once, it is a little while, and I will shake the heavens, and the earth, and the sea, and the dry land" (2:6). This earthquake was, of course, one of those of which the Lord spoke in general terms in the Olivet discourse, "And there shall be famines, and pestilences, and earthquakes, in divers places" (Matt 24:7). It may be argued that there have always been earthquakes since the time of the flood. While this is true those who study them point out that the number of earthquakes has doubled every ten years since records have been kept (see *The Shaking Earth* J. Gribben). This particular earthquake is called "great", a word that possibly indicates an earthquake on a global scale. The word "earthquake" (*seismos*) occurs seven times in this book, but the only three that are called "great" occur in the period that in the introduction to this chapter has been shown to link the sixth seal (v.12), the sixth trumpet (11:13) and the seventh bowl (16:18). A shaking earth seems to be given a very special shaking just before Christ comes. The three "great" earthquakes are as follows:-

6:12	The sixth seal	"And, lo, there was a *great* earthquake"
11:13	The sixth trumpet	"And the same hour there was a *great* earthquake"
16:18	The seventh bowl	"And there was a *great* earthquake, such as was not since men were upon the earth, so mighty an earthquake and so great"

"And the sun became black as sackcloth of hair, and the moon became as blood". Seismologists and geophysicists recognise that some catastrophe has smashed the once solid crust of earth (the Bible is clear that God did this in the flood in the days of Noah). Large sections of this crust, great plates floating on a plastic mantle, collide with each other, slip over each other and fracture. These movements have produced the shattering earthquakes of recent years. As the sixth seal is opened one word from the throne of God and of the Lamb reaches the vast network of subterranean faults and a terrifying earthquake circles the globe. Earthquakes in the past have often been accompanied by volcanic eruptions, spewing vast quantities of dust and steam and gases into the upper atmosphere. The blackened sun and the blood-like moon are the results of matter of some kind coming between these heavenly bodies and the earth; the language is figurative, the sun and moon are not actually changed. Volcanic activity is the normal cause of such darkening of the sun and discolouration of the moon. In these circumstances the prophecy of Joel 2:31 will be literally fulfilled, "The sun shall be turned into darkness, and the moon into blood". Sackcloth was the coarse rough cloth made from goat's hair and used, generally, to denote mourning. Death rampant on earth is fittingly answered by the darkness and mourning of creation.

"And the stars of heaven fell unto the earth, even as a fig tree casteth her untimely figs, when she is shaken of a mighty wind". While volcanic activity may be the cause of the matter that comes between the heavenly bodies and earth it is equally possible that it may come from some body such as a comet which, arriving from far beyond the solar system, passes between the sun and the earth. While darkening the sun and making the moon appear bloodlike, this invader would bring cosmic debris, some of which would crash to earth glowing white hot as it passes through the atmosphere. The heavens would be filled with a myraid blazing trails giving the appearance of "falling stars". The graphic metaphor is of a fig tree in a storm which, appearing to be gripped by a mighty hand, is shaken vigorously. The unripe figs which appear in winter before the leaves of spring, are hurled in all directions. This is the very language of the prophet Isaiah as he describes the day of the Lord (Isa 34:4).

"And the heaven departed as a scroll when it is rolled together". That this is not the dissolution of the solar system as described in 20:11 is clear from the different verbs used. Here the verb is "departed" (*apochōrizō*) and is the language of appearance. To an observer on earth (v. 15 describes such observers) the swirling cloud of debris would darken the sun, make the moon look blood-red, produce a cloud of meteors of such intensity that the very stars seem to be cascading to earth and give the impression that heaven (singular) itself is being rolled up like a scroll. This is the language used by Isaiah to mark the day of the Lord (Isa 34:4), "And the heavens shall be rolled together as a scroll". The rapid rolling up of an open papyrus scroll when one end is released is a fitting image of the scroll-like heavens disappearing as the comet intruder swings across the sky.

"And every mountain and island were moved out of their places". This puts beyond question the fact that these judgments cover the earth. The rippling of the earthquake tremors seem to touch its every part. In the reasoning of the "earth-dwellers" the first four seals could be explained as providential. The putting to death of men and women who refuse allegiance to "the beast" can be explained as political expediency, but this upheaval in the universe makes it abundantly clear that God is intervening in a dramatic way. There is no doubt that these cosmic disturbances are the beginning of those astronomical happenings of which the Lord spoke so plainly: "Immediately after the tribulation of those days shall the sun be darkened, and the moon shall not give her light, and the stars shall fall from heaven, and the powers of the heavens shall be shaken" (Matt 24:29). It should be re-emphasised that while the signs begin under the sixth seal and are continued and intensified under the sixth trumpet, the full climax comes in the seventh bowl just before the Lord Himself appears.

15 The reaction to these cosmic happenings of the people of earth belonging to all levels of society confirms that the literal interpretation of the phenomena is the only one tenable. The symbolic interpretation does not give a convincing picture; it is very questionable whether the collapse of governments and institutions affecting social, political and ecclesiastical life would bring the terror and panic here described. Such an idea is refuted by history. When the fabric of society crumbled in the French Revolution (1793) and every stable institution was shaken men did not betake themselves to caves and cry for the rocks to fall upon them. Men and women joined in the anarchy. On the other hand any disturbance or unusual happening in the astronomical realm causes fear and even panic; men seem to sense that here they are confronted with the divine. H. B. Swete is often quoted in this connection, "What sinners dread most is not death, but the revealed presence of God". Happenings in the universe show man his weakness and bring him face to face with God. A society embracing atheists, evolutionists, and humanists and that has publicly denied the very existence of God is now forced to acknowledge God and the Lamb. Instead of seeking mercy through repentance men call on the very rocks, whose testimony to a God of creation they have denied, to hide them from His face. If the mountains and rocks are literal, and there seems no other way of interpreting them, then it is strange exegesis to deny the same literalness to the mountains of the previous verse.

Every stratum of society is reached by this universal message. None can evade its import. The article before each of the first five classes marks out those who are regarded as leaders of society and very particularly those who normally would have had every reason to feel secure:

a. The "kings" refers to the heads of nations whatever their local designation, whether emperor, president or monarch. Protected from all the normal hazards of life by their position now they are face to face with God.
b. The term "great men" refers to the second rank nobility in states where kings rule, or to cabinet members where democracy exists. They normally would have the security of their influence. Now influence carries little weight.
c. The word "captains". The word originally described a commander of 1000 men and was the Greek word used for the Persian vizier, and for the Roman tribune, the commander of a cohort (John 18:12; Acts 21:31-33,37). Vine points out that this was the title for the commander of the Roman garrison at Jerusalem. It is equivalent to present day field-marshals and generals, but is wide enough to embrace all military leaders who normally would feel secure with the power of the military behind them.
d. The "rich men" are the leaders of industry, the managing-directors of world trading enterprises, the world bankers, financiers whose world was cushioned by their wealth and security was part of their lives.
e. The "strong men" describes those not known generally to the public, yet are the men who, behind the scenes, wield great power in politics and society. These are the leaders of the major political parties, the moguls of the media, the senators, the members of parliament and the trade union leaders. The strength of these men, in whatever realm it lay, could not now protect them.
f. "Every slave and freeman" completes the social register of Roman days. In modern days their counterparts are "'blue-collar" workers and the "white-collar" workers, men and women, for the classes cover both, earning wages or drawing salary, working in a business or owning a business; all are brought to a state of panic by these dramatic events in the universe.

16-17 Terror moves across earth. Men in all strata of society have found that their make-believe world has collapsed and they have to face God. Reality has displaced the sham of their lives. Royal lineage or humble origin makes no difference, whether a military commander or a captain of industry, all are conscious that there is a God dealing with earth. Atheism has no answer, agnosticism is inadequate in this crises. Living in a time when the blasphemy of "the beast" was rampant, knowing they had compromised their conscience for profit and wealth, they are now face to face with God. They would rather face death than God, and cry to the mountains and rocks, "Fall on us, and hide us from the face of him that sitteth upon the throne, and from the wrath of the Lamb", language reminiscent of Hos 10:8. The "face" of God is a Hebraism stemming from the reaction of Adam and Eve in the garden after the fall (Gen 3:8). Unafraid of death men are mortally afraid of the God whom through a life time they disdained, and the Lamb whom they denied. This language indicates that the witness of the 144,000, which centred on the "blood of the Lamb" (7:14), had already been borne throughout the earth. This divine cosmic intervention of God speaks to the consciences of men. Suddenly they know that, having rejected the blood of the Lamb, they must now face the wrath of the Lamb. This is a direct fulfilment of the word spoken by Isaiah in connection with the day of the Lord, "And they shall go into the holes of the rocks, and into the caves of the earth, for fear of the Lord, and for the glory of his majesty, when he ariseth to shake terribly the earth" (Isa 2:19).

Through this cosmic upheaval men on earth at last recognise that God and the Lamb are acting in judgment. The RV reading "their wrath" should be noted. The word "wrath" (*orgē*) indicates the settled displeasure of divine persons. The word "day", here, is not to be interpreted as a twenty-four hour period but as an extended period which may cover the whole of the seven-year tribulation or, more probably, describes the last three and a half years. Warnings concerning this wrath of God as an event of the end times have sounded down the ages; one of the voices was that of John the Baptist (Luke 3:7). This wrath is neither personal vindictiveness nor simply the impersonal processes of retribution in history but the direct action of God defined by F.F. Bruce as "the response of holiness to persistent and impenitent wickedness". That terrible day has arrived, made more terrible by the fact that the Lamb is associated with it. Men have refused the provision the Lamb has made and now suffer the consequences of their sin. This panic-stricken cry summarises the consciousness of men that these terrible happenings are the prelude to more terrible blows, they feel they cannot endure what they anticipate is coming. This is the implication of the last despairing cry of the chapter, "Who shall be able to stand?" In this cry is an echo of the prophet Nahum, "Who is able to stand?" (Nah 1:6) and of Malachi, "Who may abide the day of his coming? And who shall stand when he appeareth?" (Mal 3:2). God has acted so dramatically and His power has been displayed on such an astronomical scale in the shaking of earth and heaven that men recognise for the first time their weakness and nothingness. Ranged against God men must inevitably fall, they cannot possibly stand! The rhetorical question is strategically placed and the next chapter will describe those who through divine grace will be able to stand through the dark days of the tribulation period.

Notes

4 The word for "sword" is *machaira* meaning the short sword used by the Roman legions. In v.8 the word for sword is *rhomphaia* (as in 1:16) which is the broad sword of Thracian origin. Little significance should be attached to this difference as the two words were often used as synonyms as they are throughout the LXX (R.H. Mounce).

12 Literal or symbolic?

Many able and respected commentators insist that the earthquake under the sixth seal be interpreted in a figurative way as a picture of social and political upheaval. W. Scott writes, "A 'great earthquake' denotes a violent disruption of the organised state of things, a complete subversion of all existing authority". Of the other events the same writer adds, "The general idea which the metaphors present is a universal overthrow of all existing authority, a revolutionary crisis of such magnitude that kings and slaves are in abject terror. The coming crash will involve in one general catastrophe everything on earth deemed secure and strong. A vast civil, social, and political chaos will be created". Following this principle of interpretation the heaven is understood as the sphere of human government, the sun as the supreme ruler with the moon as a subsidiary and the stars as established and apparently permanent institutions. H. Ironside concurs with this interpretation and writes, "It is not therefore a worldwide, literal earthquake that the sixth seal introduces but rather the destruction of the present order – political, social and ecclesiastical – reduced to chaos, the breaking down of authority, and the breaking up of all established and apparently permanent institutions". F.A. Tatford pursues the same line of interpretation when he writes of the removal of mountains and islands, "An insensate and unreasoning wave of anarchy sweeps away all stable, settled rule (the mountains), and also the whole commercial system (the islands)".

There are very good reasons why this symbolic interpretation is entirely inadequate and does not do justice to the plain language of Scripture. In fact it detracts from the terror of the catastrophic literal judgment that the opening of this seal brings upon earth. The reasons why this scene must be taken in absolutely literal sense may be summarised:

1. Symbols are used in the previous seals but it is clear that they are symbols. There is no danger of any normal observer (or reader) mistaking the horses for anything other than symbols. However, when it comes to an earthquake, the sun and the moon there is not the slightest suggestion in the passage that they are symbols of anything. All OT earthquakes (1 Kings 19:11; Isa 29:6; Amos 1:1; Zech 14:5) are certainly literal and there is no record in other scripture of the word "earthquake" being used in other than a literal sense. When sun or moon or stars are mentioned in Scripture the literal bodies are intended. Where any other sense is required the context makes it plain as in Mal 4:2 and in this book in 9:1. The judgments of the first four seals that have depicted political deception, military destruction, widespread dearth and physical death are climaxed by the hand of God shaking the physical earth. Literal seismic disturbances and cosmic upheavals are envisaged in Joel 2:30; 3:15; Isa 13:10, 13; 24:13.
2. Much ingenuity is required to explain straightforward statements. One writer interprets the statement, "the stars of heaven fell unto the earth" as "all lesser authorities, such as individual rulers, civil and ecclesiastical, morally fell from their exalted station". The same writer interprets the statement, "and the heaven departed as a scroll when it is rolled together" as "the political, civil, and ecclesiastical systems, the constitution, bonds, and framework of society, shall as completely disappear as a book or scroll is unreadable when rolled up". It is submitted that this kind of arbitrary, subjective interpretation does not do justice to the plain language of scripture.
3. It is very much to be doubted whether even the collapse of government and constituted authorities in this moral, social and political "shake-up" could bring such abject terror as to send men to seek death under falling rocks (even commentators given to symbolic interpretation grant that these must be literal rocks). As mentioned in the verse comments,

even the complete collapse of law and order in the French Revolution did not produce this kind of panic. Interpreting the happenings literally gives a very sensible explanation for the panic on earth. Men know that only God could bring these things upon earth.

4. There are four graphic similes in the passage: "black as sackcloth of hair"; "the moon became as blood; "as a fig tree casteth her untimely figs"; "departed as a scroll". The figurative expressions must be descriptive of realities. To use similies of symbols would be unusual, and indeed confusing. In this connection it should be pointed out that these similies describe events from the point of view of the observer – what the event looks like to the eye. When reference is made to stars falling from heaven, this is the language of observation. The same language is used regularly to describe meteor showers today. When this is conceded then this judgment makes perfectly intelligible sense and no other sense need be sought.

W. Hoste summarises the matter concisely when he writes, "There does not seem sufficient reason to attempt to 'spiritualise' these happenings. Signs in the heavens are again and again associated with the last days, when 'the powers of heaven shall be shaken'. To quote from one prophet only (Joel 2:10) we read, 'The earth shall quake before them … the sun and the moon shall be dark'. And in Joel 2:31, 'The sun shall be turned into darkness and the moon into blood, before the great and terrible day of the Lord come'".

CHAPTER 7

3. *The First Parenthesis* 7:1-17

This chapter comes as a parenthesis between the sixth and the seventh seal, a structural feature repeated within the seven trumpets. It forms no part of the chronological sequence observable in the seven seals but plays a vital role in the understanding of conditions on earth during the seal judgments retrospectively, and during the trumpet and bowl judgments prospectively. The action is paused, amidst climaxing judgments, to answer the question posed by the panic-stricken society of earth at the close of the previous chapter, "Who shall be able to stand?" Questions are answered as to:

1. the nature of the testimony for God on earth during the tribulation period
2. the secret of the preservation of some saints through the tribulation while others die for their testimony and
3. the destiny of the saints who come out of the tribulation. The chapter will show that from this darkest period of earth history there will be "a great multitude, which no man could number" to stand before the throne (v.9).

Two companies are presented in the chapter and they stand in marked contrast to each other. The first company (vv.1-8) are sealed before going into the tribulation period. The only feasible explanation of the restraint of the winds is that the storm, picturing the tribulation, is delayed until the witnesses are sealed. The second company (vv.9-17) are said to be those " who come out of the great tribulation" (v.14 JND). The first company is totally Jewish in origin while the second company is multinational (v.9). The first company is limited numerically to 144,000 while the second company is beyond human enumeration.

(a) *The first company sealed (vv.1-8)*

v.1 "And after these things I saw four angels standing on the four corners of the earth, holding the four winds of the earth, that the wind should not blow on the earth, nor on the sea, nor on any tree.
v.2 And I saw another angel ascending from the east, having the seal of the living God: and he cried with a loud voice to the four angels, to whom it was given to hurt the earth and the sea,
v.3 Saying, Hurt not the earth, neither the sea, nor the trees, till we have sealed the servants of our God in their foreheads.
v.4 And I heard the number of them which were sealed: and there were sealed an hundred and forty and four thousand of all the tribes of the children of Israel.
v.5 Of the tribe of Juda were sealed twelve thousand. Of the tribe of Reuben were sealed twelve thousand, Of the tribe of Gad were sealed twelve thousand.
v.6 Of the tribe of Aser were sealed twelve thousand. Of the tribe of Naphthalim were sealed twelve thousand. Of the tribe of Manasses were sealed twelve thousand.
v.7 Of the tribe of Simeon were sealed twelve thousand. Of the tribe of Levi were sealed twelve thousand. Of the tribe of Issachar were sealed twelve thousand.
v.8 Of the tribe of Zabulon were sealed twelve thousand. Of the tribe of Joseph were sealed twelve thousand. Of the tribe of Benjamin were sealed twelve thousand".

1 The singular "after this" (RV) shows that this vision follows the vision under the sixth seal; the action itself is retrospective and goes back in time before the seals are opened. A storm is about to burst upon earth; the imagery is derived directly from the language of Jeremiah and the destruction of Elam (Jer 49:36). That it is a terrible storm of the hurricane or typhoon class is pictured in the anticipation that it will "hurt" the earth and all upon it. The verb *adikeō* in this context would be better rendered "do injury to" (see 9:10) the earth, the sea and the trees. Four angels stand on the four corners of the earth holding the four winds of heaven. As the book unfolds angels are shown in control of not only of the winds but also of fire (14:18) and waters (16:5). The scene is designed to show that, however terrible the storm winds may be, they are under divine control and cannot be released until heaven gives permission. The "four corners of the earth" is the scriptural metaphor (Isa 11:12) for the earth as a whole and says nothing about first century cosmology; it is language used by middle-eastern nations in antiquity much as the expression "the four points of the compass" is used today. The mention of "any tree" or "the trees" (v.3) seems to indicate the stillness before the storm as might be said today "not a leaf moves". Three things may be readily deduced from this picture:

1. The tribulation is seen as a terrible storm that will bring "hurt" or "damage" to the earth in its entirety. Not stated but implied is the injury it will bring to persons and in view of this there is the sealing of the 144,000 for divine preservation.
2. The threefold repetition of the word "four" – the four angels, the four corners of the earth and the four winds – suggests a universality in the storm, as the tribulation sweeps over all of earth.
3. Since the storm is restrained until the first company is sealed it is clear that the sealing must take place before the Lamb opens the seals.

2-3 Another angel, arising from the east, calls to the first four angels to hold back the storm winds till the servants of God have been sealed. Grace still moves towards responsive sinners and demands a delay to the outbreak of judgment. The east, literally the "sunrising", pictures a brightness against the dark thunder clouds of the storm. The urgency of his message is seen in the strength of the verb "cried" (*krazō*) which, with the descriptive phrase "with a loud voice", implies a shout that arrests all action until the mission of this fifth angel is concluded.

In preparation for this task this angel carries the "seal of the living God". In the Greek-Roman world the seal primarily denoted ownership. Slaves and soldiers (especially the imperial guard) had a visible tattoo on hand, or forehead, or neck to ensure that their allegiance was known. It also served to deter a slave from running away or a soldier from deserting. That cattle were similarly branded tells much about slavery in the days of the Roman empire. The basic idea was to mark one's own property. Initiates and devotees of the mystery religions also bore a brandmark to indicate their devotion and allegiance. While scriptural usage also carries the idea of ownership in the sealing of men, it also carries the idea of security. This was seen in Jerusalem (Ezek 9:1-7) when the judgment was stayed until the man with the ink-horn had marked those who mourned for sin. The mark that protected them then was the Hebrew letter "t" written as "+"; no one could harm the sealed ones without divine permission. This is emphasised when sealing is mentioned again under the fifth trumpet (9:4). God will preserve His sealed ones through the terrible days of the tribulation. The death that rides abroad under the fourth horseman cannot touch those who bear the seal of the living God. There is the additional thought of destiny implicit in the seal; God has a destined end in view for the sealed ones. This end will be seen in 14:1-4 and is there defined as entrance to the millennial kingdom when those preserved through the gloom of the tribulation will share the glory of the kingdom. W. Scott has an arresting thought in this connection (p.165): "The sealing angel ascending from the sun-rising for the preservation and blessing of Israel seems a herald of the Messiah, Who as the Sun of Righteousness shall arise with healing in His wings (Mal 4:2), and shine upon the land and people with undimmed splendour. The firstfruits of national blessing is predicated of the angel; the harvest awaits the revelation of Christ from Heaven". The designation of the living God with its OT background (Josh 3:10; 2 Kings 19:4,16) is appropriately used to describe One who stands in contrast to all idols and can intervene on behalf of His own people. As God intervened in the days of Joshua and Elijah so He will do again in the tribulation period amid the idolatrous worship of the Beast.

That believers in this dispensation of grace are sealed is seen in Eph 1:13-14 where the same verb (*sphragizō*) is used. The language is metaphorical since there is no visible mark on the believers in the church age; the Holy Spirit Himself is the seal. Nevertheless, the same ideas of ownership, preservation and destiny are all stressed in the statement, "ye were sealed, with that Holy Spirit of promise, which is the earnest of our inheritance, unto the redemption of the purchased possession". In the circumstances of this passage the sealing is literal and visible and comprises a divine logo described as "his name [of the Lamb] and the name of his Father" (14:1 RV) in their foreheads. Men can identify the followers of the Beast by his mark (13:16); God seals His own with His mark before the judgment begins.

The conjunction "till" (AV) or "until" (RV) demands a measurable time span between the rapture of the church and the commencement of the tribulation, a period when the tribulation could come but, by divine restraint, is delayed until this act of sealing has been completed. It has been pointed out previously that the rapture of the church clears the way for the beginning of the seventieth week of Daniel's prophecy. The commencement of this seven-year tribulation period, is signalled by the signing of a peace treaty between "the coming prince" and the Jewish leader of "the many" in Israel (Dan 9:27 R.V.) who will be identified as the beast out of the earth (13:11) later called the "false prophet". This moment of signing on earth parallels the moment in heaven when the Lamb begins to open the seals which marks the beginning of the tribulation period. Scripture gives no indication of the length of the interval between the rapture and the signing of the covenant. Some commentators take the view that it will be very short, perhaps days or weeks or months. Other able teachers have felt that the period could extend to years – even as much as a generation: 30-40 years. Where scripture is silent it is idle to speculate but this passage does suggest that there must be sufficient time for the salvation and the sealing of these 144,000 individuals. The length of the period is not for men to calculate. Other scriptures inferentially support the idea of a reasonable interval. Time must be granted for:

1. the impact of the rapture to give way to a period of security (1 Thess 5:3),

2. nations to be rearranged politically for the emergence of the ten-power kingdom and the rise of the Beast (13:1-2),
3. a temple to be built in Jerusalem (11:1-2)
4. a great commercial centre to be re-established on the ancient site of Babylon (implied by her destruction in 16:10).

Whether some or all of these events take place before Christ comes for the church is a matter of debate, but it seems reasonable to conclude that some substantial period is required before the prophetic clock recommences the count-down to the return of Christ to earth. Little do men realise that this unexpected calm before the storm has been brought about by a divine restraint. When the last soul of the 144,000 is saved and sealed the restraining hand will be withdrawn and the hurricane will break.

The clause "until we may seal" indicates that these "servants of our God" have yet to be sealed and so they cannot be the same as those referred to in 1:1 even though the same word "servants" (*douloi*) is used. The word describes those who in any age serve God. Saints in the church age are servants (1:1); this is another company taken from the nation of Israel who maintain testimony for God after the church has gone. Some have been perplexed with regard to a testimony after the church has gone from earth, especially when it is clearly taught that the Holy Spirit, upon whose activity men are dependent for salvation, is to be removed from earth with the church (2 Thess 2:7). It must be remembered that the Holy Spirit is God and has all the attributes of deity: omniscience, omnipotence and omnipresence. Men were saved through His activity before the church age and will be saved through His activity after the church age is closed. From Pentecost until the rapture the Holy Spirit fulfils a unique role with regard to the church and, indwelling each believer, binds all saints into one body. With the removal of the church to meet her Lord in the air this particular role is completed; the ministries that marked the function of the Holy Spirit in the church age are closed. At this point the Holy Spirit resumes the work He has done in the ages before the church came into existence. Not a soul has ever been saved in the past nor can be saved in the future apart from the activity of the Holy Spirit.

A related difficulty in the minds of some believers is how these 144,000 are reached in grace, for it must be clear that there can be no sealing without salvation. Some have suggested that they respond to the preaching of the two witnesses (11:3-12) but this poses a further problem. While the two witnesses do preach throughout the first half of the tribulation, their ministry is limited to exactly 1260 days (11:3) which would seem to correspond precisely with the first half of the tribulation; the argument of this chapter is that these 144,000 are saved and sealed before the tribulation begins. It could be that in the dramatic conversion of Saul of Tarsus, supernaturally arrested on the Damascus road (Acts 9:1-6) God has left a prototype conversion of a national Israelite. Many Jews with a knowledge of OT Scripture, already alarmed by unfolding prophetic events and with messianic expectations at fever heat, faced with the fact of the rapture of the church, may be forced to review their attitude to "the Nazarene". Such Jews learning, as Saul, that "It is hard for thee to kick against the pricks" (Acts 9:5) would be ready for the intervention of the Spirit of God and the revelation of Christ to the soul (Gal 1:15-16). Paul may have had some inkling of this truth when speaking of his own conversion in 1 Cor 15:8; he referred to himself as "one born out of due time". The Newberry translation of that verse is more accurate, "one prematurely born"; that is one born before the expected birthdate. The birthday of the nation is coming (Isa 66:8) when, in the language of Christ through Zechariah, "They shall look upon me whom they have pierced" (Zech 12:10). This is the moment of national conversion when "all Israel shall be saved" (Rom 11:26). However, this 144,000 are but the "firstfruits" (14:4) of the harvest to be reaped in that day of national rebirth. Like Saul, these Jews arrested, saved and sealed, will be sent through the world as a witness for Christ.

The substance of their preaching is summarised in 14:6-7. While preaching is not specifically mentioned in connection with this company there are implications that seem to demand it. First is the use of the word "servants" (*douloi*) or, "bondmen of our God" (JND). While this includes service generally borne through the peril and persecution of the period, NT usage suggests that a large part of the service could be preaching as seen in Acts 2:18; 4:29; 16:17; Titus 1:1; James 1:1; 2 Pet 2:19. The second consideration is that the passage suggests a continuation of the interrupted mission of the twelve disciples sent out by Christ (Matt 10:1-11). They were dispatched on a specific mission to the nation and Christ outlines the provision they would need (Matt 10:1-15), the persecution they would meet (Matt 10:16-23) and the preaching they would make known (Matt 10:24-42). He pointed out in Matt 10:23, "But when they persecute you in this city, flee ye into another: for verily I say unto you, ye shall not have gone over the cities of Israel, till the Son of man be come". This programme was interrupted by the rejection of Christ and the cross. Preaching throughout the subsequent period of grace centred on a risen Christ and the fuller and wider commission of Matt 28:18-20 came into operation. When this dispensation of grace closes at the rapture, then this older commission will be taken up again. This time the parish will include the nation of Israel first but will spread worldwide. Not twelve men but twelve thousand times twelve will carry this urgent message to all mankind. The third reason for emphasising that this company is sealed for preaching as well as preservation is that the two scenes of this chapter are obviously related; one company goes into the tribulation, the second, far larger company, comes out. It would seem to be a logical deduction that the second is the result of the first; there is the preaching first and then the harvest.

The sealing is not simply a matter of ensuring that this company remains faithful during the testing times of tribulation but it ensures physical preservation in this period. These saints are not marked to die but sealed to live. When their number is recorded again at the close of the tribulation there will still be exactly 144,000 witnesses for God to accompany the Lamb into the millennial kingdom (14:1-5).

4 This verse makes plain two matters relating to this company:

1. John heard the number. If John did see the company he was not permitted to give his own estimate, this number is a divinely-given enumeration and must be treated as such. The specified number of 144,000 stands in sharp contrast to the unnumbered host of the second company in the chapter. In keeping with all the other numbers in this book this number must be taken exactly and literally. There is no need to qualify the matter and suggest that this is a round number, or that, there will be "more or less" 12,000 from each tribe of Israel. Alford is representative of many commentators when he writes, "No one that I am aware of has taken it literally, and supposed that just this particular number and no more is imported". Post-millennial and amillennial commentators are driven to the symbolic view since they interpret this 144,000 as the church. Since the subsequent verses will show the nationality of these witnesses and rule out any possibility of this company being the church there is every reason to take the number literally. The number itself must carry symbolic overtones but this does not make it any less exact. Twelve has always been the number in Scripture to speak of governmental administration and is particularly associated with the nation of Israel. There were twelve patriarchs to found the nation; there were twelve tribes to compose the nation; the High Priest had twelve stones on His breastplate to represent the nation, and there were twelve apostles called out of the nation. It will be noted that the Holy Jerusalem, as the administrative capital of the new cosmos, has twelve gates and twelve foundations (21:12). With twelve thousand from each of twelve tribes of Israel universal administration is suggested – an adequate, sufficient worldwide ministry to cover all the earth in the time available.

2. The statement as to the identity of this company needs no clarification: "Out of every tribe of the sons of Israel" (JND). The principle that Scripture be allowed to mean what it says applied here would have saved many commentators from faulty exegesis. That Israel, as a nation, is being taken up again in the purposes of God is the clear teaching of the passage, a truth that amillennialist teachers cannot allow. W. Hendriksen is typical of such expositors when he writes, "It is very clear, therefore that the sealed multitude of Rev 7 symbolises the entire Church militant of the old and new dispensations". He writes again on the same passage, "The 144,000 sealed individuals out of the twelve tribes of literal Israel symbolise spiritual Israel, the Church of God on earth". This is a clear example of interpretation arising out of the imposition of preconceived ideas. It should be pointed out that the passage says nothing whatever about "symbols"; it is stating the literal fact of an actual company sealed to accomplish a specific mission. It should also be pointed out that when "Israel" or "Jacob" is used in the NT and

linked with his descendants, the term invariably refers to the national descendants of the patriarch. Gal 6:16 is no exception to this rule; the "Israel of God" are saved Jews who have shown that they belong to the true line of faith, the faith of believing Abraham. This company is composed of 144,000 born-again Jews sealed for a particular task. It is significant that the word used is "sons" (*huioi*) and not children as in the AV.

The common arguments against the literal identification of the tribes of Israel have been:

(a) Even in NT times there were only representatives of Judah and Benjamin in the land of Israel. It has been assumed that since the time of the Assyrian deportation of the northern kingdom of Israel in 722 BC the ten tribes have been "lost". This led men in the 19th century along the imaginative but totally unscriptural paths of British Israelism and related myths. Lurking also in the minds of many has been another notion, somewhat less popular now as the more inaccessible regions of earth are explored, that at some future date these "lost" tribes will emerge from some unknown hiding place to claim their heritage. David Baron in his book *The History of the ten "lost" tribes* has shown many years ago (1915) that those ideas display ignorance of both scripture and history.

It is true that the recovery under Zerubbabel (536 BC), Ezra (458 BC) and Nehemiah (445 BC) brought back to the land of Israel only a relatively small proportion of those in the *diaspora*, but these comprised representatives of the twelve tribes, since Babylon had taken over the earlier Assyrian Empire. In the NT individuals are named from the tribes of Judah, Benjamin, Asher and Levi. Since the land area belonged to Judah and Benjamin it has been assumed that there were representatives of only these tribes in the recovery. The majority of the whole nation remained in Mesopotamia, in the land area of the Assyrian and Babylonian Empires, until changing conditions under succeeding empires scattered them throughout the Roman Empire and then to most lands of earth. There never were ten "lost" tribes.

(b) That all tribal records have been lost. It is true that with the Roman capture of Jerusalem in 70 AD, its utter destruction and the banishment of the Jews seventy years later, the genealogical records were lost so that tribal distinctions were a matter of memory and, as a consequence, few Jews today can trace their tribe. This offers no more of a problem to faith than it did in the days of Ezra (Ezra 2:61-63). There can be no question that a God who can bring a nation back to her own land in spite of unbelief, can recover records that will provide tribal identification.

5-8 In these verses the names of the tribes are given. J.B. Smith observes that there are 29 lists of the tribes of Israel given in the scriptures in which the order of the tribes varies. A comparison of the first list of the sons of Jacob in Gen 35:23-26 may be made with this final list in Scripture:

Mother	*Son*	*Meaning*	*Place in this List*
Leah	Reuben	Behold a son	2
	Simeon	Hearing	7
	Levi	Joined	8
	Judah	Praise	1
	Issachar	Hire	9
	Zebulun	Dwelling	10
Rachel	Joseph	He will add	11
	Benjamin	Son of my right hand	12
Bilhah	Dan	Judging	Missing
	Naphthali	Wrestling	5
Zilpah	Gad	Troop	3
	Asher	Happy	4

The list as given by John is as follows: Judah, Reuben, Gad, Asher, Nepthalim, Manasseh, Simeon, Levi, Issachar, Zebulon, Joseph, Benjamin. Judah is first, of course, because it was from this tribe Christ came (5:5; Heb 7:14; Gen 49:10). It will be noticed that Manasseh, the grandson of Jacob, is included. Since Jacob had said of the two sons of Joseph, "...they are mine" (Gen 48:5) they were generally reckoned amongst the seed. It was customary, after the tribal division of the land of Israel, to include Ephraim and Manasseh amongst the tribes and omit Joseph and Levi. Joseph because he was represented in his sons and Levi, because of their priestly status. This kept the number of listed tribes to twelve.

On the omission of Ephraim and Dan from this list W. Scott writes p.166, "In the apocalyptic enumeration, Dan and Ephraim are omitted. Both these tribes were remarkable as being connected with idolatry in Israel, the probable reason for blotting out their names here (Deut 29:18-21). But in the end grace triumphs, and Dan is named first in the future distribution of the land amongst the tribes (Ezek 48:2), but while first named it is the farthest removed from the temple, being situated in the extreme north". Many commentators agree generally with this conclusion; some (as Alford) suggesting that the inclination to idolatry provides support for the ancient tradition, based on Gen 49:17, that the Antichrist will come from the tribe of Dan. This latter tradition goes back as far as Irenaeus near the close of the second century AD. A more realistic reason is that the tribe of Dan was the first to abandon their God-given heritage in Canaan and carve out with the sword a new inheritance which God had not given (Judges 18). This may have led to their scattering and eventual absorption by the other tribes. In the later years of the monarchy their numbers were considerably smaller than the numbers of Levi.

The scriptural teaching is that God has a sufficient and complete testimony.

Souls saved, sealed and sent as ideally-equipped servants from the most cosmopolitan nation on earth will preach Christ throughout the world. It could well be that the outpouring of the Holy Spirit enjoyed by the twelve (Acts 2:14-21) at Pentecost is a foreshadowing of another mission when a number, of which twelve is only a factor, will carry a message of salvation.

That this company does not represent all the saved ones of the tribulation period should not need to be stressed. This will become evident as the company at the close of the chapter is examined. It may not be quite so well understood that this company is not the "remnant" of Israel referred to later (12:17). Many from Israel will hear the message preached by this divinely preserved company and will believe. Some of those new believers will die for their faith (envisaged in 6:9); others will "endure to the end" (Matt 24:13) and in this prove the reality of their faith. There will doubtless be many of these true Israelites included in the "all nations" of v.9. There appears to be also a further remnant in the nation, who, while not believing the gospel will refuse to believe "the lie" of the Antichrist. They constitute the beleaguered remnant for whom Christ becomes the Deliverer (Rom 11:26), This is the company who, when the truth breaks upon them at the return of Christ, will use the language of Isa 53 in their confession and conversion.

(b) *The second company saved (vv.9-17)*

v.9 "After this I beheld, and, lo, a great multitude, which no man could number, of all nations, and kindreds, and people, and tongues, stood before the throne, and before the Lamb, clothed with white robes, and palms in their hands;
v.10 And cried with a loud voice, saying, Salvation to our God which sitteth upon the throne, and unto the Lamb.
v.11 And all the angels stood round about the throne, and about the elders and the four beasts, and fell before the throne on their faces, and worshipped God,
v.12 Saying, Amen: Blessing, and glory, and wisdom, and thanksgiving, and honour, and power, and might, be unto our God for ever and ever. Amen.
v.13 And one of the elders answered, saying unto me, What are these which are arrayed in white robes? and whence came they?
v.14 And I said unto him, Sir, thou knowest. And he said to me, These are they which came out of great tribulation, and have washed their robes, and made them white in the blood of the Lamb.
v.15 Therefore are they before the throne of God, and serve him day and night in his temple: and he that sitteth on the throne shall dwell among them.
v.16 They shall hunger no more, neither thirst any more; neither shall the sun light on them, nor any heat.
v.17 For the Lamb which is in the midst of the throne shall feed them, and shall lead them unto living fountains of waters: and God shall wipe away all tears from their eyes."

The recurrence of the time phrase "after these things" (meta *tauta*) followed by the usual verb "I saw" marks a further stage in the visions of John when he is shown another company who clearly are meant to stand in contrast with the first. The companies differ in three main features:

		Company 1 (vv.1-8) The Sealed Ones	Company 2 (vv.9-17) The Saved Ones
1.	Number	144,000	No man could number
2.	Nationality	Israel (Jews only)	out of every nation (mainly Gentiles)
3.	Time-period	Going into the tribulation	Coming out of the great tribulation

It has been shown that the first company are 144,000 Israelites saved, sealed and sent into the tribulation period to fulfil a missionary role for the coming Christ. It will be shown that this second company – "which no man could number"– are the saved from every nation coming out of the tribulation period. It is a valid inference that the second company is the harvest of the worldwide preaching of the first company. It will be further shown that both companies are on earth.

9-10 In connection with the first company John "heard" the number (v.4) but with this second company his eye is filled with the vista of a multitude beyond human computation. The variety of peoples seen in the crowd identifies them as "out of every nation, and of all tribes and peoples and tongues" (RV). There can scarcely be any doubt that this great company reflects the progress and power of the gospel preached throughout the tribulation period. The phrase "out of every nation (*ethnos*)" shows the cosmopolitan character of the company; the word "tribes"(*phulē*) shows their different racial background; the word "peoples" (*laos*) indicates the different cultural backgrounds and "tongues" (*glōssa*) shows the variety of languages they spoke. This fourfold description, used frequently in this book (5:9; 11:9; 13:7; 14:6; 17:15), stresses universality. All national and cultural barriers have fallen before the preaching of the gospel; salvation (v.10) has reached out to all men. It must not be thought that each national group is carefully segregated; the idea is neatly caught by the phrase of H.B. Swete, "a polyglot cosmopolitan crowd".

Four statements describe this great company:

(a) "A great multitude". The expression "which no man could number" stresses the inability of any man to calculate the number in this great crowd. The AV "stood" is the perfect participle of the verb *histēmi* and is perhaps better translated by the RV "standing". It is to be noted that this company is the answer to that cry of the panic-stricken men of earth in 6:17, "Who shall be able to stand?". After the wrath of the tribulation period has ceased there will still be on earth those able to stand, those identified by Christ in Matt 24:13, "But he that endureth to the end the same shall be saved". This company presents visually the great host of the saved ones coming out of the tribulation period in their natural bodies. It will be observed that the presence of this great company "before the throne and before the Lamb" is the cause of the worship of the angels, the twenty-four elders and the four living creatures (vv.11-12). While they do not join in the worship of the angels it is their shout of triumph and victory that causes the worship. Further points to be noted are that they are standing not seated and there is no mention of crowns.

(b) The white robes symbolise righteousness and indicate their acceptability before the throne. The term "white robes" in itself does not demand martyrdom (see 3:5), neither does it imply resurrection. This latter point is made clear by the fact that the souls of the martyrs in 6:11 are given white robes while their bodies are still in the grave. In this passage the white robes emphasise the righteous character and perfect acceptability of these saints with God. In these garments they are perfectly at home "before the throne and before the Lamb".

(c) The waving of branches of the palm tree in eastern lands symbolised victory. In Scripture too, the palm speaks of victory, but carries with it the additional note of joy after conflict. The only other occasion when this word for palms (*phoinikes*) is used in the NT is John 12:13 when the multitude symbolically acclaimed Christ as king. The rejection of that claim by the nation of Israel led Him to the cross; now palms again appear as Christ moves to take His crown. In this symbolic picture, a great company from all nations carry the palm branches in celebration of salvation by power. This is the only company in this book to carry palm branches. The scene is strongly reminiscent of the feast of tabernacles; see Lev 23:40, "And ye shall take you on the first day the boughs of goodly trees, branches of palm trees, and the boughs of thick trees, and willows of the brook; and ye shall rejoice before the Lord your God seven days". This suggests a picture of millennial blessing upon earth.

(d) The song of the twenty-four elders in 5:9-10 celebrated redemption by blood and was centred on the Lamb. This acclamation is to God and to the Lamb and celebrates redemption by power. God has wrought through the Lamb the deliverance of this great company of saved ones. "Salvation" is the comprehensive term to describe deliverance: it carries echoes of Israel's deliverance from Egypt and Pharaoh (Exod 15:2) and Jonah's deliverance from death (Jonah 2:9). This palm-waving company has known deliverance from a foe mightier than Pharaoh and a beast more terrible than the whale. Three million souls may have come out of Egypt, over a million and a quarter may have been delivered in Nineveh but here there has been a wider and greater deliverance for an innumerable company. As can be seen in 12:10 and 19:1 salvation, embracing both soul and body, is associated in this book with millennial blessing. It is a salvation which has originated in God, manifests His sovereignty as the One on the throne and has been made available to men by the sacrifice of the Lamb. It is necessarily more than deliverance from the persecution of the Beast; it embraces the blessings unfolded in subsequent verses (vv.15-17).

11-12 The sight of this host and their shout of victory stimulate worship in heaven. A comparison of this celebration with that of 5:11-12 shows that while the throne is central in each case there are significant variations. In the first scene the Lamb is the One directly addressed as Redeemer; in this scene God is central as Saviour. The mention of the twenty-four elders before the living ones may be due to the fact that the redemption of creation is the subject in ch. 5 while here the subject is the salvation of the creature. Hearing the triumphant shout (the same verb *krazō* is used as in v.2) of this great crowd angels fall instantly on their faces - the profound prostration of adoring worshippers. Since the preposition "round about" governs not only "the throne" but also "the elders" and the "four beasts" it is clear that only the angels fall on their faces. This worship is purely angelic. The worship of the living ones has been heard in 4:8; the song of the twenty-four elders has been heard in 5:9-10; now it is the host of angelic beings who respond in worship to the cry of the saved company of earth.

The praise begins with "amen" their response to, and acclamation of, the adoration of the great multitude. It ends with another "amen", the affirmation of their own worship. Seven notes of praise are sounded, repeating the seven notes of 5:12 but replacing "riches" with "thanksgiving". Some grammarians will allow the article before each noun to be translated (see W. Kelly), suggesting that quality of the highest degree is implied. Thus, attributed to God in the highest degree are the blessing and the glory and the wisdom and the thanksgiving and the honour and the power and the might. These belong to God alone. Blessing above all others (*the* blessing) is the spontaneous rising of hearts at the fulfilment of God's promises in the millennial age because of the radiance of His person (the glory), the outworking of His redemptive purposes (the wisdom) and the sovereign overruling throughout history (the power) to bring His people into such blessing. As in scriptural doxologies generally to supply the verb "be" tends to weaken in some measure the expression of praise. It is not a prayer-wish for worship to "our God" but the acknowledgement that these attributes are actually His, they belong to Him by right. The personal note of the angels as they speak of "our God" is creatorial in emphasis, while the use of this same expression by the saved ones (v.10) includes the more personal note of salvation.

13-14 That one of the twenty-four elders should intervene in this scene is no argument against their representative character. It has been shown that they represent the church in priestly function. Aaronic priests of old were both individuals and representative of the whole priesthood when they acted by course in the temple (1 Chron 27:1). The intervention of the elder is in answer to the obvious perplexity of John. John did not need any introduction to the twenty-four elders, or require further explanation of the first company but he is clearly perplexed about this new company. The verb "answered" (*apokrinomai*), besides its normal use when answering a question, has the idea of "beginning to speak"; but as W.E. Vine points out it is used "always where something has preceded, either a statement or an act to which the remarks refer, e.g. Matt 11:25; Luke 14:3; John 2:18." Here the appearance of this great company and the obvious puzzlement of John causes the elder to put into words the unspoken questions of John.

Question and answer is a common device in prophecy for the unfolding of divine revelation as in Dan 7:15-16; Zech 1:9,19; 4:1-6. The RV follows the word order more closely than the AV, "These which are arrayed in the white robes, who are they, and whence came they?" The question is clearly rhetorical and intended as a prelude to the imparting of important information to John. It must be remembered that John from the opening of the seals knows only that judgment is ahead for earth and that there will be special testimony raised up for God in the witness of the 144,000. Now he is to learn that out of these dark days there will come a great host of saved ones from every nation. John's respectful reply acknowledges the superior knowledge of the elder. "Sir" is a good translation here of *kurie* and nothing beyond respect may be read into it (see Acts 16:30). In the emphatic "thou" John admits his ignorance. The answer from the elder answers both questions but in reverse order:

Whence came they? The translation in either the RV or JND is more accurate than the AV at this point and reads, "These are they which come out of the great tribulation". Alford argues that the present participle must not be translated as a past tense, as in the AV "came"; neither must it be stressed as a present, as if they were still coming out, nor must it be used as if it were future "that shall come". He emphasises that the term designates a company and writes "their description, generically, is, that 'they are they that come.....'". It is their origin that is in view not the time of their coming. The company come "out of the great tribulation" (*ek tēs thlipseōs tēs megalēs*). If the translation were to follow the word order it would read "the tribulation, the great one". The inclusion of the article with "great" allows no other conclusion than that this is the particular period of time of which Christ spoke in Matt 24:21, "For then shall be great tribulation, such as was not since the beginning of the world to this time, no nor ever shall be". The absence of the article in the Lord's statement stresses the *character* of the period, while the duplicated article here identifies the *specific period* in view. There is one specific unique period intended. Since there cannot be two unique periods of "tribulation" these passages necessarily refer to the same specific period. As already shown this is the period of three and a half years from the time of the setting up of the "abomination of desolation" in the temple at Jerusalem until Christ comes in glory. No other period in Scripture carries the designation "the great tribulation".

Christ warned His disciples, "In the world you shall have tribulation"(John 16:33). History confirms that tribulation has been the portion of saints in all ages of church testimony. Pagan and papal persecutions have raged against the faithful in Christ at different times throughout church history. Severe and trying as these times have been this is not what is in view in this passage. Attempts to make this passage refer to the trials of believers generally can explain neither the duplication of the article nor the obviously specific nature of the period identified. This false interpretation is normally invoked by those who identify the great company as the church of this age. When the passage is rightly interpreted it is clear that this is a company of saints from the period of the great tribulation already identified as the last three and a half years of Daniel's seventieth week. This does not mean that they were all saved in the last half of the tribulation, for many of them were probably saved in the first half of the week, but that they endured through the final period and emerge triumphantly from it.

Who are they? Having shown the time-period from which they come the heavenly spokesman goes on to identify the company as those "that have washed their robes and made them white in the blood of the Lamb". Two matters may be safely deduced from this description:-

1. The gospel preached in the tribulation period is the same gospel as is preached today. The value of the death of Christ is the only foundation upon which God can save men. This truth proclaimed over earth had been the means of earth-wide blessing. W. Scott agrees and in a footnote (p.173) states, "The location of the saved Gentile company, when the testimony of God reached their consciences, must not be confined to the territorial limits of Christendom. The largeness of the scene in v.9 intimates a breadth which probably covers the whole Gentile world". Very evidently the blood of Christ was the theme of the preaching across the earth.
2. "Washing" as used in this book (1:5) includes both cleansing from the filth of sin, and clearing from the guilt of sin. The blood of Christ is the only cleansing agent for sin known to Scripture (1 John 1:7). This power of the blood is reflected in the "white robes" which symbolise the acceptability of the persons before God. This symbolism will be found again in the best texts of 22:14 (RV). The aorist tense of the verbs "washed" and "made them white" points back to the moment of individual conversion. While washing is the cleansing that removes the contamination of a Beast-ruled earth in the tribulation, the making white also implies not meritorious works but the purity of character produced by the power of the blood. It will be recalled that the washing of the clothes was an essential preparation for the descent of Jehovah in Exod 19:10-11.

15-17 Two common conclusions are drawn by commentators at this point. First that this is a company of martyrs and, second, that the scene is in heaven. These conclusions have led one commentator to entitle this section, "The heavenly bliss of the martyred saints". However, careful reading will show that the passage makes no mention of martyrdom nor hints at it in any way. A later vision (15:2-3) will show the martyrs of the tribulation period in heaven; that they are in heaven is clear from the "sea of glass" and the "harps of God". It would be somewhat surprising if, without explanation, two martyr companies were seen to come out of the same period. Martyrs from the first half of the tribulation (6:9) and those from the second half of the period are specifically mentioned as being raised and reigning with Christ (20:4-6). There is nothing of resurrection or reigning suggested in connection with the destiny of this white-robed multitude.

Martyrdom seems to depend on the fact that the multitude are "clothed with white robes" and the mention of the throne seems to place them in heaven. Now of some believers in Sardis Christ promised, "They shall walk with me in white" (3:4) where there is no suggestion of martyrdom. Nor do the "white robes" given to the souls under the altar (6:11) imply their immediate resurrection, they await the resurrection at the end of the tribulation. "White robes" simply denote, in their varying contexts, acceptability before God. It seems an insufficient argument for martyrdom unless there were other contextual evidence, which in this case is absent. These are clearly saints on earth in their natural bodies; the white robes indicate that their assessment and judgment for suffering and service is over and they have been found acceptable before Him. Now as living saints they enter into millennial blessing.

The assumption that this scene is in heaven seems to be based on the expression "before the throne"(v.9). The mention of the four living ones and the twenty-four elders clearly identifies this throne as the throne of chs. 4-5, so it seems to be generally accepted that the expression to "stand before the throne" must be confined to heaven. In answer, it is suggested that the time-frame of this scene has to be noted, for the fact that this scene refers to the very end of the tribulation period seems to have been generally overlooked. This scene is to be placed in ch. 20 at the beginning of the millennial reign of Christ. The unfolding revelation to John may be seen in the following statements:-

4:1 "Behold a door was *opened* in heaven"
11:19 "The temple of God was *opened* in heaven"
15:5 "Behold the temple of the tabernacle of the testimony in heaven was *opened*"
19:11 "I saw heaven *opened*"

Thus under an opened heaven Christ sets up His kingdom; heaven and earth, for the first time are in permanent visual communication. That visual link may overshadow the throne set up on earth (Matt 25:40), before which all those persons who have come through the tribulation will be judged. It is from this throne established in Jerusalem that Christ will reign in millennial splendour as prophesied by Zechariah, "And his dominion shall be from sea even to sea, and from the river even to the ends of the earth" (Zech 9:10). It is therefore suggested that this picture is of the saved ones of the tribulation period, who, having been judged before the throne (note the white robes), now are led by Christ into millennial blessing. They are not crowned since they are subjects of the kingdom who do not share rule with Christ as resurrected saints do. In Matt 25:32 such saints are described metaphorically as sheep, while in this passage the Lamb is seen metaphorically as the shepherd.

The "therefore"(*dia touto*) is emphatic. Their washed and whitened robes indicate their acceptability before the very throne of God and their fitness for divine service while they enjoy blessings incalculable. That these kingdom blessings belonged to Israel first is indisputable, but the point of this passage is that Gentiles, on a worldwide scale, have been brought in to share the blessings. The original promise to Abraham now has its fulfilment, "And in thee shall all families of the earth be blessed" (Gen 12:3). The blessings specifically mentioned are as follows:

(a) A Divine Standing: "Therefore are they before the throne of God". In the day of grace it is inconceivable to think of the throne of God as being located in any place other than heaven, yet it is of millennial days Jeremiah speaks "At that time they shall call Jerusalem the throne of the Lord; and all nations shall be gathered unto it, to the name of the Lord, to Jerusalem" (3:17). The visual link suggested above may well continue into millennial days where this company will have an age-long standing before that throne. T.B. Baines puts the matter concisely (p.103): "If it is on earth that they wash their robes, and make them white, why should it not be on earth that they wear them? If they are conquerors on earth, why should they not carry their palms on earth also? The multitudes in heaven are said to stand around the throne but these are said to stand before it. This position does not imply that they are in heaven. During Christ's reign God will have His earthly throne, and Christ's glory will be manifested on earth. Even now believers can 'come boldly unto the throne of grace' without being in heaven, and surely similar language might be used about God's people when His presence is vouchsafed to them as it will be at this time. Standing 'before the throne and before the Lamb' may therefore only mean special nearness of access to God, such as Moses enjoyed, in the way in which He will then be approached". W. Kelly agrees with this. A footnote p.163 may be quoted, "John's vision of them there does not imply that they are to be in heaven, rather than on the earth, when the kingdom comes. 'Before the throne and before the Lamb' is moral rather than local. It merely expresses where the prophet beholds them in the mind of God. The description with which the chapter closes conveys the idea of people delivered from bitter sorrow, and sheltered for ever. No doubt this will be inexpressible comfort to them; but nothing they say rises to the height of the joy and the intelligence which are seen in the elders, nor is anything said of them which at all sets them on equal ground with these. They are never presented with crowns nor seated on thrones like the twenty-four. They are in relationship with God when He is no longer viewed as seated on a throne of grace such as we know now, but as on a throne whence judgments proceed. All harmonises with the interval of introductory government which precedes the millennium".

(b) A Divine Service: "and serve him day and night in his temple". The verb "serve" (*latreuō*) when used with reference to deity embraces worship (22:3), which is a fitting link with the mention of the temple. In this connection W. Scott writes p.173, "Another proof is here furnished that these saints are on earth, not in Heaven, for says the Seer in a subsequent vision, 'I saw no temple therein' ". The OT Scriptures are quite insistent that there will be a magnificent temple in Jerusalem in millennial days that God will own with His presence (Isa 2:2-5; 56:5-7; Ezek 40-44). This saved company from all nations are seen on earth as worshippers serving God as Anna served (Luke 2:36-38) in an earlier day. That such earthly service is uninterrupted is the force of the expression "day and night"; Anna again provides the picture and pattern of such service. It must be conceded that, however idiomatic the expression, the mention of "day and night" is more suited to earth than a realm of which it is said "there shall be no night there" (22:5).

(c) A Divine Security: "And he that sitteth on the throne shall dwell among them". Both JND and the RV have a more exact translation, "shall spread His tabernacle over them". Either translation is at variance with a scene in heaven but is perfectly in keeping with what God promised to His people in millennial times. The reference is to Isa 4:5-6, which reads in the RV, "And the Lord will create over the whole habitation of mount Zion, and over her assemblies, a cloud and smoke by day, and the shining of a flaming fire by night; for over all the glory shall be spread a canopy. And there shall be a pavilion for a shadow in the day time from the heat, and for a refuge and for a covert from storm and from rain". What Israel had enjoyed in a national way in salvation is now the realised portion of all the redeemed of earth. In the eternal state God's tabernacle will be with (*meta*) men (21:3) but in millennial times He tabernacles over (*epi*) them. Thus He Himself is the answer to all the OT prophecies (Ezek 37:27; Zech 2:10) of shelter and security for His people.

(d) A Divine Supply. "They shall hunger no more, neither thirst any more; neither shall the sun light on them nor any heat". This further description of millennial blessing is taken from Isaiah's description of physical blessing in the millennial earth: "They shall not hunger nor thirst; neither shall the heat nor sun smite them: for he that hath mercy on them shall lead them, even by the springs of water shall he guide them" (Isa 49:10). Economic conditions during the tribulation period (13:17) were such that these believers suffered physical deprivation even to hunger, thirst and nakedness (Matt 25:37). In the bowl judgments near the close of the period earth had the water supplies disrupted (16:4-6) and felt the scorching heat of the sun (16:8). While the judgments were specifically upon the followers of the Beast these saints would have seen them and perhaps felt the repercussions indirectly. Now all that is past and on this very same earth they are assured of the fulness of divine provision.

(e) A Divine Shepherd. "Because the Lamb which is in the midst of the throne shall shepherd them" (JND). These blessings are to be enjoyed under the shepherd care of the Lamb who "shall feed them". The AV translation of the verb *poimainō* as "to feed" is too narrow; the word embraces all that is involved in the work of a shepherd in looking after and tending sheep. Of its various NT occurrences Vine writes, "'To tend' would have been a consistent rendering; a shepherd does not only feed his flock". This attention of the shepherd is particularly seen in the second verb "shall lead them" (*hodēgeō*). This verb in the R.V. is always translated "guide" (Matt 15:14; Lk 6:39; Jn 16:13; Acts 8:31; Rev 7:17) and depicts the Lamb, as an eastern shepherd, going in front of the flock to "fountains of waters of life" (JND). The "waters of life" depict those satisfying streams that meet the deepest needs of human hearts. The plural "fountains" not only involves the very sources of these supplies but describes the fulness and availability of these satisfying waters to which the Lamb guides His people. They are, indeed, "wells of salvation" (Isa 12:2). The symbolic language is better adapted to an earthly than a heavenly scene and shows that in contrast to the present earth these saints will never know either stagnation or satiation; they will ever be led by the Lamb to fresh pastures.

(f) A Divine Sympathy. "And God shall wipe away all tears from their eyes". The translation "every tear" (RV and JND) unfolds a tenderness and love that sympathetically had noted every tear of these suffering saints enduring the rage of the Beast in the tribulation years. Now every trace of sorrow is to be removed by the very hand of God. This is a further direct reference to the millennial blessing of which Isaiah spoke "He will swallow up death in victory; and the Lord God will wipe away tears from off all faces" (Isa 25:8). Similar words repeated in 21:4 indicate that millennial bliss will be carried into the eternal state. It will be noted that both passages have to do with saints on earth.

CHAPTER 8

When the time-marks within the chapters already studied are observed, it is clear that this chapter marks a crisis point in the tribulation period. As the seals were opened by the Lamb the results upon earth were immediate. The blasphemous cult of the great deceiver (the white horse) may not have been recognised instantly by men as a judgment, but when this was followed by a new quarrelsomeness of nations leading to wars and rumours of wars (the red horse) thoughtful men must have wondered. The blight of famine conditions (the black horse) and then the bane of a variety of pestilences sweeping earth (the pale horse) would put beyond question that God was acting providentially in judgment. Doubtless the mass media will present many plausible and very reasonable explanations for these wars and famines and plagues. They will argue that happenings like these have punctuated the whole of history and there is no ominous significance in their sequence. Many of the world's leading scientists will be called upon to explain the astronomical happenings under the sixth seal. It is just at this point that God acts to put the matter beyond doubt, tear away the indifference of men and shatter the philosophic calm of earth with the second series of seven judgments, the seven trumpets. By the time the sixth trumpet has sounded (9:19) there can be no remaining doubt that all men will know they are fighting against God. This is why the lack of repentance of men is mentioned after the sixth trumpet (9:20-21). Forced to recognise that they are face to face with God, men defiantly refuse to acknowledge sin and to seek the salvation being preached through every nation.

In the introduction to ch.6 it was suggested that the first six seals cover the first three and a half years of the tribulation. The effects of the sixth seal will continue and be reinforced by the similar phenomena of the seventh trumpet (11:19) and the seventh bowl (16:17-21) until the tribulation ends amid the crashing of earth's cities and the return of Christ to earth (19:11). Ch. 7 has been introduced parenthetically to show that during these seven years God will have a testimony on earth that cannot be eliminated by all the might of Satan. Israel nationally is taken up again in the 144,000 saved and sealed to bear the message of salvation to every nation (7:1-8). The white-robed multitude shows how effective that national testimony has been; an innumerable company from all nations comes out of the tribulation to go into millennial blessing under the shepherd care of the Lamb. This chapter moves to the last half of the seven year period when, in the blowing of the trumpets, God summons men to war. The chapters may be presented thus:

Ch. 6	The Commencement of the Tribulation The Opening of the six seals.		
Ch. 7	The Companies in the Tribulation		
	Going in	The Sealed Ones	vv.1-8
	Coming out	The Saved Ones	vv.9-17
Chs. 8-9	The Continuation of the Tribulation		

4. *The Seventh Seal*
8:1-5

v.1 "And when he had opened the seventh seal, there was silence in heaven about the space of half an hour.

v.2 And I saw the seven angels which stood before God; and to them were given seven trumpets.
v.3 And another angel came and stood at the altar, having a golden censer; and there was given unto him much incense, that he should offer it with the prayers of all saints upon the golden altar which was before the throne.
v.4 And the smoke of the incense, which came with the prayers of the saints, ascended up before God out of the angel's hand.
v.5 And the angel took the censer, and filled it with fire of the altar, and cast it into the earth:-and there were voices, and thunderings, and lightnings, and an earthquake."

1 It is only partly correct to say that the seven trumpets follow the seven seals. The better word to describe the relationship is telescopic, since the seventh seal opens out into the seven trumpets. If this is not so then there is nothing whatever revealed about the seventh seal. Scroggie in a concluding remark, after discussing the chronology of the book, says "The trumpets, therefore, do not double back over all or some of the seals, but lie under the sixth seal, and proceed from it. For this reason it is equally incorrect to speak of the trumpets as following the seals. They do not follow, but are the seventh seal".

The opening of the seventh seal is a climactic moment, a moment marked by the silence in heaven. If the action of the Lamb taking the book from the hand of the Throne-Sitter (5:7) is the key action of the book then the opening of the seventh seal must be seen as the key moment of the book. With the opening of the seventh seal by the authorised hand of Christ the whole scroll may now be opened and read. The title-deed of earth can now be examined and from this moment all the subsequent drama unfolds as Christ dispossesses the usurper from earth. In the same way it will be shown that the seven bowls in ch. 16 flow out of the seventh trumpet; and when the last trumpet is blown the tribulation is over, the millennium is introduced. The silence in heaven indicates that the momentous nature of the moment is recognised before the throne where even the worshipping hosts of angels fall silent. The moment is also ominous; it is the calm before the storm, the still that presages the coming tempest.

While this sudden stillness in heaven is certainly ominous, the length of the silence is suggestive. The time-scale of half-an-hour is, of course, an earthly measurement, necessary as the vision is mediated through John. This is the only occasion in the NT when the word for "half-an-hour" (*hēmiōrion*) is used. Vine's comment is helpful; he describes the half-hour as "a period corresponding to the time customarily spent in silent worship in the temple during the burning of incense". This is significant when it is noted that the offering of incense takes places (v.3) before a trumpet is blown. W. Scott may be correct when he states with reference to the action of the angel before the altar in vv.2-6, "In the meantime we are called to witness an action of an entirely different character from anything which has yet passed before us, and one which fills up the interval of the half-hour". While this assumes that the action of vv.3-5 takes place during the silence it would seem that the silence does continue until broken by the "voices, and thunderings, and lightnings, and earthquake".

2 As the silence in heaven deepens John's attention is drawn to the seven angels. It must have added to the hush in the cosmos as each angel is solemnly, and it would seem silently, presented with a trumpet. The presence of the article defines the seven as a group and their importance is shown by the expression "stood before God". Hierarchal ranking amongst the angelic hosts is implied in Scripture (e.g. Col 1:16; 1 Pet 3:22). The phrase "these that stand by" (Zech 3:7) implies a special nearness to the throne of God for some angels or men. This can be seen in Gabriel who identified himself to Mary in Luke 1:19, "I am Gabriel that stand in the presence of God". Thus from the court of heaven, from those who stand in sacred nearness to God, seven angels are commissioned to introduce what is in effect a holy war on behalf of heaven, the trumpet indicates their mission. The passive voice of the verb "give", without identifying the giver, is what Rienecker calls "the theological passive indicating that God is the One who gives". This is a form used often in this book to indicate either direct divine commission or indirect permission from God. In this case the giving is by direct commission from the throne.

3-5 The background scene for the opening of the seals was described in chs. 4-5; here the same throne-room is seen but the focus falls upon an angel and the altars instead of upon the throne itself and the Lamb. Two matters need to be addressed:

The adjective "another" (*allos*) should settle the identity of this angel (see 7:2 for the same term). It identifies another of the "angel class" but serves to distinguish him from the group of seven already mentioned. In spite of the clarity of the language many commentators insist on understanding this angel either as Christ Himself in high priestly ministry or as a representation of Him. W. Scott writes p.180, "We are satisfied that the angel-priest is Christ, our great High Priest. The service at the altars proves it, for both the brazen altar and the golden altar are referred to. No mere creature could add efficacy to the prayers of saints, for that could only be effected by One having in Himself independent right and competency". This is a misunderstanding, the AV reading is the correct translation and shows that it is the incense that he is given that the angel adds to the prayers. The angel himself adds nothing; he adds to the prayers of saints that which has been given to him, the "much incense" that speaks of Christ.

To argue as some do (see J.F. Walvoord p.152, although it must be pointed out that he is quoting the arguments of others) that the appearances of Christ in the OT, as the Angel of Jehovah (Gen 16:7; Exod 3:2; Num 22:22, Judges 2:1; 1 Kings 19:7; Ps 34:7; Isa 37:36) lend support to His appearing here as an angel-priest is false deduction. While Christophanies in the OT are part of the unfolding revelation of deity, to see such theophanies in this book is assuming what requires proof. The incarnation of Christ and His assumption of permanent manhood rule out any subsequent appearance in angelic form; a truth that is confirmed by the relationship established in Heb 1:4-13 between Christ as man and the angels.

Any thought of mediatorial or intercessory work in the office of this angel is as foreign in this passage as it is when the twenty-four elders present the vials full of the prayers of saints in 5:8. In comparing these two passages Alford remarks, "Any theological difficulty which belongs to the one belongs also to the other; and it is a canon which we must strictly observe in interpretation, that we are not, on account of any supposed doctrinal propriety, to depart from the plain meaning of words". While many able and respected expositors see this angel as Christ in angelic form it is much better to allow scripture to mean what it says; to do otherwise confuses the picture. R.H. Mounce (page 181) asks rhetorically, "Would the central figure of Revelation be introduced into the text with such an indefinite title?"

The angel came and stood at the altar. The aorist tense of the verb "stood" can be rendered "he took his place" (Rienecker) thus highlighting the moment of divine action. Alford translates the preposition "at" (*epi* with the genitive), as "over" and interprets it as indicating that the altar is seen by John as between himself and the angel. In the hand of the angel John sees a "golden censer" (Heb 9:4), a vessel used both in the tabernacle and in the temple service (1 Kings 7:50; 2 Chron 4:22). While this censer was used to carry the incense into the holy place (2 Chron 26:19; Ezek 8:11) its other use was to carry burning coals from the brazen altar to the golden altar. Upon these coals the handful of incense borne by the priest was placed when he reached the golden altar. This was the order on the great day of atonement which seems to furnish the background here (Lev 16:12-13). It is to be noticed that it is out of the "angel's hand" (v.4) that the smoke of the incense ascends, an expression that by metonymy points to the action centred on the golden censer.

The sacred incense used in the tabernacle service was made up of an equal weight of four spices: stacte, onycha, galbanum and frankincense (Exod 30:34-38). This holy perfume had its full sweetness brought out when placed on the burning coals taken from the brazen altar, delighting God and enveloping the priests. The four spices find their antitype in the perfectly balanced character of the unique person of Christ seen in His earthly ministry. Nevertheless, the full fragrance of His character can be fully enjoyed only by God and those in priestly fellowship with Him, when Christ is seen in the death of the cross. It meant death to attempt to imitate or misuse incense.

"Much incense" shows the wealth available in the worth of Christ to be added to the prayers of the saints. The passive verb "was given" is another theological passive (see v.2) to show that whatever intermediate agencies God uses, God Himself is the ultimate giver. The prayers of saints are made acceptable to God by the fragrance of Christ. It is tempting to limit the prayers here to the cries from the souls "under the altar" (6:9), a view that could find some support in the use of the article with prayers. However since the text speaks of "the prayers of all the saints" thc idea must be much wider than simply the cry of the martyred saints for the avenging of their blood. Embraced here are all the as yet unanswered longings, aspirations and hopes of the hearts of the people of God through the ages. This consideration points, not to prayers in general, but to one prayer in particular; the prayer that Christ taught His disciples, "Thy kingdom come" (Matt 6:9-13); that unanswered prayer of the ages is now about to be answered in dramatic fashion (see 11:15).

The two altars that in OT typology reflected the work and worth of Christ are before us in these verses and it is the movement of the angel between these altars that provides the pictorial background for this scene. It has been suggested that the altar in 6:9 must be the brazen altar where the sacrifices were slain and the blood poured out. This altar points to the sacrifice of Christ as the Lamb. On the great day of atonement, the tenth day of the seventh month, it was written of the high priest that: "he shall take a censer full of burning coals of fire from off the altar before the Lord and his hands full of sweet incense beaten small, and bring it within the veil: And he shall put the incense upon the fire before the Lord, that the cloud of incense may cover the mercy seat that is upon the testimony, that he die not". This is the pattern for the action in this passage. Commencing his ministry at the brazen altar (v.3a) with the golden censer full of coals from that altar, he is given the "much incense" to put on the coals when he reaches the golden altar (v.3b). The "smoke of the incense" (v.4) describes the cloud of incense rising to the throne carrying with it the prayers of the saints. Presented to God these prayers are acceptable through Christ. The angel carrying the empty censer moves back to the brazen altar, refills his censer with fire from the altar and casts the fire "into (*eis*) the earth". The action symbolises the wrath of God against sin. This fire blazed at Calvary but must now fall upon unrepentant men on a sin-stained earth. The reality is that the wrath, of which John the Baptist preached (Luke 3:7), is about to burst upon earth. The worldwide scope of the coming storm is heard in the "voices, and thunderings, and lightnings, and an earthquake". Three of these things – the "lightnings, and thunderings and voices", heralded the opening of the seals (4:5); now an earthquake is added. Under the seventh trumpet (11:19) earth's terror will be increased with the additional mention of the "great hail", while under the seventh bowl (16:17-21) unrepentant man will find all five things repeated with terrible effect. The petitions of the ages and the perfume of Christ have demanded that God be vindicated in penal judgments upon sinners.

5. *The First Six Trumpets*
8:6-9:21

v.6 "And the seven angels which had the seven trumpets prepared themselves to sound.

v.7 The first angel sounded, and there followed hail and fire mingled with blood, and they were cast upon the earth: and the third part of trees was burnt up, and all green grass was burnt up.

v.8 And the second angel sounded, and as it were a great mountain burning with fire was cast into the sea: and the third part of the sea became blood;

v.9 And the third part of the creatures which were in the sea, and had life, died: and the third part of the ships were destroyed.
v.10 And the third angel sounded, and there fell a great star from heaven, burning as it were a lamp, and it fell upon the third part of the rivers, and upon the fountains of waters;
v.11 And the name of the star is called Wormwood and the third part of the waters became wormwood; and many men died of the waters, because they were made bitter.
v.12 And the fourth angel sounded, and the third part of the sun was smitten, and the third part of the moon, and the third part of the stars; so as the third part of them was darkened, and the day shone not for a third part of it, and the night likewise.
v.13 And I beheld, and heard an angel flying through the midst of heaven, saying with a loud voice, Woe, woe, woe, to the inhabiters of the earth by reason of the other voices of the trumpet of the three angels, which are yet to sound!"

6 The audible, visible portents of the storm die away and John sees the seven angels with the trumpets put them to their lips, or as the RV translates, "prepared themselves to sound". The verb "to sound" (*salpizō*) is from the same root as the noun "trumpet". The silence of heaven had been broken by the storm signs, now the trumpets are about to shatter the stillness. The blowing of these trumpets would introduce the most shattering physical upheavals on earth since Noah's Flood. Trumpets played an important part in the affairs of Israel; they were of two different kinds. Silver trumpets (*chatsotserah*), associated with the tabernacle, were used to control Israel in their movements in peace and in war (Num 10:1-10). Fashioned from the silver redemption money the blowing of these trumpets reminded Israel that they were the redeemed of the Lord and under His direction. The second kind was the trumpet of ram's horn (*shophar*), which was first heard at Sinai (Exod 19:19) and was heard repeatedly in the conquest of Canaan (Josh 6:4). It is this word that is used metaphorically in prophetic ministry (Joel 2:1, 15). The fact that the same Greek word *salpinx* is used in the LXX for both trumpets makes the meaning here a matter of judgment. Despite the tabernacle imagery the fact that the silver trumpet was used only in relation to the people of God makes its use unlikely in this context. It is better to see here the "war trumpet" (*shophar*) used in the capture of Jericho (Josh 6:4). The OT record is dramatic, "And seven priests shall bear before the ark seven trumpets of rams' horns": when these trumpets had sounded the final note the mighty fortress of Jericho fell. When these seven trumpets have sounded (remembering that the seven bowls are the seventh trumpet) the world empire under the Beast will have been judged by God.

Trumpet One

A common feature in all the series of sevens in this book is their division into two groups of four and three. The four horsemen link the first four seals together and distinguish them from the last three. The first four trumpets affect such physical things as earth, sea, rivers and sun while the final three trumpets are different. The same four and three grouping is seen in the seven bowls.

7 The symbolic action of the casting of the coals to earth brings a terrible reality to that same earth when the trumpets are blown. With the blowing of the first trumpet, "there was hail and fire mingled with blood" (JND) – language that describes a terrible storm. It is as if every volcano of history has erupted simultaneously over one third of the earth. Mercy mingled with the judgment is seen in the fact that only one third of the earth is affected; yet within that limited area what terrible devastation! There is very good manuscript evidence for including "and the third part of the earth was burnt up" after the word "earth" (see RV; JND). The next sentence explains that it is the trees and the grass within that area that are totally "burnt up". This verb "burnt up" repeated four times (in the RV and JND) builds up to a climax so that the blaze seems to mount to heaven. Vine comments on the various occurrences of the verb , "In each place the full rendering 'burn utterly' might be used, as in Rev 18:8".

Something of this kind had happened once before in history on a smaller scale when literal hail and fire fell upon earth in the seventh plague on Egypt: "And Moses stretched forth his rod toward heaven: and the Lord sent thunder and hail, and the fire ran along the ground: and the Lord rained hail upon the land of Egypt. So there was hail, and fire mingled with the hail, very grievous, such as there was none like it in all the land of Egypt since it became a nation" (Exod 9:23-24). The consequence is described: "and the hail smote every herb of the field, and brake every tree of the field". On this occasion a storm out-ranking all the storms of the past in size and intensity brings a terrible ecological disaster upon earth. In this storm there is the added and more terrifying feature of blood. Men and animals die in the storm and their blood caught in the cyclonic winds colours the hail and the rain. An even more terrifying scene of divine judgment is painted as this blood-coloured storm leaves a blazing landscape. Destruction of a third of earth's forests is of such a scale that many must die. No mention is made of this at this stage, which may suggest the area is one of the more sparsely populated areas of earth with no major population centre included. Speculation as to the possible origin of such an unprecedented catastrophe is pointless; men on earth at the time will recognise that this must come from God acting in judgment. Some expositors limit the "earth" to the "prophetic earth", a term without any scriptural basis, that seems to have become a semi-technical term to describe the lands of the Mediterranean basin and the Middle East. Thus W. Scott writes p.185 categorically, "The western part of the prophetic earth is here designated", by which he seems to mean Europe. To limit the judgment in this way is without scriptural support.

This simple and straightforward interpretation in literal terms is to be compared with the symbolic school which only seems to create difficulties.

Perhaps the clearest expression of the symbolic method applied to this trumpet is given by John Phillips (p.129): "On the other hand, the verse can just as easily be symbolic. In this case the grass could represent the masses of mankind and the trees could represent prominent leaders and rulers (Ps 103:15; Judges 9:7-15; Dan 4:4-27). What is symbolised is a major upheaval among the nations that results in the downfall of many people in high places and a mass deportation of the globe". W. Scott (p.183) writes in the same vein when, commenting on the hail, the fire and the blood, he writes, "These are not to be understood as literal destructive agencies. They are symbols". He goes on to explain that "hail signifies a sudden, sharp, and overwhelming judgment from above, God is the executor of it (see Isa 28:2,17; Rev 11:19; 16:21). Fire is the expression of God's wrath ... Blood signifies death, both physical and moral. If the latter it would assume the form or character of apostasy, i.e. the utter abandonment of revealed truth, all religious profession given up". While the symbols may be correctly interpreted their application in this context leads to terrible confusion so that the reader becomes lost in woolly rhetoric, whereas taken in their simple literal meaning the terms describe a terrible atmospheric storm on earth that leaves an area completely devastated as a mark of its passing.

Trumpet Two

8-9 As the second angel sounds his trumpet John sees a further terrible judgment fall; this time the blow falls on the sea. The closest simile he can use to describe this fearful sight is to describe it as "a great mountain burning with fire". Since John uses a simile this is clearly not an actual burning mountain, for example the crest of an exploding volcano, but something that closely resembles this. This object hurtling into the earth's gravitational field blazes through the atmosphere and smashes into the sea. The aorist passive of the verb "to cast", used for the third time in the passage, emphasises the nature of the happening; it is almost as if this mountain-like object had been hurled from heaven to earth. As John watches a third part of earth's sea takes on the colour of blood. Immediately the marine life in that area died and ships in the same area were destroyed. The phrase "and had life" defines animal life in terms of the soul, based on Gen 2:19. The word "destroyed" (*diaphtheirō*) is the strengthened form of the word *phtheirō* and could be translated "were utterly corrupted" – the meaning it has in 11:18.

There can hardly be any question that what John sees is an extra-terrestrial body, like a great mountain hurtling towards the earth. The white heat results from the friction of the earth's atmosphere, and the igniting of the combustible materials leaves a blazing trail across the sky. A giant meteorite or a wandering asteroid caught by the earth's gravitational field would fit the picture exactly. The collision with the sea would have the impact of a nuclear bomb, the poisoned waters appearing as blood, lending terror to the scene as all the ships within the area are smashed and sink. Whether the "blood" is the result of a reaction between the chemicals carried by the invading body and the organisms in the water, or whether the water is stained with literal blood can be a matter of debate. It should be pointed out that "red tides" have been known in various places around the world as the result of millions of dead micro-organisms; these do have the appearance of blood. The same problem relates to the first plague in Egypt when the Nile was smitten and the water became "blood". There is little doubt that Scripture, as is common practice in normal conversation, uses the language of appearance to describe the visual.

In recent years there have been several occasions when an asteroid has come uncomfortably close to earth, and occasions when a comet has passed through the earth's orbit, giving rise to fears of terrible catastrophes. Before these recent happenings W. Hoste (p.66) wrote in the early years of this century, "Why should not this 'great mountain' be a gigantic meteor (like the enormous meteoric stone which struck Siberia only a few years ago, digging a huge trench between thirty and forty miles long, burning up whole forests for miles on either side, till it buried itself in a gigantic crater,) plunging into the depths of the ocean, with general damage to the fish life and enormous waves of translation, resulting in damage to shipping". Very likely the approaching meteor or asteroid will be visible for days spreading terror round the world, and while its impact point will have been calculated and evacuation procedures initiated, many people must die in the destruction of the shipping.

Those who follow the symbolic method of interpretation have great problems relating cause and effect under this trumpet blast. It is generally pointed out that a mountain in Scripture speaks of a king or a kingdom. The fact that it is burning indicates that this person or system is to be used to execute the judgment of God (W. Scott). The sea is generally agreed to be a symbol of the restless nations of the world. One commentator presents the case thus: "Ejected from its normal place, the burning mountain was cast into the restless sea of a turbulent world, with a calamitous effect on the commerce and with the result of an appalling loss of life. At the impact of the mountain, the waters became blood, and a third of the creatures in the incarnadined sea died and a third of the ships were destroyed" (F.A. Tatford p.107). The explanation of W. Scott p.188 is similar: "Now this destructive power, whether a nation or a system, violently thrown into the unformed masses of mankind not only works awful destruction, physical and moral, on peoples and persons, it wrecks also the commerce and means of communication with distant countries". It must be pointed out that many a king and many a kingdom has collapsed throughout history, and men, even within such a kingdom have scarcely noticed it. The collapse of the USSR in the last few years is a recent case; even such a world power collapsing had relatively little impact on men generally. Believers would see in it certain scriptural principles of divine retribution, but it carried no message concerning the wrath of God to the majority of mankind. This kind of interpretation does not do justice to the plain language of scripture as it symbolises away the terrifying nature of this trumpet blast. When this trumpet blows it is made absolutely clear to men that they are at war with God.

Trumpet Three

10-11 When speaking of this tribulation period Christ gave a very clear warning when He said, "Fearful sights and great signs shall there be from heaven" (Luke 21:11). Already the fearful storm (first trumpet) has left a third of the earth burnt up; the terrifying asteroid or meteorite (second trumpet) has crashed down to earth resulting in the corrupted sea bringing death to all marine life, interrupting commerce and destroying communications in a large area of earth. Men know that God is dealing judicially with them. The stress upon the third part affected in each of the first four trumpets will be a further and convincing evidence to men that these are by no means random events or simply cosmic accidents. Mercy is mixed with the judgment and a divine hand limits the destruction at this point. The failure of men to repent as the trumpets are blown (9:20-21) shows culpability; they are fitting themselves for the further unrestricted judgments under the seven bowls.

The third trumpet blast heralds the fall of "a great star from heaven". Following the principle of literal interpretation where it makes good sense there is no difficulty in seeing this star as a heavenly body, very possibly a comet, whose orbit has been altered by God to bring it within the gravitational range of earth. This would explain perfectly the difference between this happening and that under the second trumpet. The verb here is "to fall". The adjective "burning" is used for both objects but in this case it is qualified by the simile "as a lamp", indicating that it is bright enough to shed light on earth. A comet drawing near to earth, reflecting the light of the sun, gets brighter and brighter, until, if it is large enough and comes near enough, it outshines the stars and the planets. In the colloquial language of appearance it would be called a "falling star" which to the natural eye is a spectacular sight. A "falling star" to an astronomer is frequently nothing more than a piece of rock the size of an acorn caught in the earth's gravitational field and becoming white hot as it falls through the atmosphere. This comet, however, resembles a blazing torch with its tail millions of miles long. In the final stages of its approach just before collision with earth it would be a fearful sight. From the result of its fall it seems that it will smash into some high plateau or on some great water-table where rivers rise and fountains abound. This is a reasonable deduction since a third part of the water system of earth is affected by the contamination of the springs and rivers by this death-carrying comet.

Many have been puzzled by the fact that this falling star is given the name "Wormwood" (*apsinthos*). The suggestion by H.M. Morris (p.149) is most reasonable in the context: "Whatever the exact nature of the substance of this deadly star may be, it is obviously lethal to drink, and many men will die as a result of drinking water from the rivers and wells contaminated by it. As a result, the star is actually given the official astronomic (or popular) name of 'Wormwood', probably in retrospect and in commemoration of its death-dealing nature. It is certainly possible that spectrographic analysis of its light while approaching the earth will give astronomers sufficient knowledge of its composition to enable them to christen it with this appropriate name and to warn people about it even before it strikes the earth". This is in keeping with present-day scientific practice. Whether they be abnormal weather-systems building up to hurricane force in the Caribbean Sea or out of control space capsules (as happened in 1990 with the Russian Sputnik) astronomers distinguish them by appropriate names. When disaster looms over earth this approaching comet would seem to be identified by the name "Wormwood". Wormwood is a species of plant noted for its intensely bitter taste and poisonous nature (Deut 29:18; Prov 5:4; Jer 9:15; Amos 5:7; 6:12 (translated 'hemlock')). The French alcoholic drink *absinthe* is distilled from it. It is used in the OT as a symbol of bitterness and sorrow; the threat to the false prophets of Israel may be relevant in this connection: "Thus saith the Lord of hosts concerning the prophets, Behold I will feed them with wormwood, and make them drink the water of gall" (Jer 23:15). What was symbolical then is literal here, as literal as the opposite miracle at Marah (Exod 15:25). This falling star is going to make a third of earth's water supply undrinkable; those who do drink it die.

Commentators who follow the symbolic line of interpretation agree in general with F.A. Tatford: "Like the fallen wormwood, some apostate leader of a later day will become an instrument of wrath in the hands of the Almighty. His evil influence or corrupting teaching will poison morals, principles, and motives over a very wide sphere, and the spiritual death of countless numbers will plainly ensue from the infection". In answer it may be pointed out that such things have occurred frequently and their repetition, even on a unprecedented scale, would not seem to constitute the direct intervention of God to bring about the terrifying and terrible judgment that is here pictured. It is better to understand the judgment as a direct physical judgment of God upon earth.

Trumpet Four

12 The ecological and environmental disasters that have befallen earth from the first three trumpets will, doubtless, be the subject of endless debate. Scientists, astronomers, philosophers and possibly theologians will seek to explain the catastrophes that have come upon the earth. With a variety of theories they will seek to show that these events are but natural and are not the evidence of divine intervention in earth affairs. Men of course will be only too anxious to have their fears put to rest. However, as the fourth trumpet is sounded all such theories will be confounded and unbelief challenged in unmistakable fashion. God touches the sky. To men the heavenly bodies have appeared untouchable, unimpedable in their paths through an ordered universe; now they are affected. The sun, the moon and the stars feel the touch of omnipotence and to men there is nothing so terrifying. A collapsing government, an overthrown kingdom or an apostate religious leader is greeted with casual interest if not total indifference by all but the people immediately involved, but let there be the possiblity of erratic movement in a heavenly body and attention is instant. This is why the terrible storm, the blazing forest, the bloodied sea and the poisoned rivers are but preparing for the moment when God will touch the heavens. God does this under this fourth trumpet.

Those who interpret symbolically seem to have little trouble with this trumpet. One such has written in reference to the sun, moon and stars: "These are the consistent symbols of rule in government, but now with apostasy of leaders comes the darkness of anarchy, and if the light that is in thee be darkness, how great is that darkness". One simple scriptural statement shows how illogical this view is. The final statement of the verse reads "and the night likewise". Consistency in interpretation is essential; night (darkness) and day (light) cannot symbolise the same thing; if anarchy darkens the day, it is very hard to see how the night can be affected in the same way.

It is much more in keeping with the plain statements of Scripture to see described here an astronomical happening. A black body of some kind, a body that absorbs light instead of reflecting it, is allowed of God to penetrate the solar system. Some of these bodies have already been identified within our galaxy. The hand of God overrules the proportions of the body and its orbit so that, instead of total destruction, it produces one of the most dramatic signs in the heavens ever witnessed. In its passage this body causes a partial eclipse of the sun in the day, and a partial eclipse of the moon at night. As men watch in terror it darkens one third of the stars normally visible. This intruder would have the double effect of shortening the day by four hours, as if the sun had set, and extending the night by the same period. The last sentence is somewhat ambiguous yet seems to mean that as the day was shortened so the darkness of the night was deepened. There is thus a four hour time change for the duration of this astronomical happening. Other possible means of accomplishing this may be suggested but the means is really irrelevant; God is doing this miraculously and men know that it can come only from Him. This is a visible display of divine power outside the range of normal experience. To believe that God can act in this way is not gullibility but faith in a mighty God; it is neither necessary to explain it nor spiritualise it to mean something other than is stated. God does not explain how He brought the three-day darkness upon Egypt in the ninth plague (Exod 10:21-22), a somewhat parallel event; neither is it explained how God gave a long day in Joshua's time (Josh 10:12-14), nor how He caused the shadow on the sun-dial of Ahaz to go back ten degrees (Isa 38:7-8). Faith still accepts that He will bring to pass this unprecedented astronomical happening, possibly by a means not yet known to astronomers, and men will know that God is speaking. There is no doubt that Luke 21:25-26 will be fulfilled at this point: "...men's hearts failing them for fear, and for looking after those things which are coming on the earth: for the powers of heaven shall be shaken".

A review of these first four trumpet judgments indicates how rapidly God can change the environment in which men had thought themselves independent and secure.

At a superficial level men will see the beauty of the environment ravaged, the bounty of the sea diminished, the availability of water restricted and brilliance of the very heavens darkened. Beyond this the great forest fires will have had a dramatic effect on world commerce in many ways. The carbon dioxide in the atmosphere will have increased and the renewal of oxygen will be reduced as a result of the loss of so many trees; the "greenhouse effect" (of so much concern to environmentalists today) will accelerate and earth temperatures soar. The succeeding blows under the final three trumpets will leave men in no doubt that God is acting. The very fact that the judgment is limited to a third part in each case is additional evidence that these happenings are neither by chance nor accidental. The limitation of the plagues in Egypt was as much a sign of the divine hand as the plagues themselves and the same is true in this tribulation day. It must be remembered also that these happenings are the background against which the gospel is being preached, and doubtless they will form the text of many a gospel message as the witnesses of ch. 7 point men to the God they are defying.

Interlude

13 Before the last three trumpets are blown there is an interlude that allows John a short respite in the unfolding drama of divine revelation. The interlude serves a second purpose: it permits a threefold sob of "woe" to be heard from a flying eagle heralding even more terrible judgments to come.

Most textual authorities are agreed that the true reading is "eagle" (*aetos*) and not "angel" (*angelos*) as in the AV. The word can mean "eagle" or "vulture" (contrast Matt 24:28 where vultures would be the better translation) but here it is better to translate as "eagle". The flying angel in 14:6 has a ministry of a very different character. "Mid-heaven" (*mesouranēma*) in middle-eastern lands was almost a technical word to describe the noonday sky, as one looked south, when the sun was at its highest. It may be relevant to note that of the areas of creation represented by the four living ones (4:6-8) around the throne, birdlife is the only part that has not been directly affected by the trumpet judgments. Now the eagle brings a message of woe to the untouched parts of earth. The use of the eagle as a symbol of coming judgment is clearly established in the OT and points very directly to an invading enemy. Deut 28:49 warned Israel: "The Lord shall bring a nation against thee from far, from the end of the earth, as swift as the eagle flieth". The swiftness of the Babylonian invasion in Habakkuk's day (1:8) is depicted under the figure of an eagle: "They shall fly as the eagle that hasteth to eat". Hos 8:1 uses the same simile,

"He shall come as an eagle against the house of the Lord". This invasion theme symbolised in the eagle has implications for the next two trumpets.

The threefold repetition of *ouai* (pronounced ou-aye) seems from its very sound to suggest not merely a wail, but a curse that will be realised in the "voices" of the three trumpets yet to be sounded. When heaven wails earth should tremble. Those marked for judgment are described as "the inhabiters of the earth", a class already mentioned in 3:10; 6:10; 8:13. The description is moral and spiritual rather than physical; these are men who by deliberate choice have made their home under the sway of the Beast. They have chosen to be identified with him rather than with the Lamb. They must expect to share in the judgment of their chosen leader, just as Egyptians identified with Pharaoh shared the judgment that fell upon their gods.

CHAPTER 9

The Woe Judgements

The importance of the next two trumpets may be gathered from the fact that while John described the first four trumpets in six verses he takes twenty-one verses to describe the happenings under these two "woes". The first four trumpets have shown dramatically that God is dealing with earth; that it is "the day of the Lord", the day of direct divine intervention. Up to this point it has been mainly the physical things on earth that have been directly affected, trees and grass have been burned up, a third part of the sea has been turned into blood and the marine life in that area destroyed. Poisoned water supplies and the astronomical upset in the sun have doubtless added to the terror on earth. While many people may have died in the blazing forests, on the sinking ships and as a consequence of the poisoned water (8:11), most of the people on earth have not been directly affected. As the mobilised technology of earth devises treatment for the poisoned waters and philosophers find reasonable scientific explanations for the astronomical phenomena, men will happily settle down again and ignore these divine interventions. However, dramatic changes are about to take place under these next two trumpets. Men come under direct divine judgment and millions die (v.18).

5. *The First Six Trumpets (continued)* (9:1-12)

v.1 "And the fifth angel sounded, and I saw a star fall from heaven unto the earth: and to him was given the key of the bottomless pit.

v.2 And he opened the bottomless pit; and there arose a smoke out of the pit, as the smoke of a great furnace; and the sun and the air were darkened by reason of the smoke of the pit.

v.3 And there came out of the smoke locusts upon the earth:-and unto them was given power, as the scorpions of the earth have power.

v.4 And it was commanded them that they should not hurt the grass of the earth, neither any green thing, neither any tree; but only those men which have not the seal of God in their foreheads.
v.5 And to them it was given that they should not kill them, but that they should be tormented five months; and their torment *was* as the torment of a scorpion, when he striketh a man.
v.6 And in those days shall men seek death, and shall not find it; and shall desire to die, and death shall flee from them.
v.7 And the shapes of the locusts *were* like unto horses prepared unto battle; and on their heads *were* as it were crowns like gold, and their faces *were* as the faces of men.
v.8 And they had hair as the hair of women, and their teeth were as the *teeth* of lions.
v.9 And they had breastplates, as it were breastplates of iron; and the sound of their wings *was* as the sound of chariots of many horses running to battle.
v.10 And they had tails like unto scorpions, and there were stings in their tails: and their power *was* to hurt men five months.
v.11 And they had a king over them, *which* is the angel of the bottomless pit, whose name in the Hebrew tongue is Abaddon, but in the Greek tongue hath *his* name Apollyon.
v.12 One woe is past; *and*, behold, there come two woes more hereafter.
v.13 And the sixth angel sounded, and I heard a voice from the four horns of the golden altar which is before God,
v.14 Saying to the sixth angel which had the trumpet, Loose the four angels which are bound in the great river Euphrates.
v.15 And the four angels were loosed, which were prepared for an hour, and a day, and a month, and a year, for to slay the third part of men.
v.16 And the number of the army of the horsemen *were* two hundred thousand thousand: and I heard the number of them.
v.17 And thus I saw the horses in the vision, and them that sat on them, having breastplates of fire, and of jacinth, and brimstone; and the heads of the horses *were* as the heads of lions; and out of their mouths issued fire and smoke and brimstone.
v.18 By these three was the third part of men killed, by the fire, and by the smoke, and by the brimstone, which issued out of their mouths.
v.19 For their power is in their mouth, and in their tails: for their tails *were* like unto serpents, and had heads, and with them they do hurt.
v.20 And the rest of the men which were not killed by these plagues yet repented not of the works of their hands, that they should not worship devils, and idols of gold, and silver, and brass, and stone, and of wood: which neither can see, nor hear, nor walk:
v.21 Neither repented they of their murders, nor of their sorceries, nor of their fornication, nor of their thefts."

Trumpet Five - First Woe

1 The trumpet blast of the fifth angel presents John with an unforgettable sight – "a star from heaven fallen unto the earth" (RV). This translation correctly links the expression "from heaven" with the star and gives the perfect participle "fallen" its proper weight. When John sees the star it has already fallen to earth; he does not see its actual fall.

Falling stars have occurred under the sixth seal (6:13) and a falling star has been described under the third trumpet (8:10); both of these happenings are best explained as literal astronomical events. It is equally clear that the star in this passage must be taken symbolically. The lack of any accompanying physical phenomena as well as the handing over of a key demands that the star be symbolic of a person. A literal star can hardly be given a key with which to open the "bottomless pit".

Scripture leaves no doubt about the person symbolised by this star. The sphere from which he has fallen and the action permitted to him rules out any possibility of his being a man. To interpret the star as a symbol of the man of sin or the false prophet does not fit the picture; it requires heaven to be symbolic of some "moral" sphere from which an earthly leader falls to release demonic powers. Neither of the beasts in ch. 13 had been in any sphere from which he could fall, and for a man to release demons would be remarkable. Only one personage fits the picture; he is identified in Scripture as the "fallen" one. Isaiah spoke of this one, "How art thou fallen from heaven, O Lucifer, son of the morning" (Isa 14:12). Christ spoke of the same one when He said, "I beheld Satan as lightning fall from heaven" (Luke 10:18). This fallen one, stripped of the high authority that belonged to him at creation (Ezek 28:14-15) yet still possessing mighty power, is permitted access to heavenly realms (Job 2:1) until the "war in heaven"(12:7-9) at the midpoint of the tribulation. The issue of that war is that Satan and his angels are expelled from the heavens. It is suggested, that this is the event that lies behind this fallen star being on earth, for it is now that he sets about mustering his forces. By divine permission this banished being is given the key to the abyss and he uses it to release the hordes of his followers who have been locked up there.

The prison of these satanic powers is called "the bottomless pit" which is an excellent translation as the word *abussos* means "without bottom"; the RV is perhaps more graphic, "the pit of the abyss". The word pit generally depicts a well-shaft (as in Luke 14:5) but here describes the narrow subterranean passage leading to this dread abode. This bottomless pit is mentioned seven times in this book (vv.1, 2, 11; 11:7; 17:8; 20:1,3) and clearly conveys the idea of a specially-dark, deep prison house. Whether it is within hades itself as a special compartment, or distinct from it, Scripture does not reveal. It is, however, reserved for the imprisonment of spiritual and demonic beings. Doubtless this is the place that answers to the "chains of darkness" (2 Pet 2:4) where spiritual beings are confined, and the place of banishment feared by the demons on earth (Luke 8:31). It is the place from which the beast emerges (11:7; 17:8) and will be the prison of Satan himself during the millennial reign of Christ (20:3). The beings locked up here are evil spirits of some kind, and are not to be confused with the spirits of evil men which are in hades awaiting their summons before the great white throne; such can be released only by the One who has "the keys of hell and of death"(1:18).

2 Divine permission allows Satan the authority, symbolised by the key, to open this gloomy prison house of demonic spirits and there issue from it dark rolling clouds of smoke. Since it is likened to the "smoke of a furnace" the smoke is be lit up with lurid flashes of flame. This frightening picture gives an insight into what is meant by the "furnace of fire" (Matt 13:42), the destiny of unbelieving men. So dense is this smoke that the sun is shut out and darkness closes in the scene. While this swirling smoke emerging from the nether regions literally darkens the earth it heralds the release of fearsome demoniacal powers that will bring more than physical darkness. This is a deduction from the special features of the scene:

1. the region from which the eruption comes - the abyss
2. the agent of the release - a fallen star identified as Satan himself
3. the necessity for divine permission (the key given)
4. the smoke from the abyss darkening the sun and the air.

The whole action symbolises a demoniacal, Satan-directed attack upon men. It may not be entirely irrelevant that the only other time the exact expression "the smoke of a furnace" is mentioned is in Gen 19:28 in connection with the judgment upon Sodom and Gomorrah.

3-4 John watches the unfolding drama with fascinated trepidation:
out of (*ek*) heaven - a star,
out of (*ek*) the pit - smoke,
out of (*ek*) the smoke - locusts.

Literal locusts in the history of Israel were always a judgment. The eighth plague in Egypt had brought the locusts (Exod 10:3-20); the memory of which was meant to be a warning to Israel (Deut 28:38-44); sadly, they paid little attention to it. The picture of locusts rising like a cloud darkening the heavens, appearing like a mighty army with the sound of rattling chariots is familiar from the locust swarms in the prophecy of Joel (Joel 2:25). Locusts were a scourge known and dreaded in eastern lands and thus a very fit symbol of destructive enemies (Nah 3:17). They bring the darkness of an approaching storm, their unimaginable numbers mean that not a shred of green matter is left when they go. The smoke and the locust-like creatures depict literal beings just as the abyss is literal, yet there are three special features that show that these are not actual locusts. These demons may have locust features but the judgment they bring goes beyond what mere insects could bring. Myriad in numbers, mighty in power and malevolent in intention, they inflict upon men unbearable pain. It is important to notice the twice repeated "it was given"(vv.3, 5); it indicates that it was by divine permission that they carried out their penal task within limits that were clearly marked. The features that mark out these locusts as demons are:

1. Their origin. This has been shown to be the abyss from which they issued like the smoke of a furnace once their prison-house had been opened.

2. Their sting. Unlike ordinary locusts, which have no sting, these locusts have a very painful sting (v.5). The simile of the scorpion sting is very striking imagery. There is no more repulsive member of the spider family than the scorpion; the irritability of its nature, its implacability as it approaches its victim and the swiftness of its striking tail causes it to be greatly feared. Its sting is exceedingly painful and in many cases it can be deadly. The power to terrify men inherent in scorpions is given to these locusts. Whether this power is given by God directly or through Satan indirectly makes no difference to the terror they spread. God is dealing with men in judgment.
3. Their food. Locusts, by their sheer numbers and voracious appetites can devour every green thing in a whole landscape within minutes. Joel has described such a swarm: "The land is as the garden of Eden before them and behind them a desolate wilderness" (Joel 2:3). This swarm, unlike normal locusts, leave untouched the grass, the greenery and the trees, and attack only mankind. The verb "commanded" (*errethē*) is not the normal one for commands and is better translated "said" as in the RV. What God says is a binding order. It must be admitted that not all commentators agree that the orders come from God, but it is difficult to see how or why Satan should limit his own agents in this way. There is a divine limitation placed upon the locusts to protect the sealed ones just as Israelites in Egypt were protected when the plagues fell upon that land.
4. Their king. Agur, that acute observer of nature in the book of Proverbs records, "The locusts have no king" (30:27). This particular swarm of locusts differs from any natural locusts and they do have a king (v.11).

The locusts are permitted to hurt those who have not the seal of God on (*epi*) their forehead. The sealed ones, clearly the 144,000 from Israel (7:2-8), are divinely-protected since they have a divine mission to fulfil, while all others are open to this locust attack. The assumption that since the sealed ones are of Israel this attack is upon the unsealed of Israel (W.A. Still) or even the reprobate of Israel (T.B. Baines) can hardly be sustained. No such limitation is suggested in the passage where the scope seems to be worldwide. The point is that Satan, enraged at his expulsion from heaven (12:12), musters all his demoniacal forces in this second half of the tribulation to terrify men into taking the mark of the beast (13:16-17). The heralds of the coming king are divinely-protected, but, as a direct judgment of God these demons are permitted to frighten men into following the beast. What a monster Satan is seen to be; his own followers are but pawns whose suffering he ignores to further his insensate fury against heaven. Association with him brings its own retribution.

5-6 Three divine limitations are set upon these satanic agents:

1. Their victims. Those with the seal of God on their foreheads are exempt; all

others are legitimate targets of attack. The intention is that frightened men should seek protection under the miraculous powers of the beast and the false prophet (13:13-14).

2. Their power to hurt. They have the power to kill physically but permission is denied to them here; their victims may only be "tormented", a word that in this book involves divine retribution (see its usage in 14:11; 18:7,10,15); these very agents of Satan far from their own intention become agents of retributive judgment. The torment is likened to the sting of a scorpion, one of the most excruciating pains it is possible to suffer.
3. Their period of operation. These demon-locusts are allowed to attack men for only a limited period of time. Whether "five months" is the duration of that period or whether it is the length of time the pain from one attack lasts is not altogether clear. Both may be true. Commentators (see Alford) are generally satisfied that the period is based on the months (May to September in the east) when locusts normally swarm. As with all the other time periods in this book the five months are to be taken literally and seen as a five month period in the second half of the seven-year period of tribulation. Scripture yields no example of the word "month" being used in other than a literal sense.

Since these are not actual locusts the pain they inflict while largely physical may include elements of mental distress and nervous disorder, leading to the desire for death on the part of those afflicted. At the present time the link between physical and mental health is offering scientists a whole field of investigation. Scripture has always acknowledged such a link, particularly with regard to suffering (Ps 38:6-7; Matt 17:14-18; James 5:13-16) and the present day obesession with drug-addiction, alcoholism, sexual excess and occult practices will open the door for this terrible invasion from the abyss. The result is unbelievable pain for men in both the physical and the mental realms which may include demon possession. This dementia is so severe that men feel that death itself would be an escape from pain. Yet, even this is denied to these distracted souls. Job's remarks concerning a bitter longing for death that never seems to come (Job 3:20-22) may be rhetorical and indicate mere despondency, but here men are driven by excruciating pain to seek death, little realising that this would lead to a pain far more terrible (14:9-11). No longer master of their lives, men long to die and cannot. The verb "desire" (*epithumeō*) is the very strong word that describes the inward longing of the heart, the preoccupation of the mind. Death seems most enticing as an escape from the pain. The dramatic present tense of the verb "flee" paints a graphic picture; Rienecker translates "death keeps fleeing from them". Men cannot even take their own lives as an escape from this judgment.

7-10 Having shown the origin of these demon-locusts John now describes their appearance. While the language is obviously figurative the similes he uses must not be spiritualised into generalities. The similes convey pictures of terrifying reality. The similarities between this demon invasion and the literal locust invasion of Judah in the days of Joel (2:4) are to be noted.

Eight features are identified:

1. Their Shapes - "like horses prepared unto battle".
   Both ancient and more modern writers find the head of a horse an apt picture of the head of the locust. Since the horse is "prepared unto battle" resemblance lies in the shell-like scales of these creatures and the metal (or leather) protective plates commonly placed over the horses' flanks. The thought may be *invincibility;* men have no weapons able to penetrate the protective armour of these supernatural entities. By implication these things must be of some considerable size otherwise the description would be overdrawn.
2. Their Heads - "on their heads as it were crowns of gold".
   Appendages of some kind, resembling crowns (*stephanos*), glittered like gold around their heads. While pretended dignity or royalty may be involved the specific use of *stephanos* points to *victory*.
3. Their Faces - "as the faces of men".
   That these spirit-beings, described as "locusts", should be seen with the faces of men is perhaps their most terrifying feature. This suggests a claim to intelligence but with malignancy and cruelty adding terror to the picture; their *authority* is a usurped and harmful domination of mankind. Features of man, beast and insect are linked in diabolical association.
4. Their Hair - "as of a woman".
   The long flowing hair of these creatures reminds John of a characteristic feature of womanhood (1 Cor 11:15). The two short antennae of the normal locust would hardly give rise to this feature but the luxuriance of womanly hair may indicate *effeminacy*.
5. Their teeth - "as the teeth of lions".
   This is an echo of Joel 1:6. The carnivorous appearance invokes the idea of terrifying *ferocity* yet these demon-locusts inflict their hurt not with their teeth but with their tails.
6. Their breastplates - "as it were plates of iron".
   The word "breastplates" (*thōrax*) used in connection with Goliath (1 Sam 17:5 LXX) is the word that comes into English as the word "thorax" and describes the portion joining head and abdomen of the insect. These "plates of iron" protect the vital organs and suggest *impregnability*. No weapon can penetrate this armour to destroy these locusts.
7. Their wings - "the sound of their wings was as the sound of chariots of many horses running to battle".

The translation should probably be "many-horsed chariots" (Vincent). This is an echo of Joel 2:5 and describes the thunder of a charging army that strikes terror even before the battle is joined. Such an armoured charge would be *irresistible* - nothing can stand in its path.

8. Their tails - "like scorpions". The most repulsive member of the spider family, the scorpion has scarcely a redeeming feature. When its claws fasten on to its victim the tail curves back with frightening speed, its needle-like point penetrates the skin and injects the poison. The picture is one of pitiless and relentless *irritability*.

Viewed from head to tail the physical description is absolutely terrifying but recognising that they are supernatural in origin and released under satanic direction to bring such terrible pain that victims would find death a relief, adds a further dimension to their terror. God is allowing the spirit-world of demons to be seen in its true character. The mutters and the murmurs, the moving glass, the seance, the ouija board are just the playthings to entrap the gullible. Now men will reap what they have sown and bitter anguish will result. This trumpet shows evil powers in their true colours.

While some have seen in this description the invasion of a warrior army (see W. Kelly), and parallels with Joel's invasion may lend some support to this view, the whole description of the origin and character of this locust swarm is against such an interpretation. F.A. Tatford summarises the matter (p.114): "The origin of these fearsome creatures in the pit in the abyss, their emergence as a cloud to fill the air and darken the sun, their spiritual head, and various other features suggest a spiritual host rather than a material army, and the only satisfactory interpretation appears to be that the reference is to a latter-day outbreak of spiritism in a particularly-virulent form. Spirit beings, who are at present under restraint, will apparently be liberated for a short period and allowed to have their way with the unhappy descendants of Jacob". This passage does not specifically refer to any re-imprisonment of these creatures and it is possible that after the five-month period, they are still allowed their freedom until the end of the tribulation when they will be imprisoned with their master in the abyss from which they had emerged (20:3).

11 As pointed out one of the features that distinguished this invasion from a natural locust invasion is the fact that they had a "king over them" (see the comment of Agur, Prov 30:27); the word king *basileus* defines his absolute authority while the term "the angel of the abyss" (RV) defines his realm. The R.V. is clear "they have over them as king". This personage must not be confused with the fallen star who used the key. To interpret the "angel of the abyss" as Satan is a misunderstanding. R.H. Mounce agrees with this and writes, "It is unlikely that Satan would be introduced into the visions at this point in such an indefinite manner". These demon powers have, as their king, one who emerges with them while Satan stands at the head of the whole realm of evil principalities, powers and "the world-rulers of this darkness" (Eph 6:12 RV). This king is a subordinate whose special responsibility is reflected in his name – in Hebrew *Abaddon*; in Greek *Apollyon*. This bilingual identification is a characteristic of John's writing (John 6:1; 19:13, 17, 20; 20:16) and not only indicates a familiarity with both languages but hints that the scope of this invasion embraces all peoples. In Hebrew *Abaddon* means "destruction" (see Job 28:22; 31:12) while *Apollyon* means "destroyer". Many commentators see in this name a derogatory reference to the emperor Domitian who claimed to be an incarnation of the god Apollo, a name that some scholars link directly with Apollyon. God allows this demon invasion under their satanic leader to destroy the complacency of materialistic men.

12 This is a transitional verse to show that, while there may be a temporary pause in the action, two more terrible judgments lie ahead. The verb "is past" may be better expressed as suggested in the JND margin "has passed away". God dealt summarily and speedily with the locust invasion in Joel's prophecy when He promised, "I will remove far off from you the northern army and will drive him into a land barren and desolate" (Joel 2:20). The divine restraint placed on the power of these demons and their five-month time-limit shows that God is acting with a definite end in view. How God removes this invasion or nullifies its power is not explained. It is possible that the demon-locusts may be locked up again. Equally they may join the deceiving spirits preparing men for the final stage of earth's rebellion (16:14). What is sure is that they will be banished back to the abyss with their satanic overlord (20:1-3) when Christ sets up His millennial kingdom.

John's characteristic use of the exclamation "behold" makes clear that, terrible as this judgment has been, darker days lie ahead in the two woes yet to come. As H.M. Morris comments, "The first was painful, the second would be lethal". The "hereafter" (*meta tauta*) marks not only the sequence in the vision but shows that the sixth trumpet follows the fifth trumpet in time. If the trumpets open the second half of Daniel's seventieth week then it would seem that this five-month period will probably lie within the fourth year of the tribulation. It will be clear from ch. 13 that this is the period when the autocratic power of the beast is at its zenith.

Trumpet Six - Second Woe

13 The echoes of the trumpet blast from the sixth angel die away; the ensuing silence is shattered by a single (*mia*) voice from (*ek*) the four horns of the golden altar. That altar has formed part of the heavenly background from 8:3-6. From it have arisen the prayers of the saints mingled with the fragrance of Christ; now from this same altar there comes, in response, a solitary voice issuing a command that will take the judicial purposes of God on earth a step further. The four horns of the altar, in tabernacle imagery, speak of the sovereign and universal power of God. When those horns are stained with blood (Lev 16:18), the sovereignty of God can be seen in salvation - redemption purchased in blood allows salvation to be proclaimed on a worldwide scale. The absence of blood on these altar horns indicates that God is acting in universal judgment. The solitary voice seems to be that of the angel-priest in response to the prayers of the saints (8:4). The command issued sets in motion another phase of judicial action.

14 The order given to the angel who had blown the sixth trumpet is simple and yet startling. He is told to "loose the four angels which are bound in the great river Euphrates". The river Euphrates is the largest river in western Asia; rising in Turkey it flows for 1780 miles on a south-westerly course through Turkey, Syria and Iraq to the Persian Gulf. The river Tigris, rising three hundred miles further east, flows on a roughly parallel course for hundreds of miles and then converges with the Euphrates one hundred miles before entering the Persian Gulf. The area between the rivers is the ancient Mesopotamia (the land between the rivers) generally reckoned to be the cradle of civilisation and where tradition places the garden of Eden. The Nile to the west and the Euphrates to the east were the boundaries of the land-grant of Canaan promised to Abraham (Gen 15:18; Deut 11:24; Josh 1:4). For a short period, under David and Solomon Israel may have reached the Euphrates boundary (1 Chron 18:3; 2 Chron 9:26). Historically, the Euphrates protected Israel and the Middle-Eastern nations from the empires further to the east, and very particularly from mighty Assyria. This river marked the eastern border of the Roman Empire. Many of the great cities of ancient times, including Sippar and Babylon, lay on the river. Since the days of those great civilisations the course of the river has shifted so that now it runs some four miles to the west of the ruins of these cities. It was from across the Euphrates that many of the ancient enemies of Israel invaded the land (Jer 2:18; 13:4-5; 51:63). Many attempts have been made to spiritualise this reference to the Euphrates and make it represent something other than the literal river. While some OT names are used symbolically in this book as Jezebel (2:20), Sodom and Egypt (11:8) the context makes it clear when the reference is allegorical; there is no hint of such in this passage. W. Hendriksen is typical of many commentators, particularly those of amillennialist views, when he writes categorically, "This river represents Assyria, Babylon, that is, the wicked world" (*More than conquerors, p.122*). This kind of imagination forbids any sensible interpretation of Scripture. Alford is quite clear when he writes, "There is nothing in the text to prevent 'the great river Euphrates' from being taken literally". W. Scott concurs and writes p.210, "We understand, therefore, that the literal Euphrates is here signified, and not the Turkish power. So also in 16:12."

The more difficult question relates to the identity of the four angels "which are bound in (*epi*) the great river, Euphrates". Some help is afforded by noticing that grammarians are united in replacing the "in" of the AV with "at" (see JND, RV), so that the four angels are not submerged in the river but bound in some location "at the river". These four angels are, of course, different from the other group of four angels seen in 7:1. The former four were holy executors of divine purpose acting under heaven's command; these four angels have been detained by divine power for some previous transgression. Since angels are spirit beings the chain must be other than a material chain and yet be terribly real. The group of angels detained under "chains of darkness" (2 Pet 2:4) or "everlasting chains" (Jude 6) are equally literally imprisoned. The perfect participle "having been bound" is from the same verb (*deō*) as will be used later of Satan. These four angels are a specific group who, in some way, had misused either their position or the powers at their command to oppose God and His purposes. It is a scriptural deduction from Dan 10:12-14 that angels have a part to play in the affairs of the nations. It is possible therefore that these four angels, working through the political processes of nations, had stirred up the historical enemies of Israel to invade the land of Israel in the past. God used certain nations, notably Assyria and Babylon, to discipline His people Israel, but they went beyond their mandate and became objects of divine chastisement themselves. The evil angels responsible for inciting these enemies to destroy the people of God may be the ones detained at the Euphrates. Both the place of their detention (the eastern border of Israel whence invaders came) and the result of their release suggest such a link. When released these four angels set about marshalling the mightiest invasion force ever mustered.

15 While they must have realised that their release was by divine permission these angels little understand that they are to play a part in God's programme for the last days. Acting out of implacable hatred for God and His people they set about mustering an invasion force with which they plan to sweep Israel from the earth. They are but pawns in a far-wider divine purpose; a sovereignty symbolised in the four horns of the golden altar and signified in the participle "which were prepared". The "for" that follows is the AV translation of the preposition *eis* which Alford prefers to translate "in reference to", "in reservation for" or "with a view to", all expressions that suggest divine purpose in setting free these particular rebellious angels. The specific purpose for which these angels have been released is described as "the hour and day and month and year" (RV). The presence of a single article before "hour" and not repeated with the following nouns is interpreted by Alford as "the appointed hour occurring in the appointed day, and that in the appointed month, and that in the appointed year". Understood in this way the expression denotes not the length of a time-period but the specific moment when the event will take place. On that day the sovereign counsels of God through these angels will have been achieved. It is the day appointed of God when the huge invading army of the following verses begins to move. In a way that is typical of many a prophetic scripture there is now interjected a summary-result statement of the invasion even before the invading army is described: "for to slay the third part of men". The RV reading is clear: "that they should kill the third part of men". When the death-toll of this invasion is counted up one third of the population of earth will have perished. While an incalculable number of saints have died as martyrs and many more folk have died under the earlier trumpets (8:10) this is still a horrendous number. Earth's population in 1996 was around six thousand million: the death-toll based on that figure would be around two thousand million. If the reference to "one fourth part of the earth" in 6:8 describes an earlier death-toll then, the figure would be one thousand five hundred million. By comparison the total death-toll for the five years of the second world war is reckoned to have been around fifty million.

16 With great speed the scene changes and John sees the mightiest army ever set in motion. The word *strateumaton* is a plural word and should be translated "armies"(JND gives "hosts"). The word "horsemen" Vine would render "cavalry". The number of these horsemen is truly astounding. It is not a human estimate but, like the number of 7:4 which John also heard, was divinely-communicated. John heard the number "two hundred thousand thousand" or twice ten thousand times ten thousand or two hundred million (200,000,000). It is such a stupendous number that even many conservative commentators would like to modify it; W. Scott is typical of them when he writes p.211: "A literal army of 200 million of cavalry need not be thought of. The main idea in the passage is a vast and overwhelming army, one beyond human computation, and exceeding by far any before witnessed". To thus summarily dismiss a divinely-given number is a somewhat arbitrary way of treating a scriptural statement. There are more direct ways of expressing a great number (7:9), and it might be asked whether, if this is just a round number, the other numbers in this book are to be treated in the same way? It is much safer to accept that this number, while beyond our understanding, is the divine count of an invading force from the east.

Fastening on the descriptive phrases and metaphorical language used, but based particularly on the sheer immensity of the number involved in this invading force, many commentators (of which A.F. Johnston is typical) have sought to interpret this invading force as another demonic invasion following the one under the fifth trumpet. Pointing out that the combined military forces of both Allied and Axis powers at the peak of mobilisation in World War II did not exceed 70 million men Johnston argues that "an army of 200 million could not be conscripted, supported, and moved to the Middle East without totally disrupting all societal needs and capabilities". For his evidence he quotes authorities in military logistics.

This passage gives no direct statement as to:

1. the origin of such a mighty invasion force
2. the object of the attack
3. the time of the attack or
4. what happens to this invading army. There are, however, indications in the context which, when paralleled with other scriptures, may suggest some answers to these questions.

The mention of the Euphrates river has directed attention to the eastern boundary of the Roman Empire of John's day. It has already been noted that this is also the eastern boundary of the land-grant that God gave to Abraham. The only other reference to the Euphrates in this book is under the sixth bowl: "And the sixth angel poured out his vial upon the great river Euphrates, and the water thereof was dried up, that the way of the kings of the east might be prepared" (16:12). It will be shown in the comment on that passage that this implies a military invasion across the eastern boundary of the empire of the beast with the object of attacking the citadel of his power and, at the same time, destroying the nation of Israel. It is suggested that under this trumpet the gathering and equipping of the army is initiated while the actual invasion comes closer to the end of the tribulation and is part of the great gathering of the armies of earth to do battle at Armageddon (16:12-16).

This can hardly be the invasion of Israel described in Ezek 38-39. That invasion comes specifically from the north. Ezek 38:6 speaks of the "north quarters", while Ezek 38:15 speaks of the "north parts" or as RSV translates "remote parts of the north" thus putting beyond question an invasion from the far north. Another invasion of Israel described in Dan 11:40-45 is also clearly from the north, though this time from the immediate north, as it is led by "the king of the north" who in the context must be the king of Syria. Neither the attendant circumstances nor the fact that they come from the north of Israel allow a link with this passage. Under this sixth trumpet the signal is given for the gathering of a great invasion force and the mention of "the great river Euphrates" turns the eye to the east. Under the sixth bowl this same literal Euphrates is supernaturally dried up, opening the way for this great invasion force moving to Armageddon and its final destruction in 19:21.

The subjunctive mood of the verb "to slay" expresses the divine overruling that makes this invasion a judgment from God. However, the purpose in the minds of the leaders of this army is far otherwise. If the link with the "kings of the east" (16:12) is accepted then the immediate purpose in the minds of these world leaders is to resist the domination of the beast whose claims have now extended worldwide and to wipe out the nation of Israel and thus settle finally and forever the Middle-East problem. The Assyrian and the Babylonian followed this path in a past day; these invaders pursue the same object. To support the beast and the nation of Israel the western nations marshal their forces and Jerusalem becomes the geographic centre to which the armies of the world begin to move. These are the forces that will gather to Armageddon for "the battle of that great day of God Almighty" (16:14). This trumpet heralds the first movement in this gathering of the world's armies.

The suggested timing of this trumpet places the events in the fourth or even into the fifth year of the tribulation period. This may seem somewhat early for the gathering of the armies that move towards Armageddon but it should be recognised that the diplomacy required and the physical gathering of such a mighty force will demand more than a few months and possibly will occupy all the remainder of the tribulation period. Any problem related to the timing of the gathering of the armies and the invasion of "the kings of the east" (16:12) must be judged in light of the expression in 11:14, "The second woe is past and behold, the third woe cometh *quickly*". The final stages of the tribulation will be fast moving; as soon as the seventh trumpet is blown the seven bowls are emptied in swift sequence. The time span of the bowls can only be weeks and may be even days. Once the armies are gathered the end comes quickly.

It is significant that no mention is made of the final end of this invasion force. This omission along with the terrible death-toll suggests that this is only part of a larger picture. The movement of these armies from the east, across the Euphrates river, and moving towards Jerusalem indicates that they are part of the great gathering to "the battle of the great day of God Almighty" (16:14). The coming of Christ as "King of kings and Lord of lords" (19:16) deals the death blow to them at Armageddon. After the leaders have been arrested by divine power (19:21) the scriptural statement is sobering, "And the remnant were slain with the sword of him that sat on the horse". The number of those "killed" (vv.15, 18) as a result of this invasion is given as "the third part of men"; on recent population figures this could be either 1500 million or 2000 million. See page 259. This total may embrace the whole campaign from the mobilisation of the army to the destruction of the armies at Armageddon. To this count must be added the two hundred million of this army and, possibly, a number of around the same magnitude of other forces gathered to oppose them; the "supper of the great God" (19:17) will be a veritable feast for all the carrion birds of earth.

It is clear from these statements of scripture that the judgments of the tribulation will decimate the population of the earth. If 1500 million die under the seal judgments (one fourth of the population, 6:8) and a comparable number die under this sixth trumpet (one third of the remaining three quarters) this means earth's population has been halved. When to this figure is added the estimated four hundred million who die at Armageddon, the great company of the martyred saints, and all the others who die under the various judgments (6:11) and earthquakes (11:13; 16:18), the tribulation period reaps a dreadful harvest.

17 The same interpretative problem is faced with these horsemen as arose with the locusts - the relationship between what is symbolic and what is literal. In keeping with the principles of interpretation already established it is clear that John is presented with the reality of a mighty army militarily irresistible because supernaturally aided, causing death and destruction in its invasion of the territory of the beast as it moves to attack Israel. The symbols must be interpreted within the context of scripture and within their cultural background. To read modern weaponry into the expressions is to tread on the shifting sand of technology which changes from age to age. The main emphasis in the vision is manifestly the horses. The horse in scripture is ever the symbol of natural strength (Job 39:19) and natural speed (Ps 33:17). This strength and speed needs a controlling hand (Ps 32:9) if it is to be usefully employed. It is not surprising that when men rebel against God they should use the horse in military action against their fellows. In Scripture the horse is almost always linked with warfare. (The one exception to this rule is found in Isa 28:28.) When misused in this way the horse gives a false sense of power and security and thus becomes a danger to those who trust in it. In Scripture the horse was early associated with Egypt (Exod 9:3) and the might of Egypt was linked with its horses. The kings of Israel were directly forbidden to multiply horses (Deut 17:16); Israel was to be dependent upon Jehovah and not the military might embodied in horses and chariots. Here the mightiest army ever seen is equipped with horses.

That the horses are symbolic is clear from the description given. Even cross-breeding and genetic engineering will hardly produce a horse with the head of a fire-breathing lion. Not only so, but since the entire horse population of earth in 1996 was around one million it would require a population explosion amongst horses to produce two hundred million! Any idea that warfare in the future will revert to cavalry charges is simply fertile imagination. The symbol depicts the natural strength of nations harnessed militarily to put on the battlefield the mightiest invasion earth has ever seen. The allied landing on the Normandy beaches in 1944 will appear as a minor skirmish when measured against this attack.

The "breastplates" (*thōrax*) defines their defensive armour. This was a corselet, generally of metal, made in two parts which, protected the whole of the torso. The Roman breastplate covered both the chest and the back. Alford writes of the participle "having" as referring most naturally to both horses and riders, not to the riders only. The next three terms describe, not the material but the colour of the breastplates. "Of fire" could be rightly translated "fire-coloured" and was generally regarded as a bright blazing red. There is some uncertainty in the meaning of the word "jacinth" (*huakinthinos*); some early writers (Pliny) use it as equivalent to "dusky-red". However, the classical hyacinthus flower was undoubtedly blue and this is the word LXX uses for the tabernacle "blue". In 21:20 the RV margin has the weight of custom and scholarship when it renders the word "sapphire". The word "brimstone" (*theiōdōs*) describes the smoke of burning sulphur (*theion*) which beyond a blue tinge at the edges is bright yellow. The repetition of "and" between the colours suggests that separate regiments, brigades or armies were distinguished by their colours. The repetition of "fire and smoke and brimstone" in their offensive weaponry may suggest that different types of weapons were used by the different armies.

The symbolic nature of the horses is clear by the fact that John sees their heads "as the heads of lions" (RV). This symbol allies the strength of the horse with the sovereignty of the lion, the king of beasts. The teeth of the lion (v.8) spoke of ferocity; here the head indicates a claim to majesty that would defy the "King of kings". This army is Satan's great attempt to deny to Christ the sovereignty of earth. The mouth speaks of the ravenous appetite of the lion (Dan 6:21; 1 Pet 5:8), and it is fitting that these symbolic lions should spew forth "fire and smoke and brimstone". Literal fire and smoke and brimstone are seen first in Gen 19:23-28 in the destruction of the cities of the plain. It is plain that the symbol describes the offensive weaponry that wreaks havoc amongst men. It is futile to attempt to identify these with different kinds of weapons whether conventional artillery or tactical nuclear weapons. What God rained on Sodom and Gomorrah in righteous judgment Satan copies in his forces. The carnage on earth is unimaginable.

18-19 The repetition of the death-toll from this satanically inspired invasion from across the Euphrates river re-emphasises the awful carnage that results. The mention again of the fire and smoke and brimstone (sulphur) lays new stress on the death-dealing weaponry that is used by this invading army. That the massacre is wrought by the "mouths" of these lion-headed horses gives added significance to the fact that the invasion wreaks immediate destruction as soon as it strikes. The colossal numbers of this mighty army and the character of their terrible weapons bring appalling death and destruction. Under the fifth trumpet men sought death and could not find it; now they have trouble escaping from it.

We have no difficulty believing that the "power" of these horses "is in their mouth" as "fire and smoke and brimstone" issue from it, but almost as an afterthought John draws attention to their "tails". This is a further indication that the description is symbolic, for the tail of a horse is not generally associated with the fearsome or the frightening. Here, however, the tails are not like unto scorpions as with the locusts, but "like unto serpents". It is not merely the tail that startles but the fact that each tail has a "head". That old serpent from Eden has not yet had his head finally crushed and he emerges again in this last book of the Bible in a last attempt to subjugate men to his will. It is with these serpent-heads ("with them") that terrible damage is wrought ("they do hurt"). The sting of the scorpion caused pain but the bite of these slithering serpents spreads death. As it marches the army clearly leaves behind a subdued population of worshippers of the beast who have accepted his deception and are prepared to worship Satan through the beast (13:4).

As the symbols are read in the light of Scripture this vision of John portrays a mighty invading army; nationally all natural resources (the horses) are harnessed; authoritative leadership (the lion's heads) is evidenced and the subtlety of Satan (tails like serpents) follows in the wake of the army. The agents of Satan (16:13-14) have deceived men and their leaders into mounting this mighty force that with its destructive power will make "Desert Storm", the liberation of Kuwait in 1990, seem like an argument in a kindergarten. There is no need to seek to identify the means of transport, the means of communication, or the weapons that are here involved. Many commentators have seen in the symbols the tanks and the aircraft of modern warfare and others have seen strategic and tactical nuclear weapons. All attempts to interpret in this fashion unnecessarily restrict the Word. In John's day readers had a perfectly intelligible picture of an invading army backed by irresistible power. In our day, the same picture makes perfect sense. Weapons have changed in the past and may change even more in the future with the advance of technology. The picture drawn here has never changed and carries the same awesome message to the hearts of men as it ever did.

20-21 It has been pointed out that the movement of this great invasion force will be but the first military movement in the campaign that climaxes at Armageddon. These military movements will, doubtless, be pointed out by gospel preachers with Bible in hand as the evidence of the end of the age. It would be reasonable to think that with multitudes dead and many dying under "the fire and smoke and brimstone" (v.17) there would be a turning to God by the rest of mankind. Sadly this is not so. With a wilful disobedience akin to that of Egypt and Pharaoh under the plagues (Exod 9:34-35) "the rest of mankind" (RV) refused to repent. Such is the depravity of the human heart. Judgment in the early stages can lead to fear and terror (6:16-17) but, when the hardening process reaches a certain point it provokes blasphemy (16:8-10). Perhaps this is the decisive point in the lives of many, the moment when they deliberately refused the last overtures of grace and threw in their lot finally with the beast. The idolatry (v.20) and the immorality (v.21) of their society was too much a part of their lives to allow them to see sin from God's viewpoint that they might turn to the Lamb.

"The rest of mankind"(RV) are those remaining after the judgments of the seals and trumpets have taken their toll. The word "plague" is plural from the root verb "to smite"; the noun describes a "scar" left by a blow. Metaphorically it was used of a calamity. These plagues could be identified as the demon invasion and the military invasion, but since there were no deaths under the fifth trumpet, it is better to interpret them within the immediate context as the "fire and smoke and brimstone" of vv.17-18.

The challenge to the earth-dwellers was clear. To repent of their sin would demand a forsaking, immediate and instant, of the "works of their hands". The word "works"(*erga*) when it stands alone has its secondary meaning "deeds" (as in 16:11) but the qualified expression "the works of their hands" demands the meaning "idols" (see Deut 4:28; Ps 115:4-7; 135:15; Isa 2:8; Jer 1:16; 25:6, 7,14). The whole lifestyle of men, in their employment, occupations, and everyday duties, was so intertwined with idolatry in the age of the beast that they found it impossible to repent and give it up. The preposition "of" (*ek*) after the verb has the force "out of": they "repented not out of the works of their hands". They refused to abandon their lifestyle. The same preposition with the same force is repeated in v.21 before each of "murders", "sorceries", "fornication" and "thefts". The forsaking of idolatry (v.20) would have dealt with the whole problem of morality (v.21).

The deterioration in the materials of which the idols were made is significant as suggesting that every stratum of society was involved. It is possible and perhaps preferable to take the first "and" as explanatory and translate it "even", so that the material idols become merely expressions of demon worship. In the derisory comment of John about such idols, "which neither can see, nor hear, nor walk", can be heard the scorn of Isa 44:9-20 for the idol-maker.

One view of this idolatry regards it as the upsurge of the heathenism of Buddhism, Taoism, Shintoism and Hinduism sweeping into the apostate post-christian world. The idols then would be the literal idols of these and other related religions, a resurgence of OT idolatry under new names. However an alternative view is to see ancient idolatry expressed in a new way in the post-christian age. With the direct intervention of God in human affairs atheists and humanists who have formerly denied the very existence of God will find themselves confronted with the necessity of recognising that spiritual powers are at work. This recognition may well take the form of literal idols. It is remarkable that even in the present day many of the sophisticated of earth, despite scientific training and advanced education are turning more and more to occultism, astrology, spiritism and other "doctrines of demons" (1 Tim 4:1). This is but the first step in acknowledging the demoniac powers that operate under Satan "the prince of the power of the air" (Eph 2:2). Those rejecting the God of the Bible, may well follow this path to idolatry.

The preferred interpretation is to see reflected here a special form of idolatry that will claim worship of men at this point in the tribulation. Since the seven trumpets sound in the second half of the tribulation it might have been expected that there would be reference to apostate christianity under the harlot (17:1-2). The fact that no reference is made to such worship confirms, in an incidental way, that the harlot (ch. 17) is destroyed at the midpoint of the tribulation by the beast and his empire. World religion is now centred on the great image of the beast (13:14-15) in Jerusalem which men are commanded to worship. Countless copies of this idol in gold, in silver, brass, stone and wood will be sold, first as tourist mementos, but then as immediate objects of worship in the home throughout the empire of the beast. Doubtless this practice will spread over the earth and it will be wise to have one in the home or useful to have one in the office or place of work. In a very real sense idolatry will have returned to earth on an unprecedented scale when a man claims worship as God (2 Thess 2:3-5). Through an idol, through the demons behind the idol, and through a man represented in the idol, Satan is worshipped. Doubtless, miraculous happenings with these images will add to the popularity of this idolatrous cult (13:13). This gives a very literal meaning to the idolatry here and shows what a costly matter repentance would be for an earth-dweller; it would mean being ostracised in society, sacked from state corporations, and unable to "buy or sell" (13:17). Provision for a family would be difficult and the end could well be death under the relentless war of extermination against the saints waged by the beast (13:7).

The repetition of the verb "repented" in v.21 emphasises the stubbornness of the human heart. Not only are the earth-dwellers held by the idolatry of the age but they are enmeshed in a society that has given itself over to immorality. Having abandoned any recognition of the God of the Bible and having turned to idols, the moral standards of men reflect the god they serve. Scripture teaches and history confirms that idolatry and immorality go together. Four words reflect these standards, the possessive pronoun before each paints a picture of sinners hugging their sins:-

1. It almost seems from the tone of the phrase "their murders" that murder has become a way of life, a normal way of settling a problem. The standard will be set by the state in its campaign against all who refuse to conform to the state religion; the fate of the three Hebrews under Nebuchadnezzar is relevant (Dan 3:1-27); judicial murder will be too common to be news. This devaluation of human life will permeate all society.

2. The word "sorceries" (*tōn pharmakeiōn autōn*) is closely related to drugs, particularly those of a hallucinatory nature and linked with the occult; the noun "sorcerers" is used in 21:8 to define one of the groups denied entry to the Holy City. *Pharmakeia* is correctly translated "witchcraft" in Gal. 5:20 – one of the works of the flesh. It is interesting that this same word is used of the activities, not of religious Babylon, but of commercial Babylon: "By thy sorceries were all nations deceived" (18:23). Even if the word is used metaphorically in this passage it is significant that Babylon, reaching its zenith as a great commercial centre at this time and wielding mighty power over the empire of the beast, was drugging the earth-dwellers, holding them as if under the spell of witchcraft. The rampant drug abuse and the tremendous upsurge in spiritism in recent years indicate a trend that will develop so that in this tribulation period these things will be an integral part of society.

3. As part of this list of moral and social ills, "their fornication" must be taken in a literal sense. In the society under the beast the disparagement and debasement of marriage will be complete; vows, even if taken, will be honoured rather in the breaking, multiple divorce will be the norm, the family unit will be virtually a thing of the past and the rearing of children will have become a state responsibility. Television and media coverage of the most depraved sins will have exposed even the youngest to a debased way of life. Such standards will have permeated all society.

4. Despite the break-down in moral standards in present society there is still a general standard of honesty and a genuine respect of the belongings of other people. Things, however, are changing rapidly. The breakdown in law and order as shown in rising crime statistics over the world touches every strand of society. The ruthlessness and selfishness of men in the pursuit of commercial gain and personal wealth have led to a society basically ruthless and utterly selfish. Under the Beast society will have tacitly, if not openly, accepted that any malpractice or misdemeanour is permitted if undetected. Honesty and integrity will become increasingly rare and "thefts" in a very wide sense allowed if not approved.

The repetition of the preposition "of" (*ek*) after the verb "repent" and before each category indicates that true repentance demands the total deliverance "out of" that society polluted by these sins.

Notes

1 This identification and the implication of the verb "fallen" rules out any link with the angel in 20:1 who has the key of this same abyss. Here the opening is by divine permission for the release of satanic forces; at the commencement of the millennium the abyss is opened by an angelic agent of the throne for the incarceration of Satan.

7 An Arabian proverb, quoted by R.H. Mounce (p.196), describes the locust as having "A head like a horse, a breast like a lion, feet like a camel, body like a serpent, and antennae like the hair of a maiden."

CHAPTER 10

6. *The Second Parenthesis* 10:1-11:13

This chapter introduces the second major parenthesis which may be viewed against the structural background of the surrounding chapters:

Ch. 6	The Six Seals Opened	
Ch. 7	The First Parenthesis	deals with Persons
8:1-5	The Seventh Seal Opened	
8:6-9:21	The Six Trumpets Blown	
10:1-11:13	The Second Parenthesis	deals with Places

It will be observed that the first parenthesis dealt with persons; the 144,000 sealed ones are seen going into the tribulation and the innumerable company of saved ones are seen coming out of the tribulation. This second parenthesis deals with places; in ch.10, the first part of the parenthesis, the whole stage of creation is involved while in the second part the focus falls upon the city crucial to the purposes of God. This may be summarised thus:

10:1-11	The Conclusion of the Mystery	
	The Stage – Creation	God's Purpose Declared
11:1-13	The Crisis of the Messengers	
	The Stage – The City	God's Power Defined

The parenthesis between the sixth and seventh seal was comparatively brief and yet served to make clear that in this darkest period of earth's history God will have a people preserved right through those days and as a result of their witness another great company will follow the Lamb into the millennial kingdom. This longer parenthesis between the sixth and seventh trumpets will show that God has never abandoned His purpose with regard to earth and that the time has arrived when there should be no longer any delay in the working out of His plans. The groan of creation (Rom 8:22) has been heard and God will vindicate His purpose in creation. The next chapter will show that in spite of the crucifixion of Christ, the most culpable of all crimes, God will never abandon the city of His own choice. Before the storm of judgment breaks in the second half of the tribulation God will validate His place, Jerusalem.

The first parenthesis made it clear that the time period to which the visions refer is not always chronological. It was observed that the sealing of the 144,000 went back to pre-tribulation days while the "great multitude" looked forward to the very end of the tribulation. While there are no direct time-marks in ch. 10 its association with ch. 11 must place it at the midpoint of the seven-year tribulation (see 11:2). If this is so it anticipates the trumpet judgments and shows how a faithful God will never abandon His covenant promises - a very necessary assurance as earth reels under the war trumpets.

The chapter shows the descent of one called "another mighty angel" and the three paragraphs centre on him:

vv.1-4	His Advent and Appearance
vv.5-8	His Action and Announcement
vv.8-11	His Assurance and Authority

(a) *Conclusion of the Mystery (vv:1-11)*

v.1 "And I saw another mighty angel come down from heaven, clothed with a cloud: and a rainbow *was* upon his head, and his face *was* as it were the sun, and his feet as pillars of fire:
v.2 And he had in his hand a little book open: and he set his right foot upon the sea, and *his* left *foot* on the earth,
v.3 And cried with a loud voice, as *when* a lion roareth: and when he had cried, seven thunders uttered their voices.
v.4 And when the seven thunders had uttered their voices, I was about to write: and I heard a voice from heaven saying unto me, Seal up those things which the seven thunders uttered, and write them not.
v.5 And the angel which I saw stand upon the sea and upon the earth lifted up his hand to heaven,
v.6 And sware by him that liveth for ever and ever, who created heaven, and the things that therein are, and the earth, and the things that therein are, and the sea, and the things which are therein, that there should be time no longer:
v.7 But in the days of the voice of the seventh angel, when he shall begin to sound, the mystery of God should be finished, as he hath declared to his servants the prophets.
v.8 And the voice which I heard from heaven spake unto me again, and said, Go *and* take the little book which is open in the hand of the angel which standeth upon the sea and upon the earth.
v.9 And I went unto the angel, and said unto him, Give me the little book. And he said unto me, Take *it,* and eat it up; and it shall make thy belly bitter, but it shall be in thy mouth sweet as honey.
v.10 And I took the little book out of the angel's hand, and ate it up; and it was in my mouth sweet as honey; and as soon as I had eaten it, my belly was bitter.
v.11 And he said unto me, Thou must prophesy again before many peoples, and nations, and tongues, and kings."

The crucial question is the identity of the mighty angel. It must be admitted that the majority of commentators see in this angel Christ Himself. The evidence appears conclusive. First, there is His clothing and appearance. He is said to be "clothed with a cloud" which W. Scott insists is that in which deity is usually shrouded. The rainbow "upon his head" links back with the throne in 4:3; his feet as "pillars of fire" has more than a hint of the description of the Son of man in 1:15, as the description of his face "as it were the sun" echoes John's appreciation of Christ in 1:16, "His countenance was as the sun shineth in his strength". A second link is the correspondence with the "certain man" of Dan 10:4-6 who is generally agreed to be Christ in a pre-incarnate appearance. The case is generally closed by pointing to the fact that this angel seems to carry, absolute cosmic authority indicated by one foot on the land and the other on the sea. W. Scott p.180 speaks for many commentators "We are satisfied that the angel priest is Christ, our great High Priest". There can be no doubt that this picture thrills the heart of the believer. Christ as "Kinsman-Redeemer" in 5:6 pays the price of redemption and now as "Kinsman-Vindicator" (Job 19:25) displays the power of redemption and with the open book claims earth and sea for the throne.

The word "mighty" or "strong" (*ischuros*) is used also of the angels in 5:2; 18:21 and in neither of those cases can fair exegesis identify the angel as Christ. It would be very strange, to say the very least, to put Christ into any class of created beings, no matter how mighty. W. Scott sees the problem and writes with reference to 5:2: "but the only thing common to both references is the epithet 'strong'. In the earlier text a *created* being endowed with might is referred to, whereas in the passage before us an uncreated Being of divine majesty and power is witnessed. It is the Lord Himself". Unfortunately he offers no proof and the statement assumes what has to be proved. The fact that a mighty angel introduces the commencement of the tribulation period (5:2), appears again at this crisis of the tribulation (10:1) and finally appears at the consummation of the tribulation (18:21) has a certain symmetry that appears to be designed to show direct intervention from the throne by a specially-commissioned angel.

The theophanies in the OT where Christ is seen as "the Angel of the Lord" have no bearing on this argument. When Christ took manhood this type of revelation was no longer necessary; after incarnation any subsequent appearance of Christ is as man (Acts 7:55-56). The symbolic terms Lamb and Lion (5:5-6) relate to His offices and have no bearing on the matter. This is why he is seen as "Son of man" in 1:13; for Him to appear in angelic form now hardly seems appropriate and would certainly be confusing. Alford speaks clearly: "This angel is not, and cannot be, our Lord Himself. Such a supposition would, it seems to me, entirely break through the consistency of apocalyptic analogy. Throughout the book, as before observed on 8:3, angels are the ministers of divine purposes, and the carriers out of the apocalyptic course of procedure, but are everywhere distinct from the divine Persons themselves". The complete answer to the similarities that this mighty angel bears to Christ is that as a direct delegate from the throne he is acting with a divine mandate and carries the symbolic investiture that displays that authority.

1 John is now on earth as he sees this mighty angel "coming down out of heaven" (RV). The present participle graphically describes the descent with the angel taking his stand (v.5) on the earth. Four things are said about the angel:

1. "Clothed with a cloud". The imagery of the cloud wrapped around him is symbolic and shows that he is a heavenly messenger. As in each of the seven occurrences of "cloud" or "clouds" in this book (1:7; 10:1; 11:12; 14:14 (twice),15,16) it is a literal cloud. There is no reference to the OT Shekinah cloud; the symbol simply indicates heavenly authority.
2. "The rainbow upon his head" (RV). The article makes the reference to the rainbow of 4:3 certain, since it is the only rainbow mentioned thus far. It seems that the rainbow circles the brow of this mighty angel to indicate that while His commission is from the throne his activity will concern the covenant blessings that God has in mind for earth. The rainbow recalls the promise of God in Gen 9:12-17.
3. "His face as it were the sun". The metaphor shows that this angel is invested with divine glory for the execution of his task and may be compared with the far stronger metaphor in connection with Christ (1:16): "His countenance was as the sun shineth in its strength". The added words (italicised) emphasise that which belongs to Christ alone. Amidst the increasingly dark scene of the last half of the tribulation period, both spiritually (9:2) and physically (16:10), this angelic messenger is bringing a radiance of hope (v.7).
4. "His feet as pillars of fire". The relationship with the description of the feet of Christ "like unto fine brass as if they burned in a furnace" (1:15) is more apparent than real, as the two similes are quite different and convey different ideas. The simile of "military brass" conveys inward strength that gives implacability to the steps. Here the simile suggests that each step reveals the unapproachable holiness of God. Crushing judgment yet to fall on earth will reveal the punitive holiness of God. The redemptive action of Jehovah as seen in "the pillar of fire and of the cloud" (Exod 14:24) may furnish the background picture for this divine action on behalf of His divine purpose.

Foreshadowed in the very use of the symbols "cloud", "rainbow", "sun" and "fire" is the fact that all creation is involved at this point. God is about to conclude His redemptive action involving the whole creation; the angel standing astride land and sea is the picture of this universal claim.

2 What arrests John's attention is the fact that the mighty angel with the book in his hand takes his stand, with the right foot on the sea and the left foot on the earth. The stance is symbolic and shows that both realms will be affected by his mission; as the agent for the throne he is claiming possession for that throne. He is acting as a bailiff on behalf of the legal owner. Both sea and earth are to be understood literally; it is the physical creation that is in view not nations and governments.

Many commentators link this book with the seven-sealed book taken by the Lamb from the hand of the Throne-sitter in 5:7. The word here for "book" (*biblaridion*) lends itself to the translation "little book" and is adduced in support of this view. The argument is that the seven seals have been opened, the original book (*biblion*) has been diminished in some unexplained way and what is left is this little book. Apart from the inherently questionable argument as to the dimunition in the size of the book, Vine points that in Hellenistic Greek the diminutive force of the word *biblaridion* had virtually been lost by this time and no first century reader would have drawn any such inference. It should also be pointed out that the other word *biblion* is used in v.8. There is, however, a far more important argument against this identification of these two books. If as is suggested in the comments on ch. 5 the book in 5:7 is the title-deeds of the kingdom, the question arises, why had John to eat them (v.9)? There seems no reasonable answer to this question.

A much more feasible view is to see, with perhaps the majority of commentators, that the little book contains the portion of prophecy as yet unfulfilled. Some link it very closely with the sealed book of Dan 12:4 (see F.C. Jennings p.275) which is seen now opened in the hand of the angel. There is some justification for this direct link since the same aspect of prophetic truth is being dealt with at that point but, lacking direct scriptural support, it needs to be treated with caution. Whether or not there is a direct link with Daniel's book it is generally argued that this book must contain the prophetic unfolding of divine purpose for earth. It is called a "little" book because there are but three-and-a-half years of the prophetic programme to run on earth before Christ comes. On this view the eating of the book by John, under divine instruction, becomes a symbolic way of showing that while these prophetic truths are sweet to the taste of John, as he sees divine power put forth and divine purpose fulfilled, in the aftermath they are bitter as he sees the consequences on earth.

However a better interpretation of the book will be suggested when the whole picture is studied. Three matters need to be examined closely:

1. The book is open. The perfect passive participle of the verb "to open" simply draws attention to the fact that it is now open and remains open, without raising questions as to when it was opened or by whom. The symbolic import of an open book is that all may read it. This is in contrast to the sealed scroll of ch. 5.
2. The voice of the angel is not only "loud" or "great", but is described with the simile "as when a lion roareth". All the majesty and authority of the king of beasts are in that roar. The OT imagery of the roar of a lion (Hos 11:10; Joel 3:16) is that of Jehovah roused to judgment. That roar causes earth and men to tremble; God is about to act in judgment.
3. "The seven thunders uttered their voices". The instant response of the seven thunders to the lionlike voice of the angel is most suggestive. The symbolic implication is that when God acts in judgment there is an immediate response in the cosmos; as men come under divine judgment, signalled by the roar of the lion, heaven's response is the "seven thunders".

With these descriptive phrases furnishing the background another OT passage may hold the key to this passage and the interpretation of the book. In what is generally accepted as the oldest book in the Bible Job is heard to cry, "Oh that one would hear me! Behold, my desire is, that the Almighty would answer me, and that mine adversary had written a book" (Job 31:35). Job was referring to the "legal document" or "charge sheet" produced by his legal opponent in a law-suit. This book contained a list of the charges to be put to the judge in the presence of the accused. The same idea is behind Ezekiel's reference to a book: "And when 1 looked, behold, an hand was sent unto me; and, lo, a roll of a book was therein; and he spread it before me; and it was written within and without: and there was written therein lamentations, and mourning, and woe" (Ezek 2:9). The charges against the nation of Israel are made plain to Ezekiel as representing the accused and he knows that bitter grief must follow. In this closing book of divine revelation it is fitting that before the inarticulate groanings of creation (Rom 8:22) are answered by the redemption brought by the Kinsman-Redeemer, the righteous charges of the throne should be heard. On this view the word *biblaridion* should be given its technical meaning: "a small book, a document especially a petition" (see Bauer, Arndt and Gringrich). In legal terms it would thus be the indictment, the charge against the accused. It is suggested that it is the presentation of this charge which demands the lionlike voice of the angelic accuser. It is to be noticed that when that roar is heard through the prophet Amos (1:2), it is followed by the indictment of each nation around Israel and then, finally, the indictment of Israel and Judah. Thus there is a good case for seeing this "little book" as God's indictment of the nations as He lays claim to the possession of earth. The seven thunders are then explicable as heaven's response heralding judgment. In these thunders there is an echo of Ps 29:3, "The God of glory thundereth". Many commentators have linked the sevenfold mention of "the voice of the Lord" in that psalm with these seven thunders. This is certainly valid, but, it is not always recognised that that psalm is a paeon of judgment pictured in the cataclysmic flood of Noah's day. In Ps 29:3 it begins with "the voice of the Lord is upon the waters" and a closing note in v.10 is "The Lord sitteth upon the flood"; the word "flood" (*mabool*) is a word used in the OT only for the flood in Noah's day. Now the "God of glory" thunders again and, as a consequence, another cataclysmic judgment is about to engulf creation; the thunders herald the coming storm (8:5; 11:19; 16:18). This places the seven thunders in the same judgment series as the seven seals, the seven trumpets and the seven bowls.

4 The seven thunders clearly conveyed articulate messages to the ear of John. In keeping with his standing instructions (1:19) John settles down to write what he had heard from the seven thunders. This throws an interesting sidelight on the fact that John recorded the visions and messages as soon as they were given; he did not await some later opportunity. But it was not to be. John's hand was arrested by an explicit command from heaven, "write them not". The same voice of Christ that gave him his original instruction (1:19) now stays his hand. The instruction to Daniel was somewhat different (Dan 12:4), "Shut up the word and seal the book, even to the time of the end" and this envisages a time when the ban would be lifted. These unrecorded thunders pass forever. Some argue that this speaks merely of divine sovereignty. It is more likely that, given the context, it may be evidence of mercy in the midst of judgment. Whatever the explanation of the sealing, it is done at the command of Christ and with the full authority of heaven.

5-7 The mighty angel astride earth and sea raises his right hand to heaven in the familiar gesture of oath-taking, a gesture which goes back to Abram who declined the spoils of battle from the king of Sodom with the explanation, "I have lift up my hand unto the Lord, the most high God" (Gen 14:22-23). Textual authorities are agreed on the inclusion of the adjective "right" qualifying "hand" as shown in both the RV and JND. The oath is solemn and comprehensive and involves both the Creator and His creation. The oath is "by" (*en* is instrumental) the One who is the essence of deity. He is the living One: "him that liveth"; He is the eternal One: "unto the ages of the ages"; He is the mighty One who created...". This deathless, timeless One has brought into existence by His power creatures in three realms:

(a) the heaven – "and things that are therein"
(b) the earth – "and the things that are therein"
(e) the sea – "and the things that are therein"

In these comprehensive statements the whole of the material universe is embraced, from the immensity of the far-flung galaxies to the hidden beauty of the unseen denizens of the ocean depths. The evolutionary lie that for 150 years has enslaved the minds of men is dismissed in one simple statement and will be disproved in the sovereign action now announced. The significance of the creatorial title introduced here is that the One who began creation is the One who can bring that same creation to the desired goal.

In this oath there is incidental but convincing proof that the angel cannot be Christ. Scripture testifies that "men verily swear by the greater" (Heb 6:16) and this angel by the oath acknowledges that God is infinitely greater than he. For Christ to swear in this way would be out of keeping with the nature of this oath. It is not a relevant argument to quote the Lord's words in a different context, "My Father is greater than I" (John 14:28). The One involved here is God: the self-existing One ("Him that liveth"), the eternal One ("for ever and ever"); the angel swearing by the almighty Creator shows that, no matter how distinguished, he is but a creature.

The announcement comprises three matters:

1. The Declaration: "that there should be time no longer". This has often been read as if the noun "time" (*chronos*) were an abstract noun and the phrase

interpreted as if time was to be abolished and eternity to begin. In this context it simply means that the "until" that has qualified many a prophetic promise (Gen 49:10; 1 Tim 6:14; Heb 9:10) is now removed; the time of waiting is over and God is about to take decisive action. The phrase should be translated "there should be no longer delay" (JND) or "there shall be delay no longer" (RV marg). There is a close link with Hab 2:3 LXX – "it will not tarry"- quoted in Heb 10:37 as "he ... will not tarry". The waiting time is over, creation's groan (Rom 8:22) is about to be hushed.

2. The Limitation. The one limitation to this dramatic announcement concerning delay is now given. The "but"(*alla*) is strong and could almost take the meaning "except". The waiting time is to continue only until the blowing of the seventh trumpet. As soon as the seventh trumpet begins to sound the long delay of the ages will be over. As pointed out earlier the blowing of the seventh trumpet actually comprises the seven bowls and most probably these will be poured out in days. This brevity of the bowl period is the reason why "days" are mentioned in the phrase, "In the days of the voice of the seventh trumpet". The trumpet itself, embracing the bowls, will be of short duration and it is "about to sound". The word *mellō* in its twelve occurrences in the book (the first occurrence is 1:19) always indicates imminence - nothing need intervene until God's purpose is complete.

3. The Revelation. The sounding of the seventh trumpet brings to its goal what is called "the mystery of God". The verb translated "shall be finished" (*teleō*) is better rendered "shall be completed" (JND). The "mystery of God" is defined by the statement that follows: "as he hath declared to his servants the prophets". The word "mystery" in the NT never means "mysterious" but defines that which cannot be known apart from God Himself making it known; it is that which must come by divine revelation. Throughout the long ages of waiting the prophets, the servants of God, brought good tidings (the verb is *evangelizō*) to men. There is no obvious reason why "the prophets" should be restricted to either OT or NT prophets. These notes of gladness have been necessarily incomplete and partial but they will all find their completion and finally reach the goal when the seventh trumpet is sounded. This means that the "mystery of God" must be defined as being the full knowledge of Christ, which is the clear statement of Col 2:2, "The mystery of God even Christ" (RV). The manifestation of divine righteousness, holiness, power and love, all of which have been real to faith in all the ages, will now become visible and tangible, seen in the person of Christ as He takes the kingdom. Promises, prophecies and pictures that brought good news through the long centuries will all be fulfilled visibly in Him. When the trumpet is sounded in 11:15 the chorus of heaven shows the reality of this interpretation: "The kingdoms of this world are become the kingdoms of our Lord, and of his Christ; and he shall reign for ever and ever".

The ignorance, indifference and iniquity of men as a result of sin have meant that God has been denied in His own creation and apprehended only dimly by faith. Now the delay is over, and based on redemption through the Lamb, the groan of creation is hushed, the sob of the creature stilled as evil is finally dealt with by God, and creation is brought into the radiance of the millennial glory under Christ. No longer will men be able to doubt God's interest in earth or to accuse Him of indifference to their pain. No longer will questions be asked about His silence in history. What was formerly a mystery to men has reached its goal ("should be finished") and Christ takes the kingdom that has been announced and anticipated down the ages.

8-11 For the second time in this scene John hears that commanding voice from heaven; the article identifies it as the voice heard in v.4 and thus the voice of Christ. This time he is ordered to go and take the book from the hand of the mighty angel standing astride the sea and the earth, an action reminiscent of the Lamb taking the book from the hand of the Throne-Sitter (5:7). That book was sealed but this one has already been opened. As he moves to obey the command John speaks - the present participle shows John moving and speaking at the same time. The indirect speech of the original is somewhat less abrupt than the AV and is rendered by JND "saying to him that he should give me the little book". Nevertheless the infinitive of the verb "to give" after "saying" still expresses a direct command. This can be only a further incidental confirmation that this is an angel and not Christ; it would be inappropriate for John to speak thus, without greeting or recognition, to the One at whose feet he fell not so long before (1:17).

Taking the book John is commanded by the angel to eat it. In a similar situation Ezekiel received the same command (Ezek 3:1). Strength for physical activity depends on physical eating. John's eating is symbolic. What was in the scroll must be absorbed by him and so provide him with the necessary spiritual strength for the work yet to be done. Nevertheless he is given a warning, "It shall make thy belly bitter, but it shall be in thy mouth sweet as honey". John found it so when he took the book and "devoured" it; the compound verb *katesthiō* is stronger than the simple verb (*esthiō*) used in the second part of the verse. The sweetness is the language of first experience but the bitterness follows.

To the spiritual person the word of God is always sweet no matter what the content. The psalmist found it so (Ps 119:103) and this was the experience of Ezekiel having eaten the scroll given to him (Ezek 3:3). Jeremiah had a similar experience, "Thy words were found, and I did eat them; and thy word was unto me the joy and rejoicing of my heart" (Jer 15:16-18). Of John's experience Alford succinctly writes, "Its sweetness when he tasted it..... doubtless represents present satisfaction at being informed and admitted to know, a portion of God's holy will". Yet there is wrung from John an instant confession, "As soon as I had eaten it my belly was bitter". If this little book is the indictment of mankind by God, John, in agreeing with God, would find His word sweet, but as he assimilated what this entailed, especially concerning the last three and a half years of the tribulation period, bitterness wrenched at his inwards. In keeping with God's holy standards this little book demanded judgment upon mankind and very especially upon John's own nation. It was essential for John that he assimilate the holy standards that demanded righteous judgment upon men before he entered upon the closing stage of his ministry.

11 That closing stage of John's ministry is summarised in this verse. He learns that he must "prophesy again" concerning "peoples and nations and tongues and many kings" (JND). This fourfold designation of peoples worldwide occurs five times in the book (see comment on 7:9). Here "tribes" is replaced by "kings" and the adjective "many" is added, as if to emphasise that every rank of society will be involved in these endtime events.

But who is the speaker? The reading in most of the manuscripts is plural: "they say unto me" (see RV). JND quotes the practice of Luke and, treating it as a general plural, translates as a passive: "it was said to me". A possible explanation of the plural is that the message came from heaven and was repeated by the angel; John summarised by simply using the plural of the verb. He is commissioned to carry the final warnings from God to men. These warning notes will constitute the remainder of the book. They will not be delivered by John "before" (*epi*) peoples, nations, tongues and many kings. Grammarians insist that *epi* followed by the dative case must be translated "concerning" (see RV margin) or "as to" (JND) (see comments by Alford). The prophecies to follow concern the judgments and the destinies of the men of earth in all their varied racial, social, national and cultural distinctions.

Notes

10 Some commentators, of whom perhaps the best known is F.F. Bruce, hold that the first thirteen verses of the next chapter (11: 1-13) make up the content of this little book. This seems a very arbitrary conclusion without any supporting evidence. If the book is interpreted as suggested above the bitterness that John endures is self-explanatory.

CHAPTER 11

While disagreeing widely on many points of interpretation in this book there is a surprising unanimity amongst commentators in agreeing with the statement of Alford, "This chapter is undoubtedly one of the most difficult in the whole Apocalypse". It requires but the briefest survey of the variety of interpretations and the multiplicity of bizarre suggestions to see the truth of this statement. However, when the chapter is approached with the same principles that have guided interpretation up to this point it yields just as simple and straightforward teaching as the previous chapters.

The guidelines of interpretation have been discussed in the introduction to the book and may be summarised in the term "Literal-Historical-Grammatical", which means simply that the language of Scripture means exactly what it says within the historical context and using language governed by the ordinary rules of syntax and context. These are the guidelines used in sound biblical exposition generally and they yield the same clear results when applied to the prophetic portions of the Word. Literal interpretation does not mean that every statement is to be rigorously tied to its physical meaning but it does mean that prophecy is to explained in its original sense according to the normal and customary usage of language. This will include symbol and metaphor where appropriate. When these principles are applied to this chapter it will be seen that interpretation demands a literal temple with actual measurements, two literal witnesses who will witness for exactly 1260 days and then be killed and raised from the dead to be caught up to heaven. The seven thousand people slain at the close of the chapter testify to a literal earthquake in the city of Jerusalem. There is neither hint nor suggestion in the text that these matters are to be spiritualised.

It will be recalled that this chapter is the second part of the parenthesis between the sixth and the seventh seals (see introduction to ch. 10). The first part of the parenthesis dealt with creation as a whole and divine purpose regarding it; this second part has to do with the city and the divine power that will bring testimony to it in the tribulation period. This city, while not named in the chapter, is identified as "where also our Lord was crucified" (v.8) and must be Jerusalem, the only city on earth where God chose to "place his name" (Deut 12:4), – the historic capital of the nation of Israel. Focusing on this city the chapter divides readily into three main paragraphs which may be viewed as follows:

1.	vv.1-2	The Tragedy of Jerusalem	The Temple Worship
2.	vv.3-13	The Testimony in Jerusalem	The Two Witnesses
3.	vv.14-19	Trumpet Seven	The Third Woe

(b) *Crisis of the Messengers (vv.1-13)*

v.1 "And there was given me a reed like unto a rod: and the angel stood, saying, Rise, and measure the temple of God, and the altar, and them that worship therein.

v.2 But the court which is without the temple leave out, and measure it not; for it is given unto the Gentiles: and the holy city shall they tread under foot forty *and* two months.

v.3 And I will give *power* unto my two witnesses, and they shall prophesy a thousand two hundred *and* threescore days, clothed in sackcloth.

v.4 These are the two olive trees, and the two candlesticks standing before the God of the earth.

v.5 And if any man will hurt them, fire proceedeth out of their mouth, and devoureth their enemies: and if any man will hurt them, he must in this manner be killed.

v.6 These have power to shut heaven, that it rain not in the days of their prophecy:

and have power over waters to turn them to blood, and to smite the earth with all plagues, as often as they will.

v.7 And when they shall have finished their testimony, the beast that ascendeth out of the bottomless pit shall make war against them, and shall overcome them, and kill them.

v.8 And their dead bodies *shall lie* in the street of the great city, which spiritually is called Sodom and Egypt, where also our Lord was crucified.

v.9 And they of the people and kindreds and tongues and nations shall see their dead bodies three days and an half, and shall not suffer their dead bodies to be put in graves.

v.10 And they that dwell upon the earth shall rejoice over them, and make merry, and shall send gifts one to another; because these two prophets tormented them that dwelt on the earth.

v.11 And after three days and an half the Spirit of life from God entered into them, and they stood upon their feet; and great fear fell upon them which saw them.

v.12 And they heard a great voice from heaven saying unto them, Come up hither. And they ascended up to heaven in a cloud; and their enemies beheld them.

v.13 And the same hour was there a great earthquake, and the tenth part of the city fell, and in the earthquake were slain of men seven thousand: and the remnant were affrighted, and gave glory to the God of heaven".

1 The chapter division forces an unnatural break between chapters that are joined by the conjunction "and". The interruption of thought means that the significant action of the mighty angel in giving John the measuring rod is sometimes overlooked. Admittedly the passive voice of the verb "was given" does not specifically identify the one who gives John the rod, and some commentators gratuitously introduce John's conducting angel into the scene at this point. This is unnecessary when the close relationship with the previous chapter is understood. It should also be noticed that the textual evidence for the sentence, "and the angel stood", is so weak that most translations omit it altogether (see JND, RV). The mighty angel who has just claimed earth and sea for God now gives John a rod to measure the temple of God. John is to be involved actively in the vision. The voice giving John the order to measure may then be either that of the mighty angel or, more likely, the voice from heaven issuing his third command (see 10:4, 8). It has been shown that this is the voice of Christ. The "reed" (*kalamos*) given to John is to act as a measuring "rod". The word "rod" (*rhabdos*) in this kind of context is used technically to define a surveyor's rod. Reeds from the swamps of the Jordan valley, which can grow up to twenty feet long, are cut to twelve feet lengths for this purpose.

The command to John is simple and direct, "Rise and measure". The double imperative emphasises the haste necessary when heaven speaks. The reference to rising casts no reflection on John; it is not a matter of posture but, in colloquial language, stresses the immediacy of the required action, nothing else was to distract his attention. Instructions are given for the measurement of three things:

1. The temple of God,
2. The altar – the mention of the cour t in the next verse suggests that this must be the golden altar associated with the holy place.
3. The worshippers in the temple.

When John received this instruction to measure the temple near the end of the first century there was no temple in Jerusalem. The Herodian temple had been destroyed by the Roman army under Titus in AD 70. This simple fact has provided support for two diametrically-opposed systems of interpretation. The preterist interpreters (see *Introduction*) have insisted that since there must have been a temple in Jerusalem when John wrote then this book must have been written about AD 67; this early date is to fit in with their theory that all the prophecies from chs. 4-18 were fulfilled by the end of the first century. On the other hand amillennialist interpreters pointing out that the literal temple had been destroyed, insist that the "temple of God" can only be taken figuratively. They do differ as to whether it symbolises Israel (P.E. Hughes) or the church (W. Hendriksen). Hendriksen writes, "The answer is that this 'sanctuary of God' symbolises the true church, that is, all those in whose hearts Christ dwells in the Spirit. All true children of God, who worship Him in spirit and in truth are measured, that is, protected" (p.127). The simple fact that John was given a vision relating to a particular and specified time in history, the tribulation period, would have preserved from all such misleading notions.

The term "temple of God" is used figuratively on three occasions in the NT but these occasions are marked so clearly in the context that no mistake can be made. The expression, without the article, is used in 1 Cor 3:16; 2 Cor 6:16 of the local assembly and in 1 Cor 6:19 of the physical body of each believer. There is no ambiguity in any of these cases. Here the expression with the article must carry its usual meaning of a literal temple of God in Jerusalem. That there will be such a temple in the time of the tribulation Scripture leaves not the slightest doubt. The Lord's warning words about the "abomination of desolation" (Matt 24:15-18) puts this fact beyond question:-"When ye therefore shall see the abomination of desolation, spoken of by Daniel the prophet, stand in the holy place, (whose readeth let him understand) then let them which be in Judaea flee into the mountains"; the "holy place" demands a temple and Judaea fixes the location. The prophecy of Daniel from which the Lord is quoting shows that the interruption of the covenant will mean that "the sacrifice and oblation" will be caused to cease, implying necessarily that the whole sacrificial system of Judaism has been reestablished in this temple. In 2 Thess 2:3-4 the one called the man of sin reaches the pinnacle of his presumptive blasphemy: "so that he as God sitteth in the temple of God, showing himself that he is God". For this blasphemer to act like this means there must be a temple in Jerusalem.

To rebuild a temple in Jerusalem has not been remotely possible during the centuries since John wrote. This rebuilding necessarily awaits:

(a) the national regathering of Israel into their own land,
(b) the sovereignty of Israel in their own hands and
(c) the removal from the temple site of the Muslim mosques now in that area.

In recent years in spite of the bitter opposition of the Arab nations God has so ordered national and international affairs that the first two of these conditions have already been fulfilled. The last one will assuredly follow in God's time and a great temple will be built in which Judaism will recommence the blood sacrifices of a past era. There is no Scripture to deny the building of this temple even in the closing years of church testimony before the rapture. However it could be built during the period after the rapture, even before the covenant is signed that will commence the last seven years of Daniel's seventieth week. It could be built rapidly even during the first years of that seventieth week. Whenever built Scripture is clear that it exists at the midpoint of the seven-year tribulation period and in it animal sacrifices are again offered. It is this literal temple that John is ordered to measure.

The idea of taking a measurement seems to look back to the days of Joshua and the apportionment of the heritage in Canaan. It speaks of personal possession and appropriation, ideas that the Psalmist used metaphorically: "The lines are fallen unto me in pleasant places; yea, I have a goodly heritage" (Ps 16:6). When God would mark off that which belongs to Him, He sends His surveyor: Ezekiel measured the temple (Ezek 40:3) and Zechariah was to measure the city (Zech 1:16) – the sacred possessions for God in millennial times.

While the temple is a literal building and the measuring by John a physical act it is abundantly clear that both the act of measuring and the temple itself have symbolic implications. The fact that no measurements are recorded, in contrast to the measuring in 21:14-17 of the holy city, shows that there is a symbolic meaning in the act of measuring. The implication is that even in the darkest days of the tribulation there will still be a portion for God, a testimony that God can acknowledge as belonging to Him; it is His "lot" or "heritage". Men can see it but its size is known only to God. The lesson is that within the nation of Israel even in tribulation days there will be true testimony for God (symbolised in the "temple"). In this portion of His own people there is true praise reflected in the golden altar and around that altar there are worshippers engaged in priestly activity. The outer court, left out in the measuring, represents the unbelieving part of the nation of Israel.

2 The linking of a literal building with the symbolic interpretation is amply supported by the statements in this verse. The word used for "temple" (*naos*) should be translated "shrine" and refers to the innermost sanctuary where God dwelt. The court which surrounds the shrine is part of the wider temple area (*hieron*). This is the area where Mary presented her babe (Luke 2:27), where the Lord wrought many of His miracles (Matt. 21:14) and, where in His later ministry He sat to teach (Luke 21:1). In the temple of Herod there were actually three courts, the court of the priests, the court of the women and the court of the Gentiles. Solomon's temple had but one court and this seems to be the pattern for this temple. The instructions to John are explicit: the imperative "leave out" (*exballō*) means "cast out" (Newberry) while "measure it not" is absolutely prohibitive. The reason is simple – "it was given unto the Gentiles". The word "Gentiles" (*ethnesin*) may be translated "nations" (JND) but in this context it does point to Gentile nations as opposed to the Jewish nation.

The omission of the court in the measurement and the reason given for it shows that while God has a true testimony in a remnant of Israel, symbolised in the shrine, the majority of the nation, symbolised in the court, where His claims should have been similarly owned, have joined in the apostasy of the nations around. God already has the sealed company of 144,000 (7:1-8) and their converts as His witnesses in the nation. The false prophet (13:11-17) in his character of antichrist has led the majority of the nation (see the reference to "the many" in Dan 9:27) into the (false) covenant with the western leader described as the coming prince (Dan 9:26). The signing of this covenant marks the commencement of Daniel's seventieth week. In the midst of the week (Dan 9:27) this deceiver throws off the lamb-like character he had assumed and begins to speak as the dragon (13:11). He introduces the man of sin or his image, or perhaps both, into the holy place in the temple and in this way fulfils the prophecy concerning the "abomination of desolation". This brings the whole sacrificial system of Judaism to an end and those who refuse to accept the worship of the Beast have to flee or die. It is of this period that the Lord spoke when He warned, "Then let them which be in Judaea flee unto the mountains" (Matt 24:16). Those accepting the claims of antichrist are symbolised in the court given over to the nations.

The inevitable consequence of this apostasy is that the city of Jerusalem is invaded and subjugated for another time in Israel's history. The military might of the armies of the Beast is in view in the graphic metaphor, "tread under foot" the holy city. The Assyrian invasion in the ministry of Isaiah was but the pattern for this ruthless invader when God said, "I will send him against a hypocritical nation, and against the people of my wrath will I give him a charge, to take the spoil and to take the prey, and to tread them down like mire in the streets" (Isa 10:5-6). That the term "holy city" refers to Jerusalem is beyond doubt. Five times in the OT (Neh 11:1, 18; Isa 48:2; 52: 1; Dan 9:24) and on two occasions in the NT (Matt 4:5; 27:53) Jerusalem has this title. It is remarkable that every time it is used in the OT it is a Jerusalem under discipline from God for her sin and under the heel of a Gentile invader. It should be clear that the word "holy" cannot refer to the state of a city so often marked by sin, rebellion and apostasy, but to its standing in the counsels of God. No other city has borne this sacred title as a city set apart for God. When state and standing coincide in the millennial reign then will Jerusalem be indeed the holy city and "the joy of the whole earth".

The period of "treading under foot" the holy city, the symbolic way of expressing the subjugation of the whole of national Israel, is given as forty and two months. This is the first of five occasions when this period of three and a half years is mentioned in the book. It is referred to in three different ways:

11:2; 13:5 forty and two months
11:3; 12:6 a thousand two hundred and sixty days
12:14 a time, times and half a time.

The calendar year for Israel, as also for the Chaldeans and some other nations in antiquity, was based on a 360 day cycle divided into twelve months of thirty days each. This is the year that is used in prophetic Scriptures generally. With this in mind it is seen that the above periods are identical in length. Since the seventieth week of Daniel has been shown to be divided into equal portions then each half of the week could be described by any of the above terms. Some expositors believe that these periods all describe the last half of the week; W. Scott writes dogmatically, "Now these periods refer to the last half-week of the seven years of Daniel's prophecy" (p.229) but, unfortunately he does not offer any scriptural support for the statement and it seems to be a matter of assuming that which needs to be proved. It will be essential to allow the context of each passage to determine which part of the week is meant.

That this particular reference to forty-two months refers to the last half of Daniel's seventieth week is clear from the context. The signing of the covenant to introduce the week has brought a measure of peace and prosperity to Israel that allows the re-establishment of the temple worship. When, however, for political and international reasons the false prophet in Jerusalem introduces the image of the Beast or the Beast himself into the temple (13:14-15), the temple sacrifices are stopped (Dan 9:27) because of this "abomination of desolation". It has been customary to refer to this as "the breaking of the covenant" although Scripture does not use this exact term. Perhaps it is simply the implementation of a secret codicil of the treaty between the Beast and false prophet that has been there from the inception of the covenant. It makes little difference, for the result in either case is the total suppression of Judaism and a pogrom of extermination against all who refuse to conform. The military might of the Beast treads down the city for the last half of the week. With the Beast in the temple of God claiming to be God (2 Thess 2:3-4) the last great idolatrous religion of earth, patterned on Babylon, sweeps across earth and apostasy is now fully revealed. Any Israelite refusing to accept this idolatry will be forced to flee (12:14) or die. Rebellion is suppressed in blood and a military boot grinds Jerusalem in the dust.

3 The voice from heaven already identified as that of Christ as the Lamb continues to speak. John learns that even in tribulation days there will be raised up witnesses whom Christ can own as "my two witnesses". Commissioned and charged by Christ they carry an uncompromising call to repentance in Jerusalem as the national capital of the nation of Israel. Rienecker quoting R.H. Charles as his grammatical authority, translates, "I will give and they shall prophesy" and points out that is a Hebraic construction meaning "I will commission (or give permission to) my two witnesses to prophesy". The garb of these two witnesses speaks of the character of the witness they bear. Sackcloth is the traditional garb of mourning (Joel 1:13;-1 Kings 20:31; Jer 4:8). Prophets who felt the weight of their ministry (Dan 9:3)-wore it as did penitents feeling the weight of their need (Isa 37:1-2). The number "two" reflects the standard of legal witness demanded throughout Scripture (Num 35:30; Deut 19:15; Matt 18:16).

These two witnesses have provided a fruitful topic of discussion and dispute amongst commentators. Those expositors compelled by their system of interpretation to spiritualise these witnesses have judged them to be the symbolic way of describing the ministry of Israel (P.E. Hughes) or the ministry of the church. W. Hendriksen writes, "The true church is now represented under the figure of two witnesses. These witnesses symbolise the church militant bearing testimony through its ministers and missionaries throughout the present dispensation" (p.129). Fastening on the martyrdom of these two witnesses the followers of the historical school interpret them as the Waldenses and Albigenses whose witness was borne in blood under papal persecution. All these speculative fancies are ruled out when it is seen that these two witnesses have yet to arise after the church age (notice the future tense "I will give") in the tribulation period.

Premillennialist expositors who are clear about the period involved seem somewhat reluctant to accept the fact that there are but two individuals. F.A. Tatford writes, "It is more likely, however, that the number is simply indicative of an adequate testimony, and that the actual number of those bearing a faithful witness to God in the period in question will be considerable" (p.127). W. Scott, p.230, writes in similar vein: "A full and adequate testimony is the thought purposely intended in the number of the witnesses. It seems to us that a larger number than actually two is called for in the solemn crisis before us, also that verse eight supposes a company of slain witnesses". W. Kelly supports this view: "I would just remark, as to the witnesses, that there is no necessity to take them as two persons: they might be two hundred". As pointed out with reference to the numbers in ch.7, if numbers are to be treated in this way there is no reason why the thousand years of 20:3 may not be stretched, as amillennialists teach, to cover the period of church history. It is axiomatic to sound interpretation of this book that numbers are allowed to stand as God has given them. There is no doubt whatever that God has a multitude of witnesses in the tribulation period, including the 144,000 but that is not the point; He raises up and commissions two special men to a particular task that requires both divine empowerment and divine protection for the period of their testimony. The number "two" does go back to the principle of an adequate and sufficient testimony as required under law (Deut 19:15).

Having accepted the principle of two special men for a special task many commentators have gone on to speculate as to the identity of these men. The two favourite candidates are undoubtedly Moses and Elijah. That there is a close similarity with the ministry of Moses who withstood the might of Egypt represented in a Pharaoh, there is no question whatever. Turning water into blood and smiting the earth with every plague (v.6) recalls Egyptian bondage and the battle to liberate God's people. There is an equally-obvious parallel with the ministry of Elijah, in an apostate nation, doing battle with evil king Ahab. The shutting of the heavens in withholding rain (v.6) recalls the discipline of God upon the nation through Elijah. W. Hoste lends his authority to this interpretation (p.78). In support of Elijah some commentators refer to the prophecy of Malachi, "Behold I will send you Elijah the prophet before the coming of the great and dreadful day of the Lord" (Mal 4:5), and point to its fulfilment in this Scripture. This, of course, is to overlook the fulfilment of this prophecy in John the Baptist. Zechariah, the father of John the Baptist, had pointed the way to the true explanation "He shall go before him in the spirit and power of Elijah" (Luke 1:17), which the Lord Himself had confirmed in His word, "But I say unto you, that Elias is come already, and they knew him not" (Matt 17:12). Malachi's prophecy has already been fulfilled. Other commentators, recognising the difficulty posed by the truth of Heb 9:27, "It is appointed unto men once to die", with regard to Moses, would replace him in this witness with Enoch, the only other man besides Elijah taken up without dying into heaven. These speculations remain speculations and have no real scriptural support. It is better to see these two witnesses as men whom God has called and equipped for a special task. They carry out this task on the pattern of Moses or Elijah, who have borne testimony in somewhat similar circumstances in the past history of the nation of Israel.

The period of witness of these two men is given as 1260 days, which is another way of expressing forty-two months or three and a half years. It may be noted that when the period is given in days persecuted servants or suffering saints (12:6) are in view – as if God values every day of testimony or trial of His own. The divided seventieth week of Daniel provides two periods of three and a half years; the problem arises over whether to relate this period of ministry of the two witnesses to the first half of the week or to the last half. Some commentators, like W. Scott, solve the problem by assuming that all the five mentions of the period necessarily describe the last half of the week. There seems no reason why this should be so. In fact, with regard to this particular period there are a number of very good reasons why the two witnesses must witness in the first half of the seventieth week. These reasons may be summarised thus:

1. The present participle ("that ascendeth") describing the Beast as from the abyss (17:8) suggests that this evil one has just reached the pinnacle of his power (13:5), and as an evidence of his new authority he kills the two witnesses and then carries the war to their followers (see the similar language of 13:6). This means that the two witnesses die at the midpoint of the week.

2. The three and a half days that the two bodies lie in the streets of Jerusalem seem to be in a period of relative calm worldwide so that the nations have time to ponder the obvious implications of the supernatural power of the beast. It is probable that the questions of 13:4 will be asked at this point, "Who is like unto the beast? Who is able to make war with him?" Since the men who have been divinely protected for three and a half years have now fallen before him can any other stand before him? Such a time for world wide publicity seems unlikely if their death takes place when mighty armies are gathering round Jerusalem and at the time when the cities of earth are shaking under the mighty earthquake that closes the tribulation (16:19).
3. The great earthquake in Jerusalem (v.13) as heaven's warning on national apostasy would seem to be somewhat pointless at the close of the tribulation when earthquakes are rocking the earth but would carry great weight at the midpoint of the tribulation as an indication of what is in store for impious men.

Thus it is suggested that the preaching of the two witnesses occurs in the first half of the seventieth week while the second half is the time of bitter trial when the Beast reigns supreme and the climaxing events of chs. 13-19 take place.

4 The fact that these two witnesses are symbolised as "the two olive trees' points back to an OT picture where two olive trees are mentioned together for the only time in Scripture (Zech 4:3 and 11). The article points to two well-known trees. The context of that picture is the national testimony of saints who had abandoned Babylonish conditions and returned to the divine centre at Jerusalem. Amidst the world powers of that day regathered Israel was weak and defenceless. Babylon though defeated in battle was still a mighty power; Medo-Persia was a ruthless military force; Egypt was trying to expand its borders and there seemed little future for the little company in Jerusalem as a testimony for God. Questions must have been in the minds of saints as to their survival in a day of much weakness and the mighty powers around. God used Zechariah to show that the maintenance of the testimony was a divine responsibility. The lampstand of national testimony in Israel would be supplied by oil directly from the olive trees. The word of assurance was, "Not by might, nor by power, but by my spirit, saith the Lord of hosts" (Zech 4:6). Neither military might nor political power could preserve a testimony for God; the supplies needed must come from another source entirely. The olive trees were symbolic in that day of Joshua (the priest) and Zerubbabel (the prince) together presenting Christ as priest upon His throne. The primary lesson here is plain. These two witnesses would be the channels to sustain the witness for God within the nation of Israel.

But the two witnesses were to be more than channels of sustenance to others. In their own right they were to bear testimony; this is seen in the phrase "and the two lampstands" where the "and" is explanatory and should be translated "even". Most manuscript evidence favours the translation "standing before the Lord of the earth" (JND, RV). This language links the passage with Zech 4:14 as well as having an echo of the ministry of Elijah as recorded in 1 Kings 17:1, "As the Lord God of Israel liveth before whom I stand". To stand "before" a king or a throne not only expresses intimacy and fellowship with that authority but implies a readiness to act for it. In this day of grace Christ is seen by the church as "the Lord from heaven" (1 Cor 15:47), not as "Lord of the earth". In this connection W. Kelly makes a relevant point: "These [witnesses] maintained Christ's title to earth that he was 'the Lord of the earth' and this excited enmity. The beast might not have cared so much if they had said 'the Lord of heaven' but they claimed the earth not for themselves but for Him, and men will not bear it".

5 Divine protection encloses these two witnesses like an unseen but very real shield. The very wish to hurt them invites instant divine retribution. In the expression, "if any man will hurt them," the present tense of the verb *thelō* expresses desire. When that desire rising in the hearts of ill-wishers reaches towards these men it is answered by a flame – "fire proceedeth out of their mouth". This is again an echo of the divine protection afforded to Elijah (2 Kings 1:10-12) when Ahaziah sought his death. The Lord's rebuke of the disciples when they wished to see this kind of judgment on the Samaritan village (Luke 9:54) shows that this is not in keeping with the age of grace. It should be clear that these men are not preaching the gospel of the grace of God as in this dispensation, but proclaiming the truth of the coming king. Individuals will repent and be saved under the preaching of the two witnesses, but the emphasis is not on the grace of God but on the government of God. These demonstrations of divine power in protection of His own are thus perfectly in keeping with the message and, indeed, a foreshadowing of that which lies ahead when the Lord Himself returns to earth (2 Thess 1:6-10; 2:8). The word "devour" (*katesthiō*), a strengthened form of the verb "to eat", is a graphic description of these enemies being swallowed up in the flame. The physical death of their opponents in a literal flame protecting these witnesses in their preaching is the simple interpretation of the passage. The statement is emphatic: the expression "must in this manner be killed" indicates that God has established an automatic response triggered by the hatred of the enemies. The Lord's witnesses are protected by a divine law from which there is no escape.

6 These witnesses have the authority to act in two different spheres:
1. "They have power to shut heaven that it rain not". This is the Elijah-like aspect of the ministry of these men and recalls the time when rebellious Israel under their evil king were three and a half years without rain (1 Kings 17:1). The length of the period is not recorded in the book of Kings but is supplied in

James 5:17. The same judgment is brought upon earth by these witnesses in similar circumstances and for the same period. There seems to be no reason why the expression the "days of their prophecy" may not mean that the drought extended over the whole period of 1260 days while they preached. Whether this drought can be equated with the famine under the third seal is a separate issue.

2. "[They] have power over waters to turn them to blood, and to smite the earth with all plagues as often as they will". This is the Moses-like aspect of their ministry. What Moses did in the first plague in Egypt (Exod 7:16-19) they do against a mightier tyrant than Pharaoh. The second part of the description of their ministry reads in the RV, "and to smite the earth with every plague", a statement that suggests that the action of God against the gods of Egypt is repeated against the more terrible idolatry under the beast. In the verb "to smite" (*patassō*) can be heard the hammer-thuds as the blows fall on this rebellious earth. The expression "as often as they will" repeats the verb *thelō* as expressing the desire or will of the witnesses. Thus the battle is joined in a clash of wills. Men under satanic control desire to wipe out the witness for God; these witnesses acting for God defend their message by unmistakable physical blows that leave men in no doubt as to heaven's demand for repentance. These plagues also serve to confirm the faith of the saints and prepare their hearts for a deliverance that is on the way. The time is drawing near when a mightier than Moses will effect a greater deliverance from a despot mightier than Pharaoh. Then will arise not just the song of Moses but the song of Moses and the Lamb (15:3-4).

7 The AV translation, "and when they shall have finished their testimony" catches the thought perfectly. Even the great power of the Beast is ineffective until the moment when their testimony is concluded and God permits the removal of the protective shield. This permission will allow a final act of testimony but it will be through their death. God has numbered their days of public witness as 1260 and Satan cannot shorten this period by even one day. As already shown the weight of evidence places their testimony in the first half of the week.

The great enemy of these two witnesses is described as "the Beast that ascendeth out of the bottomless pit" . The word *thērion* means "an animal, a wild animal, a wild beast". Thayer points out that when the word is used metaphorically, as here, then what is stressed is not low intelligence or stupidity, but always the ferocity and savagery of the untamed animal nature. This is the word used for the four beasts of Dan 7 LXX. By the normal rules of grammar the article used with beast would refer back to a beast already mentioned, but since this is the first mention of the Beast the emphasis is more general and points to "that well-known beast"– as if no further explanation is required. The absence of any explanatory remarks is in keeping with John's practice of introducing a matter abruptly and leaving further detail until later. He does this with "the second death" (2:11) and with "the book of life" (3:5). This beast reappears in 13:1 as "a beast ... out of the sea" and in 17:8 as "the beast ... that shall ascend out of the bottomless pit". It will be shown that in both these passages the word "Beast" is used metaphorically of a personage of world stature who will appear in the tribulation period.

To explain the expression "out of the bottomless pit" it is necessary to point out that this world-leader with the title "beast" has "two comings" (*parousia*) to use the word of 2 Thess 2:9.

1. First Coming of the Beast

The coming out of the sea (13:1) where the word "beast" has no article is clearly his first appearance on the world stage. His relationship with the empire that he heads and their mutual interaction is discussed in the comments on that chapter. In the symbolic picture the sea must speak of the turmoil of the nations and from this will emerge this world-leader of imposing personality and power. This defines his ethnic and political origin and suggests that the Beast will be a Gentile and arise from the Western world. This fits in with the OT picture of a western Gentile world figure called the "prince that shall come" (Dan 9:26) and suggests that the NT identification of this one is "the Beast". Since OT and NT agree that this leader is one of the signatories of the covenant with Israel that introduces the seventieth week of Daniel, his first appearance on the world stage must be prior to the tribulation period.

2. Second Coming of the Beast

The coming "out of the bottomless pit" in 17:8 is predictive and should read as JND "is about to come out of the abyss". It will be argued in the commentary on that verse that this anticipates a world leader who, at a vital point of his career, which other scriptures suggest (particularly 13:3) will be at the midpoint of the seventieth week, receives "the deadly wound" arising possibly from an attempted assassination. While a stunned world watches it seems that the deadly wound is "healed" (13:3,12). Suddenly this world leader has become one who can claim to have been raised from the dead. After this satantically-staged pseudo-resurrection this book speaks of him as "from the abyss". This is the same location as in 9:1-12 from which the demons emerged and the very abode over which Satan, as the fallen star (9:1), has been given the key for a period. If this happens as suggested at the midpoint of the seventieth week then for the final three and a half years of the tribulation this world is ruled by a satanically-possessed and satanically-controlled man. It is not correct to speak of this as a satanic incarnation, as Satan has no power to take human flesh as Christ did, but in this man he has found a totally-yielded tool suitable for the furtherance of his plans. It is not surprising that the Beast turns upon these witnesses with satanic venom, but the amazing fact is that God allows him to kill them.

The preaching and power of these two witnesses seem to have been a constant irritant to the Beast as he moves to the peak of his power in the middle of the week. The drama of his pseudo-resurrection and the resulting world acclaim lead him to make an all-out assault upon them. The text describes this drama in the simplest of language; he "shall make war against them" and "shall overcome them" and "shall kill them". Since his complete submission to satanic power in his pseudo-resurrection the Beast has waged an unrelenting campaign to stamp out and destroy all who belong to God (13:6-7); he now turns his attention to the two witnesses who have previously been invincible. His terrible success in killing them must echo round the world. Men will feel that this man has now no rival and his power is greater than that of God, who can no longer protect His own. Men will say, "Who is like unto the beast? who is able to make war with him?" (13:4).

8-10 So significant is the victory for the Beast that, as an evidence to the whole world of his power, the bodies of the witnesses are allowed to lie in the open street of the city in contemptuous defiance of every rule of decency and morality. This is for publicity. Out of (*ek*) every sector of humanity described as peoples, tribes, tongues, and nations there will be those to see and recognise the significance of these two dead bodies. This fourfold description of people of different ethnic, cultural, social and language background denotes the world-covering publicity. Many centuries before such a thing would have been technically possible, the Holy Spirit has anticipated the scale of television coverage in these latter days. This macabre exposure of dead bodies is not ghoulish delight in death but a satanic challenge to heaven; the world press and television crews make sure, over the three and a half day period, that the news circles the globe. It is, doubtless, of deliberate policy and possibly by a directive from the head of state that the bodies are not put out of sight in a tomb or sepulchre. Satan would recall another tomb (John 19:39-42) and the issue of Christ's resurrection. The public exposure of the bodies under the gaze of the world and the period of exposure into the fourth day is because Satan, through his puppets, wants no clandestine message of resurrection to circulate and undermine the faith of his followers. Satan is setting out to prove that, even if he could not hold Christ in the grave, he can hold these two witnesses, little realising he is but setting the stage for a mighty act of God. God permits his triumph, but only for a time!

The city on the street of which the dead bodies lie is called "the great city". While admittedly Jerusalem is not elsewhere identified by this title the statements that follow leave no question that this is the holy city of v.2. Any mystical notions about Rome or Babylon are ruled out by the identification marks that follow. The word "spiritually" must not be taken to mean simply figuratively or allegorically; it is rather an interpretation given by the Holy Spirit. The Holy Spirit has given the name of "Sodom" to Jerusalem because of its immorality and its mistreatment of the heavenly messengers (Gen 19: 1-14). This is its moral identification. That same Holy Spirit has given it the name "Egypt" because of its idolatry in the worship of the beast and its persecution of those who worship God. This is its spiritual identification. That there should be no question as to the city the historical identification is added, "where also their Lord was crucified" (JND, RV). The heinousness and utter obscenity of the crimes of Jerusalem was not in crucifying "our Lord" but in crucifying "their Lord" – to the One who came with the authentic claims of a sovereign and to whom they should have given a crown they gave a cross! Could any sin be greater?

As the news of this spectacular triumph of the Beast spreads throughout the earth, a great world party begins. The description of men of earth as, "they that dwell on the earth" has been shown (see comments under 6:10) to point, not merely to physical location, but moral identification. Distinct from saints who, born from above, claim heaven as their country of origin, this phrase describes those who have made earth their home and have identified with the Beast and his empire. By this time they will have taken his mark (13:16-17) and become his worshippers. This is evident in the way that they respond to this news. The delight of the earth-dwellers seems to develop into an international thanksgiving in the expression "make merry" (Luke 15:23). Congratulations from round the world pour in for the Beast giving a carnival atmosphere of a world holiday. The sending of gifts (Prov 19:6; Est 2:18; 9:19) or the exchange of gifts in many cultures expresses mutual pleasure and delight at the news. Rulers who have been at loggerheads are united for once; politicians bury their party differences and unite in praising the might and ability of the Beast – he has triumphed even against heaven. In this worldwide joy the predominant note is relief. For three and a half years the consciences of men have been stung by the preaching of these two witnesses, supported by the evident power of God and His divine protection of them. The verb "tormented" (*basanizō* rendered "vexed" in 2 Pet 2:8) in the aorist tense sums up their ministry and it may include, not only an anguished conscience but, in addition, a tormented body from the plagues inflicted by the two witnesses. It is the same verb used in 9:5; 12:2; 14:10; 20:10 where physical pain is primarily intended. Now men are free from these tormentors; the deaths of the two witnesses tells unbelieving men that there is a limit to the power of God. The Beast, the chosen god of men of earth, seems to be in total control. The earth-dwellers anticipate peace to pursue their plans and pleasures unhindered by any voice from God.

11-12 It is easy to imagine the tension around the earth as, forbidden burial, two dead bodies lie in the open street in Jerusalem. World television crews linked by satellite beam the sight around the world. As the third day approaches, the day traditionally linked with resurrection, the tension mounts as hourly news bulletins make sure that every eye is focused here. Into the fourth day and the world breathes a sigh of relief and relaxes – not a sign of resurrection. But God's moment arrives. His witnesses have testified for three and half years; their bodies have lain exposed for three and a half days; now on the stage set by Satan himself and before a watching world is seen the mightiest miracle since the resurrection of Christ. The word is clear and concise and cannot be misunderstood: "The spirit of life (*pneuma zōēs*) from God entered into them and they stood upon their feet". The "breath of life from God" (RV) reflects a possible translation but it is apparent that in this resurrection the Holy Spirit must be involved (Rom 8:11). Arguments based on the absence of the article before *pneuma* are irrelevant, as most grammarians point out that this word does not require the article. Alford writes, "No inference of indefiniteness can be drawn from the absence of the article from such a word as *pneuma*". As the voice of television and news media commentators and reporters falls silent, a palpable hush circles the globe as men watch this mighty demonstration of God's power. With the brevity of divine restraint the record states simply "and great fear fell upon all them that saw them". The merriment of earth is stilled as it was in Belshazzar's feast (Dan 5:1-9) when the fingers of a man's hand wrote over against the candlestick. This action is just as manifestly "the finger of God". The great voice "from heaven" summons the witnesses "into heaven" and as the cloud shuts them out of sight their enemies watch spellbound. There are obvious echoes of the ascension of the Christ in Acts 1:9. The summons is in the same words used to John in 4:1 but this time the world is watching. The message to men is clear, God is not "dead" and will take action against the Beast; a sobering note as worship for the Beast is demanded ever more forcefully (13:8). Believers will see in the resurrection of these witnesses an evidence of God's mighty power and know that, even physical death at the hands of the Beast will give way to resurrection power. This action speaks of defeat for the Beast and deliverance for saints even if they die at his hand. The three and a half days of festivities on earth will be followed by three and a half years of unrestrained wrath.

13 The literal interpretation of events throughout this chapter is borne out by this literal earthquake occurring in the very same hour as the rapture of the two witnesses. No one on earth at the time could miss the supernatural significance of it and dismiss it is as coincidental. Jerusalem is shaken by an almighty hand. That only a tenth part of the city is affected indicates an exact and measured judgment sent as a further warning upon a defiant nation. "Seven thousand names of men" (see JND, RV margin) die in this earthquake. This strange method of recording the number of dead is an idiomatic way of showing a careful and precise count. It suggests that the names were put on a list, or perhaps even put on a monument of remembrance. They may well have been the particular agents of the Beast responsible for the death of the two witnesses and God deals with them as He dealt with Korah, Dathan and Abiram in an earlier rebellion (Num 16:21-33). The contrast with the 7000 witnesses for God in Elijah's day under an apostate king Ahab (1 Kings 19:18) cannot be missed. God's witnesses in that dark day were preserved, Satan's workers in this dark day are destroyed. This display of God's power in the resurrection of the two witnesses and the simultaneous earthquake strike terror to the hearts of men. The word "affrighted" (*emphobos*) is the word used of the terror of the women at the tomb (Luke 24:5) and of the disciples when confronted with the truth of the resurrection of Christ (Luke 24:37). When God acts in power men are affected like this (Acts 10:4; 22:9; 24:25). The "remnant" in the context describes the other inhabitants of the city besides the beast-worshippers. To "give glory" to God does not necessarily mean conversion to God but it does mean a recognition of God (see Luke 17:18) that admits that God is behind the earthquake. The inhabitants of Jerusalem can do no other than recognise the "God of heaven" was acting in vindication of His two witnesses. Whether this leads to repentance and faith in the Lamb depends on the individual. In general the judgments about to climax the tribulation seem to lead men, not to brokenness and repentance, but to absolute defiance as seen after the seventh bowl judgment: "and men blasphemed God" (16:21). As Pharaoh hardened his heart against the claims of Jehovah (Exod 8:15, 32; 9:34) so the Beast and his followers defy the God of heaven.

Notes

3 It is possible to argue that the 1260 days of testimony of the two witnesses do not fall neatly into either half of the tribulation period. The text gives the period of testimony but gives no direct indication of when their ministry commences or closes in relation to other events. Some have suggested that 1260 days of the ministry of these men may fall symmetrically over the midpoint of the week giving 630 days on either side. While having the advantage of linking their ministry with the third seal (the famine conditions) and the second trumpet (turning the water into blood) the same objections that ruled out the last half of the week may be raised against this suggestion. It seems much better to see the period as the first half of the week.

7. *Trumpet Seven – The Third Woe*
11:14-19

v.14 "The second woe is past; *and,* behold, the third woe cometh quickly.

v.15 And the seventh angel sounded; and there were great voices in heaven, saying, The kingdoms of this world are become the kingdoms of our Lord, and of his Christ; and he shall reign for ever and ever.

v.16 And the four and twenty elders, which sat before God on their seats, fell upon their faces, and worshipped God,

v.17 Saying, We give thee thanks, O Lord God Almighty, which art, and wast, and art to come; because thou hast taken to thee thy great power, and hast reigned.

v.18 And the nations were angry, and thy wrath is come, and the time of the dead, that they should be judged, and that thou shouldest give reward unto they servants the prophets, and to the saints, and them that fear thy name, small and great; and shouldest destroy them which destroy the earth.

v.19 And the temple of God was opened in heaven, and there was seen in his temple the ark of his testament: and there were lightnings, and voices, and thunderings, and an earthquake, and great hail".

14 The chronological movement of the book is now to be resumed. This verse like 8:13; 9:12 is transitional. It completes one section and opens another. Two of the woes announced by the flying eagle R.V. (8:13) have been described under the fifth and the sixth trumpets. The interlude or parenthetic section from 10:1-11:13 has been completed. The present tense "cometh" hints that the third woe is already on the way. The seventh angel is about to sound the final trumpet of the series of seven.

It is to be noted that it is never called the "last" trumpet and to equate it with the trumpet so described in 1 Cor 15:52 is false exegesis and ignores the context in each case. The *last* trumpet in 1 Cor 15:52 is the final summons in the pilgrimage of the Church; the last trumpet here is the last in the series of seven already mentioned. Other trumpets will sound long after this one (for example see Matt 24:31).

15 With the sounding of the seventh trumpet there is anticipated the final stage of history before the earth is brought under the dominion of Christ in the millennial kingdom. As pointed out previously the seventh seal had no distinctive characteristic judgment included under it, suggesting that it consists of the seven trumpets. The same is true of this seventh trumpet. There is no mention of any distinctive judgment, suggesting that it consists of the seven bowls (15:1-16:21). The mighty angel (10:7) had declared that in the days of the voice of the seventh angel, when he shall begin to sound, the mystery of God should be finished. The mystery of God, as previously shown, is Christ intervening dramatically in history and taking His kingdom. The telescopic effect of the climaxing judgments means that within the seventh trumpet the seven bowls are emptied very quickly upon earth, possibly within a time-span of weeks or days. This is followed by the coming of Christ to earth. Thus instead of the silence as when the seventh seal was opened (8:1) there is a veritable symphony in heaven when the seventh trumpet is blown. A "great voice" has been heard many times in this book and will be heard again but this is the only time when the plural "voices" is qualified by "great". Heaven unites to announce the import of this trumpet.

The announcement is clear and concise. JND represents the original text very closely:"The kingdom of the world of our Lord and of His Christ is come". The textual support for the singular, "kingdom of the world" is overwhelming. The idea is that world kingdoms despite claims of independence and sovereignty are all one kingdom under Satan. From this usurper and his puppets the Beast and the false prophet, Christ comes to wrest control and when He does this, earth will still be one kingdom but under a new king. W. Scott suggests p.240 that the idea is the "world kingdom" of Christ. The simple genitives "of our Lord and of His Christ" have echoes of the Jehovah of the OT and the Christ of the NT, but these are embodied in the one sovereign, one monarch, in whom all the prophecies and promises of earthly blessing and kingdom glory are centred. The aorist verb "become" (AV) is anticipatory as having been announced by God. While certain events have yet to be fulfilled, this taking of the kingdom by Christ is so certain that it may be viewed as already having taken place and hence the past tense. The plural "voices" unite as the single voice of 19:1 but the matter for celebration is the same: the overthrow of the kingdom of the beast and the establishment of the kingdom of Christ. The singular verb "he shall reign" points to the supreme and solitary dignity of this sovereign ruler to whose reign there shall be no end. The very strong Greek expression used is literally "unto the ages of the age" (*eis tous aiōnas tōn aiōnō n*) and is the normal one used to denote time without end, so it can be described as eternity. The thousand years of 20:1-6 is but the first phase of a rule that is eternal.

16-17a The announcement of the kingdom by the heavenly symphony of voices is answered by the act of adoring worship of the twenty-four elders mentioned for the eighth time in the book. Here the Throne-Sitter is identified as God and before Him the twenty-four elders prostrate themselves "upon their faces". These representatives of the raptured church in priestly ministry bend in adoring worship as they recognise that the purpose of God on earth is moving to completion in the establishment of this long-promised kingdom. The worship (*proskunō*) may involve physical prostration, the outward sign of a bowed heart in the presence of God, but it involves also thanksgiving. The thanksgiving is addressed to the Lord God Almighty. Jehovah and His purpose in the covenant, Elohim who displayed mighty power in creation and the El-Shaddai who provided for the creature are names that have revealed deity through centuries past. The "Almighty" (*pantokratōr*) used of deity nine times in the book, stresses the absolute power of God to effect His divine purposes on earth. The title is only used once elsewhere in the NT (2 Cor 6:18) where it occurs in an OT quotation. The establishment of the kingdom will not be brought about by social changes on earth but as an act of divine power of the almighty One. This almighty One is the eternal One who transcends time; the One to whom belongs eternity in the present – "who art", the One to whom belongs history in the past – "and was", for there never was time when He was not. The clause "and art to come" in manuscripts of later date seems to have been an interpolation by a scribal hand from the title in 4:8. Its omission suits the context of a kingdom which, in fulfilment of the longings of the past, has now arrived.

17b The reason for this outburst of praise is now explained. The perfect tense of the verb "hast taken" describes the permanent result of the action of Christ in taking the kingdom. The great power (*dunamis*) that Christ has taken and will never relinquish, is the power of divine intervention in the affairs of men. He has always had the authority (*exousia*) but now he displays the power. The word has OT echoes of the power that Jehovah showed in Egypt (Exod 15:6; Deut 3:24) and showed to His people in their need (Neh 1:10; Isa 10:33) but will now be demonstrated for all to see and know. The word "power" (*dunamis*) means the ability to carry into effect all the purposes of God in the establishment of the kingdom. The aorist tense of the verb "didst reign" marks the commencement of the reign as the translation offered by Robertson makes plain, "Thou hast assumed the power and didst begin to reign". This is another prophetic statement; the event itself is yet future, but since it is in the counsel of God, it can be spoken of as if it had already happened.

18 It is not very clear from the text whether this verse is the conclusion of the thanksgiving of the twenty-four elders or whether it is John's observation given by divine revelation at this point. Since its subject matter is descriptive and directly prophetic it seems better on balance to view it as a direct prophetic statement through John. Four statements showing the order of events in the establishment of the kingdom may be set out as follows:

1. "And the nations were angry". The aorist were angry *(orgizō)* should be translated "became angry". This was not just a momentary flare up of temper but a settled burning resentment directed against God. This is obviously a reaction to the trumpet and bowl judgments. With no desire to repent of sin, angry resentment against heaven (16:11) stirs the nations as they gather to Armageddon. This is the event anticipated prophetically in Ps 2:1: "Why do the heathen rage, and the people imagine a vain thing?" It is the event described in 16:16: "And he gathered them together into a place called in the Hebrew tongue Armageddon". The "great wrath" (*thumos,* "rage") of Satan (12:12) has communicated itself to the nations under his control.

2. "And thy wrath is come". Man's wrath is answered by heaven's wrath. Since this phrase follows the mention of the anger of the nations that leads to their gathering at Armageddon it points, not backward to the tribulation in general, but forward to the one great blaze of that anger at the coming of the Christ. His coming to confront the angry nations gathered around Jerusalem is described in 19:15: "And out of his mouth goeth a sharp sword, that with it he should smite the nations: and he shall rule them with a rod of iron: and he treadeth the winepress of the fierceness (*thumos*) of the wrath (*orgē*) of Almighty God". The wrath of God has come, dramatically and terribly it has burst upon men. There is no doubt that John the Baptist had preached a message particularly relevant to the coming of the Christ, "Flee from the wrath to come" (Luke 3:7). Now it is too late, the wrath has arrived and burst upon men on earth.

3. "And the time of the dead that they should be judged". The mention of "the dead" has led many commentators to link this with the wicked dead in 20:11 where the same expression recurs. Some expositors see the difficulty in this

view as expressed by F.A. Tatford, "This obviously looks on to the last great assize of Rev 20:12, but probably also has in view that at the ushering in of the millennium". W. Hoste writes in a similar vein: "The words 'the time of the dead, that they should be judged' would seem naturally to point to the final judgment of the wicked dead before the great white throne, but that will occur a thousand years later, at the close of the millennial reign". A little consideration will show that this cannot be the judgment here described. Not only is the judgment of the dead at the great white throne a thousand years later than this judgment but those judged in this passage can only be saints, a fact made clear in the terms used. Neither can this judgment be the judgment seat of Christ which is linked exclusively with the church (2 Cor 5:10) and has taken place immediately after the rapture in heaven and before the commencement of the tribulation period. The results are already seen in the seated and crowned twenty-four elders. This judgment here is at the close of the tribulation just before the establishment of the millennial reign of Christ. Neither can this be the judgment of Matt 25:31-46 where living people are judged; here it is the dead who are judged.

Since all the other sessional judgments are ruled out this must refer to the judgment of the resurrected saints of OT days and very possibly the martyred saints of the tribulation days who belong to the same line of testimony. The terms describing the saints confirm this deduction. Those who are to be judged and given their reward (singular) are described under four categories:

1. to thy servants – their service. Like king David (Acts 13:36) they had served their own generation and now the time of their recognition has arrived.
2. to the prophets – their ministry. It could reasonably be argued on the basis of Acts 2:17 and on the pattern of the two witnesses who are called prophets (vv. 3,6) that this could refer to tribulation period prophets. In fact it must include all who have stood in this line of ministry excluding the church age. Lonely men who had stood for God in dark days would now find their work revealed and rewarded.
3. to the saints – their sanctification. The term is an OT designation of those set apart for God in the midst of idolatry and immorality. While it is the common designation of believers throughout all ages, in the NT the preferred designation for church-age believers is "the saints in Christ Jesus" (Phil 1:1). The location of the term between "prophets" and "them that fear thy name" suggests OT believers.
4. to them that fear thy name – their obedience. This is a direct allusion to Mal 3:16 and the description of exercised saints prepared to live their lives in submission to the revelation of God in the Scriptures of their time.

The final expression "to the small and to the great" does not define a category but describes the world-view of God's servants, prophets, saints and God-fearers. "Small" is the contemptuous dismissal by men of some simple saints; they are of no account on the social, political or commercial scale of values. Others are judged as "great" as filling some notable place in the esteem of men; God has His saints in every stratum of society. In that day men's values will be of no account and all will be judged impartially by the king before the establishment of the kingdom. The implication is that they will share the glory in proportion as they have shared the suffering and the service. Their reward will be commensurate with the reality of their testimony for God.

To see the resurrection and judgment of OT saints at this point fits in with the OT Scriptures. Daniel places the resurrection of OT saints at the end of the tribulation as shown in Dan 12:1-2: "and there shall be a time of trouble, such as never was since there was a nation even to that same time: and at that time thy people shall be delivered, every one that shall be found written in the book. And many of them that sleep in the dust of the earth shall awake, some to everlasting life, and some to shame and everlasting contempt". The fact that a thousand years intervenes between his two statements of resurrection identifying two classes is in keeping with many OT passages as well as John 5:28-29. Hebrew grammarians (Tregelles p.164) point out that the expression "some…and…some" is never used distributively as describing two parties from the same company, rather it is used to distinguish two separate companies as meaning "these…and…those". In this passage the saved ones of the OT period are raised to be judged as they enter the millennial kingdom while the unsaved of the nation of Israel await the summons to the great white throne a thousand years later.

The fourth and last act of Christ, just before the millennial reign is introduced, is seen in the final statement and describes an act of divine judgment upon the unbelieving:

4. "And should destroy them that destroy the earth". The verb here *diaphtheirō* may be rendered "utterly bring to corruption" (Newberry marg.). This verb graphically describes retributive justice upon those whose actions have been "utterly corrupting" (the present participle of the same verb) the earth. The verb *diaphtheirō* is used literally of the action of the moth (Luke 12:33) which quietly eats into the very fabric of a garment. The "mystery of iniquity" (2 Thess 2:7) is already at work in the church age but in the tribulation period it will destroy the very fabric of society morally, socially and politically. This corruption will extend to the environment as well, since men will refuse to God His place as Creator. The puppets of Satan, the beast and false prophet will be the first to meet destruction (19:20); the armies they have gathered will next meet total destruction (19:21). A final act of destruction may be specially in view here. In Matt 25:31-46 all the people living on earth after the tribulation are gathered before the throne of Christ. Christ divides them into the "sheep" (see comments on 7:13-17) who go into the kingdom and the "goats" who are banished into everlasting fire. These "goats" who were not present at Armageddon but have shown by their actions that they were adherents of the Beast, are judged by Christ with awful solemnity in the sentence, "Depart from me, ye cursed, into everlasting fire, prepared for the devil and his angels". With

one final comment, "And these shall go away into everlasting punishment" (Matt 25:41-46) Christ destroys those who have destroyed the earth.

19 With v. 18 the end of the tribulation is reached in anticipation. The actual establishment of that millennial kingdom will be described in 20:1-6.

When the section, "things which must be hereafter", was opened in 4:1, John saw that "a door was opened in heaven" which introduced him to the throne of God (v.16). This is the throne that has furnished the background of the action until this point in the book. Now John's gaze is focused upon a temple called "the temple of God" and from this point the temple will become the focus of action (15:5; 16:1). While the throne emphasises the righteousness of divine action the temple speaks of the holiness of divine action. The final movement of the book will await the linking of the temple and the throne in 16:17 and this will be the prelude for the final unveiling of Christ when John sees "heaven opened" (19:11). For the first time heaven and earth will be in visible communication as Christ comes forth to earth. The time interval between "the temple of God opened" (11:19) and "heaven opened" (19:11) is very short; it is in fact only the time required for the pouring out of the seven bowls (chs. 15-16). The fact that these bowls will bring unprecedented terror upon earth is foreshadowed in the storm signals that are now linked with the temple. The intensifying judgments as the period nears its end can be seen in comparing these storm signs throughout the book, as follows:

4:5 "And out of the throne proceeded *lightnings* and *thunderings* and *voices*" (linked with the *throne*).

8:5 "And there were *voices,* and *thunderings,* and *lightnings,* and *an earthquake*" (linked with the *altar*)

11:19 "And there were *lightnings,* and *voices,* and *thunderings,* and an *earthquake,* and great *hail*" (linked with the *temple*).

16:18 "And there were *voices,* and *thunders,* and *lightnings;* and there was a great *earthquake,* such as was not since there were men upon earth, so mighty an earthquake, and so great", followed in v.21 with "And there fell upon men a great *hail* out of heaven" (linked with the *temple* and *throne*).

Before the storm breaks a reassuring sight is permitted to John. A rainbow round the throne in ch.4 showed that God's covenant purpose with respect to earth would never fail despite the coming storm. Here just as the storm is about to break the sight of "the ark of his covenant" (RV) reassures John that however dark "the day of Jacob's trouble" (Jer 30:7) God will fulfil His purposes with regard to Israel. The symbolic use of the tabernacle imagery, the brazen altar (6:9) the golden altar (8:3) and the ark of the covenant is now complete; John stands in the very presence of God for the final scenes of the book.

CHAPTER 12

8. *The Third Parenthesis*
12: 1-14:20

This chapter opens the second half of the book. While chapter and verse divisions of Scripture are not inspired it is still a matter of interest that vv.8,9 are the two central verses of the 404 verses which make up the Revelation. A further point of interest is that the central verse of the chs. 4-19 which cover the tribulation period is v.12 in which it seems eminently fitting that the key word should be "woe".

With this chapter the third parenthetic portion of the book embracing the three chs. 12-14 is opened. A parenthesis provides a pause in the movement of the book while related topics are explained or introduced. It is important to see that these parenthetic portions are not scattered at random but follow a very definite pattern. The first parenthesis comes between the sixth and the seventh seals; that the second parenthesis comes between the sixth and the seventh trumpet, and this third parenthesis precedes the pouring out of any of the bowls. The reason for this latter placement can be grasped when it is pointed out that the bowls will occupy a very short span of time, possibly weeks at the most, and that the seventh bowl is poured out when the tribulation is in its closing hours.

It is useful to see at a glance the actual setting of this chapter and relate it to the overall picture of events thus:-

1. The Six Seals	6:1-17	
2. The First Parenthesis	7:1-17	Deals with People (a) Going into the tribulation (vv.1-8) (b) Coming out of the tribulation (vv.9-17)
3. The Seventh Seal	8:1-5	
4. The Six Trumpets	8:6-9:21	
5. The Second Parenthesis	10:1-11:13	Deals with Places (a) The earth – divine possession 10:1-11 (b) The city – divine purpose 11:1-13
6. The Seventh Trumpet	11:14-19	
7. The Third Parenthesis	12:1-14:20	Deals with Purposes (a) The coming of God's Man – ch. 12 (b) The coming of Satan's men – ch. 13 (c) Cameos of the tribulation – ch.14
8. The Seven Bowls	15:1-16:21	
9. The Fourth Parenthesis	17:1-19:10	Deals with Powers (a) Religious power – the harlot – ch. 17 (b) Commercial power – the city – ch. 18

Chs. 12, 13 will deal with the main actors who play a major part in the end-time drama of the tribulation period. As it has done in the pre-church era the nation of Israel plays a key role in the tribulation period. This nation is presented in this chapter under the symbol of a radiant expectant mother. The key event in the history of the nation is the birth of Christ and this is seen in the manchild of this picture. Ch. 13 will show that in the tribulation two mighty personalities will emerge on earth. One will be seen symbolically as rising from the sea and the other from the earth. There will be a common link in that both are shown as wild beasts and both have major roles to play in the events of the tribulation period. Behind the emergence of these beasts and their activities and, indeed, involved in all the events of the period lurks a sinister personage seen as "a great red dragon". This dragon, plotting and planning for his own ends, is shown to have been working in total opposition to God throughout history. The three parenthetic chapters can be simply linked:

1. Ch. 12	Whence Evil Comes	The Dragon
2. Ch. 13	What Evil Produces	Beasts
3. Ch. 14	What Evil-Brings	A Harvest and a Vintage

In ch. 12 the symbols used are a woman, her child and the dragon. It will be shown that the woman speaks of Israel in history, her manchild speaks of Christ in prophecy, while the dragon portrays Satan in both history and prophecy and sees him as one implacably opposed to the woman because of the Child. The subject of the chapter is Satan and his malignant purpose.

There are three sections in the chapter which may be set out as follows:

(i) The Cameo of History
The Woman and her Child (vv.1-6)

(ii) The Conflict in Heaven
The War and its Consequence (vv.7-12)

(iii) The Confrontation on Earth
The Woe and its Character (vv.13-17)

(a) *The Purpose of Satan Disclosed (vv.1-17)*

v.1 "And there appeared a great wonder in heaven; a woman clothed with the sun, and the moon under her feet, and upon her head a crown of twelve stars:
v.2 And she being with child cried, travailing in birth, and pained to be delivered.
v.3 And there appeared another wonder in heaven; and behold a great red dragon, having seven heads and ten horns, and seven crowns upon his heads.
v.4 And his tail drew the third part of the stars of heaven, and did cast them to the

earth: and the dragon stood before the woman which was ready to be delivered, for to devour her child as soon as it was born.
v.5 And she brought forth a man child, who was to rule all nations with a rod of iron: and her child was caught up unto God, and *to* his throne.
v.6 And the woman fled into the wilderness, where she hath a place prepared of God, that they should feed her there a thousand two hundred and threescore days.
v.7 And there was war in heaven: Michael and his angels fought against the dragon; and the dragon fought and his angels,
v.8 And prevailed not; neither was their place found any more in heaven.
v.9 And the great dragon was cast out, that old serpent, called the Devil, and Satan, which deceiveth the whole world: he was cast out into the earth, and his angels were cast out with him.
v.10 And I heard a loud voice saying in heaven, Now is come salvation, and strength, and the kingdom of our God, and the power of his Christ: for the accuser of our brethren is cast down, which accused them before our God day and night.
v.11 And they overcame him by the blood of the Lamb, and by the word of their testimony; and they loved not their lives unto the death.
v.12 Therefore rejoice, ye heavens, and ye that dwell in them. Woe to the inhabiters of the earth and of the sea! for the devil is come down unto you, having great wrath, because he knoweth that he hath but a short time.
v.13 And when the dragon saw that he was cast unto the earth, he persecuted the woman which brought forth the man *child.*
v.14 And to the woman were given two wings of a great eagle, that she might fly into the wilderness, into her place, where she is nourished for a time, and times, and half a time, from the face of the serpent.
v.15 And the serpent cast out of his mouth water as a flood after the woman, that he might cause her to be carried away of the flood.
v.16 And the earth helped the woman, and the earth opened her mouth, and swallowed up the flood which the dragon cast out of his mouth.
v.17 And the dragon was wroth with the woman, and went to make war with the remnant of her seed, which keep the commandments of God, and have the testimony of Jesus Christ".

The Cameo of History – The Woman and her Child

1-2 The AV "a great wonder" (*sēmeion mega*) would have been better rendered "a great sign" as in the RV and most other translations. The word *sēmeion* is a characteristic word of John which he uses seventeen times in his Gospel and seven times in this book (12:1,3; 13:13,14;15:1;16:14; 19:20). The word "sign" draws attention to the divine purpose behind the symbol or happening. (The word *teras* ("wonder"), which John hardly ever uses in any of his writings, is used to draw attention to the awe-inspiring effect which the happening has on the mind of the observer.) The link with the last verse of the previous chapter is to be noted in the conjunction "and" and the echo of the phrase "in heaven". Against the background of the opened temple and dark thunder clouds of judgment there appears a sun-clad woman. While the repeated use of the word "and" builds up the picture the main point is to show that the sign must not be limited to the woman. It is a composite sign of sun-clothed, star-crowned woman with the moon under her feet and expecting a child. The features described are all part of the sign. The very use of the word "sign" indicates that the picture is to be taken symbolically, while the adjective "great" shows how it is to be regarded in importance.

Many strange interpretations of the sun-clothed woman have been offered. Discounting the more bizarre suggestions the favourite amongst amillennial expositors is that she represents the church. W. Hendriksen speaks for many when he writes, p.135 "That woman symbolises the church (cf. Isa 50:1; 54:1; Hos 2:1; Eph 5:32). Scripture emphasises that the church in both dispensations is one. It is one chosen people in Christ". Since the premise of this argument is wrong the conclusion is wrong and the Scriptures quoted prove the very opposite. Israel and the church have ever been distinct. Other expositors, with more credibility, have sought to literalise the woman and identify her with Mary, the human mother of Christ. Others again have held to the interpretation of the actual Mary while widening the thought to include holy mothers from Eve downward as if the symbol presented ideal "motherhood". In support they point to the promise of the seed of the woman (Gen 3:15). There is nothing in this passage to support an interpretation of this nature and it leads to very strange conclusions in the later verses (see vv.13-14). The woman reflects the nation of Israel, ideally and historically, as the particular nation through which God would bring His Son the designated Sovereign into the world.

It has previously been stressed that the symbols used in this book are taken from the Scriptures themselves and thus do not allow arbitrary interpretations to be imposed upon them. This is so in the symbol of the woman. Israel in the OT is repeatedly represented as a woman, e.g. Isa 54:5; Jer 31:32; Ezek 16:32; Hos 2:16. Because of national sin and departure she is repudiated by Jehovah her husband and is spoken of as desolate, forsaken and a harlot (Isa 54:3, 4, 6; Lam 1:1; Hos 3:1; Jer 3:6-10). In the symbolism here the emphasis does not lie upon her state but upon her standing in the counsels of God. She is presented as God intended her to be ideally, fulfilling His divine purpose in being the nation through which His Son would come into manhood. That she is not to be identified as the remnant throughout the ages becomes clear from v.17 where the woman and the remnant are seen to be distinct. She is the nation of Israel in the counsels of God. Four matters serve to confirm this identification and point out the dignity of Israel as she is in the mind of God:

1. Her clothing: "clothed with the sun". As John gazed into heaven it seemed that the sun itself was the brilliant apparel of this beautiful woman (cf. the clothing of the angel in 10: 1). There is no doubt that the detail is intended to convey to the mind the thought of supreme glory. There can be nothing greater on earth than to be clothed with the radiance of the sun. As W. Kelly writes, "All this is seen in connection with Israel; for God intends, as far as this world is concerned, all power and glory to centre around Israel".
2. Her position: "the moon under her feet". Since the moon shines by reflected

sunlight it has generally been seen as symbolising derived authority. The expression "under her feet" symbolically presents Israel has having under God supreme dominion. She is the channel of divine revelation since Scripture and the Son of God have come to men through Israel and in this rests her divine authority. The expression "under her feet" does not necessarily picture subjugation but simply subordination (see Ps 91:13; 1 Cor 15:25).

3. Her crown: "upon her head a crown of twelve stars". The crown speaks of supreme sovereignty. God intended this nation to wield sovereignty for Him on earth. The word used for crown (*stephanos*) here must reflect "royalty" and not simply "victory". Thayer points out that any distinction between *stephanos* and *diadēma* (the word in v.3) was not "strictly observed" in Hellenistic Greek. The reference to the twelve stars, not only confirms that the woman is Israel, but must also show that the twelve tribes of Israel will be the administrative channel through which the sovereignty of the nation will be exercised. The allusion is to the dream of Joseph in Gen 37:9-11 where the sun is interpreted as Jacob his father, the moon as Rachel his mother and the eleven stars as his brethren. Joseph's view is restricted to eleven stars as he himself was a participant in that action. The main point of the dream is that the Abrahamic covenant would be fulfilled in the elevation of the messianic figure of whom Joseph was only a picture. In this more complete picture, showing the place of the nation of Israel in divine counsel, the twelve stars indicate that all the twelve tribes will be involved in the sovereign status enjoyed by Israel when the purpose of God has been fully worked out on earth.

4. Her condition: "And she being with child". The most striking thing about this woman is that she is "with child", the literal reading is "having in the womb". The human situation portrays a crisis, the woman "travailing in birth" cries out in her labour pain as the moment of delivery approaches. In the background of the symbolism is the promise in Gen 3:14-16 concerning the "seed of the woman". Sorrow would be associated with childbirth for all women, yet the expectation of the ages would centre on a son who would come through this very sorrow. Succeeding ages would narrow the channel to the "seed of Abraham" (Gen 15:18) and then to the "seed of David" (2 Sam 7:12-16) so that the expectation became scripturally embodied in one nation. While the birth-moment will come under the divine camera in v.5, the whole period of gestation is in view here as down the centuries Israel waited for the coming One. From Eve to Abraham and then down to David, age after age rolled away until a babe of the line of David was born to Mary in Bethlehem. Through the centuries Israel was ever an expectant nation.

A problem arises when considering the labour pains of this woman in connection with the birth. Many commentators point out that the Roman occupation of Judaea, while severely affecting life generally, hardly answers to the picture of a mother in labour crying out in pain. To limit the travail at the time of Christ's birth to the spiritual remnant in the nation as represented by Simeon (Luke 2:25-28), Anna (Luke 2:36-38), and Joseph of Armithea (Luke

23:51), does not fit the picture of the whole nation in travail. The answer lies in the uniqueness of the birth of Christ in that the birth itself comes before the labour pains. Isaiah anticipated this unnatural birth-situation when he wrote, "Before she travailed she brought forth; Before her pain came, she was delivered of a manchild" (Isa 66:7). Thus the real travail of the nation of Israel did not occur at the time of this actual birth but still lies ahead in the terrible anguish of the tribulation period. Christ spoke of the first part of the tribulation as "the beginning of sorrows" (Matt 24:8) where the word "sorrows" (*ōdis*) is the normal word for labour in childbirth and can be translated "travail" (as in 1 Thess 5:3) or "birth pangs". The latter part of the tribulation is appropriately described by Jeremiah as "the time of Jacob's trouble" (Jer 30:7), where the Hebrew word for "trouble" should be translated "distress" (W. Wilson). Thus the actual birth of Christ, with a time-abridgement familiar in prophecy, is linked directly to His second coming when, after the anguish and pain of the tribulation, Christ comes forth as the Son-Sovereign to claim His kingdom.

3-4 The first "sign" gave John a view of Israel as the people of God seen ideally in the purposes of God. Another sign gives John a view of Satan as the enemy of God both in history and in prophecy. John's surprise is registered in the "behold" as he sees "a great red dragon". There has been some satanic subtlety in the fact that the dragon is classified in the present day amongst the mythological beasts. Scripture is perfectly clear that it was an actual known animal. In Ps 91:13 it is classed amongst other literal animals in the promise, "Thou shalt tread upon the lion and adder; the young lion and the dragon shalt thou trample under foot". Other scriptures lend their support (Isa 34:13; Ezek 29:3). It very possibly belonged to the dinosaur family in which recent research has shown certain classes had fire-breathing capacity. Here the dragon picture is used symbolically but it is interpreted in vv.8-9 as "that old serpent, the devil and Satan". The dragon character emphasises the malignancy and utter implacability of this inveterate enemy of God and His people.

The fiery-red colour no doubt symbolises the murderous activity of God's ancient enemy as he has stirred up hatred in the hearts of men from the days of Cain (1 John 3:12) to the present. Unlike any real dragon known on earth this dragon has seven heads and ten horns. The fact that these two unusual features occur again in the first beast of ch. 13 (13:1; 17:3) has led some expositors to assume that the two are identical. This is a mistake. The reproduction of the features of the dragon in the beast is not unexpected but similarity does not prove identity. Closely related, the two are utterly distinct, the dragon is the master, the beast is but the servant. Nevertheless the scriptural interpretation of these two features given in 17:9-10 is vital to our understanding since consistency of interpretation demands that the same symbols be interpreted in the same way in each case. In 17:9 it is shown that "The seven heads are seven mountains...and they are seven kings" (RV). It is not likely that the Holy Spirit would change the symbol without explanation, so it is a safe deduction that the seven heads represent seven mountains, the scriptural symbol for kingdoms, and these kingdoms are equivalent to or are represented by seven kings. The picture presents the malignancy of Satan as revealed in seven kingdoms (or kings) who have opposed Israel and sought to wipe out that nation at various times down the ages. Israel as the nation through which Christ would come has been specially hated by Satan who, as shown here, awaits the birth of the child with evil purpose.

Scanning the history of Israel it is a simple matter to pick out the nations who have been bitterly antagonistic to Israel and sought its destruction. Satan has used puppet nations and kings throughout history in the pursuit of this malignant purpose. From the birth of the nation in Egypt to the cross of Calvary there are only six nations that fill this role. These are as follows:-

1. Egypt – Represented in Pharaoh
   Egypt and Pharaoh are linked in the denunciation of Ezekiel "Behold I am against thee, Pharaoh, king of Egypt, the great dragon that lieth in the midst of the rivers." (Ezek 29:3). The dragon is used symbolically of a satanically inspired enemy of Israel, hardly possible if the dragon was only a mythological beast.
2. Assyria – Represented in Sennacherib
3. Babylon – Represented in Nebuchadnezzar
   The lament of Jehovah identified in His people is heard in the voice of Jeremiah, "Nebuchadnezzar the king of Babylon hath devoured me, he hath crushed me, he hath made me an empty vessel, he hath swallowed me up like a dragon."(Jer 51:34).
4. Medeo-Persia – Represented in Ahasuerus
5. Greece – Represented in Antiochus Epiphanes
6. Rome – Represented in Caesar

Under each of these kingdoms and kings there was a deliberate attempt to wipe out Israel and thus rule out any possibility of the Christ coming through the line of promise. This view of history given by God shows that Satan was behind each one of these attempts; they were neither accidents of history nor to be explained in terms of political expediency but were Satan-directed attacks on the line of Christ. In Egypt the edict of Pharaoh (Exod 1:22) would have destroyed every male child. In Assyrian times the last of the Davidic line, a childless Hezekiah, was besieged in Jerusalem yet the Davidic promises (Isa 7:13-14; Ps 127:1) were centred in him. The activity of Haman under Ahasuerus in the Medo-Persian times was designed to wipe out the larger part of Israel (Est 3). In the Greek period Antiochus Epiphanes becomes the spearhead of genocide (Dan 11:21-32) against Israel. In the Roman Empire Caesar's puppet king Herod carries out satanic purpose in the slaughter of the children (Matt

2:16-18), while Caesar's procurator, Pilate, in defiance of Roman law and justice, passes the sentence of death on the Christ. When the cross stood on Golgotha it seemed as if Satan had triumphed at last. If these show the nature of satanic attacks in the first six kingdoms it could be expected that there would be a specially-ferocious attack in the seventh and final empire.

The seventh empire and its emperor, from John's historical perspective, had not yet arrived. This is seen in his comment with reference to the seventh head, "The other is not yet come" (17:10). Since the whole of history is represented in this symbolic view of satanic animosity, the presence of the final head is perfectly understandable; its anticipated arrival is so sure that, in the vision, it is seen as present already. As will be shown in comments on 13:1 this final empire is the empire of the Beast that dominates earth during the tribulation years. This empire and emperor will far outrank all its predecessors in its malignancy and cruelty directed against Israel, and this hatred will be a major factor in the sufferings of Israel throughout the seven years of tribulation.

As the scriptural interpretation of the seven heads will show (17:9-10), the governments and kings that are represented are consecutive. One has followed the other across the page of history. Another and complementary aspect of satanic power is shown in the ten horns. The "horn" in Scripture has been shown to be the symbol of power (see 5:6). Associated in this context with the number "ten" completeness of administrative power is in view. While the heads are successive it will be shown that the ten horns all rule together. This would be difficult to prove from this picture alone, but the reappearance of the ten horns in the Beast in 13:1; 17:3 and the explanatory statement of 17:12 show that this must be so: "the ten horns which thou sawest are ten kings which have received no kingdom as yet, but receive power one hour with the beast". The fact that these ten horns have close correspondence also with the "ten toes" of Daniel's image (Dan 2:42) confirms this deduction. The full manifestation of satanic administrative power will be seen in the final empire and manifested in ten subordinate rulers.

Each of the seven heads is wearing a crown (*diadēma*) which describes a fillet or chaplet encircling the brow that reflects royal dignity. Every one of these heads shows that Satan makes a royal claim through the seven historical personages symbolised. The very number seven indicates Satan's claim to complete power in the kingdoms of the world throughout history. It will be noted that when the beast appears (13:1) the crowns are not upon the heads but upon the horns. Seen against the background of history these seven kingdoms (or kings) have had regal power; when the last kingdom (and king) appears that regal power will be shared with ten kings. John's time-perspective has been changed. See comment on 13:1.

4 The scorpion is feared because of the sting in its tail (9:10); this dragon has fearsome strength in its tail. In the OT the tail is used symbolically of "the end" or "that which follows" so it came to mean influence and power particularly in example and teaching (see Deut 28:13; Isa 7:4; 9:15). Symbolically presented to John's gaze is the fact that the power of the dragon drew a third part of the stars of heaven after it and threw them down to earth. The interpretation of the "stars" in v.1 in the context of the vision, shows that they were actual historical personages: the twelve patriarchs or the twelve tribes of Israel descended from these patriarchs (Gen 37:9-1 1). Thus it is possible to interpret the stars in this verse as kings or personalities on earth, one third of the rulers are so affected by satanic power as to follow Satan's man the Beast. J.F. Walvoord expresses this view: "This seems to refer to the gathering under his power of those who oppose him politically and spiritually involving his temporary subjugation of a large portion of the earth". W. Scott is somewhat similar in interpretation though he sees the stars as "Individual rulers set in outward relationship with God in positions and places of authority. These christian rulers and teachers are caught in Satan's snare and believe the devil's lies". F.C. Jennings, insisting that the similarity of language demands here a fulfilment of Dan 8:10, sees the third part cast down as referring to the apostate part of the nation of Israel who enter into alliance with the beast. None of these suggestions gives sufficient weight to the difference between stars *in* a crown (v.l) and "stars *of* heaven". It is important to notice the genitive case here; they are not stars in heaven, but stars that belong to heaven, heaven's stars. Heaven is their proper realm. Stars and angels are often equated in scripture (1:20; Job 38:7) and Satan is described as "Lucifer" the "day-star" (Isa 14:12). It is therefore suggested that what is in view is the great rebellion of Satan against the Most High, a rebellion that resulted in one third of the angels being cast down to earth. The verb "cast down" is readily explicable: Satan was the one who caused this catastrophe; he brought it about. This is doubtless the event to which the Lord Jesus referred when he said, "I beheld Satan as lightning fall from heaven" (Luke 10:18). In that fall he brought other angels with him. The casting of the stars to earth is the result of Satan leading the angels who followed him into a battle in which they were defeated when he with them was hurled down from heaven. The "third part" of the stars is to be taken with the same literalness as the mention of the same fraction in the trumpet judgments (8:7-12). The point of this detail is to make clear the might of this inveterate enemy of God; a depleted heaven and a blood-stained history of nations evidence his power. The reference to angels under satanic command in vv.8-9 when he leads them in a second battle supports this interpretation.

The two symbols are brought together to show the relationship between them. The dragon stands before the expectant woman. Not knowing the exact moment of birth, yet knowing the Scriptures and reading the signs, the dragon takes up position to destroy the child as soon as it is born. Herod the Edomite, the suspicious old king of Judaea knowing that his very life hung by the tenuous thread of Caesar's favour, had his own personal reasons for ordering the slaying of the children under two years of age in Bethlehem and the surrounding area (Matt 2:16-18), but in this barbarous act he was but the tool of Satan. In the symbolic language of the vision the dragon sought to devour the manchild. Some have questioned this interpretation on the grounds that this "murder of the innocents", the term used by historians, is not documented outside of the Gospels. The complete answer is that, on the scale of the atrocities of Herod, this was a very minor event historically. Herod's reign was one of the most blood-stained in history. Tacitus the cynical Roman historian wrote of Herod, "I had rather been Herod's pig than Herod's son; so dark and gruesome is the history of this man who murdered all his own family members". He was a fitting instrument through whom the dragon revealed his malignant nature.

5 This cameo of history is completed with the sun-clothed woman giving birth to a son. Before the dragon can act to devour the child it is caught up to God and to His throne. The expression "manchild" is most unusual, as it would be unusual in English to speak of a "male son". Since the one word *huios* is sufficient to distinguish the sex of the child, the addition of "male" suggests an emphasis on the masculinity of Christ: this is the birth of the "Man".

Much debate has centred on the interpretation of this "manchild". If the above interpretation of the sun-clothed woman is accepted as Israel, for which there is ample scriptural support, then there can be little doubt that this manchild is Christ. The only objections having any weight have been on the grounds that:

1. This retrospectively makes the sun-clothed woman the virgin Mary. However, to accept this argument is to miss the whole import of the symbol. It is true that Mary was the channel through whom Christ came; in the very nature of the case there had to be a single mother since Christ had to be born of a woman (Gal. 4:4); but in this historical cameo individuality is lost in the symbol of the nation; it is that nation that brought forth Christ.
2. No reference is made to the death, burial and resurrection of Christ. The case is put clearly by W. Hoste (page 88): "This view also demands that the Spirit of God, for some reason, which one has not heard explained, should suddenly go back to the incarnation. Would it be likely that such a transcendent and unique event should be described as here? Why, too, should no reference be made to His ministry, death and resurrection, were the Lord in view?". As explained, chronological development is not in view; neither are the historical events surrounding and within the ministry of Christ. This picture is a symbolic portrayal of the conflict between God and Satan. Israel the chosen nation would bring forth the Christ whom Satan would seek to destroy as soon as He was born. God would catch away this One to the throne. The intervening events of the ministry of Christ and His death and resurrection are all implied but are

not the object of the cameo. It fastens on one issue of history: the hatred of Satan for the woman.

Other interpretations of the manchild do not fit the picture. Some see in it the church, or, in a refinement favoured by those who subscribe to the partial rapture theory (J.A. Seiss), the overcomers of the church age. These are ruled out by earlier considerations that place the church in heaven and represented by the twenty-four elders. On other grounds the maleness emphasised here is totally at variance with the feminine idea in the church as well as the feminine gender of the word *ekklēsia*. Some see in this raptured manchild a select number from Israel raptured at the midpoint of the tribulation. All that can be said of this suggestion is that there is no scriptural support for it. That the manchild can be only Christ is confirmed by the statement, "Who was about to rule all nations with a rod of iron". This is a direct allusion to Ps 2:9 and stresses the divine purpose regarding the Christ. In 2:27 the same quotation brings promise to the overcomer in Thyatira and awaits the fulfilment of 19:15. This manchild as the royal Sovereign will wield the sceptre for God in the millennial kingdom. The verb "to rule" (*poimainō*) should be translated "to shepherd" (JND) which implies absolute power linked with care. (See discussion on the verb *poimainō* at 2:27.) The idea is a benevolent paternalism that brooks no dissent. The iron rod reflects this same idea with the added nuance that the rod will never break nor be broken. This dynasty will never be changed. The staff and the rod identify him as the Shepherd: the one is for correction and the other for protection. Here the benevolent Shepherd-King, of whom David was the picture, will shepherd all nations. That overcomers of the church age will share His rule is but an added facet of the picture.

This child the object of satanic attack is the subject of divine action. "Caught up" (*harpazō*) has in it the idea of "to seize", "to snatch" or "to take away" implying suddenness, swiftness even violence in the action. A study of its usage will show that the emphasis is not removal from danger but the speed of the action taken (see Matt 11:12; 13:19; John 10:29). It is the verb in Acts 8:39 "The Spirit of the Lord caught away Philip"; it is used of the apostle in 2 Cor 12:2-4 "caught up to the third heaven" and of the church when the Lord comes "caught up together" (1 Thess 4:17). There can be little doubt but that this refers to the ascension of Christ (Luke 24:51; Acts 1:9-11), while the main purpose of the ascension was not to escape the hostility of Satan which Christ had endured in life and death, this was in fact the end-result. The expression, "to God and to his throne" shows this child to be associated with deity and given the highest place in the universe. In the change of word from "male son" (*huios arsēn*) to "child" (*teknon*) some have sought to limit the picture to the early years of Christ and see in this statement a reference to the escape of Joseph and Mary and child (*paidion*) from the murderous intention of Herod (Matt 2:16). This cannot be so because:

1. the word "child" (*teknon*) simply means "born one" and shows his relationship to the woman even though now an adult
2. the verb "caught up" (*harpazō*) in itself does not include any idea of escape from danger
3. to be caught up "to God and to his throne" would be a strange way of describing the flight into Egypt.

Some commentators argue, on the basis of the promise to the overcomer in Thyatira (2:27), that saints of this dispensation will reign with Christ in the millennial kingdom. While this is certainly true some go further and suggest that since the word "caught up" (*harpazō*) used here of Christ is used of the church in 1 Thess 4:13-18, the rapture of the church is included in the picture with Christ. Perhaps there is some support for this view when it is recognised that between vv.5,6 there is a very large time gap that includes the whole church age from Pentecost to the rapture. Linking the ascension of Christ and the rapture of the church in this way removes the church from earth before the tribulation begins, a truth already established on other grounds. While there is some appeal in this suggestion, the best that can be said about it are the words of W. Scott, p.252 "We cannot find Scripture to warrant the assumption that the church is embraced in the rapture of the manchild".

6 The cameo of history closes with v.5, and there now follows a direct prophecy as the focus in John's vision returns to the mother of the manchild. In the symbolic picture Israel has brought forth Christ whose history on earth has closed with the ascension. Now the flight of the woman must be interpreted in keeping with the symbols and it shows not a remnant of the nation but the nation of Israel itself fleeing into the wilderness. Some expositors insist on retaining this verse as history. While admitting that no flight of Israel took place immediately after the ascension of Christ, they point out that in the years leading up to the destruction of Jerusalem by the Roman army under Titus in AD70 there was an exodus from Jerusalem to Pella, a sandstone city in the mountains of Edom. This flight is documented in Josephus and Pella has been identified by Sir Charles Marston, the antiquary and archaeologist, as modern Petra, a city purpose-built and concealed amongst rocky outcrops. Well-nigh inaccessible and now completely deserted it yields many evidences of occupation in the past. While that may have been a foreshadowing of what is prophesied here it cannot have been the fulfilment of it. Three reasons summarise the objections:

1. Only a tiny group fled from Jerusalem, mainly those who took seriously Christ's warning of the destruction of Jerusalem (Matt 24:15-18). If interpretation is to be consistent the woman must represent the whole nation or at least the major part of it.

2. This hiding place is "prepared of God" and there is a very definite hint of supernatural provision of food for the refugees. A handful of believers hiding in the rocks of Pella hardly meets these requirements.
3. The time note 1260 days has special significance and points onward to the last days (see comment at 11:3), specifically to a three and a half year period in the tribulation.

Thus between v.5 and v.6 there occurs what is not unknown in prophetic writings: an unannounced time-gap. Nothing is mentioned between the ascension of Christ and the moment when Israel as a nation flees into the wilderness. This flight can hardly take place in the first half of the seventieth week when the nation, resting in the false assurance of the seven year covenant, is relatively at peace. At the midpoint of the week, with the introduction of the "abomination of desolation" into the holy place, the whole picture is changed. The terrible rage of the Beast is focused on the nation which, as a nation, will not conform to the new worship in the temple and is forced to flee. It is here that Christ's words find their complete fulfilment, "Then let them which be in Judaea flee into the mountains" (Matt 24:16). The mountains in Christ's statement are physical, but in this passage the "wilderness", in keeping with the symbolic picture, is the spiritual identification of the place in which the fugitive nation finds shelter. The "barrenness" of their place of exile will mean they require sustenance there. What is pictorially presented here was prophetically anticipated by Isaiah: "Hide the outcasts; bewray not him that wandereth. Let mine outcasts dwell with thee, Moab; be thou a covert to them from the face of the spoiler" (Isa 16:3); or, "Come, my people, enter thou into thy chambers, and shut thy doors about thee: hide thyself as it were for a little moment, until the indignation be overpast. For behold, the Lord cometh out of his place to punish the inhabitants of the earth for their iniquity" (Isa 26:20-21). Daniel spoke in the same way of the same people of the same time: "Moab, Ammon and Edom will be safe havens" (Dan 11:36-45).

It is clear that, just as God intervened supernaturally to preserve Elijah for three and a half years when the apostate nation of Israel was under disciplinary drought in the reign of Ahab (1 Kings 17-18), so He will preserve this remnant through this latter day apostasy. The apostate of Israel, who have been deceived by the false prophet, are identified with the worship of the Beast (13:12) whose image stands in the holy place in Jerusalem (13:15). The orthodox of Israel who will not bow to the image as in the days of Elijah (1 Kings 18:13; 19:18) flee for their lives and are divinely protected and supplied. In this verse the fact of their flight is stated while v.14 describes more fully the manner of their flight. Not only are they protected, but provision is made for them, just as Elijah was directed to a brook, supplied by ravens and provided for by a widow. The verb "to feed"(*trephō*) is an all-embracive word and means to "supply all that is needed for her well-being"; it covers much more than food. There is also a divine limit set on the length of her exile; God is so careful of His people that He numbers the period in days. These 1260 days, the last three and half years of the seventieth week, are the period of "the great tribulation" (7:14), which with reference to Israel is called "the time of Jacob's trouble" (Jer 30:7).

Notes

3 Questions may be raised as to why other nations are not included here who, with equal hatred, have tried to wipe out the nation of Israel. The answer is that the church age is not the subject of direct prophecy. From Pentecost until the rapture of the church, Israel as a nation has been set aside by God, and therefore the happenings in this period are not portrayed in prophetic overviews. Dark and terrible as have been the anti-Semitic crusades and the organised outrages against the Jews in many lands (cf. the holocaust in Nazi Germany in this century), they are not the subject of prophecy and therefore are omitted in this overall picture of satanic hatred.

The Conflict in Heaven – A War and its Consequence

7-8 These six verses explain why at the midpoint of the seventieth week conditions on earth change so dramatically. The answer is that there is a battle in heaven and its results are felt on earth. The word "war" (*polemos*) here indicates a set battle. JND in his marginal notes explains the aorist tense in the "was" (*egenetō*) as "has now taken place, has begun to be". Suddenly a battle is raging in heavenly realms. It is possible that as Satan has observed the rapture of the church, the judgment seat and the marriage union about to take place in heaven he feels that the moment is ripe for him to make an assault on the throne. The success of his plans for the emergence of his agents on earth and the slaying of the two witnesses may have encouraged this delusion. On the other hand, with time running out, the dragon may take the initiative to prevent the outpouring of the final judgments upon his earthly agents. Scripture does not explain who started the battle but the word order in the sentence would suggest that the initiative may have come from Michael who, with divine authority, takes the first step to clear the universe of the instigator of rebellion. This view finds support in the statement of Dan 12: 1, which refers to the same moment in the seventieth week, "And at that time shall Michael stand up, the great prince which standeth up for the children of thy people". It may well be that in answer to the pressure upon the nation of Israel Michael is authorised to take action.

Michael whose name means "Who is like God?" is mentioned five times in Scripture. In Dan 10:13 he is called "one of the chief princes"; while in 10:21 he is called "Michael your prince". In Dan 12:1 he is named as "the great prince" and in Jude 9 is identified as "the archangel", the only one in Scripture. Here he leads a great angelic host; they are so under his command as to be called "his angels". Against the host of heaven are ranged the enemy described as "the dragon and his angels" and the result is a titanic struggle. The verb "prevailed not" descriptive of the failure of the satanic attack, reflects the supreme effort they put forth to defeat the host of heaven.

The location of this battle has given rise to much dispute since it is described as being "in heaven". The risen Lord has "passed through the heavens" (RV) clearly the aerial and astral heavens, and having become "higher than the heavens" (Heb 7:26) has entered into "heaven itself, now to appear in the presence of God for us" (Heb 9:24). The third heaven is identified with Paradise where God is and Christ dwells (2 Cor 12:2-4) and where the saved of earth gather (Luke 23:43) to be with Christ. This can hardly be the realm where this battle rages. Neither does this battle rage in "the heavenlies" of Eph 6 which conveys different teaching entirely. The words of Christ in Luke 10:18 refer to the fall of Satan from his place as "the anointed cherub that covereth" (Ezek 28:14) so very close to the throne of God. That event is history and took place between Gen 2 and Gen 3. Since this fall it is clear that Satan can dwell no longer in the very presence of God. Nevertheless it is also clear that there are certain regions in heaven identified with angelic ministration to which Satan still has access (Job 1:6; 2:1) and where as the accuser of the saints he is free to present his case before God. It is from this "place" that Satan and his angels are now expelled. This interpretation is supported by the emphasis on "their" in the sentence "neither was their place found any more in heaven", as if they had had a special realm available to them. It would seem that not only is this rebellious band now expelled from heaven but the very region where they gathered is closed to them forever as Michael acts to clear the cosmos of evil.

9 This expulsion of Satan and his hosts from heaven takes place at the midpoint of the seven-year tribulation. Many expositors have commented upon the fact that vv.8,9 are the two middle verses of the 404 verses of the Revelation (see J.B. Smith). The first half of this book thus closes with the expulsion of Satan from heaven; the second half will end with the exaltation of the Lamb so that "the throne of God and the Lamb" (22:1) will be seen eternally. This expulsion is but the first step to the moment of final doom of the enemy of God and man. The same verb "cast out" or "cast down" is used to mark the downward steps as God deals with the great adversary:-

12.9	"He was *cast out* into the earth"	Exiled from heaven.
20:3	"*cast* him *into* the bottomless pit"	Imprisoned in the abyss.
20:10	"The devil ... was *cast into* the lake of fire"	Banished to the Lake of Fire.

So that there should not be the slightest misunderstanding of the work and person who has been against God and His people throughout the ages, three of his titles are given:

1. "The old serpent" identifies him as the one who brought disaster to

mankind in the garden of Eden (Gen 3:1-24) at the very dawn of history. The literal serpent allowed itself to be used as the vehicle of this powerful enemy of God and it has paid the price since then. Subtlety and treachery are the characteristics of the serpent – fit words to describe man's most ancient and most wily foe.

2 "The Devil, and Satan" is really a double title. The word "devil" (*diabolos*) is derived from the verb *diaballō* which means "to slander" or "to defame". He is described as "the accuser of our brethren"; he accuses men before God as he did Job (Job 2:4), and he slanders God to men. The other side of his character is given by the Hebrew word *Satan* meaning "adversary". This is his uniform title in the OT where he is seen as the adversary of God, His people and all the purposes of God.

3 "Which deceiveth the whole world" is literally "the (one) deceiving the whole world". The construction shows that this one is *the* deceiver *par excellence*. Seven times in the latter part of this book he is associated with deception (12:9; 13:14; 18:23; 19:20; 20:3, 8, 10) as if to suggest that, while deception has been his characteristic work throughout history, in these closing days he reaches the peak of his deceiving work. All the great "isms" that have shut God out of His creation have been his work; now the greatest "ism", the "deism" that will demand worship for himself, will be his last great deception. The "whole habitable world" (JND) gives the scope of his plotting which includes all the population of earth. It has been argued that this "inhabited earth" must be limited to the earth known to John. This is a totally unjustified limitation placed on divine revelation; nothing in the word itself would restrict it to either the "Roman earth" or "the prophetic earth" or to the christendom of our day. Notice the use of the same word in Heb 2:5 where no possible limitation may be placed upon the scope it embraces.

The repetition of the verb "cast out" with regard to both Satan and his angels stresses the ignominy of his total defeat. From this point onward Satan and his angels have no further access to heaven and are restricted in their movements to the physical earth. When he is defeated in this earth realm (19:20) there is no avenue of retreat open to him. God has started the process of clearing the usurper from the cosmos and he will find his final doom in the lake of fire.

10-11 This war that John has just witnessed has a twofold result: in heaven there is a call to worship (vv.10-12); for earth there is the pronouncement of woe (vv.13-17). The voice calling for rejoicing and pronouncing woe cannot be that of God or Christ since in the praise they are referred to in the third person; it can hardly be angels since it refers to "our brethren"; and the twenty-four elders never speak unitedly in this way. This suggests that the company who have previously spoken in this way – the souls of the martyred saints of the first half of the tribulation (6:10) – speak again. Their shout of triumph seems to be a fitting conclusion to their long wait for vindication, as they realise that this action heralds a decisive step towards the ultimate defeat of Satan and the establishment of the kingdom. As so often in the book, they see in the first step the whole completed process. The one "loud voice" offers no problem; another great company is heard as a single voice in 19:1. The triumphant praise of this martyred company sees in the expulsion of Satan and his hosts from heaven the realisation of that for which they have waited so long. There are four related terms in their praise:

1. "*The salvation*" in the context and with the article, must be the physical deliverance of saints through the tribulation period as they have awaited the King. Christ has spoken of this salvation: "But he that shall endure unto the end the same shall be saved" (Matt 24:13). Much wider than personal salvation, the term must embrace both the creation and the creature delivered from the thraldom of sin and Satan into millennial blessing.
2. "*The strength*" ("power" RV) is essentially the opposite of "weakness" that has characterised the testimony for God down through the ages and particularly in the tribulation period. Political power, civil power, commercial power and military power have all been marshalled by Satan to destroy what has been for God. Saints in tribulation days were ostracised, persecuted, hunted and slain; weakness characterised them, now the situation is reversed in dramatic fashion.
3. "*The kingdom of our God*" is the millennial kingdom established when Christ comes to earth in the full display of His sovereign rights as heir to the throne of David. All nations bow to His authority as He takes the kingdom for God.
4. "*The power of his Christ*" is the "authority" (*exousia*) that men have disputed and denied; now there can be no question as to who has absolute control. Neither monarchy nor democracy has been able to subdue men; all ended in anarchy but now that theocracy is established in the Son of God all men must bow (Phil 2:9-11). It is no longer optional but obligatory. The words "his Christ" are an echo of 11:15 and show that Messiah of prophetic promise has always been central to the purpose of God. It is an echo too of Ps 2:2 where it is translated "his anointed".

"For" (*hoti*) should be translated "because". The reason for this triumphant anticipation of the kingdom is the defeat and banishment of Satan and his angels from heaven. This action presages the overthrow of all satanic influence and power. Satan, described as the "accuser", a word used for a legal opponent in a court of law, has been the active accuser before the bar of heaven of those spoken of as "our brethren". This is the company spoken of as "their brethren" in 6:11 and must be the saints of the last part of the tribulation who are about to die. This adversary of the saints, undauntedly carries his attack before God and does it without pausing. The phrase "day and night" is used five times in the book (4:8; 7:15; 12:10; 14:11; 20:10) to show uninterrupted action. Saints are only men at the best and have many failings; Satan, refusing to acknowledge the basis of God's blessing as established in blood, seeks by his constant accusing demands to stir up divine justice against them. Martyred they might be but defeat on earth is victory from the standpoint of heaven. The victory, which at this point has not yet taken place, anticipates the song of 15:3 and is summed up in the tense of the verb "overcame" and the emphatic pronoun "they" – these very saints who have been the subject of satanic accusation, the very ones who die.

These overcomers are the second group of martyred saints in the tribulation period. Their song is heard in 15:3 where the reason for their death is given: they refused the mark of the beast. The double use of the preposition "by" (*dia*) gives the grounds of their victory, not the means:

1. "By (*dia*) the blood of the Lamb" indicates that for the individual the guilt and filth of sin have been removed and, having peace with God, he is able fearlessly to stand against the might of the Beast. Cleansing and clearing before God are both embraced in the mention of the blood; this is the ground of their victory over Satan. That blood was the full and sufficient answer to every calumny and charge of Satan.
2. "By (*dia*) the word of their testimony" is secondary and is the result of the first; these saints, far from being discouraged by satanic accusation, were stimulated to sacrificial service for the Lamb. Giving a faithful and fearless testimony even to the point of death these saints contribute to their own victory. The expression refers to their evangelical witness even when they were dying under the Beast.

The secret strength of these martyrs was their attitude towards "their lives". Christ set the standard of discipleship when He used similar words in challenging would-be disciples, "and hate not .... his own life also" (Luke 14:26). Now this standard is met in those "who loved not their life even unto death" (RV). The aorist tense "loved not" suggests the moment of crisis when a choice had to made and they choose death. Swete puts it concisely: "Their non-attachment to life was carried to the extent of being ready to die for their faith". Earth viewed it as defeat; God and heaven view it as victory.

12 The introductory "therefore" (*dia touto*) refers back to the "now" of v.10. In the expulsion of Satan and his angels from heaven these martyred saints glimpse both the establishment of the kingdom and the vindication of those who have died for their faith. Is it any wonder that the "heavens" are addressed and called upon to rejoice (JND translates "be full of delight")? This is the only time in the book that the word "heavens" occurs in the plural, as if to show that this first note of praise includes realms now cleared of Satan and his angels. At this same time there is a party going on upon earth, men are rejoicing (the same verb *euphrainō*) at the victory of the Beast over the two witnesses (11:10). They do not know that the heavens are called to rejoice as Satan is expelled from the courts above. Heaven will be called to rejoice for the third and final time in the book at the close of the tribulation over the fall of Babylon (18:20). This summons to rejoice begins a paean of praise that swells into the "hallelujah chorus" of 19:1-6. The challenge to worship embraces not only angels who belong to the heavens, but it embraces other companies described as "ye that dwell in them". The verb "to dwell or tabernacle" (*skēnoō*), has the root idea of a "tent" as a temporary dwelling but includes the idea of "presence". Both ideas are embraced in John 1:14 when the word is used of Christ "and dwelt (tabernacled) amongst us". These heaven-dwellers are in the very presence of God and await their permanent home after the resurrection and establishment of the kingdom. This word is repeated in 13:6, where the same company or companies are in view. Since the word is never used of angels it is men from earth who await their permanent residence. Rejoicing in heaven is answered by a "woe", a word of unutterable anguish that fittingly describes what is about to fall upon earth. The voice is still that of the martyred saints expressing fearful anticipation for all who dwell on earth. This is not the third woe of 8:13 which awaits the seven bowls of ch. 16 (see 11:14) but simply a sympathetic interjection from heaven. While the RV reads "woe for the earth and for the sea" and JND "woe to the earth and to the sea", the AV gives the correct sense: "woe to the inhabiters of the earth and of the sea". The inhabitants of earth who draw out the sympathy of heaven are not those who have been formerly called "earth dwellers" (see 3:10 for the moral identification) but simply those who live on earth. The statements that follow will show that the special objects of satanic rage are Israel and the saints.

Expelled from heaven the devil has no option but to make his last stand on planet earth. Two present participles describe his state. "Having great wrath" describes his emotional state: intense rage (*thumos*) burning in the heart of the devil. "Knowing that his time is short" describes the consciousness that stirs him into such a rage. He knows full well that the plan of God in redemption is moving to completion and that the time available to him now is very short. The "season" (*kairos*) in which he can wield power is limited to three and a half years; it is only a little period compared to the centuries of the past and it corresponds to the "short space" of the eighth head of the beast in 17:10. Intuitively enlightened by the prophetic scriptures he knows (*oida*) that Christ is about to receive His kingdom. Within this short space will be seen the final outburst of satanic rage against all that represents God on earth.

The Confrontation on Earth – The Woe and its Character

13 The paragraph from vv.7-12 has provided the background for this final scene between the woman and the dragon. This is not history symbolised as in the first paragraph (vv.1-5) but prophecy presented. The flight of the woman in v.6 is taken up again in v.14 with added detail as to the cause, the character and the consequences of her flight. Satan, expelled with his angels from heaven, turns with bitter fury upon the nation that has given Christ to men. He intends at this midpoint of the seven-year tribulation to destroy this nation utterly. The sheer rage of this enemy of God is hard to describe. He is called in v.12 "the devil"; in this verse he is identified again as "the dragon" while in v.14 he is named "the serpent". He is a terrible foe for Israel and the saints. This nation is attacked because it is the nation through which Christ has come. The same word "male" (*arsēn*) is used as in v.5 but here it stands alone. Foiled in his earlier attempts on the life of Christ through Herod and Pilate Satan now attacks the mother. The verb "persecuted" (*diōkō*) has as its original meaning "to put to flight" or "to follow" and the picture is that of a nation harried from post to pillar. The aorist tense sums up the activity of this enemy throughout the three and a half years of the great tribulation period (Matt 24:15-22); he plots and plans and pursues Israel with the object of exterminating her.

14 Under the persecution the woman flees. While many in the nation will worship the beast, the nation as such will refuse his claims despite the miraculous powers of the false prophet (13:11-17). As a consequence Israel is banned internationally and has to flee. This is the flight of v.6; there the fact is stated, here the reason is given. Satanic persecution is answered by divine intervention. The verb "were given", as so often in this book, indicates divine permission without identifying the giver. In this case the giver is God; "the two wings of the great eagle" (RV) echoes another deliverance of this same people in a past day. Jehovah's assurance to Israel as they came out of Egypt has a new meaning for the nation at this juncture: "You have seen what I did unto the Egyptians, and how I bare you on eagles' wings" (Exod 19:4). This picture is used again by Moses to show the care of Jehovah for His people, "As an eagle stirreth up her nest, fluttereth over her young, spreadeth abroad her wings, taketh them, beareth them on her wings" (Deut 32:11). While the faithfulness and trustworthiness of God in caring for His people are included, the emphasis here is on the speed with which they find safety: "that she might fly into the wilderness" (v.14). In v.6 the period is given in days to show God's concern for every day that saints suffer; here it is not the personal element of suffering that is stressed but the prophetic element and the period is given as " a time, times, and half a time". The only other places where this term is used are Dan 7:25; 12:7. The word *kairos* is used as a unit of time, which in the context of Daniel is a year, so that the woman is nourished in the wilderness for three and a half years. As observed in the comments on v.6 this is the same flight as that in Matt 24:16 where the mountains are literal. Here the wilderness may also be literal but more likely describes the spiritual barrenness of the whole political and national arena where these souls have to seek shelter and sustenance during the heyday of the beast. Since they will be unable to "buy or sell" (13:17) and the giving of food or drink or clothing or care will be a highly dangerous thing for others (Matt 25:35-39), this will be a very real "wilderness" experience. Nevertheless they will be "nourished" (*trephō* rendered "feed" in v.6); they will be supernaturally supplied with all they need to survive. Like Elijah there will be a "brook" and "ravens" and a "barrel" in the darkest days of apostasy. The supernatural nature of the supply will be essential as the malignancy of the dragon changes to the subtlety of the serpent. The expression "from the face of the serpent" is to be construed with "nourished" and the preposition is to be understood in the sense of distance – "far from" or "safe from" (Alford). Israel will be scattered to the distant parts of the empire of the Beast.

15 Out of the mouth of the serpent comes "water as a flood" or as both JND and the RV translate "water as a river". A raging torrent sweeps after the woman; clearly designed to carry her to destruction. Since the picture is symbolic it is totally improbable that a symbolic mouth of the serpent could produce a literal flood. Other difficulties in interpreting the flood literally include the physical features of the land and the single direction of flight. Rather the idea is a swelling tide of satanic origin designed to destroy the nation of Israel. One suggested interpretation (presented by W. Scott) is that this flood is a tide of false teaching and deception that persuades so many of the nation of Israel to swallow the lie of the Beast (2 Thess 2:11). This would metaphorically swallow up the nation and destroy it as a testimony for God.

On the other hand the providential intervention of earth which "helped the woman and... opened her mouth and swallowed up the flood" suggests another line of interpretation. God describes the military might of Assyria about to overwhelm Israel in the days of Isaiah as "a flood of mighty waters overflowing" (Isa 28:2). Similar language is used of the Babylonian attacks on Judah in Jer 48:8; 47:2. The key passage in the action of "the prince who shall come" (Dan 9: 26) against Israel is the statement, "and the end shall be with a flood". Since this coming prince has already been identified with the Beast it is suggested that this flood is an extermination policy directed against the nation of Israel to put to death every member of that nation. Previous anti-semitic massacres and even the Nazi holocaust will have been but harbingers of the massive extermination programme against Israel. Centuries of anti-semitism reach a terrible climax at this point.

16 The dramatic intervention of "earth" is perhaps foreshadowed in what happened at the Red Sea to the flood-tide of Egyptian military might about to overwhelm Israel. The record is suggestive even if it is poetic: "Thou stretchest forth thy right hand and the earth swallowed them up" (Exod 15:12). The symbolism here indicates that some providential happening of a supernatural character intervenes to nullify the efforts of Satan. Just as the Assyrian flood-tide was about to engulf Jerusalem it was dramatically destroyed (2 Kings 19:35). If "the earth" is interpreted in strictly symbolic terms it is very likely that the nations on the fringes of the Beast's empire who, for a number of practical reasons, are already stirring in opposition, may offer a safe haven to these fugitives. F. A. Tatford saw the interpretation in similar terms and wrote, "If the interpretation of the flood as false doctrines be adopted, the expositor is in difficulties in explaining their absorption by the earth, and we prefer the more obvious interpretation of the river as a power (or powers) under satanic influence, whose inspired efforts to destroy the Jews are defeated by the attitudes taken by the other nations. The world will not allow the extermination of the Jews which will be attempted. In this way the flood is swallowed up". There is no doubt God intervenes providentially to protect His national people.

The obliqueness of the reference to deliverance may mean that this remnant is composed largely of those who, while they will not take the mark of the beast, have not as yet turned to Christ. Thus while God would act for the preservation of His people, as in the days of Esther, He cannot yet be publicly identified with them. The remnant of true believers comes into view in the next verse.

17 The clearly-providential, yet manifestly-supernatural, intervention to frustrate the "final settlement" of the national Jewish question sends the dragon into a fit of wrath. The verb "was wroth" (*orgizō*) could be translated "flew into a rage" (Rienecker). This goes beyond the emotional response of v.12 (where the word is *thumos*), to describe the blazing temper tantrum arising from implacable hatred in Satan. The cause of such fury is simply the continued existence of the woman despite all his efforts. The preposition "with" (*epi*) in the context would be better translated "over". The dragon's rage drives him to one final assault but, frustrated in his pursuit of the nation, he turns his fury upon "the remnant of her seed". The use of the verb "went" (*aperchomai*) is somewhat strange as normally it would be translated "went away" or "departed". It can be understood in almost a colloquial sense as showing the dragon abandoning every other interest and concentrating on this one matter only, the destroying of the woman. It is better to see the dragon abandoning his pursuit of the woman, and turning his wrath upon this other remnant whom he links with national Israel. From the identification clauses given these are obviously true believers. The remnant is *hoi loipoi* which simply defines "the remaining ones"; the nation itself is protected by the providential intervention of the previous verse, but he can reach these saints and turns upon them in fury. The expression "remnant of her seed" at least suggests that this is the line of faith though Christ – the true seed (Gal 3:16). The expression "make war" will be repeated in 13:7 where the object of attack is "the saints". In this chapter the dragon himself is the attacker while in the next chapter it is his agent the Beast but it is the same war of extermination. In addition to the hint about the seed there are two further identification marks of this remnant which put their identity beyond doubt:

1. "which keep the commandments of God" stresses their relationship to divine revelation in the Scriptures
2. "have the testimony of Jesus Christ" stresses their relationship with the Saviour.

These are not two groups within a remnant but two parallel and supplementary descriptions of true believers from the nation of Israel.

From this chapter it is clear that the animosity of the Beast against the nation of Israel is a special aspect of his more general war with:

1. the Lamb (see 17:14). Since the Lamb is beyond the reach of the dragon it is the followers of the Lamb who are persecuted;
2. the saints (see 13:7). As will be shown in ch.13 the term "the saints" includes all believers irrespective of whether they are Jews or Gentiles.

The persecution of the woman shows that Israel as a nation becomes the target for an extermination campaign, a new holocaust. The reason is that, though they have not trusted Christ, they know enough not to go along with the rest of the nation in the worship of the Beast. As a consequence his fury blazes against them. It will be this remnant of the nation who, when Christ is revealed in glory, will use the language of Isa 53 in heart-broken confession, and Isaiah's reference to "a nation born at once" (Isa 66:8) will be fact. In the language of Paul the great conversion miracle will have taken place: "And so all Israel shall be saved" (Rom 11:26).

However the added expression "the remnant of her seed" (v.17) describes those who have been already born again from the nation of Israel. Satan frustrated by divine intervention in his evil purpose to destroy the nation turns against these more accessible believers with redoubled fury. These are the ones identified by Christ as "my brethren" (Matt 25:40) and who become the touchstone of faith to distinguish between the "sheep" and "goats" at the judgment before the throne as the kingdom is established (Matt 25:31-46).

CHAPTER 13

The chapter division has meant that the close relationship between this chapter and the preceding one has been often missed. The conjunction "And" shows that the two are closely connected; a connection that the RV indicates by placing the first sentence of ch. 13 as the concluding verse (v.17) of ch. 12. The connection has been further obscured by a textual problem: should the verb be read *estathēn* (I stood) or *estathē* (he stood)? The manuscript evidence is divided and some textual scholars, arguing that when copying a manuscript a letter is more easily lost than added, support the AV reading "I stood". However the weight of evidence does seem to point to the reading "he stood" which is given in the RV and by JND as an alternative reading. Since "he" must be the dragon this fits the contextual picture much better. In his burning hatred of Israel and his passion to destroy her (symbolised in the woman of ch. 12) the dragon "took his stand" (the aorist tense) as if to draw out from the sea and from the land the agents who will carry out his purposes on earth. At the very least the symbolism shows that he watches, or supervises, the emergence of his men on the political scene. From the animosity of the dragon shown throughout history towards Israel (ch. 12) this chapter turns to the actual human instruments used by the dragon. The two dragon-controlled beasts that emerge, one from the sea and the other from the earth, are the agents through whom he wages his war of extermination against the seed of the woman in the last half of the tribulation.

(b) *The Puppets of Satan Described (vv.1-18)*

The False Prince

v.1 "And I stood upon the sand of the sea, and saw a beast rise up out of the sea, having seven heads and ten horns, and upon his horns ten crowns, and upon his heads the name of blasphemy.
v.2 And the beast which I saw was like unto a leopard, and his feet were as *the feet* of a bear, and his mouth as the mouth of a lion: and the dragon gave him his power, and his seat, and great authority.
v.3 And I saw one of his heads, as it were wounded to death; and his deadly wound was healed: and all the world wondered after the beast.
v.4 And they worshipped the dragon which gave power unto the beast: and they worshipped the beast, saying, Who *is* like unto the beast? who is able to make war with him?
v.5 And there was given unto him a mouth speaking great things and blasphemies; and power was given unto him to continue forty *and* two months.
v.6 And he opened his mouth in blasphemy against God, to blaspheme his name, and his tabernacle, and them that dwell in heaven.
v.7 And it was given unto him to make war with the saints, and to overcome them: and power was given him over all kindreds, and tongues, and nations.
v.8 And all that dwell upon the earth shall worship him, whose names are not written in the book of life of the Lamb slain from the foundation of the world.
v.9 If any man have an ear, let him hear.
v.10 He that leadeth into captivity shall go into captivity: he that killeth with the sword must be killed with the sword. Here is the patience and the faith of the saints."

1 While "the sea" is most likely the Mediterranean Sea strict identification is hardly relevant unless to show that the dragon, looks westwards to supervise the emergence of the first beast (v.1) and then turns eastwards to watch the emergence of the second beast "out of the earth" (v.11). Most commentators of the futurist school (see *Introduction*) insist that the imagery suggests that the first beast arises from among the nations of Europe to the west of Israel, while the second beast emerges from Israel itself. The inference is that the first beast is of Gentile origin while the second beast is a Jew. These deductions are logical but need scriptural support. Other commentators, drawing on the symbolic nature of the scene, point out that "the sea" represents the turmoil of nations while "the earth" represents, by contrast, settled human government. This is more debatable and perhaps unnecessary. In contrast to the storm "upon the great sea" in Dan 7 there is no suggestion of a storm here. The main emphasis does lie in the fact that one beast rises from the nations while the other comes from the land of Israel.

John is an eye-witness to the drama. The RV is clearer when it contrasts "he stood upon the sand of the sea" referring to the dragon, with his own position as an observer defined in the expression "and I saw". What John saw was a most dreadful monster, "having ten horns and seven heads" (RV following the word order of the text). The order in which the parts of the body are mentioned (horns, heads, body, feet) is the natural order in which John would see a beast emerge from water. The word for beast, *thērion*, is not to be confused with the word *zōa* used of the four living creatures (4:6). The word *thērion* depicts a wild, untameable, savage beast. When used metaphorically of a man, it emphasises his bestiality not his stupidity – he has a beast-like character. This beast-like character is a true reflection of human nature when it rejects divine revelation.

The correct interpretation of this beast holds the key to the understanding of this book. Scriptural identification must hold in tension several lines of thought drawn from a number of Scriptures until the whole picture comes into focus. The main points to consider are:

1. As John saw the beast emerge from the sea his first thought must have been of the similarity between it and the dragon which stood on the seashore. The beast and the dragon are obviously to be distinguished though the claim to authority (the seven heads) and the claim to power (the ten horns) are common to both. Nevertheless the scene shows that the beast is a distinct personality and not to be confused with the dragon.
2. The beast had a body like the body of a leopard, feet like the feet of a bear, and a mouth like the mouth of a lion. These animals were familiar to John from the vision of Daniel (Dan 7:1-8). Rising from the storm-tossed sea, Daniel saw a lion, a bear, and a leopard, followed by an unnamed monster with ten horns. There is no doubt that the ten horns of the fourth beast of Daniel's prophecy link it directly with this beast. However a more important identification mark is the description of its mouth: "a mouth speaking great things" (Dan 7:8). Similar words are used of this beast in v.5: "and there was given unto him a mouth speaking great things". It is readily shown that the four beasts of Dan 7 represent empires that dominate the world just before the Son of man is given dominion (Dan 7:13-14). The unnamed fourth beast must therefore be the final empire on earth before Christ comes to claim His kingdom (Dan

7:9-14). Daniel writes, "I beheld even till the beast was slain, and his body destroyed, and given to the burning flame" (Dan 7:11). The fifth and final kingdom in earth history is the messianic kingdom of Christ. Thus Daniel's prophecy enables us to identify this first beast out of the sea as the final world-empire (the fourth in Daniel's sequence) holding sway when Christ comes; this is the empire that Christ overthrows to set up His kingdom.

3. A study of this chapter as well as related Scriptures will show that often an empire is personalised as a man, or perhaps a better expression would be, epitomised in a person. (See Dan 2:38f., "Thou art this head of gold".) This was seen in the Roman Empire where it was hard to distinguish between the empire and the Caesar who controlled it; the religious cult which combined emperor and empire was enshrined in the title *Rome and Augustus*. So closely identified is this empire with its head (who might be called the emperor), that the context of each Scripture will be required to identify which aspect of the beast is in view. It will be seen in v.3 that the wounding and healing of one of the heads focuses attention on a man, who in a very real way embodies the empire in his person.

For the sake of clarity when the term "beast" is judged to refer to the emperor he will be identified with the upper case letter as "the Beast".

A beast with seven heads and ten horns appears three times in this book. Consistency of interpretation demands that the heads and the horns be interpreted in the same way throughout. Thus:

1. "Behold a great red dragon, having seven heads and ten horns and seven crowns upon his heads" (12:3).
   The seven heads have been shown to be historical kingdoms (represented by kings) who have been agents of Satan in waging bitter war against Israel the people of God. These have followed each other across the stage of history: Egypt, Assyria, Babylon, Medo-Persia, Greece, Rome. The seventh is yet to come (17:10) and will display the same satanic hatred with more terrible intensity. (It will be noted that the church age is omitted.) The horns have been shown to be ten contemporaneous kings who will emerge to further the satanic destruction of the nation of Israel.
2. "I saw a beast rising out of the sea, having ten horns and seven heads" (13:1 JND).
   As shown above this empire and its head will manifest in tribulation days that same satanic hatred first seen in the dragon but now in identifiable political form. Having historical features of past empires the empire will be rapacious and cruel and its emperor will show this fully.
3. "I saw a woman sit upon a scarlet coloured beast, full of the names of blasphemy, having seven heads and ten horns" (17:3).

> A woman identified as "Mystery, Babylon the great" sits upon this same beast. The identification marks of Satan are still there but the political manifestation of dragon power in the final empire has now become the supporter of a world-embracing religious system that has its roots in the Babylon of the past. The beast both as an empire and its head support the religious system.

As discussed in the comments on 12:3 the interpretation of the seven heads is given in 17:9 RV: "The seven heads are seven mountains on which the woman sitteth: and they are seven kings". These are further defined by the expression, "five are fallen, and one is and the other is not yet come". Various interpretations will be discussed *in loc*, but the simple explanation is that John was living under the sixth empire represented by the Caesar, the sixth in the list of those who have shown hatred and animosity to the nation of Israel – the focal nation in scriptural history. Which particular Caesar is irrelevant since Caesar is but the representation of the empire. John would not have had the slightest difficulty naming these nations as Egypt, Assyria, Babylon, Medo-Persia and Greece. These five had passed off the scene but the sixth was still in existence when John wrote – the Roman Empire. The one to come is this seventh empire, future in John's day and still future today since the church age has come in as an interlude. John here sees the beast rising out of the sea; the seventh head has arrived and the full display of satanic power will be seen in an empire and represented in the person who heads it – the Beast.

The "ten horns" are defined as "ten kings, which have received no kingdom as yet, but receive power as kings one hour with the beast" (17:12). While the seven heads are clearly successive empires (or emperors representing empires) the horns are equally clearly ten kings, bearing rule at the same time as the Beast. In the vision of the dragon (12:3) the heads wear the crowns but here the horns are crowned. The explanation is that in the cameo of history presented in ch. 12 the heads already have been or are on the world stage; they are largely historic. The horns are prophetic: the ten kings have not yet appeared on the stage of time. In this chapter, when the final empire has come onto the stage, ten horns also appear with him and the fact that they have kingdoms is shown by the crowns. This suggests that when the Beast appears not only are there also ten kings reigning, but they have not yet handed over their kingdoms to him as they do at the mid-point of the seventieth week (17:12-13).

As suggested the beast rising out of the sea describes the historical advent of the empire and its emperor upon the world stage; it is likely that both are so closely intertwined that the history of one is virtually the history of the other.

As a man the Beast will have been born years before this event and will have risen to power through normal political channels in his own country – a rise likely to be meteoric. To the news media of the world he will be "the coming man", until by sheer ability allied with personality, he will reach the highest echelons of political power in his own country. At the same time world events will likely allow him centre-stage and bring world-leadership to his own nation. Since he is the "prince that shall come" (Dan 9:26) the signing of the seven-year treaty with Israel will be the great achievement of his career up to this point and it may well be that this is the event that is symbolised in the beast "rising of out of the sea". A man and his empire have reached a world status, have moved into the centre of the world's political stage.

Since both "heads" and "names of blasphemy" are plural (see JND) it is difficult to determine whether there is a particular "name" associated with each "head" or whether there are a number of names of blasphemy on each head. The simple reading of the text rather gives the latter impression. A review of the interpretation of the heads brings into focus a spectrum of idolatry from Assyria to Rome; as will be shown in 17:3 this includes all shades of blasphemous heathendom arising from the Babylon of Nimrod and Semiramis. The deification of the Caesar, familiar in John's day, which had been growing as a serious blasphemy from the time of Caesar Augustus (27BC- 14AD) may well be the pattern for the last great blasphemy of the Beast.

2 The overall appearance of this beast, probably in its distinctive colouring and muscular build, reminds John of a leopard where the picture is litheness and speed. The feet, disproportionately large, remind John of the feet of a bear that speaks of the tenacity that refuses to let go the prey. The mouth of the lion shows the ferocity of the carnivore. The three beasts of which this beast has features are the beasts of Dan 7:1-6 which antedate the appearance of the fourth beast. In other words these kingdoms are on earth immediately prior to the emergence of the fourth beast which incorporates some of their features, suggesting strongly that the four beasts of Dan 7 are not be equated with the four metals of the image of Dan 2 and hence with the kingdoms of Babylon, Medo-Persia and Greece that have already passed into history. In other words the three beasts indicate the three kingdoms that will be identifiable on earth immediately preceding the emergence of the fourth empire. The fact that they exist, in a changed form, after the Son of man takes the kingdom is confirmation of this interpretation (Dan 7:12).

The emergence of this beast is not simply the result of political circumstances or human ability; another more sinister power is at work. The dragon provides all that is needed for his prince and his empire:

1. *His power*. The word here (*dunamis*) defines all the executive power to put his decisions into effect. This must lie in the physical realm – military might backed up by police, secret police and militia. Parallels in history are without number from the SS of Nazidom to the KGB of communism. The dragon will see to it that this ruler has all that he needs.
2. *His throne* (RV). The legitimacy of the claim of the Beast to monarchy, or royalty or even presidency will be supplied by the dragon. Ample

resources will ensure that men will accept him wholeheartedly. His own personality and ability will be backed up by all the diplomacy required and behind it all, the subtlety of the dragon.

3. *His great authority*. This could be the political power base that supports the other claims so that he is unimpeachable in the eyes of men, and the empire in human terms unshakeable.

The close identification of the empire and emperor is implied in these statements. The problem, as translators acknowledge, is that there is an inherent ambiguity in the language. The personal pronoun *autou* may be masculine or neuter so the difficulty is whether to translate it as "of it" or "of him". One translator (Marshall) writes in a footnote to this chapter, "But *thērion* is neuter. Yet as it stands for a person, as *arnion* [Lamb] does, it too should be treated as to the pronoun, as masculine." The problem becomes one of interpretation: is the "it" the empire or its head? It may well be that the Holy Spirit has allowed this ambiguity to link both aspects of the beast together inseparably. The history of one is the history of the other.

3 The beast as the final world empire dominates the earth. It is clear that at this point in the tribulation, the seventh head, the one who in John's day is spoken of as "not yet come" (17:10a), has now arrived. He continues for "a short space" (17:10) which, it may be suggested, covers the first half of the tribulation, a three and a half year period. At this point something dramatic takes place. John is allowed to focus upon one of the heads; which head is not identified in this passage but 17:10-11 makes it clear that it is the seventh head. The expression "wounded to death" is translated in the RV "as though it had been smitten to death" and in JND "as slain to death". Exactly the same word is used of the Lamb (5:6). John has seen a Lamb "as it had been slain" and now he sees a Beast "as it had been slain". If in ch. 5 the expression means a personal violent death, then the balance of probability is that the expression carries the same meaning here. It must mean something in the nature of a public putting to death or even assassination. It should be noted that it is not the beast which is slain but one of its heads, turning the thought directly from the empire to the one in whom empire is embodied, the head of that empire.

The expression "his deadly wound" is translated in the RV "his death stroke" and in JND "his wound of death". The verb "was healed" records the drama of a terrible wounding which convinced the world that he was dead, being followed by an equally dramatic recovery. The verb "wondered" (*thaumazō*) describes the moment of thunder-struck unbelief. In each of the forty-six times this verb is used in the NT what is seen goes far beyond human comprehension and gives rise to stunned wonder. It is very possible that this happening is seen world-wide on a televised state occasion and the sense of stunned disbelief circles the globe - men cannot believe what they see. It must be clear from the language used that though this man embodies an empire he is distinct from it; it is not an empire that dies or appears to die, but a man.

The dramatic event causes men first to wonder, then the whisper of the supernatural in it causes them to worship. That this is not a true resurrection but a pseudo-resurrection is made plain in the introductory word "as it were" (*hos*) – it has only the appearance of a death and resurrection. In some way Satan has stage-managed this deception for the aggrandisement of his man. This takes place at the mid-point of the seven-year period which is the point when the Beast is identified as the one "that ascendeth out of the bottomless pit" (11:7). As shown in comments *in loc* this Beast is now satanically indwelt and the change in his personality and his actions proves that he is but the tool of Satan and no longer a free-will agent. This is also the point where the seventh head becomes the eighth (17:11). Eight in Scripture speaks of resurrection and this man aims by satanic power to mimic the Christ so that he too can claim to be the risen man – alive from the dead. While the resurrection of Christ, one of the best-attested facts in history, is denied today even in professing christendom, this satanic counterfeit will be believed throughout the world.

Excursus: Resurrection of a Man or Revival of an Empire?

Some of the most able and respected expositors have seen in this event not the death of a man but the death and revival of the Roman Empire. W. Scott writes, p.273 "Here we have the political death and resurrection of the Beast. The wounded head and the Beast are evidently identified. It was the Beast in its imperial head that was slain. The empire ceased to exist AD 476. The world-wide dominion of the Caesars has lain in the iron grip of political death from that date until now. But God in His providence will call the empire again into being, out of a scene of revolutionary passion and conflict, like that out of which the empire of the first Napoleon arose – out of the sea (v.1). His wound of death had been healed". The weight of evangelical scholarship in support of this view is most impressive but there are some serious problems with it. These may be summarised as follows:

1. It is a head that is "wounded to death" not the beast. The whole context indicates that this is a person not an empire. For an empire to fall as dramatically as is envisaged here would demand an event or a battle of world-shaking dimensions that will be sought in vain in the slow decline of the Roman Empire. Even to mark the demise of the Roman Empire is a somewhat difficult task leading to questions as to what is actually meant by the expression. Did the Roman Empire receive the deadly wound when it was formally divided into east and west after the death of Theodosius the Great in AD395, or was it in AD476 when the German chieftain Odoacer forced the emperor Romolus Augustus to abdicate? The eastern half of the Roman Empire survived under largely Greek rulers as the Byzantine Empire until its capital Constantinople (now Istanbul) was conquered by the Turks in

1453. Some expositors who have noted the problem that it is the "head" not the "beast" which is "wounded to death" have suggested that the seven heads are different forms of government that have operated over the period of the Roman Republic and the Roman Empire. The most serious problem with this view is that it ignores the scriptural explanation of the heads given in 17:10. The seven forms of government suggested vary from expositor to expositor and their selection is highly subjective and demands a very close scrutiny of Roman history and, even then not all the different forms of government are recognised by accredited Roman historians. In this kind of study the history of the Republic and the history of the Empire have to be treated as one, hardly a fair way to handle the history. On this interpretation the smitten head is the imperial form of government which is to be revived under the Beast. A change in governmental method or institutions seems a somewhat trivial interpretation.

2. It has been shown that there is, of necessity, a continuity between the Roman Empire and the final empire of the Beast, but if the prophetic clock stopped at the cross and only begins again with the signing of the covenant between the Beast and the false prophet, all the intervening history is irrelevant for prophetic purposes. So the search for a wounding to death and the subsequent revival of the Roman Empire is interesting as a parallel between empire and emperor but pointless for interpretation.
3. The drama, as portrayed here, involves both the presumed death and a pseudo-resurrection of a person. Even if the revival of the Roman Empire is accepted as the interpretation, the only dramatic point is its revival, which is only half the picture. It is submitted that even if this did happen and the jurisdiction of Rome, the territory of Rome and the institutions of Rome were to be revived overnight, it would cause a certain amount of diplomatic stir and national and international media sensation but there would be very little in it to cause men to wonder and then to worship – as seen here. The Treaty of Rome (1948) was hailed by many as the revival of the Roman Empire when European nations took the first step to unity. A review of the press for that time shows there was mild world-wide interest. If the European Parliament opted overnight for a re-born Roman Empire the impact world-wide would be on a similar scale. The German nation has been revived and restored in the last decade and any "wonder" has been on a very minor scale. The event here is a world-wide televised event that has supernatural overtones and by it a man is elevated to a status hitherto unknown amongst men.

4 Overawed and thunderstruck by such a supernatural event, men "wondered after" the Beast but they "worshipped the dragon". The two aorist tenses are obviously linked with the same event and are synchronous. In doing one men did the other. What previously had been only whispered about in secret is now out in the open; the power of the occult, the reality behind astrology, the underground witchcraft is all acknowledged as belonging to Satan and its efficacy has been publicly demonstrated. Unashamedly men worship the dragon; the mask has been dropped and the power of Satan stands opposed to the power of the risen Christ. In the adulation of the Beast lies the adoration of the dragon. The textual reading accepted by JND and the RV, which gives "because" as the introduction to the next clause, shows that the dragon is recognised as the source of the authority of the Beast. While blasphemy has been identified with the heads throughout the ages (see v.1) this final apostasy is the worship of Satan himself. That the Beast is his deputy and visible representation is seen in the challenges thrown out to earth by his worshippers. These challenges relate to:

1. *His person* – "who is like unto the beast?". This is an echo of the challenge to the gods of Egypt when Jehovah had shown His power in the deliverance of Israel at the Red Sea (Exod 15:1): "Who is like unto thee, O Lord among the gods? Who is like unto thee?". Both witness and warning lie in the challenge of the Beast-worshippers. This earth-encircling cry witnesses and warns that the Beast has no rival on earth; this "miracle" bears witness to the authority vested in him by the dragon.
2. *His power* – "who is able to make war with him?" This assassination-resurrection drama takes place at the midpoint of the week (see v.5) and possibly this very miracle enables him to reach the apex of his power. In the eyes of men he is supernaturally enabled and enthroned; there is no power left either militarily, politically, religiously or commercially that can challenge his absolute rule.

The events that take place around the midpoint of the seventieth week show the power of the Beast, and consequently, how reasonable in their own eyes is this challenge that the Beast-worshippers offer to earth. Whether these events take place before the assassination-resurrection of the Beast or as a consequence of it may be debated since Scripture does not give a timetable. The view that seems to fit the picture best is that the events are the result of the assassination-resurrection experience of the Beast when he is seen as "the beast out of the bottomless pit" (11:7) and, in a very special way, has satanic authority behind him. The events that evidence the power of the Beast may be listed thus:

1. The Beast has shown his power by the slaying of the two witnesses (11:3-13). What others have failed to do and what he previously could not do he has now been able to do. Suddenly he has displayed supernatural power that can challenge heaven.
2. The harlot identified as Mystery, Babylon the great, apostate religion (17:1-18), has been totally destroyed; even nominal adherence to religious things has been outlawed. The burning of chapels and churches

(17:16) and possibly all religious buildings and the seizure of the associated wealth has opened the way for the religion of the Beast.

3. "The abomination of desolation" set up in the temple at Jerusalem (v.15) has destroyed Judaism as a coherent force. Those of the nation of Israel refusing allegiance to the Beast have fled (12:14).
4. The northern invasion of Ezek 38-39 has taken place and that mighty army has been destroyed. The subsequent power vacuum has left the Beast and his empire in complete military domination of earth.

This summary of the scene at the midpoint of the seventieth week paints the background picture of the consolidation of the power of the Beast as events move towards the final confrontation between Christ and Satan. The dragon is personally on earth (12:7-9), the Beast has reached the apex of his power and apparently there is no one to dispute his autocratic rule. The only stirrings of discontent (see 9:13-21) are found on the fringes of the Beast's empire and have not yet reached dangerous proportions. This is the moment when the Beast offers the final act of rebellion against heaven and he takes his seat in the temple in Jerusalem in fulfilment of 2 Thess 2:4, "Who opposeth and exalteth himself above all that is called God or that is worshipped; so that he as God sitteth in the temple of God, shewing himself that he is God". This is the final apostasy from "all that is called God or that is worshipped" – in other words from all that God has revealed of Himself. Men will have to make their choice; they may worship Satan through the Beast or worship God through the Lamb.

5 As the Beast reaches the apex of world power four things are said to be given to him. The aorist tense of the verb "to give" is again in the "theological passive" (Rienecker) used so frequently in this book with this same verb to describe the fact without identifying the giver. The donor in vv.2,4 where the active voice is used is Satan and he is still the donor here but God, in the outworking of divine purpose, allows him to give to his puppet prince all he needs to develop his world power. The four gifts to the Beast are as follows:

1. "There was given unto him a mouth". The reference to the mouth is a very important link with "the little horn" of Dan 7: 8 where it is recorded, "And, behold, in this horn were eyes like the eyes of man, and a mouth speaking great things", a description repeated in Dan 7:19-25. The linking of "great things" and "blasphemies" indicates that there is more than simply eloquence and oratory in view. The greatest of earth's threatening orators may have been a Nebuchadnezzar, a Mussolini or a Hitler but this man outranks them all. These *ex cathedra* statements of this man who oracularly claims deity are blasphemies of the darkest colour. In his utterances he is the satanic mouthpiece.

2. "Power was given unto him to continue for forty and two months". There is a hint here that under normal circumstances this blasphemer would have been instantly judged had God not given permission for this stated period. The verb "to continue" (*poieō*) is the verb "to act" or "to do" and may be freely translated "to carry out his work" (Rienecker). Thinking he is doing his own will or even doing the will of Satan this man little realises he acts only by divine permission and only for the set period. As in 10:2 this period of forty-two months is the last half of the seven-year tribulation. This same period is designated in Dan 7:25 as "a time, times and the dividing of time" and ends at the coming of Christ to earth (19:20).

3. " It was given unto him to make war with the saints". The two verbs in the aorist tense, "to make war" (*poiēsai polemon*) and "to overcome" (*nikēsai*), suggest the launching of an all-out war against "the saints". This is the direct link with the previous chapter where the rage of the dragon is focused on the "remnant of her seed" (12:17) which has been shown to be true believers. The Beast is but the instrument of the dragon's rage. The first statement is no surprise; it echoes the statement related to the "two witnesses"(11:7) and that in connection with "the remnant of the seed" of the woman (12:17). Here it is wider than before and embraces all who would believe the gospel preached and give allegiance to Christ. The second verb is a surprise. The verb "overcome"(*nikaō*) in the context can only mean "put to death". That God should be silent and allow His own to suffer and die under this blasphemer is a matter that tests the faith of the saints in these years that will make the terror-regimes of Nazism and Stalinism seem gentle when compared with this persecution. It is recorded of the "little horn" that, "he shall wear out the saints of the most High" (Dan 7:25). This is power in the hands of a man with the character of a beast.

4. "And power was given him over all kindreds, and tongues, and nations". Christ could say, "All power (*exousia*) is given unto me" (Matt 28:18). For this limited time God allows this usurper to be given this authority (*"exousia"*) over "every tribe and people and tongue and nation" (RV). The manuscript evidence for the inclusion of "and people" is overwhelming. It brings the fourfold designation of earth's people into line with the occurrences of this refrain throughout the book (5:9; 7:9; 10:11; 11:9; 13:7; 14:6; 16:10; 17:15). Here each of the words is singular but this makes the expression no less wide than the other occurrences and it shows the influence of the Beast reaching into every corner of the world. While it would be going beyond scripture to say that the Beast rules world-wide, the language here supported by many other scriptures indicates that his influence and power are felt throughout the earth. He is a world-ruler, if not, indeed, the world-ruler. What mighty men down the ages have vainly sought is now granted to this man for a period. Satan has produced his own version of a man-ruled kingdom.

6 Between the two gifts of v.5 and the two gifts of v.7 this verse is interpolated to show with what forbearance God acts to permit this blasphemer to complete his course. The blasphemies (plural) are primarily and essentially against God. The noun "blasphemies" and the related verb "to blaspheme" do not mean simply "to curse" or "to swear" as in colloquial English. The basic meaning is "to speak contemptuously of" or "to misrepresent" God. This is the speciality of this arch-blasphemer. Bengel notes that blasphemy is committed in three different ways:

1. When anything is attributed to God that is contrary to His holiness,
2. when anything is disowned that rightfully belongs to God and
3. when anything is ascribed to a creature that belongs to God alone.

These are the very things of which the Beast is guilty. In the expression "he opened his mouth" there is likely reference to formal state occasions or important interviews when the Beast makes deliberate attacks on God. He blasphemes in speaking contemptuously of:

1. "His name". In NT teaching the name is linked with the revelation of God in Christ. Christ addressing the Father said, "I have manifested thy name unto the men that thou gavest me out of the world" (John 17:6). All that has been revealed in Christ is now ridiculed by the atheistic rationalism propagated by the Beast.
2. "His tabernacle". The whole idea that God would dwell amongst men either in Christ (John 1:14), with his saints now in heaven, or amongst men in a day to come (21:3) is a fruitful subject of hilarious ridicule by the Beast. Such a thought is ludicrous in this society headed up in a man who claims deity. According to the Beast heaven is to be experienced now as men submit to him.
3. "Them that dwell in heaven". That God would have a company of saints temporarily dwelling ("have their tabernacle" JND) in heaven until the completion of His purposes on earth is scorned and ridiculed by this satanic usurper. In his "utterances" (pronouncements) the Beast argues that these ideas belong to a by-gone age of credulity. There is no such place nor people according to the philosophy of the Beast; the only heaven men can ever know is earth under his rule.

In these blasphemies are crystallised all the blasphemies of the centuries; they are epitomised in one person this arch-blasphemer.

8 Worship that belongs alone to God is given to this man. Those who worship are called "[them] that dwell on the earth" or "earth-dwellers". This is the seventh of the twelve occurrences of this descriptive identification in the book. As shown in comments on 2:10 it has a moral and spiritual import as describing those who have made their home on earth and are quite happy under the rule of the Beast. While his power is acknowledged throughout the world (v.7b) there is a fanatically-devoted group who actually worship this man. The term "earth-dwellers" describes a particular group of a wider class defined as those whose names are "not written in the Lamb's book of life". The population of earth is clearly divided by the Lamb's book of life; those whose names are written in it and those whose names are not written in it, in our terms called believers and unbelievers. Of this second class there is a fanatically-devoted class who worship the Beast. The battle lines on earth are drawn in this war between sinners and saints, between the dragon and the Lamb.

These earth dwellers are identified negatively by the fact that their "names are not written in the Lamb's book of life". The book of life is mentioned seven times in this book (3:5; 13:8; 20:12, 15; 21:27; 22:19). (In 22:19 many manuscripts read "the tree of life".) The same book is mentioned in Phil 4:3 and Christ alludes to it in Luke 10:20 while there are only two references to the Lamb's book of life (here and in 21:27). Some expositors suggest that the book of life is the record of all persons who live on earth, their names being entered in this register at birth, so that those who do not trust Christ in their lifetime have their names blotted out on their death (see 3:5 which is used in support of this theory). This leaves only the names of saved ones so that the Lamb's book of life is the final record of the redeemed; a record to be opened at the great white throne (20:15). Attractive as some aspects of this suggestion are, it does not distinguish clearly in their lifetime between those whose names are in the book and those whose names are not. Neither does it give sufficient weight to:

1. the value of the word "written" used seemingly to define a specific inscription (used on three occasions),
2. the implication of Christ's comment to His own (Luke 10:20) that distinguished them from the others whose names were not written,
3. the glad assurance of the apostle when writing of believers in Philippi (Phil 4:3).

The simpler interpretation giving weight to all the scripture references is to see that the book of life is the register of the redeemed whose names are entered at the moment of their conversion to Christ. This has always been the clear division running through the inhabitants of earth, and it is emphatically so in the tribulation as pressure is put on men to identify with the Beast and take his mark while saints are being persecuted unto death. The two occasions when this register is called the Lamb's book of life (here and 21:27) emphasise that what has been true for believers throughout history has become in this tribulation period an issue between the Beast and the Lamb. This emphasis is to be seen in the adjectival participle "having been slain" which is used of the Lamb (5:6) and of the Beast (v.3). Christ's claim rests on His death and resurrection and all who turn to Him will find security in that their name (name is singular see RV) is registered above. The Lamb has a record of His saints and they are those who stand aside from the current hysteria of Beast-worship.

The final phrase in the verse, "from the foundation of the world", has caused much discussion. In the word order in the sentence it stands in a somewhat ambiguous position. It could possibly modify the verb "written"- so the meaning would be "written from the foundation of the world"; an interpretation supported by JND, "written from [the] founding of the world in the book of life of the slain Lamb". Alternatively it could qualify the participle "having been slain" and give the translation as in the RV, "written in the book of life of the Lamb that hath been slain from the foundation of the world". This is a view strongly supported by Alford on grammatical grounds; he points out that the connection is "obvious and natural; and had it not been for the apparent difficulty of the sense thus conveyed, the going so far back to *gegraptai* (written) for a connection would never have been thought of". The "apparent difficulty" to which Alford refers is the understanding of how the Lamb could be slain "from" (*apo*) the foundation of the world. To solve the problem the preposition *apo* should be taken simply in its basic sense of "away from" or "since" (See *A Grammar of the Greek New Testament,* A. T. Robertson p.575). So if the starting point is the "foundation of the world" then the slaying of Christ is dated "since" then. This is perfectly in keeping with scriptural truth for Peter writes of "a Lamb..... who was foreordained before the foundation of the world" (1 Pet 1:19-20). He was foreordained before this event and slain since it. The "foundation of the world" is the ordered creation brought into existence on the six days of the creation week recorded in Gen 1-2. This is the landmark in eternity when time began. The word "world" (*kosmos*) includes all the space, time, matter and energy components that distinguish the ordered universe.

9 The absolute dominion of the Beast at this time, in influence and power, covers the earth. Not only politically and militarily but also commercially and religiously his control is complete – the only dissidents being the saints whose names are in the Lamb's book of life. The adherents of the Beast will be distinguished by having his name in hand or forehead (v.16) but heaven now issues a challenge to the people of earth. All who have physical ears should allow the message of the gospel (14:6) proclaimed by the 144,000 and their converts, to produce a spiritual response – "let him hear". Amidst all the confusing noises of earth there is the necessity to listen carefully and respond positively to the voice of God in the message. As in the Gospels where this phrase occurs frequently (Matt 11:15; 13:9, 43; Mark 4:9, 23; 7:16; Luke 8:8; 14:35), the appeal concludes an important revelation that demands careful consideration. In the messages to the seven churches Christ concludes each message with the same appeal, "He that hath an ear, let him hear what the Spirit saith unto the churches". The absence of the concluding sentence here is incidental confirmation that the churches are no longer on earth at the time when this appeal is made.

10 Minor textual variations have led to some discussion on this verse but there is no real problem. Possibly the RV expresses it most clearly; "If any man is for captivity, into captivity he goeth, if any man shall kill with the sword, with the sword must he be killed". This is a restatement of the law of sowing and reaping that is taught clearly throughout Scripture. There are various statements of it and allusions to it in many Scriptures and most obviously in Jer 15:2; 43:11; Zech 11:9. Not only the OT but the NT insists that it is written into the moral government of earth. Referred to in Gen 9:6; Matt 5:38; 26:52, it is comprehensively summed up in Gal 6:7: "Whatsoever a man soweth, that shall he also reap". The Beast, in implacable hatred of Israel and the saints, will introduce unjust detention (captivity) and unrighteous execution using legal processes (the sword) for the "crime" of refusing worship to the state. As head of state the Beast of course claims that worship – the ancient Caesar worship has been re-established on earth! This very principle, restated here, will sustain the faith of the saints in these terrible days when they see, foreshadowed even in their own suffering, the ultimate fate of their persecutors under the sword of Christ (19:21).

In the confidence that God is working out His purposes and that their persecutors are moving to just retribution from God the saints display a supernatural "endurance" and "faith", as saints have done down the ages. The definite article with each quality marks them out as characteristic of saints of all ages but which are displayed now in a very special way under tribulation conditions. Suffering right to the point of death by martyrdom these saints cling with unshakeable confidence to the fact that Christ is coming and that the wrongs of earth will be finally righted. This is the darkest hour before the dawn for a blood-stained earth and the endurance and faith of saints shines out clearly.

Vv. 9-10 are a divinely-given interpolation in the unfolding vision and should be compared with the similar interpolation of vv.12-13 in the next chapter. Here saints draw strength from the principle of divine retribution on the persecutors; in the next chapter they are sustained by the promise of divine reward for the saint whether they live or die.

Notes

1-8 There is no doubt that the ten horns must have a close link also with the ten toes of Nebuchadnezzar's image (Dan 2:31-45). The empires that would have dominion over Israel during the "times of the Gentiles" are seen as metals in the great image. From the perspective of Daniel's day looking down through history until the millennial kingdom there were to be only four world empires. The first three are identified, Babylon in the passage (Dan 2:36) and the Medo-Persian and Greek Empires in Dan 8:20. The fourth empire is neither identified nor named. This is, doubtless, divine superintendence in the record, for while it is known historically that the fourth empire was Rome, Scripture does not name it and there must be a reason for this omission. There cannot be more than four empires within this time-band because the fifth kingdom is the millennial kingdom of Christ. Thus as seen also in the prophecy of Daniel's seventy weeks (Dan 9:24-27) the prophetic clock stopped at the crucifixion of Christ under the Roman Empire. The period from Pentecost to the rapture of the church is not the subject of prophecy. Nevertheless the story is taken up again when the church has been removed, and this is where the final empire comes onto the stage. The Roman Empire has long since passed across the stage of history and gone forever; despite many attempts at various times and periods it has never been revived or restored. Nevertheless another empire with the same features and very possibly the same heartland in the continent of Europe will emerge on the world stage after the rapture. This empire will show a continuity with Rome and will complete her history. Scripture nowhere suggests that this empire will be confined to the boundaries of the old Roman Empire; in fact it strongly suggests that the boundaries will be very much wider. This empire will be far greater and mightier than Rome ever was since it will be the empire that is seen both in Daniel's "fourth beast, dreadful and terrible and strong exceedingly" (Dan 7:7) and John's "beast rising out of the sea". The Roman Empire held the seeds of development that come to fulness in this final empire which may be viewed as a continuation of the fourth prophetic empire to dominate Israel. The term "revived Roman Empire" is often used, but this can lead to misunderstanding and since it is not used in Scripture it is better to avoid it. Scripture gives no support for the re-emergence of an ancient Rome with all the pomp and circumstance of a past age attached to it or even the reversion to an empire-capital city on the Tiber. This empire under the Beast is the fulfilment or the full development of an empire that has it roots in Rome.

2 As an example of the identification of a state with its head there is the history of the German Republic from 1930, when Adolf Hitler became Reich Chancellor, to his death in 1945. The history of the Republic is virtually the history of one man.

3 Political assassinations have occurred again and again throughout history. In more recent times the assassination in Dallas in November 1963 of J. F. Kennedy, President of the U.S.A, of President Sadat of Egypt in 1981 or that of the Prime Minister of Israel in November 1995 have provided examples in this generation of such political assassinations seen on the television screens of the world. If in any of these cases the mourning had been suddenly interrupted by the reappearance of the victim alive and well, the hush, the wonder, the whisper of the supernatural would have circled the earth within moments. There would be no difficulty in men first wondering after and then worshipping such a man.

Some expositors who have seen that this event is centred on a person and not an empire have sought to link the event to someone in the past who has died and is allowed of God to return in the guise of the Beast. A number claim that the Beast is a resurrected Judas Iscariot, a view set out by Charleton Steen in his book *God's Prophetic Programme*. Insisting that the term "out of the abyss" must mean resurrection Steen goes on to point out that the term "the son of perdition" is used only twice in scripture, first of Judas by the Lord (John 17:12) and of the Beast (2 Thess 2:3). Many early expositors believed that the Roman Emperor Nero (reigned 54-68AD) would be raised to fill this satanic role. Alternative suggestions have been many and their very multiplicity is their own refutation. The scripture here does not demand it nor is there any possibility that the One who holds the "keys of hell and of death" (1:18) would permit any to return in this way to life on earth.

10 The variant readings in the text of this verse have led to other interpretations. In light of the final statement "here is the patience and the faith of saints" considerable weight should be given to the parallel readings:-

"If anyone is to go into captivity, into captivity he must go;
"If anyone is to be slain with the sword, he is to be slain with the sword"

based on the Metzger text. The acceptance of the divine will in the lives of the persecuted saints as they submit to the persecution of the Beast will result in the development of "patience" and "faith" in these difficult days.

The False Prophet

v.11 "And I beheld another beast coming up out of the earth; and he had two horns like a lamb, and he spake as a dragon.
v.12 And he exerciseth all the power of the first beast before him, and causeth the earth and them which dwell therein to worship the first beast, whose deadly wound was healed.
v.13 And he doeth great wonders, so that he maketh fire come down from heaven on the earth in the sight of men,
v.14 And deceiveth them that dwell on the earth by *the means* of those miracles which he had power to do in the sight of the beast: saying to them that dwell on the earth, that they should make an image to the beast, which had the wound by a sword; and did live.
v.15 And he had power to give life unto the image of the beast, that the image of the beast should both speak, and cause that as many as would not worship the image of the beast should be killed.
v.16 And he causeth all, both small and great, rich and poor, free and bond, to receive a mark in their right hand, or in their foreheads:
v.17 And that no man might buy or sell, save he that had the mark, or the name of the beast, or the number of his name.
v.18 Here is wisdom. Let him that hath understanding count the number of the beast: for it is the number of a man; and his number *is* six hundred threescore *and* six."

John now sees a second beast coming up out of the earth. It has already been observed that the first beast out of the sea came up under the supervision of the dragon who had taken his stance on the sea-shore. The dragon seems to turn from looking westwards to look eastwards over the land of Israel. John must have watched fascinated as another beast appeared, this time rising out of the earth. The word *thērion* is again used indicating that this beast is of the same nature as the first. They are of the same genus and share the same savage nature but, in every other respect they are very different. With the advent of this beast the evil triad is now complete, Satan has all his forces mobilised for the last three and a half years of the tribulation period.

11 The contrast between the sea (v.1) from which the first beast arises and the earth in this verse must be deliberate. If the sea symbolises the nations in general, then the earth symbolises the land of Israel. This suggests, if it does not prove, that the first beast is of Gentile origin while this second beast has a Jewish background. Out of the sea we see emerging, first an empire and then a person who epitomises that empire. On the other hand out of the stable government of the nation of Israel there arises a single individual; an individual who arrives in this position by the normal processes of politics. As has been shown with the first beast other Scriptures throw light upon these two beasts as to their origins and the means by which they reach their positions of power.

There could scarcely be a greater contrast than that between a monster and a lamb. The word "beast" (*thērion*) is a warning lest there shall be deception, for this animal looks like a lamb even to the normal two horns. Innocence, gentleness and harmlessness are words that describe a lamb and, doubtless, this lamb would like men to see in him features of the expected Lamb of God anticipated in the Scripture. It has already been shown that a horn speaks of power and Christ has been seen as the seven-horned Lamb in whom is the perfection of power (5:6). If the ten horns of the first beast tell of power in the realm of territory and envisage the extent of his dominion then the two horns of this beast must speak of power in the realm of testimony. This beast claims all the power of divine attestation. Adequate testimony will be given to the power of this beast in the signs that he gives to establish his claim (v.13).

The second descriptive note could hardly be more different. It comes with quite a shock when a lamb-like beast speaks as a dragon. "The dragon" recognisable in history through his agents and activity (ch. 12) has personally supervised the advent of these two beasts (v.1) but he can now be heard speaking through this beast. This beast "spake as a dragon". What is in view is not merely the timbre of the voice (for dragons do not usually speak) but the character of what he says. This lamb-like beast simply echoes the threatening language of the dragon. A greater contrast between sight and sound can scarcely be imagined: nobody would think to fear a little lamb but, suddenly, the lamb is echoing the language of one who is a "liar" and a "murderer" (John 8:44) and a deceiver (12:9; 19:20; 20:3). The docility of the lamb gives credence to the duplicity of the dragon. Men will be called upon to believe "the lie" (2 Thess 2:11 Newberry).

The symbolism portrays a man who comes into political prominence in Israel, very possibly through normal democratic political channels, whose apparent innocence and gentleness lead the people from all sections of the nation to trust him. His origins will be so well-known that no mystery can surround him and this assists his rise to influence and power in Israel. Winning over the diverse elements in the regathered nation of Israel so that they accept him as the Prime Minister or President will be no small matter and call for consummate political skill. It is only when he has reached this place of prominence and power that the dulcet tones will carry a message straight from the dragon. Whatever his political designation at the time may be, Prime Minister or President, this man will wield the power of a king in Israel. However the substance of his proclamations make it clear that he is not only the spokesman for the dragon but the associate of the first Beast. As public spokesman and the worker of "great signs" (v.13 RV) he earns the apocalyptic title of "the false prophet" (16:13; 19:20; 20:10),

12-14 The overwhelming note that impresses in the summary given by John of the impact of this beast is the power that he displays. There is a recurring verb in these verses that needs to be noted:

v.12 "he exerciseth (*poieō*) all the power (*exousia*) of the first beast."
v.12(b) "he causeth (*poieō*) the earth and them which dwell therein..."
v.13 "he doeth (*poieō*) great wonders..."

The variation in translation is perfectly justified in that the verb *poieō* is far more versatile that the English verb "to do" and requires different translations in different contexts. The present tense is the tense of repeated action; the beast does this again and again when opportunity offers or occasion demands. It is the characteristic work of the beast to do these very things.

In v.2 the source of the first Beast's authority has been shown to be the dragon. This second beast receives his authority from the very same source. It is not that the second beast derives his authority from the first Beast, but that the second beast has the same authority as the first Beast and from the same source. That their authorities are comparable is shown in the expression "*all* the power of the first beast", but these powers are displayed in differing realms. The expression "before him" has location in view and may be translated "in his presence" (1 Cor 1:29) or "in his sight" (as repeated in v.13c). There is no question of men being confused between the two mighty men of earth, they are not acting in competition but in co-operation. They have behind them the same satanic power base. The expression "before him" may suggest a worldwide television interview when both demonstrate their miraculous powers.

The demonstration of miraculous power has behind it one purpose: to get the earth and "them which dwell therein" to worship the "first beast". "The earth" simply means "all the people physically dwelling on earth", while the second expression describes the same group as v.8: the "earth-dwellers" who spiritually belong to the earth because they already have given at least some credibility, if not full allegiance, to the Beast. The ministry of this second beast is to "evangelise" amongst men to bring as many as possible into the satanic fold and, at the same time, bolster the "faith" of "believers" in the Beast. The person to be worshipped, whose cause is preached by this second beast, is the one "whose deadly wound was healed". There is only one living man on earth who can show in his body the evidence of a "death wound" and for him this second beast demands worship as God.

The authentication of the authority of this man is most convincing and has a very special appeal to the Jewish nation. The words "great wonders" should be translated as in the RV "great signs"; the word *sēmeion* indicating a very definite appeal on religious grounds to the nation of Israel. This man will do what Christ refused to do when the leading Pharisees demanded "a sign" (Matt 12:38). Jews still seek a sign (1 Cor 1:22) and this man will provide all the signs that they demand. The AV has omitted an important "and" after "great wonders". When translated "even" it suggests that his final authentication is seen in making fire come down from heaven. This was the sign that heaven gave in the authentication of Elijah as a true prophet (1 Kings 18:36-38; 2 Kings 1:9-12) and this man will be able to do the same. The word translated "in the sight of " (*enōpion*) could be translated "in their very presence".

There is no suggestion that these wonders, miracles or signs are in any way faked. While there is no deception in the sign itself the object behind it is a very deadly deception; he "deceiveth (*planaō*) them that dwell on the earth". The verb *planaō* describes the characteristic activity of Satan and his agents; it is used eight times in the book (2:20; 12:9; 13:14; 18:23; 19:20; 20:3, 8, 10). The noun is found in 2 Thess 2:11 concerning the great lie that will engulf men at this time "God shall send them strong delusion (*planē*)". Culpable failure to respond to the truth (Christ) leads to a yielding to the satanic lie that brings judicial blindness. This second beast, in his special religious office, is the satanic agent in deception and his miracles are the means he uses to convince the nation of Israel of his credentials. In this he is simply supplying the credentials of the false prophet of Deut 13:1-6 and if Israel were in touch with God at this time they would execute the sentence that God demanded: "and that prophet or dreamer of dreams shall be put to death". Instead the nation allows itself to be deceived.

The demonstration of the "signs" done by this beast, climaxed in the making of fire to come down on earth, established the credentials of this great deceiver as a prophet, and this allows him to make an unbelievable demand, or suggestion, to the nation. The very casualness of the language is terrifying. The verb "to say" (*legō*) does not even suggest an authoritative announcement, yet it underlines the absolute power of this man carried on such a wave of adulation that his slightest wish had to be enthusiastically adopted. Amongst the many false prophets of whom the Lord warned (Matt 24:11) this man merits being later identified as "*the* false prophet" (16:13; 19:20; 20:10). His suggestion to the deceived "earth-dwellers" is "that they should make an image to the beast". The word "image" (*eikōn*) has in it two ideas, first the idea of likeness or representation – the image represents a person; the more important idea is manifestation – the image reveals a person. Christ is the image of God (Col 1:15) and not only shows the likeness of God but manifests God because He is God. This image was to be not only a likeness of the beast, but a manifestation of one who was worshipped. The image bears the physical likeness of the Beast but it is also a visible and tangible manifestation of this mighty personality. In the same way the image of Nebuchadnezzar's day (Dan 3) is nowhere said to be a representation of the king but it was the image of a man and manifested the power of the empire. The reason why men should worship this man is again made clear; it is not because of his financial wizardry, his political acumen or his military prowess but, of all men, he is the one who has "the wound by a sword and did live". To refer this to the Roman Empire of past centuries and see in it the revival of that empire after receiving the sword stroke of the Ostrogoth invasion in the fifth century does not do justice to the dramatic language used. It has been noted above that the expression "as it had been slain" used of the Beast in v.3 is used of the Lamb (5:6); it should now be noticed that the exact expression "lived again" (*ezēsen*) has been used by Christ referring to Himself in 2:8. Christ became dead and lived again; the first Beast as the counterfeit deity makes this exact claim upon men. The "had" of the AV should be replaced by the present tense "has"(*echei*) (JND; RV), and shows that this man still bears the scar of the attempted assassination (see comments on v.3). This recalls the withered arm and the blinded right eye of the one called "the idol shepherd" (Zech 4:17). That this image plays a key role in the last three and a half years of the tribulation can be seen in the fact that not only is it mentioned four times in this chapter but it will be mentioned a further seven times before the end of the book (14:9, 11; 15:2; 16:2; 19:20; 20:4). It epitomises idolatry, a tendency inherent in the heart of fallen man (Rom 1:22-23) which Satan exploits in an ecumenical religion to draw men to himself. This second beast is the accredited spokesman of both the Beast and the dragon.

J. Phillips expresses very clearly the key role and the magnetic appeal of this man: "The role of the false prophet will be to make the new religion appealing and palatable to men. No doubt it will combine all the features of the religious systems of men, will appeal to man's total personality, and will take full advantage of his carnal appetite. The dynamic appeal of the false prophet will lie in his skill in combining political expediency with religious passion, self-interest with benevolent philanthropy, lofty sentiment with blatant sophistry, moral platitude with unbridaled self-indulgence. His arguments will be subtle, convincing and appealing. His oratory will be hypnotic, for he will be able to move the masses to tears or whip them into a frenzy. He will control the communication media of the world and will skillfully organise mass publicity to promote his ends. He will be the master of every promotional device and every public relations gimmick. He will manage the truth with guile beyond words, bending it, twisting it, and distorting it. Public opinion will be his to command. He will mold world thought and shape human opinion like so much potter's clay. His deadly appeal will lie in the fact that what he says will sound so right, so sensible, so exactly what unregenerate men have always wanted to hear." This man will be the ideally-fitted spokesman for Satan's man – the first Beast.

Some commentators, rightly observing the religious role of this second beast, and influenced by the historical school of interpretation, have here followed Alford in identification of these two beasts as:

1. the first beast representing the secular power of the pagan Roman Empire reproduced in the final empire on earth;
2. the second beast representing the sacerdotal power of papal Rome which arising later is subordinate to the first. They claim that this second beast is thus the head of apostate christianity – the Pope.

J.F. Walvoord gives some credence to this view when he writes, p.205 "There is some evidence pointing to the conclusion that the second beast is the head of the apostate church during the first half of Daniel's seventieth week. With the rise of the first beast to a place of world-wide dominion, the apostate church is destroyed according to Rev 17:16 and the worship of the whole world is directed to the beast out of the sea. The second beast, however, survives the destruction of the church which had been under his control and he assists the beast in making the transition. Facilitating this change into the final form of apostate religion, the beast out of the earth causes men to worship the first beast".

Contrary to Alford and those who follow this line of interpretation these beasts are not just the representations of abstract powers they are real persons who fill the major roles of end time politics. There is no hint in Scripture that the second beast is linked in any way with apostate christianity seen in the harlot of ch.17. The reference to "the God of his fathers" in Dan 11:36-39 makes it abundantly clear that he is a Jew. He appeals to Jewish expectations and gives the very "signs" that authenticate in Jewish eyes his "prophet" status. He has the "lamb-like" appearance that befits the expected Jewish Messiah. The whole scene is Jewish and this impostor takes the place of the Christ that the nation refused. He is the one whom Christ anticipated, "If another shall come in his own name, him ye will receive" (John 5:43). The climax of the scene is that this impostor, coming in his own name, demands worship for another; the visible symbol of that "other" is the image now introduced. The first Beast is spoken of in his proclamations "against God" (v.6); he personally claims deity (2 Thess 2:3-4) and demands the worship of men. The second beast in Jerusalem claims:-

1. royal power as "the king" who "shall do according to his will" (Dan 11:36-39).
2. the place of a prophet in the very terms of the expected prophet of Deut 18:15 when Moses said, "The Lord thy God will raise up unto thee a prophet from the midst of thee, of thy brethren, like unto me". These claims point to the fact that this is "the Antichrist" (1 John 2:18) if the prefix *anti* is given its full grammatical weight of "in place of". Refusing the true Christ the nation of Israel has fallen prey to satanic deception and has given its allegiance to one who is "in place of' Christ. The term "antichrist" occurs five times in the NT (1 John 2:18 (2), 22; 4:3; 2 John 7). Much argument has raged whether the title is applicable to the first Beast or the second. While there are cogent arguments that can be advanced on each side, the national background of this second beast and his religious authority over Israel fit him ideally for the title. The triarchy of evil, so beloved of commentators, is not infringed by this identification; if the first beast is anti-God (see v.6) and the second beast is anti-Christ then the unseen yet all pervasive power of Satan is set over against the person and power of the Holy Spirit.

15 The RV translation is more exact at this point: "And it was given unto him to give breath to it". The same verb is used of the endowments of the first beast in vv. 3-5 showing that this second beast is also the recipient of supernatural power from his satanic master. Though the first Beast is empowered by Satan there is no record of him doing any miracles; his infernal master is clever enough to see that two miracle-workers would confuse men. To give "breath" to the image of the Beast is obviously the very high point in the deceptive work of Antichrist. JND and the RV both have "breath" where the AV has "life"; and of the 385 times it occurs in the NT this is the only occasion in which the word *pneuma* is translated life (J.B. Smith). It is better to translate it "spirit" and understand it as the installation of an evil spirit in this image. No one can give life but God. This miracle in some way so surpasses what men can do that all the world recognises it as the crowning display of the supernatural power of the false prophet.

Two clauses joined by "and" make the image of the Beast do two things. The first is "that it should … speak". The second is to "cause that as many as would not worship the image of the beast should be killed". The tense of the verbs translated "speak" and "cause" shows that they are to be seen as simultaneous actions of the image. Speaking oracularly this image backs up in the clearest of language the demands of the false prophet and, in doing so, reveals the murderous intentions of Satan. Men must either worship the Beast or die. The reference to "as many" widens the scale of the war already being waged against saints. The flight of the nation of Israel (12:14), the persecution of the "remnant of her seed" (12:17) and the "war with the saints" (v.7) is now carried worldwide against all who will not bow in worship to this speaking image. The parallels from the past are suggestive. The emperor-cult of John's day was introduced as the ecumenical (world-embracing) religion binding diverse peoples together. Nebuchadnezzar had sought to do exactly this in Babylon in the sixth century BC (Dan 3:1-7). In Babylon there was a great image, a royal declaration and the state forces were standing by to deal with dissenters and the furnace was ready for the nonconformists. These satanic tactics will be seen again in the Babylonish conditions pertaining throughout the empire of the Beast as he demands the worship of earth. These are the terrible days of which the Lord spoke, "Except these days should be shortened there should no flesh be saved" (Matt 24:22). The murder campaign of the Beast will lead to genocide on an unbelievable scale. The verb "cut short" should not be understood as the shortening of the twenty-four hour day, or even the shortening of the number of days which God has given for the great tribulation period (1260 days), the verb has its secondary meaning of "to terminate". If these daily murders had continued uninterrupted earth's population would soon have been wiped out; but they will be "terminated" when Christ comes in glory. What a relief for earth!

16 The ambiguity in the subject of the verb "causeth" (*poieō*) whether "it" or "he", makes it unclear whether these actions are to be traced back to the utterances of the image or are attributable directly to the second beast. The mood of the verb suggests that it is the second beast who is responsible for these actions. There is no ambiguity about the actions. The next verb translated by JND, "that they should give them a mark", may suggest that the worshippers ask for the mark as a sign of their commitment to the Beast. They desire to be publicly identified with their "god", just as the 144,000 have been marked for God "in their forehead" (14:1). This mark (*charagma*) has its background in an old custom spoken of by Isaiah, "And another shall subscribe with his hand unto the Lord, and surname himself by the name of Israel" (Isa 44:5) or of the practice of NT times of putting a brand mark on a slave (Gal 6:17 figuratively) or an animal. It indicates ownership. The mark on the right hand would be easily accessible though it could also be readily removed by amputation. The mark on the forehead would be unremovable and permanent until death. Visibility may be part of the picture but even in the present day a mark can be put by laser beam on forehead or hand that is visible only in ultra-violet light. To say that the hand may refer to manual workers, while the head refers to the intelligentsia is to read too much into the text. Any suggestion of this nature is already covered by the six classes touching every social grouping of society. There are "the small" and "the great", the famous and the unknown are all embraced in this hysteria, "the rich" and "the poor", the millionaire magnates and poverty-stricken peasants meet on this common ground; "the free" and "the bond", the liberated and the enslaved of differing political ideologies all unite in demanding and receiving this identifying mark. The worship of the Beast crosses all the boundary lines of society. The mark of Cain (Gen 4:15) identifies the seed of the serpent (1 John 3:12). The importance of this mark of the Beast is seen in the prominence given to it in the later chapters of the book, where it is mentioned a further six times (14:9, 11; 15:2; 16:2; 19.20; 20:4). Earth-dwellers have become Beast-worshippers by their own choice and are proud to be so identified. There is no suggestion that there is any possibility of this mark being removed and it would seem that, once it is received by adult choice, the destiny of the individual is linked with that of the Beast. Such will share his doom.

17 When this mark has been given then it will be a simple matter to introduce legislation making it illegal to buy or to sell goods without it – legislation that will likely cover even the simplest domestic transaction. This will be, in effect, an economic boycott of those who do not identify with the Beast. That which began as political allegiance and through the second beast became a religious affiliation, now moves inexorably to the third stage. All the common transactions of everyday life demand the use of this mark and without it the simplest transactions are refused. In the society of the closing years of the 20th century the trend is already unmistakable; "plastic money", the multiplicity of bank cards, credit cards and debit cards makes cash cumbersome. Salaries are paid by computer transaction into personal accounts; debit cards will soon mean that money is no longer used. These transactions all demand a personal number for each individual, unique and untransferable from birth to death.

How to link that number with the individual so that it can neither be lost nor removed is under urgent study. Recent reports recommend laser identification marks on the body – hand or forehead have been suggested as possibilities. These are the trends at present but when the Beast reaches the peak of his power at the midpoint of the tribulation there will be the technology to mark his adherents.

The mark of the Beast provides both textual as well as interpretative problems. There are three ways of viewing the verse:

1. The AV reads, "he that had the mark, or the name of the beast, or the number of his name" suggesting that these are alternatives that one could have either the mark or the name or the number or the number corresponding to the name.
2. JND on very good authority omits the first "or" and translates, "save he that had the mark, the name of the beast or the number of its name" implying that the mark consists of either "the name of the beast" or alternatively "the number of his name". The implication may be that second-class citizens had only the name of the beast while first-class citizens had a personal number that identified their status in the empire with all the special privileges this would imply.
3. Some expositors insist that grammatical considerations point in the other direction and that the mark is to be interpreted as the name of the Beast inscribed simply as its numerical equivalent (R.H. Mounce). This simple interpretation is possibly to be preferred with the additional refinement suggested by the next verse that other personal identification numbers are included within an eighteen-digit base-number which would be the number of the Beast himself. The discrimination and difficulties of even normal living at this time for those without the mark can be readily imagined. Sympathetic hearts who would assist the mark-refusing saints with food, drink, clothing and shelter will be showing faith in a real way; a faith that could endanger their lives since they are challenging the power of the Beast (Matt 25:34-36). Yet by this exercise of faith they will show themselves to be citizens of the kingdom of God and fit to enter the millennial reign of Christ.

18 The word "wisdom" as used in a similar statement in 17:9 indicates that more than human intellect is involved in the unlocking of the enigma to be given. The word "understanding" implies the divinely-illuminated mind; the same idea is in the statement of Dan 12:10, "but the wise shall understand". Spirit-given insight will be able to identify a person by the cryptogram here given. It will neither be doubtful nor disputable and all saints will be able to see the self-evident rightness of it while the worshippers of the Beast will likely be totally oblivious of it. The clue will be a number, and it will be "the number of the Beast" and it will be "the number of a man". This again is incidental confirmation that the Beast is not an empire but a man.

That the number is given as 666 is the weight of all the reliable textual evidence (see RV margin for an alternative reading). Knowing that "six" is generally associated with man, since he was created on the sixth day, the triple six has generally been taken to mean man at his best, man at the height of his power, yet still short of the divine perfection seen in the triple seven. The imperative "count" has been the justification for the endless mathematical attempts to unravel the enigma of the number. The only other occasion when this verb is used in the NT is the calculation required when building a tower (Luke 14:28). The art of linking letters and numbers, called by the Jewish rabbis *gematria*, was endlessly applied to the OT Scriptures to search for hidden meanings. Assigning numerical values to letters of the alphabet is normal in Hebrew, Greek and Latin. Many have amused themselves with numbers endlessly and to little profit (see note on this verse). Various methods have been used to arrive at a meaning for this number. Typical of this kind of fruitless speculation is the comment that since the numerical values of the six Roman numerals I, V, X, L, C, D add up to 666 then the Beast must be a Roman. It is much better to leave the identification to the saints of the tribulation who will recognise, beyond the suave dynamic politician, the able statesman and the magnetic personality, the satanically-energised opponent of God and His Christ. This Scripture will put to rest every doubt and they will know how to react to him.

Summary of the Second Beast

This chapter has presented, under the symbols of "beasts" the two great evil characters who will dominate the last seven years of earth history before Christ comes to claim His kingdom. A mighty leader with dynamic personality and surpassing ability emerges to lead the end-time history of the fourth empire of Daniel's vision (Dan 7); having many of the features of the old Roman Empire this empire surpasses it in every way to become such an empire as the world has never previously seen. While this empire has its base in Europe it comes to dominate the world scene as no empire has ever done before. The first Beast dominates earth not only politically, but religiously and commercially. He has been pointed out to be "the little horn" (Dan 7:8), the prince that shall come (Dan 9:26) and "the man of sin" (2 Thess 2:3). This satanic puppet whose antecedents embrace all who have aspired to world dominion down the ages, takes the lead in opposition to God. The words used to describe his activity in v.6 are "against God".

The second beast who arises out of the earth has been shown to be a Jew. He is to be identified with:

1. The king of fierce countenance of Dan 8:23-26 of whom the "little horn" of Dan 8:9, historically seen in Antiochus IV (known as Antiochus Epiphanes, 215-163BC) was but the pattern.

2. The wilful king ("The king shall do according to his will", Dan 11:36-45). Some have argued that "the God of his fathers" does not necessarily demand a Jewish origin (see Walvoord) but the arguments are unconvincing. This is the one who has come in his own name and claimed the allegiance of the Jewish nation: he leads them into a false covenant with the first Beast which brings a false peace and which allows him to be identified as the false prophet. No one but a Jew could deceive his own people and lead them to disaster in a travesty of what they expected from their longed-for Messiah.

While John has spoken of "the Antichrist" in 1 John 2:18 he does not state precisely which of these two end-time figures fills that description. Perhaps this very fact may teach caution. However, enough has been outlined to show that as far as Israel is concerned the second beast must be "the Antichrist". The prefix *anti* must be understood as "in place of" or "instead of". When Israel rejected Christ they left the way open for a replacement and Satan makes sure he has a claimant ready. The false prophet channels worship to one who takes the place of God and acts with his authority. Behind both is the unseen one who fulfils the role of the third member of this unholy triarchy seeking to bring earth under his control. This pseudo-lamb assumes the office of a priest as he demands worship for another (v.15) and is temple guardian for the false god (2 Thess 2:3-4). In his leadership he has displayed a prophetic ministry that entitles him to be called "the false prophet" (16:13; 19:20; 20:10). In his domination and dictatorship in the land he is seen as "the king of fierce countenance" (Dan 8:23) and "the wilful king" (Dan 11:36-45). He thus replaces Christ as priest, prophet and king.

Many expositors have argued for the first Beast as filling the role of antichrist. This argument becomes almost academic when it is seen that they are using the prefix "anti" in a completely different sense. "Anti" can also mean "against", a meaning foreshadowed in Ps 2:2 to describe the rebellion of earth, a rebellion that is led by the first beast, "The kings of the earth set themselves, and the rulers take counsel together, against the Lord, and against his anointed saying, Let us break their bands asunder, and cast their cords away from us". He is the one whom Satan uses to marshal every earthly opponent against Christ and in this secondary sense may be seen also as antichrist. However NT identification points to the nation of Israel as the key nation for the identification of the one who will take the place of Christ and, in this sense, "the Antichrist" he must be identified as the second beast in this chapter.

Notes

12-14 It should be pointed out that this subservient role of the second beast supports the previous interpretation on a number of points:

1. While a mighty Empire is involved (the fourth empire of Dan 7) this is centred in an identifiable person identified as the "beast out of the sea" who is claiming worship of mankind. Empires as such are not worshipped except in so far as they are reflected in an individual; this was true of the Roman Empire.
2. The death-resurrection sequence is not the experience of an empire but of an individual in a satanic parody of the death and resurrection of Christ, it is the ground of his claim to worship.
3. The time sequence when both these satanic personalities reach the climax of their careers is at the midpoint of the tribulation period.

15 While the temple as the site for this image is not specifically mentioned here, it must be pointed out that Scripture is clear that it is introduced into the rebuilt temple at Jerusalem at the midpoint of the seven-year tribulation. The evidence is conclusive:

(a) *The place*. It is in this temple that the first Beast as the man of sin takes his place as the "one who opposeth and exalteth himself above all that is called God, or that is worshipped; so that he, as God, sitteth in the temple of God, showing himself that he is God" (2 Thess 2:4). However since this blasphemer cannot physically be present at all times it is logical that the false prophet should introduce this image to represent him there. This would be on the pattern of Antiochus Ephiphanes (175-164 BC) who introduced the idol of Jupiter Capitolinus into the holy place during his invasion of Israel. This Seleucid king of Syria, Antiochus IV, is the historical fulfilment of the "vile person" of Dan 11:21 who, on his second campaign against Israel, fulfilled the prophecy of Daniel, "and they shall pollute the sanctuary of strength, and shall take away the daily sacrifice , and they shall place the abomination that maketh desolate" (Dan 11:31).

(b) *The Person* The action of Antiochus as spoken of by Daniel was but a historical foreshadowing of the activities of the false prophet that will result in this "abomination of desolation" (Dan 9:27; 11:31; 12:11) standing in the holy place. Christ spoke specifically in Matt 24:15, "When ye, therefore shall see the abomination of desolation, spoken of by Daniel the prophet, stand in the holy place (whoso readeth let him understand;) then let them which be in Judea flee unto the mountains". It has been pointed out in comment on 12:6,14 that this is the signal for the flight of the nation of Israel. This abomination of desolation is this image of the Beast being introduced into the temple of God at Jerusalem. The seven-year tribulation has already been inaugurated by the signing of a peace covenant between the first Beast and the second beast as leader of the Jewish nation or the greater part of it ("the many" of Dan 9:27). This is the covenant which Isaiah denounced as far back as the year 725 BC when he proclaimed, "Wherefore hear the word of the Lord, ye scornful men, that rule this people which is in Jerusalem; Because ye have said We have made a covenant with death, and with hell are we at agreement; when the overflowing scourge shall pass through, it shall not come unto us: for we have made lies our refuge, and under falsehood have we hid ourselves" (Isa 28: 14,15). At the midpoint of the tribulation when this image is introduced into the holy place there is an immediate cessation of the sacrifices. This can be seen as the breaking of the covenant from the point of view of the nation or, as suggested earlier, this could be viewed as the implementation of hidden codicils by these two deceivers. In either case the result is the same. This Scripture shows the forces and the persons at work to produce this final evidence of idolatry and apostasy within the nation of Israel, a worldwide apostasy that has not only political and religious forces working for it but, as the final verses will show, powerful commercial incentives to make all people conform. Those who refuse face death.

(c) *The time* The words of Christ in Matt 24:15-18 place the "abomination of desolation" at the midpoint of the seventieth week when the "beginning of sorrows" (Matt 24:15-18), already shown to be the first half of the week, has passed and just before "the great tribulation" identified as the second half of the week begins.

18 Perhaps J.B. Smith gives the most concise statement of the science of *gematria* when he writes, "The numerical values were applied in this manner; the first ten letters of the alphabet increased by units, a-1, b-2, c-3, etc. After the tenth and up to the nineteenth inclusive they increased by tens i.e. K-20, L-30, M-40, etc. From the twentieth the increase is by one hundred, i.e. T-200, U-300 etc." Using this method Smith goes on to calculate to his own satisfaction that, using the Hebrew form for the name of Nero, the Roman Emperor, he is identified as the Beast. He writes, "The name Nero Caesar does not occur in Revelation; in fact, nowhere in the NT except in the postcript to 2 Timothy in the AV, where it occurs in the Hebrew form *Kaiser Neron*. Had John used the name, he doubtless would have written it with Hebrew endings as he does other proper names, viz. Abaddon, Apollyon, and Armageddon, in which the second letter is a long o. Using only the consonants as the Hebrew does , the numerical values of the Hebrew composing Kaisar Neron are: (K)-100; (S)=60; (R)= 200, (N)=50; (R)=200; (0)=6; (N)=50. As Nero alone totals 666, he must be the emperor intended."

This kind of speculation based on an unproveable hypothesis is both endless and unrewarding. In spite of Smith's last statement in the quotation many have shown a variety of claimants to this number. The answer to Nero is that it is totally unscriptural to imagine that a long dead emperor would be allowed to return to earth, even in his life there is no doubt that Nero was a disgrace to Satan. This Beast will be a far greater man than Nero was and when he appears spiritually enlightened saints will recognise him by this number and they will not need to be mathematicians to do this!

CHAPTER 14

This chapter is the last of the three chapters that comprise the third parenthetic section of the book. The relationship between these three chapters may be seen as follows:

Ch. 12 The Purpose of Satan Disclosed
In symbolic form the historic and prophetic evidences of the implacable hatred of Satan for Christ and hence for the nation through whom He would come are unfolded,

Ch. 13 The Puppets of Satan Described
In the symbols of the beast from the sea and the beast out of the earth the advent, the authority and the activities of these satanic agents are described,

Ch. 14 The Power of Satan Defeated
In seven pictures aspects of the conditions obtaining during the last half of the seven-year tribulation period are described with particular emphasis upon the

ultimate deliverance of the saints and the ultimate destruction of those who are identified with the Beast and the false prophet.

It will be remembered that the chronological action has been interrupted just after the blowing of the seventh trumpet at 11:15-18. It has been shown already that this trumpet comprises the seven bowls, the pouring out of which will bring the tribulation to its close in Ch. 16. Suffering and dying under the tyranny of the Beast and false prophet the saints need reassurance in the ultimate triumph of the Lamb. This reassurance is given in these seven pictures that show, no matter how dark the conditions, the ultimate triumph of the Lamb and His followers and the ultimate doom of the followers of the Beast.

These seven cameos describing conditions in the final three and a half years before the Christ comes to earth are grouped around the event that has been shown in the last chapter to mark the midpoint of the tribulation thus:

vv.1-5 *The Sealed of God*
(Presentation of God's Witnesses)

vv.6-7 *The Sound of the Gospel*
(Preaching of God's Word)

v.8 *The Fall of Babylon*
(Destruction of the harlot)

vv.9-11 *The Image and the Mark*
(The midpoint of the tribulation)

vv.12-13 *The Comfort of Saints*
(Assurance to the saints)

vv.14-16 *The Gathering of the Harvest*
(The Son of man and the sickle)

vv.17-20 *The Treading of the Witness*
(The angel and the sickle)

(c) *The Power of Satan Defeated (vv.1-20)*

v.1 "And I looked, and, lo, a Lamb stood on the mount Sion, and with him an hundred forty and four thousand, having his Father's name written in their foreheads.

v.2 And I heard a voice from heaven, as the voice of many waters, and as the voice of a great thunder: and I heard the voice of harpers harping with their harps:

v.3 And they sung as it were a new song before the throne, and before the four beasts, and the elders: and no man could learn that song but the hundred and forty and four thousand, which were redeemed from the earth.
v.4 These are they which were not defiled with woman; for they are virgins. These are they which follow the Lamb whithersoever he goeth. These were redeemed from among men, being the firstfruits unto God and to the Lamb.
v.5 And in their mouth was found no guile: for they are without fault before the throne of God.
v.6 And I saw another angel fly in the midst of heaven, having the everlasting gospel to preach unto them that dwell on the earth, and to every nation, and kindred, and tongue, and people,
v.7 Saying with a loud voice, Fear God, and give glory to him; for the hour of his judgment is come: and worship him that made heaven, and earth, and the sea, and the fountains of waters.
v.8 And there followed another angel, saying, Babylon is fallen, is fallen, that great city, because she made all nations drink of the wine of the wrath of her fornication.
v.9 And the third angel followed them, saying with a loud voice, If any man worship the beast and his image, and receive his mark in his forehead, or in his hand,
v.10 The same shall drink of the wine of the wrath of God, which is poured out without mixture into the cup of his indignation; and shall be tormented with fire and brimstone in the presence of the holy angels, and in the presence of the Lamb:
v.11 And the smoke of their torment ascendeth up for ever and ever: and they have no rest day nor night, who worship the beast and his image, and whosever receiveth the mark of his name.
v.12 Here is the patience of the saints: here are they that keep the commandments of God, and the faith of Jesus.
v.13 And I heard a voice from heaven, saying unto me, Write, Blessed *are* the dead which die in the Lord from hence-forth: Yea, saith the Spirit, that they may rest from their labours; and their works do follow them.
v.14 And I looked, and behold a white cloud, and upon the cloud *one* sat like unto the Son of man, having on his head a golden crown, and in his hand a sharp sickle.
v.15 And another angel came out of the temple, crying with a loud voice to him that sat on the cloud, Thrust in thy sickle, and reap: for the time is come for thee to reap; for the harvest of the earth is ripe.
v.16 And he that sat on the cloud thrust in his sickle on the earth; and the earth was reaped.
v.17 And another angel came out of the temple which is in heaven, he also having a sharp sickle.
v.18 And another angel came out from the altar, which had power over fire; and cried with a loud cry to him that had the sharp sickle, saying, Thrust in thy sharp sickle, and gather the clusters of the vine of the earth; for her grapes are fully ripe.
v.19 And the angel thrust in his sickle into the earth, and gathered the vine of the earth, and cast *it* into the great winepress of the wrath of God.
v.20 And the winepress was trodden without the city, and blood came out of the winepress, even unto the horse bridles, by the space of a thousand and six hundred furlongs."

The Sealed of God — Cameo 1

1 Once again John uses the exclamatory "behold" or "lo" after the verb "I saw". This time what startles him is not the sight of wild beasts but the sight of "the Lamb". The article points back to the Lamb previously introduced in the vision in 5:6 and also serves to highlight a contrast with the pseudo-lamb of the previous chapter (13:11). This is *the* Lamb, any other is counterfeit. The transition from the tyranny of the Beast to the triumph of the Lamb; from watching the dragon "take his stand" (13:1) on the sand of the seashore to seeing the Lamb "standing" (RV) on Mount Zion (RV spelling) highlights the change of perspective.

There can be little argument that the 144,000 of this chapter is the same company as in 7:1-8 and any differences can be explained by the fact that they are viewed now at a different time and under very different circumstances. Ch. 7 views them as the sealed ones going into the tribulation, this scene views them as the preserved ones coming out of the tribulation and entering the millennial kingdom. The evidence for the two companies being the same is conclusive:

1. The correspondence of the numbers must be considered a weighty point. Any argument based on the silence of Scripture must be examined carefully but one commentator (J.B. Smith) insists that if they had been different John, with his habitual carefulness, would have distinguished them with the adjective "another".
2. The very lack of any definitive identification in the passage itself suggests that this is unnecessary, as if they should be readily recognised. The term "firstfruits" and the expression "no guile" suggests that they must be from Israel. W. Scott insists that they come from the tribe of Judah but does not give any supporting evidence and the passage itself does not make any such distinction. The lack of tribal identification is not an argument against the identification of the companies; Scripture does not repeat what has already been stressed and the point here is their relationship to the Lamb, not with each other.
3. If this passage had not been included there would have been questions as to what had become of the company of ch. 7. This picture settles any question on this matter.
4. The supposed difficulty of the difference between the verbs used in the expressions "sealed in their foreheads" (7:3) and "written in their foreheads" (v.1) is more a matter of semantics than any real problem. In ch. 7 information is given about the fact of the sealing; here further detail is given of the nature of the seal – the seal comprised "his name and the name of his Father" (RV).

It may be concluded that this is the company of the sealed from Israel of 7:1-8 who have passed through the terrors of the tribulation period and are now seen at the very end of that period entering into the millennial kingdom in company with the Lamb. There is something very reassuring in the fact that after these saints have gone through the whole seven-year period of the tribulation, their number is still the same. The Beast with all his mighty power has not been able to destroy a single one of them; a very sound reason, indeed, for re-emphasising their exact number.

Mount Zion with the article points to "the well-known" Mount Zion. This is the literal Mount Zion in Jerusalem that, from the days of king David, was the centre point of kingdom rule in Israel (2 Sam 5:7). In later prophetic ministry it was clearly shown that from this literal Mount Zion Christ would reign on earth (Ps 48:1; Isa 24:23; Joel 2:32; Obad 17, 21; Micah 4:1; Zech 14:4). These Scriptures are now fulfilled and the Lamb is publicly associated with His servants; their suffering in the dark days of tribulation over, they are associated with Him as He sets up His kingdom. The very mention of Mount Zion shows that the Lamb is about to assert His royal prerogative and take His place on the throne of David.

Some commentators labour to prove that Mount Zion is a figurative expression and simply means that this company is in heaven. In answer it may be pointed out that:

1. it would be very difficult to prove that "Zion" is ever used figuratively of heaven (Heb 12:22 is the possible exception). Even in the Psalms with all their poetic imagery it would be difficult to find one occasion when Zion is used figuratively;
2. this 144,000 of ch. 7 were sealed for preservation through the tribulation so there is no question of martyrdom nor is there any record of their rapture or removal to heaven;
3. in v.2 John hears a voice "out of heaven" which, at the very least, suggests that neither he nor the 144,000 are in heaven. Rather these 144,000 witnesses, delivered from the tyranny of the Beast, now share the triumph of the Lamb as He sets up His Kingdom on earth.

While ch. 7 refers to the seal "in their foreheads" (7:3), here the seal is described: "having his name and the name of his Father written upon their foreheads" (JND). The textual variant behind this translation has overwhelming support and shows that there are two names inscribed on the foreheads. The name of "the Lamb" proclaims their redemption by blood; the name of His Father (Christ's Father) proclaims their relationship by new birth. They belong to both the Lamb and the Father (the truth of John 17:10). This visible identification has publicly declared their allegiance in dangerous times and now they carry it into the kingdom. There is an obvious contrast with the followers of the Beast who have his mark in their foreheads (13:16) and he leads them to their doom (vv.9-10).

2-3 As John surveys this glorious scene there bursts on his ear a "sound", in this context a better translation than "voice", described as being "out of heaven"; an incidental confirmation that the scene is upon earth. It is a composite sound and John is able to distinguish three elements marked by the repetition of the word "as":

1. "As the voice of many waters" – the *majesty* of the sound, all other voices are drowned. It is reminiscent of the voice of Christ (1:15)
2. "As the voice of a great thunder" – the *authority* of the sound, no other voice can compete.
3. "[As] the voice of harpers harping with their harps" – the *sweetness* of the sound, a tenderness and gentleness combine to soothe the ear.

It is to be noted that though the sound is heard the harpers and the singers are out of sight as yet. This is obviously a company in heaven who in the presence of the throne, the four living creatures and the twenty-four elders, raise this new song. It has echoes of the new song of the twenty-four elders in 5:9-10 but is clearly distinguished from it. John is hearing the company which in 15:2-4 he will see standing on the sea of glass. It will be shown that this is the full martyr band from the tribulation period who have died for their faith and now sing the new song in heaven. The company of 6:9-11 from the first half of the tribulation, have been joined by their brethren who died in the final three and a half years, and together they sing "the song of Moses and the song of the Lamb". Here they are heard; in the next chapter they will be seen (15:2-4). Apart from the twenty-four elders this is the only other company in this book who use the "harp" in their praise.

The abrupt introduction of the verb "they sing" (present tense, not the past as in the AV) shows that the singers are the "harpers" of the previous verse. "Before" (*enōpion*) the throne, the four living creatures and the twenty-four elders the song rises; the fact that it is heard on earth shows that heaven and earth are now in communication. The throne of the government of the universe (5:2-11) is now linked to Mount Zion in Jerusalem at the commencement of the millennial reign of Christ (see comments on 7:9-17). For the moment the audible link is the "new song". The old song goes back to the creation, "When the morning stars sang together, and all the sons of God shouted for joy" (Job 38:7) but this new song goes back to the cross and a paean of praise never heard before unites heaven and earth. In 5:9 the new song celebrates the person of the Lamb; here (and in 15:3) it celebrates His power.

As the song swells from heaven it is taken up on earth but a divine limitation is imposed. Only the 144,000 have the capacity (the verb *dunamai* is related to ability not authority) to learn this song, a unique way of emphasising that experiences on earth prepare for praise in the future; no one may sing beyond their experience. The link between these companies is the suffering endured in the tribulation. Unique pain brings unique praise; the tears under the Beast give way to triumph with the Lamb, they suffered therefore they reign (2 Tim 2:12). One company, now in heaven, laid down their lives for the Lamb; the other company, on earth, suffered and were preserved for the Lamb. They both join in a song of which the detail will be given in 15:2-4.

This company are "redeemed from the earth". The verb "to redeem" *(agorazō)* simply stresses the idea of "having been bought out of the slave market" with the emphasis on the price paid. The RV gives "had been purchased" while JND reads "who were bought". Christ paid the price to purchase these saints "from the earth". This earth where Satan was rampaging in rage and the Beast was ruling had yielded this company of purchased ones. Purchased "from earth" in v.3 and purchased "from among men" in v.4 are parallel expressions which highlight the conditions and company from which these saints were redeemed.

4 Three times the pronoun "these" is used to mark out features of this company:

1. *Individually* "These are they which were not defiled with women; for they are virgins". It has been argued that the first part of this statement demands that the company are all male. This would then suggest that the word "virgins" in the explanatory statement must be taken to mean "celibates" – a possible use of the word. However this argument is fatally flawed on two related matters and cannot be maintained. First, it suggests that there is something unclean in marriage, a totally unjustifiable slur on the holy relationship in marriage and an inference totally unscriptural and categorically denied in Heb 13:4. The related matter is that such an interpretation puts a totally unscriptural value on celibacy, a very early distortion of truth. The much more valid interpretation is to see that virginity should be taken in a figurative sense as referring to the spiritual purity of this company in these days when spiritual values were prostituted for profit or preservation. The symbolism of the book shows that the corruption of moral and spiritual values is described by the word "fornication" as has been seen in Jezebel (2:20) and will be seen in Babylon (17:4). It is suggested that these saints, both men and women, maintained their moral and spiritual purity in a morally corrupt scene. They had repulsed all the moral entanglements that surpassed those of Egypt for Joseph and Babylon for Daniel. The sexual symbolism of association with either religious or commercial Babylon is articulated in 17:4 and 18:3. These saints, are pure from such defilement; they have been shown to be faithful and are fit to follow the Lamb.

2. *Spiritually* "These are they which follow the Lamb whithersoever he goeth". The associations of these saints through the defiling days of the tribulation were governed by their affection for the Lamb. Purity was the inevitable result of this affection; this is now recognised and rewarded by the

Lamb; they will have the privilege of forming the guard of honour for Him in His movements on earth. The mighty men of David, proved through the years of his rejection, were honoured when he came to the throne by their nearness and right of access to him (2 Sam 23:8-39). The Lamb likewise will have His close attendants. They have earned this privilege. The only closer relationship will be between the Lamb and His Bride.

3. *Collectively* "These were redeemed from among men, being the firstfruits unto God and to the Lamb". The harvest in Israel began with the barley harvest in the first month (Nisan) of the year. Passover was a fixed date, the fourteenth of Nisan, but the feast of firstfruits fell "on the morrow after the sabbath" (Lev 23:9ff); the sabbath being the weekly sabbath that followed the fourteenth of Nisan. This made "firstfruits" a moveable feast. On that day "firstfruits" of the barley harvest were waved before the Lord in acknowledgement that the whole harvest belonged to God and that the major part of the harvest was yet to follow. It is these ideas that are carried over into the NT wherever "firstfruits" are used figuratively. Christ is the "firstfruits" from the grave (1 Cor 15:20-23) of the great host of the redeemed; Epaenetus is described as the "firstfruits of Achaia unto Christ" (Rom 16:5); the believers of the church age are spoken of "a kind of firstfruits of his creatures" (James 1:18); these 144,000 are the "firstfruits" of a great national reaping that will be harvested when "all Israel" will be saved when they embrace their once-rejected Messiah as He returns in glory (Rom 11:26-27). These 144,000 are but the pledge of a harvest to be reaped when the purposes of God have been completed.

5 In the statement "in their mouth was found no lie" (RV) is shown their association with Christ who is "the truth" (John 14:6) and their total dissociation from "the lie" (2 Thess 2:11) and the liar (1 John 2:21-23) identified in Israel as the false prophet (13:11-16). "Without fault" *(amōmoi)* is better translated "without blemish". It is a word that describes the perfection of the internal organs of a sacrificial victim; used of Christ and NT believers it means ethically blameless (see Eph 1:4; 5:27; Col 1:22; Heb 9:14; 1 Pet 1:24; Jude 19). This company has earned the very highest commendation.

Based on the weight of textual evidence both JND and the RV omit the concluding words "before the throne of God" as not having sufficient authority. Other textual scholars disagree but the inclusion of the phrase is no argument against this scene being on earth. Exactly the same expression "before the throne" is used twice in ch. 7 with reference to the great multitude (7:9-17) who are also on earth. Heaven has been opened (19:11) and heaven and earth are in communication at the installation of the King.

The Sound of the Gospel — Cameo 2

6 After the introductory tableau on Mount Zion, taking the scene to the close of the tribulation and the entrance to the millennial kingdom, the action returns to the tribulation period. The angel "flying in mid-heaven" (RV) is the first of six angels who appear in the remaining part of the chapter grouped round the appearance of the Son of man in v.14. Three appear before He is introduced (vv. 6, 8, 9) and three follow His appearance (vv.15, 17,19), a symmetry designed to give Christ the central place in the vision.

"Mid heaven" as shown in 8:13 is almost a technical expression for the southern sky viewed from Mount Zion at midday. The last angel to appear was the seventh of the trumpet-bearing angels in 11:15, so the adjective "another" simply distinguishes this one from the previous group. The dirge of the flying eagle in 8:13 is to be contrasted with the declaration of this angel who has the "everlasting gospel". The word *aiōnios* is better rendered "eternal" and, while used 70 times in the NT, is used only here in this book. Within the context the best translation would be "ageless" as showing that this message has no time limitation – it is true for all ages. The gospel is fundamentally the same in every age, the basis of the good news is the work of Christ and no one has ever been saved, or will be saved, on any other grounds. Different emphases allow men in different ages to grasp the same truths. The "gospel of the grace of God" focuses upon the cross of Christ, while the "gospel of the kingdom" focuses upon the coming of Christ but they present the same message. The "ageless gospel" (without the article) is the same message but stresses the responsibility of the creature to worship the Creator. This will be pointedly relevant in the tribulation when the Creator has been excluded from His creation and men worship a creature (2 Thess 2:3-4).

The people to whom this gospel is announced (*euangelizō*, to preach good news) are "them that dwell on the earth". This is not the group twelve times referred to in this book as earth dwellers" (3:10; 6:10; 8:13; 11:10 (twice); 12:12; 13:8, 12, 14 (twice); 17:2, 8.) who have identified themselves with the Beast. The verb "dwell" here is the verb *kathēmai* which is translated "settled" (JND) or "sit" (RV marg). It is another way of describing those who live on earth with a possible hint of being so happily settled they do not wish to be disturbed. These largely indifferent folk are now presented with their final challenge and last opportunity. The "and" does not introduce a second audience for this gospel but explains that this class of person is found right across the world in every nation and tribe and tongue and people. The fourfold designation of all peoples of earth (used in 5:9; 7:9; 10:11; 17:15) shows the worldwide proclamation envisaged by Christ in Matt 24:14, "This gospel of the kingdom shall be preached in all the world for a witness unto all nations".

Some have raised difficulties about an angel preaching the gospel. This is however an unnecessary problem. It is recognised that God has never permitted angels to bear the message of the gospel in the church age nor will He permit this in this tribulation period. This is a symbolic presentation of realities happening in the last half of the tribulation. It is unlikely that the voice of any of the six angels in this chapter is heard during the tribulation so the implication is that they represent human agents that God uses on earth. There is no doubt that this angel in a single symbol represents the gospel preached by a divinely-commissioned messenger or a body of messengers. As shown in ch.7 the 144,000 will be preachers and, doubtless, those who are saved through their ministry will also spread the message of salvation.

7 The "loud" voice emphasises that this message must take priority over all the clamorous noises of earth. Three imperatives give the substance and emphasise the urgency of this message:

1. *Fear God*. Man lost that fear of God through sin (Rom 3:18) and is recalled to it in this summons. Men are called to face the reality of a God who is acting in judgment upon the earth.
2. *Give glory to Him*. Once the reality of the fear of God has dawned upon the human heart the response is an act of recognition giving to God what has been denied Him (see comment on 11:13). The explanatory clause "for the hour of his judgment is come" may be understood in two ways. It could be a reference to the fact that for men this is the decisive hour when destinies are settled; there is no middle ground, men may worship the Beast or they may worship God, they cannot do both. A choice has to be made. However, it may be better to see a reference to the judgment of God breaking upon men in this tribulation period and, in view of this, the urgency of repentance.
3. *Worship Him*. Herein lies the choice for men, while the Beast is claiming the worship of men (13:12) there is a message sounding forth that men should turn away from the creature and bow the knee to the Creator God "that made heaven, and earth, and the sea, and the fountains of waters". It is to be noted that these are the four areas of earth that already have been touched by the trumpet judgments (8:7-12) and will be touched again by the bowl judgments (16:2-8). Men can hardly miss the point that the God who created is the same God who acts in judgment. This is the God whom they must worship.

It will be clear that while there is no specific mention of repentance and faith in Christ, all the basic gospel truths are included in this comprehensive setting forth of the message that will challenge men at this point in the tribulation.

The Fall of Babylon — Cameo 3

8 Two textual amendments need to be noted: the sequence of visions is stressed by the inclusion, on good textual authority, of the word "second" to qualify angel (see JND and the RV); the omission, again on overwhelming textual authority, of the word "city" – the RV reads, "Fallen, fallen is Babylon the great".

This is the first of six references to Babylon by name in this book (14:8; 16:19; 17:5; 18:2, 10, 21), and, it should be noted that the word "city" connected with Babylon is found only in 17:18 and in ch. 18.

The mention of Babylon refers back historically to the city of Babel (Gen 10:10), founded by the arch-rebel Nimrod, which became the centre of the first worldwide empire on earth. Associated with the city, and behind the political dominance of the empire, lay a religious system that spread across the world appearing in various guises as it covered the earth with idolatry. The city itself waxed and waned over the centuries; founded by Nimrod about 24th century BC, it flowered again under Hammurabi in the 18th century BC. It was destroyed and then rebuilt to reach a high point again under Nebuchadnezzar in the time of Daniel (6th century BC). As a literal city, a political empire and a religious system its unchanging characteristic was absolute opposition to God and to His people. In Scripture it is viewed as the very citadel of idolatry, and thus, as the satanic capital on earth. From a corruption of *babel* which means "Gate of God" it became aptly *babal* which means "confusion" and is scripturally the "city of confusion" in contrast to Jerusalem the "city of peace". The influence of Babylon has been age-long and worldwide. Its idolatry has been the satanic religion that has doomed millions. It is not surprising, therefore, that this age-long opponent of God and His people reappears in this closing book of the Bible. In this final period of earth history Babylon in all its manifestations will be dealt with by God and when earth is finally rid of this satanic encumbrance its destruction will open the way for the great hallelujah chorus of 19:2ff.

However, it is perfectly clear that not all aspects of Babylon are dealt with by God at the same time. The aorist tenses, which can only be translated into English as perfects, draw attention to the catastrophic nature of the event itself as shown by exclamation marks " Fallen! Fallen!" (see RV). These words echo Isaiah's prophetic words "Babylon is fallen, is fallen" (Isa 21:9) which likely anticipate the destruction of Nabopolassar's Babylon in the 7th century before the time of Nebuchadnezzar the great re-builder of Babylon.

In recognising the time-sequence of these pictures of the tribulation period it should be clear that the fall of Babylon must come at the midpoint of the tribulation; the time when the image of the Beast is introduced into the temple of God. Beast-worship is the theme of Cameo 4, but before this happens Babylon is judged by God. The further pictures in the sequence then detail happenings in the closing three-and-a-half years of the tribulation. The omission of the word "city" with overwhelming manuscript authority, suggests that it is the religious aspect of Babylon that is here judged. This is a reference in summary form to the destruction of the harlot described in detail in ch. 17. The word "mystery"(17:5) linked with the name Babylon indicates that it is an idolatrous, apostate religious system that is judged. Such a religious system, seen already in embryo form in the latter part of the church age as Roman

Catholicism, will develop after the rapture into an ecumenical conglomerate having all the features of the ancient Babylonish idolatry. Here are shown the reality and timing of the destruction, while in ch. 17 details of its identity and a description of its doom will fill out the picture (17:16-17). Here it is simply noted that a catastrophic judgment has befallen Babylon. This is in keeping with the oft-noted feature of this book of introducing a matter abruptly and giving the full explanation later (see 2:11).

The reason for the fall is given concisely. The omission of "because" in some texts (see JND) makes no difference – the sentence is explanatory. This Babylon has been the centre from which a dangerous drink or opiate has been passed to all nations. In v.10 the expression is "the wine of the wrath of God"; in 17:2 the description is "the wine of her fornication". Here the two ideas are combined into "the wine of the wrath of her fornication" to indicate that what this system forced on nations for her pleasure now becomes the basis of both their judgment and hers. The symbolic picture of illicit sexual relations, indicating spiritual fornication, the idolatry of earth, invites the wrath (*thumos*) of God. *Thumos*, the blaze of God's anger, is reflected in the fire that marks Babylon's end (17:16-17). In Jer 51:7-8 the prophet foretold heaven's retribution in the words, "Babylon hath been a golden cup in the Lord's hand, that made all the earth drunken; the nations have drunk of her wine; therefore the nations are mad. Babylon is suddenly fallen and destroyed".

Fornication in the literal sense is the misuse of what God intended to be holy and pure and its subsequent degradation for mere sensual pleasure. In the spiritual sense it is the same principle of misuse but in the realm of sacred revelation. When profit becomes the motive then there is prostitution or harlotry, which the scripture calls "whoredom" (see 17:1). Babylon, trading in what has been revealed by God as sacred and holy, through allurements, enticements and excitement has stirred passions by the illicit selling of sacred things to the nations. Now this false system is destroyed.

In the minds of many commentators Babylon is to be identified with the city of Rome. J.B. Smith is a fair exponent of this view: "It has become increasingly clear even to opposite schools of thought that by Babylon in Revelation, Rome is intended. The testimony of the early church fathers is so convincing and decisive in this, that anyone familiar with it knows that they take this to be an established fact. Just as Jerusalem 'spiritually is called Sodom' (11: 8), so Rome spiritually is called Babylon, and Rome is this in a twofold sense, for she is both the religious and political successor of the former Babylon". This is certainly plausible but has no scriptural support, despite the advocacy of the early church fathers. While literal Jerusalem is identified scripturally (as in 11:8) there is no such interpretative statement for Babylon. It will be shown in ch. 17 that the word "mystery" legitimately allows, even demands, that Babylon be interpreted as other than a literal city. In fact it points to something which was formerly concealed and now has been revealed by God: a religious system that is to be identified with the ancient religious system of Babylon. It will be shown that this can be no other than Roman Catholicism as a system centralised in the Vatican City in Rome but worldwide in its scope. It is this Babylon, a religious system not a city, that is here destroyed at the midpoint of the tribulation. It has been the scheme of the Beast and Satan to replace all worship on earth, even its apostate forms, with the final great apostasy embodied in the man of sin and his image in Jerusalem. Judaism having been dealt its death-blow, now apostate christianity and all associated religion is similarly destroyed by the Beast. The Beast does not realise it but in this he is but the agent of the will of God (17:16-17).

The Image and the Mark — Cameo 4

9-11 It has been shown that "the abomination that maketh desolate" (Dan 12:11) and "the abomination of desolation" (Matt 24:15), find their fulfilment in "the image of the beast" (13:15) set up in the temple in Jerusalem by the false prophet (13:14-15). Such is the propaganda associated with this event, such the supernatural powers manifested by the infernal triarchy of Satan and his puppets, that men seem anxious to be identified with this religious movement. The act of worship involved is sealed irrevocably by the receiving of the mark of the Beast in forehead or hand. While men, despite the divinely-given signs refused Christ who is "the truth" (John 14:6), they hurry to be identified with "the lie" (2 Thess 2:11) and "the liar" (1 John 2:22).

It is against this background that this third angel brings his warning. The ever changing vision of one angel following another across the divine stage gives a sense of urgency to the message. The taking of the mark by men is the crisis point in the establishment of earth's last apostasy and men have to be warned that to take the mark of the Beast is to elect to share his doom. The first angel challenged men to "worship God"; the challenge of Satan is to "worship the Beast and his image and receive his mark". Babylonish religion needs no longer the cloak of christianised terms; it is now revealed as the worship of Satan through a man. Those who would be associated with this worship need to see its consequences. Three matters are involved:

1. *The subjects of the judgment.* Individuals make their decision; an act of homage to the image and the reception of the mark seals destiny forever. These verses show that once that mark is received it can never be repudiated or erased; those who receive it are identified with the Beast eternally.

2. *The reality of the judgment* (v.10). The same symbol of drinking from the cup links this worship with Babylon, which indicates that while Babylon in its mystery form has been destroyed, as announced by the previous angel, Babylon in another form still exists. The cup held out to men offers sensual pleasure and many delightful things in earthly terms, but to share it is eventually to find that it means to "drink of the wine of the wrath of God". The word "wrath" (*thumos*)

defines the blaze of the fury of God against such presumption. Down the centuries there have been times when God's fury has been glimpsed, as in the destruction of Sodom and Gomorrah, but it has always been mixed with mercy. Now God's anger is "without mixture" (*akratos*); undiluted judgment will be the portion of the Beast-worshippers. This undiluted potion is spoken of as already "in the cup of his wrath" (JND). Here the word "wrath" (AV "indignation") is *orgē*, the characteristic hatred of God for such wilful rebellion, wrath which, while glimpsed by men down the ages from time to time, will be displayed in its fulness against the Beast-worshippers. As the symbolic language gives way to plain statements the full reality of the judgment becomes apparent. The word "tormented" (*basanizō*), a more terrible word even than that used (*odunaō*) of the rich man in hades (Luke 16:24), opens a vista of anguish. It speaks of unrelieved pain. The agent of the pain is defined as "in fire and brimstone" where "in" (*en*) is the instrumental "by". The expression recurs in 19:20; 20:10; 21:8. The addition of "brimstone" (sulphur) to the more usual "fire", has not only historical echoes of the overthrow of Sodom and Gomorrah (Gen 19:24) but echoes also the prophetic voices of Isaiah (Isa 30:33) and Ezekiel (Ezek 38:22). The ancient world used the combination of "fire and brimstone" to convey the idea of a self-sustained furnace independent of external fuel. It is the equivalent of the phrase "unquenchable fire" in the ministry of Christ (Matt 3:12; Luke 3:17).

The translation of the preposition *enōpion* as "in the presence of" carries in English an unfortunate shade of meaning as if the holy angels and the Lamb took some kind of pleasure in the punishment. This is totally foreign to the passage. It is better with JND to translate the preposition "before", or even "in the sight of" (J.B. Smith) as indicating simply that the judgment falls within the view, or within sight of the holy angels and the Lamb. There is no suggestion that they watch the scene throughout eternity; the judgment is eternal but not the viewing of it. That this interpretation is correct can be seen in 19:20 and 20:14; here John is simply shown the ultimate result of identification with the worship of the Beast.

3. *The eternity of the judgment* (v.11). That this judgment is neither temporary in duration nor reformatory in nature is seen in the language used. Expositors agree that the expression "forever and ever" is the strongest possible in the Greek language to express uninterrupted duration. It is repeated on a further ten occasions in this book. Even to link time with creation makes no difference, this expression unfolds the uninterruptedness of what is called "eternity". The dramatic "smoke of their torment" conveys the idea of conscious pain that admits no annihilation even as ages roll away. There can be neither alteration nor amelioration in this terrible burning. The language of human experience is searched to describe the indescribable. Uninterrupted continuance is expressed in the fact that "they have no rest"; what Christ offered they refused (Matt 11:28-29) and now they can never know it "day nor

night". No specious argument about "day or night" as time-related must be allowed to weaken the awful force of this eternal restlessness. The expression is used five times in this book and is simply the earthly way of expressing uninterruptedness (4:8; 7:15; 12:10; 20:10). Language cannot go further to express the thought of uninhibited, unchanging pain. The unceasing praise of worshippers of God (4:8) is to be contrasted with the unceasing pain of worshippers of the Beast. The identification marks of those who suffer in this way are repeated again to ensure that men realise the issue at stake when they listen to the call of the Beast.

The Comfort of the Saints — Cameo 5

12 Against the background of Beast-worship there are those who are called "the saints ". The present participle "that keep" defines the constancy of those keeping "the commandments of God and the faith of Jesus". They have responded to the word of God and believed in the Son of God. The authority of the Word and affection for the Son dominate their lives in the midst of satanic conditions. "The faith of Jesus" points to the faith placed in Jesus as its object; in spite of persecution they retain their confidence in Him. They hold on at the risk of their lives when everything of God and of Christ is under the ban of the Beast. Christian character will develop rapidly under such conditions as shown in the word "patience" which is better translated "endurance" (JND). Christ used the related verb when He said of conditions at this period: "He that shall endure to the end, the same shall saved" (Matt 24:13); the salvation is physical salvation into the millennial kingdom. The words of Christ in Matt 10:28 will have special relevance to saints at this period, "Fear not them which kill the body, but are not able to kill the soul, but rather fear him which is able to destroy both soul and body in hell". The word "hell" in Matt 10:28 is *gehenna* and corresponds with the "fire and brimstone" of v.10. It is better to endure physical death under the Beast than share eternal death with him.

13 The persecution and pain of these tried saints is noted by heaven. The voice that John heard "out of (*ek*) heaven" in 10:4, 8; 11:12; and in v.2 is now heard for the fifth time (the sixth and seventh times are recorded in 18:4 and 21:3). This message is not communicated through an angel but is a direct divine promise. The imperative almost seems to break into John's reverie and carries the snap of a divine command; he is told to "write". John is to write the divine assurance that those who die under the persecution of the Beast cannot, and do not, miss out on the bliss won by the Lamb. In fact they are specially favoured – men judged them worthy of death but heaven speaks of them as "blessed ones". This group are defined as "the dead which die in the Lord". The NT expression "in Christ" (1 Thess 4:16) is almost a technical expression describing the standing of believers of the church age, but the expression "in the Lord" defines a believer's state not his standing: i.e. how much place he gives Christ as Lord. To "die in the Lord" describes those who have given Jesus (see v.12) the place that God has given Him as Lord (Acts 2:36; Phil 2:11). Their public confession has brought them death. The expression "from henceforth", literally "from now" (*ap'arti*), shows that this is not a general statement, but has in view the persecuted and martyred saints from the midpoint of the tribulation until Christ comes to earth. These saints are given a special assurance.

This second of the seven beatitudes in this book (see comments at 1:3) is so important that for the first time the Holy Spirit adds His direct testimony to the voice from heaven. Only once more in this book will the Holy Spirit interject a personal word into the record; here it is an affirmation to saints, while on the other occasion in 22:17 He joins the church in a cry to the Saviour to come. "What the Spirit saith" to the seven churches is reported but these two urgent matters – a promise to saints and a plea to the Saviour – call for a direct word from the Holy Spirit. The message is simply an affirmation (Yea!) that there is both a rest and a reward for these saints who die. From the labours including the trials and the tears of tribulation conditions saints may have present rest. The verb "rest" and its noun in v.11 sets the two destinies in absolute and sharp contrast. Beast-worshippers will never rest again; those who give Christ His place as Lord may die for their faith but they will "rest" both now and forever. That rest will be enhanced by the recognition of their work for the Lord. The expression "their works follow with them" (JND) is an assurance that their position in the kingdom will be a direct result of their labours. The Lord will never allow to be forgotten what has been borne so honourably for Him in such adverse conditions.

The Gathering of Harvest — Cameo 6

14-16 With the familiar phrase, "And I looked, and behold", repeated from v.1 John sets this scene in contrast with the first scene. In the opening tableau followers of the Lamb are seen delivered, in these two closing scenes the followers of the Beast are seen doomed. There is in fact a double picture; one picture describes a harvest (vv.14-16) and the other a vintage (vv.17-19).

The question whether the harvest depicts blessing or judgment has been the subject of much debate. Many expositors have seen it as the in-gathering of saints into the kingdom. J. Heading writes positively, "In Rev 14, the angel is associated with the vintage ending in judgment, but the Son of man with the harvest. The first sickle and the harvest relate to men of faith on earth at the end of the great tribulation; see Isa 11:11 where 'the remnant of his people' are gathered in" (p. 161). Alford reaches the same conclusion but with considerable hesitation: "On the whole then, though I would not pronounce decidedly, I must incline to think that the harvest is the in-gathering of the saints, God's harvest, reaped from the earth, described here thus generally, before the vintage of wrath which follows".

The difficulty has arisen because the metaphor of the "harvest" is used in Scripture with different emphases. In some passages in the Gospels, as in

Matt 9:37-38; Luke 10:2; John 4:35, Christ used this metaphor to describe the age-long in-gathering of souls as the fruit of the sowing of Calvary. In this sense He is "the Lord of the harvest". In contrast Christ also used the metaphor in a narrower sense to describe a special period of discriminative judgment between the "wheat" and the "tares" as in Matt 13:30, "Let both grow together until the harvest: and in the time of harvest I will say to the reapers, Gather ye together first the tares, and bind them in bundles to burn them; but gather the wheat into my barn". In v.40 of this same passage the Lord interprets this as "therefore the tares are gathered and burned in the fire; so shall it be in the end of this world" (or as JND translates this last phrase "in the completion of the age"). It is suggested that this narrower aspect of the harvest is shown here to John. The harvest of Satan's sowing is to be reaped; men have become "overripe" for judgment and Christ now acts.

That this is a judgment scene is supported by three observations in the passage:-

1. The title of Christ – "like unto the Son of man". It is the same title as in 1:13 and carries the same implication of judgment; in ch. 1 the judgment is towards the churches; here it is towards the earth. There is no problem about Christ receiving orders from the angel when the symbolism of the book is understood; the angel "out of the temple" symbolises divine authentication from the holiness of God (see 11:19) for the commencement of the judgment timetable.
2. The verb "to dry" (*xēraniō*). This verb should be rendered "is withered". In none of the sixteen occurrences of the verb in the NT is it used in a good sense. Its consistent translation in connection with the seed (Matt 13:6), the fig tree (Matt 21:19, 20), the hand (Mark 3:1, 3) and the branch (John 15:6) is "withered". JND has the somewhat ambiguous "dried" but the RV "over-ripe" is clearer (RV margin "dried up"). In the longsuffering of God the tares have been permitted to ripen to the stage where holiness now demands the sickle of judgment on the harvest.
3. The Son of Man is seated on a white cloud. There is nothing in the passage to indicate that this is other than a literal cloud. The colour white stresses the righteousness of God and the parallel with the white horse (19:11) and the white throne (20:11) suggests judgment upon sinners.

The Son of man upon the white cloud reveals Christ as man, the appointed representative of deity (John 5:27) acting in the execution of divine judgment. The golden crown shows Him as the authorised ruler who through His victory over death (Heb 2:7) will bring earth to His feet in submission. The sharp sickle indicates that He is the accredited reaper. Where the adjective "sharp" is used, as in 2:12; 19:15, it indicates the incisive severity of the judgment. It is another indication that judgment is the subject of the passage.

15 Another angel, the fourth in the passage and the first of the second group of three, brings from "out of the temple" the command for executive action. This is the temple that was opened in 11:19 to show that the judgments of the last half of the week are the outcome of divine holiness being applied to earth; earth is judged from an opened temple. Angels have acted previously with the authority of the throne (8:3; 10:1-4); one is now dispatched from the temple to make clear in this symbolic way that the timing of these events is dictated by the throne and that Christ is acting with its authority. This is in keeping with Christ's own words, "But of that day and that hour knoweth no man, no, not the angels which are in heaven, neither the Son, but the Father" (Mark 13:32). The tense of the verbs "thrust" and "reap" fits in well with the RV which, with good manuscript authority reads, "for the hour to reap is come". The words "the hour" must be taken in the same sense as in v.7 and suggest that the harvest reaping takes place at the same time as the proclamation of the gospel. The harvest period is the whole of the last three and a half years of the tribulation when the great swathes of a judgment harvest are reaped. The blowing of the seven trumpets and the pouring of the seven bowls bring bundles of tares for the burning; Satan and his agents have sown and now earth must reap the terrible harvest. Consistency in translation demands that the verb "is ripe" be translated "is withered" or as in the RV "is over-ripe". There is no example in the sixteen times it is used in the NT or the fifty times it is used in the LXX of this verb being used in a good sense. "The harvest of the earth" is in itself a condemnatory phrase to be compared with "the vine of the earth" in the final cameo.

16 The Cloud-Sitter acts at the behest of the angelic messenger and in one simple statement the whole period of the judgment is covered: "and the earth was reaped". The aorist tense summarises the action in one statement while the passive voice suggests that Christ uses the agencies already described under the trumpets and the bowls. There is no doubt that at the very close of the period the angelic ministry of which Christ spoke in Matt 13:40-43 will be used to "gather out of his kingdom all things that offend, and them which do iniquity". All these actions are summed up in the one verb. To use the metaphorical language of the passage, the fields of earth are cleared of all that the enemy had sown.

The Treading of the Winepress — Cameo 7

17-19 Another angel issued from the temple (see v.15) and the sharp sickle in his hand indicates a further judgment scene. As did the Son of man, this angel awaits the direct command from heaven to commence the judgment. This is relayed by the sixth angel of the chapter who came out directly "from the altar". If the temple stresses the holiness of God which must be vindicated, the altar presents the provision of God that has been rejected by the Beast-worshippers; they will find that a God of light and a God of love must act in vindication of His own character. This altar is the brazen altar already seen in two earlier visions (6:9; 8:5). The cry of the martyred saints (6:9) for vengeance is now to be answered. The fire of the altar (8:5) is to bring the final judgment on a rebellious earth. This angel is described as having "authority (*exousia*) over fire". The article with fire may suggest that the fire previously mentioned at 8:3-5 is in view. The angels in control of the winds (7:1) speak of divine control over providential judgments on earth, while control over fire speaks of divine control over the direct judgments of God.

This command has to do with the ingathering of the clusters of grapes on "the vine of the earth". The vine has been a useful figure in Scripture to describe the testimony borne for God by the nation of Israel (Ps 80:8, 14-15; Isa 5:2-7; Jer 2:21; Ezek 17:5-8; Hos 10:1). The cultivation and care of that vine has been a major theme in prophecy. Christ used the same figure to describe the testimony on earth of Himself and believers in the church age (John 15:1-6). At the point of this vision the church has been removed from earth and the nation of Israel is under the control of the Beast (10:2) so it would be a mistake to link this vine with either Israel or the church. The article repeated in the expression "the vine of the earth" shows that it is testimony springing from earth and that belongs to earth. Israel according to Ps 80:8 was a vine "brought out of Egypt" to be the object of special care and protection. This vine is very much wider and represents the full ripening of ideas, philosophies and principles that spring from the soil of nature. Now the grapes, the fruit of this earth vine, are "fully ripe" (*ēkmasan*) or, as in JND, "fully ripened". This is to be distinguished from the word "ripe" (*exēranthē*) used of the harvest (v.15). Each fits the figure used: *exēranthē* ("dry" or "withered") depicts over-ripe grain, *ēkmasan* depicts grapes at "bursting point". In each case it is time to use the sickle.

"The harvest of the earth" and "the vine of the earth" are both described by Joel: "Put ye in the sickle, for the harvest is ripe: come, get you down; for the press is full, the fats overflow, for their wickedness is great" (Joel 3:13). The vintage in Israel was relatively short compared with the harvest, so great activity was compressed into a few weeks at the end of the summer. In the vintage the "clusters" are gathered quickly and cast into the winepress. The verb "gather" anticipates the gathering of the nations in 16:14-16. In the very closing stages of the tribulation period the nations of "the whole habitable world", or more exactly the armies of these nations, are gathered around Jerusalem "into a place called in the Hebrew tongue Armageddon". On the arrival of Christ this gathering at Armageddon will become, "the great winepress of the wrath of God". The similarity of the language of 19:15 is conclusive: "he treadeth the winepress of the fierceness and wrath of Almighty God". This is the winepress described by Jeremiah (25:30-31), by

Isaiah (63:1-4) and by Joel (3:13-16); it depicts the ultimate judgment of God executed by Christ upon the armies of earth gathered to destroy God's saints and resist God's Sovereign (19:16).

20 The symbolic picture is carried to its terrible outcome. With the grapes gathered there comes the treading of the winepress. A literal winepress was generally hewn out of the solid rock and consisted of two vats, an upper and a lower vat. Into the upper vat the grapes were thrown and were trodden upon to express the juice, which was then caught in the lower vat. The two vats are mentioned in Joel 3:13: "The press *(gath,* the upper vat) is full; the vats *(yekeb,* the lower vats) overflow". The upper vat was full of fruit and the lower vats full of the expressed juice (see Unger). Naturally the clothes of the person treading out the grapes would be stained by the juice. This is the figure used by Isaiah (63:1-6) to depict the Lord acting in judgment: "Wherefore art thou red in thine apparel, and thy garments like him that treadeth in the winefat?" (Isa 63:1-6). The word winefat *(gath)* refers to the upper vat where the grapes are thrown. The answer of the Lord makes the meaning of the winepress clear: "I have trodden the winepress alone; and of the people there was none with me, for I will tread them in mine anger, and trample them in my fury; and their blood shall be sprinkled upon my garments, and I will stain all my raiment. For the day of vengeance is in mine heart, and the year of my redeemed is come". This is clearly the prophetic picture that lies behind this scene of judgment.

The location of the winepress is given as "without the city". The city can hardly be any other than the city of Jerusalem. This city has already been seen as characterised by moral corruption (11:8); it has become the centre of the idolatrous worship of the Beast (13:14) and it becomes the centre around which the nations of earth gather (16:16). It is outside this city that the most devastating judgment in human history is to fall upon the armies of the world. The prophets in speaking of this judgment have made reference to a number of specific locations:

1. Isaiah has pointed to Bozrah in Edom, just to the east of the Jordan: "Who is this that cometh from Edom, with dyed garments from Bozrah?" (Isa 63:1-4).
2. Joel has identified the location as the valley of Jehoshaphat: "I will also gather all nations, and will bring them down into the valley of Jehoshaphat, and will plead with them there for my people and for my heritage Israel, whom they have scattered among the nations and parted my land" (Joel 3:2). Since there is no geographical valley known by this name in the vicinity of Jerusalem it could be that this is a historical reference to the great victory granted to king Jehoshaphat when surrounded by the Moabites and the Ammonites in the valley of

Berachah (2 Chron 20:26). The valley of Berachah lies just on the other side of Bethlehem towards Hebron about fifteen miles south of Jerusalem. Joel further identifies this valley: "Let the heathen be awakened and come to the valley of Jehoshaphat: for there will I sit to judge all the heathen round about. Put ye in the sickle; for the harvest is ripe: come, get you down; for the press is full, the fats overflow; for the wickedness is great. Multitudes, multitudes in the valley of decision: for the day of the Lord is near in the valley of decision" (Joel 3:12-14). Since "Jehoshaphat" means "Jehovah judges" the name may be a prophetic anticipation of the judgment to be executed here.

3. John identifies the location as Armageddon (16:16) which is interpreted in Newberry marginal note as *Har Megiddo* or "the mountain of a great multitude" or "the mountain of slaughter". If this is the Megiddo where Josiah died (2 Chron 35:24-25) to which Zechariah refers (Zech 12:11), then it is part of the plain of Esdraelon which lies about forty miles north of Jerusalem. It will be shown in comment on 16:16 that it is better to translate the word "Har-megadon" as "The mountain where troops gather" and interpret it as the mountains surrounding Jerusalem where the military forces of earth assemble.

Since all these references clearly refer to the same gathering of the nations it would seem that the whole land of Israel has become an armed camp. The city would seem to be either encircled, or almost encircled, since locations are mentioned to the east (Bozrah), to the north (Megiddo) and to the south (valley of Jehoshaphat). These armies may have gathered for differing reasons (see comments on 16:16) but they are now united in one purpose: to wipe out Jerusalem and her people and to resist the coming of the King. The winepress is indeed full; it only awaits the treading. The Lord Himself will do this in His coming.

Grape juice flowing from a literal winepress is the terrifying metaphor used to describe the effects of this judgment. The picture is of terrible carnage (19:21; 2 Thess 2:8). The AV "even unto" is a good translation of the preposition *achri* which can mean "as far as" and the picture may show the blood spurting, or splattering, as high as the horse bridles. The definite articles in the phrase "the bridles of the horses" at least suggest that John sees, symbolically, fully-equipped military forces gathered and destroyed. The final statement "by the space of a thousand and six hundred furlongs" shows how far this terrible destruction extends. The word "furlong" is the Greek *stadion* generally agreed to be about 607 feet. This gives a distance of 183.9 miles or, in round figures (given the uncertainty over the *stadion*) of 200 miles, which is the distance from Dan to Beersheba, the whole length of the present land of Israel. There is no reason to take this distance in any other than a literal sense.

CHAPTER 15

9. *The Seven Bowls Poured Out* 15:1-16:21

(a) *Interlude: The Temple Scene in Heaven (vv.1-8)*

v.1 "And I saw another sign in heaven, great and marvellous, seven angels having the seven last plagues; for in them is filled up the wrath of God.
v.2 And I saw as it were a sea of glass mingled with fire: and them that had gotten the victory over the beast, and over his image, and over his mark, and over the number of his name, stand on the sea of glass, having the harps of God.
v.3 And they sing the song of Moses the servant of God, and the song of the Lamb, saying, Great and marvellous are thy works, Lord God Almighty; just and true *are* thy ways, thou King of saints.
v.4 Who shall not fear thee, O Lord, and glorify thy name? for thou only art holy: for all nations shall come and worship before thee; for thy judgments are made manifest.
v.5 And after that I looked, and, behold, the temple of the tabernacle of the testimony in heaven was opened:
v.6 And the seven angels came out of the temple, having the seven plagues, clothed in pure and white linen, and having their breasts girded with golden girdles.
v.7 And one of the four beasts gave unto the seven angels seven golden vials, full of the wrath of God, who liveth for ever and ever.
v.8 And the temple was filled with smoke from the glory of God, and from his power; and no man was able to enter into the temple, till the seven plagues of the seven angels were fulfilled."

After the third parenthesis (chs. 12-14) the chronological movement of the book is resumed. Chs. 4-5 showed the throne in heaven as the background against which the Lamb opened the seven seals to commence the seven-year tribulation. The providential judgments of the seven seals then gave way to the seven trumpets that showed that heaven was at war with earth; the final three trumpets became the three "woe" judgments (8:13). With the seventh trumpet (11:15-19) the temple of God was opened in heaven and this temple becomes the background for the outpouring of the seven bowls which bring the tribulation to its close.

The temple scene is solemn and dramatic and is the heavenly interlude before earth's final agony. Four things are to be observed:

The Sign in heaven	v.1
The Sea in heaven	v.2
The Song in heaven	vv.3-4
The Sanctuary in heaven	vv.5-8

1 The word "sign" (*sēmeion*) recalls the earlier signs of the radiant woman

(12:1) and the great red dragon (12:3) and implies that there is a meaning in the picture beyond the merely visual. It is important to see that in this particular case the sign is composite and made up of three elements indicated by the threefold repetition of the verb "I saw" (vv.1,2,5 RV). The saints in v.2 and the song in vv.3-4 form the background for the emergence in v.5 of the seven angels with the seven bowls that are to be poured on earth from the smoke-filled temple. The meaning is clear – the punishment of sinners, in keeping with the holiness of God, may no longer be denied nor delayed and, at this stage, even priestly intercession is no longer permitted.

The previous signs (12:1,3) have presented in symbol the forces shaping history over the centuries. The sun-clothed woman symbolised the nation of Israel through whom would come the Christ; the dragon symbolised the implacable enemy of God anxious to destroy Christ and, failing this, the nation through whom He came. This third sign presents the final stages of earth's judgment drawing forth the praise of saints in anticipation of God's triumph over rebel men. Just as on the banks of the Red Sea Israel sang in triumph the song of Moses (Exod 15:1), so saints sing again when an enemy mightier than Pharaoh is defeated. The adjective "great" shows the importance of the sign (repeated from the first sign, 12:1) but the adjective "marvellous" draws attention to the awe-inspiring effect on the beholder. Apart from the repetition of this adjective in v.3 its only other occurrences in the NT are Matt 21:42; Mark 12:11; John 9:30; 2 Cor 11:14; 1 Pet 2:9. The fact that the sign is awe-inspiring ("marvellous") emphasises the composite nature of the sign. Other angels, and indeed other groups of seven angels (1:20; 8:1), have appeared previously, so this cannot be the whole sign. The repetition of the verb "I saw" in vv.2, 5 (AV translates "I looked", v.5) shows the additional factors; the saints on the sea of glass (v.2), the song in heaven (v.3) and the commissioning of the bowl-bearing angels (v.7) all form part of the sign. The sense could be conveyed in English by placing a colon after the word "marvellous".

There have been previous groups of seven angels, as the angels of the seven churches (1:20) or the seven angels with the trumpets (8:2), but there is no case for connecting these angels with any previous group. That these angels have "the seven last plagues" is their distinguishing feature. The word "plague" in Scripture is used to describe direct divine action on sin or sinners and has been used already to describe previous judgments, in the plural in 9:20 and in the singular in 11:6. The very use of this word recalls Egypt and the ten plagues that God brought on Pharaoh and the gods of Egypt, but now a far greater tyrant, of whom Pharaoh was but a picture, is to be dealt with. They are called the "last" plagues because they are the last series in the sequence of the seven seals and the seven trumpets; no others are to follow, for no more are needed. This is shown in the added explanation, "for in them is filled up the wrath of God". The verb "filled up" (*teleō*), which is translated "is finished" (RV); "is completed" (JND), implies not merely a cessation, but has the idea of "a conclusion arrived at" or "a goal reached". It means more than "ended" and implies that God's purpose in the judgment has been accomplished. The aorist tense is anticipative and indicates that what God has planned becomes a fact in history. The word for wrath (*thumos*) used ten times in the book, describes the outburst of anger or fury (sometimes translated "fierceness", 16:19; 19:15) that, in a public way, shows God's displeasure against sin; these seven plagues will be the final public demonstration of this anger of God.

2 John's eye moves to the second element in the sign, the sea of glass. Despite the fact that "sea" has no article this must be the same sea as in 4:6; it seems most unlikely that there should be two seas in heaven. In ch. 4 the sea is seen in relation to the throne; here it is seen in relation to the temple. A further difference is that this sea is "mingled with fire". The phrase "as it were" indicates that terms familiar on earth are being used to enable the picture to be conveyed more vividly. It was pointed out in the comments on 4:6 that this sea symbolises the crystallisation of the purposes of God in light of divine *righteousness,* seen in the throne of God. Here the commingling of fire shows that the outworking of these purposes on a sin-stained earth demands the execution of judgment in light of divine *holiness,* seen in the temple of God. Righteousness and holiness allow this sea to be peopled when God's goal is reached on earth by way of judgment. To have "standing" before the throne on the ground of righteousness and holiness means that those who stand here must be the redeemed. No longer need this sea stand empty as in 4:6; throne and temple are vindicated and the result is that the redeemed take their place on this sea.

Since the sea is in heaven and before the throne the company on it must be the martyrs who have died in the tribulation. The way in which the company is identified shows that it comprises not only the martyrs of 6:9 from "under the altar" (the martyrs of the first half of the tribulation), but the martyrs who have died since the image of the Beast was introduced into the temple in Jerusalem (the martyrs of the second half of the tribulation). It is to be seen as the completed martyr company just before the resurrection of 20:4; they are described as "them that had gotten the victory over the beast". This phrase in English is somewhat cumbersome; it translates a present participle (*tous nikō ntas*) that is really timeless and describes them as "victors" or "conquerors", showing heaven's assessment of those who have died under the regime of the Beast. This is a general statement which includes all who died during the seven-year period and is true even of the martyrs of the first half of the tribulation. The additional phrases expand particular aspects of that regime relating to the image, the mark and the number of the beast evident during the last half of the tribulation. These martyrs were described in 12:11 as those who "loved not their lives unto the death"; they had been engaged in that seemingly hopeless war against the Beast of 13:7: "And it was given unto him to make war with the saints, and to overcome them". Hailed now as conquerors and standing on the sea of glass, their song has been heard in 14:2 and learned by the 144,000 on earth. Having died for Christ they share their song with those who have lived for Him through the same period; a company in heaven and a company on earth sing of victory associated with the Lamb. Apart from the twenty-four elders (5:8) this is the only company in the book having harps. This enables them to be identified with the company whose voice was heard in 14:2. The word *kithara* ("harps"), which has given us "guitar" in English (see Vine), is an instrument of ten strings somewhat like the lyre (Josephus). It was noted for the sweetness of its music (Ps 81:2) and is a very fitting accompaniment to the singing of the redeemed.

Their victory is described in three ways: it is victory over the Beast and over his image and over the number of his name. The clause "over his mark" has little manuscript support and is omitted by most translations. The threefold repetition of "over" (*ek*), which would be better translated "from" (RV), shows the problems and the pressures that were put on these saints. The preposition *ek* following "overcomers" (victors) stresses the element of escape in their victory, even though the escape meant martyrdom. Multitudes on earth succumbed to the satanic imposture of the Beast; still others acquiesced politically and bowed to his image; others for purely commercial advantage accepted the number of his name. These saints stood apart and died for their separation; heaven calls them victors.

3 This dramatic moment that anticipates God's last judgments on earth demands a celebratory song and these martyred saints sing "the song of Moses the servant of God, and the song of the Lamb". The repetition of the words "the song" provide a very good grammatical reason for understanding that there are two songs in view. H.B. Swete insists that if there were only one song then the text would read "the song of Moses the servant of God and of the Lamb". The two songs celebrate two different aspects of the victory of the martyrs but they are in perfect harmony and fit the circumstances admirably. The reason so many commentators (Alford, Hendriksen) insist that there is only one song seems to be theological rather than exegetical: they suggest that Israel and the church unite harmoniously in this song of victory. It scarcely needs to be pointed out that this is faulty exegesis. The church is seen in the twenty-four elders while this company of martyrs are those from every nation who have died in the tribulation period after the church has been removed from earth at the rapture.

"The song of Moses" celebrates the *power* of redemption. The genitive "...of Moses" may be understood either as the song that Moses composed or the song that Moses sang. If the first view is taken then it could be argued that the reference is to the song of Moses (spoken of as such in Deut 31:30) recorded in Deut 32. Based on the parallels between these two songs a strong case can be presented for this identification. The faithfulness of God to His people to whom He will bring deliverance (Deut 32:9), the righteous character of God (Deut 32:4), the power of God to bring all nations under His authority (Deut 32:43) and the fact that God will avenge the blood of His people (Deut 32:41-43) all find echoes in this song. However the second view pointing back to the song that Moses sang on the banks of the Red Sea (Exod 15) seems a much more appropriate background. While language correspondences may not be so exact the theme is the same: victory over a mighty foe. In Exodus a plague-stricken Egypt is behind the people of Israel, the value of the blood of the lamb has been experienced and they have seen the mighty power of a Pharaoh overthrown in the Red Sea. What was national and historical in the past is now seen again on a far wider scale and these martyrs celebrate this mighty victory. They have escaped the plague-stricken empire of the Beast; they have experienced the value of the blood of the Lamb and the moment has arrived for the overthrow of a far mightier tyrant than Pharaoh.

This note of power is celebrated in two parallel statements which may be set out thus:

> "Great and marvellous are thy works, Lord God Almighty"
> "just and true are thy ways, thou King of saints".

The comparison between the works and the ways of deity echoes Ps 103:7: "He hath made known his ways unto Moses, his acts unto the children of Israel". "Great and marvellous" is a couplet occurring only in this chapter (see v.1) that defines the works of One who bears the title "the Almighty". The fact that this title is used nine times in the book and only once elsewhere in the NT, and that in a quotation (2 Cor 6:18), emphasises how the absolute power of deity will be displayed as never before in these tribulation times. Here it is the mighty deliverance experienced that causes such an ascription of praise from the redeemed. In the second statement the ways of God are seen as "just" and "true", words that are an echo of the character of God Himself (6:10; 19:2). The ways of God are "right" by an absolute standard and they are "real", genuinely in keeping with His character. This ascription of praise is to the "King of nations" (see JND and RV marg). "King of saints" has weak manuscript support and the RV "King of the ages" is very doubtful. The title "King of nations" is a direct quotation from Jer 10:6-7: "Forasmuch as there is none like unto thee, O Lord; thou art great, and thy name is great in might. Who would not fear thee, O King of nations?" This sovereignty over the nations becomes clearer in the following notes of praise where "fear" and the "name" are linked as in the quotation. The point emphasised is that, despite the rebellion of men, the Almighty is recognised by these saints as the supreme Ruler, who will establish His kingdom over all nations.

4 "The song of the Lamb" celebrates the *person* of the Redeemer. The works and ways of the Almighty acting through history as the King of the nations demand "fear" and "glory" from men. Israel failed nationally in this very respect (Mal 1:6). Now through what God has done in Christ the recognition of His lordship is the touchstone of fear and respect Godward. This is no longer national but worldwide in its scope as men seek salvation through the Lamb. This is why the praise in this second part of the song centres on Christ. This may be shown as follows:

> "Who shall not fear thee, O Lord,
> and glorify thy Name?
> for (*hoti*) thou only (*monos*) art holy:
> for (*hoti*) all nations shall come and worship before thee:
> for (*hoti*) thy judgments are made manifest".

The tense of the verb fear may be rendered "come to fear" (Alford) pointing to the moment of conversion from which men "will give glory" (future tense) to His name. It is reminiscent of the moment when in the experience of men the knee is bowed and Christ given His place as Lord "to the glory of God the Father" (Phil 2:9-11). The rhetorical question, in two parts, invites the answer, "No one". Not only is this true in personal conversion but these singers anticipate the day when no one can fail to respond to the exaltation of Christ. Three reasons are given for such universal acclamation, each introduced by "for" (*hoti*). First is the absolute uniqueness of deity shown in Christ. No other has such a claim to present to the nations. The Beast and the false prophet have been shown by the events at the close of the tribulation to be satanic counterfeits. The word "only" (*monos*) can readily be missed but it is the key word; none other can claim to be "holy" (*hosios*). This is the Jehovah of the ministry of Isaiah (Isa 5:16; 6:3; 57:15) seen in Christ. The word *hosios* is the most comprehensive word translated "holy" in the NT and occurs again once in this book (16:5). According to Vine it signifies "what is religiously right, holy, as opposed to what is unrighteous or polluted". It defines the unique unapproachable majesty of deity and in its meaning goes beyond what is sacred (*hieros*), what is set apart for God (*hagios*) or even what is free from defilement (*hagnos*). This word *hosios* defines an essential uniqueness that belongs to deity alone. Men turn from the blasphemy and idolatry of tribulation conditions to "fear the Lord" and "give glory to the name" for now they see that to do anything else is idolatry. His name here is not a name that He bears but refers to the acknowledgement of the revelation of who He is.

The rhetorical question in the song is answered by the second "for". The victors recognise that they are but the forerunners of a far wider company. Now the term universal applies, not to the idolatrous rule of the Beast, but to the exaltation of Christ. In tribulation days, when these martyrs died for their faith, comparatively few gave Christ His place as Lord. Now with Christ's universal exaltation all nations shall come and worship before Him. This is the theme of prophecy and is re-emphasised in this victor's song. Worship, formerly given to idols and claimed by the Beast, will be offered through Christ to God. The words of the Psalm are explicit, "Yea, all kings shall fall down before him, all nations shall serve him" (Ps 72:11).

The third "for" gives the reason for this miraculous conversion that leads to universal worship. Judgments (*dikaiōmata*) is admirably rendered in the Newberry margin "righteous judgments". This does not refer to the deliverance of these saints but to the divine actions taken throughout the tribulation period to purge the earth of the satanic usurper and his earthly puppets. The deliverance is a consequence of the judgments of the seals, of the trumpets and of the bowls, although they have not yet been poured out. "Are made manifest", rendered in the RV "have been made manifest", is the prophetic anticipation of the final righteous judgments of God in the last plagues about to be poured out. Men will see at this point that God has acted in perfect righteousness in these acts of judgment.

It is to be noted that these martyrs do not sing of their own endurance, their own experience nor even their own victory over the Beast. They are occupied rather with the power of redemption and the person of the Redeemer, and in the acknowledgement of the sovereignty, righteousness and holiness of God. He alone is worthy of worship through the Lamb.

5-6 The third and final element in this sign-scene brings from John the exclamation of surprise, "behold". In 4:1 a door was opened in heaven; in 11:19 the temple of God in heaven was opened; now "the temple of the tabernacle of the testimony in heaven" was opened to John's gaze. It would seem from the careful language used that these words describe the innermost shrine (*ho naos*) of heaven, the very dwelling place of deity. This is "heaven itself" (Heb 9:24) where a Man has entered on the ground of blood. "The temple (*ho naos*) of the tabernacle (*tēs skēnēs*) of the testimony (*tou marturiou*)" is virtually a combination of Num 10:11 with Exod 25:22. "The tabernacle of the testimony" and "the ark of the testimony" have found their answer in Christ, described as "A minister of the sanctuary, and of the true tabernacle, which the Lord pitched, and not man" (Heb 8:2). This interim abode of deity ("the tent") will give way to the eternal city dwelling of 21:1-4 when God's purposes for earth are complete. At this point in the tribulation, seven angels come forth commissioned for the execution of judgment on earth.

The seven angels of v.1 – the article identifies them as the same group – emerge in solemn stately order from the inner shrine (clearly man is not allowed to peer into that sacred place) "having the seven plagues". This expression is an identifying phrase from v.1; their actual commissioning will be given in the next verse. "Clothed" and "girded" are terms used of the Son of man (1:13); as He acted for God in priestly ministry, these angels act in the same way for God. The "linen" is "pure" and "bright" or "glistening", reflecting the "righteous judgments" of God (v.4). The golden girdles round the breasts suggest urgent priestly service not in blessing but in judgment for the glory of God.

7 Having emerged from the innermost shrine the seven angels are positioned to receive their public commissioning from the throne. In the symbolism of the book they are linked with both the temple and the throne. One of the four living creatures associated with the throne gives to the angels "seven golden vials". While the English "vial" does come directly from the word *phialē* it does not convey a correct picture of the vessel in view. A much more accurate picture is conveyed by JND and the RV translation "bowls" which should be substituted for the twelve occurrences of this word in the book. In the LXX *phialē* is found in Exod 27:3; Num 4:14 where the AV has "basons". According to W. Kelly the word describes the saucer-shaped vessels with a handle that were used to pour drink offerings over the sacrifices on the altar. A vessel of this shape could be completely emptied in one movement. With the temple background this seems a useful suggestion, while the fact that the bowls are of gold stresses that the glory of God will be revealed in their out-pouring. The prayers of the saints presented in the golden bowls (6:8) of an earlier vision are now replaced with these bowls brimming with divine judgment. The two scenes form an instructive contrast at two different time-points in the tribulation period.

The bowls are "full", a descriptive word picturing the brimming over condition, as if no more could be pressed into the vessel. The contents are described as "the wrath of God" where the word *thumos* implies an outburst of righteous indignation against sin and unrepentant sinners (see v.1) seen in these final judgments. While this blazing anger is seen in time it originates in God who is outside of time and is described as living "to the ages of ages" (JND). While the Beast and his followers will die and yet exist in pain "to the ages of ages" (14:11) the self-existing One will live timelessly.

8 The final act in this drama, preparatory to the out-pouring of the seven bowls, recalls many OT crisis scenes when God drew near to men. The temple "was filled" with smoke. This is the visible manifestation arising out of "the glory of God" and arising out of "his power". Men cannot gaze directly upon the glory of God nor scrutinise His power so the smoke while it manifests also conceals lest men be destroyed. This is the idea in Exod 19:18; 40:34 when God would show His presence to men. What was seen at the dedication of the tabernacle (Exod 40:34-35) was seen also at the dedication of the temple (1 Kings 8:10-12) and was the experience of Isaiah at a later date (Isa 6:4). The glory of God and the power of God are awesome in their manifestation.

The final note in this scene stresses the inescapable and inevitable judgment about to be poured out on the earth. The lesson to be drawn from the smoke-filled temple is spelled out very plainly: "No man was able to enter into the temple, till the seven plagues of the seven angels were fulfilled". This indicates symbolically that God will not permit any intercession in the period of the bowl judgments. The words of Lam 3:44 in the days when God judged rebellious Jerusalem are relevant: "Thou hast covered thyself with a cloud, that our prayer should not pass through". Now in this later day when God judges earth, He rules out any intercession. When the smouldering fires of God's wrath arising from His glory and His power are about to erupt in volcanic fashion God is absolutely unapproachable. This period of "no intercession" lasts until the seven plagues "should be finished" (*teleō*). The repetition of the same verb as in v.1 shows the seven plagues poured out on earth. In these plagues the purposes of God have reached their goal and are complete.

CHAPTER 16

The opening of the seals commenced the tribulation period on earth; action has been initiated by the Lamb to recover the inheritance. Of those judgments men will use the word *providential*, but after the scroll is opened and the next series of judgments begins, this mental escape will no longer be possible. The seven trumpets will show men that God has declared war on rebellious men: the word *retributive* accurately describes the judgments they introduced. Now, in this final series of judgments these seven bowls will show men the penal results of sin; men will know the *punitive* action of God upon a guilty earth. The seals produced a measure of anticipatory fear (6:15-17) without any sign of repentance; the more severe warning of the trumpets but hardened men in their sin (9:20-21); now God in the vindication of His character must act in punitive judgment. Already commissioned in the previous chapter (15:7) the seven angels prepare to pour out the judgments.

The saucer-shape of the golden bowls hints that the judgments are sudden in their onslaught and swift in their action. The out-pouring of the drink-offering (Gen 35:14: Exod 29:40; Lev 23:13) over the sacrificial victim on the altar was in a single movement. Earth is pictured as the victim ready for the sacrifice and swiftly bowl after bowl is emptied over it so that the whole period may be limited to days or at the most weeks. This sense of urgency in the successive judgments is heightened by the omission of the word "angel" in most manuscripts after v.1, so that the first, the second, the third etc. stand starkly alone; Bengel's comment on this omission is to the point, "The vials make short work".

Attention has already been drawn to the telescopic nature of the different series of judgments (see introduction to ch. 6). The seventh seal when expanded comprises the seven trumpets and the seventh trumpet expanded comprises the seven bowls. A comparison between the seven trumpet judgments and these seven bowls may be noted thus:-

		Trumpets		Bowls
1.	8:7	upon (*eis*) the earth	16:2	upon (*eis*) the earth
2.	8:8	into (*eis*) the sea	16:3	upon (*eis*) the sea
3.	8:10	upon (*epi*) the rivers	16:4	upon (*epi*) the rivers
4.	8:12	the sun was smitten	16:8	upon (*epi*) the sun
5.	9:2	the air was darkened	16:10	his kingdom was full of darkness
6.	9:14	the great river Euphrates	16:12	the great river Euphrates
7.	11:19	an earthquake	16:18	a great earthquake

While the resemblances are evident, the bowls are not to be understood as a mere recapitulation of the trumpets on a wider scale. There is both intensification and enlargement but major differences indicate that the bowls have a finality not seen in the trumpets:

1. The trumpet judgments were restricted to a third part of the areas affected but the bowl judgments affect all of earth (with the exception of the fifth bowl – the limitation there is with divine purpose).
2. Under the trumpet judgments individual men were affected indirectly; under the bowl judgments men are affected directly. In fact the last three bowl judgments make it clear that heaven is directly at war with one person – the Beast and the satanic trinity which he represents. All associated with him must face the penal consequences of accepting the claims of the Beast as the wrath of God is poured out upon earth.

(b) *The Seven Bowls (vv.1-21)*

v.1 "And I heard a great voice out of the temple saying to the seven angels, Go your ways, and pour out the vials of the wrath of God upon the earth.
v.2 And the first went, and poured out his vial upon the earth; and there fell a noisome and grievous sore upon the men which had the mark of the beast, and upon them which worshipped his image.
v.3 And the second angel poured out his vial upon the sea; and it became as the blood of a dead man: and every living soul died in the sea.
v.4 And the third angel poured out his vial upon the rivers and fountains of waters; and they became blood.
v.5 And I heard the angel of the waters say, Thou art righteous, O Lord, which art, and wast, and shalt be, because thou hast judged thus.
v.6 For they have shed the blood of saints and prophets, and thou hast given them blood to drink; for they are worthy.
v.7 And I heard another out of the altar say, Even so, Lord God Almighty, true and righteous are thy judgments.
v.8 And the fourth angel poured out his vial upon the sun; and power was given unto him to scorch men with fire.
v.9 And men were scorched with great heat, and blasphemed the name of God, which hath power over these plagues: and they repented not to give him glory.
v.10 And the fifth angel poured out his vial upon the seat of the beast; and his kingdom was full of darkness; and they gnawned their tongues for pain,
v.11 And blasphemed the God of heaven because of their pains and their sores, and repented not of their deeds.

v.12 And the sixth angel poured out his vial upon the great river Euphrates; and the water thereof was dried up, that the way of the kings of the east might be prepared.
v.13 And I saw three unclean spirits like frogs come out of the mouth of the dragon, and out of the mouth of the beast, and out of the mouth of the false prophet.
v.14 For they are the spirits of devils, working miracles, *which* go forth unto the kings of the earth and of the whole world, to gather them to the battle of that great day of God Almighty.
v.15 Behold, I come as a thief. Blessed *is* he that watcheth, and keepeth his garments, lest he walk naked, and they see his shame.
v.16 And he gathered them together into a place called in the Hebrew tongue Armageddon.
v.17 And the seventh angel poured out his vial into the air; and there came a great voice out of the temple of heaven, from the throne, saying. It is done.
v.18 And there were voices, and thunders, and lightnings; and there was a great earthquake, such as was not since men were upon the earth, so mighty an earthquake, and so great.
v.19 And the great city was divided into three parts and the cities of the nations fell: and great Babylon came in remembrance before God, to give unto her the cup of the wine of the fierceness of his wrath.
v.20 And every island fled away, and the mountains were not found.
v.21 And there fell upon men a great hail out of heaven, every stone about the weight of a talent: and men blasphemed God because of the plague of the hail; for the plague therefore was exceeding great."

1 From the opened (15:5), smoke-filled (15:8) temple where no creature may enter comes the command to the seven angels that will set in motion the final judgments of "the great and terrible day of the Lord" (Joel 2:31). Since the "great voice" comes from the temple it must be that of God; only deity can authorise these climactic judgments. This is confirmed in v.17 where the great voice is heard again and is said to come, not only from the temple, but from the throne. It is worth noting that the adjective "great" occurs eleven times in this chapter. The verb "pour out" is familiar from its association with the sending of the Holy Spirit (Acts 2:17, 18, 33) but this is a very different "out-pouring" from heaven. It has already been shown that the translation "bowls" is better than the AV's "vials" not only as a more accurate representation of the saucer-shaped vessels but as a reminder of the temple and the ark (11:19) and of the altar (v.7). These bowls contain the "wrath (*thumos*) of God" – the concentrated blaze of the righteous anger of God against sin and sinners in the earth. The "earth" here must be taken in a general sense as including all land, sea, and rivers affected by the following bowls. There is no justification in the context for placing any limitation upon it either physically or politically; it cannot be confined to either the Mediterranean earth or the Roman Empire – it is all that men understand by the expression "the planet earth".

Bowl One: Cancer of the Skin

2 The first angel did exactly as commanded, pouring his bowl "upon (*eis*) the earth". Since the sea and the rivers are the objects of the following out-pourings it seems reasonable to assume that the word earth is used here in a more restricted sense than in v.1 and should be understood as the dry land where men live. The immediate result is that men are affected by "a noisome and grievous sore". "The men" (*anthrōpos*) embraces both men and women but the plague is restricted to those identified with the Beast: "upon the men which had the mark of the beast and upon them which worshipped his image". Grammatically a case could be made for dividing this company into those having the mark and those worshipping his image. However comparison with v.9 (see JND) suggests that it is better to see simply two identification marks of the Beast-worshippers: they have his mark and they worship his image. The divine discrimination of this judgment recalls the Egyptian plagues (Exod 9:6, 11, 26 etc). The only other occurrence of the word "sore" (*helkos*) in the NT is in Luke 16:21 but the word recalls the sixth plague upon Egypt where the LXX uses this word, translated into English as "boil". The adjectives "noisome and grievous" though somewhat dated are graphic; a modern translation gives "ugly and painful"; Alford understands the combined terms as "bad in itself and painful to the sufferers". What is envisaged is clearly a boil or sore, possibly a malignant ulcer, hideous in appearance and painful in the extreme, breaking out in the skin of men. John Phillips speaks of this plague as "cancer of the skin". Developing this thought Henry Morris suggests that since it is confined to those having the mark of the Beast, it may well be that God allows the laser beam or radioactive ray used in their branding to become a tool of judgment. While the means that God uses is not given, it is clear that the plague spreads rapidly through the ranks of the Beast-worshippers.

Commentators who refuse a literal interpretation to these judgments have great problems with this plague. W. Scott (p. 323) is a representative of this school and puts the best case when he writes, "We judge that the plagues of our chapter must be understood symbolically in keeping with the general character and design of the book. What is signified is a *moral* sore which will cause intense mental suffering" (author's own italics). What is meant by "a moral sore" is somewhat difficult to understand. It is more in keeping with the design of this book to allow Scripture to mean what it says, especially when there is not the slightest hint in the language or context that a meaning other than the literal is to be sought.

Bowl Two: Corruption of the Sea

3 Without any further word from heaven, since the command has already been given, the second angel empties his bowl "upon the sea" better translated by the RV as "into the sea". It will be recalled that under the second trumpet one third of the sea "became blood". The cause of that catastrophe was a "mountain burning with fire" cast into the sea; God had allowed a heavenly body of some kind, possibly a meteorite or asteroid, to crash into the sea. No explanation of this plague is given; God may use similar means again or some other naturally-occurring catastrophe, or He may use some totally-unexpected source to cause the sea to "become blood". The language suggests a catastrophe of worldwide scope; there is no need to restrict this to the Mediterranean sea. Not only does the sea become as blood but the blood is described as that "of a dead man". The function of the blood in a living person is described in Lev 17:11: "The life of the flesh is in the blood". It carries life-sustaining oxygen to all parts of the body. In death blood becomes a congealing mass of stinking chemicals repulsive and nauseating. This is the blood pictured under this judgment where "as" emphasises that appearance and effect are in view. In this toxic sea nothing can survive. In the first plague in Egypt when the fresh waters of the river became blood, all "the fish that was in the river died and the river stank" (Exod 7:19-21). Now an ecological disaster on a world scale leaves all marine life dead. Billions of sea creatures, the vertebrates and invertebrates, the sea mammals as well as the fish, meet sudden death and their decomposing bodies strewn on all the beaches of earth must cause a stench greater than Egypt ever knew.

The symbolic interpretation is curiously unsatisfying even when presented by able expositors. W. Scott may again be quoted: "The sea 'became blood' is not a physical fact, as it is in the Egyptian plague (Exod 7:17-25), when the Nile, the justly-celebrated river of Egypt, with its canals, streams and tributaries, was turned into blood literally and actually. But in the Vial Plague the sea becoming blood points symbolically to a scene of moral death. Christianity, or at least what then represents it, is abandoned. So complete and thorough is the apostasy that the blood (life, moral or physical, as the case may be) is 'as of a dead man'". He goes on to explain "Every living soul died" as, "Each mere professor makes shipwreck of faith, of conscience, of truth, and gives up every vestige of religious profession. The apostasy and alienation from God are complete, not one left, save those that are real and whose names are in the Lamb's book of life". It may be sufficient to point out that this interpretation makes this judgment of God very little different from what has occurred repeatedly down the ages as men have turned away from truth. Men "having their conscience seared with a hot iron" (1 Tim 4:2) may reflect "moral death" in the church age but even their wide-spread prevalence in the tribulation time would hardly justify speaking of nations as becoming "blood". Such a view raises a host of unanswerable questions, does not do justice to the text and seriously weakens the impact of one of God's most terrible judgments upon earth.

Bowl Three: Contamination of Springs

4 As the third angel empties his bowl another hammer blow of divine judgment falls upon earth. This time the rivers and "fountains of waters" are smitten. Under the third trumpet a third part of earth's water supplies were affected by the fallen star which had blazed a path through the atmosphere (8:10-11), but under this plague there is no restriction and all the water supplies of earth "became blood". What John saw in the vision was the striking visible change from water to blood. Whether the language of appearance demands literal blood or whether micro-organisms introduced by meteorites bring about chemical changes to give water sources this colour is largely irrelevant. Speculation cannot solve the problem; God is judging earth and a mark of that judgment is "blood". That this plague affected the sources and supplies of drinking water of earth is clear from the comment of the angel in v.6. The judgment upon the sea in the previous plague would not necessarily interfere immediately with the processes of evaporation, condensation and precipitation which would still provide pure water for the rivers and the reservoirs and thus provide drinking water for men and animals. These rivers and reservoirs would have supplied men during the drought in the first half of the tribulation (11:6) but now they fall under divine judgment. Whether their supplies come from surface rivers or underground springs (*pēgē*) created by God Himself (14:6-7), men find that suddenly the water essential for life is undrinkable. No hint is given in the text as to what causes this contamination but the God who turned the waters bitter under the third trumpet can turn these same waters into blood under this third bowl. With all the technology of earth at his disposal the Beast will find it hard to find potable water for his kingdom just as King Ahab did in the time of Elijah (1 Kings 18:5-6). Perhaps this is the very time when the cup of cold water becomes very precious indeed (Matt 10:42). The saints that come through this terrible plague in the tribulation period and enter the millennial kingdom will have special delight in the "living fountains of waters" (7:17) to which the Lamb will lead them.

It may be pointed out that the judgment under this bowl offers incidental confirmation that the dramatic ministry of the two witnesses (11:3-8) occurs in the first half of the seven year tribulation period. In that early period the miracle of turning water into blood would be a dramatic divine confirmation of their ministry but it would also be a terrible warning of what lay ahead for earth. In these days near the climax of the tribulation when the sea is blood, rivers run with blood and springs pour out blood, such a miracle would scarcely be noticed.

A Parenthetic Interpolation

5-7 This book gives remarkable insights into the normally-hidden administration of the cosmos; angels govern the winds (7:1); an angel is said to have authority over fire (14:18) and here "the angel of the waters", the very angel possibly who has responsibility for the implementation of the plague, bows in acknowledgement of the righteous action of God. Men will bitterly complain and blaspheme (v.9) but a holy angel bows in worship. The translation of JND reflects the most authentic manuscripts and is to be preferred "Thou art righteous, who art and wast, the holy one, that thou hast judged so". This terrible judgment reflects the righteous character of God – for He is the Holy One (*hosios*). The emphasis falls upon the holy character of God, who is still the Holy One when the plague falls; He is the One who is eternally holy. The uniqueness of the essential holiness of God is embraced in this word *hosios* which is used only twice in this book (see comments on 15:4). The aorist tense of the verb "judged" along with the plural demonstrative pronoun "thus" (*tauta*) points dramatically to the out-pouring of the third bowl upon "the rivers and fountains of waters".

The principle of Scripture "an eye for an eye, and a tooth for a tooth" (Deut 19:21; Gal. 6:7) already observed in 13:10 operates again in the case of the bowls. Blood to drink is a fitting judgment upon those who have shed blood. The verb "shed" is the same verb *ekcheō* as used for the pouring of the bowls; sinners poured out blood, God pours out His judgment upon them. The scales of divine justice are evenly balanced. When men give worship to the Beast they share his guilt for the war of extermination waged against the saints and prophets in the last half of the tribulation; this is the company for whom the martyrs of the first half of the tribulation were instructed to wait (6:11). These saints who die are "fellow servants and brethren" in relation to the first company; in relation to their witness for God they are called "saints and prophets". The prophets in 11:18 have been shown to be the OT prophets and the order is "prophets and saints" as would be expected; here the order is "saints and prophets" for God would use believers of this tribulation age in this office following in the steps of the two witnesses who are called prophets (11:10). That there were true prophets will be the background for the claims of the "false prophet" (19:20; 20:10). The phrase "they are worthy" fittingly described faithful saints under Sardian conditions (3:4); it is a terrible indictment that this same phrase is used to describe sinners under the judgment of heaven. They have proved themselves worthy recipients of divine judgment.

7 Suddenly and unexpectedly John hears the voice of the altar acquiescing in this judgment of the angel of the waters. The RV and JND rightly omit the words "another out of" that suggest an angelic messenger from the altar; very possibly this was a scribe's marginal note that became incorporated into later texts. God allows the brazen altar under which had been resting the souls of the martyrs (6:9) to become the mouthpiece of all the blood that has been shed there down the ages because of sin. This altar has been associated with judgment in this book (6:9; 8:5; 14:18) and now appears for the last time to voice this testimony to a righteous God who is addressed in the fulness of His deity. There is absolute authority in the Lord, the Jehovah of old now seen in Jesus enthroned as Lord; He bears the "name that is above every name" and all will acknowledge that "Jesus Christ is Lord" (Phil 2:11), the One to whom all judgment has been committed (John 5:22-23). Humanity is joined with deity so that He is worshipped as God, absolute in His deity. The omnipotence belonging to deity is fittingly addressed as "Almighty", a suitable ascription of worship amid the crash of civilisation as the just judgments of heaven fall upon men. "True and righteous" (*alēthinai kai dikaiai*) are words that reveal that the essence (true) of the judgments as well as their very nature (righteous) and reflect God Himself. In 15:4 the word "judgments" (*dikaiōmata*) is associated with the verb "manifest" and indicates that the character of God Himself is seen in the acts of judgment themselves; in the present context, the word is *krisis* and could be translated "sentences". The sentences that God passes are always in keeping with His character – "true and righteous". Mythology is full of the vengeful and capricious acts of pagan deities but the only true God always acts in keeping with His character – righteously.

Bowl Four: Consumption by the Sun

8 Under the fourth trumpet the heavenly bodies were partially darkened so that there was a reduction in the energy reaching the earth from the sun. As the fourth bowl is poured out upon (*epi*) the sun the opposite effect is produced. The sunlight falling on earth is so increased that men are scorched "with fire". Since "men" has the article it would be normal to understand it as embracing all mankind (Alford). However the article may well point back to the men already mentioned in v.2 as "the men which had the mark of the beast". This would mean that in some way not explained God allows this plague to be directed upon Beast-worshippers only and protects others as He did under the Egyptian plagues. This interpretation has support from the next verse when "the men", presumably the same men, are seen to blaspheme. The verb "scorch" (*kaumatizō*) is used again in v.9 and in the parable of the sower (Matt 13:6; Mark 4:6) and presents a graphic picture of wheat on the rocks withering under a blazing sun. To make sure that the literal picture is plain the words "with fire" add a terrifying dimension – the very atmosphere seems to be on fire.

It is clear that the fourth trumpet and the fourth bowl judgment are part of the signs of which the Lord spoke in Luke 21:25: "And there shall be signs in the sun, and in the moon, and in the stars". There is no reason to interpret the Lord's words in any symbolic sense and here the literal understanding of the judgment is the only credible interpretation. To interpret the sun as a "supreme ruler" scorching his own subjects makes very little sense.

The temporary darkening of the heavenly bodies (8:12) and then the upsurge of radiant energy under this bowl will provide a great test of the ingenuity of the scientists of the tribulation period. Even within the last few decades theories concerning the origin of the energy of the sun and the stars have changed. Recent discoveries have caused scientists to revert to Sir Isaac Newton's theory and scientific opinion is at present divided as to whether the sun will burn out or die out. Nevertheless no matter what theories scientists use to explain these stellar phenomena Scripture simply states, "It was given unto it to scorch men with fire" (RV). The verb "given" stresses divine permission no matter what the actual mechanism may be, and in this will be the literal fulfilment of Isa 24:6: "Therefore the inhabitants of the earth are burned, and few men left". This statement from Isaiah comes in a passage of sober prose and cannot be explained away by either poetic licence or dramatic hyperbole and is fully supported by Isa 30:26: "Moreover the light of the moon shall be as the light of the sun, and the light of the sun shall be sevenfold, as the light of seven days". It may also be that Mal 4:1 deserves a more literal interpretation than is generally allowed: "For, behold, the day cometh that shall burn as an oven; and all the proud, yea, and all that do wickedly, shall be stubble; and the day that cometh shall burn them up, saith the Lord of hosts, that it shall leave them neither root nor branch". The physical blessing of those who enter the millennial earth will stand in sharp contrast to these terrible tribulation days when it is said of the followers of the Lamb, "neither shall the sun light on them, nor any heat".

9 A repetition of men (with the article) pinpoints again the Beast-worshippers, and the repetition of the scorching, this time "with great heat", stresses the dreadful severity of what has befallen them. This is far more severe than a mere heatwave, and the implied consequences, including the melting of the polar ice-caps and the subsequent flooding, must bring worldwide devastation. Men at this stage seem to have reached the point when they no longer try to explain away these things; they are under no delusion and know that God is directly responsible. Sadly even this realisation does not bring admission of sin and repentance. The evolutionary lie that allowed men to believe that the existence of a Creator-God was mere religious invention has been swept away and scientific materialism has been exposed in its helplessness, but men still refuse to bow the knee to this mighty God with whom they are now face to face. Instead they "blasphemed the name of God". The propaganda of the Beast (13:6) is taken up by his followers. Not only privately but publicly through the news media on every television screen and radio-channel men will speak disparagingly of God; refusing to accept any responsibility they will blame Him for the calamities befalling earth and use this as an excuse to support the man of sin. "They repented not" is the scriptural record as they refuse to admit their sin as the first step to taking sides with God. To do this would be "to give him glory". The everlasting gospel demanded this (14:7) and, out of fear, some had done this at an earlier stage in the tribulation (11:13) but now, like Pharaoh of old (Exod 8:32), hearts are hardened and men plunge to destruction.

As in the seven seal judgments, and again in the seven trumpets, there is an obvious break in the bowl series dividing them into four and three. The first four form one group and the final three are somewhat different. In the first four bowls different parts of creation are affected: men have skin cancer, the sea is corrupted, the streams are contaminated, the sun is stricken with a terrible catastrophe. In the last three bowls the creature is directly affected and especially the followers of the Beast; they become the special targets of divine justice. Notice how the blows fall:

Bowl 5	The Kingdom of the Beast	Darkened	vv.10-11
Bowl 6	The Power of the Beast	Disclosed	vv.12-16
Bowl 7	The Capital of the Beast	Destroyed	vv.17-21

Bowl Five: The Kingdom of the Beast Darkened

10-11 The darkening of the air under the fifth trumpet has been shown from the context to symbolise a satanic attack unleashed from the abyss upon men. Under the pouring out of the fifth bowl a terrible physical darkness settles upon the kingdom of the Beast. This darkness is just as physical as the darkness in Egypt under the ninth plague (Exod 10:21-23). Like that early plague it is centred upon a specific geographic area outside of which conditions seem to be normal. "The seat of the beast" is better translated "the throne of the beast" (JND). Of the 61 occurrences of *thronos* in the NT it is rendered "throne" 54 times. In six verses in this book it is translated "seat" (2:13; 4:4 (twice); 11:16; 13:2; 16:10). The AV translators commendably sought to emphasise centralised authority in a physical location of earth and it is this city upon (*epi*) which the bowl is poured. Thus from this as centre, a darkness engulfs the kingdom, which in this instance should be seen as more restricted geographically than the empire. The Beast to whom Satan has given a throne (13:2) finds his administrative capital in darkness. A better translation of "full of darkness" (*eskotōmenē*) would be "plunged into darkness". The dramatic language presents the picture of a city ablaze with a multitude of lights suddenly being plunged into darkness. Satan in the OT is shown to be "Lucifer son of the morning" (Isa 14:12); now his limitation of power is seen worldwide in that he is unable to keep light in the capital city of his puppet prince. It is totally meaningless to try to refer to this darkness as "moral darkness". Moral darkness has already spread across the world through Babylonish religion and it may well be in answer to that moral darkness that God sends this physical darkness upon the kingdom of the Beast to show men that choosing darkness rather than light (John 3:19) has inescapable consequences. The Creator God who "maketh darkness and it is night" (Ps 104:20) blankets this satanic kingdom with that which answers to their moral condition. While the rest of the world enjoys the normal sunlight this is striking testimony to the power of God. In the ninth

Egyptian plague the power of the sun-god Ra, of whom Pharaoh was the earthly representative, was of no avail against the power of Jehovah. Now in the darkened cabinet room of the mightiest empire the world has ever seen, the mightiest emperor and his prime-minister, the false prophet, face the fact that their satanic master is not almighty. Some commentators (of whom J. Morris is representative) have suggested that the preceding judgments, notably the water turned into blood and the blazing sun melting the ice-caps, have brought the electricity generators of the empire to a stand-still and plunged the kingdom into darkness. This is totally inadequate as an explanation since it is clearly daylight that is darkened and men, in the next verse, recognise that this is not a darkness subject to scientific explanation. They know that the only explanation is the God whom they have defied.

The capital of the Beast is not identified in this passage. On the parallel with the old Roman Empire many commentators favour Rome. F.A. Tatford is typical of many when he writes, "The Beast of whom the Apocalypse speaks is a personality not yet seen on the public stage – the great western emperor who will be opposed to all things sacred and holy. Judgment will be meted out upon that mighty power at the epiphany of the Son of man, but, prior to that, the nations of earth will turn in flattery and adulation to the powerful dictator who has his seat at Rome". The best that can be said for this suggestion is that it is a reasonable inference but lacks scriptural support. The alternative suggestions have been legion and it would seem that almost any capital would suffice except the only one given in Scripture. This mighty world-leader having reached the pinnacle of power will scarcely be satisfied with the discredited capitals of earth. There is little doubt in view of 2 Thess 2:3-4 that the religious capital of the empire of the Beast will be Jerusalem, where he can safely leave the religious matters in the hands of his prime minister, the false prophet. His administrative and commercial capital would seem to be another matter. Suggestions have been made that since the ten-powered kingdom need not be confined to Europe then a most suitable capital would be in the middle-east area and the thoughts of many have turned to the ancient capital of Babylon. Scripture offers no evidence that the great capital of Nebuchadnezzar has ever been destroyed in the way envisaged by Isaiah and Jeremiah; history too is equally silent that those prophecies have been fulfilled. It is, therefore, a valid inference that this city will be re-built to become the commercial capital of this empire and eventually be finally destroyed as shown in ch. 18 of this book. It is this city that is the focus in these bowl judgments.

The blows that have fallen so rapidly on the kingdom of the Beast might lead to expectations of individual confession of sin and a turning to God, but this is to underestimate the hardness of the human heart. The result recorded is the very opposite. The repetition of "and" six times in these two verses piles effect upon cause to show that the hearts of men have hardened irrevocably against God. Three major statements summarise the result of this bowl and the bowls generally upon men:

1. "and they gnawed their tongues for (*ek*) pain"

The verb *masaomai* means "to chew". This is a very natural reaction to extreme pain when culture demands that the slightest acknowledgement of the pain be judged a sign of weakness. The masochistic culture of the Beast could not allow the pain to be admitted. The word "pain" (*ponos*) used twice here occurs only once more in the NT in connection with the Eternal State when the scriptural assurance is given that "neither shall there be any more pain" (21:4). W. Ramsay writing of this expression says, "This is the only expression of the kind that we have in all the word of God and it indicates the most intense and excruciating agony". This distress, however, has a large element of frustration in it coupled with anger against God. The next statement shows this anger.

2. "And blasphemed the God of heaven because of their pains and their sores"

Conscious that these judgments were not providential but are "acts of God", men are challenged for the last time to face the God that they have for so long denied. Scientists will seek to explain, politicians will argue, philosophers of earth will offer panaceas of all kinds but the one thing men will not do is acknowledge their sin. Instead they point to their pains and their sores (*helkos* – as in v.2 indicating that the plagues are cumulative) and hurl insults against the God of heaven. They charge God with unrighteousness and vindictive action against helpless creatures, impunging His very character.

3. "And repented not of their deeds"

Men still steadfastly refuse to acknowledge that the cause of their pain is their sin. At an earlier stage, in the middle of the tribulation period, God displayed His power in the resurrection and rapture of the two witnesses and men were prepared to repent and give glory to the God of heaven (11:13). Now, with irretrievably-hardened hearts, they blaspheme this same God of heaven–a title used only in 11:13 and here. This is the last time repentance is mentioned in the book; after the last bowl men will still blaspheme God (v.21) but the word "repentance" is not even mentioned.

Bowl Six: The Power of the Beast Disclosed

12 It is to be remarked that the river Euphrates appearing twice in the first book of the Bible (Gen 2:14; 15:18) appears twice in this last book – under the sixth trumpet (9:13-15) and under the sixth bowl. Of the twenty-one references to the Euphrates in the Bible the majority draw attention to the fact that this mighty river serves as a boundary. It was given by God as one of the boundaries of the land grant to Abraham and to Israel (Gen 15:18). Historically it was a boundary for the westward expansion of the Assyrian Empire and served as a line drawn between Israel and the invading nations of the east. This was also its function in the times of the Roman Empire and it marked the eastern boundary of that empire. It was, in fact, a natural geographical boundary between nations. That this river needs no spiritualising is the unanimous opinion of most commentators. Almost without exception they agree that this is the presently existing literal Euphrates that pours from the Armenian mountains through Turkey, Iran and Iraq over a course of nearly 1800 miles and empties into the Persian gulf. Walter Scott is forthright in his comment with reference to the drying up of the river: "There need be no difficulty in accepting the statement in our text in its full and literal sense" (p.331).

Under the sixth trumpet divine orders were given for the release from their imprisonment at this river of the four angels who would stir up and supervise the incursion of an army two hundred million strong. Nothing was revealed at that stage of the purpose of that host except to draw attention to the terrible death toll that results from its movement. The power behind this great army and the purpose of its gathering is now made plain as the tribulation nears its close.

Since the Euphrates is a literal river the drying up of that river must be a literal, physical happening. If such a thing had happened in the days of the Roman empire civilisation then would have been shaken to its foundations. Rome watched its eastern boundary with great trepidation. Parthian armies marshalled there from time to time awaiting their opportunity to launch their hordes across the river and erupt across the Roman empire. Since it has already been pointed out that this final world-empire of the Beast will have many features of that old Roman empire, there is no doubt that what is indicated here is that God opens the way for a mighty invasion of the Beast's empire from the east. The drying up of the river is, in itself, a judgment upon the kingdom of the Beast and upon his new capital city at Babylon near or on the river, but the results of the drying up are even more terrible for the Beast. That the drying up of a river, even of a major river like the Euphrates, is shown as a divine judgment needs some explanation. To put the matter bluntly, if that river were dried up today that fact, startling though it may be, would merit little more than a casual mention in the world news-bulletins. At most there would be the dispatch of an international scientific expedition to investigate the cause. In 1993 Turkey diverted half the waters of the Euphrates to fill a new dam and the world press scarcely mentioned the matter. Clearly in tribulation times this area will have been brought into prominence and loom large in world affairs.

It is apt to be forgotten in these later centuries that this area of Mesopotamia – the land between the rivers (Euphrates and Tigris) – was the birthplace of the great historical civilisations, a fact recognised in Scripture. There the earliest cities were established by Nimrod (Gen 10:10), and the Accadian, Sumerian, and Babylonian empires followed each other down to the period of the might and prosperity of the neo-Babylonian Empire under Nebuchadnezzar (Dan 1:1). From NT times a changed weather pattern has destroyed the earlier fecundity of this area, but that agricultural potential is still there and requires only irrigation or a further change in climate to become fertile again and that very quickly. The oil wealth has already centred attention on the general area but evidence will be presented in ch. 18 to show that in the tribulation period interest in this area will be so revived, for reasons far beyond oil wealth, that it will become the focus of world media attention. It is possible that the Beast, disdaining the outworn capital cities of discredited empires, will establish his political capital in a rebuilt neo-Babylon on the banks of the Euphrates river. This new city, not necessarily in geographic extent or demographic terms to be compared with the great population centres of earth, will out-strip them all in importance. This importance derived from its charismatic founder will make it commercially and financially the capital of the empire of the Beast for it will become, for these very reasons, the *de facto* capital of the world. God, in the judgment of the previous bowl (v.10), has already struck at this heart of the Beast's empire and plunged it into darkness. Under this bowl a second stroke falls and the Euphrates river, vital to the survival of the city and the whole area, is dried up. Evaporation from a scorching sun (vv.8-9) and dwindling supplies from the diminishing ice-caps on the Armenian mountains has probably given ample warning, but now God dries it up completely. The God who opened a path through the Red Sea and dried the Jordan river with a word has put His hand on this mighty river. Whatever means God chooses to use – diverting waters by an enemy hand (as happened when Babylon fell in October 539BC on the night that Belshazzar died under the hand of the Medes), unprecedented evaporation or seismic disturbance the fact is the same – the waters are gone. Irrigation pumps seize up, power generators fall silent (note the candle in 18:23) and the great distilling plants are closed down. Darkness and drought herald a doom for all under the suzerainty of the Beast. This very stroke will bring home to all the followers of the Beast that the whole fabric of life is disintegrating under the judgments of God. The empire of the Beast is tottering to its irrevocable and final doom.

But this is only incidental. There is not only a punishment but a divine purpose in the drying up of the waters of the Euphrates. There is an enemy poised on the borders of the mighty empire of the Beast that reduces the Parthian invasion in Roman times to a mere footnote in history. The purpose of God is summarised in a brief sentence given more exactly in JND: "that the way of the kings from the rising of the sun might be prepared". Suddenly and dramatically the dry river bed offers powers (note the plural in "the kings") from the east a right of way for an invasion of Israel. It is certainly true that in the light of modern technological warfare a river, even a great river like the Euphrates, offers little problem to an invading force. Air power and ballistic missiles in particular, recognise no such old-fashioned boundaries. Nevertheless what is in view is that God, in a supernatural way, removes this riverine barrier to the physical invasion of the empire of the Beast. Men deceived by satanic power may even view the happening as a sign of the rightness of their purpose.

Two differing views are possible of the reason for this invasion from the east and commentators have taken different sides. The most favoured view, anticipating what is said in vv.13-16, is that these eastern forces are part of the worldwide gathering of the nations in support of the Beast and they move with his approval towards Jerusalem, his religious capital. No specific reason for this invasion is given by those who advocate this view, except perhaps the general suggestion that the Beast desires all possible reinforcements for his attempt to wipe out the recalcitrant nation Israel and deal with the middle eastern dilemma in a very final way. The weaknesses of this suggestion are that it does not give sufficient weight to the fact that the Beast and the false prophet in Israel are acting together and it does not explain why special mention is made of the kings from the east as a separate group from the armies of v.14.

There is much more to be said for recognising that this invasion is not to support the Beast but to attack him. The very phrasing suggests that these confederate invaders come with evil intent and their coming is, in itself, part of the judgment of God. They are seizing what they see as a God-given opportunity, in the drying up of the Euphrates, to launch an attack on the rule of a Beast they have come to fear and to hate. From the middle of the seven-year tribulation, with the defeat of the northern invasion (Dan 11:4-45), the authority of the Beast has spread beyond Europe (17:12-13) to affect the whole of earth both politically and commercially. This worldwide influence in the very nature of the human heart, would be viewed with both jealousy and apprehension. Politically, militarily and financially the world has seen emerge a man more powerful than Augustus Caesar. With the crushing of apostate christianity (the harlot of ch. 17) and the crushing of Judaism (12:6) this mighty man has taken the ultimate step and claimed deity (2 Thess 2:4). Some nations of earth have worshipped, some have wondered and some have just waited. An iron discipline has repressed dissent in the central parts of the empire as multitudes have died for their faith in Christ but possibly many, for a large variety of reasons, have fled beyond the reach of the secret police of the Beast's empire. It is possible that the east has been a haven for such dissenters and they have found refuge where Islam has ruled. Doubtless the claim to deity by a western leader in eastern parts has been fanatically rejected – they will not worship this man. Now at this point, with the empire reeling under the hammer blows of God's judgment, the disaffected peoples and nations, falling in behind the Islamic powers in their militant rejection of this claimant to deity, seize the opportunity and mount a campaign from the east against the Beast. Interpreting the drying up of the river as a sign of supernatural approval, the militant Islamic nations including Iran, Iraq, India, Malaysia, Indonesia and China, possibly backed by Japan, move against the Beast. It is interesting to remember that Japan is called "the land of the rising sun". To put in the field an army of two hundred million men (9:16) would be no problem to these nations. The population of China alone is over one thousand million (1996). Doubtless in the calculations of the leaders of this invasion there would be the subsidiary reason, not only to attack the empire of the Beast, but at the same time to deal with his puppet nation Israel once and for all. For them the time for diplomacy in the Palestinian question is long past and drastic military action is required. They little realise that they are but pawns in the hand of the great deceiver of the nations. They have their own plans and interest but Satan has a totally different programme in mind.

13-14 These two verses are a vision (introduced by the customary "I saw)" given to John to explain a movement that is about to embrace the whole earth. Without this vision a host of unanswerable questions would arise as to how this great gathering of the nations to be described in v.16 had been brought about. The vision shows that Satan is behind the gathering of the nations. The movement of the kings of the east is only a part, but a key part, of a far wider movement planned by Satan. The move from the east triggers a response from the west and the agencies behind it are now disclosed.

John is permitted in this vision to peer into the council chamber of the trinity of evil ranged against God and His Christ. In some dark cabinet room in the darkened capital city of the Beast the dragon takes the chair. His earthly puppets, the Beast and the false prophet, take their places for this crisis meeting. This is the first occurrence of the term "the false prophet" (*pseudoprophētēs*) to describe the second beast of 13:11, a title repeated in 19:20; 20:10. Christ warned of false prophets (Matt 7:15; Mark 13:22) but the article distinguishes this one from all who have gone before; this is "*the* false prophet". This one stands in contrast to the prophet that God promised to Israel in Deut 18:15, a promise fulfilled in Christ. These leaders of the earth rebellion know full well that the moment for the great confrontation with heaven has arrived; the days are running out as they recognise that Christ is coming back to earth. Doubtless the leading item on the satanic agenda for this meeting is how to gather all the armies of earth into one place to resist the return of Christ. Ever since Satan infiltrated the garden of Eden history has moved towards this climactic moment.

The result of these unholy deliberations is seen visually and symbolically by John as a spirit like a frog coming out of the mouth of each of the participants. The symbolism is graphic: "from the mouth" clearly indicates "utterances", in our language it might be called "propaganda". It is to be noted how large a part the "mouth" plays in these end-time scenes (12:15; 13:6). The "three unclean spirits" show both the nature of the propaganda – it is unclean, and the energy for the propagation of the propaganda, a spiritual power that is defined under the term "spirits of demons". The symbol is the frog, levitically unclean and an abomination to Israel (Lev 11:10-11,41); frogs only find biblical mention in connection with the second plague (Exod 8:2-14; Ps 78: 45; 105:30). Emerging from river mud and slime, especially clamorous in the darkness of the night, they are a fitting symbol of evil propaganda. From these leaders of rebellion there come deceptive statements and speeches that are carried on the worldwide radio and television to stir up nations to action. The very words are energised by evil spirits to carry conviction to all classes and all nations throughout the earth. There is a distinct reminiscence of the OT scene of 1 Kings 22:19-22 when a lying spirit was used to lure Ahab into battle.

That a great upsurge of demon activity was associated with the first coming of Christ is attested by the Gospel records. Believing hearts worship as the power of Christ is shown in these confrontations. This vision of John shows that demon power is marshalled by Satan to be the effective agency behind the world-stirring speeches of the world leaders, all of which are designed to further the satanic plan of gathering all armies of earth around Jerusalem. Lies are Satan's characteristic activity and all sorts of lies will be disseminated and believed. Satan will be able to persuade the kings of the east that it is in their best interests to attack the Beast at this critical juncture before he gains further power and, incidentally, to settle the Palestinian question finally. Doubtless in the Islamic world a holy *jihad* will form part of that lie and will gather many nations against the greatest "infidel" of all time. Other nations will be persuaded that their interest lies in gathering to support the Beast and defend Israel against this eastern invasion. The result will be that many a parliament or congress, many a monarch or dictator will persuade their nations to dispatch armies to Jerusalem. Supernatural power displayed in "signs" carried out by the demon spirits will corroborate the power that the Beast had earlier displayed (13:3-4). Perhaps the very drying up of the Euphrates will be misrepresented as the Elijah-like power that authenticates the righteousness of the cause (2 Kings 2:8). There is no doubt that all sorts of deceptive messages and miracles will convince "the kings of the earth" that they should mobilise their forces at this time. JND reflects the more reliable manuscripts "which go out to the kings of the whole inhabitable world". The word "world" *oikoumenē* implies that the movement of armies is worldwide. The movement from the east would seem to trigger responses from other nations around the earth as they muster their forces to defend the Beast.

The stark simplicity of the scriptural record gives no place to the diplomatic exchanges, the hot-line conferences, the high level summit meetings and the United Nations emergency meetings that lie behind such a worldwide mobilisation of armies. Newspapers' headlines and news bulletins will cause the peoples of earth to watch in trepidation as, once again, earth lurches towards war. Mobilisation and transportation of armies lead to unprecedented military forces converging on Israel and Jerusalem for the greatest confrontation of armed forces of all time. Some have gathered to destroy the Beast, mainly from the east; others have gathered to defend the Beast, mainly from the west. They little realise they are all, in some degree, but puppets in a terrible deception. When that deception is unmasked and it is far too late, they will find they are all enrolled under the banner of Satan in opposition to God and His Christ. They have, in fact, been gathered for "the battle of that great day of God Almighty". This gathering of the nations has been prophetically foreseen in Ps 2:1-3. This is very clear in JND: "Why are the nations in tumultuous agitation, and [why] do the peoples meditate a vain thing? The kings of the earth set themselves and the princes plot together against Jehovah and against his anointed: let us break their bonds asunder, and cast away their cords from us". As the armies arrive to confront each other it is clear that the astronomical disturbances and the sign of the coming of the Son of man (Matt 24:29-30) show the leaders that Christ is coming. Very likely urgent security council meetings in the United Nations and hastily-called summit meetings between earth leaders settle all disputes quickly in favour of a united front against God and Christ. Satan has achieved his age-long purpose and gathered his army. The word "battle" (*polemos*) would be better translated "war" as in RV. The word for a specific engagement would be *machē* (see James 4:1 for the difference between the words) but this is an age-long conflict that finds its climax on "the great day" when God Almighty confronts Satan and his hosts. It is not actually called the battle of Armageddon, for v.16 shows that Armageddon is but the gathering point; it is "the war" belonging to the day of Almighty God (see v.7) when the creature furnished with the weaponry of earth and under the leadership of Satan confronts Almighty God. Some commentators hold that "war" should be given its strict meaning as a series of engagements over an extended period, beginning with the army movement under the sixth trumpet (9:13-20), with the final engagement around Jerusalem. It is better to see that the sixth trumpet (9:13-19) heralds but the gathering of this eastern army (see comments *in loc*) which now crosses the Euphrates to be destroyed at Armageddon. The appearance of Christ as "King of kings and Lord of lords" (19:16) brings total destruction to these armies and the final outcome is described in 19:17-19 where the feast for the carrion birds of earth is called "the supper of the great God". In this gathering of armies the prophecy of Joel will have found its fulfilment: "Proclaim ye this among the Gentiles; Prepare war, wake up the mighty men, let all the men of war draw near; let them come up: Beat your ploughshares into swords, and your pruning hooks into spears; let the weak say, I am strong" (Joel 3:9-10). Earth's nations have taken up the challenge and move to war.

15 A sudden divine interjection interrupts this dark scene. Characteristic of the book, these oracular interruptions at critical junctures display the interest of God in the happenings on earth. Here the message, "Behold I come as a thief", repeats and re-emphasises an earlier statement to the church at Sardis (3:3) and can only be the voice of the Son of man. This message would have neither interest nor meaning to the armies en route to Armageddon, and even less to the demon-controlled media pandering to a war-crazed society listening with avid interest for the latest reports from the war fronts or the deliberations of the United Nations. To them He will come as a thief, unannounced and unexpected, to their immediate damage and eternal loss. To the scattered and fleeing saints persecuted by the Beast these words will bring tremendous comfort. Christ will take this corrupted world by surprise. It has been previously suggested that where the simile of the thief is used with reference to the Lord's coming (Matt 24:42-44; Luke 12:35-40; 1 Thess 5:2-4; 2 Pet 3:10) the main point stressed is the unannounced and unexpected nature of His coming. Since believers of any dispensation by definition have accepted His word and been taken into His confidence, He cannot come upon them as a thief. To unbelievers He will assuredly do so. The warning to the church in Sardis is no exception (3:3) and, in fact, strengthens the argument, since it is prefaced by the statement "If thou wilt not watch" which clearly identifies the lifeless professors within that church.

The second beatitude in the book (14:13) was directed as encouragement to saints dying as martyrs under the fury of the Beast. This third beatitude is addressed to the living saints and brings challenge as well as cheer. The blessing is for those on tip-toe of expectation awaiting their Lord. The two present participles, watching and keeping, qualified by the single article describe one class of person only; those who are "watching" are the ones "keeping their garments". The metaphor in the word "watching" depicts a householder so sure of the arrival of a friend that he sits up throughout the night (the verb *grēgoreō* is used of keeping awake). Such are unwilling to lay aside their clothes lest the arrival of the friend catch them "naked"; if they had taken off their clothes to retire to bed it would have denied their profession of confidence in the word of their friend; taken unawares in these circumstances others would see their shame. Waiting and watching saints in this dark night of earth are thus encouraged by the Christ Himself to put confidence in His word. Those saints who do this are assured of His personal blessing.

16 The conjunction "and" resumes the previous subject of the gathering armies of earth. The verb "gathered" views the whole process as one action. Much unnecessary debate has centred on whether "he" is God or Satan. The RV, in keeping with the rule that plural neuter nouns may have the verb in the singular (as in 8:3; 13:14; 14:13; 16:14), gives the subject as "they" with its antecedent the neuter plural "spirits" of v.14. These demons, of course, cannot act without the direction of their satanic master but behind this is the will of God expressed in the word of Jehovah: "For I will gather all nations to Jerusalem to battle" (Zech 14:2). Omitting the mere agents it is God who gathers these armies.

Popular usage speaks of "the battle of Armageddon" but v.14 has spoken of it as "the battle of the great day of God Almighty" without specifying location. The location given is the gathering centre of the rebellious armies of earth not the scene of the battle. The gathering centre is described as "a place called in the

Hebrew tongue Armageddon". John does not translate the Hebrew name into Greek as he did in 9:11, suggesting that the understanding of it lies in its Hebrew derivation. The great majority of scholars are satisfied that the Hebrew word should be transcribed on the lines of "Har Megiddo" (Newberry), "Harmagedon" (JND marg.) or "Harmegadoon" (F.C. Jennings). The Hebrew *Har* meaning "mountain" is the key, and many partly translate and partly transliterate the word as "mountain of Megiddo" (J.F. Walvoord and many others). The only problem is that there is no scriptural record of any such mountain nor any geographic support for a mountain of this name. Many assume that the "mountain of Megiddo" must mean the "hill country" (a possible translation of *har*) adjacent to the Plain of Megiddo with the large plain of Esdraelon lying to the north-east. It is certainly true that this area has been the scene of battles that have changed the history of Israel. Barak and the Canaanites (Judges 4), Gideon and the Midianites, and Josiah and the army of Egypt have all moved across this historic battlefield, fourteen miles long and twenty miles in width. Napoleon remarked that all the armies of the world could be deployed here; while possibly true in his day it is certainly no longer valid today. While this area has had a turbulent and intriguing history it does not, without stretching the Scripture, fit the idea of a mountain.

The solution of the problem may lie in the simple observation of F.C. Jennings some years ago (*Studies in Revelation),* p.437. He pointed out that if the first part of the word is translated "mountain" the second part of the word should be translated as well. The root of the word *megadon* is the verb "to gather" (Ps 94:21; Mic 5:1) which supplies the proper name "Gad" given to Leah's son as she exclaimed on his birth "behold a troop cometh" (Gen 30:11). The word *megadon* should therefore be translated as "the gathering of troops" or "the gathering in troops". The complete word *Har-megadon* would thus mean "the mountain where the troops gather" – which would be the correct designation of the literal mountain (or mountains) around Jerusalem where Zechariah prophesied that the proud armies of earth with impious insolence would congregate to wipe out a nation and a city (Zech 14:12). This fits well with the other prophetic word of Zechariah, "In that day there shall be a great mourning in Jerusalem as the great mourning of Hadadrimmon in the valley of Megiddon" (Zech 12:11). As Christ destroys the armies under the Beast massed against Him there is a simultaneous recognition of Him by His people that results in a national mourning that far exceeds the mourning for Josiah (2 Chron 35:25). It is to be noted that the mountain is literal – just as literal as the Euphrates river, and yet places the scene around Jerusalem – the centre of the action.

Bowl Seven: The Capital of the Beast Destroyed

17-21 The seventh bowl is poured by the angel into (*epi*) the air. This is to be taken just as literally as the air, sea, rivers and sun of the previous plagues and suggests the atmosphere surrounding the earth. It thus indicates the final apocalyptic storm that is the background for this seventh and final judgment. The touching of this atmospheric envelope means that the storm is worldwide. Alternative interpretations have been many. Some commentators have felt that since Satan is called "the prince of the power of the air" (Eph 2:2) it is his realm that is affected, but since Satan has already been confined to earth (12:9) this can hardly be a valid interpretation. Those who follow the symbolic approach suggest the judgment falls upon "the moral life-breath of the world" (W. Scott). In a realm where the heights of immorality and idolatry have already been scaled by impious men controlled by Satan this is clearly far too weak to explain the climactic nature of this plague. More modern interpreters have suggested that "the air" is the symbol of military might now available to men in military air power seen in rockets and missiles and star-war techniques, but this can hardly have been how John's readers would understand it. They would have recognised that the symbolic action was depicting a terrible storm that would affect all of earth; to touch the atmospheric aerial canopy around the globe means to allow the judgment to sweep over the earth.

The out-pouring of the bowl is heralded by "a great voice" out of (*ek*) the temple of the heaven from (*apo*) the throne (see JND). The temple of 11:19 and the throne of 4:2 are now linked by this great voice which can be no other than the voice of God. Both the holiness of God (the temple) and the righteousness of God (the throne) have been vindicated by divine judgments on earth. Now God announces that "It is done". The singular "it" points to the completion of divine purpose through the whole series of judgments. The statement is anticipatory in that it covers all action within the seventh trumpet until Christ comes in 19:11 with which event the tribulation is closed; a truth anticipated by the angelic messenger in 10:7. The perfect tense shows that the effects of the judgment will remain with respect to Israel and the nations; there is nothing more to be done to accomplish God's purpose with regard to judgment upon earth (cf. the voice of 21:6).

18 As in the seventh seal (8:5) and in the seventh trumpet (11:19) the seventh bowl has a storm picture as background. The voices and thunders and lightnings and an earthquake are common and suggest that the storm rumbling from the seventh seal has intensified under the seventh trumpet and now with the seventh bowl reaches hurricane strength. The hail that began under the seventh trumpet has now become "every stone about the weight of a talent" and the earthquake is "such as was not since men were upon the earth". Great movements of the earth's crust were the result of the flood (Ps 104:5-9) when "the fountains of the great deep" (Gen 7:11) were broken up by divine action. These movements and the associated volcanic activity have left physical scars on earth and psychological ones in the race's memory over past ages but at this point, as the tribulation closes, the most terrible earthquake of all time convulses the earth. Language seems inadequate to convey its magnitude. The AV is as dramatic as the original, "so mighty an earthquake and so great". The superlative that Christ used of the tribulation (Mark 13:19) to eclipse all previous tribulation is copied by John to show that all previous earthquakes are overshadowed by this mighty shaking. How this can be other than physical it is difficult to see when history will be scanned in vain for anything with which to compare it. The seismologists and volcanologists of earth will watch in horror as their recording instruments move right off the Richter scale – God is shaking the earth. Haggai foresaw it and spoke: "For thus saith the Lord of hosts; yet once, it is a little while, and I will shake the heavens and the earth, and the sea and the dry land" (Hag 2:6). Isaiah foretold it and wrote, "The fountains of the earth do shake, the earth is utterly broken down, the earth is clean dissolved, the earth is moved exceedingly" (Isa 24:17-21). Joel forewarned of it and cried: "The Lord also shall roar out of Zion, and utter his voice from Jerusalem; the heavens and the earth shall shake" (Joel 3:16).

Many expositors refuse to see this earthquake as literal. W. Scott p.337 may be quoted in this connection as he writes, "There will be physical earthquakes in divers places (Mark 13:8). But the vast and unparalleled upheaval under the seventh vial is not that of the elements of nature but symbolises a violent disruption of all government, the total collapse of authority from the highest down to the lowest. Under it thrones totter and fall, crowns are broken, sceptres are shivered; the whole framework of society is overthrown. It will be a revolution unexampled in the history of the race" (p. 337). It is submitted that this arbitrary and subjective interpretation not only lacks the support of Scripture but is strangely weak in the context of this climaxing judgment of earth. A social revolution, however widespread, of which earth has had many, scarcely fits a scene in which cosmic and astronomic signs are the prelude to an earth shaking under the feet of men. It would be difficult to prove that the word "earthquake" in Scripture ever carries a symbolic meaning of this kind. The statements in their simple literal sense provide a clear and terrible picture of God's wrath upon a rebel earth.

19 Cities and islands and mountains are shaken in this worldwide upheaval. Earth's cities have individually and partially been shaken by terrible earthquakes, but never has destruction been on such a scale. The simple scriptural statement is terrifying in its simplicity: "The cities of the nations fell". Centres of population like London, Paris, Rome, New York, Tokyo and many others collapse with resulting death and devastation over unimaginable areas. Attention is drawn particularly to two cities, very possibly because of their association with the Beast. One is called "the great city" and the only city so identified in Scripture is Jerusalem (11:8) which the Beast has made his religious centre. Strikingly this centre of Beast-worship is not destroyed as other cities but simply "divided into three parts". There will be topographic changes that speak of divine judgment yet, even through the judgment, there is divine preservation of the city of divine choice (Zech 1:17). God has yet a purpose for this city above all other cities and in fact it will be the capital city of the millennial reign of Christ.

The second city to which particular attention is drawn is Babylon. The description uses the familiar adjective of this chapter; an adjective linked with Babylon in this book – "great Babylon". The verb "was remembered" (RV) used concerning Babylon is Hebrew idiom; it does not mean that God had "forgotten" Babylon but rather that He was now ready to take action about it. When it is stated that "God remembered Noah" (Gen 8:1) there is no thought of God's forgetfulness but that, with His purpose achieved, God took action on behalf of Noah. Now the city that had shared her filthy cup (18:6) of debauchery with the kings of earth receives "the cup of the wine of the fierceness of his wrath". The rebellious nature of man, fostered by satanic malice, has used Babylon from the dawn of history (Gen 10) as the centre of opposition to God and all that is now focused in an earth city. The fury of God's displeasure will be seen in the single act of judgment that will befall this city. There is no more reason to make "great Babylon" a symbol than there is to make "the great river Euphrates" (v.12) a symbol. Neither is there the slightest hint that the name should be changed at an expositor's whim to mean Rome or some other of earth's cities which have already been destroyed in the earthquake. It has already been suggested that the reference to the "throne of the beast" in v.10 implied the rebuilding of this ancient city to become the capital of the Beast's empire. Further details will be seen in ch. 18. It would seem from the wording of this verse that the judgment of Babylon is apart even from the great earthquake and is a separate act of divine fury the details of which will be given in ch. 18.

It has been shown in the comments at 14:8 that Babylon has two aspects – religious Babylon and political Babylon. "Mystery", associated with Babylon in 17:5, indicates the religious aspect; in the comments there its final manifestation will be shown to be essentially Roman Catholicism developed into an ecumenical system with its capital in the Vatican city in Rome. The destruction of this religious Babylon will be by the Beast and his associate kings for their own reasons (17:16) at the midpoint of the tribulation period; a destruction described in ch. 17. The Babylon "remembered" at this point is the political and commercial empire of the Beast headed up by his capital city – a rebuilt Babylon on the banks of the Euphrates. Since a literal earthquake demands literal cities around the earth it would seem reasonable to allow God to name another literal city where man's rebellion has crystallised in so signal a way. The description and detail of this fall will be supplied in ch. 18 at the very close of the tribulation – just where it occurs under this seventh bowl. The fall of Babylon is followed by the "Hallelujah" of heaven (19:1-4).

20 Under the sixth seal the upheavals were such that "every mountain and island were moved out of their places" (6:14); in these final hours of judgment before Christ appears the upheaval across earth is even more widespread. The graphic picture verb "to flee" has been used of death (9:6) and of the woman (12:6); now it is used to show that the islands of earth, borne by the continental plates to which they are attached, actually move away from the observer as if they were fleeing. Mountains that have been landmarks for long centuries disappear and any search is vain ("not found", *heuriskō*). Both these verbs will be used again to describe the physical removal of the present cosmos in 20:11. Earth is altered radically both in its seascape and its landscape as God's judgments fall upon its rebellious tenants. There is no doubt, on the other hand, that these physical changes will open the way for the physical and geographical changes that will be seen in the millennial kingdom as anticipated in many OT Scriptures (cf. Zech 14:4). Many of the refurbishment and rehabilitation changes will take place after the arrival of Christ as the earth settles down and the seismic forces are restored to equilibrium. Under this judgment there can hardly fail to be the total disruption of any normal life left on earth and many people must die in the convulsions. The termination of these terrors envisaged in Matt 24:22 is the only escape for men and that termination will take place when Christ is revealed from the opened heaven (19:11).

21 The climaxing blow on this scene of earthly misery is a devastating blitz of great hailstones as if the heavens were bombarding the earth. The seventh Egyptian plague (Exod 9:18-26) provides a faint picture of this storm. The word "hail", used in the NT only in this book (8:7; 11:19), probably has its normal meaning even if the weight of the hailstones is unbelievable to the natural mind. "Weight of a talent" puts a divine measure on this terrifying precipitation from the atmosphere. While there have been minor variations in the talent down the ages it is generally agreed that it was about 250 kilograms (100 pounds) or the weight that a grown man can carry. The largest recorded hailstones on earth in a sustained shower have been less than a quarter-pound or 50 grams (about the size of billiard balls) and this has been found both devastating and terrifying. These are "the treasures of the hail, which I have reserved against the time of trouble, against the day of battle and war" (Job 38:22). Under such a hailstorm normal buildings will prove inadequate for cover and the armies massed in Israel will suffer a terrible bombardment. Men will take up the cry of an earlier stage in the tribulation and cry to the mountains and rocks, "Fall on us and hide us from the face of him that sitteth on the throne, and from the wrath of the Lamb" (6:16-17).

The men of this verse (with the article) are the men of v.2 so that the brunt of the storm falls on adherents of the Beast. But even this terrible final blow effects no change in their hearts; stricken with sores, burnt by a blazing sun, plunged into darkness, shaken by earthquakes, their cities crashing round them and now blitzed by the hail – they still blaspheme God. There is no room for repentance, it is not even mentioned now; all that can be heard from the men of earth is bitter abuse as they raise a blasphemous fist against God. Amid crashing cities and the thunder of the hurricane Satan's puppets and their followers cower, terrified and yet defiant, as earth history moves to its climax. The next event chronologically (after the fourth parenthesis of 17:1-19:10) will be the opening of heaven and the coming of Christ at the head of the armies of heaven (19:11).

10. *Introduction to Chapters 17 and 18*
17:1-19:10

The Setting of This Parenthesis

The chronological development of the action in the book is interrupted by a fourth parenthesis comprising this section from 17:1 to 19:10 which may also be viewed as an extended explanatory appendix, not to the seventh trumpet alone, but to the whole sequence of judgments resulting from the action of the Lamb in opening the scroll. The immediate intention is to explain more fully the term Babylon, mentioned in 14:8 and again in 16:19.

It will be shown that the events described in this section take place at climactic moments in the tribulation period and furnish the background information needed to understand the crisis nature of the final three and a half years of the period just before Christ appears on earth (19:11).

The repetition of the expression "after these things" (*meta tauta*) marks the division of the section into three visions as follows:

Vision 1	The Woman and the Beast	17:1-18
	"And after these things I saw....	18:1
Vision 2	The City and its Fall	18:1-24
	"And after these things I heard...	19:1
Vision 3	The Hallelujah Chorus	19:1-4
	The Marriage of the Lamb	19:5-10

The Subject of This Parenthesis

The subject of this parenthesis is Babylon. There have been two somewhat cryptic references to Babylon in the book already, at 14:8 and 16:19; now the chronological movement of events is interrupted while John is given a closer look at this object of divine judgment. While Babylon is necessarily defined the subject of this chapter is given in v.l "the judgment of the great whore" – the doom that God brings upon it. The consequences of this divine action are recognised in heaven itself and the response is heard in "the hallelujah chorus" (19:1-5). This final enemy of God having been judged, the way is now open for Christ to come to earth and claim His kingdom.

The historical identification of Babylon is given concisely by R. Young in his concordance as he writes under "Babylon": "The Greek mode of spelling what in the Hebrew is uniformly Babel. Perhaps when Nimrod founded the city he gave it the name Bab-il, or 'Gate of Il' or 'gate of God'. After the 'confusion' of tongues, the name was connected by the Hebrews with the root *balal*, 'to confound'. It became the principal city of the land called in Gen 11:2 'The land of Shinar', and in the later scriptures 'Chaldea' or the 'land of the Chaldean'". In Biblical history Babylon under Nimrod (Gen 10:10; 11:1-9) became synonymous with the rejection of divine revelation and rebellion against God. Thus Satan found it a useful centre and from the scriptural link between the "king of Babylon" and "Lucifer, son of the morning" (Isa 14:3-15) it would appear that Satan used it as the centre of his operations on earth. That this ancient centre of satanic power should reappear in the closing pages of Scripture is but to be expected and, in fitting acknowledgment of God's changeless purposes, John is invited to witness its doom.

The Interpretation of the Parenthesis

To many exegetes of widely-varying schools of thought there is no doubt that Babylon represents the city of Rome. Expositors who follow this line argue that the beast (13:1-8) represents the revived Roman empire, in which term they include many subject nations and provinces of whom the ten kings are the rulers in the European heart-land of that empire.

The same expositors view the Roman Catholic church under the Pope, with its ceremonies and practices clearly derived from the religion established by Nimrod and Semiramis his wife, as the religious side of the Beast's empire. They point out that Roman Catholicism, having its seat of authority in the Vatican City in Rome, confirms the theory that when John writes "Babylon" he really means Rome. These chapters are used to support this identification; in particular much weight is placed on the reference to the "seven mountains" (17:9) which is often given a double interpretation; first taken to refer to the "seven hills" of Rome it is also taken to refer to the seven Roman emperors from Augustus to Domitian (that there were more than seven means that the view has to be modified in certain respects). On this view, these two chapters present the judgment of God upon the empire-supported religious system of Roman Catholicism and its earthy capital the city of Rome. Scholars and commentators of unquestioned competence lend weighty support to this view.

It will be shown in the exposition, however, that this view is somewhat simplistic, inadequate and, more importantly, does not agree with the statements of Scripture. Ch. 17 will show that there is a "mystery" side to Babylon, which could only be recognised when God reveals it as He does here, showing that while the roots of Babylon are ancient there is a final manifestation, a religious entity supported by the Beast and described in metaphorical terms as "a harlot". It will be shown that this religious entity, while wider than Roman Catholicism, is headed up in Roman Catholicism. This is the Babylon that is destroyed at the midpoint of the tribulation (17:16-18) by the Beast and the ten kings, who up to this point had supported her. Another aspect of Babylon, which is established commercially in a city, is dealt with by God directly in ch. 18 at the very close of the tribulation. While many expositors accept that there is a literal city involved they still prefer to call it Rome. It will be shown that, on the balance of Scripture, there is much more to be said for calling the city by the name given by God, which is Babylon. That, of course, necessarily involves the rebuilding of this ancient capital on the Euphrates.

The Significance of the Two Visions in the Parenthesis

It should be pointed out that the chapter division here has a basis in the text itself. The repetition of the expression "after these things" (*meta tauta*) in 18:1 and 19:1 clearly divides the section into three distinct visions. Much learned discussion has centred on the relationship between the first two visions, particularly as to whether the chapters describe one judgment seen from two different angles, or whether two separate judgments are involved. Commentators who, in general, support a symbolic interpretation for the term "Babylon" insist that the chapters describe one judgment at the end of the tribulation (see W. Scott). Other commentators seek to show that the evidence, fairly considered, indicates two judgments at different times in the tribulation and by different agents with different results. The evidence for two judgments seems conclusive and may be summarised thus:

1. The expression "And after these things" in 18:1 divides the chapters into successive visions which, at the very least, suggests two different events.
2. The two previous mentions of Babylon, in 14:8 and 16:19, suggest separate and distinct events connected with the fall of Babylon.
   (i) As suggested in comments on 14:8, based on the time sequence of the related events, the fall of Babylon there announced must take place about the midpoint of the seven-year tribulation. Some commentators place it earlier (see J.F. Walvoord), but it can scarcely be any later. Note also the absence of the word "city" in the RV and JND.
   (ii) As suggested in comments on 16:19 this judgment upon Babylon takes place as other cities are being shaken and this occurs in the seventh bowl which is the final judgment before the coming of Christ to earth. It is clear that ch. 17 gives the detail of the judgment of 14:8 while ch. 18 gives the detail of the judgment of 16:19.
3. Corroborative evidence lies in the fact that the judgment of ch. 17 is carried out by the Beast and the ten kings under him (17:16). That God put this in their hearts is true (17:17) but they imagine they are acting for their own purpose and to further their own interests. The judgment in ch. 18, on the other hand, is directly from the hand of God. The same kings that destroy the harlot of ch. 17 mourn the destruction of the city (18:9) in ch. 18. Any difference in the expressions "ten kings" (17:12) and "the kings of the earth" (18:9) will be shown to be of minor importance – it is basically the same company. Thus these two judgments can hardly be the same.

If there are thus two separate judgments the question must then be raised as to the relationship between the chapters, for it is clear that Babylon must be understood in two different ways, symbolically and literally. Babylon as the name of a city is familiar from Scripture and from history. The references to the great river Euphrates (9:14; 16:12), in the absence of any other feasible interpretation, have been shown to be literal so there does not seem to be any reason why Babylon should not be allowed to be the name of a literal city. In NT times Peter knew the city, had visited it and wrote his first epistle from it. (That Peter used "Babylon" as a "cover-name" for Rome is scarcely worthy of comment). When this revelation was given to John, near the end of the first century AD, Babylon on the Euphrates had a larger Jewish population than Jerusalem. When the Babylonian Talmud was issued in Babylon c. 500AD this city was still a great centre of trade with a major Rabbinic School established there. In the later centuries the city declined to village status but it was neither destroyed nor totally deserted. Of the six references to Babylon in this book (14:8; 16:19; 17:5; 18:2,10, 21) four have the word "city" linked with it (17:18; 18:16,18,19). If the word "city" is to be taken in other than a literal sense the onus must be on the commentator to prove it.

The one occasion where the word "Babylon" is to be taken symbolically is clearly indicated in ch. 17 and is preceded by the word "mystery". That the harlot depicts a non-literal aspect of Babylon is clear from the passage and God reveals the mystery, but there is no mystery attached to the city. To make the city a symbol is to make the harlot a symbol of a symbol (see comments on 1:20) and this is to take a step away from sound consistent exegesis. This is confirmed by 17:18 that links the two chapters. "The woman which thou sawest" is the symbol; "the great city" (see RV) is the literal entity.

The difficulty posed by the interpretation that makes Babylon a literal city is the fact that Babylon has ceased to exist as a major city in world affairs. For several centuries it had been reduced to a few scattered villages near the Euphrates river, which itself has changed its course over the centuries. This has led many commentators to seek for an interpretation other than the literal, and they have found this in the simple device of extending the symbolism of ch. 17 into ch. 18. There can be little dispute that ch. 17 describes, under the symbol of the harlot, a religious system that has all the features of the mystery religion arising from Nimrod and his wife Semiramis in Babylon. That this system today is perfectly reflected in Roman Catholicism any unbiased mind must concede. That Roman Catholicism has its base and controlling centre in the Vatican city in Rome is simply fact. Thus many commentators have been led to assume that ch. 18 is the commercial side of religious Babylon and thus the city, in their judgment, has to be interpreted as Rome. They find support for this view in the fact that Rome was the centre of empire when the Roman Empire ruled the world, and they suggest that it comes again into prominence in the time of the final empire of the Beast.

The arguments are appealing but faulty. It should be pointed out that Babylon is mentioned about 277 times in the OT and 12 times in the NT and, apart from 17:5, it would be very difficult to show that Babylon is used symbolically on even one occasion. It was the early church fathers who took the view that the name Babylon is used, particularly in this book, as a code name for Rome as if the Holy Spirit was afraid to identify that city plainly. It would almost seem as if they imposed their fear of Rome on the Holy Spirit. It is more in keeping with the dignity of Scripture to allow it to mean exactly what it says. On this basis Scripture is perfectly clear on the two aspects of Babylon here presented:

Ch. 17 presents symbolically a religious and ecclesiastical system reflecting the ancient Babylonish mystery religion. Details of that mystery religion, its re-emergence in the period of church testimony as Roman Catholicism, will be found in *The Two Babylons* by A. Hislop . God uses the agency of the Beast and the ten kings to destroy this system at the midpoint of the tribulation.

Ch. 18 presents literally a commercial empire with its centre in a city. God Himself in direct judgment destroys this empire when He destroys its capital at the very close of the tribulation. This capital Scripture calls Babylon. Many commentators who have seen that an actual city lies at the centre of this commercial empire have been reluctant to give it the scriptural name. In fact almost any name would seem to do so long as it is not Babylon. There is a strange reluctance to acknowledge that, if Jerusalem can be restored and rebuilt, so can this ancient city of satanic influence. It will be shown in comment on ch. 18 that Scripture not only permits the rebuilding of it but actually demands it. A simple study will show that Babylon has never been destroyed as described by Isaiah (Isa 13-14) and by Jeremiah (Jer 50-51) and, that in fact, the rebuilding of Babylon is not merely an interpretative possibility but that the fulfilment of Scripture actually demands it. Both aspects are scripturally called Babylon. Just as the Babylon in Genesis is seen both as a tower (the religious aspect) and as a city (the political and commercial aspect) so Babylon in the tribulation times will be both a system of religion and a city that lies at the heart of a commercial empire. The remaining aspects of Babylon, not specifically mentioned in these two chapters, are the political and the military. These will be dealt with by Christ personally on His return to earth in ch. 19.

CHAPTER 17

10. *The Fourth Parenthesis*
17:1-19:10

(vision 1) *The Woman and the Beast (vv.1-18)*

v.1 "And there came one of the seven angels which had the seven vials, and talked with me, saying unto me, Come hither; I will shew unto thee the judgment of the great whore that sitteth upon many waters:
v.2 With whom the kings of the earth have committed fornication, and the inhabitants of the earth have been made drunk with the wine of her fornication.
v.3 So he carried me away in the spirit into the wilderness: and I saw a woman sit upon a scarlet coloured beast, full of names of blasphemy, having seven heads and ten horns.
v.4 And the woman was arrayed in purple and scarlet colour, and decked with gold and precious stones and pearls, having a golden cup in her hand full of abominations and filthiness of her fornication:
v.5 And upon her forehead was a name written, MYSTERY, BABYLON THE GREAT, THE MOTHER OF HARLOTS AND ABOMINATIONS OF THE EARTH.
v.6 And I saw the woman drunken with the blood of the saints, and with the blood of the martyrs of Jesus: and when I saw her, I wondered with great admiration.
v.7 And the angel said unto me, Wherefore didst thou marvel? I will tell thee the mystery of the woman, and of the beast that carrieth her, which hath the seven heads and ten horns.
v.8 The beast that thou sawest was, and is not; and shall ascend out of the bottomless pit, and go into perdition: and they that dwell on the earth shall wonder, whose names were not written in the book of life from the foundation of the world, when they behold the beast that was, and is not, and yet is.
v.9 And here *is* the mind which hath wisdom. The seven heads are seven mountains, on which the woman sitteth.
v.10 And there are seven kings: five are fallen, and one is, *and* the other is not yet come; and when he cometh, he must continue a short space.
v.11 And the beast that was, and is not, even he is the eighth, and is of the seven, and goeth into perdition.
v.12 And the ten horns which thou sawest are ten kings, which have received no kingdom as yet; but receive power as kings one hour with the beast.
v.13 These have one mind, and shall give their power and strength unto the beast.
v.14 These shall make war with the Lamb, and the Lamb shall overcome them: for he is Lord of lords, and King of kings: and they that are with him are called, and chosen, and faithful.
v.15 And he saith unto me, The waters which thou sawest, where the whore sitteth, are peoples, and multitudes, and nations, and tongues.
v.16 And the ten horns which thou sawest upon the beast, these shall hate the whore, and shall make her desolate and naked, and shall eat her flesh, and burn her with fire.
v.17 For God hath put in their hearts to fulfil his will, and to agree, and give their kingdom unto the beast, until the words of God shall be fulfilled.
v.18 And the woman which thou sawest is that great city, which reigneth over the kings of the earth."

The Scheme of the Chapter

(a) The Woman – The Mother Figure (vv. 1-6)
The mystery and the divine identification

(b) The Beast – The Monster Figure (vv.7-14)
The meaning and the divine interpretation
(c) The Woman and the Beast (vv.15-17)
The judgment – the subject of the chapter (v.1)
(d) The Woman and the City (v.18)
The relationship between the woman and the city

(a) The Woman – The Mother Figure (vv. 1-6)
1 The two occasions when one of the "bowl" angels invites John to a special vision are clearly meant to be set in contrast. Here John is invited to view "the great whore" while in 21:9 he is invited to view "the bride the Lamb's wife". The symbolic terms "whore" and "bride" describe two companies of people; the whore is the product of satanic action on earth and is doomed, the bride is the result of redemption by the Lamb and is destined for eternal glory. The whore has her home in Babylon; the bride has her home in the Holy Jerusalem.

The present participle translated "which had" (the bowls), leaves uncertain whether the bowls have been poured out or not. J. Heading takes the view that the bowls have not yet been emptied but this seems to read too much into the tense of the verb. It fits the picture better to see the bowls as already emptied when the angel gives John this retrospective illumination – what judgment has meant for Babylon. Readers are now seeing what has already taken place. As shown earlier, the judgment on Babylon closes the tribulation and the next event is the coming of Christ to earth.

The angelic invitation is for John to see the judgment of the great whore. Of the various meanings of the word "judgment" (*krima*) the only one that fits the context is "the execution of a sentence already passed" (see Vine). The first two sections of the chapter, one descriptive (vv.l-6) and the other interpretative (vv.7-15), are but preliminary to the final climax when the monster turns on the harlot (vv.16-17) and destroys her. This is the subject of the chapter.

The word "whore" (*pornē*) in its seven other NT occurrences outside this chapter (and the related reference in 19:2) is always translated "harlot". JND and the RV also use the word "harlot" in this passage but the AV translators may have had a valid point in seeking to make a distinction in that the harlotry here is not physical, as in the other passages, but is symbolic of spiritual prostitution. The word *pornē* is derived from a verb meaning "to sell". In the physical sense it describes one who sells the body for gain, but in general usage it came to describe anyone who betrayed personal purity for selfish pleasure or profit. A woman could give delight to her husband scripturally and legally within the marriage bond, but for her to betray her husband and allow herself to be used by another for pleasure or profit was to place herself in the class of the harlot.

The OT prophets used the picture of the intimacy of the marriage bond to describe Israel as the wife of Jehovah owing Him absolute fidelity with attendant purity. To be associated with or give allegiance to other gods was described as harlotry. This picture is inherent in the stern words of Isaiah, "How is the faithful city became a harlot" (Isa 1:21), when Jerusalem permitted idols to be introduced. Ezekiel used the same graphic imagery, "Thou hast played the whore with the Assyrians, because thou wast insatiable, yea, thou hast played the harlot with them and yet couldst not be satisfied. Thou hast, moreover, multiplied thy fornication in the land of Canaan unto Chaldea" (Ezek 16:28-29). Jeremiah joins in this condemnatory chorus, "Hast thou seen what backsliding Israel hath done? She is gone up under every high mountain and under every green tree and hath played the harlot" (Jer 3:6). The betrayal of the revelation of Jehovah was implicit in the alliances with the nations around Israel. For Israel to ally herself with another nation meant the acceptance of their gods. When the motive for such alliances was commercial gain then the charge was harlotry – a spiritual harlotry since the divine revelation that set Israel apart was ignored. Harlotry is never a charge laid against the Gentile nations; it is a charge against Israel as being the only nation brought into such an intimate relationship with Jehovah. In light of this OT usage this harlot symbolises a system that has misused divine truth for its own pleasure or profit or to gain power on earth; in such a charge it is the corruption and debasement of truth that is in view.

This whore has earned the adjective "the great". Israel may have committed "whoredom" but this harlot stands out above all others. The scale of her influence is seen symbolically in that she "sitteth upon many waters". There is an echo of Babylon here even before she is specifically identified. The "many waters" were historically an identification mark for Babylon situated on the Euphrates river with the network of canals and irrigation channels spreading out in all directions. In the glitter of the morning or evening sun Babylon literally seemed to be squatting on many waters. Jeremiah had this picture in view when he spoke, "O thou that dwellest upon many waters, abundant in treasures, thine end is come and the measure of thy covetousness" (Jer 51:13). Nevertheless in light of the angelic interpretation in v.15, the "many waters" must be taken symbolically as describing the worldwide influence of this harlot. The metaphor of "sitting" is used three times of the harlot in this chapter. In this verse she sits on "many waters", in v.3 she sits on "the beast" and in v.9 she sits on "seven mountains". None of these describes a physical location but each depicts in symbolic terms that which supports the harlot. There may also be a hint of the control that she thinks she exercises – particularly with regard to the symbol of the beast. Supported by "peoples and multitudes and nations and tongues" the harlot may assume she controls them.

2 The domination of earth by this harlot is seen in two matters:

1. the pollution she promotes – with "the kings of the earth". The verb "committed fornication" is in the aorist tense; grammarians call it the *constative* aorist. It sums up the lifetime pursuit of these kings in buying

from the harlot that which she had no right to sell and, in this way, they share her sin. They were quite prepared to accept her spiritual claims so long at these did not conflict with their debauchery and sin. The men of earth and particularly those in high position here called "the kings", have no objection to religion so long as it does not interfere with the exercise of their autocratic power. The religious experiences offered by this woman are certainly pleasurable and offer no threat to their authority.

2. the pleasure she proffers – to "the inhabitants of the earth". The metaphor of drunkenness describes the suspension of the mental faculties that leads to irrational behaviour. This is characteristic of those who have drunk of the wine proffered by the whore. The symbolic language, taken from Jer 51:7, gives a graphic picture of the debauchery associated with the harlot. She uses religion to bring about the suspension of the rational faculties of men that they may be the more under her control. Men have no objection to religion so long as it does not interfere with their pleasure and their sin.

3 On two previous occasions (1:10; 4:2) John was "in the spirit" and received the visions. In this passage as also later in 21:10 John expresses what happened to him somewhat differently and writes, "And he carried me away in the spirit". From the context the "he" must be the angel in conversation with him. The verb implies transportation and perhaps involves time as well as distance. While the "spirit" is his own spirit, indicating that his body was still on Patmos, the whole vision demands the presence of the Holy Spirit to introduce him ecstatically into new scenes. "...the wilderness" is a fitting location for this vision of harlot and beast, while "a great and high mountain" (21:10) is a suitable location from which to view a descending city. The absence of the article before "wilderness" indicates that the desolation of the landscape is emphasised not a particular geographic location, despite the advocacy of Alford for the desert around literal Babylon. A wilderness (or a desert) is a very appropriate background, indeed, for the monster that John is to see.

From his vantage point of a desolate wilderness John sees the woman who already has been identified to him as "the great whore". She is seen to be sitting on a wild beast (*thērion*), and what a wild beast it is! Three unusual features distinguish it from any wild beast in nature:

(i) Its colour. It is scarlet-coloured. Nature does not go in for colours like this in its fauna and this marks it out as unnatural and different from all other beasts. A blazing crimson that will be seen again in the clothing of the woman is seen in this beast. While the colour has priestly connections (Lev 14:4; Num 19:6; Heb 9:19) it is the word used for the robe that the soldiers in mockery placed on Christ (Matt 27:28). There is no mockery here; the brilliant colour is a claim to world attention; this colour cannot be missed. In the interpretation it will be seen that both the empire and the religious system she supports will demand world attention

(ii) Its names. This beast is "full of names". That they are "names of blasphemy" indicates that whatever names men have used against God are all found in the beast and all are insulting to or misrepresentations of deity.

(iii) Its heads and horns. This beast has "seven heads and ten horns". This identifies it as the first beast of 13:1-9 already shown to symbolise an empire and its head. The fact that it rose out of the sea suggested the Gentile origin of both empire and head. "Seven heads and ten horns" was the characteristic feature of the dragon pictured moving through history (12:3), but this beast is Satan's earthly representative in the tribulation period. It has already been shown in comment on 13:1 that the seven heads are symbolic of satanic power in dictatorial world governments following each other successively down through history. The administrative power of the final empire is seen in the ten horns symbolic of the ten rulers who will unitedly yield their kingdoms to the Beast (vv.12-14). The details will be discussed when the angel interprets the symbols from v.9 onwards. The composite picture of woman and beast shows the relationship between the two; sitting on the beast she is supported by it. The idea cannot be physical location and any idea that she controls it is secondary. Simply interpreted there is presented a religious and ecclesiastical system supported by a satanically-energised political power.

4 Clothing as so often in Scripture answers to character (1 Tim. 2:9-10). When Israel adopted Babylonish practices the daughters of Zion began to copy the dress and ornamentation of the daughters of Babylon (Isa 3:18-26). This harlot proclaims her trade in her dress, her decoration and her deportment:

1. Her Dress. The purple in the days of the Roman Empire was confined to royalty. The scarlet colour similar to that of the beast (v.3) is the blazing crimson that spoke of ostentatious splendour. The implication is that the woman claimed royalty allied with an earthly magnificence.
2. Her Decoration. The passive participle "decked", better translated by Newberry "gilded" and by JND as "ornaments of gold", describes the dazzling array of gold and precious stones and pearls worn by the woman. Harlots have always thought this kind of decoration essential to their trade. The flaunting of wealth in this way has always been a sign of voluptuous and licentious debauchery.
3. Her Deportment. She is clearly plying her trade. The cup speaks both of her personal debauchery and her public invitation to others to join her revels. The cup being golden shows that what she proffers was originally from divine revelation but now the contents have become totally corrupted. "Full of abominations" describes the idolatrous principles that she offers for the

pleasure of men. The word "filthiness" (*ta akatharta*), translated by JND as "the unclean things", describes the filthy practices that flow from the principles of idolatry. Behind the principles and the practices is the sin that gives rise to them. It is named again as "fornication" (see v.2) and describes the spiritual betrayal of divine revelation. In Scripture physical fornication is degrading but the severest censure is reserved for the spiritual betrayal of the holy and divine. History confirms that the most degrading and unholy practices can and do result from the abandonment of divine truth.

5 The woman is identified by the name on her forehead. H.B. Swete, quoting Seneca the Elder (55 BC-41 AD), produces some evidence, that prostitutes were identified in this way in Rome. Positive confirmation of this practice has not been forthcoming. There is no thought of this woman flaunting her name; she is not courting publicity but God has put the name there for identification in the interests of His people. She is unlikely to be even aware of the name being on her forehead. Referring to the fact that the name is "on the forehead" A. Hislop has an interesting note in his book *The Two Babylons* when he writes, "What means the writing of that name 'on the forehead'? Does it not naturally indicate that just before the judgment overtakes her, her real character was to be so thoroughly developed, that everyone who has eyes to see, who has the least spiritual discernment, would be compelled, as it were, on ocular demonstration, to recognise the wonderful fitness of the title which the Spirit of God has affixed to her". The implication is that those with spiritual discernment, with Scripture in hand, can put a name on this harlot.

That the name on the forehead is by divine act for identification is supported by the fact that the title is introduced by the word "mystery". This book has spoken of "the mystery of the seven stars" (1:20) and the "mystery of God" (10:7) and the word must carry the same meaning in this passage. It is defined by Vine as "That which being outside the range of unassisted natural apprehension can be made known only by divine revelation". Thus the identification of this woman with Babylon lies outside human comprehension until God reveals it in His word. It is not a matter for surprise, therefore, that unbelieving historians and antiquarians of the world miss this identification. Now God reveals it and no one need have any further problem. It should be noted that the word "mystery" does not form part of the title; it is not an adjective but a noun that introduces, or possibly, stands in apposition to the title. The capitalisation in many translations, including the RV, makes it part of the title which is misleading. The word "mystery" should thus be treated as appositional and read as in the RV margin "mystery, BABYLON THE GREAT".

The name of Babylon is traceable across the pages of Scripture from its origin in Gen 10:10 as the city founded by Nimrod. The history of this city forms a fascinating backdrop to and a contrast with the history of Israel as unfolded throughout the OT until Christ. The highlights of that history move from

Nimrod (c.2230 BC) through the Old Babylonian Empire under Hammurabi of the famous Hammurabi code (1728 – 1686 BC), to the Neo-Babylonian Empire of Nebuchadnezzar of the sixth century before Christ. After its capture by the Medes in 539 BC it passed virtually unchanged through the Medo-Persian Empire, the Grecian Empire under Alexander the Great, right down to the times of the Roman Empire. A fading yet a fascinating city that amidst all the vicissitudes and changing fortunes of many empires had endured to outlast them all. History will show that despite many sieges and many battles it was never completely destroyed. From its association with Nimrod, whose name means "the rebel", the city is viewed in Scripture as the centre of rebellion against God, resistance to His purposes and the persecution of His people. It became the "city of confusion" (Isa 24:10; 34:11) whence all idolatry spread across the earth, and as such stands in evident contrast to Jerusalem, the city of the Christ from which God meant truth and light to radiate over the earth.

The introductory word "mystery" in her title indicates that the woman represents not literal Babylon but the religious aspect of Babylon; a most appropriate symbolisation since the merest acquaintance with the history of the religion emanating from Babylon recognises the importance of the female element. From the records of archaeology and antiquity it is known that the key figure in the establishment of this mystery religion was Semiramis, the wife of Nimrod, a very beautiful and clever woman. She had established in Babylon a system of idolatrous worship which, because it was in direct contradiction to divine revelation, had to be conducted in secret. Within a century of the Noachic flood that destroyed a world, rebellion against God had to be carefully concealed. Initiatory rites precluded all but selected persons from being permitted to engage in these mysteries. When her husband Nimrod was killed unexpectedly while hunting, she claimed miraculous conception for her posthumously born son called Tammuz. He was acclaimed as the "saviour" and the fulfilment of the promise of the seed made to Eve (Gen 3:15). The legend of the "mother and child" was a basic tenet of the Babylonian mysteries; images and drawings pictured the mother as "Queen of Heaven" (Jer 7:18; 44:17, 18, 19, 25). The mother-and-child motif is common to all pagan religions and shows the worldwide influence of Babylon. An initiated, celibate and tonsured priesthood assisted by vestal virgins devoted to religious prostitution carried out animal sacrifice as the basis for sin-cleansing. Sprinkling with holy water, eating of a sacrificial meal and incense-burning processions were the backbone of a religious system that originated with Semiramis. The death of Tammuz, killed by a boar, presented not a problem but an opportunity. The forty-day mourning for Tammuz is referred to by Ezekiel: "And, behold there sat women weeping for Tammuz" (Ezek 8:14). This lenten mourning was turned to joy in the spring resurrection from the dead celebrated in the Feast of Ishtar (Easter). There is found in this Babylonish mystery cult the oldest and most powerful satanic deception of all time. Satan had established a religion in antiquity upon which he could draw to challenge Christ in every messianic claim. In this cult Satan would challenge the virgin birth of Christ,

His sacrificial death and His glorious resurrection; all were foreseen and foreshadowed in this ancient deception. This whole system became the basis for the spread of idolatry, under different names, into every nation of the ancient world. It is in this worldwide sense that Babylon in its religious system is given the title "the great".

Described as "the mother of harlots and abominations of the earth", this woman stands in obvious contrast to the mother in 12:1-5. There the nation of Israel, seen ideally in the purpose of God, becomes the divine channel by which Christ comes to earth; here this mother reflects the purpose of Satan and she produces offspring that are the very antithesis of Christ, They are called "the harlots" as describing those systems produced across earth taking character from their debased mother in that they too would prostitute sacred things for profit or pleasure or power. Her progeny are further described as "the abominations (*bdelugmata*) of the earth"; the same word in v.4 describes the character of the debased practices stemming from this false religion. The article is better included as in JND and the RV. All the idolatrous systems belonging to earth and the vile practices stemming from these systems have their origin in this Babylonish mother. Abraham was delivered from the very home of idolatry in Babylonia; Israel had to be rescued from the gods of Egypt and in their Canaan inheritance it was a constant battle to preserve them first from the idolatry of Canaan, Phoenicia, and Assyria and finally the idolatry of the Neo-Babylonian empire under Nebuchadnezzar. All these idolatrous systems came from the same source. Eastwards the development of Hinduism, Buddhism and Shintoism were all distortions of the same revealed truth and its debasement into animism and spiritism. North and west and south as men moved they carried the false cult with satanically-inspired local variations to appeal to all races and cultures. The family of this mother covered the globe.

Despite the stress on the religious aspect of Babylon, two matters must be made plain:

1. that it is not the historical religious system that is principally before John in the harlot; while Babylon is the ancient name she bears she has yet to appear in her final guise in the tribulation.

2. John is being shown a harlot and beast that have not yet appeared on the world stage; he sees them prophetically. This woman has ancient origins but she sits on a beast that has not yet appeared on the stage of history (see 13:1).

From the perspective of the present day, near the close of the church age, the only religious system that fits this picture, and it does fit the picture in amazing detail, is the Roman Catholic church. This religious system, though it has emerged only in the centuries following Pentecost, will still be on earth after every true believer is removed from earth at the rapture. This will be the system that, absorbing other religious systems will be the final manifestation of a religion that has its roots in Babylon. That this is so lies in a truth made plain in Scripture – that when truth is distorted and Scripture abandoned Babylonish conditions are the result. This was true of:

1. the post-diluvian civilisation in Gen 10-11 when the early truths of creation and a Creator were rejected and the gospel that God had put in the stars was distorted and misused for astrological purposes. The end was Babel and its tower.
2. the time when Israel as a nation rejected the truth of prophetic revelation and was carried away to spend seventy years in Babylon.
3. the abandonment of truth in this church age results in the emergence of the Babylonish conditions of confusion and corruption (2 Cor 6:14-18). The end result is a return to Babylonish idolatry with christianised names that has emerged in Roman Catholicism through the abandonment of the truth. It is in this system that the full flower of Babylonian teaching and practice is found today. This woman is the end result of forces already at work throughout christendom where the abandonment of scriptural truth in Protestantism will result in a union of denominations into an ecumenism that will be truly Babylonish in character. Many of the denominational successors of those who abandoned as corrupt Roman Catholicism at the Reformation, have already returned to the fold of Rome, and many others are moving in this same direction. The Pope will lead the greatest religious body on earth up to the midpoint of the tribulation. Believers today may raise only a feeble voice of protest at the harlotry involved in the prostitution of divine truth, but their removal at the rapture will but accelerate the union and emergence of this harlot. Roman Catholicism is the worthy daughter of Babylon but she, herself, is a mother to many denominations who in greater or lesser measure reflect her teaching. In its final form of the harlot, this system will unite all the ancient religions of Babylon as well as apostate christianity; Rome will be the umbrella under which even that which formerly was called heathendom will find a shelter. What began with the introduction of leaven into the meal by the woman in the parable (Matt 13:33) and the activity of "that woman" Jezebel (2:20), are church-age developments that have flowered already into Roman Catholicism that is essentially Babylonish. The declared aim of the World Council of Churches is to unite all protestant denominations with Rome. Already it has achieved union with the Eastern Orthodox Church which is but Roman Catholicism under another name. Committees exist for the incorporation into this same union of the original religions stemming from ancient Babylon as Hinduism, Buddhism and Shintoism. It would seem that all the daughters are returning to the mother figure and this end-time

harlot, while mainly and emphatically Roman Catholicism, will certainly embrace the older heathen religions of the world.

6 The unique position this harlot has claimed, the unholy profligacy that has displayed her sin gives way to the most terrible note of all – the unparalleled persecution of which she has been guilty. The drunken debauchery with which she has beguiled her paramours (v.2) does not satisfy her depraved tastes. The present participle "drunken" describes her state as a result, not of wine, but of blood. To be drunk from (*ek*) the blood of the saints is a gruesome metaphorical way to describe the fact that this harlot has revelled in putting men and women to death. She has been intoxicated with what is normally repulsive to any right-thinking person. The repetition that follows:

"drunken with (*ek*) the blood of the saints and"

"[drunken] with (*ek*) the blood of the martyrs of Jesus"

suggests that there are two different groups who have suffered from this harlot:

1 "The blood of the saints". John is shown in prophetic perspective a final manifestation in the tribulation of one who is as old as history, but he is given to see that throughout history she has never changed her character. These saints suffered from the idolatrous systems before the time of Christ. The summary of Heb 11:32-38 gives the record of some who through faith refused the idolatry of their day and as a result suffered and died. Babylon is guilty of their blood.

2. "The blood of the martyrs (*martures*) of Jesus". A little consideration will show that this second group of martyrs must be much wider than even the blood-stained history of papal Rome during the church age. Pagan Rome, particularly during the Smyrna period of church history, put multitudes to death long before papal Rome emerged in history. The statement includes all who have died for Christ throughout the church age. It will embrace also those who still bear testimony for Jesus (12:17) throughout the first half of the tribulation period. Many will die at the instigation of the harlot up to the time of her judgment at the midpoint of the tribulation. The blood of such martyrs is traced to the satanic religious system having its origins in Babylon. The statement in 18:24 is even wider in its scope and, going back before Babel in history, comes right down to the genocide and wholesale murder of the closing years of the rule of the Beast.

The RV accurately catches the relation between the verb and noun with the translation, "I wondered with a great wonder". "Admiration" in the AV is misleading, if it be taken to mean that John admired or respected this woman. The idea is rather of "shock" or "astonishment" (the verb *thaumazō* is translated often in the Gospels "to marvel") that a woman of such a clearly depraved character finds a place in prophecy.

(b) The Beast – The Monster Figure (vv. 7-14)

7 The amazement that John showed at the sight of the woman causes the angel to ask of John a reason for this shock; the "wherefore?" could be more idiomatically presented as "why?" Whether this question is purely rhetorical makes little difference for the angel does not wait for a reply but uses the question to introduce the interpretation. There could be various explanations as to why John is lost in wonder at this point. Since he had seen the Beast in a previous vision (13:1) John would hardly find its re-appearance a matter of wonder. Perhaps the name Babylon borne by the woman shocked him. More likely the shock arose because the beast carried the woman instead of devouring her. It is with this relationship between the woman and the Beast that the angel begins his interpretation and calls it, "the mystery of the woman and of the beast". The word "mystery" (*mustērion*) again has its usual NT meaning of a divine revelation that could not be known by unaided human intelligence. It is God who reveals that apostate religion (symbolised by the harlot) will be supported and upheld and carried by the Beast (symbol of a world political power) in the time of the tribulation. The final phase of the mystery of this relationship will come in vv.16-17 where it is shown that the very Beast that carries her will devour the woman. This latter point is the subject of the chapter (see v.1).

The angelic description of the Beast repeats the part of the description of v.3 that is relevant for the interpretation. The fact that no mention is made of crowns on the horns (cf. 13:1) suggests that the ten subsidiary rulers are viewed at a time-point when they have already surrendered their authority to the beast (see v.12). If this is a legitimate deduction then the point of time under review is the midpoint of the tribulation. Other considerations in the following verses will support this deduction.

The section may be divided as follows:

The Arrival of the Beast	v.8
The Ancestry of the Beast	vv.9-11
The Actions of the Beast	vv.12-14

8 For the clear exposition of this difficult verse a number of matters must be kept in mind:

1. The correlation between the Empire and its Emperor. It was clear in 13:1-10 that the symbol of the beast was used to refer both to a world empire and to an individual in whom this world empire would be represented or embodied. Under whatever name he will eventually use, whether king, president or emperor this individual is for all purposes seen to be identified closely with the empire he represents. Scripture says the same things about both and the context must show whether the empire or its leader is meant. In many cases there is no need for distinction to be drawn but for simplicity of reference it was

decided to use the capital letter when it was judged that the man (Beast) is in view.

2. The coming of the Empire and of its Emperor. The Beast has been shown to have two "comings" onto the world stage. In the first coming the beast rises up "out of the sea" (13:1) where the language and context clearly suggest the emergence of this final world empire from amongst the nations. In the second coming, referred to in 11:7 the Beast is said to ascend "out of the abyss". As has been shown this language is not appropriate for an empire and points to the Beast as a world leader who, having received the "deadly wound" (13:3), appears to die and as a result there is the pseudo-resurrection and the satanic presentation to the world of a man who has defeated death itself. The two aspects of empire and emperor and the two comings are the necessary background for the understanding of this passage. The fact that earlier references have placed this assassination-resurrection drama at the midpoint of the tribulation offers guidance when the Beast here is spoken of as "out of the abyss" (RV).

3. The connection between the woman and the Beast. This passage does not deal with the history of the woman and only incidentally with the history of the beast. When John is shown the vision in v.3 he is shown the woman already seated on the Beast. So the interpretation by the angel must be understood as related to this point in time. The woman symbolising world-religion in Roman Catholicism, is seen at the midpoint of the tribulation supported by this Beast. The name Babylon does look back to Nimrod (Gen 10) and the ancient mystery religion originating with his wife Semiramis but this is for historical and Biblical identification. A worldwide apostate religion, mainly apostate christianity, will be supported by the world power at this point in the tribulation. The beast symbolises an empire (or its leader), at the same time-point in the tribulation giving full support to the woman; the political power is sustaining the religious system. John is given a prophetic glimpse of this strange relationship; history only comes into the picture in vv.9-10 as explanation of the strange appearance of this Beast.

That the Beast had an existence before this time-point when he is carrying the woman is shown by the emphatic "was" in the statement "the beast…was". It will be shown that all the four statements are best understood as referring to the Beast as the mighty head of this last empire. The statements summarise the history and destiny of the Beast:

a. The Beast "was". Looking back from the midpoint of the tribulation, the Beast has already had a meteoric rise in popularity and power until he had reached the highest pinnacles of empire (see 13:1-2). He has already had at the very least three and a half years of world leadership and possibly quite a few years even before this period. What is emphasised is that he had a history before this midpoint of the tribulation.

b. The Beast "was..... and is not" . Dramatically and suddenly he is gone at the very moment when he reaches this pinnacle of power. The present tense is a dramatic present that allows the onlooker to scan the surroundings to assure himself that he is gone. It also implies that something dramatic has happened. Commentators who interpret this beast as the Roman Empire have a problem here as this would seem to be a very odd way of describing the Roman Empire under which John was suffering banishment at this moment. The statements that follow put beyond doubt that this present tense is to be interpreted as the moment when this world-leader receives the "wound to death" (13:3) and is suddenly gone from the scene. There is a very big gap on the earth-scene as this mighty charismatic figure "is not".

c. The Beast .... "shall ascend out of the bottomless pit". The descriptive phrase "out of the bottomless pit" links this man and this moment to the same man and the same moment in 11:7. At this point the power of Satan is involved in the greatest deception ever to be foisted upon men. The Beast appears to emerge from death itself in a re-enactment of the resurrection of Christ. Recalling that Satan, at this very time, has been permitted to hold the key to the bottomless pit (9:1) it would appear that he conducts the Beast to that realm and then brings him back again on to the world-stage as his special agent on earth. It would seem that from this midpoint of the tribulation the Beast is satanically indwelt.

d. The Beast shall "go into perdition". There is a textual variation with considerable authority behind the RV marginal reading, "and he goeth into perdition". In the word "perdition" (*apōleia*) the final destiny of the Beast is summarised and it can only refer to the judgment executed on this man when the Christ comes to earth. That end is described as the lake of fire (19:20).

Statements c. and d. above put beyond question the interpretation that the Beast as a man is in view and not the beast as an empire. Figurative language could possibly explain statement c. as teaching that an empire emerges with full satanic support, though it is somewhat difficult to see how an empire could be said to come up out of the abyss. It is even more difficult to envisage an empire going into perdition. Some commentators see the problem and suggest that it is the empire as seen in its head that is consigned to the lake of fire, an explanation that does not do justice to the four balanced statements describing the existence, the removal, the return and the end of a man.

This identification of the symbolic beast as the head of empire is supported by the startled reaction of the "earth-dwellers" as shown in the verb "shall wonder" (see vv.6-7 where the same verb has described John's personal reaction to the scene). The use of this verb links this passage with 13:3 when it is said "And all the world wondered after the beast". This startled reaction is much more explicable in terms of the amazement roused by the dramatic events that have happened to a world leader, very possibly in sight of the whole world via television, than the revival or re-emergence of any ancient kingdom even that of the mighty Roman Empire.

The people who wonder are described as the earth-dwellers, an expression which, as previously pointed out (see 13:8), identifies persons who have chosen to be identified with the Beast. They are shown in the next statement to stand in contrast to the saints. Manuscript authority which seems conclusive (see JND footnote on this verse) gives the R.V. reading, "Whose name hath not been written in the book of life". In other words the register of heaven, the book of life, will confirm that their names are missing and emphasise the truth that heaven is not taken by surprise by the action of the creature. These citizens of earth have no citizenship of heaven – having refused eternal life they have settled down to a home on earth and the record of "the book of life" when it is opened at the great white throne (20:12) will prove that this is so. The phrase "from the foundation of the world" modifies "written" and, as in 13:8 (see comments *in loc*), is to be translated "since the foundation of the world" and thus defines the complete register of saints from the creation (Gen 1:1) until the close of earth history at the great white throne.

The point of time when the earth-dwellers wonder is defined as the moment "when they behold the beast". This is the AV rendering of the present participle of a quite common verb "to see" (*blepō*); a verb which, on occasions, is used to convey an apprehension that goes beyond physical sight. It is the verb used in Heb 2:8-9 in the statement "But we see Jesus". The verb seems to be used in this dramatic way here; the moment when those whose interest has already been engaged by the meteoric rise and overpowering personality of this mighty emperor, see this latest evidence of his supernatural power, and it dawns upon them that this is "the man" for whom they have been waiting. Instantly they are won over completely and give him their undivided allegiance. This moment of " satanic conversion" is the reason for the repetition of the description of the Beast from the first part of the verse – to show that the focus is settled firmly upon the man in whom empire is embodied. JND supports this view of a "conversion" experience (in an evil sense): "Seeing the beast, that it was, and is not, and shall be present". The manuscript evidence for JND's translation of the final clause is quite convincing. The amazed citizens of the Beast's kingdom will have watched with horror that assassination attempt; the apparent resurrection will convince them of his supernatural power and they bow to worship a man (13:4) who before their very eyes "was" and "is not" and yet is still present. This visual evidence is enough; they will argue that this man must be God and worship follows (13:4).

9 The angelic interpreter acknowledges that more than natural understanding is required to grasp what he has now to explain. There is no case for referring this statement back to the previous verse; it must relate to what follows. Wisdom in Scripture generally implies an insight into the true nature of things and this requires divine illumination. The somewhat similar statement in 13:18 offers a challenge to the identification of the person of the Beast; here the challenge is to see this beast in the light of history. The interpretative key lies in following the original word order which is best presented by the RV: "The seven heads are seven mountains on which the woman sitteth: and they are seven kings" (also JND margin). The expression "there are seven kings" (AV) is less likely, if only because it spoils the double symbol. The sequence is perfectly plain – the seven symbolic heads (on the beast) picture seven metaphorical mountains which represent seven actual kings. The statements to follow will show that these are seven actual personages who have moved in succession across the page of history.

The mention of "seven mountains" has led many commentators to see nothing beyond the literal city of Rome. W. Scott puts it clearly when he writes, "The seven-hilled city of Rome is here indicated as the seat and centre of the woman's almost universal authority and influence. It is where the papacy has been located and has flourished, more or less for 1500 years" (p.351). J.B. Smith puts the corroborative evidence: "The city intended is undoubtedly Rome on the following evidence: as many as a dozen of the old Roman authors speak of Rome as the city of seven hills; Roman coins (still preserved) bear the imprint of Rome as built on seven hills; Victorinus, the first commentator on Revelation, in his notes on the present verse, says 'that is, the city of Rome'". All this is interesting but irrelevant and a serious misinterpretation. It should be noted:

1. that the seven mountains are not given as the identifying mark of any city. This is an interpretative interpolation by commentators which only serves to distort the picture.
2. if this expression was meant to describe Rome the wrong word is used. Rome was spoken of as *urbs septicollis*. The Latin word *collis* means "hill" or "slope" an appropriate term for the ten hills identified in Rome (historians have great problems selecting seven out of the ten named by various authorities). The highest of these hills was the Janiculum which at 275 feet was scarcely a mountain, while all the others varied between 150-250 feet. The Greek equivalent for the Latin *collis* would be *bounos* while the word used here is *oros* the normal word for mountain.
3. the word "mountain" is used metaphorically and is interpreted in the text. The seven mountains symbolise seven kings. To interpret them as literal hills is to misunderstand the angelic message.
4. when the woman sits on the "many waters" (v.1) this must be taken as metaphorical since it is interpreted in v.15; when the woman sits upon "a scarlet coloured beast" this again is symbolic; thus when she sits upon the "seven mountains" this too must be figurative. In none of these cases is there any justification for taking the location as literal.

The angelic interpretation is plain: "The seven heads (symbolic) are seven mountains (metaphorical)...and they are (RV) seven kings (historical)". The word "mountain" is a normal scriptural metaphor for a kingdom. Such kingdoms stand out in the historical landscape as mountains do in the physical landscape. David uses such a picture poetically to describe Israel (Ps 30:7) and Jeremiah uses it pictorially of Babylon (Jer 51:25). The Messianic kingdom is described as a "stone which became a great mountain and filled the whole earth" (Dan 2:35).

Seven great kingdoms represented by their kings then should stand out in the landscape of Biblical history. An imperial power is represented in an imperial person in each kingdom. A uniting link is seen in that these particular seven support the woman or, to put the point another way, judging from the outward appearance she seems to be in control of these kings. The angel clarifies the picture when he refers to five of the kings as fallen, one as presently existing and one as not yet come. The five fallen looks back into history from John's time, the aorist tense of the verb "fallen" summarises the history of the five kings – they have passed from the stage of time. The reference to the present, "one is", allows John to look around at the existing Roman empire; the reference to the seventh, "the other is not yet come", lifts his eye to the future.

It is not history in general that is presented to John in these seven kingdoms. It is history from the Biblical viewpoint and, when Biblical history is examined, it is a startling fact that there have been only five empires that have moved across the Biblical page up to the time of John. These empires have come into Biblical prominence because of their link with Israel. These five nations are as follows:-

1.	Egypt	personified in	a Pharaoh
2.	Assyria	represented by	a Sennacherib
3.	Babylon	symbolised in	a Nebuchadnezzar
4.	Medeo-Persia	identified in	a Cyrus
5.	Greece	personified in	an Alexander

In the time of John all these empires and their kings had passed off the world stage. The one that then existed in the time of John is clearly the sixth

6.	Rome	personified in	a Caesar

The seventh, "the other" which "is not yet come", points beyond the church age to the appearance of the final world-empire and the man representing it. In this book this empire and its leader are both pictured as the beast (or Beast).

7.	Final Empire	represented in	the Beast

It is clear that the time-gap between the sixth and the seventh head is the same as the time-gap between Daniel's sixty-ninth and seventieth week. The church age is omitted again; Scripture moves from the time of the Caesar and the Roman Empire to the time of the Beast and the endtime empire. The fact that the seventh empire is not a revived Roman Empire is implicit in this picture.

Commentators who interpret the Beast as the revived Roman Empire must seek an alternative interpretation for the heads. There are two main suggestions from which to choose:

1. Some see the heads as Caesars of the Roman Empire. If this book was written as suggested about 96AD then Domitian must be the sixth head ("one is"). Looking backwards the difficulty is to select five from his eleven predecessors all called "Caesar" (*vide* Seutonius and his history of the twelve Caesars). It takes some historical dexterity as well as detailed knowledge to select five from the list (see J.B. Smith) even if the criteria are limited to their "blasphemy" or their "violent deaths" or their "persecution of the Jews". The theory depends too much on the subjective choice of the historian and demands extensive historical research.
2. Some see the heads as seven forms of government within the Roman Empire. W. Scott writes (p.351) "The seven heads on the Beast represent seven successive forms of government from the rise of the fourth universal empire on through its history till its end". The six forms of government up to the time of John are generally listed as kings, consuls, dictators, deceivers, military tribunes and emperors. In answer it must be pointed out that:

    a. it seems somewhat strange to impose an arbitrary interpretation when the heads have already been interpreted as kings;
    b. to get the seven forms of government the history of the Roman Empire must be extended back beyond Caesar Augustus into the Roman Republic. The Empire as such had basically only one form of government until long after John's time – the Caesar.
    c. A further problem arises if the sixth form of government is the imperial rule of the Caesar; then the seventh must be the imperial rule revived, which leaves a difficulty with the eighth form of government. Few clear explanations are forthcoming as to the form of the eighth kind of rule.
    d. It should also be pointed out that the verb "to fall" (*piptō*) is the verb used in the Septuagint to describe the violent fall or overthrow of kings or kingdoms (Isa 21:9; Jer 50:15; 51:8; Ezek 29:5; 30:6). It is difficult to find an example of its use in connection with a change in method of government. These do not generally "fall" in the usual sense of the word, but are modified or changed over a period.

The connection between the seven heads as seven imperial powers and the seven kings as seven imperial personages, becomes clearer in the mention of the seventh. He is identified as "the other" (*ho allos*) which "is not yet come". The use of *allos* shows he is of the same kind as his predecessors. "When he cometh" is an indefinite temporal clause (Robertson) equivalent to "whenever he comes". The masculine pronoun indicates that it is a person and not a new form of imperialism coming unto the scene. This imperial personage stands in the line of a Pharaoh, a Sennacherib, a Nebuchadnezzar, a Cyrus, an Alexander and a Caesar but greater than all of them. He is the "little horn" of Dan 7:8 arising from the mightiest empire in world history pictured in the fourth beast with the ten horns in Dan 7:7. The expression "must continue" points to the place this ruler fills in divine purpose. His stay however is limited and is summarised in the statement "a short space" given in the RV as "a little while". While this seventh world-ruler must have been on the world stage perhaps for some years before he signs the covenant this is the point when he takes on a world-dominant role. The signing of the covenant with the national leader in Israel also brings him into the prophetic picture as inaugurating the seventieth week. From this point this period of his rule is described as "a little while" and covers only the three and a half years up to the midpoint of the week. The following verse will describe how his rule will continue to the end of the seven-year period but he will then be seen as the eighth head.

11 One further fact has to be added to the symbolic picture to allow it to represent the complete history of the Beast. The language of v.8 is repeated, "the beast that was" looks back to his first appearance on the world-stage (13:1); the second statement "and is not" points to his dramatic assassination and disappearance for a time. In place of the third statement of v.8 "shall ascend out of the pit" the point is made that he is just not the seventh head restored, but he must now be seen as the eighth. That this is not a different person entirely is carefully guarded for he is still "of (*ek*) the seven"; nevertheless he is distinct. This refers to the change brought about in this man when, after his "death" and "resurrection", he is not merely the agent of Satan but a Satan-controlled man. The number "eight" is associated in Scripture with resurrection and the Beast claims to be the risen man. The word "eighth" must point to the man, since it is masculine, while both "head" and "kingdom" are feminine. In this claim as a man risen from the grave he will make his bid for world-worship (2 Thess 2:4) and many will believe the lie (2 Thess 2:11). After this additional explanation the history of this man is closed with the statement repeated from v.8: "he goeth into perdition". Three and a half years later, at the end of the tribulation, the fuller detail of 19:20 explains this clearly, "And the beast was taken, and with him the false prophet…these both were cast alive into a lake of fire burning with brimstone".

12 The perspective from which John has viewed the Beast is confirmed by the angelic interpretation of the ten horns. As shown previously (see comments at 13:1) these are ten kings who all hold power simultaneously. The point that is emphasised now is their relationship with the beast. They hold their power collectively but in association with the Beast and not independently of him. When the Beast appears in 13:1 he has ten horns and each horn has a crown, showing that as the Beast emerges on the world-stage (as when he signs the seven-year covenant with the false prophet) he brings with him ten associated kings. Before this point the angelic word is, "they have no kingdom as yet", but with the emergence of the Beast they receive both their "kingdom" and their "authority" as kings. To use the metaphor they receive their crowns. This interpretation is supported by the fact that "kingdom" is singular, which suggests that the rights (*exousia*) of these ten kings come into existence simultaneously by a decree or resolution, perhaps from a world-body like the United Nations. Scripture gives no information as to whether these kingdoms are confined to Europe as suggested by commentators who subscribe to the idea of a "revived Roman Empire". The world-embracing view of the kingdom of the Beast would suggest a kingdom on a world-scale. These kings receive their kingdom with the Beast at the time of his emergence as the dominant world-leader; an inference from the fact that in 13:1 the beast emerges from the sea with the crowns on the horns. Their kingdom, however, has only a limited time-span and is divinely given as "one hour" – a metaphorical way of expressing a short-lived kingdom. Their kingdom is linked to the Beast personally and their period of associated rule can therefore be only the three and a half years of the first half of the week until they reach the decision to yield their kingdoms to him. In the event the period allowed by God for their reign both in association with the Beast and then under him is exactly seven years.

13 These ten kings, at the midpoint of the seven-year period, with cold calculation decide that it is in their interest to renounce their individual kingships and hand over control to the Beast. That they have "one mind" in the matter leaves no room for any dissenting voice as they recognise their future is bound up with this man. The tremendous events linked with this midpoint of the tribulation as set out in ch. 13, have convinced these kings of the supernatural power of the Beast and they are determined to be on the winning side. This handover of their kingdoms involves both the might (*dunamis*) of powerful military machines as well as the sovereignty (*exousia*) vested in the individual states. This is a calculated political response to the personal magnetism and charismatic claim of the world figure who claims to have been "raised from the dead" (13:3). These kings are caught up in the movement of adulation sweeping the earth and resign their individual sovereignty.

14 Whether it was the calculated intention of these kings to join forces with the Beast against God is not clear, but the fact is that they find themselves engaged immediately in the war with the Lamb (11:7;13:7) in which the "resurrected" Beast seeks to stamp out the testimony for Christ. These kings have been recruited into the forces of the Beast to carry out the satanic programme. Without going into detail John simply points triumphantly to the end of that war in the terse statement, "and the Lamb shall overcome them"; a reference to the moment of revelation of Christ as "Lord of lords and King of kings" when the armies of earth are gathered to Armageddon (16:16; 9:16). This glorious victory dealing with the confederated enemy will establish for all time that Christ is Lord over all who would claim lordship, and King over all who would claim sovereignty on earth. In the OT the title of deity is "God of gods and Lord of lords" (Deut 10:17; Dan 2:47) but in the NT the title belongs to Christ (19:16; 1 Tim 6:15). To the saints suffering in this war the Lordship of Christ is the vital matter and this will be confirmed by sight of the King, hence the order in the title. When Christ comes to earth sinners see him as King first and then have to bow the knee to Him as Lord (Phil 2:11); this order corresponds to the title in 19:16.

To the terrible shock of unbelievers Christ will not return alone to earth in this moment of triumph. The expression "with the beast" in v.12 shows the power ranged on the side of Satan, while the similar expression "with him (Christ)" describes the host allied to Christ. On earth despised, hunted and slain now the tears are over and the triumph has arrived; the saints share in the triumph of Christ. Three characteristic words are used of these saints; they are the "called" as to their salvation, they are the "chosen" referring to their service and they are the "faithful" referring to their stewardship. The single article shows there is but one company of saints. The RV reading, "And they also shall overcome that are with him, called and chosen and faithful", shows that the saints are not merely spectators of the triumph but actually share in this triumph of Christ.

(c) The Woman and the Beast (vv. 15-17)

15 Having described the woman (vv.1-7) and the beast (vv.8-14) John is now shown the judgment that he was invited to witness in v.1. First the angel shows to John the world-wide support that the harlot enjoyed before the sentence falls, by interpreting the "many waters" (v.1) on which the woman sat as "peoples, and multitudes and nations and tongues". This interpretation is given to ensure that there was no confusion with the literal waters on which literal Babylon did sit (see comment on v.1). Men from every national background, from every grade of society, of every political opinion and of every language give her unqualified support. This is the sixth and final listing of these familiar earthly demarcation lines in the book (5:9; 7:9; 10:11; 13:7; 14:6) and shows the worldwide support of this religious system symbolised in the harlot. This trans-national support has ever been characteristic of Roman Catholicism and will become even more pronounced when she gathers denominational protestantism and heathendom under her ecumenical umbrella. Supported by men internationally and, in the first half of the tribulation, by the Beast (v.3) this harlot is a mighty tool of satanic deception.

16 However at the moment of her greatest triumph, and apparently invincible, the harlot meets her doom. Having a worldwide power that ancient

Babylon sought and with a religious syncretism that had long abandoned any pretence of scriptural authority, she has developed the ancient mysteries into a veritable "tower" centred in the Pope and the Vatican City. Non-conformity is no longer a problem since non-conformists are no longer allowed to live. Using the secular arm of the empire, as the papacy has ever done, she has stamped out all opposition. Chapels and churches are channels to funnel wealth into her coffers. Nuncios and ambassadors give her a political power that rivals that of the Beast. Through her educational programmes and the worldwide communications she sits proudly as queen-consort of the world-ruler. The world is at her feet and ancient plottings of Semiramis the wife of Nimrod have been fulfilled at last.

Her end comes suddenly and catastrophically and from a most unexpected quarter. The ten kings with the support of the beast turn upon the harlot and destroy her utterly. That the kings and the beast act together, with the kings taking the lead, is shown by both the RV and JND, "And the ten horns which thou sawest and the beast" – a reading with overwhelming manuscript support. The ten satellite kings under the Beast have grown restive at the pretension and arrogance of this harlot and have begun to covet the wealth she possesses. Now with the support of the Beast they move to destroy her quickly and completely. A parallel in history is the moment when Henry VIII, with political and military power in his hands, decided he no longer needed the support of the Roman Catholic church in England and proceeded with the dissolution and destruction of the monasteries and the seizure of their wealth. The Beast, in a stunning act of betrayal, will turn on the Roman Catholic church and destroy her utterly. From the Vatican city the destruction will spread to every corner of the earth; the future tenses in the verbs of destruction graphically describe this spreading devastation. The first verb is "hate" and indicates the utter loathing and disgust with which her late confederates view her. This burning hatred drives them as they "make her desolate". Stripped of all that she valued her treasures are ransacked and her antiquities smashed or stolen. Literal acts of robbery and vandalism leave her "naked" when the scarlet and purple robes of ecclesiastical finery are stolen or burned; but there must also be a moral element as the news media expose from her long-hidden records the scandals of the ages and the catalogue of her harlotry and shame. She will indeed be naked! The symbolic cannibalism in the expression "shall eat her flesh" shows the bitterness of former friends who now set about tearing her limb from limb, satisfying depraved human nature by what they can tear from her in death. It is easy to envisage the exposure of the media as metaphorically they "make a meal" of this once-so-reclusive harlot. The final act of destruction is to "burn her with fire". This is surely a literal burning that leaves churches, chapels, abbeys, monasteries and convents in flames across the earth; a burning that leaves not a vestige of the glory that was Roman Catholicism which for many centuries darkened the light of revelation and brought men into slavery. This woman was the final manifestation of that which had its roots in ancient Babylon. It had reached its apogee and God saw to it that it was destroyed, utterly and completely.

17 The ten kings had their own reasons for destroying the harlot. The incalculable wealth of the Vatican (estimated very conservatively in 1993 as in the range of seven thousand billion pounds sterling in realisable assets and not including land values) would be an attraction to supplement national budgets in the various nations and covetous eyes would be fastened upon it. Add the resentment against a discredited religion, which in the judgment of men is no longer needed, and it is clear that the kings would only await a suitable opportunity to embark on this orgy of destruction. The Beast too had his reasons for allowing the destruction of the harlot. In the years of his rise to power she had been a useful ally and a staunch supporter throughout the nations; she may well have organised diplomatically the bloodless coup that allowed him world dominance and control of the ten-powered kingdom. Now he no longer needs this influence and may well have resented the state trappings of Vatican power as a challenge to his authority. But behind both of these puppets there is no doubt that Satan, the master deceiver, has decided that the moment has arrived for his man, the Beast, to claim divine honours as outlined in 2 Thess 2:2-4, "Who opposeth and exalteth himself above all that is called God, or that is worshipped, so that he, as God; sitteth in the temple of God, shewing himself that he is God". The removal of the harlot from the world- stage leaves the way open for the last religion of earth – the worship of a man and through him the worship of Satan. The mystery is stripped away, the sham has gone and unashamedly the final form of Babylonian worship is established on earth for the final three and a half years of the tribulation. Judaism has been proscribed, apostate christianity and the religions ecumenically embraced in it are now destroyed and worship is directed through this man of sin to Satan. The ten kings, the Beast and Satan are working to their own agenda thinking they were free to make their own decisions, but they little realise they are working out the will of God. There is a well-substantiated textual variation, reflected in the RV, that makes this point even clearer, "For God did put in their hearts to do his mind, and to come to one mind, and to give their kingdom unto the beast, until the words of God should be accomplished". That united mind of the ten kings and the Beast was simply, yet unknowingly, to carry out the mind of God. The expression "give their kingdom" is a stronger expression than the expression "to give their power and strength to the beast" (v.13) – they have become at this point dependent monarchs under his absolute control and the destruction of the harlot would seem to be their first united action. Throughout history men have acted out of their own will thinking to oppose God, little realising that they were actually carrying out divine purpose. God described the Assyrians as "the rod of mine anger" (Isa 10:5) when He used them to chastise disobedient

Israel; the Babylonians carried Israel into captivity in the sixth century BC, little realising that they were but the instrument of the divine purpose. So the Beast and the ten kings are but the unwitting instruments to execute the mind of God on this false religious system. The final statement in the verse shows the divine limitation on these godless agents of judgment; they can only act "until the words of God shall be fulfilled", in other words, until all the written records of Scripture "should be accomplished" (RV). The record of 14:8 echoes around the earth "Babylon is fallen, is fallen". God has done what He promised to do.

(d) The Woman and the City (v.18)

18 This final verse of the chapter is the link with the next chapter. It concludes the judgment of the harlot and begins the second vision of the judgment of the city. The chronological relationship of the visions is indicated in the statement of 18:1, "after these things I saw". The woman is of course the symbol of a religious system that has its roots in a city while the city is the reality. To make the city a symbol of something else is to make a symbol of a symbol which is contrary to normal scriptural usage (the single exception seems to be in v.9 of this chapter where the double symbol is explained). The woman, introduced by the word "mystery", represents the ecclesiastical aspect of Babylon, while the city reflects the reality behind the symbol. There is no mystery attached to this city; it is simply described as "that great city, which reigneth over the kings of the earth" which is neatly rendered by JND, "hath a kingship over the kings of the earth". The kings of the earth, an expression which must be wider than the ten kings of v.12, come under the dominion of this city, which, by implication if not direct statement, makes it the capital city of earth. The destruction of this city is the subject of the next chapter.

Notes

8 The revived Roman Empire

It must be pointed out that many respected commentators interpret the beast as the Roman Empire. Acknowledging the fact that the Roman Empire has long disappeared they refer to this beast as the Revived Roman Empire. They interpret the first statement "The beast...was" as the Roman Empire existing in the time of John. W. Scott writes (p.348); "The ancient empire beheld in vision 'was', that is, it existed in its imperial form in John's day, and on till its destruction in AD476". The following expression "and is not" is then interpreted as the church age subsequent to the destruction of the Roman Empire. The ascending out of the abyss is interpreted as the revival of the empire by satanic power under the Beast and then its final doom sees it go unto perdition. Some of the older commentators were so sure that this was the picture that great discussion centred on the exact boundaries of the empire; a real problem indeed, since virtually every decade saw Rome with different boundaries throughout its history. On this view it is the revival of this ancient empire that gives rise to the worldwide wonder that grips the earth.

There is much that can be said in favour of this interpretation and it has been taught for many years by able, learned and godly men. That there are clear links between the Roman Empire and the final empire of the Beast is readily conceded. This can be seen from the fact that there are only four worldwide empires within the scope of the times of the Gentiles commencing with Nebuchadnezzar and Babylonian empire. Yet while the first three empires of Babylon, Medo-Persia and Greece are named in Scripture the fourth empire is not; a point which must have some significance. It is therefore to be expected if the church age is lifted out of the chronological picture (the period from Pentecost to the rapture forming an interregnum between Daniel's sixty-ninth and seventieth week) then the final world-empire forms a continuum with the Roman Empire. It is thus to be expected that the features of the Roman Empire will be reproduced in this final empire but on a far greater worldwide scale. Any death-wound to the Roman Empire must, of necessity, fall in the church age and, in any case is almost impossible to find historically and this seems a rather a dramatic way to refer to the many strokes received by the Roman Empire as it tottered over decades to its demise. Startled wonder also seems rather dramatic language to apply to the revival or reappearance of an empire on the world-stage. Even if the federation of European powers in the present day led to the re-emergence of an empire based on Rome there would likely be vast media coverage and mild interest from a historical perspective but nothing to merit the language of wonder here recorded.

However, the real problem for this view is that the scriptural language does not fit an empire. If John is seen as viewing the beast and woman from the midpoint of the tribulation (as suggested above) the statement, "the beast...was", can be understood as the Roman Empire having already passed into history, but the second statement, and "is not", can hardly describe the empire of the beast at that point. On the other hand if John is viewing the beast from his own time, as is the common interpretation, then the problem is greater still for the "was" implies that the Empire has existed and is now passed away while the statement, "and is not" seems a very strange way to refer to the great empire under which John is presently suffering. To speak of an empire as ascending out of the abyss and going into perdition is also rather strange and difficult to understand.

When all the problems are examined in light of Scripture it is suggested that it is much more satisfactory to see the four descriptive statements as referring to the Beast as the embodiment of the final great empire of the tribulation period and, in this summary form, describing his history and destiny as shown in the comments on the text.

10 It is to be noted that all these world powers symbolised as heads of the beast have been in close touch with Israel and take their importance historically from this fact. Other mighty kingdoms have existed on earth but they are unimportant from the prophetic standpoint of the purposes of God. Again all these six kingdoms at one time or another in their history had attempted to destroy Israel. The scriptural records embrace the attempts of Egypt, Assyria, Babylon, Medo-Persia, Greece and Rome. The apparent exception of Medo-Persia is no real exception when it is seen that Satan, as the book of Esther shows, plotted to use Haman to wipe out the greater part of the nation.

12 It is interesting to note that commercially world economists have divided the earth into ten discrete trade zones. Already these trade zones are controlled by supreme councils drawn from the member states and it is not difficult to see emerging the frame-work of a world trade body backed up by the authority of the United Nations.

CHAPTER 18

10. *The Fourth Parenthesis continued* 17: 1-19:10

(vision 2) *Babylon the Great – The City and its Fall (18:1-24)*

The opening phrase of this chapter provides initial evidence that the events described follow the destruction of the harlot in ch. 17. The expression "after these things" occurs ten times in this book and on four occasions (1:19; 4:1; 9:12; 20:3) the context leaves no doubt that the events are chronologically subsequent to what has gone before. On the other six occasions when the expression is followed by a verb of perception (4:11; 7:1, 9; 15:5; 18:1; 19:1) it has sometimes been argued that it is the visions only that are in sequence. However, as each case is examined it soon becomes clear that it is because the events follow each other in time that the visions are given in this order. It is suggested therefore as something to be considered, in the light of other evidence, that the events of ch. 18 follow those of ch. 17 in time.

1. The Argument for Two Distinct Judgments

It would however be faulty exegesis to allow such an important point to be established on the interpretation of an introductory phrase and it will be pointed out that there are a number of weighty reasons why the destruction of the city of Babylon described in this chapter is to be seen as distinct from the destruction of the harlot in the previous chapter. These reasons may be summarised as follows:

a. There are two different entities judged

In ch. 17 the subject of judgment is symbolised as a woman identified as a "harlot" with the word "mystery" introducing the title given to her, "Babylon the great". It has been shown that this is the judgment of the great ecclesiastical system of apostate christianity headed up in Roman Catholicism as the final manifestation of religious Babylon. The subject, however, of the judgment in ch.18 is "that great city" (five times so named). There is no hint that the word city is to be taken other than literally and it should be noted that the word "mystery" does not occur in the book after 17:7. Commerce and not religion is the subject of this chapter.

b. There are two different agents used in the judgments

Both judgments are from God. In 17:16-17 God used the Beast and the ten kings as His agents who, while they imagine that they are acting for their own purposes, carry out the divine purpose in judgment. In ch. 18 the judgment of the city comes directly from the hand of God. It is clear that this is a direct divine judgment from the hand of God even before the world-shattering earthquake of the last bowl judgment (16:19). The fact that "the kings of the earth" (v.9) bewail the destruction of the city shows that they are not the agents of the overthrow. The fall of the city is mourned universally; monarchs, merchants and mariners are all appalled at this action, a reaction that stands in stark contrast to the very obvious pleasure taken in the destruction of the harlot (17:16).

c. The times of the judgments are different

It has been shown from the internal evidence in ch. 17 that the despoiling and death of the harlot takes place at the midpoint of the seven-year tribulation when the Beast has reached the apex of his power. This corresponds to the fall of Babylon announced by the angel in 14:8, a time-note confirmed by the independent internal evidence of that chapter. In this chapter the destruction of the city takes place at the very end of the tribulation corresponding to the moment under the seventh bowl when "great Babylon came in remembrance before God" (16:19). There must be three and a half years between the two judgments.

A clear and full presentation of the case for the one judgment viewed from two different angles on both religious and commercial Babylon is presented by Charles H. Dyer in "The identity of Babylon in Revelation 17-18" in *Bibliotheca Sacra* (Vol. 145). Some of the main arguments presented are noted as follows below.

2. The Argument for One Judgment

It should be pointed out that many commentators do not accept the arguments presented for two separate judgments on Babylon in its different forms and insist that there is only one judgment of Babylon at the very end of the tribulation period. They suggest that the difference in the chapters arises from the viewing of that judgment from two different angles and argue as follows:

a. Ch. 17 presents the judgment from man's side while ch. 18 shows the judgment from God's side.
b. The different emphasis in each chapter is because the religious side of Babylon is in view in ch. 17 and the commercial side of this same religious system is dealt with in ch. 18. They argue that the commerce here presented is commerce inherent in the worship of religious Babylon.
c. The mention of the burning with fire in both chapters (17:16; 18:8) must link the two judgments.
d. The difference between the action of the kings in 17:16 and their reaction to the judgment in 18:9 is explained either as different groups of kings involved or a sudden reversal of feeling once they have taken the irrevocable action of ridding themselves of this religious incubus.

e. The emphasis on commerce in this chapter is explained by postulating that it is the commerce dependent on Roman Catholicism that is in view, and it must be conceded that the destruction of the wealth and commerce of the Roman Catholic church would have serious worldwide consequences and cause many to mourn.

Weighty scholarship and many able commentators identify the judgments with these arguments. A.F. Johnston is typical of many commentators when he writes, "It is important not to separate this chapter from the portrayal of the prostitute in ch. 17, since there is no warrant for making the prostitute in ch. 17 different from the city in ch. 18 (cf 17:18). Under the imagery of the destruction of a great commercial city, John describes the final overthrow of the great prostitute, Babylon" (p. 163).

However it is very difficult to gather scriptural support for these arguments or to feel that they present a coherent case. There seems to be a very large measure of special pleading and more fundamentally, an ignoring of the different contexts in which the judgments are found. It seems that sufficient weight has not been given to the facts already mentioned which may be summarised thus:

a. There are clearly two different agencies used in the judgments. No special pleading can really distinguish between the "ten kings" of 17:12 and "the kings of the earth" of 18:9, nor can a change of feeling be sufficient reason to explain the different reactions to the fall of Babylon.
b. The double mention of Babylon (14:8 16:19) points to different times for the two judgments: judgments separated by three and a half years.
c. While the collapse of Roman Catholicism commercially would be a serious matter for many individuals and the world stock markets it is hard to see it as bringing about such mourning as envisaged in this chapter.

It is therefore suggested that these two chapters present a double judgment of two different aspects of Babylon at two different times in the tribulation period. The word "mystery" is required in ch. 17 to emphasise that this requires divine revelation while the city is self-evidently proclaimed as Babylon and requires no such identification.

3. The Argument for a Literal City

Most commentators are agreed that ch. 17 deals with the religious side of Babylon and this chapter deals with the commercial side of Babylon. While a majority also agree that there are two different judgments as discussed above, a greater difference of opinion lies in the interpretation of the city. Some see the city merely as the symbol of a commercial empire while others insist that such an empire demands a financial heart – in other words a literal city. Since religious Babylon has its capital in the city of Rome, it has been accepted by many commentators, misinterpreting the reference to the "seven mountains" of 17:8, that Rome becomes the capital of the Beast's commercial empire. Reading Scripture in the light of modern history it is often claimed that the Treaty of Rome (1948) laid the political foundation for the European Union, which, it is argued, could well become the ten kingdom empire of the Beast. On this understanding the city in this chapter symbolises a literal city but it is called "Rome" so that by a happy correspondence, the city of Rome the capital of the old Roman Empire comes back into prophecy, not only through its religious association with the Vatican city, but as the capital of the revived Roman Empire under the Beast. Rome becomes, in fact, the commercial capital of world trade. While the argument is attractive it assumes too much without any solid scriptural basis and uses the word "Babylon" symbolically without sound scriptural basis. It has already been shown that:

a. While the empire of the Beast has links with the old Roman Empire it is much wider and infinitely more powerful; the new empire outranks the Roman Empire just as the Beast outranks the Caesar. This empire is neither confined to the old Roman Empire's boundaries nor need it have the same capital city.
b. The reference to the "seven mountains" in 17.9 has no reference to the city of Rome. The symbol is interpreted in the passage as "seven kings".
c. To assume that Babylon is the scriptural code name for Rome is totally without warrant. There is no hint in this chapter that the word Babylon is anything other than a reference to a literal city of that name. The reason for the existence of this city is neither religion nor even politics, but commerce. It seems reasonable that the Beast will see the necessity of having a compact, centralised, computerised control-centre for the commerce of earth. Disdaining the discredited capitals of earth there seems to be no reason why he should not find it useful to return to an ancient site in a strategic location in his empire for a new Babylon to emerge suddenly on the world scene. There is no indication in the chapter that the word "city" is employed symbolically and the graphic language of destruction demands a literal city. It is very difficult to explain the desolation of the site after the destruction (vv.21-23) unless a literal city is involved. Small in comparison with the great metropolitan capitals of earth, this city would rapidly outrank all others as it represents the financial control that makes the Beast such a mighty power on the world scene. When God calls this city Babylon it requires compelling scriptural reasons to substitute a different name.

Commentators who dispute the identification of this city as the rebuilt literal Babylon do so on one main argument. They insist that the prophecies of the destruction of Babylon, particularly of Isaiah and Jeremiah, have been fulfilled and the old Babylon has gone forever. Making this assumption the logical deduction is that either "Babylon" must be a code name for Rome or the city must be interpreted symbolically as the embodiment of the commercial empire of the Beast. Since the initial assumption is wrong, the deduction based on it is wrong. It must be stated very clearly that it is a complete misreading of history to say that the OT judgments on Babylon have been fulfilled. A survey of the history of Babylon taken from reliable authorities will show quite clearly that Babylon has never been destroyed in the complete and literal way with the catastrophic overthrow that Scripture demands. Babylon certainly decayed over centuries but was never suddenly nor utterly destroyed; in fact Babylon has been a city until comparatively recent times. In the last century or so it has been reduced to village proportions but it does not seem to have been ever utterly abandoned. To say that the prophecies of Isa 13-14; Jer 50-51 have been fulfilled in the same way as, for example, the prophecy concerning Tyre (Ezek 26), demands either a distortion of history or a devaluing of Scripture. To claim absolute fulfilment requires that these Scriptures have to be spiritualised or treated as poetic rhetoric and neither of these approaches appeals to those who believe in the inspiration of all Scripture. The only alternative is to accept that they have yet to be fulfilled. This chapter presents the judgment of a rebuilt and restored Babylon and it is in this judgment, yet future, that the prophecies of Isaiah and Jeremiah find their literal fulfilment.

It is somewhat strange that there has been such a reluctance amongst commentators to accept the possibility of a rebuilt Babylon. Jerusalem has been destroyed and rebuilt a number of times, so it might reasonably be asked why not Babylon. The OT prophecies, when studied without reading into them prejudgments by nineteenth century travellers, leave no doubt that the judgment of Babylon as described is not to be found in recorded history. Thus these Scriptures not only allow, but actually demand for their authentication, the rebuilding and final destruction of this ancient city. There is no doubt that the city will be rebuilt rapidly. The meteoric rise of the Beast to world dominion will be matched by the sudden rise of the commercial heart of his empire rebuilt on the ancient site on the Euphrates river.

The chapter is readily divided into four paragraphs set out as follows:

1. The Stroke upon Babylon vv.1-3
2. The Summons from Heaven vv.4-8
3. The Sob of Earth vv.9-20
4. The Symbolised Doom of Babylon vv.21-24

v.1 "And after these things I saw another angel come down from heaven, having great power; and the earth was lightened with his glory.

v.2 And he cried mightily with a strong voice, saying, Babylon the great is fallen, is fallen, and is become the habitation of devils, and the hold of every foul spirit, and a cage of every unclean and hateful bird.

v.3 For all nations have drunk of the wine of the wrath of her fornication, and the kings of the earth have committed fornication with her, and the merchants of the earth are waxed rich through the abundance of her delicacies.

v.4 And I heard another voice from heaven, saying, Come out of her, my people, that ye be not partakers of her sins, and that ye receive not of her plagues.

v.5 For her sins have reached unto heaven, and God hath remembered her iniquities.

v.6 Reward her even as she rewarded you, and double unto her double according to her works: in the cup which she hath filled, fill to her double.

v.7 How much she hath glorified herself, and lived deliciously, so much torment and sorrow give her; for she saith in her heart, I sit a queen, and am no widow, and shall see no sorrow.

v.8 Therefore shall her plagues come in one day, death, and mourning, and famine; and she shall be utterly burned with fire: for strong *is* the Lord God who judgeth her.

v.9 And the kings of the earth, who have committed fornication and lived deliciously with her, shall bewail her, and lament for her, when they shall see the smoke of her burning,

v.10 Standing afar off for the fear of her torment, saying. Alas, alas that great city Babylon, that mighty city! for in one hour is thy judgment come.

v.11 And the merchants of the earth shall weep and mourn over her; for no man buyeth their merchandise any more:

v.12 The merchandise of gold, and silver, and precious stones, and of pearls, and fine linen, and purple, and silk, and scarlet, and all thyine wood, and all manner vessels of ivory, and all manner vessels of most precious wood, and of brass, and iron, and marble,

v.13 And cinnamon, and odours, and ointments, and frankincense, and wine, and oil, and fine flour, and wheat, and beasts, and sheep, and horses, and chariots, and slaves, and souls of men.

v.14 And the fruits that thy soul lusted after are departed from thee, and all things which were dainty and goodly are departed from thee, and thou shalt find them no more at all.

v.15 The merchants of these things, which were made rich by her, shall stand afar off for the fear of her torment, weeping and wailing,

v.16 And saying, Alas, alas that great city, that was clothed in fine linen, and purple, and scarlet, and decked with gold, and precious stones, and pearls!

v.17 For in one hour so great riches is come to nought. And every shipmaster, and all the company in ships, and sailors, and as many as trade by sea, stood afar off,

v.18 And cried when they saw the smoke of her burning, saying, What city is like unto this great city!

v.19 And they cast dust on their heads, and cried, weeping and wailing, saying, Alas, alas that great city, wherein were made rich all that had ships in the sea by reason of her costliness! for in one hour is she made desolate.

v.20 Rejoice over her, *thou* heaven, and ye holy apostles and prophets: for God hath avenged you on her,

v.21 And a mighty angel took up a stone like a great millstone, and cast it into the sea, saying, Thus with violence shall that great city Babylon be thrown down, and shall be found no more at all.

v.22 And the voice of harpers, and musicians, and of pipers, and trumpeters, shall be heard no more at all in thee; and no craftsman, of whatsoever craft *he* be, shall be found any more in thee; and the sound of a millstone shall be heard no more at all in thee;

v.23 And the light of a candle shall shine no more at all in thee; and the voice of the bridegroom and of the bride shall be heard no more at all in thee: for thy merchants were the great men of the earth; for by thy sorceries were all nations deceived.

v.24 And in her was found the blood of prophets, and of saints, and of all that were slain upon the earth."

1-2 The separate vision introduced by the phrase "after these things" is introduced by "another angel". This is clearly a different angel from the one in 17:1 and there is nothing to insist that it is even another one of the seven angels of 15:1. The things said about the angel cast light on the importance of his mission. He comes directly from heaven as if divinely commissioned from the throne. He carries great authority as if directly delegated from God. It is thus no wonder that the earth is illuminated by his radiant glory. H.B. Swete sums up the matter, p.226 "So recently has he come from the Presence that in passing he flings a broad belt of light across the dark earth". Elsewhere in Scripture God is seen to dwell in light unapproachable (1 Tim 6:16) and as covering Himself with light as with a garment (Ps 104:2) so it is little wonder that those who come directly from His presence carry something of this radiance with them (Exod 34:29-34). The darkened kingdom of the Beast (16:10) might well be stilled by the magnificence of this herald of divine judgment. While the description of the angel emphasises the greatness of his mission it would be just as much a mistake, as in 8:3; 10:1, to see this angel as Christ Himself. Angelic messengers reflect a glory attached to their office in the outworking of divine plans but this must not be confused with the resplendent glory inherently belonging to Christ. It is not in keeping with the glory of the ascended Man to assume the relatively humble role of a divine messenger – an angel. Any such thought is ruled out by the word "another" – the angel is only one of a class, Christ is absolutely unique.

The RV reading is dramatic: "He cried with a mighty voice". Earth is compelled to listen to this message. The drama of the message is in the word order: "Fallen! Fallen! Babylon the great", which is an echo of the cry of Isaiah (Isa 21:9). Isaiah's prophecy anticipated the capture of Belshazzar's Babylon by Cyrus in 539 BC, but only at this stage is it finally fulfilled in this destruction of this end-time Babylon. The repetition of the verb is simply for emphasis and finality and has little to do with the double fall of Babylon. The aorist tense anticipates what is to be described in the remainder of the chapter; a method of revelation used previously in connection with the kingdom (11:15).

This anticipation describes the site of Babylon after the fall – a graphic method of conveying the completeness of the destruction of Babylon. This physical ruin will become the place of confinement of satanic powers awaiting their final judgment and thus will be the one geographic location on the millennial earth under a divine interdict. During this same period Satan himself is confined in the "bottomless pit" (20:1-3). In the words of the divine sentence Babylon "is become":

1. "A habitation of devils". The word "habitation' (*katoikētērion*, "dwelling place") may be contrasted with the "habitation of God" (Eph 2:22). The word "devils" (*daimonia*) is better translated "demons" (JND).
2. "A hold of every unclean spirit" (JND). The word *phulakē* ("hold") is translated "cage" in the following statement but the usual translation in

the NT is "prison". Thus this is not a voluntary residence for these subjects of Satan's kingdom but their prison house. While the word "demons" describes their origin, the word "unclean" (*akathartos*) describes their operations as the foul and degrading spirits that have influenced and degraded mankind through Babylonish practices.

3. "A hold of every unclean and hateful bird" (RV). The AV translation "cage" fits the picture of the birds, even though the same word for "prison" is used. Jeremiah had used the symbol of birds to portray picturesquely deceitful practices in his day when he said, "As a cage is full of birds, so are their houses full of deceit" (Jer 5:27). Isaiah uses the same kind of picture (Isa 34:11-15) as did the Lord in the parable of the sower (Matt 13:4). The presence of these kinds of birds in a region is an OT indication of abandonment and desolation (Isa 34:11; Jer 50:39; Zeph 2:13-14). However in this passage the word must be more than simply a symbol and seems to indicate all the agencies in nature that have willingly co-operated with Satan in his rebellion against heaven. The adjectives "unclean" and "hateful" describe heaven's assessment of them. "Unclean" obviously describes the nature of the agency and "hated" (JND) accurately describes heaven's attitude to such.

All the demons, all the spirit forces and all that in the world of nature has yielded to Satan are now, after the destruction of the literal city of Babylon, to be confined to the site as a literal prison-house. This abandonment of the site to these demons and evil spirits is part of the divine sentence pronounced upon Babylon by Isaiah: "It shall never be inhabited, neither shall it be dwelt in from generation to generation:... But wild beasts of the desert shall lie there and their houses shall be full of doleful creatures" (Isa 13:19-22). While there was, undoubtedly, some foreshadowing of this seen in the decay of historic Babylon, the complete fulfilment awaits the judgment of this chapter. The wild beasts, the doleful creatures, the owls, the satyrs and the dragons define all that in the realm of nature has succumbed to satanic influence and become linked with their demon masters. The reference of Christ to the gathering out of the kingdom "all things that offend" (Matt 13:41) may point to the internment of these agencies in this site of desolation. The proud city which claimed world dominance is now not only a monument of judgment, but a place to be shunned in the millennial age as the prison house of demons.

3 Three reasons are given for the judgment: -

1. The Magnitude of Babylon's sin. "All nations" measures the scale of the influence of Babylon. The perfect tense "have drunk" summarises the past; the pleasure of the "wine...of her fornication"- that intoxicating lifestyle of sin, now brings its penalty in "the wrath of her fornication" – the judgment her sin brings. The word "wrath" (*thumos*) is better translated "fury" (JND) to describe the blaze of God's anger against their

fornication with Babylon. Wine and wrath stand opposed as reflecting sin and its sentence. Fornication must be taken primarily in the spiritual sense of 17:2 as defining the prostitution of holy things for gain or pleasure. Since the harlot, symbolising apostate christianity, has already been destroyed this must be the final form of Babylonish deception in the worship of the Beast (13:4). In the final years of the tribulation to worship the Beast is the only way to survive and grow prosperous (13:16-17), and all nations have succumbed to the allurements of this path of spiritual corruption.

2. The Nature of Babylon's sin – This second reason, "and the kings of the earth have committed fornication with her", points to the political intrigues of Babylon. This goes beyond the selfish personal interest of individuals and points to the selfish political interest of rulers who traded every moral principle for position and power under the Beast. Whatever they had of spiritual light and moral principle was bartered in the worship of mammon. The kings were willing partners with Babylon in this sin of fornication and now they must share her judgment. The aorist tense "committed fornication" sums up their past; this was not just the matter of a moral slip but the practice of a deliberate policy over the whole period.

3. The Result of Babylon's sin. All the earth has been involved with Babylon: And the merchants of the earth are waxed rich through the abundance of her delicacies. First the nations made up of individuals, then the kings of the earth pointing to the rulers and finally the powerful commercial barons of earth all had a part in Babylon's sin. These merchants are a new class who have waxed rich through the commercial practices of Babylon. The AV's "the abundance of her delicacies" is better translated "the might of her luxury" (JND). The word "delicacy" (*strēnos*) is defined by Thayer as "excessive strength which longs to break forth, luxury" and points to the uncountable riches of Babylon that finance the luxurious lifestyle characteristic of commercial Babylon. Power now lies in the hands of the managing directors, the financial controllers and the merchant-bankers who owe their positions and their prosperity as well as their sensual pleasures to this commercial regime. This movement of world capital and commerce back to Babylon is in fulfilment of Zechariah's prophecy of the ephah (Zech 5:5-11).

4 From the desolation of the satanic prison-site John is taken back in time to hear the final summons of heaven before the judgment falls. The voice is "another" voice, not the voice of the angel of v.2. Since the call is addressed to "my people" and God is spoken of in the third person it is clear that Christ is summoning His own. This call seems to come after the destruction of mystery Babylon and just before the seven bowls are poured out in the closing days of the tribulation period. There is not any reason to doubt that the "seven last plagues" (15:1) are here referred to as "her plagues" since they affect the persons and places associated with Babylon (see 16:1-12). It can be inferred from this call that some true believers, while refusing the mark of the Beast, are resident in the city itself or at least are associated with the commercial empire of the Beast even in the last months of the tribulation. Just before the judgment falls Christ summons His own to leave the city and the system it represents.

While not a direct quotation from Jeremiah the call echoes the summons of the prophet to the people of Israel in Babylon at the close of the seventy years of captivity. The call of Jeremiah is direct and unequivocal: "Remove out of the midst of Babylon, and go forth out of the land of the Chaldeans" (Jer 50:8); the urgency of the summons is echoed in the cry, "Flee out of the midst of Babylon and deliver every man his soul, be not cut off in her inquity" (Jer 51:6). Isaiah also called for the physical abandonment of the city of Babylon: "Depart ye, depart ye, go ye up from hence, touch no unclean thing, go out of the midst of her, be ye clean that bear the vessels of the Lord" (Isa 52:11). The words of Christ recall these OT pictures as He summons His own to leave this latter day neo-Babylon on the banks of the Euphrates. A literal flight from a doomed city is certainly envisaged, but the call goes much further and demands not only a physical, but a total moral and spiritual rejection of the commercial empire of the Beast. No saint will accept the mark or number of the Beast on forehead or hand but there will be the temptation to belong to Babylon's associations and be a part of her society. Success in life will depend on this association but so will security; to obey Christ's summons will be to put life at risk. Emphasising the spiritual side of the withdrawal one commentator has said that "the saints are called to a spiritual withdrawal from Vanity Fair" (M. Kiddle). This call to spiritual separation will be just as necessary in this future day as it is vital now (2 Cor 6:17). Saints will find it profitable to be associated with the prestige of this mighty commercial empire, and to be in its professional associations will be the only path to material prosperity. The ordinary transactions of life demanding credit and debit cards link individuals with the commercial system of Babylon and to obey this call of Christ will be costly. On the merely physical level greed for gold, lust for power, and pride in possessions could lead many a believer to reside in this great commercial metropolis and thus become entangled in its society. Christ's summons is absolute and demands instant obedience. Failure invites disaster for it means sharing in the sins of Babylon – accepting her principles and following her practices. The word "partakers" (*sunkoinōneō*) is used three times in the NT (Eph 5:11; Phil 4:14; and here and means "to share in"). To have "fellowship in her sins" (JND) will mean to receive of her plagues – the judgments about to burst upon her as the seven bowls are poured out (15:1).

5 What drew the attention of God to Babel was the tower "whose top may reach unto heaven" (Gen 11:4). To use the metaphorical picture this end-time

Babylon has built another eye-catching structure – a tower of sins which demand divine action. The AV has followed the TR, reading *ēkolouthēsan* (of which the normal meaning is "to follow"); "have reached unto heaven", is a very suitable translation in the context and is in keeping with the tower of Babel picture. The variant reading, *ekollēthēsan* meaning "to glue or stick together" is, however, very well attested (see JND margin "joined together") and perhaps gives a more graphic picture of the brick-by-brick construction of this edifice. The word "sins" describes the principles and the word "iniquities" the unrighteous acts and misdeeds that are unmistakable evidence of her guilt. In the expression "God hath remembered" is an echo of 16:19, "Great Babylon came in remembrance before God". This is a Hebraism for God taking action with regard to some person or thing (see Gen 8:1); God taking action with regard to Babylon's misdeeds seals her doom; her time has run out.

6 This summons is not to saints but to undesignated agents of divine judgment. These executors of the wrath of God may well be those who are called "the watchers" who featured in the judgment upon an earlier Babylon (Dan 4:17). Christ Himself is calling for absolute justice in connection with the OT law of retribution: an eye for an eye, a tooth for a tooth (Lev 24:17-22). It cannot be men that are addressed here since men do not know the record of Babylon's sin and they are never called upon to execute this kind of divine retribution. The majority of textual authorities omit "you" in the first sentence and the RV reproduces the Hebrew parallelism, "Render unto her as she rendered, and double [unto her] the double according to her works". This law of divine retribution is perfectly righteous and shows that the sins of Babylon will be repaid exactly (F.A.Tatford p.203 replaces the noun "double" with "counterpart'). It is not to be understood as going beyond what is due and giving back a double portion to Babylon. This would not be in keeping with the character of God, despite the special pleading of some commentators (see J. Morris); and it neither allows for the parallelism in the verse nor does it fit the demand for equal payment that follows. Christ is here but reiterating what Jeremiah had demanded in this very connection: "Recompense her according to her work; according to all that she hath done, do unto her" (Jer 50:29). The punishment fits the crime. This sentence of heaven is symbolised in the cup; in her hand the cup contained a brew of intoxicating spiritual and sensual depravity of which the nations had drunk (14:8); now that same cup holds a very different cocktail. JND's translation is somewhat clearer: "In the cup which she has mixed, mix to her double". She mixed a drink for men; now God orders another mixing – a very different portion for her – mixed for her judgment.

7 The above interpretation of the corresponding judgment is confirmed by the first part of this verse. "How much" (*hosa,* literally "what things") is balanced by "so much". Her punishment corresponds exactly to the self-glorification and luxurious lifestyle she had displayed. Two verbs define the pride of Babylon. In absolute contrast to Christ who "glorified not himself" (Heb 5:5), Babylon "glorified herself": she revelled in self-glorification – what she was and what she had achieved. The political domination and the military subordination of earth opened the way to commercial exploitation witnessed by the magnificence of her buildings, the richness of her merchants and the wealth of her resources. The second verb, "lived deliciously" (*strēniaō*) repeated in v.9, means to "run riot, to revel or be wanton" (the intensified form is used in 1 Tim 5:11) and describes the hedonistic, sensual, luxurious way of life that leaves out all spiritual values. The divinely-commissioned assessors of judgment are asked to weigh the boastful pride and sensual pleasures of Babylon and assign the corresponding retribution. Measured to Babylon will be "torment" (*basanismos*) a word used to describe all that the body can bear in physical pain as in 9:5; 14:11. "Sorrow" is the anguish and grief brought by the pain. The pain is God's answer to the pride and pleasure-mad career of this licentious city.

The last part of the verse is really the introduction to v.8. The verse division tends to obscure the connection between the "for", introducing what Babylon is saying quietly in her heart, and the "therefore" introducing the sentence of heaven. In arrogant pride Babylon sees herself as mistress of the world (queen); this in itself is sufficiently serious to invite divine judgment, but she goes much further. "I sit a queen and am no widow and shall see no sorrow" is a deliberate, defiant challenge to God to fulfil the OT prophecies about the destruction of Babylon. In Isa 47:5 God's sentence through the prophet was, "Sit thou silent, and get thee into darkness, O daughter of the Chaldeans: for thou shalt no more be called, The lady of kingdoms". The defiant answer was, "I shall be a lady forever" (Isa 47:7) and, "I shall not sit as a widow, neither shall I know the loss of children" (Isa 47:8). God's answer was clear: "But these two things shall come to thee in a moment in one day, the loss of children, and widowhood; they shall come upon thee in their perfection" (Isa 47:9). These Scriptures indicate how, in this latter day, Babylon will seize again her power over nations and defy God to fulfil His word. Jerusalem at this same point in the tribulation will again be seen in her widowhood (Lam 1:1) with no Messiah to deliver her, but Babylon in overweening arrogance defies God to rob her of her status (queen) or of her "husband" or to bring upon her the sorrow that has been threatened. God will do exactly this. Within the figurative context it would seem as if Babylon in her defiance of heaven assumes that she is the "consort" of the Beast – so closely are they linked at this point in the tribulation; she defies God to rob her of his protection.

8 "Therefore" is the answer of heaven to the "for" in the previous verse introducing the secret thinking of Babylon. The defiance of this proud city will be answered by the sudden judgment of heaven summarised as "her plagues";

the use of this word links the bowl judgments with the judgment on Babylon. "In one day" is an echo of Isa 47:9 and, while it is a term that can simply imply suddenness (as does the term "in one hour" in vv.10, 17,19), there is no reason why it should not be accepted as a literal day of twenty-four hours. Suddenly and devastatingly, death and mourning and famine shall come upon this proud city. "Utterly burned" is a graphic translation of *katakaiō* where *kata* intensifies the action; all that is left is a smoking ruin: in ancient times the rising smoke was the irrefutable sign of a city sacked and burnt. "With fire" is not needless repetition but heightens the terrible reality of the picture and brings to mind the prophecies of Jeremiah where Babylon is seen as a burnt mountain (Jer 51:25), a city in which the houses and walls and the gates are all utterly consumed (Jer 51:30-58). While Belshazzar's Babylon (Dan 5:30) fell in one night it was never destroyed like this; the prophetic word awaits fulfilment in this end-time city. A smouldering ruin testifies to the fact that the Lord God has acted in direct divine judgment upon Babylon.

The whole earth is affected by the fall of this great city. The commercial and economic systems of the nations are so closely linked with the empire of the Beast that this capital city is the hub of world trade. The sudden overthrow of this financial centre causes a wail of anguish to rise from earth. Other cities have been destroyed in the earthquakes of the seventh bowl (16:18-20), but it would seem some confidence remained that the world leaders, the Beast and the false prophet drawing upon their obviously-supernatural powers, would be able to deliver their own capital city from the crisis. Now with the Beast's kingdom darkened and his capital city destroyed a wail of anguish rises; first from the monarchs of earth, the world-leaders who have succumbed to the immoral inducements of Babylon, then from the merchants (vv.11-17a) whose markets have collapsed, and finally from the mariners (17b-19) whose livelihoods depended on the trade of Babylon. The dirge is patterned on the mourning for the city of Tyre, the great commercial capital of the Phoenician empire in Ezek 27; the same three groups of mourners bewail the destruction of Tyre – the kings (v.35), the merchants (v.36) and the mariners (v.29).

The kings of the earth is a general term which, while embracing the ten kings under the Beast (17:12), is more general and more embracive as in v.3 and in 17:2. These are the governing heads of the nations of earth who have engaged in illicit relations ("committed fornication") with this trading empire. The "fornication" is the betrayal of every principle of righteousness by the kings that they might enjoy the luxurious, voluptuous lifestyle that Babylon offered in return. The verb "lived deliciously" is repeated from v.7, and summarises the whole sensual lifestyle of these courtesans of Babylon. Now as the television screens of the world are filled by this blazing pyre of all their hopes a terrible wail rises to heaven. The word "bewail" (*klaiō*) is used of any loud expression of pain or grief hence is often translated "to sob openly". The verb *koptō* (meaning "to cut"), when used in the middle voice as here, conveys the idea of beating the breast as an act of mourning. Their grief is real. What has stirred this terrible anguish is the sight of "the smoke of her burning" – the funeral pyre of the greatest commercial centre the world has ever seen.

Mingled with the grief of these world leaders there is a clear note of fear. Some of these kings on their way with their armies to Armageddon may well be within sight of the blazing city, as they cross the Euphrates, and visibly draw back ("standing afar off") from the inferno. There is no rush to her aid; emergency plans are cancelled, ships on the river dare not approach the burning city, planes cannot land as the world leaders stand in helpless horror. Around the earth television screens carry the terrifying pictures and "the fear of her torment" grips the hearts of men. The physical destruction of a city is but the visible evidence of what association with Babylon and the Beast means for men in time. In the death of this city men can read their own doom.

The English word "alas" is a good translation of the Greek word *ouai*, in which can be heard the very wailing that is wrung from hearts that are deeply moved. The word order of their cry shows how central Babylon was in their thinking, "The city – the great Babylon – the city – the strong". Only the mighty Lord God (v.8) can deal with this "mighty city", but when He does act one hour is sufficient; and earth's might succumbs before heaven's power. While "one hour" can be used on occasions figuratively there is no reason why here it should not be literal.

11-13 The dirge is taken up by the merchants of earth. They join in this universal mourning not out of sympathy for the city and its citizens but out of selfish interest since, with the destruction of this city, the source of their wealth is destroyed. The word *klaiō* ("weep") was translated "bewail" in v.9; the verb "to mourn" (*pentheō*) is related to the noun "sorrow" (*penthos*) of v.7. Those linked with her are enduring what Babylon boasted she would never see – widowhood; a partner is gone. It is clear that despite the judgments bursting upon earth, the physical phenomena and the political turmoil, a world commerce had developed under the control of Babylon that had brought prosperity to many. Now with Babylon blazing the great merchant princes of earth know that this commerce is at an end. These men are described in v.23 as "the great men of the earth" and they know that there is no one now to buy their wares. The word "merchants" (vv.3, 11, 15, 23) is used once only in the NT outside this chapter (Matt 13:45); the cognate word *emporion* denotes a trading place and is the word which comes into English as "emporium". It is clear that these men are the bulk-buyers, the great wholesalers whose control of prices on the world markets dictates currency fluctuations, shipping policies and insurance rates and all the allied business of the commercial world. They are not the shop-keepers but the managing directors of the great international combines, the bankers who have controlled the currencies of nations, the captains of industry and the financial magnates behind world commerce. With the destruction of Babylon their world is shattered and there are no buyers for their merchandise (*gomos*); the latter word originally denoted the freight or lading of a ship (Acts 21:3) but came to mean bulk cargo in general. These men know that with Babylon gone world commerce will collapse and their goods remain unsaleable; the bulk carriers around the world suddenly have no buyers for their cargoes.

In the list of merchandise given in vv.12-13 historical interpreters have seen a very close correspondence with the trade of Rome as the world capital in John's day. The tremendous volume of this trade, recorded by a number of contemporary writers, particularly Pliny (23-79 AD), was not confined to basic materials but was meant to furnish the imperial court with items of unbelievable luxury. It should also be noted that seventeen of the items of the merchandise of Tyre, recorded in Ezek 27, are identical with those in this list. The point is that the great trading centres of the past are used simply as background pictures to explain in intelligible terms how great a trading centre Babylon had now become and what a disaster it is when God judges it. The merchant princes of earth have every reason to mourn – their markets are gone.

There are twenty-eight items of merchandise in this list (twenty-nine in the RV). Some find significance in the number twenty-eight in that it is the product of seven (completeness) and four (universal) – thus they would say this describes a complete universal trade. In the absence of clear separation marks in the text any proposed grouping is somewhat arbitrary; nevertheless it is possible to see eight groups as follows:

1 Gold, silver, precious stones, pearls – the investment market
The RV is correct in translating "precious stone" in the singular. In the Roman world these were the items in which wealth was stored and transported. In modern times it is the stock market and the bullion market dealing in the imperishable goods which retain value as inflation soars. Men invest in these goods as a "hedge" in times of rampant inflation. This will have been a vital market in the tribulation years but, suddenly, the metals themselves are of no further use – the trade collapses.

2 Fine linen, purple, silk, scarlet – the commodities market
These fabrics clearly cover the whole textile trade. From Roman times until now linen and silk have been earth's most valued materials and the colours scarlet and purple are associated with the religious side of Babylon (17:3-4) as well as the commercial side (v.15) to mark wealth and ostentation. Outward show is suddenly no longer popular and these costly goods are valueless.

3 All thyine wood, all manner of vessels of ivory, and all manner of vessels of most precious wood, and of brass and iron, and marble – the materials market.

In Roman times these materials were utilised in the nobles' homes to display wealth and set them apart from the homes of the common people. The rich furniture was made of thyine wood – a hard aromatic wood from citron trees much valued in Rome. The elaborate vessels of imported ivory and the construction in marble all speak of wealth and ease and comfort. These materials reflect the ostentation and wealth enjoyed by the profiteers under Babylonian commerce.

4 Cinnamon, spice (RV), ointment, frankincense – the luxury market
These luxuries, mostly transported from distant lands, were top-of-the-range goods for the wealthy Romans. For food, for the cosmetic industry, for the home these things were meant to deliver from the all-pervading stench of city life. Some manuscripts include "incense" between spice and ointment giving the twenty-ninth item in the RV. It is clear that the aromatic and cosmetic industry will develop under Babylon.

5 Wine, oil, fine flour, wheat – the food market
The judgments of the early years of the tribulation (note the "drought" of 11:6) could place the food-producing areas of earth under such strain that it may be easy for the Beast to bring the basic food-stuffs under his control.

6 Beasts and sheep – the livestock market
While the word "beasts" (*ktēnos*) sometimes means "beasts of burden" (Luke 10:34; Acts 23:24) its general meaning is "cattle" and, when linked with "sheep" would seem to refer to the livestock trade and thus the meat and wool markets.

7 Horses and chariots – the transport market
The word for "chariot" (*rhedē*) denotes a four-wheeled wagon used for the transport of people or goods. The two-wheeled war-chariot is referred to in 9:9. In modern terms this would refer to the air and sea transport of persons and goods, both the travel and the transport business would be involved.

8 Bodies and souls of men – the manpower market
The two words used together simply mean that Babylon has complete control of men. A similar expression is used in English when a business is said to take over a person "body and soul". The AV translation of *sōmata* as "slaves" is taken from extra-Biblical sources; it has led some commentators to refer it to a resumption of the slave-trade or to the development of the white-slave trade (prostitution). The figurative interpretation of the statement suits this context very much better.

14 In the hour of judgment heaven addresses Babylon and summarises all that she has now lost and lost forever: "The fruits that thy soul lusted after". The word "fruit" describes all that is gathered in the fruit harvest (Bauer, Arndt and Gingrich) and is a fitting word to describe all that Babylon could expect to gather from its policies and practices in the mercantile world. This harvest fruit is defined as "the lust of thy soul" (JND) which is the base desire of a fallen human nature divorced from the higher things of the spirit. This fruit that Babylon desired is defined in the next sentence.

"All things which were dainty and goodly". "Dainty" describes the sumptuous and luxurious things that the unregenerate heart of man loves. The word occurs only here in the NT but in the LXX is equivalent to "fat" (Judges 3:29; Neh 9:35; Isa 30:23) and may refer to gourmet tastes in expensive food. "Goodly" refers to the bright things that give pleasure to the eye; from its use in James 2:2 it is a fair deduction that it points to expensive and ostentatious dress. Sumptuous, lavish, gorgeous are adjectives appropriate to Babylon. Expressed in modern terms this refers to the luxurious villas, the expensive lifestyle, the private planes and yachts that are the tangible goals of the materialism of the age. Babylon supplied all these abundantly but now, in divine judgment, all these tokens of wealth "are departed". Two different verbs are translated in the same way in the AV; the first verb *aperchomai* means simply "are gone" (RV), are no longer to be found, while the second verb *apollumi* is much stronger and better translated "are perished" (RV). These things have gone forever and, as men watch the conflagration in Babylon, they dare not even hope that this is a disaster from which earth may recover. The sentence of heaven is final: "Thou shalt find them no more at all". The "no more" is an echo of v.11 but now the very things of luxury and pleasure for which men sold themselves "body and soul" are gone forever. No search can bring them back; they are not to be found.

15 The dirge of the merchants is resumed from v.11 after the digression of vv.12-14 describing the merchandise of Babylon. The expression "the merchants of these things" is a graphic way of indicating that these merchant princes of v.11 are not only commodity traders but they have held the monopoly of the very things men lusted after – the luxurious things and the attractive things of the previous verse. Further identified as those "which were made rich" by Babylon, they are the business magnates from the great multinational companies and the world financial controllers, the Rockefellers and the Rothschilds of that future day. The fact that they "stand afar off" and that they are marked by "fear" indicates that they are aware that they cannot dismiss this catastrophe as a natural disaster; they know that this is from God. The knowledge that the situation is irrecoverable is the reason for the bitter "weeping and mourning" (RV).

16-17a The lament of the merchants echoes that of the kings (v.10) but the differences are instructive. To the kings Babylon was "the mighty city"; to the merchants she was "clothed in fine linen" and "decked with gold". Each company sees her fall in terms that affect their interests. The interest of the world-leaders is in the political might of Babylon based on her wealth; the merchants mourn the luxury and prosperity that stemmed from her wealth. The fact that the symbolic description of Babylon echoes the description of the harlot (17:4) should occasion no surprise. Any differences are in fact very minor, such as the inclusion of "fine linen" and the singular "pearl" (RV). There is no doubt that the similarity is designed to show that the features of Babylon that appeal to the flesh are the same whether in the realm of religion or in the realm of commerce. In each case there are the ostentatious claims of royalty, "arrayed in fine linen and purple and scarlet", and the voluptuous display of wealth, "decked with gold and precious stone and pearl" (RV). The sudden sweeping away ("in one hour") by divine judgment evokes from the financial controllers of earth not a wail of repentance, but a terrible wail over the wealth that has been lost. The final verb "is come to nought" (*erēmoō*) was used of the harlot in 17:16 and should be rendered "made desolate". Here the subject of the verb is "so great riches" or "wealth"; the merchants mourn not for the city but for their lost wealth.

17b-18 The dirge grows in volume as the third group, linked to the transport and shipping industry, joins in the wail over Babylon. There are four categories mentioned;

1 Shipmasters: "Strictly speaking *kubernētēs* points to the steersman or pilot (Acts 27:11). It may point symbolically to the shipping magnates.
2 Passengers: "All the company in ships", translated literally by JND as "every one who sailed to any place", points to the passengers transported: all who used the facilities provided by Babylon both by air and sea.
3 Sailors are those whose livelihood depended on the transport industry and provided the manpower for Babylon's facilities.
4 Workers: "As many as trade by sea" translated by RV "as many as gain their living by sea". This term includes the wider groups of related industries like shipbuilding and cargo-handling which depended, not on the immediate facilities of Babylon, which was a river port and not a seaport, but on the financial nerve centre of Babylon: in the language of the first century, it embraces the worldwide transport industry. Without going beyond the language of Scripture, but interpreting the picture in present day terms, it is perfectly valid to see a worldwide transportation network having its centre in Babylon, the crossroads of the world. Assuming that this world trade centre is rebuilt exactly on the ancient site and thus is not a seaport, the emphasis falls on the control it has over the worldwide transport industry: the language of the first century describes this in terms easy to be understood. Control stems from its commerce and the fact that it is close to the oil-producing centres. Many industries with highly specialised technology will be dependent upon this nerve-centre

and multitudes of people will make their living through it, each contributing in his own way to the prosperity of this mighty city.

Again "the smoke of her burning" tells the story and evokes the same wail from the workers of Babylon. The intensity of their grief is reflected in the verb "cried" (*krazō* as in v.2) as they fling a challenge to earth in the rhetorical question, "What city is like unto this great city?"; an echo of the lamentation at the fall of Tyre (Ezek 27:32). Cities have risen and fallen throughout earth's history from the time of Cain (Gen 4:17) but these workers know that never before has technology united with civilisation to produce a city of this character. It seemed to epitomise all that men could wish of wealth and luxury. Men had calculated that it was destined to last forever, but the smoke cloud now rising from it indicates the end not only of their livelihoods, but of their hopes. No wonder that they wail. The extent of their grief is seen in the very old, somewhat bizarre, custom of gathering up a handful of dust and pouring it over the head. This action expressed the hopelessness of a situation, and in symbol declared that the grave was the only answer. It is referred to in Job 2:12; Lam 2:10; Ezek 27:30. At the same time they were "weeping and mourning" (RV), their cry of "alas, alas" joining that from the monarchs and merchants. Again there are special emphases in the cry that show that these workers had their own interests at heart. The wealth that they particularly mourned was the wealth by which "were made rich all that had ships in the sea" i.e. those who were in the transport industry and had been made wealthy by the great enterprises of Babylon. The motive behind these wealth-creating enterprises lies in the word "costliness" (*timiotēs*), which means "worth". In secular literature it is used to define "an abundance of costly things" (Bauer, Arndt and Gingrich). Babylon demanded the very best things of life and created the wealth to achieve them; men caught her spirit, became slaves to it, and sold themselves "body and soul" to it. Now they weep as "in one hour" the judgment of God sweeps away all that they had valued in life. The final verb "made desolate"(*erēmoō*) is translated "come to nought" in v.17.

20 The sob of earth is followed by the song in heaven; the dirge of earth is replaced by the delight of heaven; for while earth is grieved by Babylon's fall, heaven is gladdened. The speaker is not identified but it would seem to be the final call from Christ who, in v.4, summoned His saints on earth to separate; now He summons His saints in heaven to rejoice. The RV translation, on good manuscript authority, follows the summons to heaven with the descriptive phrases, "and ye saints, and ye apostles and ye prophets" (see also JND). The verb "rejoice" (*euphrainō* as in 11:10; 12:12) is frequently rendered "make merry" (as in Luke 15:29,32) and implies the vocal expression of overflowing joy in the heart. The destruction of this wicked city, the very heart of satanic opposition to God and His people, demands an outburst of joy. This summons will be answered by the outbreak of the chorus of "hallelujahs" in 19:1-6. The call to rejoice is based upon the justice that God has meted out to Babylon; saints who have suffered at the hands of Babylon may now rejoice in the justice of heaven. The AV's "avenged" is a paraphrase of the literal expression, "[God] hath judged your judgment upon her". G.B.Caird, proposing a legal setting where God has found Babylon guilty of perjury and passes on her the sentence she passed on the saints, translates, "God has imposed on her the sentence she passed on you". While it is possible to argue that the "prophets" mentioned are OT prophets who suffered under historical Babylon, that would make the mention of "apostles" problematic. The mention of "apostles and prophets" in that order (cf. Eph 2:20) suggests very strongly that it is the glorified church in heaven who is called to rejoice. Since her apostles and prophets suffered under pagan Rome and not under papal Rome this is an incidental confirmation that the raptured church is in heaven at this point and that Babylon is found throughout history, reaching its full development only in the harlot and the city. John and the believers in his day, knowing that the other eleven apostles and many NT prophets had all suffered martyrdom, would rejoice in anticipation of God's just government.

21 The mighty Lord God of v.8 commissions a mighty angel to deal with this mighty city. Whether this is the same mighty angel of 5:2 or 10:1 is not stated but he is certainly of the same class. A symbolic action by the angel provides the background for the doom-song that rises over Babylon. The action recalls the days of Jeremiah when Seraiah was taken captive along with king Zedekiah to Babylon. Jeremiah had written in a book the doom of Babylon shown to him by God and had instructed Seraiah, "And it shall be, when thou hast made an end of reading this book, that thou shalt bind a stone to it, and cast it into the midst of Euphrates; And thou shalt say, Thus shall Babylon sink, and shall not rise from the evil that I will bring upon her..." (Jer 51:61-64). A sudden catastrophic destruction by God is envisaged in the action, just as sudden as the destruction of the might of Egypt at the Red Sea of which exactly the same figure is used in Neh 9:11. The usual household millstone was four to five feet in diameter, one foot thick, and weighed at least a thousand pounds. The "millstone" in this context may refer back to the words of Christ in Matt 18:6 when He warned that the offender against one of His "little ones" should have a millstone "hanged about his neck" and be drowned in the depth of the sea. Here the bitter opponent of the people of God throughout the ages is dealt with in summary fashion. The smash of Babylon can almost be heard in the adverb *hormēmati* (translated "with violence"): it is derived from the verb *hormaō* ("to rush") and is used in Mark 5:13 in connection with the herd of swine, and in Acts 19:29 in connection with the mob in the theatre. The RV translates the adverb "with a mighty fall", which allows the rumbling crash of the city to be heard. A study of the history of Babylon shows that no judgment of this character has yet overtaken the city of Babylon. Jeremiah's prophecy of the stone with all the associated detail awaits this action at the close of the tribulation when all the prophecies of Babylon's destruction will be finally fulfilled.

22-23 It is clear from what follows in these verses that the symbolic action of the stone hurled into the sea does not demand the total elimination of the site of Babylon The sob of Babylon's commercial allies is answered by a deathly silence over the scene of devastation. This is the fulfilment of Jeremiah's words, "Then shalt thou say, O Lord, thou hast spoken against this place, to cut it off that none should remain in it, neither man nor beast but that it may be desolate forever" (Jer 51:62). This terrible silence is due to the fact that all normal noises of life are stilled. The expression "no more at all", repeated six times with minor variations, seems like the intoning of a death-knell throughout the years of the millennium. City life has a large variety of sounds and noises from the deafening clanging of industrial factories to the raucous musical entertainment of social occasions; none of this will be heard any more in Babylon. Even in the happy days of millennial peace, one site on earth will remain ominously and eerily silent; a site that God leaves as a silent witness to His judgment of sin. God had meant Jericho to fulfil this role in Canaan (Josh 6:26). Perhaps preachers in the years of the millennium will use it as a text for warning messages to those born during that period. Life that was normal in Babylon is now gone:

1. Music: "The voice of harpers, and musicians, and of pipers and trumpeters"
   This list of instruments is representative rather than exhaustive. It embraces the whole of the great entertainment industry that had found its home in Babylon (see Isa 24:10 where Babylon is called the "city of confusion"). It is clear that God gave man the ability to enjoy and employ music but man, away from God, has used this in a sensual way so that modern music with its powerful beat has largely been used of Satan to destroy generations of young people. Babylon had become the centre of this seductive industry – and suddenly there is silence, no longer are the air-waves polluted by the music and mirth of Babylon. God has acted and silence broods over the site.
2. Craft: "No craftsman, of whatsoever craft he be"
   The wealth of Babylon had allowed it to become the home of every diverse craft that would indulge the artistic and lavish tastes of the dabblers in the world of fine art. Wealth had led these craftsmen to ignore the appeal of Christ (v.4). The workshops are burned: silence reigns.
3. Domestic: "The sound of a millstone"
   The normal domestic noises may well be in view in this statement. The word used is *mulos* means a handmill, which was used only by women or slaves in the Roman world. There may be therefore an oblique reference

to the fact that wealth demanded "slaves" and Babylon, despite social charters and trade union legislation, would depend upon the working class for its prosperity. No longer will economic slavery pander to the needs of the wealthy; all society has gone from Babylon and even the handmill is silent.

4. Physical: "The light of a candle shall shine no more at all in thee"
The sunshine that made life delightful in Babylon was eclipsed in the darkness of the fifth bowl judgment (16:10); it carried a terrible and prophetic warning. The great solar panels for the generation of electrical power had suddenly become valueless and useless. The drying up of the Euphrates (16:12) under the sixth bowl silenced the power-generating plants upon which the air-conditioned luxury of Babylon depended. This once sun-bathed city, highly illuminated and resplendent in artificial light at night, now under divine interdict has not even the light of a lamp (*luchnos*). The silence and the darkness testify to God's judgment upon sin. It seems a logical deduction that there is one site throughout the millennium where the sun is not permitted to shine.

5. Social "The voice of the bridegroom and of the bride"
Just as the millstone evokes memories of normal domestic chores so the voice of bridegroom and bride evoke memories of happy family occasions, but these too are gone forever. However the setting here may suggest not just a simple marriage occasion, but a licentious orgy such as a wedding in Babylon would have been with all the glitter, opulence and display that Babylon could command. The immorality lies in the fact that men use a divine institution for sensual and possibly even political and commercial ends – as weddings have been used in the past amongst royalty and the high society of earth. God has brought such licentious luxury to its final end.

In these results of God's judgment on Babylon an echo can be heard of the prophecy of Jeremiah. Although he was speaking of the desolation of Jerusalem during the seventy-year captivity the terms are the same: "Moreover I will take from them the voice of mirth, and the voice of gladness, the voice of the bridegroom, and the voice of the bride, the sound of millstones, and the light of the candle. And this whole land shall be a desolation and an astonishment"(Jer 25:10-11). What Babylon meted out to Jerusalem God metes out to Babylon. That judgment was for a brief seventy years with ultimate recovery but there is no recovery for Babylon – the dirge has a note of finality, "no more at all".

23b-24 Three reasons are now given for this judgment upon Babylon. These repeat the characteristics that have marked Babylon throughout her history, but which find their full display in this endtime city that reflects an empire.

1. Her Pride: "For thy merchants were the great men of the earth"

Pride in the might of empire was always characteristic of Babylon. This runs from Nimrod through Nabopolassar to Nebuchadnezzar (Dan 4:30) and ends in the Beast. The control of commerce and trade had enabled Babylon as the capital of the Beast's empire to dominate earth. This is reflected in the word "merchants" used three times in this chapter: they are the great merchant princes of the commercial world who have displaced both politicians and royalty to become "the great men" of the earth. This latter word is translated "lords" in Mark 6:21 and is used in extra-Biblical literature to refer to princes, nobles or magnates (Bauer, Arndt and Gingrich). Elsewhere the word is used only in 6:15 which may confirm that the sixth seal, in its effects, runs to the end of the tribulation. These merchant princes were the men who counted on the world scene: Babylon was proud of them.

2. Her Power: "For with thy sorcery were all the nations deceived"(RV)

The word "sorcery" (*pharmakeia*) suggests that the power-base of Babylon was not only her formidable military might under the Beast, and her commercial control of the world money markets, but that she plied another trade that gave her access to the power of the great deceiver Satan himself. The primary meaning of *pharmakeia* is "drug" or "medicine" or "potion". Through the popular practice of seeking healing by charms, magic potions and spells it came to have a direct link with the occult. In Gal 5:20 it is translated "witchcraft". Its use here suggests that Babylon was the source of hallucinatory drugs that made men an easy prey to deception. This combination of drug addiction and occult power explains the extraordinary success of the deception by the harlot, and was equally useful in the propagation of the last world religion when men worshipped the Beast. Satan himself is the great deceiver (12:9) and used Babylon simply as his tool to deceive men. God deals here with Babylon the satanic agent.

3 Her Persecutions: "And in her was found the blood of prophets and of saints, and of all that were slain upon the earth"

There could hardly be a more sweeping indictment in all Scripture. Taken at face value it indicates that all the blood that has stained the earth is traceable to the plottings of this God-opposed Babylonish system. It is interpretation, not grammar, that limits the slain to those martyred for God and for Christ. Alford has an interpolated comment in this vein: " [this refers] naturally, to all slain for Christ's sake and his word. Compare the declaration of our Lord respecting Jerusalem (Matt 23:37)". Babylon is here charged with responsibility for the blood of the prophets of the past ages, the martyrs who died under paganism, the death of Christ, and the martyrs who died under Rome whether pagan or papal. These all have left their bloodstains on the history of testimony for God. Believers of the present church age are aware of the years of the inquisition and the presence of the many martyr graves in our land. Even when Christ has taken the church away Babylon will still be putting saints to death in her harlot character and, finally, in the last three and a half years of the great tribulation she will slay many who refuse the mark of the Beast;

Babylon is blood-stained to the end. The blood "of prophets and of saints" must include prophets and saints from both OT and NT periods, such is the sweep of the statement. The sense of the word "found" would appear to be that, on her destruction, such indisputable evidence of her guilt will come to light that the whole universe will acknowledge the justice of the divine action against this evil city.

Notes

While it is a fact that in 1996 much of ancient Babylon has already been rebuilt by Saddam Hussein, complete with Isthar gate, the temple of Marduk and the palace of Nebuchanezzar, the interpretation of Scripture does not depend on the existence of this tourist-oriented city. While a matter of interest for believers yet the truth of a rebuilt Babylon rests on Scripture and not on something that could readily be destroyed in another middle-east war.

8 Pictures of the burning oilfields of Kuwait in 1991 were both terrifying and frightening, and had apocalyptic overtones, but they only foreshadow a more terrible holocaust; the smoke of Babylon's burning is yet to cause a wave of mourning to circle the earth.

13 While the word "oil" must be interpreted in the context of the first century as "olive oil" (as in 6:6) there is no reason to exclude a prophetic mention of "fuel oil" which will form a large part of the trade and wealth of Babylon. Babylon's fall will mean that the fuel distribution upon which so much of earth's commerce will still depend will be totally disrupted.

CHAPTER 19

10. *The Fourth Parenthesis continued* 17:1-19:10

(vision 3) *The Hallelujah Chorus and the Marriage of the Lamb (19:1-10)*

The first two visions of this fourth parenthesis have shown the end of mighty Babylon both in her religious guise, symbolically as the harlot (ch. 17), and in her commercial guise as an actual city (ch. 18). The destruction of this city in the closing days of the tribulation echoes to heaven itself and the immediate consequence is the marriage of the Lamb. Heaven's delight in Babylon's overthrow is followed by heaven's joy in the union of Christ and His bride, an event that takes place just before Christ returns to earth for the final confrontation with the Beast at Armageddon.

(a) *The Hallelujah Chorus (vv.1-4)*

v.1 "And after these things I heard a great voice of much people in heaven, saying, Alleluia, Salvation, and glory, and honour, and power, unto the Lord our God:
v.2 For true and righteous are his judgments: for he hath judged the great whore, which did corrupt the earth with her fornication, and hath avenged the blood of his servants at her hand.
v.3 And again they said, Alleluia. And her smoke rose up for ever and ever.
v.4 And the four and twenty elders and the four beasts fell down and worshipped God that sat on the throne, saying, Amen; Alleluia."

1 The repetition of the expression "after these things" from 18:1 introduces the third vision in this parenthesis but it also moves events forward chronologically. Babylon's doom on earth causes delight in heaven, expressed in the fourfold "hallelujah", the only time this word appears in the NT. It is the transliteration into English of the Greek *hallelouia* which in turn comes directly from the combined Hebrew words *hallel* ("praise") and *Jah* ("Jehovah") meaning "praise the Lord". In the Book of Psalms it is found twenty-four times but in the AV it is always translated, "Praise ye the Lord". The group of Psalms 113-118 is known to Judaism as the "Hallel of Egypt" because of its association with Israel's deliverance from Egypt. A far greater deliverance here raises a heavenly anthem of praise.

"Much people" recalls the "great multitude" (7:9) on earth. This heavenly company are heard in a single united voice of praise; in holy harmony their "hallelujah" rises to the throne. There is no reason to restrict this company to the martyred dead (seen by John on the sea of glass in 15:2-4); nor is there any contextual hint that this is a company of angels. From the content of the praise this is evidently the host of all the redeemed in heaven showing their delight at the overthrow of this ancient enemy of God.

Three majestic notes of praise are sounded by this redeemed host:-

(a) Salvation is much more than the personal salvation of individuals and includes the whole programme of God brought to the moment of realisation (1 Pet 1:5).

(b) Glory is the revealed excellence of deity displayed in redemption through the Lamb, the basis of the salvation.

(c) Power is the might required to bring the benefits of redemption to earth, dispossess the Beast and bring men into blessing.

A fourth word "honour" occurs between glory and power in some manuscripts but the RV and JND agree on its omission. They also agree that the ascription of praise is to "God" (omitting "the Lord"). This echoes the song of the great company on earth in 7:9-10 where God is addressed and salvation is the theme. It is clear that a great host on earth and a great host in heaven unite in praise as the tribulation ends and Christ is about to establish His millennial kingdom. Praise echoed throughout the universe with respect to creation (4:11), and with respect to redemption when the Lamb took the book (5:9), and now, the book opened, the emphatic word in the praise is salvation!

2-3 There are two reasons given for the "hallelujah" that has echoed in heaven; each reason is introduced by the preposition "for":

1. "for true and righteous are his judgments". This is the general reason, true for all the actions of deity. "Judgments" describe actions whose essence is truth and whose righteous standard is God Himself; the same confession has already been heard from the altar (16:7) amidst the crashing thunders of the bowl judgments.
2. "for he hath judged the great whore". This is the specific example of the general truth of the first statement. The testimony of heaven is that judgment on Babylon displays truth and righteousness and the result is the shout of praise. The word "whore" is used (see 17:1) to define the characteristic sin of Babylon when she traded the general revelation given to man and built a religious system for her own self interest and pleasure. "Judged" and "avenged" point back to the blazing pyre of Babylon (18:8). The imperfect tense of the verb "did corrupt" points to what was characteristic of Babylon; she did this throughout the ages and continued until God judged her. The word shows the effect Babylon has had on society: she has corrupted every divine institution. She corrupted the family and destroyed society; she corrupted the nation of Israel and destroyed a national testimony; she corrupted scriptural teaching and led men back into paganism. Now God has finally judged this harlot.

The verb "avenged"(*ekdikeo-*) describes an action "arising out of (*ek*) justice (*dikē*)"; if justice was to be executed on earth Babylon could not escape. The first charge which makes judgment inevitable is the corruption she spread, but a second and related charge is her persecution of saints. The martyred dead cried for this very thing three and a half years before (note the same verb in 6:10) and God takes vengeance (*ekdikēsis*) on behalf of His people (Rom 12:19; Heb 10:30). God has now called Babylon to account for the way she treated His servants. The language is taken from 2 Kings 9:7, when God passed sentence on Ahab and his wife Jezebel who were the agents of a Babylonish-type persecution in their age. From its beginning Babylon has hated testimony for God with an implacable hatred and has tried to destroy the saints. God has now acted to settle the account; the "day of vengeance of our God" has arrived (Isa 61:2).

A second "hallelujah" like a heavenly encore echoes around heaven as the company views the visible evidence of the judgment of God upon Babylon – "and her smoke rose up forever and ever", a reference to "the smoke of her burning" in 18:9,18. The present tense of the verb "rose up" tells of the permanent memorial left on earth to the judgment of God. The language is taken from Isa 34:8-10 (which describes the judgment of God upon Idumea): "It shall not be quenched night nor day; the smoke thereof shall go up forever; from generation to generation it shall lie waste". This is God's final judgment on Babylon, the smoke ascends "forever and ever". The message is plain: there will never again be a restoration of Babylon.

4 In the opening throne-scene in 4:4 the twenty-four elders made their first appearance in the book; in 5: 6-10 with their harps and vials they prostrated themselves before the Lamb as He took the scroll to open the seals. Their song was the new song of redemption based on the worth of the Lamb. In this last mention in the book (the twelfth reference), once again in company with the four living creatures, they prostrate themselves before the throne and worship. The destruction of this ancient enemy of God is the signal for an outburst of praise in the "Amen, Hallelujah" (Ps 106:48) as elders and living creatures recognise that the purposes of God are moving to their consummation. J.B. Smith suggests that the living creatures cry "Amen" while the twenty-four elders respond with "Hallelujah"; a suggestion with merit since "Amen" repeats the earlier cry of the living creatures (5:14). The living creatures, having a special link with the earth that Babylon has corrupted (see v.2), gladly acquiesce in her judgment (in their "amen"), while the twenty-four elders representing the church, which had known Babylonish persecution in the days of both pagan Rome and papal Rome, gladly raise the third great "hallelujah" in heaven.

It is interesting that this is the last appearance of both the four living creatures and of the twenty-four elders in the book. The twenty-four elders represent the church in heaven in the period between the rapture and the establishment of the millennial kingdom. With the appearance of the bride (v.7) ready for the wedding ceremony, this priestly representation of the church is no longer needed and hence the elders are not mentioned again. The bride will be associated with Christ from this point onward. The living creatures were shown to be actual spirit beings representing features of deity in creation, so when Christ is unveiled in His own creation (v.11) they are no longer prominent. Christ is the full revelation of deity throughout creation and His bride is with Him.

(b) *The Marriage of the Lamb (vv.5-10)*

v.5 "And a voice came out of the throne, saying, Praise our God, all ye his servants, and ye that fear him, both small and great.
v.6 And I heard as it were the voice of a great multitude, and as the voice of many waters, and as the voice of mighty thunderings, saying, Alleluia: for the Lord God omnipotent reigneth.
v.7 Let us be glad and rejoice, and give honour to him: for the marriage of the Lamb is come, and his wife hath made herself ready.
v.8 And to her was granted that she should be arrayed in fine linen, clean and white: for the fine linen is the righteousness of saints.
v.9 And he saith unto me, Write, Blessed are they which are called unto the marriage supper of the Lamb. And he saith unto me, These are the true sayings of God.
v.10 And I fell at his feet to worship him. And he said unto me, See thou do it not: I am thy fellowservant, and of thy brethren that have the testimony of Jesus: worship God: for the testimony of Jesus is the spirit of prophecy."

5-6 In 16:17 a voice from the throne cried "it is done" – the judgments were finished. Here that same voice, likely the voice of Christ, issues a summons to the saints on earth. Since the authority of God in the throne has been fully vindicated in Babylon's destruction, now saints are called upon to praise God. The present imperative of the verb may be translated "keep on praising"; they must begin and never cease to praise the God who has acted in this way. The omission of the "and" (see RV and JND) shows that only one company is addressed. Coming from every stratum of society (great and small) they are called "his servants", clearly the bondslaves of God (the seventh mention of them in the book). Having shown in their lives a reverential fear of God that kept them apart from the Beast-worship of their day, they are called to join in heaven's praise. This they willingly do and John hears the fourth hallelujah of the passage rise to heaven. To describe this mighty roar John links three similes; he hears "as it were":

(a) [the] voice of a great multitude
(b) [the] voice of many waters
(c) [the] voice of mighty thunderings.

Beginning like the low murmur of a great crowd, deepening to become like the roar of cascading waters (see 1:15) it swells until its thunders crash around the hearer and drown out every other sound. The saints on earth, relieved of the nightmarish oppression of Babylon, respond in a full-hearted way to heaven's summons and echo back the hallelujah of heaven. This is the real "Hallelujah Chorus" rising from both heaven and earth.

While the "for" of v.2 shows that saints in heaven are occupied with the destruction of Babylon, the "for" in this verse shows that the saints on earth see in the destruction of Babylon the first act of kingly power. The aorist tense of the verb "reigneth" is best reflected in JND, "has taken to Himself kingly power", showing that the destruction of Babylon is the first act in the establishment of the kingdom. The titles of deity, "the Lord our God, the Almighty" (RV) stress the power of God displayed in this judgment that opens the way for the king. This is the seventh of nine references to the "Almighty" (*pantokratōr*) and Babylon's end has demonstrated His might in no uncertain way. Now the next event will be the arrival of the King (v.11).

7-9 This great company not only recognises the might that God has shown on earth but grasps the next step in the divine programme and in view of it they summon their own hearts to further notes of praise. "Be glad" (*chairō*) and "rejoice" (*agalliaō*) are synonymous verbs (found together again only in Matt 5:12) that describe the welling up of praise as they "give glory" to God in anticipation of the joy that lies ahead . Another "for" points to the ground of praise as they anticipate the joy in the marriage of the Lamb. This is the high point of the great chorus that unites heaven and earth; with Babylon destroyed and the kingdom about to be established the moment has arrived for the greatest of earth's joys – a marriage feast. The "blood of the Lamb" (7:14; 12:11) has pointed back to Calvary; the "wrath of the Lamb" (6:16) has pointed upward to the throne; now the "marriage of the Lamb" points forward to days of gladness and joy.

Marriage as a divine institution pre-dates both Israel and the church (Gen 2:21-24) and was meant by God to be monogamous and permanent. This is why it could be used as a picture of the bond between Jehovah and His covenant people, the nation of Israel. In numerous scriptures Israel is referred to as "wife" (Jer 3:14; Isa 54:5; Ezek 16:8) and in others Jehovah speaks of Himself as "husband" (Jer 31:31-32; Isa 54:5); in the use of these terms it is clear that the covenant relationship is viewed as a marriage bond. The unfaithfulness of Israel, when betrayed into idolatry, is called fornication; yet despite such sin Jehovah refuses to give His erring wife a divorce (Isa 50:1). With patient and unchanging love He has sought to recover this unfaithful wife. (See Hos 1-3).

A question that has engaged the minds of commentators is the identity of the one called metaphorically "his wife" in the marriage of the Lamb. Some commentators argue, as does Sir Robert Anderson, that this marriage involves the recovery and restoration of Israel. Others who are not clear on the distinction between Israel and the church contend that the wife mentioned here must include all the redeemed of all ages who have been brought into covenant relationship with God. It should be quite clear that both these ideas are untenable and only serve to introduce confusion. This very passage makes it obvious that there are great companies both in heaven (v.l) and earth (v.6) who are redeemed and rejoice at the arrival of the marriage but their separate mention indicates that they cannot be the bride. Again the passage makes it clear that this is "the marriage of the Lamb" not "the marriage of Jehovah". It is shown in Isa 50:1 that Jehovah has never divorced his unfaithful wife, and it is neither possible nor logical to apply the figure of marriage to the restoration of an erring wife. While the Lamb has been expected from the dawn of history (Gen 22:7-8), Christ Himself bears this character only from His incarnation and, thus His bride can hardly pre-date the incarnation. The church was hidden in the counsels of God until NT times, so while the bride may be foreshadowed in the OT in certain pictures this is irrelevant to the present discussion. As the church appears historically as a divine entity at Pentecost so the picture of Christ as bridegroom and the church as bride becomes relevant. This pattern of Christ and His bride becomes the pattern for NT marriage (Eph 5:22-32) and Paul uses the same picture illustratively in 2 Cor 11:2. This wedding ceremony is the moment anticipated in Eph 5:27 when the church is presented to Christ as His blood-bought bride. The aorists "is come" and "made herself ready", do not need to be treated as anticipating a happening yet to take place as Alford suggests. Translated as perfects (AV, RV and JND) they point to the fact that, Babylon being judged, the time for the wedding ceremony has arrived. Anticipating that moment the bride has already made herself ready.

The aorist tense "made herself ready" shows that the process of preparation is complete. The verb *hetoimazō* which is used seven times in the book (8:6; 9:7,15; 12:6; 16:12; 19:7; 21:2) is explained figuratively in v.8 as the donning of her bridal dress. The symbolic use of the term "fine linen" is interpreted as "the righteousness (*dikaiōmata*) of saints". The RV translation as "the righteous acts of saints" is more literal and points, not to the forensic righteousness declared by the throne on the basis of the work of Christ that clears the guilty, but the righteous deeds in the lives of the saints. The preparation of this glorious bridal garment has involved every member of the church from Pentecost to the rapture. It is the preparation of these years that is recognised in the emphasis on her personal action "made herself ready" – the robe she wears is the result of her own actions on earth which, as other Scriptures show, are the result of the operations of divine grace. Nevertheless, in a very real way, she makes her own preparation for the marriage. It is clear that the donning of the dress shows that the judgment seat of Christ is already past and the outcome is apparent in this glorious dress. The righteous acts of believers during their lifetime on earth have become the glorious bridal attire for her day of nuptial bliss. Scott sums it up beautifully (p.381) in memorable words: "Our lives have to be reviewed at the bema of Christ (2 Cor 5:10). The light of the throne will be cast over and upon every moment of our lives, discovering the hidden, and bringing out the true character of act, word and service. The enigmas of life will be explained, unsolved problems cleared up, and all mistakes and misunderstandings rectified. This and more is the application of the judgment seat of Christ to the heavenly saints, and precedes the marriage: 'His wife hath made herself ready'. The light of the throne had done its work, bringing into bold relief the whole story of her history on earth". Note that the verb "granted" (translated "given" in AV, JND) is another aorist, referring back to that judgment seat when all testimony through the ages has been divinely evaluated. Now the bride is fittingly adorned for presentation to her bridegroom in the marriage ceremony (Eph 5:27).

9-10 So absorbed is John in these soul-stirring scenes that he has to be commanded by the voice of his conducting angel to "write". On three occasions in this book (14:13; 19:9; 21:5) it would seem that John has to be awakened out of a reverie and this time it is to record the fourth beatitude of the book. This blessing is upon those that have been called to the "marriage supper of the Lamb". It should be clear that the angel is making a distinction between the marriage (v.7) of the Lamb in heaven and this marriage supper. No one with cultural knowledge of wedding custom could confuse the marriage and the marriage supper. They were different events, at different times and in different places. The marriage of v.7 takes place in the Father's house in heaven, thus it seems, without specific statement, that this summons is to the marriage supper on earth. A second point to be considered in this connection is that the other six beatitudes in the book (1:3; 14:13; 16:15; 20:6; 22:7,14), refer without exception to men on earth and the same is true of this blessing. God is bestowing blessings on particular groups of people on earth, and in this case the blessing is linked with the call to the marriage supper. The teaching of the parables in the Gospels shows that there are those who will be excluded from the festivities (Matt 22:1-13; 25:10-11).

The persons called to the marriage supper are the invited guests. Christ as bridegroom has with Him His blood-bought bride, and together they share the central place, but others are called to share in the festivities. "They which are called" translates the same word used in the parables of the great supper and translated "them that are bidden" (Matt 22:3; Luke 14:17). This is the "calling" of the gospel preached throughout the tribulation and the souls who responded and received salvation are now welcomed to the festal gathering of the marriage supper at the beginning of the millennium. This explains the use of the term "blessed" as referring specifically to men and women on earth who have believed the gospel; those who refuse it will be banished into the outer darkness (Matt 25:30). There is no doubt that there will be other guests as well, those whom John the Baptist identified figuratively as friends of the bridegroom (John 3:29). The first resurrection will just be completed at this point (20:4-6) so this feast will be open to all who, down the ages, have responded to the divine revelation concerning the Christ. The antediluvian saints will be there including Abel and Enoch, the pre-Abraham saints embracing all from Noah and Job, then the great company from Israel who all looked forward to kingdom glory right down to the resurrected martyrs of the tribulation period. What a festal gathering this will be! All the anticipations and expectations of the ages are realised in the shared joy of Christ and His bride at the marriage supper.

Such a tremendous event seems so far beyond human experience as to stretch human credibility, so that the communicating angel feels it necessary to give a word of assurance first to John and through him to his readers: "These are the true words (*logoi*) of God" (JND). The truth is conveyed in the very words that bear the stamp of divine authenticity. Overwhelmed and overawed, in a very natural reaction, John falls down before the feet of the angel. Homage to a superior is in order but John's spirit is so moved, either by the excitement of the moment or by the feeling that the angel represented God, that he is in danger of giving to the angel the worship which belongs to God alone. Arrested in the action and rebuked by the angel ("see thou do it not") he is instructed in the right relationship between God and His creatures. Angels and men are all simply servants (*douloi*): the RV translation is much clearer, "I am a fellow-servant with thee and with thy brethren". The angel takes his rightful place as a servant and one servant does not worship another; each must worship God alone. John's brethren are identified as those "that have the testimony of Jesus". The use of this descriptive phrase in 12:17 (see RV) indicates that these are a special class of John's brethren. If it had been "the testimony of Christ" then it would have embraced all the saints down the ages including the church age. However the expression "testimony of Jesus" indicates that it is tribulation saints who are in view; those who in the darkest days of the tribulation bore witness to the despised Jesus at a time when there seemed little prospect that He would ever be recognised on earth. This interpretation is supported by the explanatory "for" that follows. That the prophetic spirit shows itself in testimony to Christ is the record of Scripture (1 Pet 1:11) but this is not what is in view here. The truth emphasised by the angel is that those who have the testimony of Jesus, believe as Jesus did that, in spite of all the present evidence to the contrary, Jesus will rule on earth. These saints give witness even to the point of death that God will fulfil all the promises concerning Jesus; in Him God will display His faithfulness and His might and this despised One will be revealed publicly as "King of kings and Lord of lords" (v.16). This is the very essence of prophecy and this very prophecy (the whole book) given through John will be the mainstay of the faith of many in the closing days of the tribulation. Whether "spirit" is taken to mean the essence of prophecy or interpreted as the Holy Spirit the truth is the same; only the Holy Spirit can reveal the truth by which men can live and for which men will die.

Notes

7 The whole sequence of events relating to the marriage of Christ and His church becomes clearer against the social background of marriage in NT times. It is, of course, true that wedding customs varied in the ancient world from society to society and underwent changes from age to age. Generally, however, in Jewish society there were three distinct events associated with a marriage of which Scripture gives glimpses. These three major events associated with a wedding in NT days may be set out as follows:

1. *The betrothal.* A marriage contract was entered into by parents when the parties were children. Generally a suitable dowry was paid to seal the contract (Matt 1:18). This pictures the period of the church age and the espousal of the church to Christ. Redeemed by the blood of the Lamb as the great dowry price, espoused to her absent Lord, she awaits His coming to the air to claim her for Himself.
2. *The ceremony.* When the parties had reached an appropriate age the second stage took place. The bridegroom accompanied with his friends, went to the home of the bride and escorted her back to his home, where the wedding ceremony took place.
   This corresponds to the moment of the rapture when Christ comes to call away His bride and take her to the Father's house for the wedding ceremony. It is clear that the coming of Christ for the church is very much His personal act, as 1 Thess 4:16 stresses that it is the Lord "himself" who summons her, so that the friends of the bridegroom (John 3:29) must wait in heaven for the return of Christ and His bride. The preparation of the judgment seat must take place at this point to be followed by the marriage ceremony (v.7).
3. *The supper.* The wedding ceremony over, the bridegroom introduced the bride to her home which they were to share together and it is there that the marriage feast took place. This is variously called the "marriage feast" and the "marriage supper" and was not merely one meal, as in many western cultures, but a series of festivities that could go on for several days. It is this third stage of the marriage that is referred to in the story of the marriage in Cana of Galilee (John 2:1-11) and it is also the background of the picture in Matt 25: 1-10. It will be noted that the word in Matt 25:10 is not "marriage" (AV) but "marriage feasts" (*tous gamous*) (see Newberry margin and refer also to JND, RV).

Some will question why the judgment seat is only introduced indirectly without a positive statement.

The answer is once again that the church is not the subject of this prophecy except in so far as she is linked with Christ. Returning to earth with Him as His bride is the main point here. The judgment seat is dealt with in other Scriptures (Rom 14:10-12; 1 Cor 3:10-17; 2 Cor 5:9-10).

IV. Vision 3: Christ Conquering (19:11-20:6) Christ Comes – The Sovereign

In this passage the climax of the book is reached, the point to which all the previous events have moved step by step. In the first vision Christ has been seen in the midst of the churches (1:9-3:22), in the second vision He has been seen in the midst of the throne (4:1-19:10), now in this third vision at the head of the armies of heaven He is revealed to earth as "King of kings and Lord of lords".

The central event in this vision, the revelation of Christ to earth, must be seen as:

1. The consummation of prophecy.

Zechariah had this moment before him when he announced: "Then shall the Lord go forth, and fight against those nations, as when he fought in the day of battle. And his feet shall stand in that day upon the mount of Olives, which is before Jerusalem on the east, and the mount of Olives shall cleave in the midst thereof toward the east and toward the west, and there shall be a very great valley; and half the mountain shall remove toward the north, and half of it toward the south" (Zech 14:3-4). The words of Christ Himself pointed to this same moment: "Immediately after the tribulation of those days shall the sun be darkened, and the moon shall not give her light, and the stars shall fall from heaven, and the powers of the heavens shall be shaken: and then shall appear the sign of the Son of man in heaven: and then shall all tribes of the earth mourn, and they shall see the Son of man coming in the clouds of heaven with power and great glory" (Matt 24:29-30). Paul adds further detail: "when the Lord Jesus shall be revealed from heaven with his mighty angels, In flaming fire taking vengeance on them that know not God, and obey not the gospel of our Lord Jesus Christ" (2 Thess 1: 7-8). This is the moment of which John has already written: "Behold, he cometh with clouds; and every eye shall see him, and they also which pierced him: and all kindreds of the earth shall wail because of him" (1:7).

2. The climax of history.

From the time when sin entered the earth the history of men has been one of departure from God and defiance of God. In light of the seed promised by God immediately after the fall (Gen 3:14-15) earth has awaited the coming of a man. Eve's assurance concerning her firstborn was premature: "I have gotten a man from the Lord" (Gen 4:1); a disappointment that was to be repeated through the centuries as men of all kinds proved to be failures. When Christ came they did not recognise Him and gave Him a cross. Another man of different origin and character, identified in this book as the Beast, has deceived men and marshalled them under his banner in the great gathering of armies around Jerusalem. This rebellion of earth is answered by the revelation from heaven of the Christ who leads forth His armies to confront the deceiver and claim His inheritance. This is the ultimate climax to which all ages have moved; heaven is opened as if in answer to that cry from the heart of Isaiah, "Oh that thou wouldest rend the heavens, that thou wouldest come down...to make thy name known to thine adversaries, that the nations may tremble at thy presence!" (Isa 64:1-2). The great "how long?" (Hab 1:2) wrung from many a faithful heart down the ages is now answered, Christ comes as the Man from glory.

3. The crisis of earth.

Earth has had many a crisis in the past but none to compare with this moment. The armies of earth by various satanic stratagems (see 16:13-16) have been gathered around Jerusalem (Zech 14:2), and stretch in a menacing crescent from Armageddon (16:16) to Edom (Isa 63:1) in a battle line almost 200 miles long (14:20). Stirred by satanic power, beguiled by the masterly oratory of the Beast and the supernatural power of the false prophet, the nations of earth unite for the last time in the unholy union revealed in Ps 2:1-3, "Why do the heathen rage (Newberry margin 'tumultuously assemble'), and the people imagine (RV margin 'meditate') a vain thing? The kings of the earth set themselves, and the rulers take counsel together, against the Lord, and against his anointed, saying, Let us break their bands asunder and cast away their cords from us". It is at this moment of crisis that God acts: heaven is opened and Christ is revealed at the head of the armies of heaven. Earth faces the greatest crisis of its history.

This second coming of Christ to earth is shown to be visible to every soul on earth as Christ described it in dramatic language: "For as the lightning cometh out of the east, and shineth even unto the west; so shall also the coming of the Son of man be" (Matt 24:27). On earth in the political realm there will be conferences, consultations and all the media coverage of the gathering of these mighty armies gathered around Jerusalem. There is the background noise and horror of the crash of collapsing cities in the earthquakes under the seventh bowl (16:19); the news carried by live television coverage throughout the world. In the heavens there are the astronomical disturbances (Matt 24:29) climaxed by the sign of the Son of man (Matt 24:30), which in this context seems to be some dramatic visible indication that puts beyond doubt the fact that Christ is coming personally to earth. It is of this moment that John writes "and I saw heaven opened". The very simplicity of the words convey the solemnity of the moment as earth stands in confrontation with heaven. Christ confronts His satanic antagonist, the Beast.

1. *The Revelation of the King* 19:11-21

(a) *I saw – the Sovereign (vv.11-16)*

v.11 "And I saw heaven opened, and behold, a white horse; and he that sat upon him was called Faithful and True, and in righteousness he doth, judge and make war.

v.12 His eyes were as a flame of fire, and on his head were many crowns: and he had a name written, that no man knew but he himself.
v.13 And he was clothed with a vesture dipped in blood: and his name is called The Word of God.
v.14 And the armies which were in heaven followed him upon white horses, clothed in fine linen, white and clean.
v.15 And out of his mouth goeth a sharp sword, that with it he should smite the nations: and he shall rule them with a rod of iron: and he treadeth the winepress of the fierceness and wrath of Almighty God.
v.16 And he hath on his vesture and on his thigh a name written, KING OF KINGS, AND LORD OF LORDS."

John had seen a door opened in heaven (4:1), and the temple of God opened (11:19); here he sees heaven opened. The perfect participle would be better translated "standing open" as it describes the result of the opening rather than the act of opening. There is no suggestion that heaven is closed again (see comments on 7:9; 14:2-3) throughout the millennial reign. John's exclamation of surprise ("behold") is understandable when from this opened heaven he sees a white horse, and its rider. While on earth Christ entered Jerusalem on an ass in keeping with the prophetic word, "Behold thy King cometh unto thee: he is just and having salvation: lowly and riding upon an ass, and upon a colt the foal of an ass" (Zech 9:9). This time, riding a white horse, the traditional symbol of conquest and victory, His mission is not peace but to "judge and make war". White symbolises the righteousness of His cause. Formerly He sat on a white cloud (14:14) and later will sit upon a white throne (20:11), symbolising the fact that His actions in judgment always reflect the standards of absolute righteousness. He stands in absolute contrast to the previous rider on a white horse (6:2) who appeared on the opening of the first seal. J.B. Smith sums up concisely the differences in the two pictures, "This rider comes from heaven; the former from earth. This one has five names indicating His deity, the former is unnamed. This one has on his head many crowns (*diadēma*); the former has no crown in his own right, but a crown (*stephanos*) is given him. A number of other descriptive terms are here mentioned, all indicating the deity of this rider in unmistakable terms, none of which are ascribed to the former". It was shown that the rider of 6:2 is the personification of the deception sweeping earth and centred in the Beast; like everything about that deceiver the white colour in his horse is part of the lie he represents.

Four names (the double name of "Faithful and True" may be treated as one) identify Christ and indicate the offices He bears at this moment of revelation. The first is "Faithful and True" which is not only a title but His name, as the participle "called" suggests. Christ has already been identified as "faithful" (1:5) with regard to His witness, and as "true" (3:7) with respect to His person, and to the church in Laodicea he identified Himself as both "faithful and true" (3:14). During His sojourn on earth He was faithful to God and true to His own nature; now this same One returns to earth to confront the Beast who is the personification of faithlessness and falseness. This particular title is most relevant to the tasks He has now to execute for God. The tenses of the verbs "judge" and "make war" are dramatic presents and show that the action begins as heaven is opened, while the modifying phrase "in righteousness" precedes the verbs and thus places the emphasis on the manner in which He sets about the work. Isaiah's prophecy looked forward to this moment: "He shall not judge after the sight of his eyes, neither reprove after the hearing of his ears: But with righteousness shall he judge the poor, and reprove with equity for the meek of the earth: and he shall smite the earth with the rod of his mouth, and with the breath of his lips shall he slay the wicked. And righteousness shall be the girdle of his loins, and faithfulness the girdle of his reins" (Isa 11:3-5). The reference is not to any sessional judgment (as in Matt 25:31-46), but to the decisions and actions of this warrior-king as He acts righteously for God in the execution of divine justice on the nations. This justice was foreseen by the psalmist: "He shall judge among the nations, he shall fill [all places] with dead bodies, he shall smite through the head of a great country" (Ps 110:6 JND). Earth's challenge: "Who is like unto the Beast? who is able to make war with him?" (13:4) is now answered from heaven.

12-13 John's eye is drawn to four features of this majestic Sovereign: His eyes, His head, His name and His clothing. The blazing eyes of this warrior-king have been seen in 1:14; 2:18 but here the statement is even more direct, "His eyes are a flame of fire"(RV), which describes the incandescent blaze of the eyes before which rebellious men will shrink and shrivel. The head that John had seen wear a crown of thorns (John 19:5) now wears many diadems. The diadem is the crown of royal dignity. The dragon had diadems on his seven heads (12:3); the Beast had diadems on his ten horns (13:1). From the time of his fall Satan has coveted this regal authority; men throughout history have struggled and died to seize it but Christ here is crowned with many diadems. W. Scott (p.387) puts it memorably, "There is but One who can be entrusted with the exercise of absolute authority and dominion, and he is the Son of man (Ps 8). Seven diadems on the dragon, ten on the Beast, but 'many' upon the head of the conqueror Christ denote that every form and kind of government is vested in Him". His name, the second name given to Christ in this passage, is clearly visible; whether He bears it on the forehead is not specifically stated, but recalling the parallel of the redeemed 144,000 (14:1) this may be inferred, particularly when v.16 mentions another name on His vesture and thigh. While it is clearly visible this name is also, in some way, incomprehensible: "no one knows" suggests that divine illumination is needed. When God reveals Himself by His name He puts the power implied in that name at the disposal of those who receive the revelation. The fact that only Christ knows this name shows that there are resources of infinite power in deity available only to Christ as He acts for God in this judgment on earth; men even redeemed men, may not share in this aspect of divine power.

His blood-stained garment (RV), too, arrests John's eye. Indeed the language is most graphic, for the participle "dipped" is from the verb *bapto-* (translated "baptise" in the Gospels) as if the garment or part of it had actually been plunged into blood. (The RV reading *rhantizō*, "sprinkled", has insufficient manuscript support.) There is nothing in the text to suggest a link with the purple robe (John 19:5) that Christ wore before Calvary and which was stained with His own blood. Nor is it a symbolic reference to the work of the cross. It shows that Christ the warrior has newly come from previous battles and the blood of His enemies has stained his garment. The battle of "the great day of God Almighty" (16:14) has already begun; one phase has passed or is passing and John sees the mighty victor deal with the last group of the enemy forces. Only the climax is described, the final act of confrontation with the Beast. The intervening acts of judgment in the sweep of His coming are not given in detail. This agrees with Isaiah's prophecy: "Who is this that cometh from Edom, with dyed garments from Bozrah? this that is glorious in his apparel, travelling in the greatness of his strength?" and the question that follows, "Wherefore art thou red in thine apparel, and thy garments like him that treadeth in the winefat? I have trodden the winepress alone; and of the people there was none with me: for I will tread them in mine anger, and trample them in my fury; and their blood shall be sprinkled upon my garments, and I will stain all my raiment. For the day of vengeance is in mine heart, and the year of my redeemed is come" (Isa 63:1-4). This is the final stage of the battle of the great day of God Almighty.

The third name Christ bears is "The Word of God". It is given to Christ only in John's writings and links this warrior-king with the prologue to John's Gospel (John 1:1-18). The pre-existent Son is the Word who in God's time became incarnate and dwelt amongst men. Christ revealed God as to His purpose in salvation while He tabernacled with men, now He reveals God as to His power, when He judges and makes war. God was revealed in Christ in the days of His flesh acting in grace; now that same God is revealed in Christ acting in truth (John 1:17). He is the Word of God.

14 This verse, introduced somewhat parenthetically in the description of Christ, gives the majestic train of this mighty conqueror. Behind Him come the armies from heaven, mounted as He is on white horses. The symbol shows they share in His triumph. Many commentators understand these armies to be angelic hosts; Christ did refer to "twelve legions of angels" (Matt 26:53) and angels are associated with the coming of Christ to earth in Matt 16:27 and in 2 Thess 1:7. Nevertheless since this moment was anticipated in 17:14 and those that are with Christ are there identified as the "called, chosen and faithful" then these armies must include the saved ones of all ages joining Christ in His moment of triumph. The fact that they ride on white horses symbolic of victory is appropriate for saints but scarcely appropriate for angels. Their clothing too, described as " fine linen, white and clean", is similar to that of the bride (v.8) and must carry the same interpretation, ie it must symbolise the righteous acts of the saints. In v.8 the word "white" is *lampros*, bright, reflecting the glorious splendour of the bridal attire; here the word is *leukos* which, with the colour of the horses, is in stark contrast to the darkness of earth under a darkened sun, a stricken moon and falling stars (Matt 24:29-30). Since the bride and these armies are similarly clothed some have suggested that this is the church militant going into battle with Christ. This is too limited an interpretation; the church will be present (see 1 Thess 4:14) but other companies of saints from past ages who have been in heaven will come with Christ as He claims His throne. The splendour of such a coming was glimpsed in early history in the ministry of Enoch when he preached, "Behold the Lord cometh with ten thousands of his saints" (Jude 14). Zechariah joined in this anticipation, "And the Lord my God shall come, and all the saints with thee" (Zech 14:5) and Paul adds his voice when he writes of "the coming of our Lord Jesus Christ with all his saints" (1 Thess 3:13). The church and the saints of all the different ages share in the triumph of Christ and, since it is clear from 6:11 that white robes do not necessarily demand resurrection, this is possibly the company of all saints who are described as "them that dwell (tabernacle, JND) in heaven" (13:6; 12:12).

15 Three figures are used to describe the impact of the coming of Christ at this moment: the sword (the warrior), the rod (the shepherd) and the winepress (the farmer). He will wield the sword. This Warrior-King has a sword (*rhomphaia*), not in His hand but proceeding out of His mouth. This word for sword is peculiar to this book (except for a figurative use in Luke 2:35) and describes the large, broad, tongue-shaped sword of Thracian origin. In the Roman world the sword symbolised magisterial authority backed up by military power. These belong to Christ inherently (1:16) and He reminded the compromising elements in Pergamum (2:12,16) of His ability to act in keeping with this authority. Now this same sharp sword (some manuscripts include "two-edged" but the evidence suggests it has been copied from 1:16; 2:12) is used against the gathered armies of a rebel earth. The figure of a *sword* proceeding from His mouth is not found in the OT; it shows that Christ acts and conquers by His word. Paul writes of this same occasion but uses a slightly different figure: "Whom the Lord shall consume with the spirit of his mouth, and shall destroy with the brightness of his coming" (2 Thess 2:8). Both are based on a prophetic word in Isaiah, "He shall smite the earth with the rod of His mouth, and with the breath of his lips shall he slay the wicked." (Isa 11:4). While Isaiah and Paul had in view particularly the rebel leader this same sword of Christ will deal with the armies that have gathered in his support.

He will use the rod. The reference is to Ps 2:8-9: "Ask of me, and I shall give thee the heathen for thine inheritance, and the uttermost parts of the earth for thy possession. Thou shalt break them with a rod of iron; thou shalt dash them in pieces like a potter's vessel". It has been pointed out at 2:27 that this same quotation is an example of Hebrew *parallelism* in which the second statement restates and reinforces the first. This means that the verb "rule" (*poimainō*), instead of its normal meaning of "rule as a shepherd" should have its extended meaning of "destroy", in keeping with the Hebrew *rahgag* ("break them with a rod of iron"). Ruling as a shepherd involves care for the sheep but includes ruthless destruction of the enemies of the sheep; the two senses interlock. Both verbs refer to the destruction of the rebel armies as Christ comes to earth, in fact the very moment that is described here. The shepherd-rule of Christ will extend through the millennium (7:17) but that is not in view at this point. That the rod is of "iron" indicates that the stroke given by this mighty King will deal summarily with all opposition; there is no danger of its breaking.

He treads the winepress. Further detail is now added to the "winepress without the city" already mentioned in 14:20. In the earlier passage the passive "was trodden" left open the identity of the one who would tread the winepress. Here Christ, in the emphatic "he", is pointed out as the executor of "the fierceness and wrath of Almighty God". This thundering phrase combining "fierceness" (*thumos*) and "wrath" (*orgē*) stresses the blaze of anger of an indignant God whose patience has been tried throughout the ages by the wickedness, rebellion and blasphemy of men. In this simple statement is summed up the terrifying picture painted by the OT prophets; Isaiah wrote in messianic language, "I have trodden the winepress alone; and of the people there was none with me" (Isa 63:3); Joel's cry becomes a terrible reality: "Put ye in the sickle, for the harvest is ripe: come, get you down, for the press is full, the fats overflow; for their wickedness is great. Multitudes, multitudes in the valley of decision: for the day of the Lord is near in the valley of decision" (Joel 3:13-14). The gathered armies around Jerusalem are but as grapes in the winepress and Christ is about to tread that winepress. The "battle of the great day of God Almighty" (16:14) is the realisation of the "fierceness and wrath of Almighty God"; Christ is the treader of the winepress.

16 The psalmist, when addressing the warrior-king in Ps 45:3 cries, "Gird thy sword upon thy thigh, O most mighty, with thy glory and thy majesty". When Christ fulfils His mission for God the sword proceeds from His mouth; but in the place where a sword would normally be worn there is a name written and written here it cannot be missed. The name is not written in two places as the AV may suggest, the "and" is explanatory and should be translated "even" as Alford explains: "Written at length, partly on the vesture and partly on the thigh itself, as the part where, in an equestrian figure, the robe drops from the thigh". Behind the action of the sword lies all the authority of the mightiest Sovereign in the cosmos. The answer to Pilate's mocking question, "Art thou a king then?" (John 18:37) is given now from heaven: He is "King of kings and Lord of lords". Paul wrote in anticipation, "he shall shew, who is the blessed and only Potentate, the King of kings, and Lord of lords" (1 Tim 6:15); the angel in 17:14 identified this same moment: "and the Lamb shall overcome them; for He is Lord of lords, and King of king". Moses (in Deut 10:17) and Nebuchadnezzar (in Dan 2:47) spoke of deity in these terms but now deity is manifest in Christ and He is the absolute Sovereign.

(b) *I saw – The Supper (vv.17-18)*

v.17 "And I saw an angel standing in the sun; and he cried with a loud voice, saying to all the fowls that fly in the midst of heaven, Come and gather yourselves together unto the supper of the great God;
v.18 That ye may eat the flesh of kings, and the flesh of captains, and the flesh of mighty men, and the flesh of horses, and of them that sit on them, and the flesh of all men, both free and bond, both small and great."

17-18 No detail is given of the flash of the divine sword, the smiting by the shepherd rod or the treading of the human winepress. "The battle of that great day of God Almighty" (16:14) is seen only in its aftermath. In fact it is not a battle in the normal meaning of the word. No evenly matched forces are locked in a death struggle with the tide of battle ebbing and flowing; this is simply a complete and utter destruction of the gathered armies by the sword out of the mouth of Christ (v.21). The sword figure shows that at just one word from Christ the rebels are vanquished. The completeness and the utter physical destruction of the enemy forces is graphically illustrated by the summoning of the fowls of the air to "the supper of the great God". In the east the vultures and other birds of prey gathered to a field of battle to feast on the dead bodies, blood-stained and broken, left behind after the battle. Often their presence as the only moving things amid silence and death indicated the site of the carnage. This is the graphic picture given to John to illustrate the most terrible massacre, the greatest devastation, that has ever befallen mankind. Having rejected Him who is the truth men have followed the liar to their destruction.

If this summoning angel stands in (*en*) the sun there can be no doubt about the brilliance with which he is clothed to outshine it. It should be remembered, however, that at this period there has been unprecedented disturbance of the heavenly bodies. The kingdom of the Beast was described as " full of darkness" (16:10); Christ warned of such happenings, "Immediately after the tribulation of those days shall the sun be darkened" (Matt 24:29); Zechariah added his voice, "And it shall come to pass in that day, that the light shall not be clear, nor dark" (Zech 14:6). On this terrible day standing stark against the subdued orb on which every human eye is focused, this angel issues his terrible summons to "the fowls that fly in the midst of heaven". Those birds that circle through the atmosphere are now summoned to "the supper of the great God". The word "supper" (*deipnon*) is used in v.9 of the bridal feast and a contrast is certainly intended. God provides for His Son and His bride a marriage supper of festive joy; all that Satan can provide is a feast for the unclean birds of earth.

The language of this summons is clearly derived from Ezek 39:17-20: "Speak unto every feathered fowl, and to every beast of the field, Assemble yourselves and come; gather yourselves on every side to my sacrifice that I do sacrifice for you, even a great sacrifice upon the mountains of Israel, that ye may eat flesh, and drink blood. Ye shall eat the flesh of the mighty, and drink the blood of the princes of the earth". Many commentators, misled by the similarity of the language, have thought that Ezek 39 describes this occasion. In discussing this point J.F. Walvoord acknowledges that while the language is similar, "Care must be exercised in interpreting passages so similar by following the rule that similarities do not necessarily prove identity. Birds of prey are always in evidence where there is death" (page 279). A little consideration will show that the battle of Ezek 39 is undertaken by one foe, Gog and Magog coming from lands to the north of Israel; it interrupts a period of unusual peace in Israel and takes place in the early part of the tribulation. The battle here described closes the tribulation when all nations gather round Jerusalem for the final confrontation with heaven. The language is borrowed from that earlier battle but the events themselves are distinct.

18 This summons is issued in anticipation of the feast to be enjoyed by the fowls when the judgment falls in vv.19-21. A macabre table is spread, gruesome even to contemplate. The word "flesh" (plural) repeated five times is translated by Robertson "pieces of flesh". All the social distinctions of earth upon which men placed such importance are obliterated in this terrible supper spread for the fowls; the greatest men of earth are just "pieces of flesh". The leaders are there; kings, captains and mighty men lie among the slain. Neither political power, military skill nor physical strength afforded the slightest protection against this mighty Sovereign. Their followers are there; slain horses and their riders who have been drawn from every stratum of society, the freemen and the bondmen, the slaves and their masters, the small and the great, have all met the same doom. In terms of the Roman world of John's day the picture describes a gathering of all classes of men. So it will be in the days of the Beast, all of earth will be united in opposition to the Lamb and will be united again in the doom they share. The sword of the Lord wielded by a mightier than Gideon (Judges 7:20) takes terrible toll upon the rebels of earth.

(c) *I saw – The Slaughter (vv.19-21)*

v.19 "And I saw the beast, and the kings of the earth, and their armies, gathered together to make war against him that sat on the horse, and against his army.

v.20 And the beast was taken, and with him the false prophet that wrought miracles before him, with which he deceived them that had received the mark of the beast, and them that worshipped his image. These both were cast alive into a lake of fire burning with brimstone.

v.21 And the remnant were slain with the sword of him that sat upon the horse, which sword proceeded out of his mouth: and all the fowls were filled with their flesh."

19 The arrival of the Sovereign (v.11) followed by the summons of the angel (v.17) to the fowls has prepared John for this third sight ("I saw") of the chapter – the confrontation between the Beast with his armies from earth and Christ with His army from heaven. "The kings of the earth" (17:2; 18:9) is a comprehensive term describing the world-leaders who have given allegiance to the Beast. As shown in the comments at 16:16 some of these kings have gathered to attack the Beast and others have gathered to defend him; however, as the crisis deepens they recognise that their common enemy is Christ and unite in a great confederate army (Ps 2:1-3) to defy heaven. Satan deceived men and planned this gathering of armies (16:16) but God allowed it (Zech 14:2); now the forces of earth under the Beast and the false prophet are united in disputing the claim of Christ to the sovereignty of earth. The plural "armies" of the Beast may suggest the disparate nature of the forces gathered in opposition while the singular "army" shows that all the redeemed are united under their Sovereign Lord.

20 The serried ranks of earth's armies stand opposed to the advancing host of heaven, when suddenly and without warning the ring-leaders are arrested. The verb "was taken" (*piazō*) is used frequently in John's Gospel of the efforts to lay hands on Christ (John 7:30, 32, 44; 8:20; 10:39; 11:57) when the AV renders it "lay hands on" (John 8:20) or "apprehend" (Acts 12:4; 2 Cor 11:32). The idea in the verb is to "seize with hostile intent". In one dramatic moment this great host is left leaderless; the satanically-empowered leaders in whom men had placed such trust have gone. Even at this crisis it is possible men had imagined that satanic power would come to their aid through the puppet prince and prophet; now they see them seized and hurled into the lake of fire.

The Beast is the one whose coming, character and career has been studied throughout this book. From his first mention in 11:7, to his manifestation in 13:1-10 he has stalked across the prophetic page as the epitome of satanic power in a man. The final empire of earth was embodied in this man who from his emergence from the abyss (11:7) at the midpoint of the tribulation has been yielded totally to Satan. He is the "anti-God" (see the expression is 13:6) in the very fullest use of that term and claimed the worship that belonged to God alone (2 Thess 2:4). The charismatic personality of the political world leader found ample support in one who epitomised the power of religion on earth and called here the "false prophet", a term first used of him in 16:13. As the beast out of the earth (13:11-18) he is a Jew who leads his nation, or the apostate part of it; he is the Antichrist, where the prefix "anti" is used in the sense of "in the place of". Israel refused the Christ whom God sent and they had received one who came in his own name (John 5:43) so that he is, in fact, a replacement Christ. The ability of this man to perform miracles (*sēmeia*, "signs") lends credibility to his deception as he leads men to take the mark of the Beast (13:16) and to worship the image of the Beast (13:15). The features identify him as the one whom John calls "the Antichrist" (1 John 2:18). Under the darkening skies, on a shaking earth and amid the circling fowls of the air, these men are seized by divine power and hurled into the lake of fire. Suddenly the two most feared and powerful men who have ever been seen in history are removed dramatically from the very head of their armies. Left leaderless and helpless the vast armies of earth have only moments to savour the mind-numbing terror of the measured approach of Christ and His army. What terrible moments those will be until that dread sword does its mighty work (v.21).

This is the first of five mentions of the "lake of fire" in the book (20:10,14,15; 21:8). It is clear from these references that the lake of fire is the final and eternal abode of stubborn and rebellious creatures who have refused God's grace in salvation. First to enter there are the Beast and the false prophet, followed a thousand years later by their master Satan (20:10). The full complement will only be realised when the great white throne judgment is over and Death and Hell are followed by "whosoever was not found written in the book of life" (20:14-15). The terror of this place is presented, not only by the reference to its size as being a "lake", but by the intensity of its "burning". The word "burning" qualifies "lake" (feminine) not "fire" (neuter) and this "burning lake" burns with the intense blue flame of burning sulphur, mentioned in three of the references (19:20; 20:10; 21:8). It may be argued that the language is symbolic, to convey to us in the language of earth, the terror of this awful place. This could well be so but, if the terror of the symbolic is so great, what will be the reality? There is little comfort for any soul in such an argument. It is better to bow to revelation and recognise that God has a place in the universe, originally prepared for the devil and his angels (Matt 25:41), which will be forever a burning lake where the bodies and souls of rebellious creatures will be incarcerated and from which there can be no escape. This is the reality behind the "hell fire" (Mark 9:47) and the "everlasting punishment" (Matt 25:46) of which Christ warned.

21 Once the leaders have been seized and removed, Christ deals with "the rest" (RV, JND), which in this case is the whole array of armies gathered around Jerusalem. The guilt of the leaders is patent to the whole universe and instant and immediate banishment to the lake of fire is their sentence. For them no question arises of resurrection and judgment at the great white throne. On the other hand deceived men are dealt with physically in judgment by that sword from the mouth of the Sovereign so that their bodies become carrion for the birds. There is no thunder of gunfire, no clash of armour in this battle; swiftly and silently that death-dealing sword from the mouth of the Sovereign sweeps through the ranks of earth's military might. Bengel calls it "a spiritual weapon of resistless might" and the armies of earth lie in physical death. As individuals these men will stand before the great white throne (20:11) and with heaven's justice vindicated will find their place in the lake of fire with the men they followed. It can only be with bowed heart that this closing scene of the tribulation period is viewed as the full outworking of sin is contemplated. The birds of prey swoop down upon this terrible battlefield; they rest gorged to repletion in the eerie twilight of the darkest day in human history. The text of James 1:15 is appropriate, "And sin when it is finished bringeth forth death".

CHAPTER 20

2. *The Establishment of the Kingdom* 20:1-6

This chapter presents, in summary form, the events associated with the millennial reign of Christ on earth. Remarkably few details are given of the reign itself for the focus falls rather upon the preparations for the reign, the events that bring it to a close and the events that follow it as the divine programme moves on to introduce the eternal state. In fact the chronological sequence of events is presented as a series of scenes marked out by John's use of the verb "I saw" from its first occurrence at 19:11 until its tenth and final occurrence at 21:22. There is every reason to understand these scenes as marking chronological stages in the final visions of the book. A summary of the ten occurrences may be set out as follows:-

1.	19:11	I saw	The revelation of Christ
Before the establishment of the millennial kingdom			
2.	19:17	I saw	The summons to the supper
3.	19:19	I saw	The slaying of the armies of the Beast
4.	20:1	I saw	The seizure of Satan
In the millennial kingdom			
5.	20:4	I saw	The reign of Christ with His saints
After the millennial kingdom			
6.	20:11	I saw	The great white throne
7.	20:12	I saw	The lake of fire
8.	21:1	I saw	The new heaven and the new earth
9.	21:2	I saw	The holy city
10:	21:22	I saw	No temple within

The chronological development of these ten scenes has an important bearing on the understanding of the final vision in the book.

In this chapter the method of interpretation adopted throughout the book receives its most critical test and stands up to the severest scrutiny. It has been pointed out (see Introduction) that there are three different methods of approaching the interpretation of the book and when they are applied to the eschatological events surrounding the millennial reign of Christ they give three different results. These methods of interpretation may be summarised as follows:

1. The Amillennial View. This view emphasises the symbolic element in all the prophecies of this book and, in particular, rejects any literal interpretation of the thousand years, insisting that the idea of Christ reigning is figurative language to describe spiritual realities. This view denies that a literal reign of Christ on earth is intended in this passage or any other passage of Scripture. While there are many variations amongst those who are amillennialist in outlook, the main tenets of the theory may be summarised as follows:

(a) Satan was defeated and bound as a result of the cross of Christ and His subsequent resurrection and ascension.
(b) The thousand years are not to be taken literally but are a symbolic way of describing the gospel age, when saints who are born again (the first resurrection), reign spiritually now with Christ.
(c) All the OT prophecies of kingdom blessing have their complete fulfilment not in Israel but in the church. The rebellious nation of Israel has been set aside by God forever and is suffering judgment for its sin in rejecting Christ so that there can never be any restoration of this nation to divine favour. In summary such expositors view the curses as belonging now to Israel on account of their rejection of Christ and all the blessings as belonging to the church.
(d) The return of Christ will be to earth at the end of the church age and will be followed by a general judgment of both saints and sinners.

This chapter shows in very clear terms that these notions do not do justice to the plain language of this Scripture.

2. The Post-millennial View.This view has some things in common with amillennialism but by denying any clear distinction between Israel and the church, it rejects any thought of a rapture for the church. Expositors of this school insist that there is only one stage to the coming of Christ which takes place after the millennial reign of Christ. This millennial reign is not to be understood as a literal period but a term describing the closing phase of the church age just before Christ comes to introduce the new heaven and the new earth. In common with amillennialists they see Christ and the church as reigning spiritually in this gospel age. The thousand-year period is to be established by the changing of society as the gospel is preached worldwide in fulfilment of the great commission of Matt 28:18-20. Admitting that, from the viewpoint of our day, this is neither a present

reality nor a realistic prospect post-millennialists blame the failure of the church. Such interpreters look for mighty revivals to change society and establish righteousness on earth so that Christ can come again. This is essentially a 19th-century view that has had to receive serious modification in light of two world wars and all the happenings of the 20th century which have displayed in a very real way, that society, instead of becoming steadily better, is becoming increasingly corrupt. The binding of Satan and the resurrection of saints when interpreted in the normal scriptural way refute absolutely this kind of theory.

3. The Premillennial View. It has been argued throughout this study that Scripture should be allowed to mean what it says without the addition of men's presuppositions. This leads inevitably to the premillennial view of eschatology. The term describes the view that Christ comes personally to earth with His saints at the close of the tribulation period to establish the millennial kingdom and that this kingdom will last for exactly one thousand years. There are many variations within the general scheme but the great majority of premillennialists would agree with the following summary:

(a) The millennial kingdom has its foundation in the promise of the land-grant to Israel as the seed of Abraham and the promise of the throne to one of the line of David. Thus the view gives to Israel their key role in the kingdom promised to them throughout the OT.

(b) This kingdom will be a literal kingdom on earth centred on Israel with the capital Jerusalem. Christ will share this theocratic reign with His saints. The Lamb's wife, the bride, the church of this dispensation, will fill a special place of nearness to the reigning Christ while other resurrected saints have thrones under Christ.

(c) This reign will not be limited to Israel but will embrace the whole of earth (Zech 9:10). All the OT prophecies of worldwide blessing through Abraham (Gen 12:1-3) will then be fulfilled.

(d) All who enter this kingdom to dwell on earth will be redeemed. These will be the "sheep" of Matt 25:33, the unnumbered multitude of 7:9-17. The 144,000 (14:1-5) will form a special company as a guard of honour for Christ in His earthly movements.

(e) This kingdom is established by the personal return of Christ at the close of the tribulation period as described in 19:20. The Beast and the false prophet are arrested and their armies destroyed, the people of Israel are delivered, Satan is bound and the kingdom established.

(f) The "born again" ones, the redeemed who enter the kingdom, will find their redeemed condition reflected in new conditions on earth. New climatic conditions will favour the changes that Christ brings to the flora and fauna in keeping with the new geography of earth (Zech 14:4) so that all things are made new (Isa 35:1-10).

(g) This kingdom lasts for one thousand years. It ends with the rebellion of the Satan-led hosts, as described in 20:7-10, whose destruction by God opens the way for the new heaven and the new earth that introduces the eternal state.

It is submitted that the premillennial descent of Christ to earth to establish a literal kingdom for one thousand years is the only view that gives full weight to the plain language of this chapter. It allows Scripture its crowning development and undermines all the fanciful and subjective interpretations that have clouded the teaching of Scripture on these issues. The exposition will deal with the specific points that reinforce the premillennial teaching of the chapter.

(a) *I Saw – the Restraint and Removal of Satan (vv.1-3)*

v.1 "And I saw an angel come down from heaven, having the key of the bottomless pit, and a great chain in his hand.
v.2 And he laid hold on the dragon, that old serpent, which is the Devil, and Satan, and bound him a thousand years,
v.3 And cast him into the bottomless pit, and shut him up, and set a seal upon him, that he should deceive the nations no more, till the thousand years should be fulfilled: and after that he must be loosed a little season."

1 The arrest of Satan and his binding with the chain follows immediately upon the destruction of the armies of the Beast. The puppets of Satan have been summarily seized and ignominiously dispatched to the lake of fire and their armies destroyed. Now Christ deals with Satan the master-plotter himself: an angel from the opened heaven acting with all the authority of the throne arrests Satan. This angel is neither Christ in angelic guise (see comments at 8:3; 10:1) nor the "fallen star" of 9:1 but simply a commissioned angel with the nature of his commission symbolised in the key and the chain. This is not the key of hades, entrusted to Christ alone (1:18), but the key of that dark dungeon where spirit-beings are imprisoned and called "the bottomless pit" (see 9:1, 2, 11). The great chain dangling on (*epi*) the hand of the angel indicates his mission and even though Satan is a spirit-being the symbol is plain. To insist that a literal chain is demanded by the literal approach is to misunderstand the normal use of symbolic language. Satan bound is the reality, the symbol is the chain.

2-3 The four names of Satan repeat the names of identification of 12:9. W. Scott distinguishes the names (p.397), "As the dragon he is the embodiment of cruelty. As the serpent he is the personification of guile. As the devil he is the arch-tempter of man. As Satan he is the declared opponent of Christ and His people". All his machinations and plottings down the ages have brought him to this moment of truth.

The imprisonment of Satan is described in five verbs (all in the aorist tense) that tell the dramatic story. He is seized (AV "laid hold on") and bound; he is then cast into the abyss. The pit is closed (AV "shut him up"). Doubtless with the use of the key and the final action is the sealing of the abyss. The seal is clearly upon the pit and JND translates "and shut [it] and sealed [it] over him". This latter action, reminiscent of Daniel in the den of lions (Dan 6:17) and of Christ in the tomb (Matt 27:60-66), is the pledge of responsible authority that this prisoner will be held in secure custody; no unauthorised hand may break this divine seal. That Satan is both bound by the chain and shut up under seal is a graphic way of describing that Satan, banished to the abyss, is no longer allowed the personal freedom he has been permitted down the ages since his fall. While this passage makes no mention of the angels who have followed Satan in rebellion, or of the demonic hosts released in 9:1-11, it would seem that all follow him into the abyss. Confirmation may be in the fact that the fear of the demons in Luke 8:31 relates to the abyss and not the lake of fire, the final abode of the devil and his angels (Matt 25:41). It would be somewhat strange if Satan himself was imprisoned and his followers left free to pursue their evil ways in the kingdom age. In the incarceration of Satan it would seem that all his hosts are similarly confined. The personal chain on Satan would keep him apart even in the abyss.

The period of Satan's imprisonment is to be one thousand years. In keeping with the exact and literal usage of numbers in this book there is no reason why this number should not be taken in the same way. In these first seven verses this period is mentioned six times. Three times it refers to the imprisonment of Satan (vv.2,3,7); twice it is used of the period of the reign of the saints (vv.4,6), and once it used of the period between the first resurrection and the resurrection of the unsaved dead (v.5). This thousand years begins with the removal of Satan, is marked by the reign of the saints with Christ and closes with the release of Satan.

The millennium commences with the binding of Satan. Amillennial teaching asserts that this took place through the death, resurrection and ascension of Christ. Following Augustine (4th century AD) amillennial expositors claim that Christ's statement, "I beheld Satan as lightning fall from heaven" (Luke 10:18), anticipated the cross; they use Christ's illustration of the binding of the strong man (Matt 12:29) in the same way to show that Satan was bound as a result of the first coming of Christ. Thus Satan is now bound and the whole of the period between His two comings is the millennium. The thousand years is seen as the symbolic way of expressing a lengthy, yet indeterminate, period. Augustine and other commentators living during the first few hundred years of church testimony had no problem in assuming that Christ would come at the end of the first thousand years to fit their theory. In this second millennium present-day expositors who follow this line of interpretation have to insist that the thousand years is the figurative way of describing a long period. Human experience alone is sufficient to show the fallacy of such teaching regarding Satan while the Scripture knows absolutely nothing of it. The NT shows beyond argument that Satan is not only active now, but that his activity will increase as this age moves towards its end. Satan filled the heart of Ananias and Sapphira (Acts 5:3), blinds the minds of sinners (2 Cor 4:3-4); attacks an assembly (2 Cor 11:3); hinders the servant (1 Thess 2:18); takes men captive (2 Tim 2:26) and walks through the earth as a roaring lion (1 Pet 5:8). Divine sovereignty has always put a limit on satanic power and it is clear that since the cross he is a defeated foe (Heb 2:14), but there is not a vestige of scriptural support for believing that he is bound. The binding of Satan at the commencement of the millennium begins the only period from Eden to the close of history when Satan will be physically restrained from his deceptive activities amongst men and this is, of course, essential for the peace and tranquillity of the kingdom age. The particular reason why he must be removed is the fact that he deceives the nations. As "the father of lies" (John 8:44) he has ever been characteristically the deceiver (12:9; 13:14; 18:23; 19:20; 20:3, 8, 10); he and his agents have deceived men in every age, but in this last, tribulation, age his deception was particularly successful (2 Thess 2:11) and led men to their ruin in the worship of the Beast. Now for one thousand years men will no longer have to withstand this deceiver.

"After that" (*meta tauta*) is John's usual phrase as he moves chronologically to the next event. There is nothing more startling than the recurrence of the verb *dei* (rightly translated "must") in the unfolding of a divine programme. This is the seventh of eight times it occurs in the book, and shows that in the outworking of the purposes of God for earth it is necessary that this deceiver be loosed from the abyss. The reason for the loosing, while not specifically stated, may be deduced from the result as seen in vv.7-10. When Satan was cast down to earth (12:7-12) at the midpoint of the tribulation he knew that he had only "a short time" and in his rage he set about persecuting the nation of Israel. That short time was limited to three and a half years. Now the divine programme allows him freedom but only "for a little time" (RV). No indication is given as to the length of the period and to parallel it with the previous period lacks any firm evidence. While by human reckoning it is only a short period nevertheless it is fraught with dire consequences for men.

Notes

3 It is from this passage that the word "millennium", which is not found in Scripture, is derived. It seems to have been first used in written English commentaries around 1638 based on the Latin *mille* (a thousand), and *annus* (a year), as a shorthand way of describing the thousand-year period. It may be pointed out incidentally that, if the binding of Satan means, as amillennialists teach, his restraint through the cross, it may reasonably be asked what his release means. To ask the question is but to answer it; his release is as literal as his binding.

(b) *I Saw – the Resurrection and Reign of Saints (vv.4-6)*

v.4 "And I saw thrones, and they sat upon them, and judgment was given unto them: and I saw the souls of them that were beheaded for the witness of Jesus, and for the word of God, and which had not worshipped the beast, neither his image, neither had received his mark upon their foreheads, or in their hands; and they lived and reigned with Christ a thousand years.
v.5 But the rest of the dead lived not again until the thousand years were finished. This is the first resurrection.
v.6 Blessed and holy is he that hath part in the first resurrection: on such the second death hath no power, but they shall be priests of God and of Christ, and shall reign with him a thousand years."

4 With the binding of Satan, and thus the clearing from earth of all the forces that have opposed God and His plans down the ages, the way is opened for the establishment of the kingdom of Christ – the goal to which this book has been moving. This kingdom has been the goal of the ages and details of its character and course are to be found in many Scriptures. Its establishment will involve changes in every facet of life. There will be geographical changes (Zech 14:4; Isa 11:15-16), botanical changes (Isa 35:1-2), zoological changes (Isa 11:6-9), national changes (Isa 11:10-14) and changes in the human body (Isa 35:5-7). Other physical changes are implied in these new conditions that will be found on the restored earth. Glorious though they are these physical changes but reflect the most radical change of all – the change in the nature of men through the new birth.

The change to which John directs particular attention is the new government of earth which he introduces simply with the statement "I saw thrones". These are clearly not the thrones of the twenty-four elders (4:4) since those thrones were in heaven (and were twenty-four in number) while the thrones here are on earth (and no number is given). The verb "they sat" does not identify the throne-sitters but it is apparent that they are the saints of the church age of whom the twenty-four elders were the heavenly representatives. This is the time of which Christ spoke to His disciples, "Verily I say unto you, that ye which have followed me, in the regeneration when the Son of man shall sit in the throne of his glory, ye also shall sit upon twelve thrones, judging the twelve tribes of Israel" (Matt 19:28). The fact that the twelve apostles have links with Israel and are also in the church may well indicate that all the resurrected saints of the church and Israel have a share in the administration of the kingdom at various levels. Paul recognises the same truth when writing to Corinthian believers who would have liked to anticipate the kingdom age (1 Cor 4:8), "I would to God ye did reign, that we also might reign with you". For the OT saints Daniel is equally specific: "Until the Ancient of days came, and judgment was given to the saints of the most High; and the time came that the saints possessed the kingdom" (Dan 7:22). Thus it might be suggested that the saints who accompanied Christ from heaven to earth have now exchanged the horses of the previous chapter for the administrative thrones of the kingdom.

The "judgment given unto them" must be understood as the power of administration in the sense of a divine commission to act for Christ in the kingdom. Alford interprets the grammar and translates as "they were constituted judges". "Judging" is but one particular aspect of the reigning of v.4; both 1 Cor 6:2 and Dan 7:22 support this interpretation. All the sessions of judgment (2 Cor 5:10; Matt 25:31-46; Rev 11:18; 20:11) are the prerogative of Christ Himself; He alone will judge "the quick and the dead" (2 Tim 4:1) but in the administrative rule of the kingdom He associates His people with Him (3:21).

The grammar of the passage indicates that John saw:

1. The throne sitters to whom judgment was committed
2. The souls of the faithful witnesses .... who lived and reigned with Christ a thousand years (see verse note).

   John uses the word "souls" to describe persons very much as he did in 6:9. To find the verb it is necessary to move to the end of the verse, "and they lived and reigned with Christ a thousand years"; it is almost as if John saw them rise from the graves. This resurrected group of saints are the martyred dead of the tribulation period who are described in familiar terms:

(a) They "were beheaded for the witness of Jesus, and for the word of God". The word "beheaded" in the Roman world meant beheading with the lictor's axe, as distinct from beheading with the sword which was used for Roman citizens only. However, like the word "execution" in the English of today, it had long lost its original literal significance and came to mean "put to death". (*Expositor's Greek Testament*). Two reasons are given for their martyrdom; in their lives was a

(i) commitment to a person – for (*dia*, "on account of") the witness of Jesus

(ii) conviction – for (*dia*, "on account of") the word of God.

The language is very similar to that used of the martyrs in 6:9 and points specifically to those who perished in the first half of the tribulation.

(b) They "had not worshipped the beast, neither his image, neither had received his mark upon their foreheads or in their hands". The "and" here points to a second group of martyrs, those from the last half of the tribulation who died after the setting up of the image of the Beast. During the Beast's cruel and demanding reign testimony which had been positive in the first half of the week seems to have necessarily become more negative in the second half and the saints are identified by what they refused to do. The two verbs "worship" and "receive", each in the aorist tense, may point to a crisis moment in the life of each saint when they were faced with choice between the Beast and the Lamb. Like the three Hebrews in Babylon (Dan 3:16-18) they would not bow to the Beast or his image and refused his mark. They stood apart from the satanic deception and died for their fidelity to Christ. This language relates only to the second half of the tribulation (13:16-17) after the Beast had reached the apex of his power.

Both groups of martyrs from the tribulation period share the same blessing, "they lived and reigned with Christ". The aorist tense of "lived" may be translated "come to life", and since the subject of the verb is "souls", this must be interpreted as the receiving of their bodies in resurrection. Those whose earthly bodies had been so cruelly treated now receive resurrection bodies that fit them to reign with Christ. Amillennialists who interpret this verb as describing the impartation of spiritual life at conversion are quick to point out that the verb *zaō* itself does not mean "to be resurrected" but simply "to live". They fail to note that this verb is used of Christ in 1:18; 2:8 where it must involve resurrection and it is also used in the next verse of the unbelieving dead. The only possible interpretation is the resurrection of the body. It is faulty exegesis to make the same verb mean different things in the same context.

The aorist tense of the verb "reigned" (because of the modifying time period) sums up in one word the thousand years of the reign. It has been pointed out that many Scriptures speak in detail of the kingdom reign of Christ on earth but this is the only passage where we are told the length of that reign. While the verbs "lived" and "reigned" are confined grammatically and contextually to the martyred dead of the tribulation period it has already been shown that the thrones are filled by resurrected saints of the church and Israel. In fact all those who are raised in the first resurrection will be shown in v.6 to be associated with Christ in His reign on earth, This is the administrative side of the kingdom reign while those faithful saints, the "sheep" of Matt 25:33 along with the 144,000, all of whom have come though the tribulation, become the citizens of the kingdom on earth.

5 To ensure that there is no misunderstanding on the issue of who are raised in this resurrection an abrupt clarification is inserted. It might have been thought that all the graves of earth were emptied at this point as in a general resurrection. That this is not so is made abundantly clear. The resurrection of the martyred saints completes what is called "the first resurrection" while the bodies of the wicked dead will remain in their graves and their souls remain in hell for another thousand years until the close of the millennium kingdom. The abruptness of the statement (most reliable manuscripts omit the "but" of the AV) makes it stand out – "the rest of the dead lived not again". The very silence of the graveyards of earth becomes awesome; silent and largely forgotten they will remain as the centuries pass in the peace and tranquillity of Christ's glorious reign. Death will be a rare occurrence during this period and will be seen as the execution of divine justice for deliberate rebellion (Ezek 18:20).

Yet there is a very solemn note in the verse and it lies in the consideration of the word "until". God has not yet finished with those who have lived and died unrepentant and unforgiven despite His grace made available in Christ. The wicked dead await the moment of which Christ spoke, "Marvel not at this, for the hour is coming, in the which all that are in the graves shall hear his voice and shall come forth; they that have done good unto the resurrection of life; and they that have done evil unto the resurrection of damnation" (John 5:28-29). The "resurrection of life" is the first resurrection completed in the resurrection of the martyred dead: "the resurrection of damnation" or, as the better translation (RV) reads, "the resurrection of judgment" will be fully described in vv.11-12. It has already been pointed out (v.4) that the verb "lived again" (*zaō*) can only mean in this context the physical bodily resurrection of the unsaved dead.

The fact that souls lived and reigned with Christ a thousand years is now explained in one brief statement, "This is the first resurrection". That a resurrection is called "the first" implies one to follow. Even if the name is not directly used in Scripture it is in fact the second resurrection, just as the "second death" implies a first death, without actually naming it. The term "first resurrection" necessarily implies a time sequence, but there is more than just time sequence; it is a different kind of resurrection. The first and pattern resurrection of this order is the resurrection of Christ (1 Cor 15:20). This is followed by the resurrection of the church age saints on the pattern of Christ (1 Thess 4:16). The resurrection of the OT saints and of the martyred dead of the tribulation period at the commencement of the millennial reign completes this resurrection in which it is "blessed" (v.6) to share. This resurrection is complete before the millennial reign of Christ: all the bodies still remaining in the grave belong to the wicked dead awaiting the summons to the great white throne (v.11).

6 The fifth beatitude in the book is introduced by John to show the superlative blessing of those who have a part in this first resurrection. To the normal "blessed" (*makarios*) John adds the word "holy" (*hagios*) as if to show how God has set such saints apart in their blessedness. Having their "part" in this resurrection ensures their eternal bliss of which three matters are mentioned. First is an assurance in the negative followed by two positive assurances:

1. Life is their portion forever; over (*epi*) them the second death has no power (*exousia*). The second death is the eternal separation from God which lies beyond physical death (merely the separation of soul and body). Assurance that overcomers would not be hurt by this second death was given to the saints in Smyrna who were threatened by physical death (2:11). Its character will be fully explained as "the lake of fire" in v.14; 21:8 but here the assurance is given that this dread state has absolutely no authority over these resurrected saints – in no sense will they ever die again.
2. They will be priests of God and of Christ. These resurrected saints, enjoying a never-dying state through Christ, will not only have the privilege of intimate access to God and Christ but in the administration of the kingdom they will act in a mediatorial capacity as "priests of God and of Christ". The rule associated with this millennial kingdom will be in their hands.

3. They will reign with Christ. Not only will they be priests but they will share the rule of Christ and in a real way be "royal priests" as the sons of David acted in his kingdom (2 Sam 8:18). The period of the millennial kingdom is restated as a thousand years as if to emphasise the extended blessedness of these saints. When the millennial kingdom issues in the eternal state it is evident from 22:5 that the reign of Christ and His saints will continue – this reign will, in fact, never have an end.

Notes

4 The AV insertion of the italicised words "I saw" is to draw attention to the fact that the martyrs are distinct from the throne sitters. The "and" with "souls" in the accusative case, is decisive. If the "and" had been explanatory, as it is later in the same sentence, then souls" would have been in the nominative case.

3. *The End of Earth History* 20:7-15

(a) *Release of Satan and Rebellion of Sinners (vv.7-10)*

v.7 "And when the thousand years are expired, Satan shall be loosed out of his prison,
v.8 And shall go out to deceive the nations which are in the four quarters of the earth, Gog and Magog, to gather them together to battle: the number of whom is as the sand of the sea.
v.9 And they went up on the breadth of the earth, and compassed the camp of the saints about, and the beloved city: and fire came down from God out of heaven, and devoured them.
v.10 And the devil that deceived them was cast into the lake of fire and brimstone, where the beast and the false prophet are, and shall be tormented day and night for ever and ever."

7 For the third time in this chapter the verb *teleō* is used though it is translated into English by three different words thus:-

"Till the thousand years should be *fulfilled*" v.3
"Till the thousand years were *finished*" v.5
"And when the thousand years were *expired*" v.7

For consistency the verb would be better translated "completed". The verb *teleō* has implied in it the idea of "reaching a goal", so that it would be perfectly legitimate to translate: " should be brought to its goal or end" hence "should be finished". The goal that God has planned for the millennial age has been reached and the final test of men is about to begin. As a result Satan is released.

The release of Satan "for a little season" (v.3) is just as literal as his chaining. When the results of his release are seen the reason for it becomes evident. All who enter the millennium in earthly bodies are possessors of eternal life; all others have been removed in the establishment of the kingdom (Matt 25:31-46). For the first time since the garden of Eden conditions on earth will be ideal and with sin subdued, sickness banished and no death from natural causes, there will be a population explosion that fulfils the original creation mandate, "Be fruitful and multiply and fill the earth and subdue it" (Gen 1:28 JND). For the whole period of the millennial reign (described in Ps 72) righteousness will flourish and peace will be enjoyed under the dominion of Christ; Israel will be in her place as head of the nations and every other nation will be worshipping the King. However the children born, even under these ideal conditions, have still a fallen nature and need to be born again. The opportunity will be offered in the preaching of the gospel of the kingdom when Christ is presented as Saviour and King. Every influence in the home, in society and through the preaching of the gospel, as well as the compulsory attendance three times a year at the feasts in Jerusalem, would lead souls to personal faith in the Christ. It might be expected that all born during this thousand years will gladly accept Christ and share in the spiritual blessings as well as the physical blessings of the kingdom. This might also be expected since Satan is no longer active to deceive men. However the sequel shows that this expectation is not to be realised. The children born in the millennial kingdom will far outnumber their parents as the centuries pass, and earth will undoubtedly have a population of many billions at its close. Alas! human nature even under ideal conditions is still the same – utterly opposed to God. Knowing that open defiance to the rule of Christ leads to instant death (Ezek 32:20) under the rod of iron, the rejection of His claims will be hidden under outward conformity to the society in which they live. The Psalms have a foreshadowing of a feigned submission to divine rule that may point to this millennial period; the verb "submit" in Pss 18:44; 66:3; 81:15 can be rendered "yield feigned obedience" (RV margin and Newberry margin). Such outward conformity without inward reality offers a great opportunity for Satan, and as soon as he is released and gets to work the inward rejection becomes outward rebellion. The aim of heaven has been to show that even under the peace, prosperity and divine protection of millennial conditions, men's hearts have not changed for the better, nor can they grow naturally into children of God even in the absence of satanic deceivings. As W. Hoste writes (p. 161), "Alas! It will be proved once more that man whatever his advantages and environment, apart from the grace of God and the new birth, remains at heart only evil and at enmity with God".

8 Having learned nothing from his thousand-year imprisonment Satan sets out on his final attempt to rally men to his banner against God. That all nations on earth have come under the rule of Christ in the millennial reign is the clear testimony of Scripture: "The kings of Tarshish and of the isles shall bring presents. The kings of Sheba and Seba shall offer gifts. Yea all kings shall fall down before him; all nations shall serve him" (Ps 72:10-11). Other Scriptures support this universal rule of Christ as can be seen in Isa 2:2-4; 65:20-22; 66:18-24; Ezek 36:38; Zech 8:4-5, 20-23; 14:16-18. Nevertheless Satan finds a response in the "four corners of the earth" (RV) which may be interpreted as suggesting the widespread nature of the rebellion or, perhaps, as indicating that the dissidents come from the outlying regions of the kingdom. It has always been recognised that the geographic centre of earth is the land of Israel and Jerusalem which has become the capital of Christ's kingdom. It is possible that dissidents and rebels who refuse to bow to Christ will move to the outlying regions on the periphery of the kingdom for shelter and succour, and it is amongst these nations that Satan finds his response and gathers his rebel army.

In describing this scene of rebellion the words "Gog and Magog" are introduced without any explanation. One very reasonable explanation is to see the phrase as standing in apposition to the "four quarters of the earth" and then to translate the words instead of simply transliterating them. Since "Gog" means "extension" and "Magog" means "expansion" the words then simply describe the widespread sweep of the satanic effort to gather forces against the capital of Christ's kingdom. (See comments at 16:16 for a similar interpretation of the word "Armageddon".)

However, the words do occur in Ezek 38-39 in the same kind of context and it has tempted many expositors to see a link between the invasion of Israel there described and this final rebellion under Satan. But closer consideration shows that the two invasions are different in a number of major respects and cannot be seen as the same:

1. Ezekiel speaks of the invasion of Israel by a great northern power called Gog belonging to the land of Magog. Hebrew scholars, particularly Gesenius, from incidental and geographic references in Ezekiel, identify the northern power as Russia. In this passage the invasion does not come from the north but is from "the four quarters of the earth".
2. Ezekiel places an earth ruler, "the chief prince of Meshech and Tubal", at the head of the invasion forces. Here it is Satan himself who gathers this army but nothing is said of the actual human leader.
3. Ezekiel shows that the main purpose of the invasion is "To take a spoil and to take a prey" (Ezek 38:12) so that the invasion is a predatory attack against a people who recently have been brought into peace and security. Here the attack is on the capital city of a kingdom established for a thousand years and upon a company far wider than the nation of Israel, called "the saints".
4. Ezekiel shows that the result of the invasion is a judgment that leaves Israel so many dead bodies that it takes seven months to bury them (Ezek 39:11-16) – the land stinks as it becomes a vast open graveyard. Here the

armies of Satan are engulfed in fire from heaven – there does not appear to be any need for burial.

5. Possibly the most important distinction between the two passages is the timing. What happens in Ezekiel is a sign to Israel (Ezek 39:22) and the subsequent language (Ezek 39:23-28) places the whole invasion in the period of the tribulation before the millennium. Here it is at the very close of the millennium.

It should be clear from the above considerations that the invasion of which Ezekiel speaks is an invasion of the land of Israel in the tribulation period. God delivers His people by a signal destruction of the invading army that demonstates His power on their behalf. The extent of the destruction of the invading army, evidenced in the time required to bury the dead, is seen as testimony to other nations (Ezek 38:23) of the power of Israel's God. This attack is by a mighty host gathered from all nations by Satan against God's King and His saints in their capital city, and it takes place after the thousand-year millennial kingdom. When God acts to destroy these rebels by fire the destruction is complete and no burials are required. The echo of "Gog and Magog" is a reminder of an earlier invasion and the mighty deliverance God wrought then for His people; now God delivers His people again in a deliverance that is final and need never be repeated.

What particular deceptive lie Satan will use to gather such a company is not directly revealed. The "rod of iron" (2:27; 12:5; 19:15) descriptive of the rule of Christ in absolute justice and righteousness will scarcely appeal to unregenerate hearts; resentment and opposition will build up against all that is good and holy and make many ripe for rebellion. F.A. Tatford (p. 223) makes a reasonable suggestion along the same lines but stresses the national aspect when he writes, "It is probable that the satanic appeal to these nations was to establish their own government and to overthrow that of Messiah. Galled by the superior position of Israel and their own subordination, they would readily respond to such an appeal".

The gathering of these nations is "to the war" (RV). This translation rightly stresses the article, which suggests that this war was expected and threatened, possibly planned, perhaps for a long period. Alford suggests "to the well-known war" but this may make a little too much of the article. At least this war will take precedence over all others in history, it will actually be the "war to end wars". Satan is making his final effort against God and Christ, and rebel sinners fall in behind his banner. When these hosts begin to move under satanic direction the normal assessment of numbers seems to fail and John simply says, "the number of whom is as the sand of the sea". In the first book of the Bible Abraham's seed were viewed thus (Gen 22:17); now in this last book Satan shows the same figurative fecundity. The conditions in the millennial kingdom have encouraged population growth and the numbers on earth very likely will be counted in the billions (much higher than the world's population in 1996 of around six billion) so that this huge company of the disaffected need be no surprise.

9 It should be noted that the prophetic future tense of the verbs in vv.7-8 is now changed in this verse to the historic aorist and events are described as having already taken place. The use of the term "went up" echoes the term used to describe the pilgrimage of Israelites who made their thrice annual visit to Jerusalem as in Ps 122:3-4 LXX: "Jerusalem ... whither the tribes go up". The physical elevation of Jerusalem lies in the origin of the expression as in the NT usage "to go up to Jerusalem" (used over 20 times). During millennial times the nations will all be expected to go up, or perhaps send delegations to Jerusalem especially to the Feast of Tabernacles (Zech 14:16). It has been suggested (see Govett) that this going up could well be the time here in view. The fact that all nations would thus be doing the same would offer some cover for the gathering in the early stages of the rebellion and would be fully in line with the satanic duplicity behind the movement.

The expression "the four quarters of the earth" has shown the wide area from which this army has been drawn; the expression in the RV reading, "over the breadth of the earth" shows the surging tide of the enemy as they converge on the camp and the city. Their stategy has been determined previously and, as an encircling tide, they sweep round the "camp of the saints and the beloved city". The word "compassed" evokes a memory of Israel encircling Jericho (Heb 11:30) and of Christ's prophetic warning to Jerusalem (Luke 21:20). The word "camp" (*parembolē*) is translated "castle" six times in the Acts (Acts 21:34, 37; 22:24; 23:10, 16, 32) but the general idea is more "citadel" or "fortress" and with an army in the field it was generally taken to mean "headquarters". This is the idea behind its use in Heb 11:34 in the expression the "armies (*parembolē*) of the aliens" or its use in Heb 13:11,13 with reference to "the camp" of Israel. Christ as ruler has His headquarters amongst his saints and the location is explained as "the beloved city". This takes the "and" (*kai*) as meaning "even" (Alford). The headquarters of divine rule is located in the beloved city which must be Jerusalem. It is an interesting fact that Jerusalem, the earthly capital of Israel, is not named in this book until the name is found in the New Jerusalem (3:12; 21:2) and the Holy Jerusalem (21:10); nevertheless it is referred to in unmistakable terms as the "holy city" (11:2) and the "great city" (11:8; 16:19) and now the "beloved city". It is the only city of which it could be spoken, "the mount Zion which he loved" (Ps 78:68) or "The Lord loveth the gates of Zion" (Ps 87:2). In divine wisdom God permits this vast satanically-mustered army to encircle the headquarters of the millennial administration in the city of Jerusalem. To a watching universe it must appear as if Satan is about to triumph and Christ must sue for terms.

Appearances are deceiving. This confrontation again (as at Armageddon, over a thousand years before) issues in no battle. Writing in a past age an author might have said, "ere a sword was drawn"; today it would be said, "before a shot was fired", God intervened dramatically. The very simplicity of the language lends weight to the awesome judgment, "And fire came down from God out of heaven, and devoured them". God had acted in this way in the matter of Sodom and Gomorrah (Gen 19:24) and in the judgment on the emissaries of Ahaziah sent to take Elijah (2 Kings 1:10); the disciples would have liked to invoke a similar judgment on the Samaritan village (Luke 9:54). All these pale into insignificance as fire "from God" and "out of heaven" engulfs this rebel army. The besiegers of the beloved city are destroyed and with them the last attempt of Satan to usurp the place of God is defeated. Those who have been deceived by Satan and followed him now share his doom.

10 The wicked of earth who followed Satan in his last attempt to overthrow the throne of Christ die physically in the fire that devoured them; the ashes of the bodies lie on earth while their souls join the wicked dead in hell until they are all summoned before the great white throne. However "the devil that deceived them" is allowed no such respite in receiving his final sentence. Satan, called the devil and, because of his activities down the ages, symbolised in the dragon and in the serpent, appears here in Scripture for the last time. His final designation as "the devil" reveals the character in which he has been so successful with men – men in fact gave him plenty of opportunity to act as their accuser before God. Self-deceived (Isa 14:14) he claimed deity; he deceived Eve in Eden (1 Tim 2:14) and brought down mankind. An innumerable company down the ages suffered from his deceivings, and very especially during the tribulation (13:14; 18.23; 19:20) he showed the extent of his powers. Now in this final post-millennium bid he has been at his ancient work and men and nations have been deceived (v.8) to their eternal loss. As the great deceiver with character unchanged he takes this name with him to the lake of fire. This place, already prepared for him and his angels (Matt 25:41), now opens to embrace him eternally. His course for the last three and a half years has been downward; cast out of heaven (12:9) to earth, cast into the abyss for a thousand years (20:3) now he is hurled into the lake of fire forever. For him as for those he deceived there is no repentance and no reprieve. In this lake of fire he joins his former agents, the Beast and the false prophet who already have spent one thousand years in this dread place (19:20). Their very presence in the lake after such a lengthy period proves that any thought of annihilation is without scriptural foundation, and it further shows that time brings no alleviation or amelioration of conditions. It is possible that the devil deceives himself as to the nature of the doom that he knows awaits him; it is certainly true that he deceives men. The verb "shall be tormented" is plural and thus must include the Beast and the false prophet in its subject; the RV correctly translates "they shall be tormented". The expression "day and night" (4:8; 7:15; 12:10; 14:11) is a common metaphorical way of expressing something that goes on endlessly or ceaselessly – there is never any intermission. "Forever and ever", literally "to the ages of the ages", is the strongest possible expression in the Greek language to express emphatically that the punishment lasts eternally. Ceaselessly and endlessly until the mind reels at the concept this torment must be the portion of the devil and those associated with him. After commenting on the everlasting nature of this punishment and pointing out that "it is as long as God lives", J.B. Smith adds an apposite warning "better to believe it here than to find it out hereafter".

(b) *Resurrection of Sinners and the Great White Throne (vv.11-15)*

v.11 "And I saw a great white throne, and him that sat on it, from whose face the earth and the heaven fled away; and there was found no place for them.
v.12 And I saw the dead, small and great, stand before God; and the books were opened: and another book was opened, which is the book of life: and the dead were judged out of those things which were written in the books, according to their works.
v.13 And the sea gave up the dead which were in it; and death and hell delivered up the dead which were in them: and they were judged every man according to their works.
v.14 And death and hell were cast into the lake of fire. This is the second death.
v.15 And whosoever was not found written in the book of life was cast into the lake of fire."

The scene that closes the sad history of earth is presented in this paragraph. In simple words, devoid of all the melodrama of earth, is described the most solemn scene ever witnessed if only in vision form. It is the final judgment of men and presents:

1. the place of judgment,
2. the person of the Judge,
3. the people who are judged and
4. the penalty of the judgment when the individual sinners of earth, unredeemed and unchanged in the very bodies in which they sinned, meet the Judge of all the earth.

11 The sixth "I saw" in the sequence from 19:11 introduces the great white throne. The absence of the article before noun or adjectives makes this throne stark and clear; through the eyes of John is seen – a throne! Great! White! Men have flaunted their independence of God throughout history, they have denied Him a place in His own creation, now they must stand before the throne and its authority is absolute. That the throne is "white" reflects the absolute righteousness with which judgment is dispensed. When Christ dealt with wicked men He was seen seated on the "white cloud" (14:14); He has been seen on the white horse (19:11) and now He is seen on the white throne. The first two visions contain a symbolic element but there is no symbolism here: this is reality. This final judgment of sinners will be carried out in accordance with the strict principles of righteousness and absolute justice.

The throne of ch. 4 has dominated the main section of the book (chs. 6-16); it has already been referred to over thirty times and has conveyed the picture of God's government and sovereignty amongst men by One who is the Immutable and the Eternal. The throne here, is distinguished by the adjectives "great" and "white" from any previous throne mentioned in the Scriptures and would seem to be established for a particular purpose and for a specified time. W. Scott agrees and writes, "Not the throne of the Sovereign, but that of the Judge, not regal but judicial. Neither is it permanently set up, but temporally; and for a special purpose" (footnote on p.410).

The awesome majesty of the Judge is described very simply as "the One sitting on it". That it is deity in the person of Christ is clear from many relevant Scriptures:

1. Christ's own words leave little doubt in the matter, "For the Father judgeth no man, but hath committed all judgment unto the Son" (John 5:22);
2. Christ added in the same passage, "For as the Father hath life in himself; so hath he given to the Son to have life in himself; And hath given him authority to execute judgment also because he is the Son of man" (John 5:26-27);
3. Christ is spoken of as the One "who shall judge the quick and the dead" (2 Tim 4:1). The living (the quick) have been judged (Matt 25:31-46) and now the dead are to be judged.

The terror of the scene for the human heart is the fact that from the face of the Throne-sitter the earth and the heaven fled away. It is perfectly true that Christ has filled a throne in the millennial kingdom on earth (3:21) and graciously has identified His own with Himself in that royal state (vv.4-6) when as the King-Priest kindness and blessing flowed from Him. Now as the Judge, representing neither mercy nor blessing but absolute justice, the earth and the heaven flee from before Him. The next statement is explanatory and shows the completeness of the action, "and there was found no place for them". Earth that had no place for Christ in His first coming as Saviour (Luke 2:7) now flees from before Him as Judge. There is nothing but a throne and limitless space. The very face that men spat upon (Matt 26:67), that in cruel mockery they covered (Mark 14:65), that they struck with the rod (Luke 22:64) now strikes terror to the cosmos. This is the One before whom the dead must stand.

The flight of the earth and the heaven has provided ground for much debate in the light of the words of Christ in the Gospels, "Heaven and earth shall pass away, but my words shall not pass away" (Matt 24:35; Mark 13:31; Luke 21:33), and the extended description in 2 Pet 3:10, "But the day of the Lord will come as a thief in the night, in the which the heavens shall pass away with a great noise, and the elements shall melt with fervent heat, the earth also and the works that are therein shall be burned up". Much scholarship has been flaunted and not a little heat (if little light) has been generated in attempting to show that words mean not what they say (see note on v.11). The point that many expositors labour is that what God intends is not a new creation but a regeneration and reassembling of the constituents of the old creation. It is submitted that neither the language of 2 Pet 3:10-11 nor the more explicit fact stated here of the fleeing away of the earth and the heaven will allow such a construction to be put on the words. The words of Peter describe the detail of the cataclysmic end to this creation; the heavens, both the atmospheric and the stellar, will pass away with a great noise. Unbelieving evolutionists say the cosmos began with a "big bang"; God says it will end with it. The elements, the basic building units of the material universe right down to the constituent particles of the atom, will have their binding forces released (the scriptural word is "dissolved", 2 Pet 3:11). The accompanying energy release provides the "fervent heat" that engulfs creation. The statement is explicit, "the earth also and the works that are therein shall be burned up". Words could scarcely be clearer. Ps 102:25-27 and the quotation from that Psalm in Heb 1:10-12 use the poetic language of discarding a worn-out garment and its replacement by the new to bring out exactly the same message. This passage states in language that can bear no other interpretation that the first creation has gone and it will be replaced by another – a new (*kainos*) one (21:1).

It is important to see just where this great white throne judgment comes in the chronological order of events; the material creation has just fled from before the face of the Judge. The new heaven and the new earth have not yet been introduced (21:1). Since Scripture indicates that time belongs to the creation (Gen l:1) then the flight of this creation, or to use the language of Peter its dissolution, must introduce eternity (see note on v.10). Since time, space, matter, and energy are the constituent elements in a unitary cosmos (Gen 1:1-2) there cannot be one element without the others. The inference is that at the moment that earth and heaven fled, time (as known to this cosmos) ceased. Thus the great white throne is established in a period (if it may be spoken of like this) when there is no time – in other words it is in eternity. If this is so then the consequences that flow from the great white throne must be eternal too; the lake of fire has already been shown to be eternal (v.10). The location of this throne has often been said to be "in space"; this can hardly be so since space is part of the cosmos which has fled. A further question has often been raised as to the place of the redeemed at this point. The simple answer is that God has given no direct information on either of these matters.. It should be remembered that the fleeing of this cosmos cannot effect "heaven itself" (Heb 9:24) the very presence of God. If this judgment takes place there in "heaven itself" then there would seem to be no reason why it should not be witnessed by the whole host of the redeemed.

12 For the seventh time (since 19:11) John uses the verb "I saw", and shifts the focus from the throne to those who stand before that throne. These are described as "the dead"; the article describes a class who need no further identification; the plural is obvious even in English but for emphasis it might be written as "the dead ones". The phrase, "the small (ones) and the great (ones)" (used earlier in 11:18; 13:16; 19:5,18), shows that the distinctions of earth no longer apply; these dead come from all social strata and all walks of life; the royal and the noble stand side by side with the mean and the lowly. The reversal of the normal word order (see RV) may suggest the scriptural truth that there is no respect of persons with God. Earth's honours are irrelevant; men stand "before the throne" (see JND) as sinners. These dead are all who have been left in the graves after the first resurrection and are described in v.5 as "the rest of the dead". The first resurrection has taken from the graves of earth the redeemed of the church age, the OT saints, and the martyred dead of the tribulation period. Those left in the grave for this resurrection are the wicked who have died from the dawn of history until the cataclysmic judgment of the fire from heaven that destroyed the rebellious army of Satan (v.9). Any who died under judgment in the millennial age are also included.

The solemn judicial nature of this judgment comes into prominence when attention is drawn to the books, which as the records of the works of sinners will form the basis of the judgment. These *records of earth* are the personal records of each individual sinner from birth to death with all the facts that contribute to a just assessment of privilege, opportunity and responsibility. Justice will be dispensed, even to those who have rejected grace in their lifetime. The general teaching of Scripture is that there are degrees of guilt (see note on v.12) and consequently grades of punishment. It is clear that every fact will be weighed and every mitigating factor taken into account so that every soul will know they have received absolute justice. The book of life is the *register of heaven* containing the names of all those who during their lifetime have received eternal life through Christ (see comments on 3:5; 13:8; 17:8; 21:27; 22:19). The first book will show the basis of the sentence given by the judge, the book of life will be produced as evidence that the sentence is in keeping with divine righteousness. The opening of the book of life implies that the name could have been in it, that life was available, but it also implies that the name is missing – the life offered was never accepted. This is but confirmation of the divine judgment and closes the matter forever and there can be no appeal. Alford tellingly points out that the two books are independent witnesses to the same thing; the record of earth shows from the works that there was no divine life in evidence; the register of heaven shows that there never had been life.

13 Resurrection refers to the body which normally, when death claims it, is buried in the earth. To ensure there can be no misunderstanding on such a solemn matter further statements are added to ensure that it is perfectly understood that treatment of the body after death does not affect the truth of the bodily resurrection of all unbelievers. No matter how the body is treated, all the wicked dead of all ages will stand before the great white throne. Atheistic human reasoning in rebellion against the truth of God may insist that the body once destroyed, as in cremation, can never be raised again, as a step to denying the fact of judgment. Two statements refute such a lie:

1. "The sea gave up the dead which were in it" is a recognition that all the dead are not in the earth; many have drowned and never been buried; others have been cremated and the ashes scattered at sea. This will not make the slightest difference as, whether from the soil or from the sea (the only two possibilities), the wicked dead will be raised to stand at the great white throne. It may well be that there is also here an implicit reminder concerning the millions who perished in the catalysmic judgment of the Noahic flood, that they too must stand before this throne. All sinners will stand before the throne in the bodies in which they sinned.
2. "Death and hell delivered up the dead which were in them". Every person is made up of two parts: the body is the material part; the soul comprising mind and spirit is the immaterial part. While the material body is given to the soil or sea, the immaterial soul of the unbeliever at death passes into hell. (For the believer in this age the soul, at death, is instantly with Christ, 2 Cor 5:6-8; Phil 1:23.) Resurrection demands the reunion of body and soul so that the material part and the immaterial part are linked again in the complete person. For believers this has already taken place in the first resurrection. Since it is the wicked dead alone who are in view in this passage reference is made to hell (*hadēs*) where their souls have been detained. Now at this moment of resurrection the earth and the sea that received the bodies of men are emptied as is hell that received their souls. As complete persons once again they stand before the great white throne to receive their judgment. *Hadēs* is the realm of the unseen (see discussion on 1:18), and for the unsaved ones it is the place of torment (Luke 16:23); the intermediate state that ends for the wicked with the summons to the great white throne. *Hadēs* is used by Christ on four occasions in the Gospels but He reserves the word *gehenna* (also translated "hell" in the AV and used eleven times) for the final destiny of the wicked. *Gehenna* of the Gospels is now given its definitive name "the lake of fire".

The construction of the last sentence is somewhat unusual. Between the plural verb "they were judged" and the expression "according to their works" is placed a singular pronoun "each one". The meaning however is perfectly plain: while all the company are judged this does not happen *en masse*, each person is judged individually.

14 The last enemy death has been stripped of its power and is now banished to the lake of fire; *hades* has been emptied of its souls and, no longer needed, is also consigned to the lake of fire. This evil pair, the terror of mankind through history, were robbed of their terror for the believer by the resurrection of Christ, a truth symbolised in the keys which the risen Christ holds (1:18). Having fulfilled their permitted role down through the ages and into the church age (see 2:8b), they had been allowed to rampage over earth during the tribulation (6:7). Now their role over and with no further part to play in the purposes of God they are cast into the lake of fire. Death and hell for the wicked have been the two sides of the one reality; there could not be one without the other, death touching the body and hell embracing the soul. Thus while death may be thought of as intangible this is scarcely relevant to the fact that the reality named in the expression as "death and hell" is banished to the lake of fire forever.

The lake of fire is the place described by Christ as "everlasting fire prepared for the devil and his angels" (Matt 25:41). The first to enter there are the Beast and the false prophet (19:20) at the very end of the tribulation. They will be joined there by their followers judged by Christ before the throne in Matt 25:34-46 (see verse note). At the end of the millennium these sinners are joined by the arch-enemy of God and of men – the devil himself (v.10) – and with him, no doubt, all his angel followers. Now death and *hades* find their final resting place in this dread abode where they are joined by that terrible procession of sinners from the great white throne (v.15).

Atheism denies absolutely any question of eternal punishment; agnosticism and humanism replace it with annihilation. Even some who profess to believe the Bible seek to dilute the truth by making the fire a symbol. Even this is to admit the truth while seeking to deny it, for the symbol must be a symbol of some terrible and terrifying reality. The Scripture leaves no shadow of doubt that there is a physical location in the cosmos that God has specially prepared for the devil and his angels (Matt 25:41) and because of sin men will share that place. In light of recent scientific discoveries respecting "black holes" in the universe it would be a rash infidel who would deny the physical element in this raging inferno called in this book the lake of fire. Scripture is also plain that those incarcerated there are in conscious torment (Matt 13:42; Mark 9:43-45 *et al*) that will endure forever. The believing soul bows before the absolute righteousness and inflexible justice of God.

Again with startling simplicity the lake of fire is defined as the second death. Introduced in the promise to the overcomer in Smyrna (2:11) this term has awaited further explanation. The first death was spiritual and its consequence for the body was physical death. Through Christ God made life available (Rom 6:23); this is the life called eternal life (John 3:16; 17:3 etc.) and must be received during the lifetime of the individual. To die physically without this eternal life from God means that at the great white throne the nature of death as separation from God becomes absolute. To pass to the lake of fire means that there takes place a separation from which there is no recovery; a death called the second death from which there is no resurrection. Possessed of eternal life, saints find after resurrection there is no more death (21:4); having refused life in Christ sinners find that in this death there is no more life.

15 The final act of the Judge on the great white throne is to provide the irrefutable evidence of the righteousness of the judgment – the book of life is scanned. The earlier books have shown individual culpability that has merited the death sentence but at this point an independent witness is opened to show that there has been no miscarriage of justice. It has been shown in the earlier references to this book of life (see under the first reference at 3:5) that this is the register of all those from creation who have received life through Christ. The works (vv.12, 13) of these sinners have made it plain that there was no evidence of divine life; this register confirms that they never had divine life. The search over ("not found" suggests a search) and the name missing, nothing remains but the execution of the sentence and the sinner is cast into the lake of fire. There can be no appeal from the sentence of this righteous Judge. The "whosoever" points to the fact that any status enjoyed on earth is irrelevant now. What matters is that the name is not in the book of life.

Much has been written to seek to prove that even at the great white throne there will be those shown to be amongst the saved. Some commentators have tried to support this from use of the word "whosoever" (*ei tis*) which can be more literally translated "if any", which they suggest must mean that some names will be found in the book of life. This is a false and unwarranted deduction and misunderstands the grammar. The use of "whosoever" does not suggest the presence of another class whose names are written in the book of life. The whole phrase "whosoever was not found written" is descriptive of a class and is the conclusive proof that there is no respect of persons with God. No matter how high the standing of sinners on earth the fact that their names are not in the book of life means for them the lake of fire. This is confirmed by noticing that this whole phrase is the subject of the verb "cast". Additional confirmation lies in the whole context. It is only the wicked dead who are being judged; every saint has been raised and judged a thousand years before this scene. The issue is to make clear that God is righteous and just in the sentence meted out to sinners and this is done by the opening of the books, with the final witness the book of life. There is a terrible finality about the scene as one by one sinners pass from the great white throne to the lake of fire. The Scriptures have been shown to be true: "The wages of sin is death" (Rom 6:23).

Notes

10 J.B. Smith is somewhat typical of a number of commentators who refuse to accept the words of Scripture on this point. He writes (page 278), "That the language employed does not signify the vanishing of the former heaven and earth into nothingness is proved by the language of pertinent passages elsewhere cf 2 Cor 5:17; James 1:10; Rom 9:23; 2 Pet 3:10,13". However a thorough study of each of the references given lends no support whatever to his interpretation, in fact rather the contrary. He follows his theory to its logical conclusion and writes in a subsequent paragraph, "So the new heaven and the new earth of Rev 21:1 are not a new creation added to the sum total of existing things but a change from the bondage of corruption due to sin of its inhabitants into a new heaven and earth wherein dwelleth righteousness". This comes very close to a direct contradiction of scriptural statement. W. Scott agrees with this interpretation. He writes, "The earth and Heaven fled – not passed out of existence, not annihilated. The next clause carefully guards against any such an unscriptural deduction – "place was not found for them". It does not intimate the complete disappearance of the millennial earth and Heaven. Consequent upon the removal of these, new heavens and a new earth fitted, furnished, and constituted for eternity take their place – are made, not created" (page 411). It is very difficult to see the distinction he makes between "complete disappearance" and "removal" of earth and heaven. It is much simpler and safer to take the text as meaning what it says – the earth and heaven as they have been known have gone and will be replaced with the new heaven and the new earth (21:1). The very scene where sin ruled, Satan raged and saints died has gone forever and a new order of things is introduced.

11 It is worthy of comment that many of earth's leading scientists no longer believe in the eternity of matter. The lie of evolution is being undermined by inescapable scientific facts that are forcing a radical scientific rethink. Stephen Hawking, claimed to be the greatest thinker in the world of science since Einstein, shows in his book *A Brief History of Time* that creation had a beginning in finite time and must have an end in finite time. Thus even unbelieving minds are forced to accept what the Bible has made clear all along. Scientific argument may not be used to interpret Scripture but it is worthy of note that the present laws that without any known exception operate in the universe, the first and second laws of thermodynamics, give creation a built-in life-span. These can hardly be the laws that operate in an eternal state, the new heaven and the new earth will have different laws governing their operation.

12 Neither this passage nor any other Scripture lends support to what is commonly spoken of as "a general judgment", by which is meant a judgment to assess who is saved and who is lost and, as a consequence, who are to be admitted to heaven and who are to be consigned to hell. This kind of theory is based on religious imagination rather than Scripture. The matter of salvation, and hence destiny, is settled on earth by an individual's response to Christ presented in the gospel. Judgment for believers is not for salvation but for service. Saints are judged with respect to service according to their time-period of testimony as follows:

1. The judgment seat of Christ (1 Cor 3:10-14; 2 Cor 5:10; Rom 14:7-12) is for believers of the church age and takes place in heaven immediately after the rapture.
2. The judgment of all OT saints, the judgment of saints from Israel and the judgment of the saints who have died in the tribulation, takes place between the end of the tribulation and the establishment of the millennial kingdom (11:18). With the completion of the first resurrection the judgment of saints is complete in view of the kingdom.

That the judgment of sinners is totally separate from the judgment of saints is clear from the following Scriptures:

1. "And shall come forth, they that have done good unto the resurrection of life, and they that have done evil unto the resurrection of damnation" (John 5:29). That a thousand

years separate the resurrections mentioned in this verse is explained in v.5 of this chapter. At the great white throne Christ is dealing with those "that have done evil".

2. "There shall be a resurrection of the dead both of the just and the unjust" (Acts 24:15). The same time distinction is to be observed in this verse. The just have their part in the first resurrection before the millennium; the unjust are raised after the millennium and judged at the great white throne.

3. "And many of them that sleep in the dust of the earth shall awake some to everlasting life and some to shame and everlasting contempt" (Dan 12:2). This is the physical resurrection of saints of Israel and the same time distinction is seen here with the "some" raised in the first resurrection and some not raised until the end of the millennium.

It is the wicked dead who are judged at the great white throne, not to see whether they are saved or not (that has been settled on earth), but to award the exact judicial sentence for the measure of their guilt and sin.

It comes as no surprise to those who accept divine revelation that twice the passage stressed that the dead are judged "according to their works". Every final sessional judgment of Scripture is a judgment on the ground of works, whether of saint or sinner (2 Cor 5:10; Matt 25:34-46; Rev 11:18). The statement of Rom 2:6 is all-embracing and applies to both believers and unbelievers, as Paul writes concerning, "The righteous judgment of God who will render to every man according to his deeds". Scripture teaches and the gospel emphatically declares that salvation is not to be obtained by works (Gal 2:16; 3:2; Eph 2:8; Titus 3:5); it can be obtained only through faith on the ground of the work of Christ. Nevertheless the justice of God is revealed in the fact that when He deals with men in judgment He does so on the ground of what they have done. Even those who have refused the grace of God in Christ have had different opportunities and privileges and all of these will be justly assessed; the personal record of sin and wickedness will be judged righteously. Scripture teaches that punishment for sin is real and eternal but it never teaches that it will be uniform – as if the kind or amount of sin did not matter. Christ enunciated the principle of varying degrees of punishment when in Luke 12:47-48 He spoke of one beaten "with many stripes" and another beaten "with few stripes". He confirmed it by His reference to the variation in judgment when He upbraided the cities of the plain: "It shall be more tolerable for Tyre and Sidon at the day of judgment than for you" (Matt 11:22). Thus in strict justice this final judgment is on the basis of what men have done, a fact made plain in the twice-repeated statement, "according to their works" (vv.12, 13). What a terrifying contemplation when men are confronted with a complete record of all that they have thought and done as responsible creatures; what a terror-filled silence as the record of each is examined and the soul knows there can be but one issue from this revelation of the past. The soul that refused mercy from the cross must now face justice from the throne.

14 The judgment before the throne in Matt 25:31-46 is the judgment of persons who have come through the tribulation; by their actions they have given proof either of faith in Christ or of their rejection of Him. Clearly it is not nations as such that are judged but the individuals who comprise the nations. These are divided by Christ into the "sheep" who enter the kingdom and the "goats" of whom Christ said "these shall go away into everlasting punishment". Some commentators argue that the individuals judged before that throne on earth are first banished to *hades* and then stand in resurrection bodies at the great white throne. Amongst other problems posed by this view is the fact that it suggests that the same individuals stand before Christ as judge on two separate occasions. While the end result is the same on either view, the term "everlasting punishment" used of their judgment seems perfectly sufficient to warrant the deduction that these sinners judged by Christ Himself pass directly in their bodies to the lake of fire.

CHAPTER 21

Vision 4: Christ in Consummation (21:1-22:5)
Christ Reigns - the Throne of God and the Lamb

1. *The New Creation*
21:1-8

v.1 "And I saw a new heaven and a new earth: for the first heaven and the first earth were passed away; and there was no more sea.
v.2 And I John saw the holy city, new Jerusalem, coming down from God out of heaven, prepared as a bride adorned for her husband.
v.3 And I heard a great voice out of heaven saying, Behold, the tabernacle of God is with men, and he will dwell with them, and they shall be his people, and God himself shall be with them, and be their God.
v.4 And God shall wipe away all tears from their eyes; and there shall be no more death, neither sorrow, nor crying, neither shall there be any more pain: for the former things are passed away.
v.5 And he that sat upon the throne said, Behold, I make all things new. And he said unto me, Write: for these words are true and faithful.
v.6 And he said unto me, It is done. I am Alpha and Omega, the beginning and the end. I will give unto him that is athirst of the fountain of the water of life freely.
v.7 He that overcometh shall inherit all things; and I will be his God, and he shall be my son.
v.8 But the fearful, and unbelieving, and the abominable, and murderers, and whoremongers, and sorcerers, and idolaters, and all liars, shall have their part in the lake which burneth with fire and brimstone: which is the second death."

The chapter division tends to blur the chronological sequence of events. Immediately following the great white throne John is introduced to "a new heaven and a new earth". For the eighth time since 19:11 John uses the verb "I saw" and will repeat it on two further occasions in the chapter (vv.2, 22) to complete the ten stages in this final vision. It was pointed out in the comment on 20:11 that, when the earth and the heaven fled away, time as related to this present creation ceased and John is introduced into a period for which it is customary to use the word "eternal". While the great white throne judged men in view of their life on earth the judgment itself takes place when time has gone and therefore the sentence from it must also be eternal. The judgment of men now complete, John is shown a new era opening wherein all is different. Commentators, with unusual unanimity, agree with this conclusion and are satisfied that the first eight verses of this chapter describe what has come to be referred to as the "eternal state". Most also agree that, all the stages of man's probationary testing now completed, God brings all His purposes to the designed end and these verses describe that end to which God has been working throughout all time.

This eternal state is not to be confused with the millennial kingdom. Reference is frequently made to the OT prophecy, "For, behold, I create new heavens and a new earth: and the former shall not be remembered nor come into mind" (Isa 65:17) and to a parallel passage in the same prophecy, "For as the new heavens and the new earth, which I will make shall remain before me, saith the Lord, so shall your seed and your name remain" (Isa 66:22). A closer study will show, however, that these passages refer to the period of the millennial kingdom where spiritual regeneration of men and the physical renewal of earth are in view. In the millennium, blessing in every sphere of life will be so enjoyed as to warrant the adjective "new" but even under such ideal conditions the ultimate goal of history is not reached as yet. Sin and death and corruption will still be present in the millennial age (Isa 65:20; 66:24) so that there can be no perfection until God finally makes all things new (v.5). It is this final goal of the ages that is described here. This eternal state is introduced only when man's final test in the millennial age is over, the great white throne has settled the destiny of sinners of all dispensations, and the old heavens and the old earth have passed away.

While NT references to this eternal state are few in number two passages place it within the divine timetable: 1 Cor 15:24-27 shows that the expression "then cometh the end" describes the period when God will be all in all, and this comes after the kingdom age (v.24), and the subjugation of all enemies (v.25) with death as the last enemy destroyed (v.26). At this stage these events have taken place and the last chapter closed with death cast into the lake of fire. 2 Pet 3:10-13 shows that "the day of the Lord" which includes the millennial age closes with the passing away of the heavens and the burning up of the earth to begin "the day of God". This action is the prelude to the introduction of the "new heavens and the new earth" (v.13). The same sequence of events leads to the eternal state in this passage.

1 The word "new" (*kainos*) shows the totally-new character of this new heaven and new earth. It is not only "new in time" but a fresh departure very different from all that has been previously known. The first heaven and the first earth passed away and with them their characteristic features that made them what they were; the new heaven and the new earth will have distinguishing characteristic features of their own. As discussed in comments on 20:11 the language does not allow either a renovation or even a purging of the present material of the cosmos but suggests a completely-new creation. The verb "passed away" (*aperchomai*) is the one linked with this dramatic event in several Scriptures (eg Matt 5:18) and in its 31 references in the NT always means an action that takes a thing or person completely away from the observer so that in some cases the primary idea is "pass completely out of sight". The same verb in v.4 describes the passing away of the "former things"; tears, death, sorrow and crying are not changed but pass away entirely. While "passed away" points to the fact, the verb "fled away" (20:11) describes the action from the point of view of the observer.

Only one physical feature of the new earth is mentioned and yet it is of major significance – "and the sea exists no more" (JND). Life on earth is dependent on the hydrological cycle and water plays a major role in its ecology as well as a vital part in the physiology of animals and men. On the third day of creation (Gen 1:9) when God separated the dry land and the waters it would seem that fifty per cent of earth's surface area became "seas" – a deduction based on the analogy of God dividing the light from the darkness (v.4). Since the seas are specifically said to have been all gathered in one place they would not convey any idea of separation to the antediluvian people. At the flood "the waters that were above the firmament" (Gen 1:7) came down, and almost seventy-five per cent of the earth's surface is now covered by sea as a witness to the fact that this is a judged earth. Even in the refashioned earth in the millennium the seas will remain (Ps 72:8; Isa 11:9, 11; Ezek 47:10-20; 48:28; Zech 9:10; 14:8) but in the new earth all marks of judgment are gone forever and all of the earth's surface is available for man. The statement should not be taken to mean the absence of water. This cannot be, since from the throne in 22:1 there flows the "river of the water of life" and it will be shown that this is real water from a real throne. This river from the throne in the capital city could be the source of countless rivers and streams spreading out to irrigate the new earth. In a physical sense this means that the water from the throne is, in a very real way, "the water of life". At present the sea is an essential link in the hydrological cycle; enough water evaporates from its large surface area to provide the subsequent rain and snow necessary to sustain life. While clearly there will be an abundance of water the missing surface area for evaporation suggests that other laws must operate or else God establishes an ecology for earth and a physiology for the creature that is radically different from what is known at present.

2 The last time John referred to himself by name was in 1:9 (JND, RV omit "John"). Now so overwhelming is the vision that he feels it necessary as the last of the apostolic company to give his personal affirmation to this vision. For the ninth time in this series he says, "I saw". With the new heaven and the new earth now in place John sees coming down to the new earth a magnificent city; following the order of the text, he identifies it as "out of heaven" and "from God". Its original sphere was heaven and its source was God; now it comes down to settle upon earth. The words "holy city" are followed by the phrase "new Jerusalem" as explanation. The earthly Jerusalem is called "the holy city" seven times in Scripture, five times in the OT (Neh 11:1, 18; Isa 48:2; 52:1; Dan 9:24) and twice in the NT (Matt 4:5; 27:53) and it has been pointed out in the comments at 11:2 that the word "holy" indicates that God set this city apart from all others in His divine purpose. However, the national Jerusalem failed so abysmally that finally God called it "Sodom" (11:8). Now in absolute contrast there comes to earth another city that bears the ancient title "the holy city"; the word "new" (*kainos*) in the explanatory title "new Jerusalem" consigns all the failure of the past to history. Yet in the very name "Jerusalem" there is a continuity with the past that implies that God's original purpose is now fulfilled in this city in the eternal state.

Foreshadowings of such a city are not wanting in earlier NT Scriptures. Paul wrote "Jerusalem which is above is free" (Gal 4:26). The writer of Hebrews spoke of "the city of the living God, the heavenly Jerusalem" (Heb 12:22; cf 11:10). John is now given a sight that for centuries has been a matter of faith to believers, and what a sight it is! The splendour of this city is reflected in the figure of a radiant bride ready for her wedding. The first participle, "prepared", qualifies "city" and shows what preparation has been done before this city stands forth in all its splendour. The second, "adorned", qualifies "bride" and illustrates the preparation and its purpose. The city is prepared with the care taken in the adornment of a bride for her husband on her wedding day. It is a mistake to confuse the figure with the reality. Many commentators insist that the city symbolises the bride and what John sees is the church under the figure of a city. This is to turn the figure upside down. The simile is an effective way of illustrating the preparation of the city and its resulting freshness and radiance. J.F. Walvoord writes (p.313), "What we have here is not the church *per se* but a city or dwelling place having the freshness and beauty of a bride adorned for marriage to her husband".

There is no reason to believe that this is not a real city. In John 14:1-3 Christ spoke of a place that He would go "to prepare" for His own and it is this same verb that is used to describe the city. Abraham looked for a city, "which hath foundations whose builder and maker is God" (Heb 11:10). For saints who had lost their natural homeland because of faith in God's promises the assurance is given, "for he hath prepared for them a city" (Heb 11:16). The same assurance is given to saints of this dispensation, "But ye are come unto mount Sion, and unto the city of the living God, the heavenly Jerusalem" (Heb 12:22). The stranger status of saints in this dispensation is recognised in Scripture as being only a temporary condition, "For here we have no continuing city but we seek one to come" (Heb 13:14). This city is the answer of heaven to the promises to both OT and NT saints and crystallises in a real way the purposes of God for His redeemed people. To spiritualise this city or make it a symbol of something else does not do justice to the language used, yet to call it a "literal" city is hardly the right use of language, since that leads to a mental picture of the "literalness" of earth cities and particularly an earthly Jerusalem. The better word is "real" or "true" (*alēthinos*) – a city having the very essence of city character. An essential part of any city is the community that lives in it; the word "city" in normal use necessarily embraces the people who are part of it. This city will actually exist, comprising a visible structure along with its inhabitants, these two combining in the word "city". That the "new Jerusalem" is a real city seems to be implied very plainly in the promise to the overcomer in the church in Philadelphia (3:12). Satanic purpose reached its climax in the most unholy city of all time, Babylon the great, which this book shows had the character and conduct of a harlot (18:3). Here the purposes of God crystallise in this holy city and it is fitting that this city is seen in all her purity as a bride adorned for her husband.

The identity of those who have their home in this city has caused much discussion amongst commentators. Failing to see that the bride figure is merely descriptive, many insist that this city is a figurative way of depicting the bride which they rightly interpret as the church of this dispensation (see 19:7-8). As has been shown above it is a mistake to press a descriptive simile into an interpretative role, and it distorts the picture. The city is not figurative but real and must necessarily embrace a community. The question is the identity of the community who make the city their home. Accepting that the church has links with this city (Heb 12:22; 13:14; Rev 3:12), as do the saints of a past dispensation (Heb 11:10, 16), it would seem that all the saints raised in the first resurrection have their home there This role as the home of all the resurrected saints may be further supported by the fact that the gates are linked with Israel (v.12) while the foundations are linked with the church (v.14). There can be no question, particularly with v.9 in view, that the bride of Christ, the church of this dispensation, has the very special place of honour in this city both in her nearness to Christ and in her place in the administration. Nevertheless it seems plain that the bride will not be alone in the city; others share it with her. While all commentators do not agree F.C. Jennings writes, "This heavenly Jerusalem is not exactly equivalent or co-terminous with the church, but includes all who, partakers of grace, have no earthly place". F.W. Grant writes in the same strain (page 231), "Why should it not be the bride-city, named after the bride-church, whose home it is, and yet contains other occupants?" It is suggested that the other occupants are the resurrected saints of Israel.

3 John's attention is now drawn to the most significant feature of the new creation and its new capital city. In Eden before the fall of man God had enjoyed communion with His creatures (Gen 2:8; 3:8). Sin interrupted that communion and only in grace, based on redemption through blood, could God fulfil the desire of His heart and have fellowship with men. On this ground God took up typical residence in the tabernacle and temple with Israel (Exod 25:8); once again sin brought disaster, and Ezekiel watched the glory depart (Ezek 9-10). That God should draw near to sinful men in the person of Christ is the glory of the gospel; John had written of Him, "And the word was made flesh and dwelt (*skēnoō*) amongst us" (John 1:14), where the verb "dwelt" could readily be translated "tabernacled" (Newberry, RV margin). God desired fellowship with men but they gave Christ a cross. Now with redemption complete and men changed God can fulfil the purpose of His heart and have communion with men on a permanent basis. The importance of this moment is emphasised as John hears the "great voice out of heaven" for the twenty-first and the last time in the book. The purpose of God in creation is now fulfilled.

With the familiar cry "Behold" John, and through him all readers, are summoned to wonder at the amazing truth that God dwells with men. The tabernacle of God has been referred to twice before in the book (13:6; 15:5) where it is linked with heaven but here it is seen on earth. The descending city and the explanatory voice must be seen together as showing that the city will be the vehicle of the presence of God in the new creation. The very word "tabernacle" recalls the presence of God dwelling with national Israel in a past day so that now, when dispensations have gone, that OT picture has a fulfilment on a far greater scale than could ever have been considered possible. "With men" encompasses all mankind; all redeemed and changed men will know forever the presence of God dwelling with them.

What it will mean for God to dwell with men is set out in five statements each of which is introduced by the conjunction "and" thus:

1. "And He will dwell (*skēnoō*) with them". No longer in type but in reality the personal presence of God is known amongst men, The verb *skēnoō* is cognate with the noun "tabernacle". All men will have access to and communion with God. This is God's presence with men.
2. "And they shall be his people". The terms of the new covenant will not now be limited to Israel nationally (Jer 31:31-34) or restricted to the church spiritually (Heb 10:15-18) but will be enjoyed by all men eternally as individually they recognise that they belong to God. This is God's possession of men.
3. "And God Himself shall be with them, their God" (JND). The words "and be" of the AV are not in the text and their omission allows the presence of God to be seen in the manifestation of His power in their interests. Israel's failure allowed men to wonder "Where is their God?" (Joel 2:17); this will never be so again: men will enjoy "their God" and say, "This God is our God"; in a real way Immanuel has taken up residence with them (Isa 7:14; Matt 1:23). This is God's power in the midst of men.
4. "And God shall wipe away all tears from their eyes". The same verb "wipe away" used of millennial conditions in 7:17, is a very tender note; the singular "every tear" and the plural "eyes" picture the tender care of God to remove every last trace of the tears which have stained the faces of His people on earth for so many millennia. This does not suggest that there can be tears in the new creation, but is a retrospective look to ensure that it is understood that every last trace of the old creation has gone forever, lost in the presence of a tenderhearted God.
5. "And there shall be no more death, neither sorrow, nor crying, neither

shall there be any more pain". As a consequence of sin men have known these in abundance down the years; death, the sentence upon sin in Eden, has brought sorrow, crying and pain in its wake. Now with the sin dealt with through redeeming grace the consequences will be removed forever so that never again will men sit in tears. Against the background of the old creation these negatives enhance the bliss of the new.

The translation of the word *prōta* as "former" is perfectly correct but rather obscures the link with v.1 where it is translated "first". The explanatory "for" shows that because of sin, death, sorrow, crying and tears belong to the first creation; with that creation now gone forever all things will be "new". The finality of the passing of the "old things" is seen in the verb "passed away", used of the old creation in v.1. The word "new" is repeated from v.1 by the voice from the throne in the next verse.

5 This voice of assurance from the Throne-Sitter explaining the scene would seem to be different from the earlier voice from heaven. The great white throne, the last throne mentioned, was seen to a be special throne set up for the judgment of the dead; it is unlikely that the voice speaks from that throne. It is possible that this voice comes from "the throne of God and the Lamb" (22:1) within this holy city. However since that throne has not yet been introduced and the city is still viewed externally it is better to see this as the throne that has dominated the book from 4:2. The content of the message supports this suggestion.

While the exclamation "Behold" in v.3 pointed to the presence of God with His people, this second "Behold" draws attention to the power of God manifested in the newness of all things; a point made by the fact that *kainos* ("new") is the first word in the sentence. As in v.1 *kainos* involves not only newness in time but also the freshness of having a completely different character. The use of the verb "make" (*poieō*) where, if a completely new creation was in view, the verb "create" (*ktizō*) might have been expected has led some commentators to argue that the materials of earth are simply purged in the fire and reassembled. J.F. Walvoord has answered this assertion fully in his comment (p. 315): "[This argument] is building too much on too little. The same word *poieō* is used in Matt 19:4 where God is said to have 'made' Adam and Eve using both the word 'create' (*ktizō*) and the word 'made' (Gr., *poieō*) for the same act". Any lexicon will point out that the two verbs are simply synonyms with *poieō* the word of wider significance. The use of *poieō* here describes more accurately the fact that God has not only created a new material realm, but also brings into this realm men from the first creation made new.

The abrupt interjection "And he said" seems to suggest a different voice interrupting the reverie of John to insist that this vision should be recorded.

(JND refers to the words "unto me" as "doubtful" on the basis of the manuscript evidence.) This is the third time (see 14:13; 19:9) that John's absorption in the scene has had to be interrupted by his conducting angel to remind him of his original mandate to "write in a book" (1:11). These words must not be lost because that they are "faithful and true". The words refer to the message "out of heaven" (v.3) and the message from the Throne-Sitter (v.5); they reflect the very character of Christ (19:11) and show the absolute trustworthiness ("faithful") and genuineness ("true") of the revelation given to John (a matter that will be re-emphasised for the last time in 22:6).

6 The familiar formula, "He said unto me", introduces another voice and this time there is no question about the identity of the speaker. God has spoken from the throne (v.5) and now the Lamb adds His personal assurance. Echoing through the new creation the voice of the Lamb cries, "It is done". On an earlier occasion this same word had been heard in the old creation to signal the end of the outpourings of judgment upon earth (16:17); now it is heard for the last time. A comprehensive plural (*gegonan*) summarises all that now has been completed to bring the purposes of God to fruition. This word embraces a wider scope than the triumphant, "It is finished" (*tetelestai*) of the cross; the cross was the foundation, the new creation is the fulfilment. In this word past history is scanned and the workings of God through the ages have now reached completion. All is done!

These purposes of God have been completed in the person of Christ, who identifies Himself in an unmistakable way. The book opened (1:8) with Christ using this title of deity, "I am Alpha and Omega, the beginning and the end", and He will close the book using the same title (22:13). At this establishment of the new creation He shows Himself central to it. History and time are linked with earth but in the eternal state the old creation and the new creation have a common link in Christ whose absolute deity is central in that He is:

(a) outside of history "the Alpha and the Omega". Within the compass of the alphabet lies hidden all the wealth of knowledge that it is possible for man to know. In Christ God has revealed Himself fully and the exploration of this knowledge will require eternity.

(b) outside of time "the beginning and the end". The Creator of time, He will be when time (in the old creation) has gone, but the title conveys more than mere existence and shows that He is both the originator (*hē archē*) and the goal (*to telos*) to which time moves. The throne of deity in the new creation will be seen as "the throne of God and of the Lamb" (22:3).

From the Lamb seen as the focus and climax of history echoes the great evangelistic call that speaks of the divine provision made available in Christ. Before sin entered, the heart of man was satisfied with the fellowship enjoyed with God; after the fall thirsty souls could find satisfaction only in responding to the call expressed by Isaiah, "Ho, everyone that thirsteth, come ye to the waters" (Isa 55:1). The metaphor of thirst is a common scriptural one to express earnest longings begotten through a sense of spiritual need. Even so men have been very ready to seek satisfaction elsewhere, as Jehovah lamented through Jeremiah: "For my people have committed two evils; they have forsaken me the fountain of living waters, and hewed them out cisterns, broken cisterns, that can hold no water" (Jer 2:13). Christ in prophecy and, through the cross, in history becomes the source from which all the spiritual longings in the hearts of men are satisfied (John 4:14; 7:37). The emphatic "I" shows that Christ alone is the source of this provision. This call shows that all the spiritual longings in the hearts of men can be satisfied forever by Christ. Men will drink eternally from an inexhaustible fountain. Christ here gives "the water of life" (a term found only in these two chapters (22:1,17)) and He gives it freely (*dōrean*), an adverb repeated in 22:17 to show that saints receive it in the same way that Christ gives it – gratuitously, without payment or price.

7 As the Lamb is the source of the divine provision that alone can satisfy the hearts of men, so now it would seem that the voice from the throne breaks in to add His promises of the further bliss of saints in the new creation. The first promise has to do with the scale of the possession into which saints will be brought and is simply stated as, "He that overcometh shall inherit all things". Those who inherit are described individually as "he that overcometh" an expression that looks back through all ages to include every soul exercising faith down those ages. Such individuals, overcoming the current unbelief of their day, witnessed to the fact that they believed God. Thus every true believer was an overcomer; it would be hard to conceive a believer not sharing in the new creation. In the church age the seven promises to the overcomers show how believers in this age can be seen to overcome in every spiritual situation. Heirship through being linked with Christ has ever been the anticipation of saints, whether of Israel (Rom 4:13-14) or of the church (Rom 8:17; Gal 4:7; Titus 3:7; James 2:5). Christ as the "appointed heir of all things" (Heb 1:2) deigns to share His inheritance with His saints and as the new creation comes into view what wealth this unfolds.

The second promise has to do with the status that saints will have in the new creation. They will not only be wealthy heirs but they have the status of sons. One of the terms of the new covenant ratified by Christ in His sacrifice of the cross was, "I will be to them for a God, and they shall be to me for a people," a relationship that implies service and testimony. In this new creation "his servants shall serve him" (22:3) implying a yielded willing service as JND suggests, "I will be to him God"; no alien claim will ever rise in the heart of one of these servants. But the relationship promised here is closer still; not only the status of a servant but the status of a son, "He shall be my son (*huios*)". The word that John has used throughout his writings to express the new relationship into which believers are brought through the new birth is "child" (*teknon*; see John 1:12 RV) and he has been careful to reserve the word "son" (*huios*) for Christ alone. This is the only occasion in all John's writings when this word is used of the relationship between the believer and his God. Now the voice from the throne takes up this precious word as if to indicate that the believer will now share a standing with Christ that reflects His uniqueness. God delights to own this servant-son in public acknowledgement.

8 The same voice from the throne now paints a solemn backdrop to the scenes of blessing amongst this new community on the new earth. Far from the bliss of this new community there will be a far different community who experience the conditions they have earned by their life on earth. Eight terrible words describe the character of those who have fitted themselves for their place in the lake of fire. Acts of sin may be forgiven and there is mercy for sinners without limit (Isa 55:7) but when practices become habitual then character is formed and destiny must be reaped. It is character that identifies this other community in this dread abode. The eight character descriptions are as follows:

Fearful. Those who regarded believing God as too great a risk and to be too costly in the things they valued in life. When used as a noun it defines cowardice and timidity and is never used in the NT in a good sense. These people shrank back from identification with Christ; they had the character of the cowardly.
Unbelieving. Having heard the message of their day they found it more reasonable to give credence to the things seen, rather than things not seen, and disbelieved the message. Once this message is rejected then the character of the unbeliever takes shape.
Abominable. The use of the perfect passive participle indicates this is something these persons have become at a time in the past. Related words are linked with the religious activity of the harlot (17:5) which has both idolatrous and sexual overtones. Lev 18:26 LXX and other passages link this word with the unnatural sexual vices of depraved human nature; all of which are morally offensive to God. This kind of conduct fashions its own character.
Murderers. Murder originated with Satan who was a "murderer from the beginning (John 8:44). This family trait has been manifest down the ages on the pattern of Cain (1 John 3:12) and carries the warning that all who show this character will share the doom of Satan (1 John 3:15). God has always made it plain that the unjustified taking of a human life was the defacing of a divine image and as such demanded justice (Gen 9:5-6). Justice has finally caught up with the murderers.
Whoremongers. A better translation would be "fornicators", the widest word possible to embrace sexual licence and depraved lust of all kinds. Those who engage in such things form character that ends in this lake of fire. The degradation

of sex through human lust carries a special note of warning (Heb 13:4). These sinners had paid no attention to any warnings while they lived; now they reap the consequences eternally.

Sorcerers (*pharmakoi*). W.E. Vine defines the adjective as signifying "devoted to the magical arts" which, when used as a noun, describes those who use drugs, potions, spells, and enchantments. It embraces all those who profess intercourse with the unseen world of spirits and demons. Men turn to this, almost by instinct, when the truth of God is refused; this was a practice meriting the death penalty in Israel (Deut 18:10-12). The manifestation of such practices in all heathen religions and its resurgence in our day in lands where the gospel has been preached widely in power is an evidence of the rejection of God and His truth. To form links with satanism means to be identified with the doom of Satan.

Idolaters. Men have made gods in their own likeness and then, on a downward scale of values, have made gods in the likeness of "four-footed beasts and creeping things" (Rom 1:23) so that there seem to have been few things, animate or inanimate, to which men have not bowed in worship at some time or another. The final apostasy on earth under the Beast will be the final great act of idolatry (13:12). Those whose character has been formed by idolatry cannot be where "God is all in all" and their final banishment is seen to be into the lake of fire.

Liars. Christ described Satan as the one who "speaketh a lie" since "he is a liar and the father of it" (John 8:44). Those who show this character of Satan share his doom. The "all" embraces all kinds of men, whatever their social standing, who have been false to the truth.

The absence of any verb ("shall have" is added in the AV for clarity) makes the following statement concerning the lake of fire the more dramatic. Those who had part in the first resurrection were described as "blessed and holy" (20:6) and they form a contrast to these sinners whose part or portion is the lake of fire. This is the fifth and last mention of this dread place (19:20; 20:10; 20:14, 15). The descriptive words are all repeated: this is a "lake" without limitation as to size, it is a burning lake (19:20), where the present participle is timeless and shows that this lake is inexhaustible, it will burn unquenched forever. "With fire" fastens on that terrifying blaze which for man has always touched some primeval chord of fear; "with brimstone" (*theion*, "sulphur") echoing 19:20; 20:10, uses a metaphor of earth to suggest that which makes the fire more agonising and more terrifying, needing no external fuel supply.

The final word from the throne identifies this awful place as "the second death", the fourth and final mention in the book (2:11; 20:6, 14); a place (the lake of fire) has now become a fixed state forever. The first death meant separation between soul and body which, as two parts of the one entity, may be rejoined in the resurrection of the person. The second death is separation between God and man which is eternal. In the presence of God a life is enjoyed, called in the NT "eternal life"; separation from God means a death experienced from which there can be no recovery and this book calls it "the second death". This is not annihilation as unbelieving minds would love to assume, but conscious, unending pain forever. The words from the throne allow no other meaning.

2. *The New City*
21:9-22:5

As pointed out in the introduction to vv.1-8 expositors are virtually unanimous in agreeing that the first eight verses of this chapter describe the eternal state and most would also agree that the city of v.10 is the city seen in v.2. At this point the unanimity ends and a division of thought takes place. Many believe that John is now invited to take a closer look at the capital city of the new creation in the eternal state. Other equally able expositors believe that at this point there is a final parenthesis (they call it the fifth parenthesis in the book) in which John is taken back in time to view the city of v.2 but in the time period of the millennial kingdom. The arguments need to be carefully examined.

The arguments for reversion to the millennial kingdom.

The arguments for believing that John is taken back to the millennial kingdom to view this city are cogently presented by commentators such as W. Kelly, W. Scott, J.N. Darby, F.A. Tatford, A.C. Gaebelein and many others. The main arguments are as follows:

1. The angel who introduces John to the city at this point is one of the seven angels commissioned to pour out the bowl judgments. Since an angel from the same group had introduced him to the fall of Babylon (17:1) it is logically deduced that this second angel is commissioned to show him the answer to earth's great city and he is shown God's city under millennial conditions. This would imply that time and not eternity is in view.
2. It is argued that the mention of "the kings of the earth", as well as the mention of "nations" in v.24 and 22:2 demands millennial conditions. The implicit assumption in this argument is that kings and nations as such no longer persist into the eternal state. (See comment on v.24 for the explanation of the mention of "kings" and "nations" in the eternal state).
3. It is claimed that "the healing of the nations" (22:2) is again a time related phrase since healing will no longer be required in the eternal state. (See 22:2 for the explanation of the use of this word where it will be pointed out that the word "healing" (*therapeia*) is more accurately translated as "health"; a translation that transforms the meaning of the phrase).

The arguments for seeing this city as in the eternal state.

On the other hand there are a number of weighty considerations that show that this scene belongs to the eternal state; a view ably argued by J.F. Walvoord and W. Hoste amongst many others. The main arguments are as follows:

1. While admittedly there are occasions in this book when John is allowed to view things retrospectively as in ch. 7 or as in chs. 17-18, there is no indication in the text itself that there is any reversion to the millennium. What is given in this vision seems to be simply a more detailed examination of the city of vv.1-2. The idea is amplification rather than reversion.
2. From 19:11 John is given a series of ten visions each introduced by the statement "I saw". The ninth vision is in v.2 and he is shown "the holy city", but since the words "I saw" are not repeated in v.9 it is suggested that what he is now given is but a closer look at that same city. To introduce a reversion in time based on inferences seems somewhat unjustified, particularly so when the visions have moved chronologically thus far from 19:11. The climax will be reached with the tenth and final "I saw" (v.22). Having reached the eternal state it seems arbitrary without clear statement to return to the millennium.
3. The major problem with viewing this city as belonging to the millennium is that no such city seems to be expected nor is such a city described in any of the detailed OT prophecies of millennial conditions. Jerusalem as the re-established capital city from which Christ reigns on earth is the uniform expectation of the prophets. J.F. Walvoord writes, "The apportionment of the Holy Land and the description of the temple as found in Ezekiel's description of the millennial earth (Ezek 40-48) are entirely different". These prophecies leave no room for such a glorious city. That it is in existence throughout the millennium there is no doubt, but it is not upon earth. It belongs to the new heaven and the new earth and its coming down is to show its association with both. Originating in heaven as its sphere it takes its station upon the new earth; this can only be in the eternal state.
4. The prophecy of Isaiah makes it plain that, even under the ideal conditions of the millennial reign of Christ, there will still be rebellious hearts, "But the sinner being a hundred years old shall be accursed" (Isa 65:20). Yet of this city John writes, "There shall be no more curse" (22:3). These statements do not appear to be describing the same conditions. To limit the "no more curse" to the city does not fit the language and savours of special pleading.

In countering some of the arguments for this being the eternal state a compromise solution is sometimes advocated that this city should be seen as a satellite city placed by God in stationary orbit over the earthly Jerusalem and furnishing the canopy of glory of which Isaiah speaks (Isa 4:5). This has been suggested as the administrative base from which the resurrected saints would rule "over the earth". Its coming down to the new earth on this view is its second descent as it must have withdrawn after the millennium when judgment fell on the old creation. There is too much human speculation in this view without sufficient scriptural support. It is better to see this city as coming down once to the new earth and seen as the city of God in the eternal state.

(a) *The City Externally (vv.9-21)*

v.9 "And there came unto me one of the seven angels which had the seven vials full of the seven last plagues, and talked with me, saying, Come hither, I will shew thee the bride, the Lamb's wife.
v.10 And he carried me away in the spirit to a great and high mountain, and shewed me that great city, the holy Jerusalem, descending out of heaven from God,
v.11 Having the glory of God: and her light was like unto a stone most precious, even like a jasper stone, clear as crystal;
v.12 And had a wall great and high, and had twelve gates, and at the gates twelve angels, and names written thereon, which are the names of the twelve tribes of the children of Israel:
v.13 On the east three gates; on the north three gates; on the south three gates; and on the west three gates.
v.14 And the wall of the city had twelve foundations, and in them the names of the twelve apostles of the Lamb.
v.15 And he that talked with me had a golden reed to measure the city, and the gates thereof, and the wall thereof.
v.16 And the city lieth foursquare, and the length is as large as the breadth: and he measured the city with the reed, twelve thousand furlongs. The length and the breadth and the height of it are equal.
v.17 And he measured the wall thereof, an hundred and forty and four cubits, according to the measure of a man, that is of the angel.
v.18 And the building of the wall of it was of jasper: and the city was pure gold, like unto clear glass.
v.19 And the foundations of the wall of the city were garnished with all manner of precious stones. The first foundation was jasper; the second, sapphire; the third, a chalcedony; the fourth, an emerald;
v.20 The fifth, sardonyx; the sixth, sardius; the seventh, chrysolyte; the eighth, beryl; the ninth, a topaz; the tenth, a chrysoprasus; the eleventh, a jacinth; the twelfth, an amethyst.
v.21 And the twelve gates were twelve pearls; every several gate was of one pearl: and the street of the city was pure gold, as it were transparent glass."

9 The great truths of the eternal state have been set out in the first eight verses. John has been shown the new creation with its capital the holy city in which God will dwell with His saints and amongst His earthly people. Now John is invited to come and be shewn the bride, the wife of the Lamb.

It is important to note the symmetry between this invitation and the invitation he received in 17:1. Using the same language as he had heard previously one of the same seven angels summons John and as a result he is "carried away". The modifying phrase "in the spirit" shows that what is in view is not merely physical but a spiritual transportation with the Holy Spirit acting through John's own spirit. The contrast with the previous scene is the destination; in 17:1 John was carried into a wilderness but in this second experience he is carried into a "great and high" mountain. The omission of the article in each case indicates that no specific wilderness or mountain is intended. The wilderness is an appropriate setting for the harlot and the beast while the elevated mountain allows him a view of the holy Jerusalem. In 17:1 John is shown a harlot linked to an ancient city, here he is to see a bride linked to the new city. The purposes of Satan for earth were evidenced in time and on earth in a harlot figure and the city of Babylon, which John has seen swept from the scene in judgment (chs. 17-18). Now he sees the purposes of God evidenced in the bride and the holy city established for eternity. The contrast is to be observed.

The identity of the bride is made plain in the explanatory expression, "the wife of the Lamb". As pointed out in v.2 the figure of a bride is used of the city as a *simile* to indicate the freshness and the sparkling beauty of that city. Here it is not a simile but a *metaphor* that is used to describe the church of this dispensation (identified in 19:7) bought by the blood of Christ and won during the period of His rejection on earth. There is no need for any confusion with Israel, who is referred to as the "wife of Jehovah" in many OT passages. Estranged now but not divorced (see Isa 50:1 RV) Israel is to be restored in her covenant relationship with Jehovah (see Hos 2:1-23), a relationship which the Scripture views as eternal. During the period of rejection by His own nation Christ sought and won His bride and John is given this view to assure persecuted believers of this church age of the glory that belongs to them in their association with Christ in the eternal state. Hidden in divine counsel but no afterthought with God, since the idea of the Lamb goes back even before creation (see 1 Pet 1:1-2, 18-21), believers of the church age have a glorious future. The "Lamb" is the metaphorical term that speaks of the Redeemer while the "bride" is the metaphorical term that speaks of relationship. The linking of the two in the expression "the Lamb's wife" shows the permanence of the relationship established on the ground of redemption. The same term was used in 19:7 when the marriage was in prospect; now the marriage is over but the church bears still her bridal character.

10 For the second time John is carried away "in spirit" (see also 1:10; 4:2; 17:3). The RV reading of "the holy city Jerusalem" reflects compelling manuscript evidence and identifies it as the same city as in v.2. The adjective "holy" stands in contrast with the failure of a former Jerusalem and with the polluted city of Babylon which had been the summing up of satanic purposes on earth. The same descriptive phrase "coming down out of heaven from God" (R.V.) and the same word order as in v.2 (R.V.) identifies the same city at the same moment of descent. John is being given a closer look at this city.

Much unnecessary difficulty has been made of the fact that John was invited to see a bride and is shown a city. Failing to see that "bride" must necessarily be a metaphor, since it describes the church, many expositors insist that the "city" is the metaphor. The result of this reasoning is that a metaphor is made to describe a metaphor something that inevitably leads to confusion. This confusion is evident from the ingenious speculation and imagination needed to spiritualise the "walls" and "gates" and "foundations" of this city. That these features of the city do carry spiritual significance is self-evident but for this to be true, they must first be features of a real city. The simple answer is that the metaphor of the "bride" is used to describe the church in her special relationship with Christ and that the city is a real city, the home of the bride.

The problem has been made worse in the minds of many by failing to see also that in the word "city", the people and the place necessarily go together. The word "city" does not in normal language refer only to material buildings; conversely it makes no sense to describe a company of people as a "city", however well organised they are. A city and its inhabitants are inseparable (see Luke 13:34). If the bride whom John is invited to see is a metaphor for the church then the city cannot also be a metaphor; in such a case interpretation loses meaning and imagination takes over. This city is a real city and is the home of the bride. The name "Jerusalem" shows historical links with both a place and a people and, it may also be pointed out, the adjective "holy" is never used in Scripture with a symbol but only with what is real. This is the city for which Abraham looked, the city "which hath foundations whose builder and maker is God" (Heb 11:10), the very city that God hath prepared (Heb 11:16). None of these terms can describe any earthly Jerusalem but they fit superbly the city called "the city of the living God" whose population is described in Heb 12: 22-24 and whose permanence is emphasised in Heb 13:14. The aspirations and expectations of the ages are focused in this city where God and His people dwell.

A further problem relates to the inhabitants of the city (see discussion under v.2). From the invitation to meet the bride it is clear that she is the chief resident in the city as would be expected from her place by the side of Christ. However it is equally clear that others have an interest in this city and particularly Abraham as shown in Heb 11:10, 16; 12:22-24; 13:14. While the names of the twelve tribes on the gates of the city may have an alternative explanation they offer some evidence that OT saints have a place in the city. One suggestion is that the city is the home of all saints who have been raised from the dead. This might be difficult to prove absolutely from Scripture yet there can be no doubt that the bride of Christ has a unique place in this glorious home.

John describes what was shown to him in terms familiar from earth. Thus he writes of walls, gates, foundations and materials to bring the vision within the scope of human understanding. That these terms are inadequate is shown in the repeated use of similes introduced by the word "like" that imply that the real and the heavenly transcends the literal and the earthly.

11 The glory of God shines through this city. The Shekinah that dwelt in the tabernacle (Exod 40:34) and in the temple of Solomon (2 Chron 5:14) has taken up residence and imparts a "light" ("radiance", Newberry) that shines through the new universe. The word *phōstēr* denotes a source of light and is used of believers in the moral darkness of earth (Phil 2:15) but God is the ultimate source. As John searches for suitable language to describe this radiance he piles simile upon simile. It is "like" a stone "most precious" which describes the scintillating sparkle of a diamond for which men would give incalculable riches. It is like a "jasper stone" which refers to the clear quartz crystal that sparkles and shimmers in the light. The word "jasper" takes the thought back to 4:3 and shows that deity has taken up residence in this city. The final word of the verse "clear as crystal" emphasises the transparency of the diamond whose sparkling glory is seen in this city.

12-13 The wall of the city is "great and high" (the actual measurement is given in v.17), an expression that echoes the description of the mountain in v.10. The OT sees a wall round a city as offering security but also proclaiming separation; these two ideas are pictured in the wall that Nehemiah built round Jerusalem (Neh 1:3). In NT days a wall spoke of security and protection. This wall conveys the related ideas of separation to God and security that can never be breached. In the new heaven and the new earth there will be special privilege associated with access to the throne of God and the Lamb, hence the wall. The gate in a city wall spoke of communication and commerce. Jerusalem had twelve gates historically and John sees twelve gates in the wall of this city placed symmetrically round the four sides. This city is in communication with the new earth but all that comes from the city and all that enters it must come through the gates. At (*epi*) the gates were twelve angels and on the gates were written the names of the twelve tribes of Israel. The repetition of the number twelve is remarkable; in addition to the twelve gates, the twelve angels, and the twelve tribes of Israel there are the twelve foundations (v.14), the names of the twelve apostles (v.14), the twelve pearls (v.21) and twelve kinds of fruit (22:2). It is also to be noted that the dimensions of the wall (v.17), 144 cubits, and the dimensions of the city itself (v.16) of 12,000 furlongs, are multiples of twelve. The scriptural significance of the number twelve is perfect administration. Thus there is no doubt that this city is the administrative capital of the universe now under direct divine administration. The fact that this city has the names of the twelve tribes associated with the gates suggests that the earthly side of this new eternal administration will be through the agency of that ancient people of God. Whether servants exit (22:3) or sovereigns enter (v.24) there will be an everlasting reminder of God's dealings with the nation of Israel in the past. The fact that three gates look out on each of the four main compass points may indicate that the tribes of the new Israel are stationed round the city as the tribes were stationed round the tabernacle of old (Num 2). The angel at each gate may suggest an angel guard and some commentators write of an "honour guard" (J.F. Walvoord) at each gate. However in the perfect setting of the eternal state it is more likely that they fulfil their title role as messengers in the service of the administration.

14 While the foundations are specifically spoken of in connection with the wall, it is logical to deduce that John sees the ends of horizontal layers of foundational material that run right under this great city. What catches his eye is the fact that there are twelve of these horizontal layers and that they bear the names of the twelve apostles of the Lamb. In practical terms these layered foundations show where the city rests upon the new earth and imply that this is not a satellite city. In spiritual terms the foundations speak of security; this city will never be shaken by any earthquake. Some commentators take a different view of the foundations and see them as vertical supports of the city. H.M. Morris presents this picture based on the analogy of the tabernacle and the sockets of silver and writes (p.448), "One foundation at each corner, plus two in each wall (located between the wall's three gates), is no doubt the pattern employed". From an engineering point of view there is no doubt that the horizontal layering would be the preferred structure for safety and stability. In either case, whatever the particular configuration of foundations, there is no question but that this is the city "which hath foundations" for which Abraham looked (Heb 11:10). That the names of the twelve apostles of the Lamb are on the foundations supports the idea of a link between the earthly people (Israel) and the heavenly (the church). These twelve men were a unique link between an earthly Israel and the church; they were a remnant of a nation that through their link with Christ became the nucleus of the church. Their names inscribed on the foundations suggests that resurrected OT saints will have their home in the city as well as the bride. The language of Heb 12:22-24 agrees with this in that the city population includes not only "the church of the firstborn" but also "the spirits of just men made perfect". Thus both the church as the bride and resurrected saints of the OT share a citizenship in the city without the slightest danger of confusion. The fact that the names of the twelve tribes and the names of the twelve apostles are linked with different structures which have different functions in the city shows that while both companies have the city as their home there is a clear distinction between them.

15-16 To show John the vastness of this city his angelic conductor now takes a reed to measure its external dimensions. In 11:1-2 when John is given the reed to measure the temple of God on earth no dimensions are recorded, showing that the act was a symbolic assessment of divine testimony and God alone knew the size of that testimony. Here the angel uses a golden reed to show that the measurement is in keeping with the glory of God and since the measurements are recorded there is no reason not to take them as literal measurements of a real city.

The length and breadth of the city are equal. The word "foursquare" (*tetragōnos*) means "four-angled" a term which can be used for a square or a rectangle, in this case a square. The length, breadth and height of this city are equal and the normal deduction is that the city is a cube which in the ancient world was the shape used to denote perfection. Of more relevance is the fact that this is the shape of the holy of holies in both the tabernacle and the temple (1 Kings 6:20). Other shapes have been suggested as in keeping with the given data as perhaps a sphere or a pyramid. The pyramid has had considerable support since it would allow the throne to be at the apex of the pyramid and the river to flow down the four planes. When all the possibilities are examined it is still better to see the city where God dwells as fulfilling the OT pictures of a cubic structure.

The actual dimensions of this city are both breathtaking and awe-inspiring. The measurement given is 12,000 furlongs (*stadion*). The *stadion* varies somewhat but is generally considered to be around 600 feet, so the length, breadth and height of this city are about 1500 miles. Such a city would reach from Rome in the west to Jerusalem on the east and from the Baltic Sea in the north to the southern boundary of the Sahara desert.

Those who reject the literal interpretation in favour of the symbolic ridicule the idea of a real city of such size. It has often been pointed out that earth's resources would be inadequate to build such a city, and that earth itself could not sustain the weight of such a city. They seem to have forgotten:

1. that God is the builder of this city and not man (Heb 11:10),
2. that this city is not on the present earth but on the new earth of which no dimensions are given,
3. that the new heavens and the new earth are unlikely to be bound by the same principles as govern life on the present earth.

Commentators committed to a symbolic interpretation find great difficulties with these details. The measurements have to be dismissed as irrelevant or interpreted to mean something other than is conveyed by ordinary language, which is hardly fair interpretation. H.M. Morris puts the matter plainly (page 449), "Even so, with all its detailed measurement and description, most commentators still refuse to believe the account means what it says, seeking by many and varied stratagems of interpretation to make it an allegory or a parable of some kind. All these devices flounder, of course, upon these very details of measurement and description". There is no doubt that the simplest and clearest view is to accept that this is God's city prepared for His own and dominating the new heavens and the new earth. From this administrative centre His servants serve Him eternally.

17 The angel continues to measure and reports his findings in human terms, "the measure of a man" which is "of an angel" – in other words the measurement taken by the angel is reported in terms of a unit based on the human frame. The unit is given as the "cubit" which comes into English through the Latin word *cubitus* meaning "elbow". Historically the cubit was the length of a man's forearm, from elbow to middle finger tip, and generally reckoned to vary between eighteen and twenty-one inches. Reckoning the cubit as eighteen inches the 144 cubits is equivalent to about 216 feet. Since the city is 1500 miles high a wall of 216 feet is disproportionately small especially since it was described in v.12 as being "great and high". Against a city almost seven million feet high 216 feet is miniscule; it could scarcely be seen. The mistake has arisen by not noting that there is no reference whatever in the verse to height and the idea has certainly arisen through carrying the word "height" from the previous statement into this verse. The measurement of 216 feet is not the height of the wall but its thickness: its height is clearly commensurate with the height of the city. It should also be noted from the measurement of cities in Jeremiah and Ezekiel that this is a feature of a wall normally measured (Jer 51:58; Ezek 41:9).

18 The word "building" (*endōmēsis*) is an unusual word not used elsewhere in the NT and seems to refer not to some feature of the wall, as for example the coping, but to the material of the wall which is described as "jasper". In v.11 the radiance of the glory of God was compared to the sparkling diamond-like brilliance of this clear crystal rock-like material. Here the wall is made of this very same material.

John, seeking to convey to human minds the reality of this city speaks of it as "gold" but not gold belonging to the old creation. John knew well that "pure gold" is almost transparent but even this is not close enough and he adds "like unto clear glass". The same adjective *katharos* ("clean"), is translated "pure" with reference to gold, and "clear" with reference to glass; the material of this city is completely transparent, it is without impurities and flawlessly perfect. Attention will be drawn again to the gold of the new creation in connection with the street of the city (v.21); here it refers to the buildings.

19-20 The ends of the foundational layers under the city are visible from every side in a rainbow spectrum of prismatic colours. Each layer seems to be of one particular type of stone but is "garnished" or "adorned"(JND) with all the other stones so that the whole forms a dazzling array of colour. The word "adorned" (*kosmeō*) has been used to describe the city under the figure of the bride (v.2) where the language was metaphorical; here it is literal. The twelve layers along with the colours normally associated with them are as follows:

1.	Jasper	The clear crystal of the city itself seems to merge into this brilliant foundation stone. The sparkling glitter of the diamond has been mentioned in vv.11,18 and seems to be characteristic of the city. The colour is crystal.
2.	Sapphire	The colour of this stone is agreed to be a beautiful blue.

3.	Chalcedony	The only reference in the Bible; it seems to have been an agate stone from Calcedon in Turkey. Its colour seems to have been a shade between blue and green – thus blue-green.
4.	Emerald	A radiant green
5.	Sardonyx	A variety of onyx with red layers mingled with white so may be classed as a shade of brownish-red.
6.	Sardius	Possibly the same stone as in 4:3, a brilliant red quartz.
7.	Chrysolyte	Would seem to have been a gold colour.
8.	Beryl	Very likely our modern beryl which is yellow though some accounts would make it sea-green.
9.	Topaz	Reported as a brilliant and deep yellow, though possibly not the modern stone of this name.
10.	Chrysoprasus	The only reference in the Bible; it seems to have been a particular shade of green. The word itself means "green as leek" (F.A. Tatford).
11.	Jacinth	Believed to be an aquamarine or turquoise colour.
12.	Amethyst	Probably the same beautiful purple colour as it shows today.

Though the precise colours are not always certain, through the transference of names in the records of antiquity, yet the overwhelming impression is of a dazzling splendour and beauty transmitted through the whole spectrum of colour from the red to violet, with the mingling of colours giving fresh shades to entrance the eye of the beholder. Materials that cannot be touched by time, and colours that will never fade, reflect the high point of the mighty creative power of God. This city is to be the home of the saints eternally.

21 Set in the jasper walls were twelve gates, each one of them a pearl. While the height of a gate, as of the walls, is not given it is certainly feasible as suggested by H.M. Morris (page 454) that each gate extended upward through the entire height of the wall so that there was entry to the city at many levels. The iridescent nature and translucence of these flawless gates remind John of the pearl. To suggest that the city cannot be real because such a pearl could not be produced on earth is almost to mock Scripture. John describes what he sees in terms we can grasp. Pearls were the most valuable of all precious stones in the Roman world (note Matt 7:6) and were amongst the treasures of the wealthy (1 Tim 2:9). Pearls were valued because of their intrinsic beauty. At that time they could not be produced artificially, nor could they be improved upon by human skill. The fact that the removal of the pearl from the oyster caused death may have a scriptural lesson in it as it is recognised that the redemption of men demanded the death of Christ. Perhaps these facts suggest why God chose this material for the gates of the city.

The final note concerning the materials used in this great city draws attention to the "street"; the word itself is singular and obviously describes the broad avenues and boulevards that intersect this capital city. The "street" is of gold, yet gold of this kind is unknown on earth. The colour intended in the adjective "pure" (*katharos*) repeated from v.18 is put beyond doubt by the simile "as it were transparent glass". "Translucent" may be more accurate than "transparent". *Diaugēs* (AV "transparent") is another word used only this once in the NT, it is as if John were searching for words to convey the beauty of the city. Clearly the street has the sheen of gold and yet at the same time transmits the brilliant and radiant light from the glory of God.

Notes

12-13 In the millennial reign of Christ there will be a new Jerusalem upon earth which is described in Ezek 40-48. It has little in common with this city from heaven except possibly the fact of having twelve gates arranged in threes in the square configuration. In Ezek 48:31-34 the names of the gates and the tribes outside are given in millennial order. Whether the order is the same when this city comes to earth in the eternal state can only be an inference but it is certainly possible that the ancient tribal order will be re-established for the men and women of the new Israel in the new earth. This understanding would suggest that nations will persist into the eternal state alongside an earthly Israel which, having come through the millennium, will still have its place at the head of the nations.

14 The argument as to whether the twelfth name amongst the apostles is that of Matthias or Paul is interesting but irrelevant and cannot be settled by this reference alone. There would seem to be enough evidence in the writings of Paul himself (1 Cor 5:3-8) to show that he saw himself as distinct from those who companied with Christ in His earthly sojourn.

15 To see this city as a pyramid does allow the throne to be at the apex and the river to flow down through it assuming that gravity acts as it does on earth. It is however a matter to be considered that the pyramid is not a shape used in Scripture in any structure and it is a favourite structure in paganism. It is seen in Egypt and in Mexico and is the basic shape in the stepped pyramid or ziggurat of Babylonia with the truncated apex dedicated to the worship of the heavenly bodies. It is unlikely that God would allow this heavenly city to have had foreshadowings in Babylon. It is more likely that the cubic holy of holies in the OT was the pattern (1 Kings 6:20). This city is surely a cube. Recent calculations have shown that in such a cube there would be ample living space for the totality of earth's population from Adam to the present day with plenty of space to spare.

19 Much time and ingenuity have been used trying to relate these stones to the stones in the breastplate of the high priest of Israel (Exod 28:17-20; 39:10-14). Eight stones seem to be identical but the four not mentioned (sardonyx, chalcedony, chrysoprasus, jacinth) are unknown in the LXX. There is no scriptural clue to any such connection and, along with attempts to associate a particular stone with a particular apostle, must be abandoned as belonging to the realm of speculation. The attempt to relate foundational truths to the colours is equally speculative and detracts from the sheer dazzling beauty of this iridescent city.

(b) *The City Internally (vv.22-27)*

v.22 "And I saw no temple therein: for the Lord God Almighty and the Lamb are the temple of it.
v.23 And the city had no need of the sun, neither of the moon, to shine in it: for the glory of God did lighten it, and the Lamb is the light thereof.
v.24 And the nations of them which are saved shall walk in the light of it: and the kings of the earth do bring their glory and honour into it.
v.25 And the gates of it shall not be shut at all by day: for there shall be no night there.
v.26 And they shall bring the glory and honour of the nations into it.
v.27 And there shall in no wise enter into it any thing that defileth, neither whatsoever worketh abomination, or maketh a lie: but they which are written in the Lamb's book of life."

22 For the tenth time in this sequence of visions from 19:11, and indeed for the last time in the book, John uses the expression "I saw". This therefore seems to be the climax of the sequence that has led from the manifestation of Christ upon earth to the arrival of the New Jerusalem in the new creation. Earthly Jerusalem had been dominated by the temple overlooking the city from the temple mount. From the days of king Solomon, apart from the seventy years "desolations" (Jer 25:12-14), until the Roman army destroyed the city (70AD) a temple had overlooked the city. In tribulation days a temple (11:1-2) had stood on the same site, and in the millennial reign of Christ the great temple described by Ezekiel (Ezek 40-48) had dominated the skyline. As John scans this city the difference is apparent – there is no temple in it! The material temple has gone and yet there is a temple! The word "temple" (*naos*, "shrine") is used in Scripture of God's dwelling place and since the Lord God Almighty and the Lamb are dwelling in this city no further shrine is needed. The city itself is the temple. Access to Him and acceptance before Him goes with the citizenship of the city that permits uninterrupted fellowship and unrestricted worship of "the Lord God Almighty and the Lamb". The absence of the article before temple shows that the city takes the character of temple and becomes to the cosmos what the holy of holies was to Solomon's temple, the place where God had chosen to dwell. This is a very powerful argument for understanding the city as a cube. The title "Almighty" has echoed through this book from the first mention (1:8) to this ninth and final mention. His power and purposes have been displayed and now He takes up residence within His new creation. Since this new creation is filled by men from the old creation it is not based on power alone but founded on redemption, so with the "Lord God Almighty" the Lamb too is worshipped. Thus the Lamb is prominent in these closing scenes; the Lamb is worshipped (v.22); the Lamb is the light of the city (v.23); to the Lamb belongs the register of citizenship (v.27) and the Lamb shares the throne (22:1, 3). Thus Christ has completed His great redemptive role and in this eternal state the word of 1 Cor 15:27-28 is fulfilled, "that God may be all in all".

23 John is struck by another contrast with earth and with time. On earth as John had known it man was dependent upon the sunlight and enjoyed the moonlight; in this city there is "no need of the sun, neither the moon". Commentators in attempting to prove that this is a millennial scene have pointed out that the form of expression does not necessarily demand that the sun and moon have disappeared from the cosmos but simply that their light is not needed in the city. This is certainly true yet the simple reading of the passage conveys the idea that these luminaries so essential to earth are no longer there to fulfil their function. If the interpretation already given is correct then the sun and moon have gone with the old cosmos and God has established some other source of illumination for earth. Perhaps this city is the new source of earth's light. In any case the sun and moon are obsolete for this city has an infinitely superior light. "The glory of God", as it did with the tabernacle of Moses (Exod 40:34-35) and the temple of Solomon (1 Kings 8: 10-11), "did lighten it". The aorist tense of the verb *phōtizō* points to the moment when God took up residence in the city. The Lamb is said to be the "light" (*luchnos*) which is better translated "lamp" (RV, JND), and shows that as the Lamb presents the worship Godwards so He focuses the light of the revealed glory of God manward. The words of Isaiah are now fulfilled not figuratively but literally, "The sun shall no more be thy light by day, neither for brightness shall the moon give light unto thee; but Jehovah shall be thine everlasting light, and thy God thy glory" (Isa 60:19).

24 The light of this city will illuminate earth; nations will walk in the light of it and kings of the earth will bring their glory and honour into it. Many commentators argue that since nations and kings are mentioned the scene must be millennial. This is to assume what has to be proved; there is no scriptural evidence to show that kings and nations will not exist after the millennium. In fact the stress in many Scriptures on the everlasting nature of Israel's status as head of the nations would argue otherwise. Why national identities should be obliterated at the close of the millennium is not clear. It is certainly possible that in the transference from the old creation to the new creation, of which transference Noah and family in the ark may be a picture, national identities are retained; this would explain the reference here to the nations and the kings. The phrase "of them that are saved" used to describe the nations is omitted by JND, RV as a late scribal emendation on very clear manuscript evidence. The phrase was included by Erasmus in the text of his Greek New Testament (1516 edition) on very weak manuscript evidence and thus became incorporated into the Textus Receptus and hence came into the AV. If it was meant to make clear the nature of these nations this is unnecessary as all on the new earth will be saved.

This great city is the light centre for earth and nations can conduct their business and order their daily living "by means of" (*dia*) the light streaming from this radiant city. "Walk" is the normal scriptural metaphor for the whole business of living. That this city is also the administrative capital of earth is seen in "the kings of the earth do bring their glory and honour into (*eis*) it." The mandate for all rule comes from this city and the kings acknowledge this as they pay homage to God and the Lamb. The present tense of the verb "bring" stresses that the action is habitual, that this is the normal procedure. The glory they bring into the city is the glory of their association with it. Many of the most reliable manuscripts omit the words "and honour" (see RV, JND). Some commentators (W. Scott, W. Kelly with others) would like to change the preposition from "into" to "unto" or "to" and suggest that the kings brought their glory up to the city and left it outside. This breaks a normal grammatical rule that where eis follows a verb of motion (as it does here) that it must be translated "into" and conveys the idea of penetration inside. There is no problem when this city is seen in the context of the eternal state when all those on earth, while they have no citizenship in the city, yet have perfect access to it.

25 This right of access for all the inhabitants of earth is made clear in two ways. The very emphatic "by no means" that has echoed on various occasions in this book is heard again in connection with the shutting of the gates. The negative in the verb "shut" indicates that there can arise no possible emergency when the gates would have to be closed by day, and the following statement beginning with "for" explains why these gates would never be closed; they stand open forever. John knew that city gates were normally closed at sunset but these gates that would never face an emergency by day would stand open always for the very obvious reason that "there shall be no night there". For this city, distinguished from earth's cities by the things missing from it, this is the most triumphant negative of all! The literal translation is graphic "for night shall not be there." It should be clear that time measurements have gone, the eternal day has dawned and that light from the very presence of God and the Lamb will never be dimmed or eclipsed. Likewise all that belonged to the night has gone forever.

26 The thought of v.24 is repeated in a wider context. It is possible to interpret the "they" as the kings mentioned in v.24 but it is better to treat it as an impersonal statement of what will occur in the future. The "glory and the honour" of the nations arise from their association with this city and in fitting tribute they acknowledge this in their attendance. The position they hold, the power they wield and the prosperity they enjoy all stem from the grace received from God and the Lamb on redemption ground. This they will show in the tributes they bring. The same verb and preposition repeated from v.24 indicate that they will not be stopped at the gates but will have access to the very presence of God and the Lamb. J.F. Walvoord makes a valid point when he writes (page 328), "Here again the word nations should be translated 'Gentiles' referring to the Gentile glory in contrast to the glory of Israel or of the church". This fits the picture in the eternal state: the city-dwellers are the resurrected saints of the church and of Israel; the earth-dwellers around the city, overlooked by three gates in each geographical direction belong to Israel; while spread over the new earth are Gentile nations now in a right relationship with Israel, the church, Christ and God. These earth-dwellers of Israel and the multitude of Gentile nations who have come through the millennium have been transferred to the new earth. Theocratic rule has been established throughout the cosmos at last.

27 Such a fair scene as is unfolded in this eternal state recalls the first creation as it was established in Edenic bliss. Yet into that scene there came disaster through sin (Gen 3). Now it is made absolutely plain that no such possibility even exists any more. The strongest negative in Greek grammar (*ou mē*) is again used to show that this city will never be invaded by "any thing that defileth" where the verb "to defile" (*koinoō*) means to render common or unclean in the ceremonial sense (Matt 15:11, 18, 20; Acts 21:28; Heb 9:13). Nothing of this character will ever enter this city. Similarly excluded is the one "that worketh abomination and maketh a lie". There is no suggestion that such persons exist outside the city or that any attempt has to be made to keep them out. The gates are never closed and such a thought is alien to the passage. In this emphatic negative way it is made clear that sin itself and all its contamination have been dealt with and excluded from this creation and the possibility of another fallen creation does not arise. Satan and his minions and his followers have been banished forever. Between the garden of Eden and this chapter there lies the whole history of redemption.

Those who do have entry are those whose names are in the Lamb's book of life (see comments at 3:5; 17:8; 20:12). The Lamb's book of life must not be confined to this church age but is the complete register of the redeemed from creation to eternity. The church linked with Christ and resurrected saints have citizenship in this city, the capital of the new cosmos; the saints changed and transported from the millennial earth live on this new earth, all share in redemption and have their own place in the worship and work of the new creation.

CHAPTER 22

(c) *The City Eternally (vv.1-5)*

v.1 "And he shewed me a pure river of water of life, clear as crystal, proceeding out of the throne of God and of the Lamb.
v.2 In the midst of the street of it, and on either side of the river, was there the tree of life, which bare twelve manner of fruits, and yielded her fruit every month: and the leaves of the tree were for the healing of the nations.
v.3 And there shall be no more curse; but the throne of God and of the Lamb shall be in it; and his servants shall serve him:
v.4 And they shall see his face; and his name shall be in their foreheads.
v.5 And there shall be no night there; and they need no candle, neither light of the sun; for the Lord God giveth them light: and they shall reign for ever and ever."

In the first five verses of this last chapter of the book John is given his final view of the city. He has viewed it externally (21:1-21), he has been introduced to it internally (21:22-27) and now he is permitted a final look at the central feature of this glorious city – the throne. It is fitting that the phrase that closes the vision in v.5 is a repetition of the strongest expression in the Greek language to describe that which never ends, this city endures – "forever and forever". This is truly the "eternal city".

It will be noted that in general terms the Genesis picture of Edenic conditions is fulfilled and expanded:

a new creation has replaced the old (Gen 1: 1)
a new river (Gen 2:10) has replaced that which flowed from the garden of Eden
a new tree of life has replaced its ancient forerunner (Gen 3:24)
the curse (Gen 3:17-18) is gone and communion between God and man is restored.

It should also be observed that this passage moves to a climax. The repetition of the conjunction "and" (*kai*) twelve times moves the vision from stage to stage thus:

1. And he shewed me a pure river of water of life ....
2. And on either side of the river .... a tree of life....
3. And the leaves of the tree ....
4. And there shall be no more curse ....
5. And the throne of God and the Lamb ....
6. And his servants shall serve him ....
7. And they shall see his face ....
8. And his name shall be in their foreheads ....
9. And there shall be no night there ....
10. And they need no candle ....

11. And they (have no need) of light of the sun ....
12. And they shall reign for ever and ever ....

1-2 The river and tree represent the endless supplies available from the throne to delight and satisfy redeemed humanity. This river from the throne answers to the water of earth as the city itself does to the cities of earth; it is "real" water but such as has never been available on earth. The adjective "pure" (*katharos*) while missing in some manuscripts is singularly appropriate as showing the purity of this uncontaminated river. The same adjective has been used to describe the "fine linen" of the saints (15:6; 19:8) and the gold of the city (21:18, 21). This river is not to be confused with the river flowing through Jerusalem (Zech 14:8), nor with the river flowing from the temple (Ezek 47:1-2), both of which belong to millennial days. The sparkling purity of this river is seen in the expression "clear as crystal" which fittingly answers to the crystal-like clearness and scintillating splendour of the material of the city (21:11).

This river comes from the throne. The verb "to proceed" could be more simply rendered "coming forth" or "going out" (JND) from the throne. Since the throne is described as "the throne of God and of the Lamb" some commentators insist that this must be a millennial scene. F. A. Tatford writes, "The fact that the throne is described as 'the throne of God and of the Lamb' is a clear indication that the kingdom had not yet been given up by the Son to the Father, and that the period under review is still the millennium and not the eternal state". This is a misunderstanding and indeed the description of the throne suggests the very opposite. To describe the throne in this way shows that the eternal state must be in view. In the millennium the throne is the throne of Christ and Christ speaks of it as "my throne" (3:21). Here it is the throne of God and of the Lamb, not two thrones (note the two genitives) but one throne. The language reflects God in Christ to whom all redeemed creation give worship and service eternally.

The next expression "in the midst of the street of it" has presented difficulty in interpretation with respect to the tree of life. While grammatical arguments can be ranged on either side, the simplest way to take the expression is to treat it as the concluding statement of v.1 as descriptive of the river. This presents the picture of the cascading waters from the throne flowing down the middle of the street of the city. The second statement of v.2 then begins naturally "and on either side of the river" as the picture changes to the tree-lined banks of this crystal river. As pointed out in comment on 21:21 the word "street" is singular but covers the whole complex of avenues and boulevards. The word "tree" is to be understood in the same way; while singular it describes the trees along each bank of the river. Again this is not to be confused with the millennial scene of Ezek 47:12 where many features of the description indicate that the perfection here described has not yet been reached. Access to the tree of life (Gen 3:24) was denied to man after Adam sinned; now in this new creation that tree is freely available to all citizens of the city.

The fruit of this tree is in keeping with the new conditions. "Twelve manner of fruits" is a good rendering of the two words "twelve fruits", even if the word "manner" is supplied by the AV translators. It is possible to interpret the expression as "twelve crops of fruits" but the AV translation gives more meaning to the following comment "in each month yielding its fruit" (JND) as if each month sees a fresh crop of a different kind of fruit. In light of the absence of sun and moon (21:23) it is clear that John uses "month" as a familiar reference to illustrate the changing variety of the supplies from the tree of life. Fecundity and variety are both in view.

That the nations of the new earth also share in the blessings presented in the tree of life is seen in the reference to the leaves of the tree. These are said to be for the "healing" (*therapeia*) of the nations. The word *therapeia* is the one from which we get the English word "therapy" and its primary meaning is the "care" or "attention" (Luke 12:42) lavished on another. The verb is used in the Gospels (Luke 9:11) of the healing that Christ brought to the sick and Vine suggests that the noun perhaps here with the meaning "health". As J.F. Walvoord writes p.330, "In other words the leaves of the tree promote the enjoyment of life in the new Jerusalem, and are not for correcting ills, which do not exist." Just as the expression "wipe away every tear" (21:4) means that saints will never weep again so the "health of the nations" shows that the illnesses endemic to earth have all gone and will never trouble men again.

3 The ideal consummation of earth's history is emphasised in the fact that the curse that was brought upon earth by the entrance of sin (Gen 3:14-19) is banished forever. During the millennium its full effects were suspended but sin was still possible and "the sinner being a hundred years old shall be accursed" (Isa 65:20). Now "there shall be no curse any more" (RV). The curse itself is forever gone (see JND and marginal note), blessing uninhibited and unhindered is the portion of saints forever. The very fact that the curse has been removed has enabled the throne of God and of the Lamb to be established in the new cosmos where God and the Lamb reign eternally. The service to the throne is rendered by those to whom John does not hesitate to apply the despised word "slaves". While it carried terrible opprobrium in the Roman empire, it has been ennobled by NT use to describe believers in their relationship to God. Used frequently in the book (1:1; 10:7; 11:18; 15:3; 19:2, 5; 22:6, 9) it here reaches its most glorious meaning as descriptive of those who serve the throne in the new creation in the holy Jerusalem. No slave labour or arduous toil is in question but glad service to the Lord God Almighty and the Lamb. The verb translated "shall serve" (*latreuō*) should be translated "they will keep on serving Him" (R.L. Thomas). The NT use of this word (it occurs 21 times) implies priestly service and its six occurrences in Hebrews (8:5; 9:9, 14; 10:2; 12:28; 13:10) should be particularly noted. Now Christ's quotation from Deut 6:13 will be universally true: "Thou shalt worship the Lord thy God and him only shalt thou serve (*latreuō*)" (Matt 4:10). The singular pronoun "him" reflects the unity of deity to whom this service is rendered.

4 "They shall see his face" is an expression denoting unrestricted access and acceptance that implies perfect communion and communication. Never again will God have to use intermediaries to convey His directions and desires; from the throne room of the cosmos His servants will come and go unrestricted; what Moses desired (Exod 33:18-23) will now be the portion of every saint in the city. "His face" must be interpreted in the same way as "him" in the previous verse. Deity is revealed visually in the Lamb. This is the fulfilment of the assurance of Christ, "Blessed are the pure in heart: for they shall see God" (Matt 5:8). In their service before the throne and throughout the cosmos these servants are accredited representatives of the throne and, as such, bear His name on their foreheads. As with all previous mentions of such marks (7:3; 13:16; 14:1) this name is both indelible and visible. This is the fulfilment of the Lord's promise to the overcomers in the church at Philadelphia (3:12).

5 What was incidental and explanatory in 21:25 is now stated simply as fact, "There shall be no night there" or, as in the more graphic JND translation, "And night shall not be any more". Since there is no night no artificial lighting is required, no lamp (*luchnos*) is needed now (the AV "candle" is misleading). No natural light is required either "for the Lord God giveth them light". The same verb *phōtizō* is used as in 21:23 but this time in the future indicative which should be translated "will shed light"; an assurance that He will continue to do this eternally.

The final note of this final vision is the expression "forever and ever" or more literally "unto the ages of the ages". This expression with minor variations occurs fourteen times in this book and is the strongest way in the Greek language of indicating something that is never-ending or unceasing: we use the word "eternal". This is to be contrasted with the thousand-year reign in the millennial kingdom (20:5). When Christ hands back the millennial kingdom to God (1 Cor 15:27-28) He does not cease to rule but the character of the rule changes, the mediatorial reign of the millennium is over, and from that point the Lamb is seen to share the throne with God, indeed as God. This reign has no end. It is with this reign of God and the Lamb that the visions of John close.

VI. Epilogue: Christ Challenging (22:6-21) Christ Speaks – The Morning Star

The visions given to John closed with the glorious description of the holy Jerusalem in which eternal bliss and absolute perfection are to be enjoyed forever. All the purposes of God are now realised in redemption, resurrection and glory. His saints are shown to be His servants in the administration of that new cosmos from the eternal city. There are now appended to the book three paragraphs that bring together major themes and final reassurances in the light of the next event on the divine calendar from the point of view of John the receiver of this revelation – the coming of the Lord to the air for His saints of this dispensation. These paragraphs may be scanned thus:-

1.	Human Responsibility	vv.6-11
	"Behold I come quickly"	(v.7)
2.	Divine Reward	vv.12-17
	"Behold I come quickly"	(v.12)
3.	Spiritual Response	vv.18-21
	"Surely I come quickly"	(v.20)

In each paragraph two matters are stressed:

(a)	The Worth of the Scripture	-	The reliability of the Word
(b)	The Waiting for the Saviour	-	The certainty of the Coming

1. *Human Responsibility* 22:6-11

v.6 "And he said unto me, These sayings are faithful and true: and the Lord God of the holy prophets sent his angel to shew unto his servants the things which must shortly be done.
v.7 Behold, I come quickly: blessed is he that keepeth the sayings of the prophecy of this book.
v.8 And I John saw these things, and heard them. And when I had heard and seen, I fell down to worship before the feet of the angel which shewed me these things.
v.9 Then saith he unto me, See thou do it not: for I am thy fellowservant, and of thy brethren the prophets, and of them which keep the sayings of this book: worship God.
v.10 And he saith unto me, Seal not the sayings of the prophecy of this book: for the time is at hand.
v.11 He that is unjust, let him be unjust still: and he which is filthy, let him be filthy still: and he that is righteous, let him be righteous still: and he that is holy, let him be holy still."

For clarity it should be pointed out that three different voices are heard in this first paragraph. These are as follows: the angel speaks (v.6); Christ speaks (v.7); John speaks (v.8); the angel speaks again (vv.9-11).

6 The conducting angel who has been taking John through the scenes of the book speaks to reiterate the reliability of what has been shown to John. It could be argued that this angel is the angel of 21:9 who has been showing John the holy Jerusalem (see also 21:15; 22:1). However his reference to his own mission suggests that it is the conducting angel of 1:1. So magnificent and so overwhelming to the human spirit have been these scenes that he feels it necessary to give

John a word of reassurance. The "sayings" (*logoi*) in this context must be the whole book. Echoing his own words from 21:5 the angel stresses the dependability of the revelation "faithful and true"; terms descriptive of Christ in 19:11, are now used of the words of this book; "faithful" in the context means "trustworthy", while "true" means "genuine". That this revelation can bear such divine approval is only to be expected as the line of communication is traced from the Lord God through the angel to His servants. The line is the same as in 1:1 except that here John's name is omitted but the interjection of his voice ("I John") in v.8 makes it complete. JND has major manuscript support for the translation "and [the] Lord God of the spirits of the prophets, sent his angel" which is also substantially the reading of the RV. The point made by the angel is that the God who acted through the OT prophets and so controlled them as to bring His word to men, is the same God who has acted again in this dispensation to show future events to those called "his servants". These recipients of this revelation have been shown to be the believers of the church age of whom John is a representative and for whom he becomes the channel of communication (1:1). The revelation concerns the "things which must shortly be done". "Must" indicates that the divine programme is already fixed; "shortly" (*en tachei*) could be translated "at speed", indicating that when the programme begins it will be swiftly executed. The idea of imminence while not stated is implied so that no event need intervene until the programme is begun. Contrast the adverb *tachu* in v.7 which is rightly translated "quickly".

7 Christ Himself breaks in at this point with an assurance in the light of what the angel has just said about the divine programme ahead. It is as if He wished to lift the eyes of believers from future events to Himself and He bridges the gap between His ascension and return in one brief promise. In the promise there is His own personal assurance that His coming will be "quickly" (*tachu*) – there will be no delay. Speaking in this way to John the Lord makes it plain that He has the rapture in view. His coming to the air for the church is the next event on the divine calendar and the event that opens the way for the count-down to the consummation of events on earth set forth in this book.

It is Christ Himself who pronounces the sixth beatitude in the book. The blessing is for the one who keeps "the sayings (*logoi*) of the prophecy of this book". The "sayings" mentioned in the previous verse by the angel are given the stamp of Christ's personal approval. The verb "keepeth" is the normal word to describe one who allows the life to be controlled by the Word or, to put it in the active sense, lives in the light of the Word. The truth of this book, if believed, would control lives. For this reason this often-neglected and misunderstood book carries very special blessing for those who give weight to its prophecies, its promises and its warnings. The vital matter is not simply the knowledge of events given in the book but the revelation of the person of Christ: that lends this book its vitality and importance. That is the secret of the added blessing in the reading and keeping of the sayings of this book.

8 John identified himself in the opening verses of this book (1:1-4) but only in 21:2 and here in this epilogue has he used the emphatic personal pronoun. So overwhelming have been the sights and sounds that have burst upon him in these visions that in light of the angelic statement and the Saviour's promise, there bursts from him a personal note of authentication. The personal experience of "hearing" and "seeing" allows him to give a note of testimony which is reminiscent of the testimony he gave of the cross (John 19:35). What John had "heard" and "seen" (called "these things" at the end of the verse) could be the vision of the eternal city or could embrace the four visions of the book. In any case John is so overwhelmed that, in a very natural reaction, he falls at the feet of his angel-guide. When he fell at the feet of Christ in the first chapter (1:17) it would seem that John's action was involuntary; here he acts deliberately, and he admits that he had worship in mind. However a comparison with 19:10 where John had his first angelic rebuke in similar circumstances will show that the pronoun "him" is missing here, and John's intention seems to be to worship God at (*emprosthen*, "before") the angel's feet. John has learned something from his first rebuke and knows that a creature is not to be worshipped; yet such a prostration is dangerous and John receives a second rebuke from the angel.

9 The sharp rebuke from the angel comprises two imperatives. The first abrupt imperative is negative, "see thou do it not" and John is arrested in mid-action. The second imperative is positive, "worship God." However exalted the responsibility given to an angel he is nothing more than a fellowservant of all those in the service of God. This angel speaks of himself as a fellowservant of John, a fellowservant of those having a prophetic ministry, and finally a fellowservant of those who keep the words of this book. An angel takes his status and dignity from the service entrusted to him and he is but a servant of God. Worship must not be given to a servant; it belongs by right to God alone.

10-11 For the fourth time in five verses the "sayings" (*logoi*) of this book are mentioned and John is commanded, "seal not" these words of divine revelation. This command stands in contrast to the command in 10:4 in connection with the seven thunders. Men are allowed to know what lies ahead for earth for two reasons. This revelation serves as a warning to sinners but also it serves as an encouragement to saints as the triumph of Christ is revealed. There is also a contrast with the command given to Daniel in connection with his prophecy, "And thou, O Daniel, shut up the words and seal the book, even to the time of the end" (Dan 12:4). Centuries had to roll away and history unfold before the endtime prophecies of Daniel could be fulfilled. All the events associated with Christ and the cross had to take place first. In the scriptural sense Daniel's prophecies were not imminent; other events had to intervene. In John's case with all events centred on Christ's first coming now history, the prophecies given to him were imminent in the sense that no major event had to take place before they could be fulfilled. This interpretation is confirmed by the final sentence of the verse, "the time is at hand", which echoes one of the earliest statements in the book (1:3). The word "time" (*kairos*), which would be better translated "season", has almost a technical sense in the NT when it refers to the future (see Acts 1:7; 3:19; 1 Thess 5:1) and with the article points to a particular set season. This is the season when God will bring all things to completion and it is described as "near". From the prophetic standpoint the towering peaks of endtime events cast their shadows across the ages.

The absolute reliability of the Word and the nearness of the season when these events will take place puts the responsibility upon men. There are only two possible reactions:

1. Men can reject that Word, but to do this results in conduct that forms character, a character that issues in a destiny. Such a Word-rejecter is described in two ways: manward he is described as "the one acting unrighteously"; Godward he is spoken of as "the filthy one".
2. Men can believe that Word, and to do this issues in conduct that forms character, a character that issues in a destiny. Such a Word-believer is described in two ways: manward he is called "the righteous one"; Godward he is seen as "the holy one".

In the case of those who believe the Word it is not their standing that is in view but their conduct. From other Scriptures we know that the believer acts before men righteously (his conduct) because he is righteous (his standing) and he is acts holily before God (his conduct) because he is holy (his standing). It is the character-forming side of conduct that is in view here.

The four imperatives are rightly translated by the English "let" and may be set out as follows:

1.	The one acting unjustly	let him act unjustly still
2.	The filthy one	let him act filthily still
3.	The righteous one	let him do righteousness still
4.	The holy one	let him be hallowed still.

As pointed out by grammarians (Dana and Mantey) these are not imperatives of command but imperatives of permission. It is as if divine permission is being given to withdraw any attempt to change men. They have chosen in life for good or ill by their response to the Word and the frightening thing is that Christ accepts that decision; the choice having been made the consequences are inevitable. In this case "still" shows that the character formed on earth will be taken into eternity whether for good or ill.

2. *Divine Reward* 22:12-17

v.12 "And, behold, I come quickly; and my reward is with me, to give every man according as his work shall be.
v.13 I am Alpha and Omega, the beginning and the end, the first and the last.
v.14 Blessed are they that do his commandments, that they may have right to the tree of life, and may enter in through the gates into the city.
v.15 For without are dogs, and sorcerers, and whoremongers, and murderers, and idolaters, and whosoever loveth and maketh a lie.
v.16 I Jesus have sent mine angel to testify unto you these things in the churches. I am the root and the offspring of David, and the bright and morning star.
v.17 And the Spirit and the bride say, Come. And let him that heareth say, Come. And let him that is athirst come. And whosoever will, let him take the water of life freely."

Again for clarity it is necessary to distinguish the speakers in the paragraph: Christ speaks (vv.12-13); John speaks (vv.14-15); Christ speaks (v.16); John speaks (v.17).

12 Christ intervenes in the scene abruptly, an abruptness emphasised by the omission of the conjunction "and" in many manuscripts. As in v.7 the present tense should be translated "I am coming"; "quickly" (*tachu*) but shows how little time men have left before the world-shaking events of this book take place. That Christ has the coming to the air in view there can be no doubt since this is the next event in the divine programme to introduce the "season" of which He spoke in v.10. This time Christ stresses, not the responsibility of men to keep the Word in view of His coming, but the reward that He brings to men at His coming. The word "reward" may be used of any recompense whether for good or for evil (see its use in the latter sense, Acts l:18) and in the context of the previous verse may indicate the division that will take place between believers and unbelievers when He comes. It is better, however, though the introduction of the subject is abrupt, to see this reward as a direct reference to the judgment seat of Christ associated with His coming to the air. Believers find much encouragement in difficult days in knowing that when Christ comes their suffering and service will be rewarded immediately. "My reward" must be interpreted as the reward that He Himself will bring "with Him" meaning that it comes from Himself alone. It is both an individual reward to "each man" (RV) and it is a just reward in light of the " work" of the individual saint. The singular "work" (*ergon*) sums up a lifetime of service as it does in a similar context in 1 Cor 3:12-15.

13 The Christ who will bring reward to His saints at His coming is God. The titles of deity that Christ uses here have been associated with Him a number of times in the book (see comments at 1:8, 11, 17; 2:8; 21:6). As "the Alpha and the Omega", a title embracing the first and last letters in the Greek alphabet, all revelation of deity and communication by deity is complete in Christ (see at 1:8). He who was outside of history became part of history to bring men the revelation. As "the First and the Last" Christ's relation to creation is seen, He was before it and will be after it, He is the One who created it and the One for whom it was created (Col 1:15-17); He is both the origin and the goal of creation. He who was outside of time stepped into time. As "the Beginning and the End" all began with Him and all will be finalised in relation to Him. When the eternal One says, "Behold I come quickly", it is evident that earth is moving to the endtime events.

14 It is possible that this is still the voice of Christ speaking to John. However on the general grounds that John is frequently used of the Holy Spirit to apply truth to the conscience of the readers it is better to see John himself as the speaker here. The fact that this is the seventh and last beatitude in the book gives no guidance as to the speaker since there has been a beatitude pronounced by the voice from heaven (14:13), one by the angel (19:9), two by John (1:3; 20:6) and two by Christ Himself (16:15; 22:7).

There is a textual problem in this verse. The AV describes those blessed as "they that do his commandments" while the RV and JND have "they that wash their robes" (*hōi plunontes tas stolas autōn*). While most textual authorities agree that the RV has the correct reading, JND comments that the scribal change must have occurred very early for many of the earliest manuscripts have the AV reading. In light of NT teaching in general as to the basis of salvation (Titus 3:5 *et al*) the RV reading "wash their robes" is to be preferred. It might, however, be reasonably argued that since doing the commandments is the result of washing the robes no doctrinal implication need be drawn from the disputed reading. Obedience to the Word is the reality of which washing the robes is the metaphor. The fact that this metaphor has already occurred in 1:5; 7:14 suggests very strongly that the RV has the original reading and that it is used in this closing benediction to show that all the redeemed may enter the city and have a right to the tree of life. To have "the right (*exousia*) over (*epi*) the tree of life" means simply that they are entitled to partake of this tree as those who share in the life of God. This tree contributes to their eternal well-being. Having this right they have automatic entry into the city. The marvel is that cleansed sinners (the metaphor is in the washing of their robes) enjoy life eternal (the symbol is the tree of Life) and have the freedom of the eternal city.

15 The contrast with this bliss of the redeemed is dramatic; made more so by the fact that most texts omit the introductory "for". To be "without" this city means more than simply physical location; the "without" has already been defined as the lake of fire (21:8). The blessedness of the citizens of the city stands in deliberate and stark contrast with this abandoned realm. Unbelievers, as in 21:8; 21:27, are described by the character formed by their subservience to sin and Satan. Metaphorically they are spoken of as "dogs" (see Phil 3:2), animals that in eastern lands would never be permitted to cross the threshold of a home; by their very nature they belonged "without" and this is where they had to stay. The repeated "and" is cumulative and adds wider categories to those already identified as belonging "without". It is not that men have fallen into these sins but rather that these sins, from which they were never delivered, characterise their lives. Five particular character-forming sins are mentioned:

1. sorcerers (*pharmakoi*) describes those who use drugs, potions, spells and enchantments as a link with the occult and the magical arts. Satanism and spiritism are included.
2. whoremongers describes all who habitually indulge sexual licence and depraved lust. The debasement of sex, a feature of present-day society, goes far beyond the sexual licence of past ages and holds multitudes in its snare.
3. murderers describes those who have reproduced the character of Satan (John 8:44) as a family feature; now they share His doom. Those who plotted against the saints of God down the ages now find just retribution, and all who shared the moral responsibility for murder now find that their true character draws down upon them absolute justice (Acts 7:52).
4. idolaters describes those who refused to give God the worship that belongs to Him and gave this to another. In the days of Israel's theocracy it was Baal and Ashtaroth who disputed Jehovah's claims upon His people; in the days of Israel's monarchy it was Molech who rivalled Jehovah; in the Christ's day it was Mammon; in our day all the ancient deities have been reinstated under new names but the idolatry is the same and God is displaced. Evolution has become a god at whose shrine atheists worship; business and wealth have their devotees and the result is the same – men have fallen into idolatry. The last apostasy under the Beast (2 Thess 2:3-4) in the tribulation period will show that idolatry becomes a basic issue of life in the tribulation.
5. "whosoever loveth and maketh a lie" is a more embracive description than the "all liars" of 21:8. It shows that the character that has not learned to loath what is false, or that co-operates in the propagation of a lie comes under this eternal banishment.

16 It is truly moving to hear from the lips of the Lord Himself the emphatic words, "I Jesus", a name that for John, as for us, recalls the lonely path of the Saviour through a hostile world. The revelation is complete and the Lord is pleased to put on it the impress of His integrity. As that personal name fell upon John's ear he must have recalled many an occasion and happening from the earthly sojourn of the Saviour, but now from His place in glory the Lord speaks to seal this revelation of His triumph and glory. No other book in the sacred canon carries this approval; it places on the reader a special responsibility.

The transmission of the revelation with its source in Christ Himself comes via the angel mentioned in 1:1 where the participle from the verb *apostellō* suggests a special commission. Here the simple verb "to send" (*pempō*) is used since the One who sends is Jesus and this is sufficient authentication. (Both verbs occur in John 20:21.) The verb "testify" in the aorist tense shows the testimony borne in this book is now finished and complete and the whole of the book summed up in the phrase – "these things". "To you" refers first of all to the believers in the seven churches in the province of Asia but through them to all saints. While there were specific letters to each church even these were meant to be seen as a unit and the whole book was intended for each church. This is the first mention of the churches from 3:22.

The historical Jesus further identifies Himself as one who has links with the past and the future. The "I" is again emphatic as Christ claims the very title that belongs exclusively to the great "I am" – the self-existing One. As "the root and the offspring of David" He is linked to the nation of Israel, "And there shall come forth a rod out of the stem of Jesse, and a branch shall grow out of his roots" (Isa 11:1). The more complete title here as compared to 5:5 suggests that "root" may be taken in the sense of the One from whom David sprang so that, as the root of David he was David's ancestor and then, as the offspring of David He was David's descendant according to the flesh (Rom 1:3). This paradox could be fulfilled only in One who voluntarily stepped into manhood (Matt 22:41-45). Historical purpose and messianic promise are fulfilled in Christ.

As "the bright and morning star" Christ links Himself with the church. The night is always followed by the day. In general terms during the night ages of earth when sin darkened the scene the anticipation has been of the day of millennial glory leading to the eternal day. The morning star anticipates the day. From the time of Balaam's prophecy (Num 24:17) the star has been a general promise of the expected one to come, a promise that has been fulfilled in Christ. But Christ to the church is the "bright and morning star", an emphasis, not on the brightness of the star, but on the fact that it precedes and thus heralds the dawn of day. The promise to the overcomer in the church in Thyatira (2:28), and Christ's own identification here, show that in this role He is the anticipation of the hope of the church-age believers. As believers look through the darkness of the night "the bright and morning star" (Christ seen in His coming for the church) heralds the dawn of day. When He subsequently comes to earth with His saints it will be as "the sun of righteousness" (Mal 4:2) shining in His strength throughout the millennial day.

17 The verse division interrupts the scene so that it is not immediately apparent that there is an instantaneous response to this revelation of Christ as the bright and morning star. John is taken up by the Spirit to become the voice of the Spirit and the bride in crying, "Come". This is not an evangelistic call to sinners but the response of the Spirit and the bride to the truth of the coming of Christ. John expresses that longing of the bride-church, in fellowship with her Holy Spirit conductor, in the cry "Come!" Just as Rebecca in the care of the unnamed servant must have anticipated Isaac coming to meet the caravan (Gen 24:62-67), the church longs to see Christ.

John now invites all who hear, meaning all who have responded positively to the message of this book, to join him in this call to Christ. Every believer who responds to the soul-stirring message of this book is expected to join in the cry of the bride-church awaiting her Lord. John is the pattern of just such a believer in v.20.

While the first two sentences in the verse are a call to Christ, from the church collectively and then from the individual saint, the last two statements are a call to sinners. This is evident since the call is not simply an appeal, but the appeal is to satisfy a need – the thirsty one and the longing one have needs that can be satisfied only in Christ. This change in the nature of the call is also seen in the fact that the verb changes from the second person (addressed to Christ) to the third person (addressed to the sinner), "let him come" and "let him take". The thirsty sinner can be satisfied only by the living water available through Christ (John 7:37). The thirsty one ("him that is athirst") describes the sinner with the urgent consuming need whose deepest longings have been stirred. "Whosoever will" is a somewhat weaker expression to describe those whose realisation of need and whose stirrings of desire have not yet deepened to the urgency of a consuming thirst. Both may come and find in Christ freely available the water of life (Isa 55: 1), that which satisfies every need. Delay must not be contemplated for any reason whatsoever; the coming of the Lord is so very near.

3. *Spiritual Responsibility*
22:18-21

v.18 "For I testify unto every man that heareth the words of the prophecy of this book, If any man shall add unto these things, God shall add unto him the plagues that are written in this book:

v.19 And if any man shall take away from the words of the book of this prophecy, God shall take away his part out of the book of life, and out of the holy city, and from the things which are written in this book.

v.20 He which testifieth these things saith, Surely I come quickly. Amen. Even so, come, Lord Jesus.

v.21 The grace of our Lord Jesus Christ be with you all. Amen."

There are only two speakers in this paragraph: Christ speaks (vv.18-20a); John speaks (vv.20b-21).

18-20a For the third time Christ uses the emphatic "I" (v.16 twice) in this passage which underlines the sacred nature of this revelation given to John; a revelation again summed up in "the words (*logoi*) of the prophecy of this book".

These "words" have already been mentioned four times (vv.6,7,9,10) but now they are identified again as:

> "the words of the prophecy of this book" (v.18),
> "the words of the book of this prophecy" (v.19).

The changed word order means that in the first statement attention is directed to the content of the book while in the second statement the emphasis falls on the completeness of the book lying before John. With regard to both the content and the completeness Christ solemnly warns that to tamper with either aspect of this divine revelation is to invite personal judgment.

What Christ warns against is not the inadvertent mistakes of scribal copyists as they laboured to produce accurate copies of the Word. Irenaeus as quoted by Eusubius mistakenly understood the passage in this way; it is far more than a threat to a copyist. In an amazing way God has preserved the text down the ages in miraculous fashion through the labours of dedicated men who have given their lives in the accurate transmission of the text. Neither is Christ warning against straightforward disobedience to the truth of the book; that warning has been heard repeatedly throughout the book; as ever, disobedience carries its own inherent penalty. Christ recognised that this book so unfolds the purposes of God in Christ and the triumph of Christ over every foe, including Satan himself, that the enemy would make a special attempt to keep men from it (1:3). When this failed, Satan would want to alter the contents either by addition to it or subtraction from it so that its truth would be invalidated. As believers near the end of the age we are indebted to God for the preservation of the content of this book.

Tampering with the content of this book could be done in either of the two ways identified by Christ as follows:

1. Addition to the book – "If any man shall add to these things". This kind of prohibition runs through Scripture from Deut 4:2 where the instruction is plain, "Ye shall not add unto the word which I command you". It is echoed again in Deut 12:32; Prov 30:6. The arrogance that would add to the sacred word of God invites God to do His "adding" (the same verb is used) but of "the plagues that are written in this book". This refers back to the judgments in the tribulation period on men, the seals, the trumpets and the bowls, but very particularly the bowls which are called the seven last plagues (15:1), an incidental confirmation of the fact that the plagues are to be interpreted literally and not symbolically. This threat is not difficult to understand when it is remembered that this book was given in the church age, that the coming of Christ is seen as imminent, and that the tribulation follows the coming of Christ at the rapture. A person who treated the Word in this fashion would demonstrate his unbelief; it is certain that he

would be left for the tribulation plagues. These judgments would become personal retribution from God upon such a person. God guards the revelation He has given of Christ.

2. Subtraction from the book – "If any man shall take away from the words of this book". Again this is a quotation from Deut 4:2 with its echo in Deut 12:32. To "take away" means to remove those parts that the proud intellect of man judges unsuitable, or inexplicable, or unpalatable, an action which displays the arrogance of unbelief in the opposite way. In this case God would do His own subtraction and two things would be lost by such an arrogant unbeliever. God would in fact:

   a. "take away" (the same verb) his part "from (*apo*) the tree of life" (JND, RV)
   b. ["take away his part] out of (*ek*) the holy city".

The final phrase is more accurately rendered in the RV margin " [even] from the things which are written in this book" and should be understood as an explanatory phrase to define the tree of life and the holy city as matters already revealed in this prophecy. The blatant declaration of unbelief in taking away from this Word would show that such had no "part" or "portion" in the two things that believers will enjoy. As sinners, through grace, they had a potential right to a part in the tree of life and a place in the holy city but their arrogant pride cost them these blessings. This Scripture must not be read as if God would take away personal salvation once enjoyed; such a thought would be contrary to the whole teaching of the NT. The AV, based on the Textus Receptus, reads "the book of life" while virtually all manuscript support is for "the tree of life". One textual authority says "the manuscript support for the AV reading is virtually non-existent". The right to the tree of life and entry to the city are the inalienable right of those who have "washed their robes" (v.14) – the metaphorical description of believers. Those who have no part in this blessing are unbelievers and their treatment of the Word shows into which class men fall. The final expression "the things written in this book", indicating the blessing of saints, stands in contrast to the "plagues that are written in this book" (v.18), indicating the judgments upon sinners.

Christ bears final testimony to the fact that the book comes directly from Himself and John is only the human channel. The participle of the verb "to testify" with which He began His final testimony in v.18 sets forth Christ as the final witness ("he that testifieth") to the reliability of the things revealed. To that testimony Christ gives a final authentic word that has rung down the ages and stirred the hearts of generations of saints: "Surely I come quickly". This is Christ's response to the cry of the Spirit and the bride and the saint in v.17. The word "surely" is a particle of affirmation used when the truth stated will not admit any shadow of doubt. The present tense of the verb *erchomai* dramatically pictures Christ on the way – "I am coming". The addition of the familiar word "quickly" (*tachu*) that in its usage throughout this book has ever stressed the imminence of the coming shows how the Lord Himself views that moment. With no Scripture to be fulfilled until He comes for His own blood-brought bride He awaits that moment with all the longing of His heart and will allow no delay.

20(b)-21 As this final assurance falls on the ear of John his heart responds in a way that it did not do when Christ had given similar promises in vv.7,12. On those previous occasions other important matters linked to the coming had been added which had, in a certain sense almost intruded: in v.7 responsibility is enjoined, in v.12 reward is expected. Now the simple fact that Christ is coming personally moves him deeply and John responds. There comes a cry (or even a sigh) that has echoed down the centuries and in which all saints of the present dispensation gladly join, "Amen. Even so, come, Lord Jesus". We know from the NT that the return of Christ for the church will only be the commencement of end-time events that will bring earth through the pain of the tribulation and through the millennial bliss to the consummation of the ages in the eternal state. This is doubtless all involved in this response of John, but while the programme is glorious something far brighter grips the heart of the trembling believer. It is the fact that the Lord Himself is coming and John longs to see Him. Every believer joins with John in this heart-felt sigh.

The last note in the book is a benediction reminiscent of Paul's epistles and confirms the fact that the book as a whole was to be sent to each of the seven churches. JND points out that only two manuscripts read "with all" and prefers the better attested reading "with all the saints". While the OT closes with a warning concerning a curse, the NT closes with witness concerning a coming. The Lord Jesus Christ who suffered grief for us, now bestows grace upon us, and to be associated with Him will mean glory eternally. No other book sets forth more fully the doom of Satan and of sinners, nor describes more fully the destiny of saints in their association with the Saviour. We can only join with John in crying, "Even so, come, Lord Jesus".